# the Unofficial Guide® to

## the Best RV and Tent Campgrounds in the Northeast

### Connecticut, Maine, Massachusetts, New Hampshire, Rhode Island & Vermont

**Other Titles in the Unofficial Guide**
**Best RV and Tent Campgrounds Series**

California & the West

Florida & the Southeast

Great Lakes States

Mid-Atlantic States

Northwest & Central Plains

Southwest & South Central Plains

U.S.A.

# Other Unofficial Guides

Beyond Disney: The Unofficial Guide to Universal, SeaWorld,
and the Best of Central Florida

Inside Disney: The Incredible Story of Walt Disney World
and the Man Behind the Mouse

Mini Las Vegas: The Pocket-Sized Unofficial Guide to Las Vegas

Mini-Mickey: The Pocket-Sized Unofficial Guide to Walt Disney World

The Unofficial Guides to Bed & Breakfasts and Country Inns:
California Great Lakes New England
Northwest Rockies Southeast Southwest

The Unofficial Guides to the Best RV and Tent Campgrounds:
California & the West Florida & the Southeast Great Lakes
Mid-Atlantic States Northeast Northwest Southwest U.S.A.

The Unofficial Guide to Branson, Missouri

The Unofficial Guide to Chicago

The Unofficial Guide to Cruises

The Unofficial Guide to Disneyland

The Unofficial Guide to Disneyland Paris

The Unofficial Guide to Florence, Rome, and the Heart of Italy

The Unofficial Guide to the Great Smoky and Blue Ridge Region

The Unofficial Guide to Golf Vacations in the Eastern U.S.

The Unofficial Guide to Hawaii

The Unofficial Guide to Las Vegas

The Unofficial Guide to London

The Unofficial Guide to New Orleans

The Unofficial Guide to New York City

The Unofficial Guide to Paris

The Unofficial Guide to San Francisco

The Unofficial Guide to South Florida, including Miami and the Keys

The Unofficial Guides to Traveling with Kids:
California Florida Mid-Atlantic New England and New York
Walt Disney World

The Unofficial Guide to Walt Disney World

The Unofficial Guide to Walt Disney World for Grown-Ups

The Unofficial Guide to Washington, D.C.

The Unofficial Guide to the World's Best Diving Vacations

# the Unofficial Guide® to

# the Best RV and Tent Campgrounds in the Northeast

### 1st Edition

Connecticut, Maine, Massachusetts,
New Hampshire, Rhode Island & Vermont

Diane Bair, Pamela Wright,
and Daniel Kline

**Hungry Minds™**

Best-Selling Books • Digital Downloads • e-Books • Answer Networks • e-Newsletters
Branded Web Sites • e-Learning

*New York, NY • Indianapolis, IN • Cleveland, OH*

Please note that price fluctuate in the course of time, and travel information changes under the impact of many factors that influence the travel industry. We therefore suggest that you write or call ahead for confirmation when making your travel plans. Every effort has been made to ensure the accuracy of information throughout this book and the contents of this publication are believed correct at the time of printing. Nevertheless, the publishers cannot accept responsibility for errors or omissions or for changes in details given in this guide or for the consequences of any reliance on the information provided by the same. Assessments of attractions and so forth are based upon the author's own experience and therefore, descriptions given in this guide necessarily contain an element of subjective opinion, which may not reflect the publisher's opinion or dictate a reader's own experience on another occasion. Readers are invited to write to the publisher with ideas, comments, and suggestions for future editions.

Your safety is important to us, so we encourage you to stay alert and be aware of your surroundings. Keep a close eye on cameras, purses, and wallets, all favorite targets of thieves and pickpockets.

**Published by Hungry Minds, Inc.**
909 Third Avenue
New York, NY 10022

Produced by Menasha Ridge Press
COVER DESIGN BY MICHAEL J. FREELAND
INTERIOR DESIGN BY MICHELE LASEAU

ISBN 0-7645-6253-3

ISSN 1536-9676

Manufactured in the United States of America

10 9 8 7 6 5 4 3 2

# Contents

# the Unofficial Guide® to

## the Best RV and Tent Campgrounds in the Northeast

# Introduction

## Why Unofficial?

The material in this guide has not been edited or in any way reviewed by the campgrounds profiled. In this "unofficial" guide we represent and serve you, the consumer. By way of contrast with other campground directories, no ads were sold to campgrounds, and no campground paid to be included. Through our independence, we're able to offer you the sort of objective information necessary to select a campground efficiently and with confidence.

### Why Another Guide to Campgrounds?

We developed *The Unofficial Guide to the Best RV and Tent Campgrounds in the Northeast* because we recognized that campers are as discriminating about their choice of campgrounds as most travelers are about their choice of hotels. As a camper, you don't want to stay in every campground along your route. Rather, you prefer to camp only in the best. A comprehensive directory with limited information on each campground listed does little to help you narrow your choices. What you need is a reference that tells you straight out which campgrounds are the best, and that supplies detailed information, collected by independent inspectors, that differentiates those campgrounds from all of the also-rans. This is exactly what *The Unofficial Guide to the Best RV and Tent Campgrounds* delivers.

### The Choice Is All Yours

Life is short, and life is about choices. You can stay in a gravel lot, elbow to elbow with other campers, with tractor-trailers roaring by just beyond the fence, or with this guide, you can spend the night in a roomy, shaded site, overlooking a sparkling blue lake. The choice is yours.

The authors of this guide have combed the Northeastern states inspecting and comparing hundreds of campgrounds. Their objective was to create a hit parade of the very best, so that no matter where you travel, you'll never have to spend another night in a dumpy, gravel lot.

The best campgrounds in each state are described in detail in individual profiles so you'll know exactly what to expect. In addition to the fully profiled campgrounds, we provide a Supplemental Directory of Campgrounds that lists hundreds of additional properties that are quite adequate, but that didn't make the cut for the top 350 in the guide. Thus, no matter where you are, you'll have plenty of campgrounds to choose from. None of the campgrounds appearing in this guide, whether fully profiled or in the supplemental list, paid to be included. Rather, each earned its place by offering a superior product. Period.

### Letters, Comments, and Questions from Readers

Many who use the Unofficial Guides write to us with questions, comments, and reports of their camping experiences. We appreciate all such input, both positive and critical. Readers' comments are frequently incorporated into revised editions of the Unofficial Guides and have contributed immeasurably to their improvement. Please write to:

*The Unofficial Guide to the Best RV and Tent Campgrounds*
P.O. Box 43673
Birmingham, AL 35243
UnofficialGuides@menasharidge.com

For letters sent through the mail, please put your return address on both your letter and envelope; the two sometimes become separated. Also include your phone number and email address if you are available for a possible interview.

## How to Use This Guide

Using this guide is quick and easy. We begin with this introduction followed by "Campground Awards," a list of the best campgrounds for RVers, tenters, families, and more. Then we profile the best 350 campgrounds in the Northeast. Next is a supplemental list of hundreds of additional campgrounds including details about prices, hookups, and more. Bringing up the rear is an alphabetical index of all campgrounds included in the guide.

Both the profiled section and the supplemental directory are ordered alphabetically, first by state and then by city. To see what campgrounds are available:

- Find the section covering the state in question.

- Within that section, look up the city alphabetically.

- Under the city, look up the campgrounds alphabetically.

You can choose and locate campgrounds in four different ways.

1. **Use the Map**   If a city appears with a black, solid bullet on our map, at least one of our profiled or listed campgrounds will be located there. The converse is also the case: if the city has a hollow, outlined bullet, you can assume that we do not cover any campgrounds in that city.

2. **Check the Campground Profiles**   In the section where we profile campgrounds, look up any city where you hope to find a campground. If the city isn't listed, it means we do not profile any campgrounds there.

3. **Check the Supplemental Directory of Campgrounds**   Check for the same city in the supplemental listings.

4. **Use the Index**   If you want to see if a specific campground is profiled or listed in the guide, look up the name of the campground in the alphabetical index at the back of the book.

When looking up campgrounds, remember that the best campgrounds are found in the profiled section; always check there first before turning to the Supplemental Directory of Campgrounds.

# Understanding the Profiles

Each profile has seven important sections:

**Campground Name, Address, and Contact Information** In addition to the street address, we also provide phone and fax numbers as well as website and email addresses.

**Ratings** Using the familiar one- to five-star rating with five stars being best, we offer one overall rating for RV campers and a second overall rating for tent campers. The overall rating for each type of camper is based on a rough weighted average of the following eight individually rated categories:

| Category | Weight |
| --- | --- |
| Beauty | 15% |
| Site Privacy | 10% |
| Site Spaciousness | 10% |
| Quiet | 15% |
| Security | 13% |
| Cleanliness/upkeep | 13% |
| Insect Control | 10% |
| Facilities | 14% |

*Beauty* This rates the natural setting of the campground in terms of its visual appeal. The highest ratings are reserved for campgrounds where the beauty of the campground can be enjoyed and appreciated both at individual campsites and at the campground's public areas. Views, vistas, landscaping, and foliage are likewise taken into consideration.

*Site Privacy* This category rates the extent to which the campsites are set apart and/or in some way buffered (usually by trees and shrubs) from adjacent or nearby campsites. The farther campsites are from one another the better. This rating also reflects how busy the access road to the campsites is in terms of traffic. Campgrounds that arrange their sites on a number of cul-de-sacs, for example, will offer quieter sites than a campground where the sites are situated off of a busy loop or along a heavily traveled access road.

*Site Spaciousness* This rates the size of the campsite. Generally, the larger the better.

*Quiet* This rating indicates the relative quietness of the campground. There are three key considerations. The first is where the campground is located. Campgrounds situated along busy highways or in cities or towns are usually noisier, for example, than rural or wilderness campgrounds removed from major thoroughfares. The second consideration relates to how noise is managed at the campground. Does the campground forbid playing of radios or enforce a "quiet time" after a certain hour? Is there someone on site at night to respond to complaints about other campers being loud or unruly at a late hour? Finally, the rating considers the extent to which trees, shrubs, and the natural topography serve to muffle noise within the campground.

*Security* This rating reflects the extent (if any) to which management monitors the campground during the day and night. Physical security is also included in this rating: Is the campground fenced? Is the campground gated? If so, is the gate manned? Generally, a campground located in a city or along a busy road is more exposed to thieves or vandals than a more remote campground, and should more actively supervise access.

*Cleanliness*   This rates the cleanliness, serviceability, and state of repair of the campground, including grounds, sites, and facilities.

*Insect Control*   This rating addresses questions regarding insect and pest control. Does management spray or take other steps to control the presence of mosquitoes and other insect pests? Does the campground drain efficiently following a rain? Are garbage and sewage properly collected and disposed of?

*Facilities*   This rates the overall variety and quality of facilities to include bath house/toilets, swimming pool, retail shops, docks, pavilions, playgrounds, etc. If the quality of respective facilities vary considerably within a given campground, inconsistencies are explained in the prose description of the campground.

**Campground Description**   This is an informative, consumer-oriented description of the campground. It includes what makes the campground special or unique and what differentiates it from other area campgrounds. The description may additionally include the following:

- The general layout of the campground.

- Where the campground is located relative to an easily referenced city or highway.

- The general setting (wilderness, rural, or urban).

- Description of the campsites including most and least desirable sites.

- Prevailing weather considerations and best time to visit.

- Mention of any unusual, exceptional, or deficient facilities.

- Security considerations, if any (gates that are locked at night, accessibility of campground to non-campers, etc.).

**Basics**   Key information about the campground including:

- *Operated By* Who owns and/or operates the campground.

- *Open* Dates or seasons the campground is open.

- *Site Assignment* How sites are most commonly obtained (first-come, first served; reservations accepted; reservations only; assigned on check-in, etc. Deposit and refund policy.

- *Registration* Where the camper registers on arrival. Information on how and where to register after normal business hours (late arrival).

- *Fee* Cost of a standard campsite for one night for RV sites and tent sites respectively. Forms of payment accepted. Uses the following abbreviations for credit cards: V = VISA, AE = American Express, MC = MasterCard, D = Discover, CB = Carte Blanche, and DC = Diner's Club International.

- *Parking* Usual entry will be "At campsite" or "On road," though some campgrounds have a central parking lot from which tent campers must carry their gear to their campsite.

**Facilities**    This is a brief data presentation that provides information on the availability of specific facilities and services.

- *Number of RV Sites* Any site where RVs are permitted.

- *Number of Tent-Only Sites* Sites set aside specifically for tent camping, including pop-up tent trailers.

- *Hookups* Possible hookups include electric, water, sewer, cable TV, phone, and Internet connection. Electrical hookups vary from campground to campground. Where electrical hookups are available, the amperage available is stated parenthetically, for example: "Hookups: Electric (20 amps), water."

- *Each Site* List of equipment such as grill, picnic table, lantern pole, fire pit, water faucet, electrical outlet, etc., provided at each campsite.

- *Dump station, laundry, pay phone, restrooms and showers, fuel, propane, RV service, general store, vending, playground* Are these items or services available on site? Their respective fields indicate the answer.

- *Internal Roads* Indicates the road type (gravel, paved, dirt), and condition.

- *Market* Location and distance of closest supermarket or large grocery store.

- *Restaurant* Location and distance of closest restaurant.

- *Other* Boat ramp, dining pavilion, miniature golf, tennis court, lounge, etc.

- *Activities* Activities available at the campground or in the area.

- *Nearby Attractions* Can be natural or manmade.

- *Additional Information* The best sources to call for general information on area activities and attractions. Sources include local or area chambers of commerce, tourist bureaus, visitors and convention authorities, forest service, etc.

**Restrictions**    Any restrictions that apply, including:

- *Pets* Conditions under which pets are allowed or not.

- *Fires* Campground rules for fires and fire safety.

- *Alcoholic Beverages* Campground rules regarding the consumption of alcoholic beverages.

- *Vehicle Maximum Length* Length in feet of the maximum size vehicle the campground can accommodate.

- *Other* Any other rules or restrictions, to include minimum and maximum stays; age or group size restrictions; areas off-limits to vehicular traffic; security constraints such as locking the main gate during the night; etc.

**How to Get There**    Clear and specific directions, including mileage and landmarks, for finding the campground.

## Supplemental Directory of Campgrounds

If you're looking for a campground within the territory covered in this guide and can't find a profiled campground that is close or convenient to your route, check the Supplemental Directory of Campgrounds. This directory of hundreds of additional campgrounds is organized alphabetically by state and city name. Each entry provides the campground's name, address, reservations phone, fax, website, number of sites, average fee per night, and hookups available.

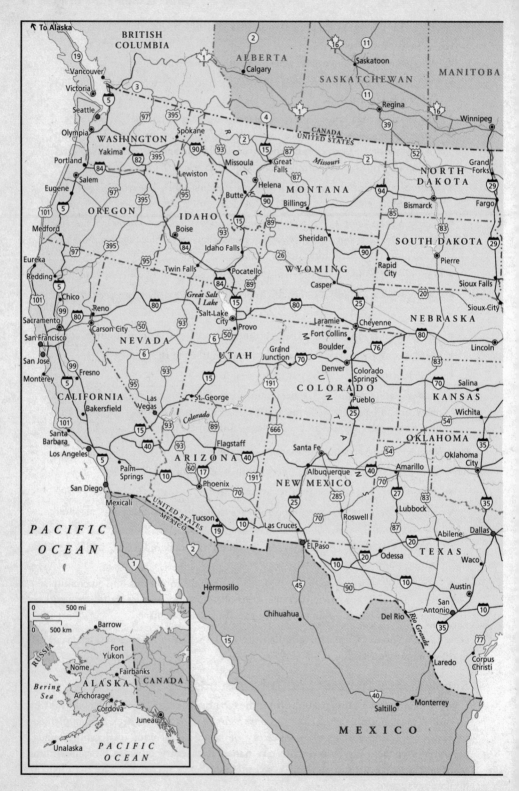

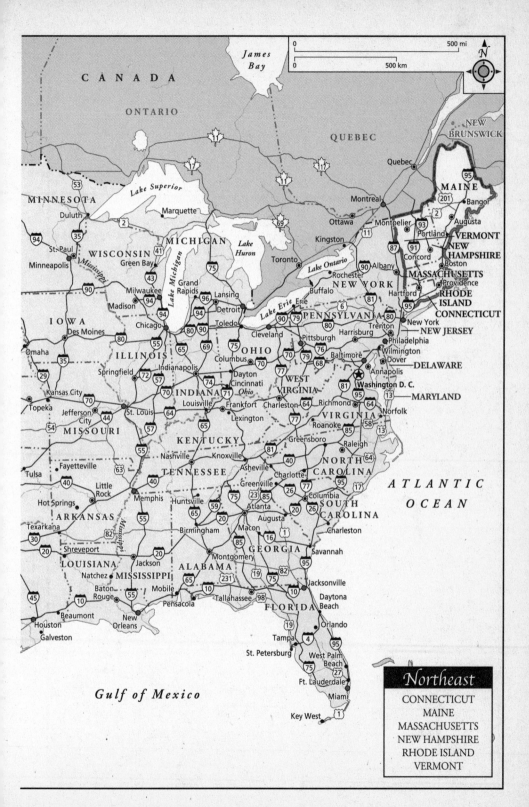

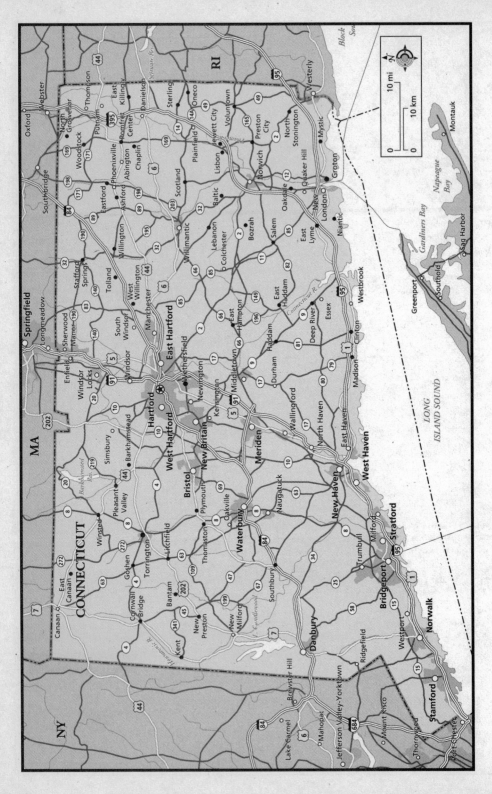

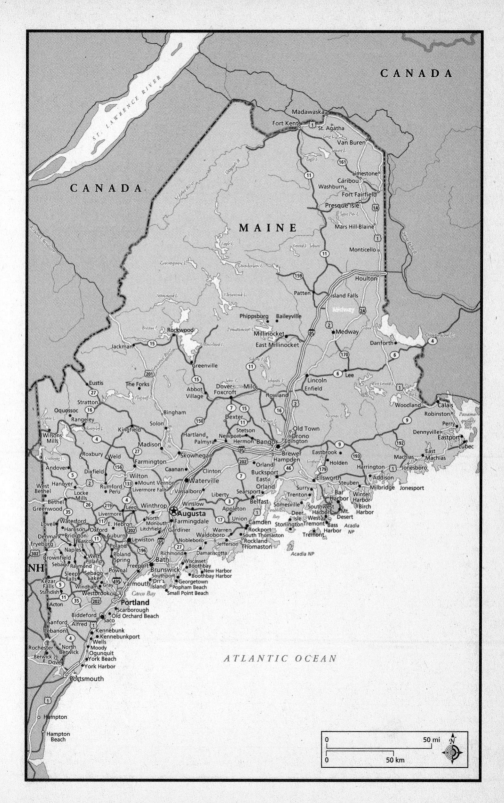

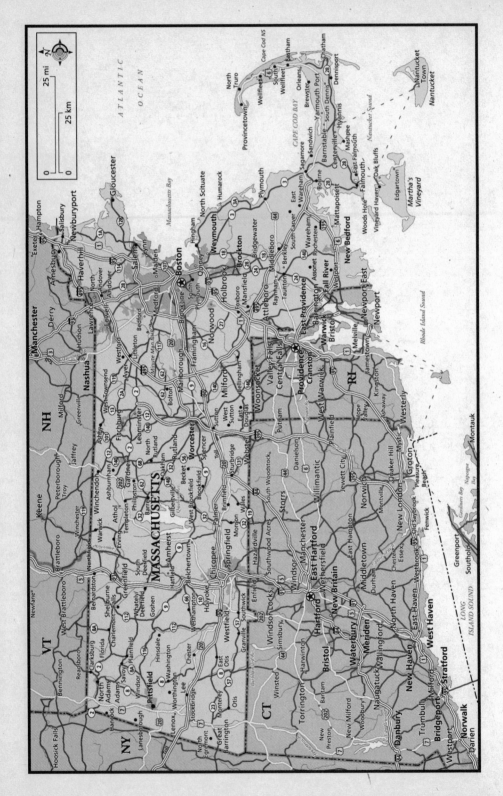

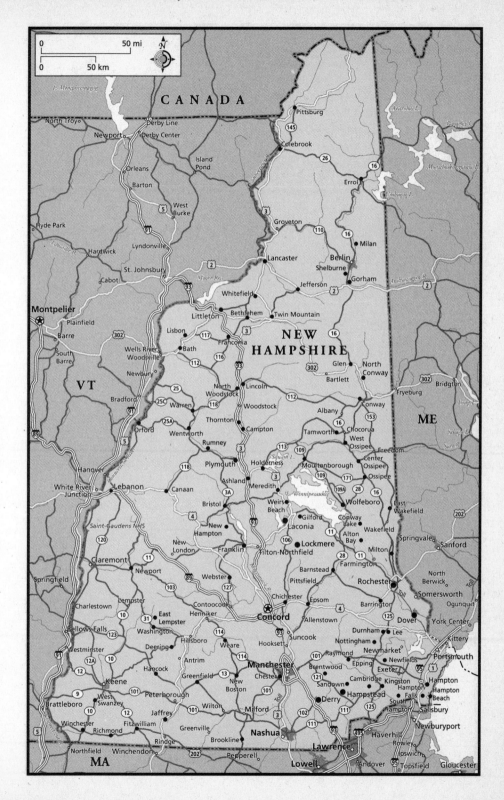

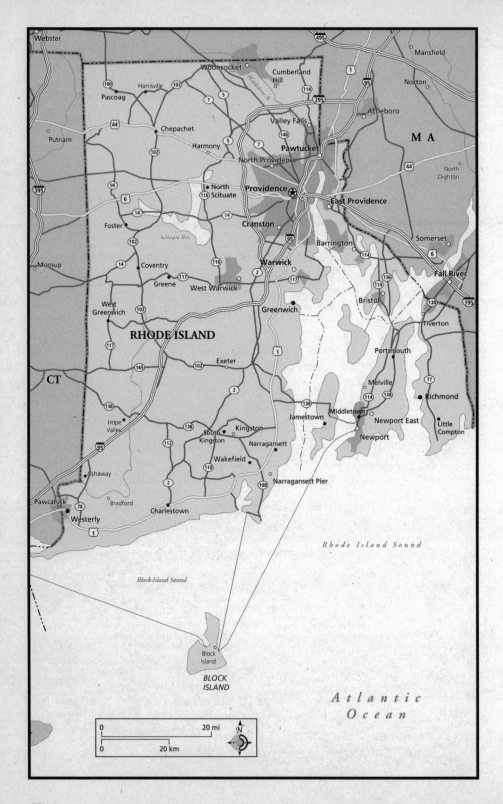

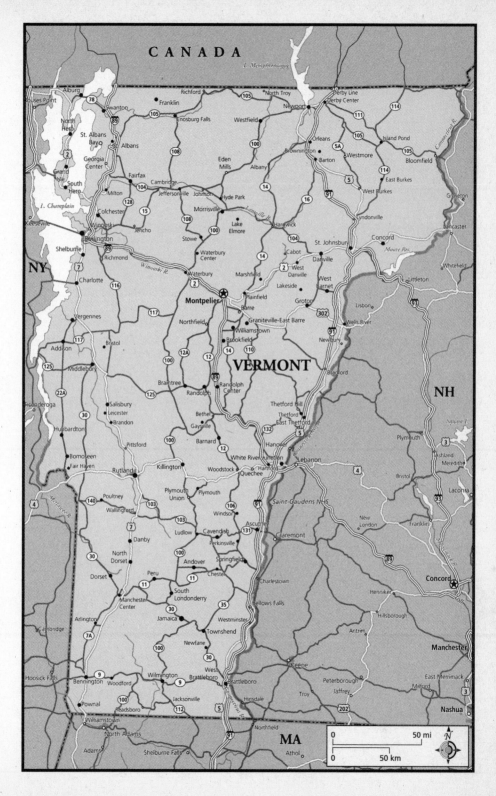

# Campground Awards

## CONNECTICUT

**Most Beautiful Campgrounds**

Highland Campground, Scotland

Island Campground & Cottages, East Lyme

**Most Private Campsites**

Beaver Pines Campground, Woodstock

Countryside Campground, Voluntown

Peppertree Camping, Oakdale

**Most Spacious Campsites**

Aces High RV Park, East Lyme

Lake Williams Campground, Lebanon

Seaport Campgrounds, Mystic

**Quietest Campgrounds**

Countryside Campground, Voluntown

Peppertree Camping, Oakdale

**Most Secure Campgrounds**

Highland Orchards Resort Park, North
Stonington

Seaport Campgrounds, Mystic

**Cleanest Campgrounds**

Countryside Campground, Voluntown

**Best Campground Facilities**

Hemlock Hill Camp Resort, Litchfield

Seaport Campgrounds, Mystic

**Best Rural, Farm, or Ranch Settings**

Island Campground & Cottages, East Lyme

**Best Waterfront Settings**

Countryside Campground, Voluntown

**Most Romantic Campgrounds**

Countryside Campground, Voluntown

Island Campground & Cottages, East Lyme

**Best Family-Oriented Campgrounds**

Beaver Pines Campground, Woodstock

Brialee RV and Tent Park, Ashford

Deer Haven Campground, Lisbon

Hemlock Hill Camp Resort, Litchfield

Hidden Acres Family Campground, Preston

Seaport Campground, Mystic

**Best Swimming Pools**

Charlie Brown Campground, Eastford

## MAINE

**Best RV Camping**

Bar Harbor Campground, Bar Harbor

Barcadia Campground, Bar Harbor

Bayley's, Scarborough

Cathedral Pines, Eustis

Mount Desert Narrows, Bar Harbor

Narrows Too, Trenton

Palmyra Golf and RV Resort, Palmyra

Papoose Pond Resort & Campground, Waterford

Patten Pond Camping Resort, Ellsworth

## MAINE (continued)

Saco/Portland South KOA, Saco
Searsport Shores Camping Resort, Searsport
South Arm Campground, Andover

### Best Tent Camping
Bar Harbor Campground, Bar Harbor
Camden Hills State Park, Camden
Cathedral Pines, Eustis
Katahdin Shadows, Medway
Mount Desert Narrows, Bar Harbor
Mt. Desert Campground, Somesville
Rangeley Lake State Park, Rangeley
Searsport Shores Camping Resort, Searsport
South Arm Campground, Andover

### Most Beautiful Campgrounds
Bar Harbor Campground, Bar Harbor
Camden Hills State Park, Camden
Cathedral Pines Campground, Eustis
Chewonki Campgrounds, Wiscasset
Hermit Island Campground, Small Point
Horseneck Beach State Park, Westport
Katahdin Shadows, Medway
Lily Bay State Park, Greenville
Megunticook Campground by the Sea, Rockport
Mount Desert Narrows, Bar Harbor
Mt. Desert Campground, Somesville
Orr's Island Campground, Orr's Island
Searsport Shores Camping Resort, Searsport
Sebago Lake State Park, Casco
South Arm Campground, Andover
Barcadia, Bar Harbor
Lily Bay State Park, Greenville

### Most Private Campsites
Blackwoods Campground, Acadia National Park
Cathedral Pines, Eustis
Lily Bay State Park, Greenville
Mt. Desert Campground, Somesville
Seawall Campground, Acadia National Park

### Most Spacious Campsites
Blackwoods Campground, Acadia National Park
Cathedral Pines, Eustis
Lily Bay State Park, Greenville
Mt. Desert Campground, Somesville
Orr's Island Campground, Orr's Island
River Run, Brownfield
Seawall Campground, Acadia National Park
Woodland Acres Camp N Canoe, Brownfield

### Quietest Campgrounds
Camden Rockport Camping, Rockport
Orr's Island Campground, Orr's Island
Seawall Campground, Acadia National Park
Whispering Pines, East Orland
Woodland Acres Camp N Canoe, Brownfield

### Most Secure Campgrounds
Acres of Wildlife, Steep Falls
Bayley's, Scarborough
Beaver Brook Campground, North Monmouth
Blackwoods Campground, Acadia National Park
Camden Hills State Park, Camden
Family and Friends Campground, Standish
Four Seasons Family Camping, Naples
Hid 'n Pines, Old Orchard Beach
Honey Run Beach & Campground, Peru
Kezar Lake Camping Area, Lovell
Kokatosi Campground, Raymond
Lake Pemaquid Camping, Damariscotta
Little Ponderosa Campground, Boothbay
Old Orchard Beach Campground, Old Orchard
  Beach
Orr's Island Campground, Orr's Island
Point Sebago Golf and Beach Resort, Casco
Powder Horn Family Camping Resort, Old
  Orchard Beach
Rangeley Lake State Park, Rangeley
River Run, Brownfield
Saco/Portland South KOA, Saco
Sea-Vu Campground, Wells
Seawall Campground, Acadia National Park
Shady Oaks, Orland
Shore Hills Campground, Boothbay Harbor
Silver Springs, Saco
Thomas Point Beach , Brunswick

### Cleanest Campgrounds
Camden Hills State Park, Camden
Camden Rockport Camping, Rockport
Honey Run Beach & Campground, Peru
Libby's Oceanside Camp, York Harbor
Meadowbrook Camping, Phippsburg
Megunticook Campground by the Sea, Rockport
Mount Desert Narrows, Bar Harbor
Mt. Desert Campground, Somesville
Narrows Too, Trenton
Palmyra Golf and RV Resort, Palmyra
Patten Pond Camping Resort, Ellsworth
Point Sebago Golf and Beach Resort, Casco

## MAINE (continued)

Poland Spring Campground, Poland Spring
Powder Horn Family Camping Resort, Old Orchard Beach
Saco/Portland South KOA, Saco
Saltwater Farm Campground, Thomaston
Searsport Shores Camping Resort, Searsport
Sennebec Lake Campground, Appleton
Skowhegan/Canaan KOA, Canaan
Thomas Point Beach, Brunswick

### Best Campground Facilities
Bayley's, Scarborough
Megunticook Campground by the Sea, Rockport
Mount Desert Narrows, Bar Harbor
Narrows Too, Trenton
Palmyra Golf and RV Resort, Palmyra
Patten Pond Camping Resort, Ellsworth
Point Sebago Golf and Beach Resort, Casco
Powder Horn Family Camping Resort, Old Orchard Beach
Searsport Shores Camping Resort, Searsport
Thomas Point Beach, Brunswick

### Best Rural, Farm, or Ranch Settings
Balsam Woods Campground, Abbott Village

### Best Urban and Suburban Settings
Paul Bunyan Campground, Bangor
Pleasant Hill Campground, Hermon
Wassamki Springs, Scarborough

### Best Mountain Settings
Katahdin Shadows, Medway
Lily Bay State Park, Greenville
Mount Blue State Park, Weld
Natanis Point Campground, Eustis

### Most Romantic Campgrounds
Bar Harbor Campground, Bar Harbor
Lily Bay State Park, Greenville
Searsport Shores, Searsport
South Arm Campground, Andover

### Best Family-Oriented Campgrounds
Acres of Wildlife, Steep Falls
Bayley's, Old Orchard Beach
Lake Pemaquid Camping, Damariscotta
Mount Desert Narrows, Bar Harbor
Narrow Too, Trenton
Papoose Pond Resort and Campground, Waterford
Point Sebago, Casco
Powder Horn, Old Orchard Beach
Wild Acres, Old Orchard Beach

### Best Swimming Pools
Bar Harbor Campground, Bar Harbor
Megunticook Campground by the Sea, Rockport

## MASSACHUSETTS

### Best RV Camping
Normandy Farms Family Camping Resort, Foxboro
Pine Acres Family Camping Resort, Oakham
Pinewood Lodge, Plymouth
Salisbury Beach State Reservation, Salisbury

### Best Tent Camping
Clarksburg State Park, Clarksburg
Pine Acres Family Camping Resort, Oakham
Pinewood Lodge, Plymouth
Shawme-Crowell State Forest, Sandwich
Wells State Park, Sturbridge

### Most Beautiful Campgrounds
Boston Northwest/Minuteman KOA, Littleton
Cape Ann Camp Site, Gloucester
Clarksburg State Park, Clarksburg

Myles Standish State Forest, South Carver
Nickerson State Park, Brewster
Normandy Farms Family Camping Resort, Foxboro
Pine Acres Family Camping Resort, Oakham
Pittsfield State Forest, Pittsfield
Salisbury Beach State Reservation, Salisbury
Shawme-Crowell State Forest, Sandwich
Wells State Park, Sturbridge

### Most Private Campsites
Shawme-Crowell State Forest, Sandwich
Wompatuck State Park, Hingham

### Most Spacious Campsites
Peppermint Park Camping Resort, Plainfield
Shady Pines Campground, Savoy

## MASSACHUSETTS (continued)

### Quietest Campgrounds
Harold Parker State Forest, North Andover
Lake Dennison State Recreation Area,
  Winchendon
Myles Standish State Forest, South Carver
Normandy Farms Family Camping Resort,
  Foxboro
Peppermint Park Camping Resort, Plainfield
Prospect Mountain Campground, Granville
Shady Acres Family Campground, South Carver
Shawme-Crowell State Forest, Sandwich
Wells State Park, Sturbridge

### Most Secure Campgrounds
Boston South/Middleboro/Plymouth KOA,
  Middleboro
Campers Haven RV Resort, Dennisport
Canoe River Campgrounds, Mansfield
Cape Cod Campresort, East Falmouth
Circle CG Farm, Bellingham
Ellis Haven Camping Resort, Plymouth
Jellystone Park Sturbridge, Sturbridge
Outdoor World—Gateway to Cape Cod,
  Rochester
Peppermint Park Camping Resort, Plainfield
Peters Pond Park Family Camping, Sandwich
Pine Acres Family Camping Resort, Oakham
Rusnik Campground, Salisbury
Scusset Beach State Reservation Camping Area,
  Sagamore
Shady Pines Campground, Savoy
Shawme-Crowell State Forest, Sandwich
Sippewissett Campground and Cabins, Falmouth
Sodom Mountain Campground, Southwick
Sunsetview Farm Camping Area, Monson

### Cleanest Campgrounds
Bay View Campgrounds, Bourne
Boston Northwest/Minuteman KOA, Littleton

Circle CG Farm, Bellingham
Ellis Haven Camping Resort, Plymouth
Maurice's Campground, Welfleet
Otter River State Forest, Templeton
Outdoor World Sturbridge Resort, Sturbridge
Pine Acres Family Camping Resort, Oakham
Pinewood Lodge, Plymouth

### Best Campground Facilities
Bay View Campgrounds, Bourne
Jellystone Park Sturbridge, Sturbridge
Normandy Farms Family Camping Resort,
  Foxboro
Outdoor World Sturbridge Resort,
  Sturbridge
Outdoor World—Gateway to Cape Cod,
  Rochester
Pine Acres Family Camping Resort, Oakham

### Best Rural, Farm, or Ranch Settings
Circle Campground Farm, Bellingham

### Best Urban and Suburban Settings
Boston Northwest KOA Minuteman
  Kampground, Littleton
Harold Parker State Forest, North Andover
Pinewood Lodge, Plymouth
Winter Island Park, Salem
Wompatuck State Park, Hingham

### Best Family-Oriented Campgrounds
Pine Acres, Oakham
Pinewood Lodge, Plymouth
Sweetwater Forest, Brewster

### Best Swimming Pools
Jellystone Park Sturbridge, Sturbridge
Normandy Farms Campground, Foxboro
Outdoor World Sturbridge Resort,
  Sturbridge

## NEW HAMPSHIRE

### Best RV Camping
Circle 9 Ranch, Epsom
Cold Springs Camp Resort, Weare
Friendly Beaver Campground, New Boston
Glen Ellis Family Campground, Glen
Mi-Te-Jo Campground, Milton
Moose Hillock Campground, Warren
Pine Acres, Raymond

### Best Tent Camping
Beech Hill Campground, Twin Mountain
Glen Ellis Family Campground, Glen
Greenfield State Park Campground, Greenfield
Lafayette Campground, Franconia
Lost River Valley Campground, North Woodstock
Mi-Te-Jo Campground, Milton
Moose Hillock Campground, Warren

## NEW HAMPSHIRE (continued)

Pawtuckaway State Park, Nottingham
Swain Brook Campground, Wentworth
White Lake State Park, Tamworth

### Most Beautiful Campgrounds

Glen Ellis Family Campground, Glen
Lost, River, North Woodstock
Mi-Te-Jo Campground, Milton
Swain Brook Campground, Wentworth
Umbagog Lake Campground, Cambridge
White Lake State Park, Tamworth
Swain Brook Campground, Wentworth

### Most Private Campsites

Beech Hill Campground, Twin Mountain
Lost River Valley Campground, North Woodstock
Moose Hillock Campground, Warren
Passaconaway Campground, Bartlett

### Most Spacious Campsites

Beech Hill Campground, Twin Mountain
Glen Ellis Family Campground, Glen
Lost River Valley Campground, North Woodstock
Moose Hillock Campground, Warren

### Quietest Campgrounds

Living Water Campground, Twin Mountain

### Most Secure Campgrounds

Ayers Lake Farm, Barrington
Barrington Shores, Barrington
Chocorua Camping Village, West Ossipee
Circle 9 Ranch, Epsom
Clearwater Campground, Meredith
Cold Springs Camp Resort, Weare
Ellacoya State Beach and RV Park, Gilford
Exeter Elms, Exeter
Glen Ellis Family Campground, Glen
Harbor Hill, Meredith
Hillcrest Campground, Chichester
Living Water Campground, Twin Mountain
Loon Lake, Newport
Lost River Valley Campground, North Woodstock
Meredith Woods, Meredith
Mi-Te-Jo Campground, Milton
Oxbow Campground, Deering
Roger's Family Camping Resort and Motel, Lancaster
Saco River Camping, North Conway
Tamworth Camping Area, Tamworth
Tidewater Campground, Hampton

Timberland, Gorham
Tuxbury Pond Camping Area, South Hampton
Twin Tamarack, New Hampton
Westward Shores, Ossipee
White Lake State Park, Tamworth

### Cleanest Campgrounds

Circle 9 Ranch, Epsom
Cold Springs Camp Resort, Weare
Friendly Beaver Campground, New Boston
Glen Ellis Family Campground, Glen
Hillcrest Campground, Chichester
Lantern Motor Inn and Campground Resort, Jefferson
Littleton/Lisbon KOA, Lisbon
Living Water Campground, Twin Mountain
Lost River Valley Campground, North Woodstock
Mi-Te-Jo Campground, Milton
Twin Mountain KOA, Twin Mountain

### Best Campground Facilities

Chocorua Camping Village, West Ossipee
Circle 9 Ranch, Epsom
Cold Springs Camp Resort, Weare
Friendly Beaver Campground, New Boston
Glen Ellis Family Campground, Glen
Gunstock Campground, Laconia
Hillcrest Campground, Chichester
Lantern Motor Inn and Campground Resort, Jefferson
Meredith Woods, Meredith
Mi-Te-Jo Campground, Milton
Moose Hillock Campground, Warren
Pine Acres, Raymond
Roger's Family Camping Resort and Motel, Lancaster
Tuxbury Pond Camping Area, South Hampton
Yogi Bear's Jellystone Park, Ashland

### Best Rural, Farm, or Ranch Settings

3 Ponds, Raymond
Ames Brook, Ashland
Ayers Lake Farm, Barrington
Ferndale Acres, Lee

### Best Urban and Suburban Settings

Circle 9 Campground, Epsom
Epsom Valley, Epsom
Hillcrest Campground, Chichester
Pine Acres, Raymond

## NEW HAMPSHIRE (continued)

### Best Mountain Settings
Beech Hill, Twin Mountain

Cannon Mountain RV Park, Franconia Notch
State Park

Crazy Horse, Littleton

Gunstock Campground, Laconia

Lafayette Campground, Franconia Notch
State Park

Lantern Motor Inn and Campground Resort,
Jefferson

Living Waters Campground, Twin Mountain

Rogers Family Camping Resort, Lancaster

Tarry Ho Campground, Twin Mountain

Timberland Campground, Gorham

Twin Mountain KOA, Twin Mountain

Twin Mountain Motor Court and RV Park,
Twin Mountain

White Lake State Park, Tamworth

### Most Romantic Campgrounds
Glen Ellis, Glen

Lost River, North Woodstock

Umbagog Lake Campground, Cambridge

### Best Family-Oriented Campgrounds
Chocurua Camping Village, West Ossipee

Cold Springs, North Woodstock

Friendly Beaver, New Boston

Glen Ellis, Glen

Gunstock, Laconia

Lantern Motor Inn & Resort, Jefferson

Mi-Te-Jo, Milton

Moose Hillock, Warren

Pine Acres, Raymond

Tuxbury Pond Camping Area, South Hampton

Yogi Bear's Jellystone, Ashland

### Best Swimming Pools
Cold Springs Camp Resort, Weare

Friendly Beaver, New Boston

Moose Hillock, Warren

Pine Acres, Raymond

## RHODE ISLAND

### Best RV Camping
Card's Camps, Wakefield

Hickory Ridge Family Campground, Greene

Timber Creek RV Resort, Westerly

### Best Tent Camping
George Washington Management Area,
Chepachet

### Most Beautiful Campgrounds
George Washington Management Area,
Chepachet

Oak Embers Campground, West Greenwich

Peeper Pond Campground, Exeter

Whispering Pines Family Campground, Hope
Valley

### Most Private Campsites
Peeper Pond Campground, Exeter

Whippoorwill Hill Family Campground,
Foster

### Most Spacious Campsites
George Washington Management Area,
Chepachet

Peeper Pond Campground, Exeter

### Quietest Campgrounds
Legrand G. Reynolds Horsemen's Camping Area,
Hope Valley

### Cleanest Campgrounds
Legrand G. Reynolds Horsemen's Camping Area,
Hope Valley

### Best Campground Facilities
Timber Creek RV Resort, Westerly

### Best Urban and Suburban Settings
Legrand G. Reynolds Horsemen's Camping Area,
Hope Valley

### Most Romantic Campgrounds
Legrand G. Reynolds Horsemen's Camping Area,
Hope Valley

### Best Family-Oriented Campgrounds
Card's Camp, Wakefield

Wawaloam Campground, Richmond

Timber Creek RV Resort, Westerly

### Best Swimming Pools
Timber Creek RV Resort, Westerly

Wawaloam Campground, Richmond

## VERMONT

### Best Tent Camping
Gifford Woods State Park, Killington
Green Mountain National Forest Campgrounds, Rutland
Kettle Pond State Park, Marshfield
Knight Island State Park, St. Albans Bay
Mount Moosalamoo Campground, Middlebury

### Most Beautiful Campgrounds
Belview Campground, Barton
Brighton State Park, Island Pond
Burton Island State Park, St. Albans Bay
Camp Skyland on Lake Champlain, South Hero
Elmore State Park, Lake Elmore
Gifford Woods State Park, Killington
Green Mountain National Forest Campgrounds, Rutland
Half Moon Pond State Park, Fair Haven
Kettle Pond State Park, Marshfield
Kings Bay Campground, North Hero
Knight Island State Park, St. Albans Bay
Mount Moosalamoo Campground, Middlebury
Mountain View Campground & Cabins, Morrisville
Sugar Ridge RV Village & Campground, Danville

### Most Private Campsites
Half Moon Pond State Park, Fair Haven
Kettle Pond State Park, Marshfield
Knight Island State Park, St. Albans Bay
Mount Moosalamoo Campground, Middlebury

### Most Spacious Campsites
Falls of Lana, Middlebury
Goose Point, Alburg
Green Mountain National Forest Campgrounds, Rutland
Kettle Pond State Park, Marshfield
Mount Moosalamoo Campground, Middlebury

### Quietest Campgrounds
Burton Island State Park, St. Albans Bay
Champlain Adult Campground, Grand Isle
Falls of Lana, Middlebury
Green Mountain National Forest Campgrounds, Rutland
Kettle Pond State Park, Marshfield
Knight Island State Park, St. Albans Bay
Mount Moosalamoo Campground, Middlebury

### Most Secure Campgrounds
Half Moon Pond State Park, Fair Haven

### Cleanest Campgrounds
Brighton State Park, Island Pond
Covenant Hills Christian Camp, Marshfield
Half Moon Pond State Park, Fair Haven
Mount Moosalamoo Campground, Middlebury

### Best Campground Facilities
Mountain View Campground & Cabins, Morrisville

### Best Rural, Farm, or Ranch Settings
Brighton State Park, Island Pond
Kettle Pond State Park, Marshfield

### Best Urban and Suburban Settings
Brewster River Campground, Jeffersonville
Burlington's North Beach Campground, Burlington
Fireside Campground, Derby
Lone Pine Campsites, Colchester

### Best Mountain Settings
Camp Skyland on Lake Champlain, South Hero
Mountain View Campground & Cabins, Morrisville

### Best Waterfront Settings
Alburg RV Resort, Alburg
Belview Campground, Barton
Gold Brook Campground, Stowe
Knight Island State Park, St. Albans Bay
Lakeside Camping, Island Pond
Mill Pond Campground, Franklin

### Most Romantic Campgrounds
Burton Island State Park, St. Albans Bay
Camp Skyland on Lake Champlain, South Hero
Champlain Adult Campground, Grand Isle
Kettle Pond State Park, Marshfield

### Best Family-Oriented Campgrounds
Apple Tree Bay Campground, South Hero
Hide-A-Way Cove Family Campground, East Killingly
Lone Pine Campsites, Colchester
Sugar Ridge RV Village & Campground, Danville

### Best Swimming Pools
Sugar Ridge RV Village & Campground, Danville

# Connecticut

A small state with a surprising variety of terrain, Connecticut offers an impressive array of camping options. Though even the most remote parts of the state aren't far from civilization (or a mall), campgrounds range from isolated to right in the middle of a town. There's almost no type of camping that you can't find here, and if you're looking for variety, you could easily spend one day at a rural site, another near the ocean, and the next one by a small mountain.

Since it takes at most three hours to drive across Connecticut, you're never that far from anything. Of course, the big attraction for most people are the **Foxwoods** and **Mohegan Sun** casinos. These gigantic Native American–run facilities are accessible from nearly anywhere in the state and are close to numerous campgrounds.

The other big attraction in Connecticut is the town of **Mystic** with its aquarium, seaport, and numerous quaint attractions. There's also an uncountable number of towns with lively downtowns full of little shops, restaurants, and attractions. Much of the state is traditional New England, where the center of town is still the center of activity.

In addition to the varying terrain of the state's campgrounds, its cities and towns tend to vary quite a bit within a small distance. Take the capital of **Hartford** as an example—you have a city with most of the amenities of its bigger counterparts that's also a five-minute ride from open space. And if you go in different directions you get a wide choice of towns that cater to different needs. Some offer gourmet dining and theater while others have great pizza places, movie theaters, and bowling alleys.

For campers, the main appeal of Connecticut has to be that it's easy to do anything from anywhere in this state, but there's enough to do to keep you busy for a while. In general, if you're looking for rustic, you'll want to stay away from the southern parts of the state, and there might be less to do outside your campground in the west. But, with the small size and many highways, you're never more than half-hour ride from pretty much anything.

## ASHFORD

### Brialee RV and Tent Park

174 Laurel Ln., P.O. Box 125, Ashford 06278. T: (800) 303-CAMP; F: (860) 429-5930; www.briar lee.net;brialee@gocampingamerica.com.

🚐 ★★★★                    ▲ ★★

Beauty: ★★★★              Site Privacy: ★★★★
Spaciousness: ★★★★        Quiet: ★★★★
Security: ★★★★            Cleanliness: ★★★★
Insect Control: ★★★       Facilities: ★★★★

A very active seasonal community, Brialee focuses most of its energy on pleasing seasonal guests and their RVs. Tent campers can still find a good site here, but they are definitely in the minority. With state forests all around and large, private sites, the scenery is definitely pleasant. There are also stone walls around the campground, a sparklingly clean lake, and a water fountain.

#### BASICS

**Operated By:** Brian, Addie, & Ed Specyalski. **Open:** Apr. 1–Dec. 1. **Site Assignment:** Reservations recommended. **Registration:** At office. **Fee:** $55 for 2 nights; 1-week min. stay in season, 2 nights otherwise. **Parking:** At site.

#### FACILITIES

**Number of RV Sites:** 180. **Number of Tent-Only Sites:** 0. **Hookups:** Electric (30 amps), sewer, cable TV. **Each Site:** Fire pit, picnic table. **Dump Station:** Yes. **Laundry:** Yes. **Pay Phone:** Yes. **Rest Rooms and Showers:** Yes. **Fuel:** No. **Propane:** Yes. **Internal Roads:** Paved. **RV Service:** No. **Market:** Bubba T's **General Store:** 259 Ference Rd., Ashford, CT (4.4 mi.). Take a left onto Rte. 89 & follow for 4.4 mi. **Restaurant:** Snack bar, Midway Restaurant & Pizza, 174 Ashford Center Rd., Ashford, CT (4.1 mi.). Take a right onto Rte. 89 followed by a left onto Rte. 44. **General Store:** Yes. **Vending:** Yes. **Swimming Pool:** Yes, heated. **Playground:** Yes. **Other:** Beach, pond, stocked fishing, arcade, walking trails. **Activities:** Band or DJ on Saturday nights, bingo. **Nearby Attractions:** Great Natchaug Forest, Sturbridge Village. **Additional Information:** Northeast Connecticut Visitors District,

(860) 779-6383 or (888) 628-1228, www.ctquietcorner.org.

#### RESTRICTIONS

**Pets:** On leash only. **Fires:** Allowed. **Alcoholic Beverages:** Allowed. **Vehicle Maximum Length:** 40 ft. **Other:** No smoking.

#### TO GET THERE

Take 84 east to Exit 69 and follow Rte. 74 east for 6 mi. to Rte. 44. Take a left onto Rte. 44 east and follow for 1 mi. At the junction of Rtes. 89 and 44 take a left onto Rte. 89 north, then take the first left onto Perry Hill Rd. and the second right onto Laurel Ln., which leads to Briarlee.

## BARKHAMSTEAD

### White Pines Campsites

232 Old North Rd., Barkhamstead 06063. T: (800) 622-6614; www.whitepinescamp.com; campwp@whitepinescamp.com.

🚐 ★★★★                    ▲ ★★★

Beauty: ★★              Site Privacy: ★★
Spaciousness: ★★★       Quiet: ★★
Security: ★★★★          Cleanliness: ★★★
Insect Control: ★★★     Facilities: ★★★★

With tons of activities and planned events, this is not the campground for quiet contemplation or for people who want to keep to themselves. A visit to White Pines is definitely for those who want an active vacation but don't want to do much themselves. However, despite the summer-camp feel, you'll find fishing and other outdoor activities, which makes White Pines a nice compromise between the resort campgrounds and those that offer a decidedly rustic experience.

#### BASICS

**Operated By:** Owners Peter Lawrence & Pete Finkel. **Open:** Mid-Apr.–mid-Oct. **Site Assignment:** Reservations. **Registration:** At office. **Fee:** $25–$32. **Parking:** At site.

#### FACILITIES

**Number of RV Sites:** 200. **Number of Tent-Only Sites:** 9. **Hookups:** Electric (30 amps), cable TV. **Each Site:** Water, electric. **Dump Station:** Yes. **Laundry:** No. **Pay Phone:** Yes. **Rest Rooms and Showers:** Yes. **Fuel:** No. **Propane:** Yes. **Internal Roads:** Stone. **RV Service:** No, but on-site handyman can do some repairs. **Market:** Pleasant Valley. **General Store:** Take a right on CT-101 & follow for 0.4 mi. **Restaurant:** Sophie's Pizza Restaurant, 200 New Hartford, Rd., Winsted, CT. Take a right on CT-181 & follow until it becomes CT-318. Stay straight on CT-318 until CT-44. Take a right on CT-44 & follow for 1.4 mi. **General Store:** Yes. **Vending:** Yes. **Swimming Pool:** Yes. **Playground:** Yes. **Other:** Paddle boat rentals. **Activities:** Every weekend has a theme & special activities, such as the mid-Aug. Las Vegas weekend & the early Sep. Mexican fiesta. **Nearby Attractions:** Fishing & tubing. **Additional Information:** Litchfield Hills Visitors Bureau, (860) 567-4506, www.litchfield hills.com.

## RESTRICTIONS

**Pets:** Yes. **Fires:** Allowed. **Alcoholic Beverages:** Allowed. **Vehicle Maximum Length:** None. **Other:** No bicycles after dark, keep only two fish per day.

## TO GET THERE

Take US 44 Old North Rd.

## BOZRAH

### Acorn Acres

135 Lake Rd., Bozrah 06334. T: (860) 859-1020; F: (609) 886-8228; www.acorncampground.com.

| 🚐 ★★★★ | ⛺ ★★ |
|---|---|
| Beauty: ★★★★ | Site Privacy: ★★★★ |
| Spaciousness: ★★★★ | Quiet: ★★★★ |
| Security: ★★★★ | Cleanliness: ★★★★ |
| Insect Control: ★★★ | Facilities: ★★★★ |

Tucked into a hill, this campground offers large sites. Though its literature claims it's a quiet spot, the sometimes large number of kids means that's not the case during the day. At night things settle down, but Acorn Acres is definitely more of a family place than a secluded spot for grown-ups. The campground caters to RVs, although the sites along the river make a nice place to pitch your tent.

## BASICS

**Operated By:** Private operator. **Open:** May 1–Columbus Day. **Site Assignment:** Reservations required. **Registration:** Office. **Fee:** $27–$33. **Parking:** At site.

## FACILITIES

**Number of RV Sites:** 200. **Number of Tent-Only Sites:** 0. **Hookups:** Water, electric (50 amps), phone, cable TV. **Each Site:** Picnic table, stone fireplace. **Dump Station:** Yes. **Laundry:** Yes. **Pay Phone:** Yes. **Rest Rooms and Showers:** Yes. **Fuel:** No. **Propane:** Yes. **Internal Roads:** Paved. **RV Service:** No. **Market:** Main's Country Store Inc., 318 Fitchville Rd., Bozrah, CT (5.5 mi.). Turn left onto Lake Rd., followed by a left onto Rte. 136, then a left onto Haughton Rd. & a left onto Fitchville Rd. **Restaurant:** Exit 23 Restaurant, 318 Fitchville Rd., Bozrah, CT (5.5 mi.). Follow above directions. **General Store:** Yes. **Vending:** No. **Swimming Pool:** Yes. **Playground:** No. **Other:** Swimming & fishing pond, trout stream, rec hall. **Activities:** Organized sports. **Nearby Attractions:** Gardner Lake. **Additional Information:** Southeastern Connecticut Tourism District, (860) 444-2206 or (800) TO-ENJOY, www.mysticmore.com.

## RESTRICTIONS

**Pets:** Yes. **Fires:** Allowed. **Alcoholic Beverages:** Allowed. **Vehicle Maximum Length:** 40 ft. **Other:** No cutting live trees.

## TO GET THERE

Take Rte. 2 east to Exit 22 and make a right at the end of the ramp. Go 2 mi. and make a left at the "T", take the next right and go down the second hill on your left to the campground.

## CLINTON

### Nickerson Park

Rte. 198, Chaplin 06235. T: (860) 455-0007; www.nickersonpark.com.

🚐 ★★★              ⛺ ★★★

Beauty: ★★                  Site Privacy: ★★
Spaciousness: ★★            Quiet: ★★
Security: ★★★               Cleanliness: ★★★★
Insect Control: ★★★         Facilities: ★★

Though the campground is nothing special, it makes an excellent home base for hunting in the Nautchag State Forest (in season, of course). The forest also offers great cross-country skiing trails for winter visitors. Since the campground is open year-round, those who don't hunt may want to try an off-season visit. Campsites are wooded and fairly private but aren't very big and could be farther apart. Note: When making a reservation here, be sure not to confuse it with a similarly named campground in Massachusetts.

### BASICS

**Operated By:** The Nickerson family. **Open:** All year. **Site Assignment:** Reservations recommended; required during holiday weekends. **Registration:** At office. **Fee:** $45–$50; 3-day min. stay. **Parking:** At site.

### FACILITIES

**Number of RV Sites:** 80. **Number of Tent-Only Sites:** 32. **Hookups:** Water, electric, sewer, cable TV, phone. **Each Site:** Fire ring, picnic table. **Dump Station:** Yes. **Laundry:** Yes. **Pay Phone:** Yes. **Rest Rooms and Showers:** Yes. **Fuel:** No. **Propane:** Yes. **Internal Roads:** Paved. **RV Service:** Yes. **Market:** Ted's Mini Market, 315 Boston Post Rd., North Windham, CT (5.5 mi.). Go south on Rte. 198 towards Pumpkin Hill Rd. by turning right, then take a slight right onto Rte. 6. Rte. 6 becomes N. Windham Rd. & then becomes Boston Post Rd. **Restaurant:** Chaplin Pizza, 52 Willimantic Rd. Chaplin, CT. Follow above directions to Willimantic Rd. **General Store:** No. **Vending:** Yes. **Swimming Pool:** No. **Playground:** No. **Other:** Rec hall. **Activities:** Trout fishing, swimming, river tubing, hiking, mountain biking, wildlife, scheduled events during peak season, hunting in season. **Nearby Attractions:** Natchaug State Forest. **Additional Information:** Connecticut River Valley & Shoreline Visitors Council, (860) 347-0028 or (800) 486-3346, www.visitctrivershore.org.

### RESTRICTIONS

**Pets:** Yes. **Fires:** Allowed. **Alcoholic Beverages:** Allowed. **Vehicle Maximum Length:** Sites vary, check ahead. **Other:** Check w/ park regarding firearms.

### TO GET THERE

Take 84 to Exit 59. Follow Rte. 384 onto Rte. 6 toward Providence and Willimantic. Take Rte. 6 east to the junction of Rte. 198 and take 198 north for 4.5 mi.

## EAST CANAAN

### Lone Oak Campsites

360 Norfolk Rd., East Canaan 06024. T: (800) 422-2267; F: (860) 422-2267; www.loneoakcampsites .com; loneoakinc@aol.com.

🚐 ★★★★              ⛺ ★★

Beauty: ★                   Site Privacy: ★★
Spaciousness: ★★            Quiet: ★★
Security: ★★★               Cleanliness: ★★
Insect Control: ★★          Facilities: ★★★★

More of a summer resort that happens to have camping and RV facilities, Lone Oak targets families looking for a camping experience without too much "roughing it." Like a summer camp for families, the campground has a daily schedule of activities that inlcude arts and crafts, ping-pong, various sports, and more conducted by the staff. For adults, there's the Hayloft Lounge, which has a full bar and a dance floor. All of these amenities make Lone Oak a good place for a family vacation but not the place for a real outdoors experience. For those who don't even want to brave the elements, Lone Oak also rents cabins and trailers.

### BASICS

**Operated By:** The Brown family. **Open:** Apr. 15–Oct. 15. **Site Assignment:** Reservations accepted; otherwise first come, first served. **Registration:** At office. **Fee:** $19–$35; V, MC, D; 2-night min. stay June, July, & Aug.; 3-night min. stay Columbus Day weekend. **Parking:** At site.

## FACILITIES

**Number of RV Sites:** 70. **Number of Tent-Only Sites:** 430. **Hookups:** Water, electric (30 amps), sewer, cable TV. **Each Site:** Picnic table, fire ring. **Dump Station:** Yes. **Laundry:** Yes. **Pay Phone:** Yes. **Rest Rooms and Showers:** Yes. **Fuel:** No. **Propane:** Yes. **Internal Roads:** Gravel. **RV Service:** No. **Market:** Stop & Shop Supermarket, Rte. 44 & East Main St., Canaan, 1.3 mi. away. **Restaurant:** The Chipmunk Deli is located on the premises. The Collins Diner is found at Rte. 7 & 44, Canaan, 1.3 mi. away. **General Store:** Yes. **Vending:** No. **Swimming Pool:** Yes. **Playground:** Yes. **Other:** Volleyball court, softball field, rec hall w/ planned activities (bingo, movies, card games). **Activities:** Fishing in the state stocked Blackberry River, which runs through the property, special events (like 50s/60s Weekend & the Country Music Double Header) nearly every weekend during the summer. **Nearby Attractions:** Appalachian Trail, Lime Rock Race Park, Norman Rockwel Museum, golf courses, Tanglewood canoe & tube rentals. **Additional Information:** Litchfield Hills Visitors Bureau, (860) 567-4506, www.litchfieldhills.com.

## RESTRICTIONS

**Pets:** Yes. **Fires:** Allowed in specified area. **Alcoholic Beverages:** At site, sold in recreation areas. **Vehicle Maximum Length:** None. **Other:** Partial handicap access.

## TO GET THERE

Lone Oak is off of route 44 and is clearly visible from that road. From Hartford the trip takes approximately 1 hour. From Springfield and Boston take the Mass Pike to Exit 2 (Lee). Follow Rt. 102 to Stockbridge. Take Rt. 7 South (at the Red Lion Inn). Follow Rt. 7 to the center of Canaan. At the junction of Rt. 7 and Rt. 44 take a left (heading east on 44). Lone Oak is 4 mi. on the right.

## EAST HADDAM
### Wolf's Den Family Campground

256 Town St., East Haddam 06423. T: (860) 873-9681; F: (860) 873-1248; wolfsdencampground.com; information@wolfsdencampground.com.

🚐 ★★★★                           ▲ ★★★

Beauty: ★★★                Site Privacy: ★★★
Spaciousness: ★★          Quiet: ★★★
Security: ★★★★            Cleanliness: ★★★★
Insect Control: ★★★★      Facilities: ★★★★

A popular campground due to its many on-site family acitivities, Wolf's Den never has a dull moment, which makes it a good place for kids. Because it's located in an area with plenty to do, Wolf's Den is an excellent place to park your RV and enjoy the surrounding sights. Since the campground tends to be booked solid throughout the entire tourist season, reservations are absolutely required for weekends and are a good idea even during the week.

## BASICS

**Operated By:** Judt Kulisch (manager), Glen Gustine (owner). **Open:** First weekend in May–last weekend in Oct. **Site Assignment:** Reservations. **Registration:** At office. **Fee:** $27 (includes electricity & water). **Parking:** At site.

## FACILITIES

**Number of RV Sites:** 209. **Number of Tent-Only Sites:** 0. **Hookups:** Water, electric (30, 50 amps), phone, cable TV. **Each Site:** Picnic table, fireplace. **Dump Station:** Yes. **Laundry:** Yes. **Pay Phone:** Yes. **Rest Rooms and Showers:** Yes. **Fuel:** No. **Propane:** Yes. **RV Service:** No. **Market:** Adams Super Food, 5.6 mi. away. Go southeast on Town St. towards River Ed. by turning left, turn right onto River Rd., River becomes Geer Hill Rd., which becomes CT-148. Follow until Middlesex Turnpike & take a left. Follow until Turnpike becomes Main, & make a left onto Essex. **Restaurant:** Hale 'N Heart Restaurant, 381 Town St. (take a right on town & follow for 1.2 mi.). **General Store:** Yes. **Vending:** Yes. **Swimming Pool:** Yes, olympic-sized. **Playground:** Yes. **Other:** Game room, rental cabin, tennis courts, basketball, mini-golf, group & club areas. **Activities:** Each weekend has a theme, such as mid-September's "toga party" & late August's "Christmas in August". **Nearby Attractions:** Essex Steam Train (1 Railroad Ave., Essex). **Additional Information:** Middlesex County Chamber of Commerce, (860) 347-1043, www.middlesexchamber.com.

### RESTRICTIONS

**Pets:** Yes. **Fires:** At site only. **Alcoholic Beverages:** Allowed. **Vehicle Maximum Length:** None. **Other:** Ask on arrival.

### TO GET THERE

From New York (north) or Rhode Island (south) take 95 to Rte. 9 North. Rte. 9 North to Exit 7, east on Rte. 82, then go 4 mi. From Massachusetts take 91 South to Rte. 9 South to Exit 7, then go east on Rte. 82 for 4 mi.

## EAST KILLINGLY

## Hide-A-Way Cove Family Campground

North Rd., P.O. Box 129, East Killingly 06243. T: (860) 774-1128; hide-awaycove@webtv.net.

🚐 ★★★            ▲ ★

| | |
|---|---|
| Beauty: ★★ | Site Privacy: ★★ |
| Spaciousness: ★ | Quiet: ★★ |
| Security: ★★★ | Cleanliness: ★★★ |
| Insect Control: ★★★ | Facilities: ★★★ |

On the positive side, the campground is located on Hide-a-Way lake, an otherwise undeveloped body of water that's fairly nice to look at. The lake allows for boating (motors up to seven horsepowers) and has some pretty good fishing. On the other hand, the campground is not much to look at. The sites are packed tightly and some of them are just plain ugly. Many of the best, lakefront sites are snapped up by seasonal customers, so you'll want to move quickly or else you'll end up with a crowded site looking at another RV. There's not much for tent campers here.

### BASICS

**Operated By:** Edward & Jacquelyn Benoit. **Open:** May 1–Oct. 15. **Site Assignment:** Reser-

vations required in season; best sites often reserved seasons in advance. **Registration:** Store. **Fee:** $18. **Parking:** At site.

### FACILITIES

**Number of RV Sites:** 300. **Number of Tent-Only Sites:** 0. **Hookups:** Water, electric (20 amps). **Each Site:** Picnic table, fire ring. **Dump Station:** Yes. **Laundry:** Yes. **Pay Phone:** Yes. **Rest Rooms and Showers:** Yes. **Fuel:** No. **Propane:** Yes. **RV Service:** No. **Market:** A&P Food Stores 1058 N. Main St., Dayville, CT (3.8 Miles). Turn right onto Rte. 101 & follow for 3.7 mi., before making a sharp left onto Rte. 12. **Restaurant:** Pizza King, 430 Ledge Rd., Dayville, CT. Go east on Rte. 101 by turning left, then turn right onto East Killingly Rd. & then right onto Shippee Schoolhouse Rd., which runs into Ledge Rd. **General Store:** Yes. **Vending:** Yes. **Swimming Pool:** Yes. **Playground:** No. **Other:** Volleyball courts, horseshoe pits, lake, rec hall. **Activities:** Lots of organized activities, including bingo & arts & crafts. **Nearby Attractions:** Inquire at campground. **Additional Information:** Northeast Connecticut Visitors District, (860) 779-6383 or (888) 628-1228, www.ctquietcorner.org.

### RESTRICTIONS

**Pets:** On leash only. **Fires:** At site only. **Alcoholic Beverages:** Allowed. **Vehicle Maximum Length:** 35 ft. **Other:** Ask on arrival.

### TO GET THERE

395 to Exit 83 onto Rte. 101 east. Go 3.5 mi. to North Rd. (Turn left onto North Rd. just prior to the blinking light). Follow North Rd. a short distance to campground on right.

## EAST LYME

## Aces High RV Park

301 Chesterfield Rd., East Lyme 06333. T: (860) 739-8858; www.aceshighrvpark.com; sales@aceshighpark.com.

🚐 ★★★★            ▲ n/a

| | |
|---|---|
| Beauty: ★★★★ | Site Privacy: ★★★ |
| Spaciousness: ★★★★★ | Quiet: ★★★★ |

Security: ★★★  Cleanliness: ★★★
Insect Control: ★★★  Facilities: ★★★

An RV-only park, Aces High manages to remain attractive despite the fact it's basically a grass field surrounding a pond and bordered by forest. Sites are large but fairly close together for such a large park. There are plenty of family activities, including movies and some things for adults only.

## BASICS

**Operated By:** Private operator. **Open:** Apr. 1–Oct. 31. **Site Assignment:** Reservations recommended. **Registration:** At office. **Fee:** $34 for pop-ups, $37 for all others. **Parking:** At site.

## FACILITIES

**Number of RV Sites:** 43. **Number of Tent-Only Sites:** 0. **Hookups:** Water, electric (50 amps), sewer, cable TV. **Dump Station:** Yes. **Laundry:** Yes. **Pay Phone:** Yes. **Rest Rooms and Showers:** No. **Fuel:** Yes. **Propane:** Yes. **RV Service:** Yes. **Market:** Oakdale Market, 430 Chapel Hill Rd., Oakdale, CT (5.5 mi.). Take a right onto Rte. 161, then a slight left onto Rte.85, followed by a right onto Chesterfield Rd. & a left onto Chapel Hill Rd. **Restaurant:** Flanders Fish Market, 22 Chesterfield Rd., East Lyme (2.7 mi.). Follow above directions through Chesterfield Rd. **General Store:** No. **Vending:** No. **Swimming Pool:** No. **Playground:** Yes. **Other:** Game room, stocked trout pond, volleyball court. **Activities:** Paddle boats, surf bikes. **Nearby Attractions:** Inquire at campground. **Additional Information:** Southeastern Connecticut Tourism District, (860) 444-2206 or (800) TO-ENJOY, www.mysticmore.com.

## RESTRICTIONS

**Pets:** Yes. **Fires:** Allowed. **Alcoholic Beverages:** Allowed. **Vehicle Maximum Length:** 45 ft. **Other:** No tents.

## TO GET THERE

Take 95 to Exit 74 and go north on Rte. 161 for 3 mi. Campground will be on your right.

## EAST LYME

## Island Campground & Cottages

P.O. Box 2, Islanda Court, East Lyme 06333.
T: (860) 739-8316.

🚐 ★★★  ⛺ ★★★★

Beauty: ★★★★★  Site Privacy: ★★★★
Spaciousness: ★★★  Quiet: ★★★★
Security: ★★★★  Cleanliness: ★★★★
Insect Control: ★★★  Facilities: ★★

This isolated campground that's basically an island on Lake Pattagansett doesn't offer much to do, but it's perfect for grown-ups looking to get away from it all. Most of the shaded sites overlook the lake and are perfect for quiet contemplation. You can fish and swim in the lake, but most of the activity here is of the hat-tipped-over-your-eyes variety. All sites allow tents and RVs, but you might be better off leaving the RV at home and just pitching a tent and enjoying the simple life.

## BASICS

**Operated By:** Private operator. **Open:** May 1–Oct. 30. **Site Assignment:** Reservations absolutely necessary; campground is small & fills up fast. **Registration:** At office. **Fee:** $18 & up. **Parking:** At site.

## FACILITIES

**Number of RV Sites:** 35. **Number of Tent-Only Sites:** 0. **Hookups:** Water, electric. **Each Site:** Table. **Dump Station:** Yes. **Laundry:** No. **Pay Phone:** Yes. **Rest Rooms and Showers:** Yes. **Fuel:** No. **Propane:** Yes. **RV Service:** No. **Market:** Adam's Super Food Stores, 58 Pennsylvania Ave., Niantic, CT (4.4 mi.). Go south on Islanda Ct. towards Pattangnasett Dr., making a left onto Rte. 1, then a right onto Rte. 161, followed by a slight left onto Pennsylvania Ave. **Restaurant:** Bee Bee Dairy Restaurant, 324 Flanders Rd., East Lyme, CT (1.4 mi.). Go south on Islanda Ct. towards Pattangnasett Dr., making a left onto Rte. 1, followed by a slight right onto Flanders Rd./Rte. 161. **General Store:** No. **Vending:** No. **Swimming Pool:** No. **Playground:** Yes. **Other:** Private beach. **Activities:** Swimming, fishing.

**Nearby Attractions:** Mystic is pretty remote but relatively accessible. **Additional Information:** Southeastern Connecticut Tourism District, (860) 444-2206 or (800) TO ENJOY, www.mysticmore.com.

<u>RESTRICTIONS</u>

**Pets:** On leash only. **Fires:** Ask on arrival. **Alcoholic Beverages:** Allowed. **Vehicle Maximum Length:** None. **Other:** Ask on arrival.

<u>TO GET THERE</u>

95 to Exit 74. Turn left onto Rte. 161 to junction of Rte. 1 and Rte. 161 and turn left. Go for 1 mi. until you see Islanda Court Rd. on your right. Follow to campground.

## EASTFORD

## Charlie Brown Campground

Rte. 198, 98 Chaplin Rd., Eastford 06242. T: (860) 974-0142.

| 🚐 ★★★★ | ▲ ★★★ |
|---|---|
| Beauty: ★★★★ | Site Privacy: ★★★★ |
| Spaciousness: ★★★★ | Quiet: ★★★★ |
| Security: ★★★ | Cleanliness: ★★★★ |
| Insect Control: ★★★ | Facilities: ★★★★ |

The campground uses fences to separate sites in some areas, while other areas have bushes or open grassy spaces to protect privacy. The swimming hole is better than your average Olympic-size pool and is almost as clean—without the chlorine. Sites are mostly flat and nearly all are shaded.

<u>BASICS</u>

**Operated By:** Steve & Gary St. John. **Open:** Apr. 15–Oct. 15. **Site Assignment:** Reservations recommended. **Registration:** Store. **Fee:** $20 & up. **Parking:** At site.

<u>FACILITIES</u>

**Number of RV Sites:** 100. **Number of Tent-Only Sites:** 25. **Hookups:** Water, electric, sewer. **Each Site:** Picnic table, fire barrel. **Dump Station:** Yes. **Laundry:** Yes. **Pay Phone:** Yes. **Rest Rooms and Showers:** Yes. **Fuel:** No. **Propane:** Yes. **RV Service:** Supply shop. **Market:** Eastford Village Store, 192 Eastford Rd., Eastford, CT (6.5 Miles). Take Rte. 198 until it becomes Rte. 171 &

look for store in 0.2 mi. **Restaurant:** Midway Restaurant & Pizza, 174 Ashford Center Rd., Ashford, CT (4.5 mi.). Take a left onto Rte. 198 & follow it until Rte. 44. Take a left onto Rte. 44 & follow for 2 mi. **General Store:** Yes. **Vending:** Yes. **Swimming Pool:** No. **Playground:** No. **Other:** Picnic area, rec hall, basketball courts, fields. **Activities:** Band performances, planned activities, mountain biking. **Nearby Attractions:** Natchaug State Forest. **Additional Information:** Northeast Connecticut Visitors District, (860) 779-6383 or (888) 628-1228, www.ctquiet corner.org.

<u>RESTRICTIONS</u>

**Pets:** On leash only. **Fires:** Allowed. **Alcoholic Beverages:** Allowed. **Vehicle Maximum Length:** None. **Other:** Ask on arrival.

<u>TO GET THERE</u>

Take 84 to Exit 69 and follow 74 east to Rte. 44, east to 198 south.

## JEWITT CITY

## Campers World of Connecticut

P.O. Box 337, Jewitt City 06351. T: (860) 376-2340.

| 🚐 ★★★ | ▲ n/a |
|---|---|
| Beauty: ★★ | Site Privacy: ★ |
| Spaciousness: ★ | Quiet: ★ |
| Security: ★★ | Cleanliness: ★★ |
| Insect Control: ★★★ | Facilities: ★★★★ |

Given the adults-only policy, one wonders why this crowded campground set on a tiny beach has a playground. Seasonal campers make up most of the clientele here, so maybe the joy of this fairly bleak, RV-packed setting is the camaraderie. Some sites do have their own boat docks, and many are shaded.

<u>BASICS</u>

**Operated By:** George Barr. **Open:** May 1–Oct. 7. **Site Assignment:** Reservations recommended. **Registration:** At office. **Fee:** $16. **Parking:** At site.

## FACILITIES

**Number of RV Sites:** 92. **Number of Tent-Only Sites:** 0. **Hookups:** Water, electric (30, 50 amps), sewer, phone. **Dump Station:** No. **Laundry:** No. **Pay Phone:** No. **Rest Rooms and Showers:** Yes. **Fuel:** No. **Propane:** No. **RV Service:** No. **Market:** Plainfield Food Mart, 518 Norwich Rd., Plainfield, CT (4.8 mi.). **Restaurant:** Altone's Italian American, 47 Main St., No. A, Jewett City, CT (1.4 mi.). Take a right onto Carely Ave., followed by a right onto Ashland St. & a left onto Rte. 12. **General Store:** No. **Vending:** No. **Swimming Pool:** No. **Playground:** Yes. **Other:** Beach, pond, boat docks. **Activities:** Fishing, swimming. **Nearby Attractions:** Inquire at campground. **Additional Information:** Northeast Connecticut Visitors District, (860) 779-6383 or (888) 628-1228, www.ctquietcorner.org.

## RESTRICTIONS

**Pets:** Yes. **Fires:** Ask on arrival. **Alcoholic Beverages:** Allowed. **Vehicle Maximum Length:** None. **Other:** No children.

## TO GET THERE

Take 395 to Exit 86 and go east on Rte. 201 for 0.5 of a mi. Take a right onto First Rd. and look for campground on the left.

## LEBANON

### Lake Williams Campground

1742 Exeter Rd. (Rte. 207), Lebanon 06249. T: (860) 642-7761; F: (860) 642-4602; www.lakewilliamscampground.com; lakewilliamscampgd@snet.com.

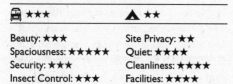

🚐 ★★★          ⛺ ★★

| | |
|---|---|
| Beauty: ★★★ | Site Privacy: ★★ |
| Spaciousness: ★★★★★ | Quiet: ★★★★ |
| Security: ★★★ | Cleanliness: ★★★★ |
| Insect Control: ★★★ | Facilities: ★★★★ |

Despite being on an enormous plot of land, the sites at Lake Williams are crowded. However, this does allow the campground's staff to better serve its visitors. In some ways, Lake Williams feels more like a hotel than a campground, as you see the employees more than you do at most places—which is generally a good thing. The entire area feels a bit too industrial to be described as "pretty" or to seem like you're taking an outdoors vacation. Still, the lake offers plenty of recreation, including fishing and boating.

## BASICS

**Operated By:** Lee & Sandra Rider. **Open:** Apr. 15–Oct. 15. **Site Assignment:** Reservations in season. **Registration:** At office. **Fee:** $32.95 (in season), $19.95 (off-season). **Parking:** At site.

## FACILITIES

**Number of RV Sites:** 87. **Number of Tent-Only Sites:** 0. **Hookups:** Water, electric (30, 50 amps), cable TV. **Each Site:** Picnic table, fire ring. **Dump Station:** Yes. **Laundry:** Yes. **Pay Phone:** Yes. **Rest Rooms and Showers:** Yes. **Fuel:** No. **Propane:** Yes. **Internal Roads:** Paved. **RV Service:** No. **Market:** Ted's Food Center, 127 Main St., Hebron, CT (4.5 mi.). Go northwest on Exeter Rd./CT-207 towards Levita Rd. by turning right. Turn right onto Rte. 85, then right onto Main St. **Restaurant:** Gina Marie's Family Restaurant, 71 Main St., Hebron, CT (4.8 mi.). Follow same directions as above. **General Store:** Yes. **Vending:** Yes. **Swimming Pool:** No. **Playground:** Yes. **Other:** Rec. hall, horseshoe pits, pool room, swimming beach. **Activities:** Bass fishing, waterskiing, boat rentals. **Nearby Attractions:** Dr. William Beaumont House (West Town St. , Lebanon). **Additional Information:** Northeast Connecticut Visitors District, (860) 779-6383 or (888) 628-1228, www.ctquietcorner.org.

## RESTRICTIONS

**Pets:** Yes. **Fires:** Allowed. **Alcoholic Beverages:** Allowed. **Vehicle Maximum Length:** 40 ft. **Other:** Ask on arrival.

## TO GET THERE

From 95, take 85 north through Colchester. About 3.5 mi. north of Colchester take a right onto Rte. 207 East. Go about 2.4 mi. and the campground will be on the left.

## LISBON

### Deer Haven Campground

15 Kenyon Rd., Lisbon 06351. T: (860) 376-1081;
F: (860) 376-3240; deerhaven@gocamping
america.com.

🚐 ★★★★          ⛺ ★★★

Beauty: ★★★              Site Privacy: ★★★
Spaciousness: ★★★         Quiet: ★★★
Security: ★★★★            Cleanliness: ★★★★
Insect Control: ★★★       Facilities: ★★★★

With both open and wooded sites as well as a
separate area for tent camping, Deer Haven has a
bit of everything. There's a nice mix of adult and
family activities here, so this might be a good
place to bring older kids who can occupy themselves at night while you head off to the adult
lounge.

#### BASICS

**Operated By:** Jane & Randy Pawlikowski.
**Open:** May 1–Oct. 18. **Site Assignment:** Reservations recommended. **Registration:** Store. **Fee:**
$17–$28. **Parking:** At site.

#### FACILITIES

**Number of RV Sites:** 50. **Number of Tent-
Only Sites:** 30. **Hookups:** Water, electric (30
amps), sewer. **Each Site:** Picnic table, fire ring.
**Dump Station:** Yes. **Laundry:** Yes. **Pay Phone:**
Yes. **Rest Rooms and Showers:** Yes. **Fuel:** No.
**Propane:** Yes. **RV Service:** No. **Market:** Russ's
Market, 754 North Main St., Norwich, CT (4.5
mi.). Turn right onto Kenyon Rd., which becomes
Strand Rd., which becomes Kendall Rd. Ext. Take
a sharp right onto Rte. 169, followed by a left
onto Rte. 97, then a slight right onto Rte. 12. Follow Rte. 12 until it becomes Main St. **Restaurant:** Corner Restaurant, 337 Old Canterbury
Turnpike, Norwich, CT (3.1 mi.). Turn right onto
Kenyon Rd., which becomes Strand Rd., which
becomes Kendall Rd. Ext. Take a sharp right onto
Rte. 169, followed by the I-395 south ramp. Get
off 395 at Exit 83, turning left onto Rte. 97. Turn
left onto Rte. 97 & go straight onto the Old
Canterbury Turnpike. **General Store:** Yes. **Vending:** Yes. **Swimming Pool:** No. **Playground:** Yes.
**Other:** Rec hall, arcade, pool tables, swimming
pond. **Activities:** Planned activities, basketball,
horseshoes. **Nearby Attractions:** Public golf
course, casinos, Norwich Navigators baseball.
**Additional Information:** Southeastern Connecticut Tourism District, (860) 444-2206 or
(800) TO-ENJOY, www.mysticmore.com.

#### RESTRICTIONS

**Pets:** Yes. **Fires:** Allowed. **Alcoholic Beverages:**
Allowed. **Vehicle Maximum Length:** None.
**Other:** Ask on arrival.

#### TO GET THERE

Take 395 north to Exit 83A (Exit 83 from 395
south), then take a left onto Rte. 169. Follow
for approximately 0.5 mi. to the Kendall Rd.
Exit and bear left onto Strand, following signs
to campground.

## LITCHFIELD

### Hemlock Hill Camp Resort

P.O. Box 828 Hemlock Hill Rd., Litchfield 06759.
T: (860) 567-2267.

🚐 ★★★          ⛺ ★★★

Beauty: ★★★              Site Privacy: ★★★★
Spaciousness: ★★★         Quiet: ★★★★
Security: ★★★             Cleanliness: ★★★
Insect Control: ★★★       Facilities: ★★★★★

Sites are set on a hillside (don't worry, the sites
themselves are flat) shaded by large hemlock
trees. Fairly spacious but not enormous, some
overlook the brook that runs through the campground. Canoes can be used on the brook, but
the real attraction at Hemlock Hills are its
planned activities. There's a lot going on during
weekends, making this a good choice for families.
People can own sites here, so many RV campers
stay the entire summer or split ownership of a
site. Since many of the guests here already know
each other, Hemlock Hills is a very friendly place.
Tent campers are welcome but find themselves in
a heavy minority.

#### BASICS

**Operated By:** Jerry & Mary Hughes. **Open:** Apr.
29–Oct. 23. **Site Assignment:** Reservations w/
deposit suggested; sites can be purchased. **Registration:** At office. **Fee:** $20–$29. **Parking:** At
site.

## FACILITIES

**Number of RV Sites:** 125. **Number of Tent-Only Sites:** 10. **Hookups:** Electric (20, 30 amps). **Each Site:** Fire pit, picnic table. **Dump Station:** Yes. **Laundry:** Yes. **Pay Phone:** Yes. **Rest Rooms and Showers:** Yes. **Fuel:** No. **Propane:** Yes. **RV Service:** No. **Market:** Stop & Shop Supermarket, 331 West St., Litchfield, CT (4.5 mi.). Take a left onto Maple St., followed by a left onto Milton Rd. Make a left onto Rte. 202, which becomes West St. **Restaurant:** Snack bar, Ming's Chinese Restaurant, Rte. 202, Litchfield, CT (3.4 mi. Follow directions above. **General Store:** No. **Vending:** Yes. **Swimming Pool:** Yes. **Playground:** Yes. **Other:** Bocce, whirlpool, sports area, fishing pond, hot tub. **Activities:** Every weekend has a heavy schedule of planned family activities. **Nearby Attractions:** Town of Litchfield has shopping & other activities. **Additional Information:** Litchfield Hills Visitors Bureau, (860) 567-4506, www.litchfieldhills.com.

## RESTRICTIONS

**Pets:** On leash only. **Fires:** Allowed. **Alcoholic Beverages:** Allowed. **Vehicle Maximum Length:** 40 ft. **Other:** Ask on arrival.

## TO GET THERE

Take 84 east to Exit 7. Follow Rte. 7 north to Rte. 202 east for 19 mi. to Maple St. Follow Maple St. for 4 mi. to Hemlock Hill Rd.

## MYSTIC

### Seaport Campgrounds

P.O. Box 104, Hwy. 184, Mystic 06372. T: (860) 536-4044; F: (860) 536-4461; www.seaportcampground.com; seaport@go campingamerica.com.

 ★★★★      ★★

| | |
|---|---|
| Beauty: ★★ | Site Privacy: ★★★ |
| Spaciousness: ★★★★★ | Quiet: ★★★ |
| Security: ★★★★★ | Cleanliness: ★★★★ |
| Insect Control: ★★★ | Facilities: ★★★★★ |

A wide-open campground with nicely sized sites but not much in the way of shade, Seaport is a well-run facility with many activities and impressive facilities. But the biggest attraction might be the easy accessibility to Mystic and its multitude of activities. There are more RVs than tenters here, but the layout makes it a pleasant place for both.

## BASICS

**Operated By:** Private operator. **Open:** Varies, call ahead. **Site Assignment:** Reservations generally required Memorial Day–Labor Day. **Registration:** Store. **Fee:** $28. **Parking:** At site.

## FACILITIES

**Number of RV Sites:** 130. **Number of Tent-Only Sites:** Undesignated sites. **Hookups:** Water, electric (30, 50 amps). **Each Site:** Picnic table, fire pit. **Dump Station:** Yes. **Laundry:** Yes. **Pay Phone:** Yes. **Rest Rooms and Showers:** Yes. **Fuel:** No. **Propane:** Yes. **RV Service:** No. **Market:** Central Market, 118 Fort Hill Rd., Groton, CT (3.7 mi.). Take a right onto High St., followed by a right onto Rte. 1. Follow Rte. for about 3 mi. until it becomes Fort Hill Rd. **Restaurant:** 41 Degrees North Restaurant, 21 W. Main St., Mystic, CT (0.6 mi.). Take a right onto High St. followed by a slight left onto Rte. 1. **General Store:** Yes. **Vending:** Yes. **Swimming Pool:** Yes. **Playground:** No. **Other:** Mini-golf, rec room, fishing pond. **Activities:** Live music on weekends. **Nearby Attractions:** Town of Mystic. **Additional Information:** Southeastern Connecticut Tourism District, (860) 444-2206 or (800) TO-ENJOY, www.mysticmore.com.

## RESTRICTIONS

**Pets:** On leash only. **Fires:** Allowed. **Alcoholic Beverages:** Allowed. **Vehicle Maximum Length:** 55 ft. **Other:** Ask on arrival.

## TO GET THERE

Take 95 to Exit 90 and go 1.25 mi. to Rte. 72, then take a right and go 0.5 mi. east on Rte. 184. The campground is on the left.

## NIANTIC

### Camp Niantic by the Atlantic

271 Main St. (Rte. 156), Niantic 06357. T: (800) 739-9308; www.campniantic.com; campniantic@aol.com.

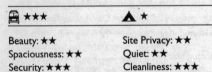

★★★    ▲ ★

Beauty: ★★              Site Privacy: ★★
Spaciousness: ★★        Quiet: ★★
Security: ★★★           Cleanliness: ★★★
Insect Control: ★★★     Facilities: ★★★★

Though tent camping is allowed here, we can't see why anyone would choose to pitch their tent at Camp Niantic. RVs absolutely fill the entire place and a tent would get lost among them. Despite all the RVs, the campground manages to remain attractive, as most of its hillside is wooded. Free passes are offered to McCook Point Beach, located a short drive away.

### BASICS

**Operated By:** Terell & Carole Rice. **Open:** May 1–Oct. 15. **Site Assignment:** Reservations recommended. **Registration:** At office. **Fee:** $23–$27. **Parking:** At site.

### FACILITIES

**Number of RV Sites:** 100. **Number of Tent-Only Sites:** 0. **Hookups:** Water, electric, sewer. **Each Site:** Fireplace, picnic table. **Dump Station:** No. **Laundry:** Yes. **Pay Phone:** Yes. **Rest Rooms and Showers:** Yes. **Fuel:** No. **Propane:** Yes. **RV Service:** No. **Market:** Colonial Market, 243 Main St., Niantic, CT (0.1 mi.). Take a left onto Main St. **Restaurant:** Constantine's, 252 Main St., Niantic, CT (0.1 mi.). Take a left onto Main St. **General Store:** No. **Vending:** No. **Swimming Pool:** No. **Playground:** No. **Other:** Free access to town beach, game room, basketball courts. **Activities:** Planned weekend activities, sports tournaments. **Nearby Attractions:** Rocky Neck State Park & McCook Point Beach. **Additional Information:** Southeastern Connecticut Tourism District, (860) 444-2206 or (800) TO-ENJOY, www.mysticmore.com.

### RESTRICTIONS

**Pets:** On leash only. **Fires:** Allowed. **Alcoholic Beverages:** Allowed. **Vehicle Maximum Length:** None. **Other:** Ask on arrival.

### TO GET THERE

95 to Exit 72. Turn right onto Rte. 156 south and follow to campsite.

## NIANTIC

### Rocky Neck State Park

244 W. Main St., Niantic 06357. T: (860) 739-1339; www.reserveamerica.com.

★★★    ▲ ★★★

Beauty: ★★★             Site Privacy: ★★★
Spaciousness: ★★★★      Quiet: ★★★★
Security: ★★            Cleanliness: ★★★
Insect Control: ★★★     Facilities: ★★★

Rocky Neck State Park is a big place. Yet despite its 700 acres, it seems fairly quiet and cozy. Its proximity to Long Island Sound, the salt marsh, and the forest make it a prime choice for birdwatching; there's a nature center on the grounds, and you'll want to take time on your way down the walking/biking trail to the beach to enjoy the salt marsh you'll pass. You may even want to do some fishing or try netting some blue crabs. The park's big, open grassy areas are great for playing Frisbee or tossing a football; lots of people are just walking about, biking, or in-line skating. (Consequently, drivers should be cautious!) There's a community fire ring, so you may make some new friends there. Tent campers will be hard pressed to find a softer surface on which to pitch their sleeping bags.

### BASICS

**Operated By:** CT Dept. of Environmental Protection. **Open:** Memorial Day–Labor Day. **Site Assignment:** Reservations or first come, first served. **Registration:** Reserve America. **Fee:** $15. **Parking:** At site.

### FACILITIES

**Number of RV Sites:** 120. **Number of Tent-Only Sites:** 48. **Hookups:** None. **Dump Station:** Yes. **Laundry:** No. **Pay Phone:** Yes. **Rest**

**Rooms and Showers:** Yes. **Fuel:** No. **Propane:** No. **Internal Roads:** Paved. **RV Service:** No. **Market:** No. **Restaurant:** No. **General Store:** Concessions. **Vending:** Yes. **Swimming Pool:** No. **Playground:** No. **Activities:** Hiking, picnicking, shellfishing, swimming, scuba diving, saltwater fishing, field sports. **Nearby Attractions:** McCook Point Beach, casinos. **Additional Information:** Southeastern Connecticut Tourism District (860) 444-2206 or (800) TO-ENJOY, www.mysticmore.com.

## RESTRICTIONS

**Pets:** No. **Fires:** In fire ring. **Alcoholic Beverages:** No. **Vehicle Maximum Length:** None. **Other:** Ask on arrival.

## TO GET THERE

From Rte. 95, take Exit 72 and follow the signs to the park.

# NORTH STONINGTON

## Highland Orchards Resort Park

P.O. Box 222, North Stonington 06359. T: (800) 624-0829; F: (860) 599-8944; www.highland orchards.com; camp@highlandorchards.com.

| 🚐 ★★★★ | 🏕 ★★★ |
|---|---|
| Beauty: ★★★ | Site Privacy: ★★★★ |
| Spaciousness: ★★★★ | Quiet: ★★★ |
| Security: ★★★★★ | Cleanliness: ★★★★ |
| Insect Control: ★★★ | Facilities: ★★★ |

Mostly grassy rolling meadows with trees here and there, Highland Orchards does have a few wooded areas that are dedicated to the tent sites. A combination destination park and travel park, Highland Orchards is a good home base for excursions to the local beaches, Mystic, and, of course, the Connecticut casinos. It's quieter than many RV-dominated campgrounds because the staff zealously enforces its quiet policy. There aren't as many planned activities here as at some places, but there's always something scheduled for Saturday evenings in season. Make weekend reservations well in advance during summer, but you'll usually find a space during the week.

## BASICS

**Operated By:** Bob, Elaine, & Joe Boissevain. **Open:** All year. **Site Assignment:** Reservations. **Registration:** At office. **Fee:** $30–$41.50. **Parking:** 1 car at site; other cars in lot.

## FACILITIES

**Number of RV Sites:** 250. **Number of Tent-Only Sites:** 20. **Hookups:** Water, electric (30, 50 amps), sewer, cable TV. **Each Site:** Picnic table, fire ring, some w/ phone. **Dump Station:** Yes. **Laundry:** Yes. **Pay Phone:** Yes. **Rest Rooms and Showers:** Yes. **Fuel:** No. **Propane:** Yes. **Internal Roads:** Paved, some gravel. **RV Service:** Yes. **Market:** A&P Super Food Market, 179 Stonington Rd., Stonington, CT. **Restaurant:** Ashby Restaurant, Rte. 27 Stonington, CT. **General Store:** Yes. **Vending:** Yes. **Swimming Pool:** Yes. **Playground:** Yes. **Other:** Fishing ponds, mini-golf, basketball court, shuffleboard, rec room, fireplace lounge. **Activities:** Free shuttle to Foxwoods casino, special events every weekend during the summer. **Nearby Attractions:** Mystic seaport, Mystic aquarium. **Additional Information:** Southeastern Connecticut Tourism District, (860) 444-2206 or (800) TO-ENJOY, www.mysticmore.com.

## RESTRICTIONS

**Pets:** Yes. **Fires:** Allowed. **Alcoholic Beverages:** Quietly at site. **Vehicle Maximum Length:** None. **Other:** Quiet hours begin at 10:30 p.m.

## TO GET THERE

95 to Exit 92. Take a left onto Rte. 2, passing under 95, and turn right onto the service road for Rte. 49. Turn left onto Rte. 49 and enter the first driveway on the right.

# OAKDALE

## Peppertree Camping

Rte. 198, Chaplin 06235. T: (860) 974-1439; www.campconn.com/peppertree.

| 🚐 ★★★★ | 🏕 ★★★ |
|---|---|
| Beauty: ★★★ | Site Privacy: ★★★★★ |
| Spaciousness: ★★★★ | Quiet: ★★★★★ |
| Security: ★★★★ | Cleanliness: ★★★★ |
| Insect Control: ★★★ | Facilities: ★★★ |

Nicer than neighboring Nickerson Campground, Peppertree Camping also borders the Natchaug

State Forest but features more attractive sites that offer a little more privacy. There are no tent-specific sites here and any site should work fine for both tents and RVs. Quite a few planned activities are offered, but your best bet might be to just spend time walking the numerous forest trails.

## BASICS

**Operated By:** Dan & Camille Wilson. **Open:** Apr. 15–Oct. 15. **Site Assignment:** Reservations recommended. **Registration:** Store. **Fee:** $22–$23.50. **Parking:** At site.

## FACILITIES

**Number of RV Sites:** 55. **Number of Tent-Only Sites:** 0. **Hookups:** Water, electric, sewer. **Each Site:** Picnic table, fireplace. **Dump Station:** Yes. **Laundry:** Yes. **Pay Phone:** Yes. **Rest Rooms and Showers:** Yes. **Fuel:** No. **Propane:** Yes. **RV Service:** No. **Market:** Ted's Mini Market, 315 Boston Post Rd., North Windham, CT (5.5 mi.). Go south on Rte. 198 towards Pumpkin Hill Rd. by turning right, then take a slight right onto Rte. 6. Rte. 6 becomes N. Windham Rd. & then becomes Boston Post Rd. **Restaurant:** Chaplin Pizza, 52 Willimantic Rd. Chaplin, CT. Follow above directions to Willimantic Rd. **General Store:** Yes. **Vending:** Yes. **Swimming Pool:** No. **Playground:** Yes. **Other:** Baseball field, horseshoe pits, basketball court. **Activities:** Swimming, rafting, river tubing, hiking, biking, bingo, pot-luck suppers. **Nearby Attractions:** Natchaug State Forest. **Additional Information:** Northeast Connecticut Visitors District, (860) 779-6383 or (888) 628-1228, www.ctquiet corner.org.

## RESTRICTIONS

**Pets:** On leash only. **Fires:** Allowed. **Alcoholic Beverages:** Allowed. **Vehicle Maximum Length:** None. **Other:** Ask on arrival.

## TO GET THERE

84 to Exit 69. Right onto Rte. 74 east to Rte. 44 east. Take 44 east to Rte. 198 south. Campground is on the left.

## PLYMOUTH

### Gentiles Campground

Rte. 262, Mt. Tobe Rd., Plymouth 06782. T: (860) 283-8437; F: (203) 755-3582.

🚐 ★★★          ⛺ ★★

| | |
|---|---|
| Beauty: ★ | Site Privacy: ★ |
| Spaciousness: ★★ | Quiet: ★★ |
| Security: ★★★ | Cleanliness: ★★★★ |
| Insect Control: ★★★ | Facilities: ★★★ |

If you're looking for nature, the actual campground here might not be the place to find it. Sites are packed close together, and it seems like most of the RVs parked here plan to remain for the season, so your view is likely to be of the side of someone's RV. However, you don't have to go far to find nature, because Gentiles borders Mattatuck State Forest, which offers stocked fishing, trails, and a chance to commune with nature. Gentiles has a lot to offer—especially if you plan to get away from your campsite a bit.

## BASICS

**Operated By:** Irene & Ray Gentile. **Open:** May 1–Oct. 15. **Site Assignment:** Reservations required. **Registration:** Store. **Fee:** Rates available by request only. **Parking:** At site.

## FACILITIES

**Number of RV Sites:** 110. **Number of Tent-Only Sites:** 0. **Hookups:** Water, electric (30 amps), sewer. **Each Site:** Picnic table, fire ring. **Dump Station:** Yes. **Laundry:** No. **Pay Phone:** Yes. **Rest Rooms and Showers:** Yes. **Fuel:** No. **Propane:** Yes. **RV Service:** No. **Market:** Village Mart, 1815 Thomaston Ave., Waterbury, CT (2.4 Miles). Left onto Rte. 262 & then a left onto Thomaston Ave. **Restaurant:** Giovanni's Restaurante, 1622 Thomaston Ave., Waterbury, CT (2.6 mi.). Follow directions above. **General Store:** Yes. **Vending:** Yes. **Swimming Pool:** Yes. **Playground:** No. **Other:** Picnic area, tennis courts, bocce, mini-golf, volleyball courts, basketball court, petting zoo, 2 rec halls. **Activities:** Tennis, swimming, hiking. **Nearby Attractions:** City of Waterbury (3 mi. south). **Additional Information:** Litchfield Hills Visitors Bureau, (860) 567-4506, www.litchfieldhills.com.

## RESTRICTIONS

**Pets:** Yes. **Fires:** Allowed. **Alcoholic Beverages:** Allowed. **Vehicle Maximum Length:** None. **Other:** Ask on arrival.

## TO GET THERE

Take 84 to Rte. 8 north to Exit 39. Go east on Rte. 6 for 2 mi., take a right at the light onto Rte. 262, and follow for 3 mi. until you see the campground on the left.

## PRESTON

## Hidden Acres Family Campground

47 River Rd., Preston 06365. T: (860) 887-9633; F: (860) 887-6359; hacampgd@aol.com.

🚐 ★★★★          ▲ ★★

| | |
|---|---|
| Beauty: ★★ | Site Privacy: ★★★ |
| Spaciousness: ★★ | Quiet: ★★ |
| Security: ★★★★ | Cleanliness: ★★★ |
| Insect Control: ★★ | Facilities: ★★★★ |

Not the place to go if you're camping with a tent, this loud campground is dedicated to RVs. Despite bordering the Quinebaug River, the scenery here is nothing special, though most sites at least have fairly large trees on them. This is also not the place to go for a quiet weekend away, but it might be a good place to take the kids, as there are many children around and numerous planned activities.

## BASICS

**Operated By:** The Migliaccio Family. **Open:** May 1–Columbus Day. **Site Assignment:** Reservations. **Registration:** At office. **Fee:** $20–$26. **Parking:** At site.

## FACILITIES

**Number of RV Sites:** 180. **Number of Tent-Only Sites:** 0. **Hookups:** Water, electric (20, 30, 50 amps). **Each Site:** Picnic table, fire ring. **Dump Station:** Yes. **Laundry:** Yes. **Pay Phone:** Yes. **Rest Rooms and Showers:** Yes. **Fuel:** No. **Propane:** Yes. **RV Service:** No. **Market:** Russ's Market, 754 N. Main St., Norwich, CT (2.8 mi.). **Restaurant:** Snack bar on site. Eli's Pizza Place, 500 Norwich Ave., Taftville, CT (2 mi.). **General Store:** Yes. **Vending:** Yes. **Swimming Pool:** No.

**Playground:** No. **Other:** Stocked fishing pond, animal-visiting area, horseshoe pits, basketball & volleyball courts, craft shop w/ ceramics, rec hall, game room. **Activities:** Hayrides, weekend entertainment, bingo. **Nearby Attractions:** Quinebaug River (offers tubing & fishing). **Additional Information:** Southeastern Connecticut Tourism District, (860) 444-2206 or (800) TO-ENJOY, www.mysticmore.com.

## RESTRICTIONS

**Pets:** On leash only. **Fires:** At site only. **Alcoholic Beverages:** At site. **Vehicle Maximum Length:** None. **Other:** Ask on arrival.

## TO GET THERE

Rte. 395 to Exit 85. Go south 1 mi. on Rte. 164 and turn right on George Palmer Rd. Continue 3 mi. to campground, bearing right the whole way.

## SALEM

## Indianfield Campground

Gardner Lake, Rte. 354, 306 Old Colchester Rd., Salem 06420. T: (860) 859-1320; F: (860) 859-1320.

🚐 ★★★          ▲ n/a

| | |
|---|---|
| Beauty: ★★★ | Site Privacy: ★★★ |
| Spaciousness: ★★★ | Quiet: ★★★ |
| Security: ★★★ | Cleanliness: ★★★ |
| Insect Control: ★★★ | Facilities: ★★★ |

A large RV-based campground located on Gardner Lake, Indianfield makes for an excellent family camping destination. The entire clientele seems to be families in enormous RVs who come for extended vacations, and the campsite caters to that. There are many planned activities as well as spontaneous ones that pop up due to the sheer volume of people here. The campground itself is actually quite large and the lakefront offers a large beach. There's also boat docks and every other kind of waterfront activity imaginable.

## BASICS

**Operated By:** Larry & Marlene Harrington. **Open:** May 1–Oct. 30. **Site Assignment:** At time of Registration. **Registration:** Store. **Fee:** $12–$28. **Parking:** At site.

### FACILITIES

**Number of RV Sites:** 228. **Number of Tent-Only Sites:** 0. **Hookups:** Water, electric (30 amps), phone. **Dump Station:** Yes. **Laundry:** Yes. **Pay Phone:** Yes. **Rest Rooms and Showers:** Yes. **Fuel:** No. **Propane:** Yes. **RV Service:** No. **Market:** Oakdale Market, 430 Chapel Hill Rd., Oakdale, CT (3.9 mi.). Turn left onto Rte. 354, then take a right onto Rte. 82, followed by an immediate left onto OldColchester Rd. Follow until Forsyth Rd. & make a right, followed by a left on Chapel Hill Rd. **Restaurant:** Grumpy Joe's Restaurant & Bar, 627 Rte. 82, Oakdale, CT (2.1 mi.). Go left onto Rte. 354 & then left onto Rte. 82. **General Store:** Yes. **Vending:** Yes. **Swimming Pool:** No. **Playground:** Yes. **Other:** Rec hall, open pavilion, dock slips. **Activities:** Planned events on weekends. **Nearby Attractions:** Inquire at campground. **Additional Information:** Southeastern Connecticut Tourism District, (860) 444-2206 or (800) TO-ENJOY, www.mysticmore.com.

### RESTRICTIONS

**Pets:** Must be leashed, quiet, & cleaned up after. **Fires:** Ask on arrival. **Alcoholic Beverages:** Allowed. **Vehicle Maximum Length:** 40 ft. **Other:** Ask on arrival.

### TO GET THERE

395 to Exit 80. Go west on Rte. 82 for 8 mi. to Rte. 354. Turn right and go 1 mi. looking for campground sign on the right.

## SCOTLAND

## Highland Campground

Toleration Rd., P.O. Box 305, Scotland 06264. T: (860) 423-5684; F: (860) 456-2697; www.highlandcampground.com; info@highlandcampground.com.

🚐 ★★★★          ▲ ★★★

| | |
|---|---|
| Beauty: ★★★★ | Site Privacy: ★★★★ |
| Spaciousness: ★★★★ | Quiet: ★★★★ |
| Security: ★★★★ | Cleanliness: ★★★★ |
| Insect Control: ★★★ | Facilities: ★★★★ |

A beautiful campground, Highland is set back well off the road. Each site has ample space, and most sites are well hidden by the forest. Unlike many campgrounds that cater to RVs, this one is also a friendly place for tent campers, as the privacy of the sites means you won't be pitching your tent too close to an RV. A well-situated campground, Highland is near a lot of recreation, both within walking distance (hiking and fishing) and within a short drive.

### BASICS

**Operated By:** The Davis family. **Open:** All year, but limited in winter. **Site Assignment:** Reservations necessary in season, though sites are sometimes available. **Registration:** Store. **Fee:** $24 & up. **Parking:** At site.

### FACILITIES

**Number of RV Sites:** 160. **Number of Tent-Only Sites:** 0. **Hookups:** Electric (20, 30 amps). **Each Site:** Fireplace, picnic table. **Dump Station:** Yes. **Laundry:** Yes. **Pay Phone:** Yes. **Rest Rooms and Showers:** Yes. **Fuel:** No. **Propane:** Yes. **RV Service:** No. **Market:** Yadiras Grocery Store, 157 Valley St., Windham, CT. **Restaurant:** Snack bar, Liberty's Restaurant, 451 Main Windham, CT. **General Store:** Yes. **Vending:** Yes. **Swimming Pool:** Yes. **Playground:** Yes. **Other:** Stocked fishing pond, mini-golf, rec hall, adult lounge, bocce court. **Activities:** Catch & release fishing, hiking, potluck suppers, volleyball, bingo, dancing. **Nearby Attractions:** Foxwoods, USS Nautilus, Plainfield Greyhound Park. **Additional Information:** Northeast Connecticut Visitors District, (860) 779-6383 or (888) 628-1228, www.ctquietcorner.org.

### RESTRICTIONS

**Pets:** On leash only. **Fires:** Allowed. **Alcoholic Beverages:** Allowed. **Vehicle Maximum Length:** 40 ft. **Other:** Ask on arrival.

### TO GET THERE

395 to Exit 83. Follow Rte. 97 north for 7.5 mi. to Toleration Rd. and take a right onto Toleration Rd.

## THOMASTON

### Branch Brook Campground

435 Watertown Rd., Thomaston 06787. T: (860) 283-8144.

🚐 ★★★          ▲ ★★

Beauty: ★★               Site Privacy: ★★★
Spaciousness: ★★★        Quiet: ★★★
Security: ★★★★           Cleanliness: ★★
Insect Control: ★★★      Facilities: ★★★

Filled mostly with seasonal campers, Branch Brook has a "lived in" feel. Though the campground has a pretty brook and some other nice scenery, it's hard to get past the feeling that you're staying in a trailer park. However, you're near Mattatuck State Forest, so walking trails and less-spoiled nature are only a little way down the road.

#### BASICS

**Operated By:** Kip & Denise Brammer. **Open:** Apr. 1–Nov. 1. **Site Assignment:** Reservations recommended. **Registration:** At office. **Fee:** Around $20 & up; 3-day min. stay required for holiday weekends. **Parking:** At site.

#### FACILITIES

**Number of RV Sites:** 63. **Number of Tent-Only Sites:** 0. **Hookups:** Water, electric (20, 30, 50 amps), sewer. **Each Site:** Picnic table, fire ring. **Dump Station:** Yes. **Laundry:** Yes. **Pay Phone:** Yes. **Rest Rooms and Showers:** Yes. **Fuel:** No. **Propane:** Yes. **RV Service:** Yes. **Market:** New Daily Mart, 9 N. Main St., Thomaston, CT (2 mi.). Go northeast on Rte. 6, following it until it becomes Waterbury Rd., then turn back to Rte. 6 & finally N. Main St. **Restaurant:** Goose & The Gander Inc., 370 Watertown Rd., Thomaston, CT (0.1 mi.). Take a right onto Watertown Rd. **General Store:** No. **Vending:** Yes. **Swimming Pool:** Yes. **Playground:** No. **Other:** Rec hall. **Activities:** Fishing. **Nearby Attractions:** Black Rock State Park. **Additional Information:** Waterbury Region CVB, (203) 597-9527, www.waterbury region.com.

#### RESTRICTIONS

**Pets:** On leash only. **Fires:** Allowed. **Alcoholic Beverages:** Allowed. **Vehicle Maximum**

**Length:** None. **Other:** Ask on arrival.

#### TO GET THERE

From Rte. 8 take Exit 38 and go 1 mi. west on Rte. 6. Campground is across from Black Rock State Park.

## TOLLAND

### Del Aire

Shepsit Lake Rd., Tolland 06084. T: (860) 875-8325.

🚐 ★★★          ▲ ★★★★

Beauty: ★★★★            Site Privacy: ★★★
Spaciousness: ★★         Quiet: ★★★
Security: ★★★            Cleanliness: ★★★★
Insect Control: ★★★      Facilities: ★★★

Del Aire caters to seasonal campers, and you can generally get a reservation. RV sites are somewhat close together, but they're flat and dotted with a reasonable number of trees offering shade. Tent sites are a little more remote, which makes them seem bigger. Two brooks run through the grounds, adding to the scenery, and the neighboring lake offers boating, fishing, and swimming. There's also an easily accessible trail up Soapstone Mountain that offers access to a lookout tower and some spectacular views.

#### BASICS

**Operated By:** Albert & Germaine Ouelette. **Open:** May 1–Oct. 15. **Site Assignment:** Reservations recommended July–Labor Day. **Registration:** Store. **Fee:** $14–$18. **Parking:** At site.

#### FACILITIES

**Number of RV Sites:** 100. **Number of Tent-Only Sites:** 25. **Hookups:** Water, electric (15, 20 amps). **Each Site:** Picnic table, stone fireplace. **Dump Station:** Yes. **Laundry:** No. **Pay Phone:** Yes. **Rest Rooms and Showers:** Yes. **Fuel:** No. **Propane:** Yes. **RV Service:** No. **Market:** Tolland IGA, 200 Merrow Rd. 208, Tolland, CT (1.3 mi.). Go right on Rte. 74 & make a sharp left onto Rte. 195. **Restaurant:** Lee's Garden, 200 Merrow Rd., Tolland, CT (1.3 mi.). Follow directions above. **General Store:** Yes (limited). **Vending:** Yes. **Swimming Pool:** No.

**Playground:** Yes. **Other:** Rec hall, sports field. **Activities:** Fishing, swimming. **Nearby Attractions:** Shenipsit Lake. **Additional Information:** Greater Hartford Tourism District, (860) 244-8181 or (800) 793-4480, www.enjoyhartford.com.

RESTRICTIONS

**Pets:** On leash only. **Fires:** Allowed. **Alcoholic Beverages:** Allowed. **Vehicle Maximum Length:** None. **Other:** Ask on arrival.

TO GET THERE

Take 84 to Exit 67. Go north on Rte. 31 for 0.25 mi. to Rte. 30. Take a right at the light and go 4 mi. to Brown Bridge Rd. Follow signs to campground.

## VOLUNTOWN

### Circle "C" Campground

RFD 1, P.O. Box 23A Bailey Rd., Voluntown 06384. T: (860) 564-4534; F: (860) 564-4339; www.campcirclec.com; circleccampground@prodigy.net.

🚐 ★★★★          ▲ ★★★

| | |
|---|---|
| Beauty: ★★★ | Site Privacy: ★★★ |
| Spaciousness: ★★★ | Quiet: ★★★ |
| Security: ★★★ | Cleanliness: ★★★★ |
| Insect Control: ★★★ | Facilities: ★★★★ |

Whether you prefer wooded sites or wide-open ones, Circle "C" has the site for you. The open sites are grassy, and some overlook Bailey Pond, which is located on the premises. You can power-boat on Bailey (up to 10 mph) and swim and fish in the other two ponds at the campground. There's a decent mix of tent and RV campers who stay here, and a handful of sites are definitely best suited for tents.

BASICS

**Operated By:** John & Jeanette Richard. **Open:** Apr. 19–Oct. 16. **Site Assignment:** Reservations recommended. **Registration:** Store. **Fee:** $22 tent, $25 hookups. **Parking:** At site.

FACILITIES

**Number of RV Sites:** 100. **Number of Tent-Only Sites:** 0. **Hookups:** Water, electric (30, 50 amps), sewer. **Each Site:** Picnic table, fire pit. **Dump Station:** Yes. **Laundry:** Yes. **Pay Phone:** Yes. **Rest Rooms and Showers:** Yes. **Fuel:** No. **Propane:** No. **RV Service:** No. **Market:** Better Val-U Supermarket, 104 Beach Pond Rd., Voluntown, CT 06384 (10.7 mi.). Turn left onto Bailey Pond Rd., followed by a right onto Hazard Rd., which becomes Escoheag Hill Rd. Turn right onto Rte. 165, which becomes Beach Pond Rd. **Restaurant:** Town Pizza & Restaurant, 104 Beach Pond Rd., Voluntown, CT (10.7 mi.). Follow above directions. **General Store:** Yes (mini-store). **Vending:** Yes. **Swimming Pool:** No. **Playground:** Yes. **Other:** Rec hall, arcade, basketball court, badminton court, mini-golf, horseshoe pits. **Activities:** Boat rentals, fishing, lots of planned activities, including "Murder Mystery" weekend. **Nearby Attractions:** Plainfield Greyhound Park. **Additional Information:** Southeastern Connecticut Tourism District, (860) 444-2206 or (800) TO-ENJOY, www.mysticmore.com.

RESTRICTIONS

**Pets:** Yes. **Fires:** Allowed. **Alcoholic Beverages:** Allowed. **Vehicle Maximum Length:** 40 ft. **Other:** Ask on arrival.

TO GET THERE

Take 95 to Exit 5A and make a right onto Rte. 3, followed by a right into Rte. 165. Follow until Rte. 40 north. Go 2.6 mi. and take a right onto Brown Rd. Follow to end and make a right onto Gallup Homestead Rd. Follow to end and make a right onto Bailey Pond Rd.

## VOLUNTOWN

### Countryside Campground

75 Cook Hill Rd., Voluntown 06384. T: (860) 376-0029; F: (860) 376-3120; countrysidecamp@email.com.

🚐 ★★★★          ▲ ★★★★

| | |
|---|---|
| Beauty: ★★★★ | Site Privacy: ★★★★★ |
| Spaciousness: ★★★★ | Quiet: ★★★★★ |
| Security: ★★★★ | Cleanliness: ★★★★★ |
| Insect Control: ★★★ | Facilities: ★★★ |

Quiet is the operative word here—the goal is to keep the noise level to a mimimum. Trees shield the sites from each other (and add to the beauty of the place). The spring-fed swimming pond is at the center of the camp, and occassional whoops of joy while taking a dip are acceptable during the day. The private sites are ideal for tent campers who don't want to feel like they're penned in by RVs.

## BASICS

**Operated By:** Linda Mackin. **Open:** May 1–Oct. 15. **Site Assignment:** Reservations w/ nonrefundable deposit recommended. **Registration:** At office. **Fee:** $18 tent, $20 hookups. **Parking:** At site.

## FACILITIES

**Number of RV Sites:** 59. **Number of Tent-Only Sites:** 9. **Hookups:** Water, electric (30, 50 amps). **Each Site:** Picnic table, stone fireplace. **Dump Station:** Yes. **Laundry:** No. **Pay Phone:** Yes. **Rest Rooms and Showers:** Yes. **Fuel:** No. **Propane:** No. **RV Service:** No. **Market:** Sunny Supermarket, 129 Main St., Voluntown, CT (1.1 mi.). Turn left onto Cook Hill Rd., followed by a slight left onto Sheldon Rd. & a right onto Rte. 138, which becomes Main St. **Restaurant:** Town Pizza & Restaurant, 104 Beach Pond Rd., Voluntown, CT (1.7 mi.). Follow above directions, staying on Main St. until it becomes Beach Pond Rd. **General Store:** No. **Vending:** No. **Swimming Pool:** No. **Playground:** No. **Other:** Swimming pond, fishing pond. **Activities:** Swimming, fishing. **Nearby Attractions:** Next to Pachaug State Forest. **Additional Information:** Southeastern Connecticut Tourism District, (860) 444-2206 or (800) TO-ENJOY, www.mysticmore.com.

## RESTRICTIONS

**Pets:** On leash only. **Fires:** Allowed. **Alcoholic Beverages:** Allowed. **Vehicle Maximum Length:** 36 ft. **Other:** Ask on arrival.

## TO GET THERE

Take 395 to Exit 85. Go east on Rte. 138 for 4 mi., then take a right onto Rte. 201 south. Follow for 1 mi. to Cook Hill Rd. on the left. Campground will be 0.5 mi. down on the right.

## WOODSTOCK
### Beaver Pines Campground

1728 Rte. 198, Woodstock 06281. T: (860) 974-0110; www.beaverpinescampground.com; e-mail form on website.

🚐 ★★★                 ▲ ★★★★

Beauty: ★★★★          Site Privacy: ★★★★★
Spaciousness: ★★★★    Quiet: ★★★★
Security: ★★★★         Cleanliness: ★★★★
Insect Control: ★★★    Facilities: ★★★★

A tent camper's paradise, Beaver Pines offers enormous sites in an attractive wooded setting. Though the regular sites are reasonably private, anyone wanting complete seclusion can reserve a remote site set away from the rest of the campground. The RV facilities are relatively limited in number, and the entire campground is somewhat small, which gives it a family feel—that's mostly what you find here.

## BASICS

**Operated By:** Private operator. **Open:** Apr. 15–Oct. 15. **Site Assignment:** Reservations recommended, required for secluded sites. **Registration:** Store. **Fee:** $22–$25. **Parking:** At site.

## FACILITIES

**Number of RV Sites:** 8. **Number of Tent-Only Sites:** 14. **Hookups:** Water, electric, cable TV. **Each Site:** Picnic table, fire ring. **Dump Station:** Yes. **Laundry:** No. **Pay Phone:** Yes. **Rest Rooms and Showers:** Yes. **Fuel:** No. **Propane:** No. **RV Service:** No. **Market:** La Bonne's Epicure Market, 544 Straits Turnpike, Watertown, CT. **Restaurant:** Anthony's, 308 Main St., Watertown, CT. **General Store:** Yes. **Vending:** No. **Swimming Pool:** No. **Playground:** Yes. **Other:** Sports field, pond, game room. **Activities:** Fishing, kayaking, hiking, mountain biking. **Nearby Attractions:** Bigelow Hollow State Park. **Additional Information:** Northeast Connecticut Visitors District, (860) 779-6383 or (888) 628-1228, www.ctquiet-corner.org.

## RESTRICTIONS

**Pets:** Yes. **Fires:** Allowed. **Alcoholic Beverages:** Allowed. **Vehicle Maximum Length:** Large vehicles must make reservations. **Other:** Ask on arrival.

## TO GET THERE

Take 84 to Exit 73 and follow Rte. 190 for 2 mi. Turn left onto Rte. 197 and follow for 2 mi., then make a left onto Rte. 198. The campground is 1.5 mi. on the left.

# WOODSTOCK

## Chamberlain Lake Campground

1397 Rte. 197, Woodstock 06281. T: (860) 974-0567; www.gocampingamerica/chamberlain; chamberlainlakecampground@yahoo.com.

🚐 ★★★★                    ▲ ★★★

| | |
|---|---|
| Beauty: ★★★ | Site Privacy: ★★★★ |
| Spaciousness: ★★★ | Quiet: ★★★★ |
| Security: ★★★★ | Cleanliness: ★★★★ |
| Insect Control: ★★★ | Facilities: ★★★★ |

While the wooded sites here aren't particularly large (around 25–35 feet), they're fairly private, with trees and other growth shielding you from your neighbors. Sites on the lakefront cost a bit more, but the others are almost as nice. Tent campers should enjoy the relative seclusion and quiet of this campground, and nature lovers will appreciate that all fishing done at the campground's lake is catch and release.

## BASICS

**Operated By:** Private operator. **Open:** May 1–Oct. 15. **Site Assignment:** Reservations rec-ommended. **Registration:** Store. **Fee:** $26–$28; 3-night min. stay required in season. **Parking:** At site.

## FACILITIES

**Number of RV Sites:** 120. **Number of Tent-Only Sites:** 30. **Hookups:** Water, electric (30, 40 amps), phone. **Each Site:** Fireplace, picnic table. **Dump Station:** Yes. **Laundry:** Yes. **Pay Phone:** Yes. **Rest Rooms and Showers:** Yes. **Fuel:** No. **Propane:** Yes. **RV Service:** No. **Market:** Xtra Mart, 251 West Main St., Dudley, MA (4.5 mi.). Turn left onto Rte. 197 & follow for 4.5 mi. **Restaurant:** No. **General Store:** Yes. **Vending:** Yes. **Swimming Pool:** Bogey's Restaurant, 80 Airport Rd., Dudley, MA (5.2 mi.). Turn left onto Rte. 197 & follow until Dudley Hill Rd. Make a left onto Dudley Hill Rd. & follow for 1.7 mi. **Playground:** No. **Other:** Rec hall, basketball court, volleyall courts, lake. **Activities:** Boat & canoe rentals, fishing. **Nearby Attractions:** Brimfield flea markets, Old Sturbridge Village. **Additional Information:** Northeast Connecti-cut Visitors District, (860) 779-6383 or (888) 628-1228, www.ctquietcorner.org.

## RESTRICTIONS

**Pets:** On leash only. **Fires:** Allowed. **Alcoholic Beverages:** Allowed. **Vehicle Maximum Length:** 40 ft. **Other:** Ask on arrival.

## TO GET THERE

Take 84 to Exit 73 and go east on Rte. 190. Take a right onto Rte. 171 and follow for 2.2 mi., then take a left onto Rte. 197 and follow for 3.5 mi. until you see the campground on the left.

# Maine

Six moose, four rabbits, a Native American gravesite, and a little bit of Canada: that's what we saw on our campground-to-campground road trip from Rangeley Lake to the Moose River. (They don't call Maine's Route 16 "Moose Alley" for nothing!) From there, we followed the silvery-blue glimmer of Moosehead Lake to spectacular Lily Bay, where Mt. Kineo rises out of a sea (OK, lake) of blue. We took the long way around the lake, since, at 117 square miles, every way is the long way, and set up camp along the shore. Just another day of camping in Maine.

As camping grounds go, Maine is outrageously attractive. Just when you think you've seen the most incredible vista of rockbound coastline, pine-shrouded mountain, or sea-meets-sky, you take another turn in the road and see something even more ahh-inspiring. And we are understating this. Good news for the camper: Maine boasts more than 200 places to take it all in. These vary widely, from upscale camping resorts like **Point Sebago** and **Megunticook-by-the-Sea** with golf courses and gourmet coffee, to rustic retreats (and in Maine, when they say rustic, they mean "the generator goes out at 11 p.m"). Some are so remote, the road in is six suspension-testing miles long; ask 'em if they have a website, and they'll snort, "We don't even have a phone."

Everybody, everybody heads to the south coast and mid-coast regions, for good reason: the beaches and the lobster shacks are there. Count on plenty of traffic in summer, and woe to those who show up in July or August, on a weekend, sans reservation! Keep driving, though, and the glories of Downeast Maine and Acadia await, with a landscape that rivals the most beautiful anywhere.

True Maine insiders know, however, that some of the best camping spots in the state are far from the Atlantic. The **Sebago Lake-Long Lake** chain, in the Western Lakes and Mountains region, offers wonderful lakeside camping, along with boating (many campgrounds offer rentals, or BYOB), fishing, even paddle-wheeler trips. This is camping like you remember it from your childhood, complete with those allowance-busting snack bars. (Hint: come in the fall for the **Fryeburg Fair,** among the best events in Maine.) Heading north, **South Arm** (at Richardson Lake), and **Eustis** (where you'll find an amazing stand of towering red pines, where Benedict Arnold once trod), and **Chain of Ponds** are well worth seeking out. (Just check out our 'best' list.) The Jackman-Moose River area, nudging Canada, is a paradise for sports-loving campers, and everybody who's ever been there loves Greenville, a taste of Montana near Moosehead Lake. Then there's **Katahdin,** and **Caribou**—enough said. Just know that the south coast of Maine is only the beginning.

*The following facilities accept payment in checks or cash only:*

Bar Harbor Campground, Bar Harbor

Camden Rockport Camping, Rockport

Cupsuptic Campground, Oquossoc

Gray Homestead Campground, Southport

Hermit Island Campground, Small Point

Honey Run Beach & Campground, Peru

Sherwood Forest Campsite, New Harbor

Shore Hills Campground, Boothbay Harbor

Somes Sound Campground, Mt. Desert Island

South Arm Campground, Andover

The Moorings, Searsport

Whispering Pines, East Orland

Wolfeboro Campground, Wolfeboro

# Campground Profiles

## ABBOT VILLAGE

### Balsam Woods Campground

112 Pond Rd., Abbot Village 04406. T: (207) 876-2731; www.balsamwoods.com; info@balsamwoods.com.

🚐 ★★★★              ⛺ ★★

Beauty: ★★★                 Site Privacy: ★★★
Spaciousness: ★★★★          Quiet: ★★★★
Security: ★★★★              Cleanliness: ★★★
Insect Control: ★★★★        Facilities: ★★★

Located just 18 miles south of outdoorsy Greenville and Moosehead Lake, Balsam Woods (despite its name) has a totally different vibe. Set in tiny Abbot Village, almost dead-center in the state, the campground has a rural, countryside feel. Freshly-mown grass surrounds a swimming pool and playground area, dotted with picnic tables. Sites in the center of the park are open and grassy, while those at the perimeter are wooded with pines, with plenty of shrubbery buffer for privacy. The property connects with a hiking trail, and the owners will point you toward berry bushes if you want to pick some fresh fruit for dinner. Nothing goes better with Maine blueberries than lobster, and they'll sell you some here. (Shouldn't every Maine campground have its own lobster pound?) Best sites, with hookups, are F3 through 5, and F7, 9, 10, and 11, backing up into the pines. Tenters might find the campsites here too exposed for their taste. In any event, avoid the privies (ugh!) and plan to hike up to the nice, clean rest room behind the rec hall.

**BASICS**

**Operated By:** Jay Eberhard. **Open:** Memorial Day–Oct. **Site Assignment:** Reservations recommended. Deposit equal to 1-night stay required for bookings of less than 1 week; 25% deposit for stays of 1 week or longer. Refunds for cancellations w/ 14-day notice. **Registration:** At office. **Fee:** $21–$23 based on family of 4. V, MC (No checks.). **Parking:** At site.

**FACILITIES**

**Number of RV Sites:** 50. **Number of Tent-Only Sites:** 0. **Hookups:** Water, electric (30 amps). **Each Site:** Picnic table, fire ring. **Dump Station:** Yes. **Laundry:** Yes. **Pay Phone:** Yes. **Rest Rooms and Showers:** Yes. **Fuel:** No. **Propane:** Yes. **Internal Roads:** Gravel, in good condition. **RV Service:** No. **Market:** 10 mi. south. **Restaurant:** 18 mi. north. **General Store:** Yes. **Vending:** No. **Swimming Pool:** Yes. **Playground:** Yes. **Other:** Rec hall. **Activities:** Hiking, berry picking, horseshoes, volleyball, planned activities. **Nearby Attractions:** Appalachian Trail, Moosehead Lake, S.S. Katahdin steamboat cruises, Moosehead Marine Museum, Eveleth-Crafts-Sheridan Historical House, Lily whitewater rafting, boating, fishing. **Additional Information:** Moosehead Lake Region Chamber of Commerce, (207) 723-4443.

**RESTRICTIONS**

**Pets:** Must be leashed, quiet, & cleaned up after. Must not be left unattended. **Fires:** In fire rings only. **Alcoholic Beverages:** Yes. **Vehicle Maximum Length:** 45 ft. **Other:** Maximum of 6 people per campsite.

## To Get There

From junction of Rtes. 15 and 16, go 1 mi. north on Rte. 15, then 3 mi. west of Pond Rd. Campground entrance is on the left.

## ACADIA NATIONAL PARK
### Blackwoods Campground

P.O. Box 177, Bar Harbor 04609. T: (207) 288-3274; www.nps/gov/acad/blackwoods.

🚐 ★★               ⛺ ★★★★

Beauty: ★★★            Site Privacy: ★★★★★
Spaciousness: ★★★★★      Quiet: ★★★★
Security: ★★★★★         Cleanliness: ★★★
Insect Control: ★★★       Facilities: ★★

Blackwoods is one of only two campgrounds in Acadia National Park (also see Seawall Campground) and offers a rustic, no frills base for campers exploring the area and visiting park sights and attractions. The woodsy campground is just 5 miles south of popular Bar Harbor and within a ten minute walk to the ocean. Though there are no showers at the campground (there is cold running water), you'll find hot showers and groceries a half-mile down the street. Typical of national park properties, this has roomy sites and lots of privacy. RVs are limited to 35 feet in length and sites are separate from the tent-only area. Evening slide shows and ranger programs are held in the campground amphitheater during July and Aug. This is a great bargain (under $20 a night) for those looking for a traditional camping experience.

## Basics

**Operated By:** Acadia National Park. **Open:** Year-round. **Site Assignment:** Reservations required mid-June-mid-Sep.; reservations are accepted beginning in Feb. by calling (800) 365-2267 or online (see above website.) Full amount deposit required; cancellations subject to $13.25 service fee; same-day cancellations also subject to 1-night fee; MC, V, no checks. **Registration:** At ranger station on-site. **Fee:** $18. **Parking:** At site.

## Facilities

**Number of RV Sites:** 117. **Number of Tent-Only Sites:** 193. **Hookups:** None. **Each Site:** Picnic table, fire ring. **Dump Station:** Yes. **Laundry:** No. **Pay Phone:** Yes. **Rest Rooms and Showers:** Yes, no showers. **Fuel:** No. **Propane:** No. **Internal Roads:** Paved, gravel (good). **RV Service:** No. **Market:** Bar Harbor (5 mi). **Restaurant:** No. **General Store:** No. **Vending:** No. **Swimming Pool:** No. **Playground:** No. **Other:** Amphitheater, group area, island shuttle bus pickup & dropoff, ranger station. **Activities:** Planned park activities, including nature programs, slide shows, & sing-alongs. **Nearby Attractions:** Bar Harbor, Acadia National Park. **Additional Information:** Acadia National Park, P.O. Box 177, Bar Harbor, ME 04609 (207) 288-3338, www.nps/gov/acad. Also, Acadia Information Center, P.O. Box 139, Mount Desert, ME 04660 (207) 667-8550 or (800) 358-8550, www.acadiainfo.com & Bar Harbor Chamber of Commerce, 93 Cottage St., Bar Harbor, ME 04609 (207) 288-5103, www.barharborinfo.com.

## Restrictions

**Pets:** Must be on a leash, never left unattended. **Fires:** In grills, stoves, & fire rings only. **Alcoholic Beverages:** At site only. **Vehicle Maximum Length:** 35 ft.

## To Get There

From junction Rtes. 3 and 233 (in Bar Harbor), go south 5 mi. on Rte. 3; the campground is on the left.

## ACADIA NATIONAL PARK
### Seawall Campground

P.O. Box 177, Bar Harbor 04609. T: (207) 244-3600; www.nps/gov/acad.

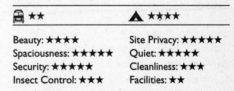

🚐 ★★               ⛺ ★★★★

Beauty: ★★★★           Site Privacy: ★★★★★
Spaciousness: ★★★★★      Quiet: ★★★★★
Security: ★★★★★         Cleanliness: ★★★
Insect Control: ★★★       Facilities: ★★

This is one of only two campgrounds in Acadia National Park (also see Blackwoods Campground) and perfect for those who like a traditional, rustic setting. Seawall is just a few miles south of Southwest Harbor on the park's "quiet" side, and within walking distance of the ocean. Showers and a camping supply store are within a half-mile of the campground. Sites are all roomy, situated in the woods along four separate loops. One loop is reserved for RVs only, where cars and trailers are placed on pull-through aisles among the trees. Two loops accommodate drive-in tent sites and another pod is reserved for walk-in tenters, offering the most privacy. We like the granite and boulder rock fire pits with grills at each site and the nightly ranger programs offered in the amphitheater throughout the summer months. For under $20 a night, it's one of the best bargains around but be sure to arrive early in the morning to snag a site.

## BASICS

**Operated By:** Acadia National Park. **Open:** Late-May–late-Sept. **Site Assignment:** first come, first served. **Registration:** At ranger station on site. **Fee:** Drive-in, $18; walk-in, $12. **Parking:** At site or at general lot to walk-in sites.

## FACILITIES

**Number of RV Sites:** 43. **Number of Tent-Only Sites:** 170. **Hookups:** None. **Each Site:** Picnic table & fire ring. **Dump Station:** Yes. **Laundry:** No. **Pay Phone:** Yes. **Rest Rooms and Showers:** Yes, no showers. **Fuel:** No. **Propane:** No. **Internal Roads:** Paved (good). **RV Service:** No. **Market:** Southwest Harbor (4 mi). **Restaurant:** No. **General Store:** No. **Vending:** No. **Swimming Pool:** No. **Playground:** No. **Other:** Amphitheater, group area, island shuttle bus pickup & dropoff, ranger station. **Activities:** Planned park activities, including nature programs, slide shows, & sing-alongs. **Nearby Attractions:** Bar Harbor, Acadia National Park. **Additional Information:** Acadia National Park, P.O. Box 177, Bar Harbor, ME 04609 (207) 288-3338, www.nps/gov/acad. Also, Acadia Information Center, P.O. Box 139, Mount Desert, ME 04660 (207) 667-8550 or (800) 358-8550, www.acadiainfo.com & Bar Harbor Chamber of Commerce, 93 Cottage St., Bar Harbor, ME 04609 (207) 288-5103, www.barharborinfo.com.

## RESTRICTIONS

**Pets:** Must be on a leash, never left unattended.

**Fires:** In grills, stoves, & fire rings only. **Alcoholic Beverages:** At site only. **Vehicle Maximum Length:** 35 ft. **Other:** 6 people & 2 small tents or 1 large tent are allowed per site; 1 vehicle per site.

## TO GET THERE

From junction Rtes. 102 and 102A, go south 5 mi. on Rte.102A; campground is on the right.

## ANDOVER

### South Arm Campground

P.O. Box 310, Andover 04216. T: (207) 364-5155 or (978) 465-5427 (winter); www.southarm.com.

| 🚐 ★★★★★ | 🛖 ★★★★★ |
|---|---|
| Beauty: ★★★★★ | Site Privacy: ★★★★ |
| Spaciousness: ★★ | Quiet: ★★★★ |
| Security: ★★★★ | Cleanliness: ★★★ |
| Insect Control: ★★ | Facilities: ★★★ |

The owner calls it "Maine's Most Beautiful Campground." No argument here. Set amidst a thousand-acre wilderness area in Western Maine, the campground nudges the south arm of Richardson Lake, with mountains providing a backdrop. Seventeen miles of lakes are accessible here; adventurous campers can choose from remote sites along the lake, reachable only by boat or canoe. The main campground is on a peninsula, with 65 wooded sites set in a loop. At least half of these are on the beach and waterfront. These prime sites require a two-night stay, but you'd want to stay that long anyway. It's a long haul to this campground, and it takes a couple of days to explore the waterways and soak in all the beauty here. Sites 1 through 51 (odd numbers) are shoreside. They're all great, but sites 29A and 29B are set back a bit, with amazing views. Site 31 is beautiful, too. These get snapped up quickly. Off the beach, we like sites 2 through 12 and, especially site 24, near the point. Book early for July and Aug., but don't even consider June, when black flies are out in force. Rainy days, borrow a book, puzzle, game, or novel. For laughs, read the over-the-top prose in their brochure.

## BASICS

**Operated By:** Scott Mitchell. **Open:** May 15–Sept. 15. **Site Assignment:** Reservations recommended. Deposit of 1 nights' fee required; check or cash acceptable. Heavily booked in July & Aug. Refunds for cancellation w/ 1-month notice. **Registration:** At office. **Fee:** $21–$27 for 2 adults & their children under age 18. Wilderness sites, $5 per family/couple. No credit cards. **Parking:** At site.

## FACILITIES

**Number of RV Sites:** 65. **Number of Tent-Only Sites:** 0. **Hookups:** Water, electric (30 amps) Note: Generator goes off at 11 p.m. nightly, comes back on at 6:30 a.m. **Each Site:** Picnic table, fireplace. **Dump Station:** Yes. **Laundry:** Yes. **Pay Phone:** No. **Rest Rooms and Showers:** Yes, coin-op. **Fuel:** No. **Propane:** Yes. **Internal Roads:** Gravel, in fair condition. **RV Service:** No. **Market:** 15 mi. south. **Restaurant:** 15 mi. south. **General Store:** Yes. **Vending:** No. **Swimming Pool:** No. **Playground:** No. **Other:** Marina, boat ramp, dock. **Activities:** Appalachian Trail hiking, fishing, (licenses available), lake swimming, boating (rentals available), boat cruises, planned activities. **Nearby Attractions:** Coose Canyon, White Mountain National Forest, historical museums. **Additional Information:** River Valley Chamber of Commerce, (207) 364-3241?.

## RESTRICTIONS

**Pets:** Must be leashed, quiet, & cleaned up after. Must not be left unattended. Current rabies vaccination certificate required. **Fires:** In fire rings only. **Alcoholic Beverages:** Yes. **Vehicle Maximum Length:** 35 ft. **Other:** 2-night min. stay for waterfront & beach sites (remote or other sites are available by the day); 3-night min. on holidays.

## TO GET THERE

From junction of Rtes. 5 and 120, go 0.5 mi. east on Rte. 120, then 11 mi. north on South Arm Rd. Campground entrance is on the left.

## APPLETON

### Sennebec Lake Campground

Rte. 131, P.O. Box 602, Appleteon 04862. T: (207) 785-4250; www.sennebeclake.com.

🚐 ★★★★          ⛺ ★★★

Beauty: ★★★★     Site Privacy: ★★★
Spaciousness: ★★★     Quiet: ★★★★
Security: ★★★★     Cleanliness: ★★★★★
Insect Control: ★★★     Facilities: ★★★★

This neat, well-kept campsite is set in a rural area in mid-coast Maine, about 12 miles northwest of Camden. It may not be on the ocean, but it's a great spot, with grassy, terraced sites overlooking Lake Sennebec. RV sites are side-by-side along the lakefront; wooded site 72 (electric and water) is the nicest, in our view. Lakeside sites include sites 62 through 73 and 74 through 80. Tent sites are walk-in, with a footpath leading over a stream to a secluded, piney grove. Best tent sites are 94 and 95; beware of lumpy site 93. There's a sandy beach with a float, and they sell bait and fishing gear if you want to have a go at the lake's bass, perch, and pickerel population. We'd be tempted to rent a canoe and paddle around the placid lake. A lodge, overlooking the lake, is the venue for Saturday night dances with live bands. This campground makes a dandy, centralized base for Maine adventures.

## BASICS

**Operated By:** Lorraine & Jim Bender. **Open:** May–Oct. **Site Assignment:** Reservations recommended. 50% deposit required. Refunds for cancellation w/ 14-day notice, minus $10 service charge. **Registration:** At office. **Fee:** $19–$28 for 2 adults & up to 3 children under age 18. V, MC. **Parking:** At site.

## FACILITIES

**Number of RV Sites:** 97. **Number of Tent-Only Sites:** 9. **Hookups:** Water, electric (30 amps), sewer, modem access. **Each Site:** Picnic table, fireplace. **Dump Station:** Yes. **Laundry:** Yes. **Pay Phone:** Yes. **Rest Rooms and Showers:** Yes. **Fuel:** No. **Propane:** Yes. **Internal Roads:**

Gravel, in good condition. **RV Service:** No. **Market:** 3 mi. south. **Restaurant:** 3 mi. south. **General Store:** Yes. **Vending:** Yes. **Swimming Pool:** No. **Playground:** Yes. **Other:** Rec hall, boat ramp. **Activities:** Lake swimming, fishing (license required), boating (rentals available), basketball, volleyball, planned activities. **Nearby Attractions:** Camden (12 mi. southeast, w/ its harbor, galleries, museums & shops), windjammer fleet, Penobscot Bay cruises, Conway Homestead & Mary Cramer Museum (28th century restored farmhouse & gardens), Camden Hills State Park, Merryspring Park, Owl's Head Transportation Museum, golf. **Additional Information:** Union Chamber of Commerce, (207) 785-3200.

## RESTRICTIONS

**Pets:** Must be leashed, quiet, & cleaned up after. Must not be left unattended. **Fires:** In fire rings. **Alcoholic Beverages:** At sites only. **Vehicle Maximum Length:** 45 ft. **Other:** 2-night min. stay required in July & Aug.; 3-night min. stay required on holiday weekends.

## TO GET THERE

From junction of Rtes. 17 and 131, go 3 mi. north on Rte. 131. Campground entrance is on the right.

# BANGOR

## Paul Bunyan Campground

1862 Union St. , Bangor 04401. T: (207) 941-1177 or (207) 947-3734; www.paulbunyan.com; paulbunyancampground@aol.com.

🚐 ★★★          ▲ ★★

Beauty: ★★★            Site Privacy: ★★★
Spaciousness: ★★★      Quiet: ★★★
Security: ★★★          Cleanliness: ★★★
Insect Control: ★★★    Facilities: ★★★

Of the two campgrounds off the interstate in the Bangor area (also see Pleasant Hill Campground), this one is livelier and a bit noisier, attracting a regular clientele of families during summer weekends and weeklong vacations. The campground offers plenty of entertainment, live bands and DJs, potluck dinners and parades, ice cream socials, contests, and tournaments. There's

also free pancake breakfast for campers every Sunday morning throughout the summer. Come fall, the campground calms down a bit, hosting more one-night travelers. The campground feels spacious due to the surrounding fields and expansive public areas, but individual sites are average to small in size. There's a small, separate tent-only area along the road; pull-through, full hookup sites are clustered in the open field toward the back of the campground. There's a pond on the property, aptly dubbed Babe's Bathtub. Don't expect much: it's barely more than a mosquito incubator but small kids have fun tossing stones and navigating paddleboats around its tiny perimeter.

## BASICS

**Operated By:** Dennis & Shirley Hachey. **Open:** May–Oct. **Site Assignment:** Reservations suggested. 1 night deposit required for reservations of 3 days or less, $40 for 4 or more days; 2-week cancellation policy w/ $5 service charge; MC, V, checks. **Registration:** At office. **Fee:** Full hookups, $26 (50 amp), $23 (30 amp); water & electric, $18.50; no hookups, $14, based on 2 adults & 2 children. **Parking:** At site.

## FACILITIES

**Number of RV Sites:** 77. **Number of Tent-Only Sites:** 18. **Hookups:** Water, electric, sewer (30, 50 amps). **Each Site:** Picnic table, fire ring. **Dump Station:** Yes. **Laundry:** Yes. **Pay Phone:** Yes. **Rest Rooms and Showers:** Yes. **Fuel:** No. **Propane:** Yes. **Internal Roads:** Dirt, gravel (fair). **RV Service:** No. **Market:** Bangor (2 mi). **Restaurant:** No. **General Store:** Yes. **Vending:** No. **Swimming Pool:** Yes. **Playground:** Yes. **Other:** Small pond, paddleboat rentals, picnic shelter, game room, sports field. **Activities:** Swimming, live entertainment, potluck dinners, planned activities, including children's programs, hayrides, socials. **Nearby Attractions:** Bangor, Bar Harbor, Acadia National Park, Maine coast. **Additional Information:** Bangor Regional Chamber of Commerce, 519 Maine St. , P.O. Box 1443, Bangor, ME 04402 (207) 947-0307, www.bangorregion.com.

## RESTRICTIONS

**Pets:** Must be on a leash, never left unattended. **Fires:** In grills, stoves, & fire rings only. **Alcoholic**

**Beverages:** At site only. **Vehicle Maximum Length:** 40 ft.

## TO GET THERE

From I-95, exit 47, go 2.8 mi. west on Rte. 222 (Union St.); campground is on the left.

## BAR HARBOR
### Bar Harbor Campground

RFD 1, Box 1125, Bar Harbor 04609. T: (207) 288-5185; www.barharborcamping.com.

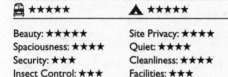

Beauty: ★★★★★         Site Privacy: ★★★★
Spaciousness: ★★★★     Quiet: ★★★★
Security: ★★★           Cleanliness: ★★★★
Insect Control: ★★★     Facilities: ★★★

This is the closet campground to Bar Harbor and one of the prettiest in the area. They like to keep it simple here: all sites are first come, first served. Campers can drive through the campground and select their site and then register. You might have a difficult time choosing; there are plenty of spacious, private spots with sweeping views of Frenchman's Bay. In fact, the entire campground has a roomy, expansive feel. There's a large secluded area for tents and small pop-ups (we like the woodsy privacy in the "s" loop) and a cluster of tent-only ocean view sites (Q1, Q2, and R1-4 are especially nice.) Water and electric sites and full hookups are scattered throughout, many with ocean views. We especially like the swimming pool area at this campground, set high on an point, overlooking the Maine coastline.

## BASICS

**Operated By:** Craig Robbins. **Open:** Memorial Day–Columbus Day. **Site Assignment:** First come, first served, cash only. **Registration:** At office. **Fee:** Full hookups, $27; water & electric, $25; no hookups, $20. **Parking:** At site.

## FACILITIES

**Number of RV Sites:** 155. **Number of Tent-Only Sites:** 145. **Hookups:** Water, electric, sewer (30, 50 amps). **Each Site:** Picnic table, fire ring. **Dump Station:** Yes. **Laundry:** Yes. **Pay Phone:** Yes. **Rest Rooms and Showers:** Yes

(coin-op). **Fuel:** No. **Propane:** Yes. **Internal Roads:** Paved, gravel (good). **RV Service:** No. **Market:** Bar Harbor (4 mi). **Restaurant:** No. **General Store:** Yes. **Vending:** Yes. **Swimming Pool:** Yes. **Playground:** Yes. **Other:** Ocean frontage, game room, TV room. **Activities:** Swimming, horseshoes, shuffleboard, basketball. **Nearby Attractions:** Bar Harbor, Acadia National Park. **Additional Information:** Acadia National Park, P.O. Box 177, Bar Harbor, ME 04609 (207) 288-3338, www.nps/gov/acad. Also, Acadia Information Center, P.O. Box 139, Mount Desert, ME 04660 (207) 667-8550 (800) 358-8550, www.acadiainfo.com & Bar Harbor Chamber of Commerce, 93 Cottage St. , Bar Harbor, ME 04609 (207) 288-5103, www.barharborinfo.com.

## RESTRICTIONS

**Pets:** Must be on a leash, never left unattended. **Fires:** In grills, stoves, & fire rings only. **Alcoholic Beverages:** At site only. **Vehicle Maximum Length:** None. **Other:** No skateboards, rollerblades allowed.

## TO GET THERE

From junction Rtes. 102 and 3, go south 5 mi. on Rte. 3; campground is on the left.

## BAR HARBOR
### Barcadia Campground

RR1 Box 2165, Bar Harbor 04609. T: (207) 288-3520; F: (207) 288-2840; www.campbarcadia.com; barcadia@acadia.net.

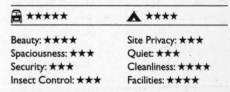

Beauty: ★★★★          Site Privacy: ★★★
Spaciousness: ★★★      Quiet: ★★★
Security: ★★★          Cleanliness: ★★★★
Insect Control: ★★★    Facilities: ★★★★

This pretty property, a stone's throw from Bar Harbor and Acadia National Park, boasts 3,500 feet of oceanfront with stunning panoramic views of the rocky Maine coastline. We love to sit on the oceanfront patio, watch the sun slip to the other side of the world while seals play on offshore rocks. Another nicety: the campground serves up a traditional fresh lobster dinner nightly during the summer. Campers can rent kayaks on site to explore area waters and coves or sign up for a guided excursion. A variety of tours are available from the campground, ranging from a few hours to all day. There's a rocky oceanfront beach for tidepooling and toe dunking, too. There are plenty of oceanfront sites, a separate tent-only area in the trees (site 405 set on a point overlooking the ocean is primo!) and level, open RV sites clustered near the front, many with ocean views.

## BASICS

**Operated By:** Pete & Lynn Desrochers. **Open:** Memorial Day–Columbus Day. **Site Assignment:** Reservations accepted year-round, recommended in Jul.–Aug. 1 day deposit required, 14-day cancellation policy with $10 service charge; MC, V & checks. **Registration:** At office. **Fee:** Full hookups, $39; water & electric, $39 (oceanfront); $38 (premium); $33 (30 amp); $31 (20 amp); tent sites: $39 (large oceanfront); $32 (oceanfront); $30 (premium); $27 (wooded); $19 (tent); based on 2 adults & 2 children under 18. Seventh night is free. **Parking:** At site, 1 vehicle per site.

## FACILITIES

**Number of RV Sites:** 200. **Number of Tent-Only Sites:** 30. **Hookups:** Water, electric, sewer (20, 30 amps), modem. **Each Site:** Picnic table, fire ring. **Dump Station:** Yes. **Laundry:** Yes. **Pay Phone:** Yes. **Rest Rooms and Showers:** Yes (coin-op). **Fuel:** No. **Propane:** Yes. **Internal Roads:** Paved, gravel (good). **RV Service:** Yes. **Market:** Bar Harbor (2 mi). **Restaurant:** No. **General Store:** Yes. **Vending:** No. **Swimming Pool:** No. **Playground:** Yes. **Other:** Ocean frontage, beach, game room, kayak rentals & guided kayak excursions, boat launch area, sunset viewing patio, free bus shuttle to Bar Harbor, trailer rentals. **Activities:** Swimming, boating, lobster bakes, basketball, volleyball, badminton, horseshoes. **Nearby Attractions:** Bar Harbor, Acadia National Park. **Additional Information:** Acadia National Park, P.O. Box 177, Bar Harbor, ME 04609 (207) 288-3338, www.nps/gov/acad. Also, Acadia Information Center, P.O. Box 139, Mount Desert, ME 04660 (207) 667-8550 (800) 358-8550, www.acadiainfo.com & Bar Harbor

Chamber of Commerce, 93 Cottage St., Bar Harbor, ME 04609 (207) 288-5103, www.barharborinfo.com.

## RESTRICTIONS

**Pets:** Must be on a leash, never left unattended. Only 2 dogs per site. **Fires:** In grills, stoves, & fire rings only. **Alcoholic Beverages:** At site only. **Vehicle Maximum Length:** 43 ft.

## TO GET THERE

From junction Rtes. 3, 102 and campground road, go southwest on campground road.

## BAR HARBOR

### Hadley's Point Campground

RFD No. 1, Box 1790, Bar Harbor 04609. T: (207) 288-4808; www.hadleyspoint.com.

🚐 ★★★          ▲ ★★★

| | |
|---|---|
| Beauty: ★★★ | Site Privacy: ★★★ |
| Spaciousness: ★★★ | Quiet: ★★★ |
| Security: ★★★ | Cleanliness: ★★★★ |
| Insect Control: ★★★ | Facilities: ★★★ |

This campground, just four miles from the Acadia National Park entrance, is a clean, pleasant base for campers visiting the area. There are plenty of nearby attractions and activities and a public saltwater beach within walking distance of the campground. The plain-jane property offers minimal frills (swimming pool, laundry, ultra clean rest rooms and showers) but you'll have a choice of sites. There's a separate tent-only area with wooded sites and adequate room and privacy. Other sites are located in an open field, ringed in a circle; these don't offer much privacy but they're good for campers who like sunny, open spaces. The staff is exceptionally friendly and come Sunday there's no need to head into town for church, if you're so inclined: church service is held each week at the campground throughout July and Aug.

## BASICS

**Operated By:** Robert & Suzanne Baker. **Open:** May 15–Oct. 15. **Site Assignment:** Reservations suggested in Jul.–Aug. $30 deposit for stays of less that 5 days, $50 deposit for stays of 5 days or more, 48-hour cancellation policy, minus $5

service charge, no refunds on holiday weekends; MC, V, checks. **Registration:** At office. **Fee:** Full hookups, $26; water & electric, $23; no hookups, $18, based on a party of 4. **Parking:** At site.

## FACILITIES

**Number of RV Sites:** 155. **Number of Tent-Only Sites:** 45. **Hookups:** Water, electric, sewer (20, 30 amps). **Each Site:** Picnic table, fire ring. **Dump Station:** Yes. **Laundry:** Yes. **Pay Phone:** Yes. **Rest Rooms and Showers:** Yes (coin-op). **Fuel:** No. **Propane:** Yes. **Internal Roads:** Gravel (good). **RV Service:** No. **Market:** Bar Harbor (5 mi). **Restaurant:** No. **General Store:** Yes. **Vending:** Yes. **Swimming Pool:** Yes. **Playground:** Yes. **Other:** Sunday church service on site. **Activities:** Swimming, horseshoes, shuffleboard. **Nearby Attractions:** Bar Harbor, Acadia National Park. **Additional Information:** Acadia National Park, P.O. Box 177, Bar Harbor, ME 04609 (207) 288-3338, www.nps/gov/acad. Also, Acadia Information Center, P.O. Box 139, Mount Desert, ME, 04660 (207) 667-8550, (800) 358-8550, www.acadiainfo.com & Bar Harbor Chamber of Commerce, 93 Cottage St., Bar Harbor, ME 04609 (207) 288-5103, www.barharborinfo.com.

## RESTRICTIONS

**Pets:** Must be on a leash, never left unattended. **Fires:** In grills, stoves, & fire rings only. **Alcoholic Beverages:** At site only. **Vehicle Maximum Length:** None.

## TO GET THERE

From junction Rtes. 102 and 3, go east 3 mi. on Rte. 3, then north 0.25 mi. on Hadley Point Rd.; the campground is on the right.

## BAR HARBOR

### Mount Desert Narrows

Rte. 3, RR 1, Box 2045B, Bar Harbor 04609. T: (207) 288-4782; www.narrowscamping.com.

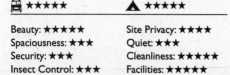

| 🚐 ★★★★★ | ▲ ★★★★★ |
|---|---|
| Beauty: ★★★★★ | Site Privacy: ★★★★ |
| Spaciousness: ★★★ | Quiet: ★★★ |
| Security: ★★★ | Cleanliness: ★★★★★ |
| Insect Control: ★★★ | Facilities: ★★★★★ |

This oceanfront campground is one of the most popular in the Bar Harbor/Acadia National Park area for both RVers and tenters, offering modern facilities, a great location, and pretty scenery. You'll find 2,100 feet of shoreline, plenty of oceanfront and ocean view sites, on-site recreation and a free bus shuttle to downtown Bar Harbor. Tenters have their own 25 acre section (first come, first served) and several prime oceanfront sites with sweeping views (sites 14 and 15 are favorites.) Tent site 30 at the end of a point on the shoreline also offers great views and plenty of space. Full hookup sites are set side-by-side near the front of the campground. There are also a handful of water and electric sites and water only sites on the ocean, too. If you're looking for a water and electric hookup, sites 88-94 on the shoreline, can't be beat.

## BASICS

**Operated By:** Pat Stanley. **Open:** May–Oct. 25. **Site Assignment:** Reservations accepted year-round, suggested in Jul.–Aug. All sites require a 2 night min. reservation w/ a 3-night min. on holiday weekends; holidays are paid in full & non-refundable. Oceanfront sites have a 3-night min. stay in July & Aug. There are no sewer sites on the ocean. No reservations taken for basic tenting sites; these are first come, first served. $50 deposit for 2 nights, $100 for 3 nights, $150 for 4–7 nights, $200 for 8 or more nights; 30-day cancellation policy w/ a $10 service charge; MC, V, D, checks for reservations; no checks upon arrival. **Registration:** At office. **Fee:** Premium full hookups, $40 (early & late summer) $60 (peak season); premium water, electric (50 amp) phone & cable, $30–$45; water, electric & sewer, $33–$45; best water & electric on ocean, $35–$50; water & electric on ocean, $33–$45; Narrows best water & electric, $28–$35; water & electric, $25–$33; oceanfront tenting, $28–$40; Narrows best tenting, $24–32; Narrows tenting, $20–$23. **Parking:** At site.

## FACILITIES

**Number of RV Sites:** 219. **Number of Tent-Only Sites:** 20. **Hookups:** Water, electric, sewer (20, 30, 50 amps), cabel TV, modem. **Each Site:** Picnic table, fire ring. **Dump Station:** Yes. **Laundry:** Yes. **Pay Phone:** Yes. **Rest Rooms and**

**Showers:** Yes. **Fuel:** No. **Propane:** Yes. **Internal Roads:** Gravel, dirt (good). **RV Service:** Yes. **Market:** Bar Harbor (4 mi). **Restaurant:** No. **General Store:** Yes. **Vending:** Yes. **Swimming Pool:** Yes. **Playground:** Yes. **Other:** Ocean frontage, entertainment pavilion, game room, shuttle bus service to Bar Harbor, canoe rentals, boat launch. **Activities:** Swimming, boating, horseshoes, basketball, volleyball, planned activities, including hayrides, movies, storytelling, & more. **Nearby Attractions:** Bar Harbor, Acadia National Park. **Additional Information:** Acadia National Park, P.O. Box 177, Bar Harbor, ME 04609 (207) 288-3338, www.nps/gov/acad. Also, Acadia Information Center, P.O. Box 139, Mount Desert, ME 04660 (207) 667-8550 (800) 358-8550, www.acadiainfo.com & Bar Harbor Chamber of Commerce, 93 Cottage St. , Bar Harbor, ME 04609 (207) 288-5103, www.barharborinfo.com.

## RESTRICTIONS

**Pets:** Must be on a leash, never left unattended. **Fires:** In grills, stoves, & fire rings only. **Alcoholic Beverages:** At site only. **Vehicle Maximum Length:** None.

## TO GET THERE

From junction Rtes. 102 and 3, go east 1.5 mi. on Rte. 3; campground is on the left.

## BAR HARBOR

### Spruce Valley Campground

RR 1, Box 2420, Rte. 102, Bar Harbor 04609. T: (207) 288-5139; www.sprucevalley.com; sprucval@midmaine.com.

🚐 ★★                    ▲ ★★★

| | |
|---|---|
| Beauty: ★★★ | Site Privacy: ★★★ |
| Spaciousness: ★★★ | Quiet: ★★★★ |
| Security: ★★★ | Cleanliness: ★★★ |
| Insect Control: ★★★ | Facilities: ★★ |

This campground, close to Acadia National Park, is best for tenters and smaller trailer campers who prefer peace and quiet to action and activities. It's low-key and family-oriented, complete with country gospel concerts on Saturday evenings during July and Aug. There are the basic conveniences: a pool for warm-day dunks, store and free hot showers, with easy access to Bar Harbor and national park sites. The Acadia National Park Visitor Center is only five miles away. Tent sites have some elbow room, set in the trees for shade and seclusion. Full hookups, including a cluster of 15 or so seasonal renters, are both open or shaded.

## BASICS

**Operated By:** Harry & Paula Luhrs. **Open:** May–Oct. **Site Assignment:** Reservations suggested in July–Aug.; 2-night deposit required, 1-night fee charged w/ less than 48-hour notice, $3 service charge for all cancellations. No refunds on holiday reservations; MC, V, D, checks. **Registration:** At office. **Fee:** Full hookups, $27; water & electric, $25; no hookups, $19, based on family of 4, 2 adults & 2 children under 16. **Parking:** At site, 1 vehicle per site.

## FACILITIES

**Number of RV Sites:** 60. **Number of Tent-Only Sites:** 40. **Hookups:** Water, electric, sewer (30 amps), cable TV. **Each Site:** Picnic table, fire ring. **Dump Station:** Yes. **Laundry:** Yes. **Pay Phone:** Yes. **Rest Rooms and Showers:** Yes. **Fuel:** No. **Propane:** Yes. **Internal Roads:** Gravel, dirt (good). **RV Service:** No. **Market:** Bar Harbor (3 mi). **Restaurant:** No. **General Store:** Yes. **Vending:** Yes. **Swimming Pool:** Yes. **Playground:** Yes. **Other:** Game room, man-made pond, country gospel concerts on Saturday evenings in July-Aug., trailer rentals. **Activities:** Swimming, horseshoes, basketball, volleyball. **Nearby Attractions:** Bar Harbor, Acadia National Park. **Additional Information:** Acadia National Park, P.O. Box 177, Bar Harbor, ME 04609 (207) 288-3338, www.nps/gov/acad. Also, Acadia Information Center, P.O. Box 139, Mount Desert, ME 04660 (207) 667-8550 (800) 358-8550, www.acadiainfo.com & Bar Harbor Chamber of Commerce, 93 Cottage St. , Bar Harbor, ME 04609 (207) 288-5103, www.barharborinfo.com.

## RESTRICTIONS

**Pets:** Must be on a leash, never left unattended. **Fires:** In grills, stoves, & fire rings only. **Alcoholic Beverages:** At site only. **Vehicle Maximum Length:** 40 ft.

<u>To Get There</u>
From junction Rtes. 3 and 102, go south 1.5 mi. on Rte. 102; campground is on the left.

## BASS HARBOR
### Bass Harbor Campground

P.O. Box 122, Rte. 102A, Bass Harbor 04653.T: (207) 244-5857 (800) 327-5857; www.bassharbor.com; info@bassharbor.com.

🚐 ★★★          ⛺ ★★★★

Beauty: ★★★          Site Privacy: ★★★
Spaciousness: ★★★    Quiet: ★★★★
Security: ★★★★        Cleanliness: ★★★
Insect Control: ★★     Facilities: ★★★

Loyal campers return to Bass Harbor Campground year after year, using it as a base to explore Acadia National Park and the surrounding area. Most come for a week or two and appreciate the peace and quiet of the campground, away from the hustle, bustle, and traffic in the Bar Harbor area. Livin' is easy and slower, here; days spent visiting Bass Harbor Lighthouse, biking and hiking area paths, or day trips into Acadia National Park attractions. Full hookups sites are set in rows behind the office and pool area; water and electric and tent sites (some with platforms) are off a loop road in the woods. There's also a separate tent-only area across the street with shaded sites and its own bathhouse and showers.

<u>Basics</u>
**Operated By:** Mike & Sue Clayton. **Open:** Memorial Day–Columbus Day. **Site Assignment:** Reservations suggested in Jul.–Aug. 1-night deposit, 14-day cancellation policy with $10 service fee; MC,V, D,AE, checks. **Registration:** At office. **Fee:** Full hookups, $30; water, electric, cable, $28; water & electric, $28; no hookups, $23. **Parking:** At site.

<u>Facilities</u>
**Number of RV Sites:** 94. **Number of Tent-Only Sites:** 36. **Hookups:** Water, electric, sewer (30, 50 amps), cable TV, modem. **Each Site:** Picnic table, fire ring. **Dump Station:** Yes. **Laundry:** Yes. **Pay Phone:** Yes. **Rest Rooms and Showers:**

Yes. **Fuel:** No. **Propane:** Yes. **Internal Roads:** Gravel, dirt (good). **RV Service:** No. **Market:** Bass Harbor (1 mi). **Restaurant:** No. **General Store:** Yes. **Vending:** No. **Swimming Pool:** Yes. **Playground:** Yes. **Other:** Cabin, trailer & motor home rentals. **Activities:** Swimming, basketball. **Nearby Attractions:** Bar Harbor, Acadia National Park. **Additional Information:** Acadia National Park, P.O. Box 177, Bar Harbor, ME 04609 (207) 288-3338, www.nps/gov/acad. Also, Acadia Information Center, P.O. Box 139, Mount Desert, ME 04660 (207) 667-8550 (800) 358-8550, www.acadiainfo.com & Bar Harbor Chamber of Commerce, 93 Cottage St., Bar Harbor, ME 04609 (207) 288-5103, www.barharborinfo.com.

<u>Restrictions</u>
**Pets:** Must be on a leash, never left unattended. **Fires:** In grills, stoves, & fire rings only. **Alcoholic Beverages:** At site only. **Vehicle Maximum Length:** None.

<u>To Get There</u>
From junction Rtes. 102 and 102A, in Southwest Harbor, go south 5 mi. on Rte. 102A; campground is on the right.

## BELFAST
### The Moorings

191 Searsport Ave., Searsport 04915.T: (207) 338-6860.

🚐 ★★★          ⛺ ★★

Beauty: ★★★          Site Privacy: ★★
Spaciousness: ★★★    Quiet: ★★★
Security: ★★★        Cleanliness: ★★★
Insect Control: ★★★   Facilities: ★★★

The smell of ocean, cool sea breezes, and views of picturesque Penobscot Bay dominate this modest mid-coast Maine campground. There's not a lot happening on this tiny slice of Maine coastline (kids will be bored and teens will die!) There's a small rocky beach, better for walking and beachcombing than swimming, and a small recreation area (volleyball, tetherball, horseshoes.) All sites are in the open, great for ocean viewing, but not very private. The staff lights a bonfire at water's edge each summer evening but most campers are content to relax at the campsite, watch the sun set over the bay and plan the next day's excursions. From here, you have all of mid-coast Maine to explore.

## BASICS

**Operated By:** Ben Hill. **Open:** May–Oct. **Site Assignment:** Reservations suggested Jul.–Aug., no deposit requirements, no credit cards, checks. **Registration:** At office. **Fee:** Water & electric, $30; no hookups, $10 per person. **Parking:** At site.

## FACILITIES

**Number of RV Sites:** 27. **Number of Tent-Only Sites:** 13. **Hookups:** Water, electric (30 amps). **Each Site:** Picnic table, security light. **Dump Station:** Yes. **Laundry:** Yes. **Pay Phone:** No. **Rest Rooms and Showers:** Yes. **Fuel:** No. **Propane:** No. **Internal Roads:** Gravel (good). **RV Service:** No. **Market:** Belfast (.5 mi). **Restaurant:** Yes. **General Store:** No. **Vending:** Yes. **Swimming Pool:** No. **Playground:** Yes. **Other:** Ocean frontage, beach, car rentals on site, game room. **Activities:** Swimming, beachcombing, volleyball, tetherball, horseshoes, basketball. **Nearby Attractions:** Belfast, Searsport, Deer Isle Peninsula, coastal beaches. **Additional Information:** Searsport Economic Development Committee, Reservoir St., Searsport, ME 04974 (207) 54807255, www.searsportme.com.

## RESTRICTIONS

**Pets:** Must be on a leash, never left unattended. **Fires:** In grills, stoves only. **Alcoholic Beverages:** At site only. **Vehicle Maximum Length:** None.

## TO GET THERE

From Rte. 1 (in Belfast), go north 2.1 mi. beyond bridge over Belfast Harbor; campground is on the right.

## BOOTHBAY

### Little Ponderosa Campground

R.R. 1, P.O. Box 915, Boothbay 04537. T: (207) 633-2700; www.littleponderoas.com; camp@littleponderosa.com.

 ★★★★           ★

| | |
|---|---|
| Beauty: ★★★★ | Site Privacy: ★★★ |
| Spaciousness: ★★★ | Quiet: ★★★★ |
| Security: ★★★★★ | Cleanliness: ★★★★ |
| Insect Control: ★★★★★ | Facilities: ★★★★ |

Mini-golf and a snack bar—two sure signs that Little Ponderosa caters to the family crowd. Of all the campgrounds in the Boothbay area, this one has the most child-friendly vibe. Saturday night concerts, ice cream sundae nights (Sundays), and non-denominational church services are among the happenings here. Then, there's nearby Boothbay Harbor, a great place to hang out, eat, shop, and take a boat cruise. This nicely-wooded campground is set on a tidal inlet, with a small, squishy-bottomed beach (wear your water shoes) and a swim raft. About one-third of the campsites are situated along the waterfront. Campsites are grass and gravel, set in a loop. The two tent-only sites are fairly exposed; we'd opt for a water/electric site, perhaps 17, 18, or 19, offering more privacy and better views. The best full hookup sites are 63 through 65, backed into the woods. We'd skip site 4, since it's right by the beach path. And Little Ponderosa gets extra points for aggressive insect management: they've installed six "Mosquito Magnets" to rid the place of pesky pests.

## BASICS

**Operated By:** Jeff & Allison Lowell. **Open:** May 15–Oct. 15. **Site Assignment:** Reservations recommended. Deposit of 1 nights' fee required. Refund for cancellation w/ 7-day notice, minus 30% service fee. **Registration:** At office. **Fee:** $18–$28 for 2 adults & 2 children. V, MC, D. **Parking:** At site.

## FACILITIES

**Number of RV Sites:** 95. **Number of Tent-Only Sites:** 2. **Hookups:** Water, electric (20, 30 amps), sewer, modem access. **Each Site:** Picnic table, fire ring. **Dump Station:** Yes. **Laundry:** Yes. **Pay Phone:** Yes. **Rest Rooms and Showers:** Yes, coin-op. **Fuel:** No. **Propane:** Yes. **Internal Roads:** Gravel, in good condition. **RV Service:** No. **Market:** 4 mi. south. **Restaurant:** 2 mi. south. **General Store:** Yes. **Vending:** Yes. **Swimming Pool:** No. **Playground:** Yes. **Other:** Mini-golf, rec hall. **Activities:** Swimming, fishing (no license required), volleyball, horseshoes, boating (canoe & kayak rentals available), planned activities. **Nearby Attractions:** Boothbay Railway Village, Maine Resources Aquarium, Boothbay Harbor restaurants, shops & galleries, deep-sea fishing, whale-watching cruises, golf. **Additional Information:** Boothbay Harbor Region Chamber of Commerce, (207) 633-2353 or (800) 266-8422.

## RESTRICTIONS

**Pets:** Must be leashed, quiet, & cleaned up after. Must not be left unattended. **Fires:** In fireplaces only. **Alcoholic Beverages:** At sites only. **Vehicle Maximum Length:** 40 ft. **Other:** Ask on arrival.

## TO GET THERE

Take Maine Turnpike to exit 9, then take I-95 to Rte. 1 in Brunswick (exit 22.) Stay on Rte. 1 through Wiscasset, then turn right on Rte. 27 south to Boothbay Harbor Region. Campground is 5 mi. on the right.

## BOOTHBAY HARBOR

### Shore Hills Campground

Rte. 27, P.O. Box 448, Boothbay 04537. T: (207) 633-4782; www.shorehills.com.

| 🚐 ★★★ | ⛺ ★★★ |
|---|---|
| Beauty: ★★★ | Site Privacy: ★★★★ |
| Spaciousness: ★★★ | Quiet: ★★★ |
| Security: ★★★★★ | Cleanliness: ★★★★ |
| Insect Control: ★★★ | Facilities: ★★★ |

It's very quiet—that's why I keep coming! says Peggy, a happy camper at Shore Hills. That sums it up. Although this wooded, coastal campground is only four miles from bustling, touristy Boothbay Harbor, all is quiet here. The far western edge of this campground sits on the Cross River. The river runs south to the sea. From site 84, guests can take a woodsy walk to the marsh and 'fishing rocks', a great spot to cast a line or just gaze out to the river, where there's bound to be a paddler or two. (Nice touch here: use of canoes is free.) Most sites are back-in, with excellent buffer for privacy. The Family Circle area is wide open, suitable for the largest rigs, while sites 66 and 67 are closest to the water. Site 57, for tenting, boasts awesome views, while hillside site

11 overlooks the marsh, very nice. Some tent sites offer a crushed-rock surface for good drainage in case of rain. All sites have water. Another great feature here, if you hate cruising for a parking place: they'll shuttle-bus you to Boothbay Harbor. This peaceful place caters to an older clientele, many of whom (like Peggy) have been coming for years.

## BASICS

**Operated By:** Peggy Fuller. **Open:** Apr. 15–Columbus Day. **Site Assignment:** Reservations recommended. $15 deposit required. Refunds for cancellations w/ 7-day notice. **Registration:** At office. **Fee:** $16–$28 for 2 adults & 2 children. No credit cards. **Parking:** At site.

## FACILITIES

**Number of RV Sites:** 85. **Number of Tent-Only Sites:** 20. **Hookups:** Water, electric (30, 50 amps), sewer, cable TV. **Each Site:** Picnic table, fire ring. **Dump Station:** Yes. **Laundry:** Yes. **Pay Phone:** Yes. **Rest Rooms and Showers:** Yes, coin-op. **Fuel:** No. **Propane:** Yes. **Internal Roads:** Paved & gravel, in good condition. **RV Service:** No. **Market:** 4 mi. south. **Restaurant:** 4 mi. south. **General Store:** Yes. **Vending:** Yes. **Swimming Pool:** No. **Playground:** Yes. **Other:** Rec hall. **Activities:** Saltwater river fishing, boating (canoes available), swimming (at high tide), horseshoes. **Nearby Attractions:** Boothbay Railway Village, Maine Resources Aquarium, Boothbay Harbor restaurants, shops & galleries, deep-sea fishing, whale-watching cruises, golf. **Additional Information:** Boothbay Harbor Region Chamber of Commerce, (207) 633-2353 or (800) 266-8422.

## RESTRICTIONS

**Pets:** Must be leashed, quiet, & cleaned up after. Must not be left unattended. **Fires:** In fire rings only. **Alcoholic Beverages:** At sites only. **Vehicle Maximum Length:** None. **Other:** 3-day min. stay on holidays.

## TO GET THERE

From Portland, take 195 north to Coastal Rte. 1 for 47 mi. From Edgecomb, take Rte. 27 south 8 mi. to campground, on right.

## BROWNFIELD

## River Run

P.O. Box 90, Brownfield 04010. T: (207) 452-2500; F: (207) 452-2500;
www.riverruncanoe.com;
canoe@riverruncanoe.com.

🚐 ★★                    ▲ ★★★

Beauty: ★★★★           Site Privacy: ★★★★
Spaciousness: ★★★★★    Quiet: ★★★
Security: ★★★★★        Cleanliness: ★★★★
Insect Control: ★★      Facilities: ★

What do you get for your money? Not much in the way of facilities—well, there's a row of porta-potties—but you do get a nice spot on the Saco River, and experienced folks who'll be happy to rent you a canoe and set you up on a paddling trip. When you've had enough of that, or your shoulders give out, stretch out on a strip of sand on one of their private beaches, or jump in for a dip. Besides, you won't get a shower otherwise, if you're tenting. This primitive area is beautifully wooded, except for the grassy field reserved for the largest RVs. Like Woodland Acres Camp 'N' Canoe (see listing), these folks offer shuttle services upstream to put in, then you can paddle downstream, and end up at River Run. Although the camping part of this operation is sort of a sideline to the canoe business, we include it here because this is such a pretty natural area, and the campsites are surprisingly appealing. And cheap. The Moose Crossing and Sandy Pine areas are right on the beach, but no doubt livelier than some other spots; we like Tall Pines, featuring a nice footpath to the beach. Best of all is Big Bend Beach (site 7), secluded, but right on the river. Sites 8, 10, and 11 are peaceful and private. The two campgrounds we've included in this book are the nicest among several along this stretch of river. The people are friendlier at Woodland Acres, but this one's got a great sandy beach. You choose.

## BASICS

**Operated By:** Bob & Joyce Parker. **Open:** Memorial Day–Labor Day. **Site Assignment:** Reservations accepted. No deposit for camping; for canoe rentals, $25 deposit due for canoes reserved for Friday, Saturday, or Sunday; 2-week notice required for refund on cancellation. **Registration:** At office. **Fee:** $5 per person; 12 & under, free. V, MC. **Parking:** At site.

## FACILITIES

**Number of RV Sites:** 22. **Number of Tent-Only Sites:** 0. **Hookups:** None. **Each Site:** Picnic table, fire ring. **Dump Station:** No. **Laundry:** No. **Pay Phone:** Yes. **Rest Rooms and Showers:** Yes, No. **Fuel:** No. **Propane:** No. **Internal Roads:** Gravel, in good condition. **RV Service:** No. **Market:** 19 mi. west, in North Conway. **Restaurant:** 8 mi. north, in Fryeburg. **General Store:** No. **Vending:** Yes. **Swimming Pool:** No. **Playground:** No. **Activities:** River fishing (license required), swimming, canoeing. **Nearby Attractions:** Narramissic 19th century working farm, Shawnee Peak Ski Area (hiking, mountain biking), outlet shopping (North Conway, N.H.). **Additional Information:** Bridgton Lakes Region Chamber of Commerce, (207) 647-3472.

## RESTRICTIONS

**Pets:** Must be leashed, quiet, & under control at all times. **Fires:** In fire rings only. **Alcoholic Beverages:** Yes. **Vehicle Maximum Length:** None. **Other:** Ask on arrival.

## TO GET THERE

From Portland, take Rte. 25 west to Rte. 113 north to Rte. 160 north. Campground is 0.75 mi. north of intersection of Rtes. 113 and 160, across the bridge and on the right.

## BROWNFIELD

## Woodland Acres Camp N Canoe

Rte. 160, R.R. 1, P.O. Box 445, Brownfield 04010. T: (207) 935-2529; www.woodlandacres.com; campcanu@nxi.com.

🚐 ★★★★                  ▲ ★★★

Beauty: ★★★           Site Privacy: ★★★
Spaciousness: ★★★★★    Quiet: ★★★★★
Security: ★★★          Cleanliness: ★★★★
Insect Control: ★★      Facilities: ★★★

Just 25 miles from North Conway, New Hampshire, and 45 miles from Portland, this Western

Lakes-area campground is a perfect choice for Saco-bound paddlers. The Saco River is a mecca for canoe and kayak enthusiasts, offering a blend of leisurely floats and short stretches of rapids (depending on the trip you choose) and scenery that includes clay cliffs and covered bridges. This peaceful riverfront campground is a great base for exploring the river. Sites are gravel, mostly wooded, and the choicest spots (94 through 104, even numbers) sit alongside the river. If those are taken, ask for something among sites 47 through 50, or 13 and 14, nice and quiet. The paddling is the thing here, and these folks know what they're doing. Bring your own boat, and you can launch it here, or they'll shuttle you to a put-in point on another part of the river. Or, rent one of their canoes or kayaks and have them set you up on a trip lasting two hours or two days (an overnight and wilderness camping along the river) or something in between.

## BASICS

**Operated By:** Chris & Trudy Gantick. **Open:** May 15–Oct. 15. **Site Assignment:** Reservations recommended. Reservations open Jan. 1. 50% deposite required; full payment required for holiday weekends (3 night min. stay required.) Refunds granted for cancellations made 14 days or more prior to arrival date, minus $5 service charge. **Registration:** At office. **Fee:** $22–$30 per night for 2 adults & children under age 18. V, MC, D. **Parking:** At sites or as designated.

## FACILITIES

**Number of RV Sites:** 109. **Number of Tent-Only Sites:** 0. **Hookups:** Water, electric (20, 30 amps), sewer. **Each Site:** Picnic table, fireplace. **Dump Station:** Yes. **Laundry:** Yes. **Pay Phone:** Yes. **Rest Rooms and Showers:** Yes, coin-op. **Fuel:** No. **Propane:** Yes. **Internal Roads:** Gravel (sandy), in good condition. **RV Service:** No. **Market:** 18 mi. west, in North Conway, N.H. **Restaurant:** 7 mi. north, in Fryeburg. **General Store:** Yes. **Vending:** Yes. **Swimming Pool:** No. **Playground:** Yes. **Other:** Boat ramp, rec hall. **Activities:** Paddling, fishing (license available at general store). **Nearby Attractions:** Narramissic 19th century working farm, Shawnee Peak Ski Area (hiking, mountain biking), outlet shopping

(North Conway, N.H.). **Additional Information:** Bridgton Lakes Region Chamber of Commerce, (207) 647-3472.

## RESTRICTIONS

**Pets:** Must be leashed, quiet, & cleaned up after. Must not be left unattended. $5 per dog per stay. **Fires:** In fireplaces only. **Alcoholic Beverages:** Yes. **Vehicle Maximum Length:** None. **Other:** 7-night min. stay required for river sites during July & Aug.

## TO GET THERE

From Maine Turnpike, take exit 11 to Rte. 202 to Rte. 115 west for 3 mi. Connect w/Rte. 35S at junction of Rte. 302 for 9 mi. Turn right onto Rte. 25 West for 2 mi., then go right onto Rte. 113 north. Follow Rte. 113 north 23 mi. into Brownfield. Head right onto Rte. 160. Campground is 0.5 mi. on the left, just before green iron bridge.

## BRUNSWICK

### Thomas Point Beach

29 Meadow Rd., Brunswick 04011. T: (207) 725-6009 or (877) TPB-4321; www.thomaspoint beach.com; summer@thomaspointbeach.com.

🚐 ★★★★　　　▲ ★★★

| | |
|---|---|
| Beauty: ★★★★ | Site Privacy: ★★ |
| Spaciousness: ★★ | Quiet: ★★ |
| Security: ★★★★★ | Cleanliness: ★★★★★ |
| Insect Control: ★★★ | Facilities: ★★★★★ |

If this pretty, oceanfront spot looks familiar, maybe you've been here before, say, sitting on the lawn at the annual Bluegrass Festival, or the Maine Arts Festival, or, perhaps, the tartaned goings-on of the Maine Highland Games. Set on Thomas Bay in mid-coast Maine, between the towns of Brunswick and Bath, this property is stunning. Manicured green lawns slope to a tidal beach, flanked by lofty pines. No wonder this is a popular site for big community events and festivals. Thomas Point was an old salting bay, used by native people; some of the old salt stones still exist. The property also features odd historic bits like the totem pole from the 1964 World's Fair (when Alaska became a state), millstones, and the handsome old cupola from St. Mary's Church. The public areas, including a pine-panelled rec hall and bathhouse, are extra-nice. Look for pretty, wooded campsites to the right of the main lodge; sites 1 through 3 (RVs only) are among the best. Sites 1 through 64 are set along the marsh, with plenty of tall pines but little privacy; another camping area is located on the other, more forested side of the property. Among these, tent site L is a super spot. This whole area, including sites B through M, give or take, are quiet and wooded.

## BASICS

**Operated By:** Patricia Crooker. **Open:** Mid-May–Oct. **Site Assignment:** Reservations recommended. Deposit of 1-day fee required. Full payment due for weekends & holidays. Refunds for cancellations w/ 7-day notice, minus $10 service fee. **Registration:** At office. **Fee:** $20–$25 for 2 adults & 2 children under age 12; additional older child/adult is $5 per night. Shipping/handling fee of $2.50 added to telephone charges. V, MC. **Parking:** At site.

## FACILITIES

**Number of RV Sites:** 75. **Number of Tent-Only Sites:** 0. **Hookups:** Water, electric (15, 30 amps). **Each Site:** Picnic table, fire ring. **Dump Station:** Yes. **Laundry:** Yes. **Pay Phone:** Yes. **Rest Rooms and Showers:** Yes. **Fuel:** No. **Propane:** No. **Internal Roads:** Gravel, in good condition. **RV Service:** No. **Market:** 7 mi. east. **Restaurant:** 7 mi. east. **General Store:** Yes. **Vending:** Yes. **Swimming Pool:** No. **Playground:** Yes. **Other:** Rec hall. **Activities:** Ocean swimming, ball field. **Nearby Attractions:** Reid State Park, Popham Beach State Park, Morse Mountain Sanctuary, Maine Maritime Museum, Bowdoin College Museum of Art, Peary-MacMillan Arctic Museum, deep-sea fishing. **Additional Information:** Chamber of Commerce of the Bath-Brunswick Region, (207) 725-8797 or (207) 443-9751; www.midcoastmaine.com.

## RESTRICTIONS

**Pets:** No. **Fires:** In fire rings only. **Alcoholic Beverages:** At sites only. **Vehicle Maximum Length:** None. **Other:** 14-day max. stay per site.

## TO GET THERE

From junction of Rtes. 1 and 24, go 3.75 mi. south on Rte. 24, then 0.5 mi. southeast on Board Rd., then 0.5 mi. east on Meadow Rd. Campground entrance is on the right.

## CAMDEN

## Camden Hills State Park

280 Belfast Rd., Camden 04843. T: (207) 236-3109 or (207) 236-0849 (off-season); www.state.me.us/doc/prkslands/reserve/htm.

🚐 ★★★          ⛺ ★★★★★

Beauty: ★★★★★          Site Privacy: ★★★
Spaciousness: ★★★★          Quiet: ★★★
Security: ★★★★★          Cleanliness: ★★★★★
Insect Control: ★★★          Facilities: ★★★★

Psst. Want to enjoy some of the best views in Maine, or (we'll go out on a limb here) all of New England? Camp here, and drive, or hike to the summit of 800-foot Mt. Battie. From there, climb 26 steps up a stone tower for panoramic views of Penobscot Bay, dotted with sailboats and gem-like islands. You'll feel like you're on top of the (very gorgeous) world. Look for the Edna St. Vincent Millay poem etched on ar rock here, inspired by this spot. There are 25 miles of hiking trails here, including another mountain summit, Mt. Megunticook, elevation 1380 feet. Bring those hiking boots. On one side of the park is Mt. Battie; on the other side is the camping area. Some sites are woody, others are open and grassy. Some, alas, are stony. Site 60L, known as the "Honeymoon Suite," is huge and secluded. We like sites 75M through 81M, on the far side of the property, for tenting. 75M and 81M are real beauties. Good features include new countertops and baby changing stations in the ladies' rest room. Bad features are the black flies, who take over in May.

## BASICS

**Operated By:** Maine Dept. of Conservation, Bureau of Parks & Lands. **Open:** May 15–Oct. 15. **Site Assignment:** In spring & fall, camping is on a first-come, first-served basis. For summer stays, reservations open on the first business day in Jan. From June 15 to the night before Labor Day, sites may be reserved for a min. of 2 nights & up to 2 weeks. Reservations recommended in July & Aug., at least 2 weeks in advance. Full payment is charged to credit card when reservation is processed. Refund with $15 cancellation fee. 24 sites are non-reservable, & available on a first-come, first-served basis. **Registration:** At office. **Fee:** $13, Maine residents; $17, nonresidents, plus $2 fee if you reserve in advance. V, MC. **Parking:** At sites & hikers lot only.

## FACILITIES

**Number of RV Sites:** 107. **Number of Tent-Only Sites:** 0. **Hookups:** None. **Each Site:** Picnic table, fireplace. **Dump Station:** Yes. **Laundry:** No. **Pay Phone:** Yes. **Rest Rooms and Showers:** Yes. **Fuel:** No. **Propane:** No. **Internal Roads:** Gravel, in good condition. **RV Service:** No. **Market:** 2 mi. south. **Restaurant:** 2 mi. south. **General Store:** No. **Vending:** No. **Swimming Pool:** No. **Playground:** Yes. **Other:** Rec room. **Activities:** Hiking (25 mi. of trails), scenic drive or hike to summit of Mt. Battie. **Nearby Attractions:** Camden galleries, museums & shops), windjammer fleet, Penobscot Bay cruises, Conway Homestead & Mary Cramer Museum (28th century restored farmhouse & gardens), Camden Hills State Park, Merryspring Park, Owl's Head Transportation Museum, golf, ocean swimming. **Additional Information:** Rockport-Camden-Lincolnville Chamber of Commerce, (207) 236-4404; (800) 223-5459.

## RESTRICTIONS

**Pets:** Must be leashed, quiet, & cleaned up after. Must not be left unattended. **Fires:** In fireplaces. **Alcoholic Beverages:** No. **Vehicle Maximum Length:** None. **Other:** No pets on beach.

## TO GET THERE

From junction of Rtes. 105 and Rte. 1, go 2 mi. northeast on Rte. 1. Campground entrance is on the left.

## CANAAN
## Skowhegan/Canaan KOA

P.O. Box 87, Canaan 04924. T: (207) 474-2858 (800) 562-7571 (reservations); www.koa.com; skowkoa@kynd.net.

🚐 ★★★★   ⛺ ★★★

| | |
|---|---|
| Beauty: ★★★★ | Site Privacy: ★★★ |
| Spaciousness: ★★★ | Quiet: ★★★ |
| Security: ★★★ | Cleanliness: ★★★★★ |
| Insect Control: ★★★ | Facilities: ★★★ |

This woodsy campground in central Maine is a perfect base for exploring Maine's western lakes and mountains or mid-coastal beaches. There's also whitewater rafting, top-notch stream and lake fishing, hiking and biking, and plenty of good antiquing nearby. The country setting, spread over 60 acres, is pleasant in the summer (try blueberry picking along the trails) and gorgeous in the fall, when the mountains and valleys are awash in fiery hues. Hiking and biking trails take off from the property and, during the summer, there are planned activities to keep families happy. Facilities are white-glove clean, staff helpful and friendly, and atmosphere decidedly low-key. There are 45 spacious pull-throughs, and a separate tent-only area, nestled in the woods. The campground is a pleasant great woods getaway and jumping off point for lots of outdoor recreation.

## BASICS

**Operated By:** Tom Kennedy. **Open:** May 15–Oct. 15. **Site Assignment:** Reservations not required; credit card will hold site, 24-hour cancellation policy. **Registration:** At office. **Fee:** Full hookups, $28; water & electric, $26; no hookups, $20, based on 2 adults & 2 children under 10; additional adult, $5; additional child, $3. **Parking:** At site.

## FACILITIES

**Number of RV Sites:** 86. **Number of Tent-Only Sites:** 14. **Hookups:** Water, electric, sewer (20, 30, 50 amps), cabel TV, modem. **Each Site:** Picnic table, fire ring. **Dump Station:** Yes. **Laundry:** Yes. **Pay Phone:** Yes. **Rest Rooms and**

**Showers:** Yes. **Fuel:** No. **Propane:** Yes. **Internal Roads:** Gravel, dirt (good). **RV Service:** No. **Market:** Skowhegan (10 mi). **Restaurant:** Yes. **General Store:** Yes. **Vending:** Yes. **Swimming Pool:** Yes. **Playground:** Yes. **Other:** Game room, TV room, sports fields, pavilion, nature trails, bike rentals, cabin rentals. **Activities:** Swimming, hiking, biking, softball, volleyball, basketball, horseshoes, badminton, planned activities, including socials, contests, & group hikes. **Nearby Attractions:** western mountains & lakes, midcoast parks & beaches, Bangor. **Additional Information:** Skowhegan Area Chamber of Commerce, 10 Russell St., Skowhegan, ME 04976 (207) 474-3621, www.skowheganchamber.com.

## RESTRICTIONS

**Pets:** Must be on a leash, never left unattended. **Fires:** In grills, stoves, & fire rings only. **Alcoholic Beverages:** At site only. **Vehicle Maximum Length:** None.

## TO GET THERE

From I-95, exit 36, go north 6 mi. on Rte. 201, then north 7 mi. on Rte. 23, then 0.6 mi. east on Rte. 2; campground is on the right.

## CASCO

## Point Sebago Golf and Beach Resort

261 Point Sebago Rd., Casco 04015. T: (207) 655-3821 or (800) 655-1232; F: (207) 655-3371; www.pointsebago.com; info@pointsebago.com.

| 🚐 ★★★★ | ⛺ ★★★ |
|---|---|
| Beauty: ★★★★ | Site Privacy: ★★ |
| Spaciousness: ★★★★ | Quiet: ★★ |
| Security: ★★★★★ | Cleanliness: ★★★★★ |
| Insect Control: ★★★ | Facilities: ★★★★★ |

One look at busy Chippy's Pavilion on the beach, and you'd swear you were at a theme park. "Number 32, your onion rings are ready," a voice chirps over the P.A. system. Meanwhile, groups of T-shirt-clad counselors are lining up small fry for scooter races. Just another summer day at Point Sebago, set on southwestern Maine's Lake Sebago, where adults can play golf on one of the finest courses in the state, while the kids chum around with their own kind in an award-winning program, from 9 to 5, if you choose. Kids' programs are split into five groups, by age, and supervised by 40 energetic young counselors. And if you think the fun stops when night falls, you've never been to Point Sebago's Vaudeville Night or the family bonfire. So what's the camping like? Sites are shaded, gravel, and mostly back-in; size and levelness vary. Tents and RVs are intermingled; we noticed that their rental units get the prime spots. If you like to be near the action, sites 801 to 811 are good for RVers, while sites along Red Rd., numbered 601 to 621, are pretty and wooded. Sites 901 to 929 back up into woods and seem fairly quiet. The place is sprawling, people are everywhere, and the place smells like French fries, not woodsmoke. But, how often do you find a camping place with a boutiques, a cybercafe, and great golf?

## BASICS

**Operated By:** Larry & Anna Gould. **Open:** May 1–Oct. 31. **Site Assignment:** Reservations recommended. Opens up for following year in mid-June. 50% deposit due within 10 days of making reservation. Refund for cancellation w/ 45-day notice prior to arrival date, minus $25 service charge. **Registration:** At office. **Fee:** $168–$378 per week (during Family Value Weeks) or $280–$420. V, MC, D. **Parking:** At site.

## FACILITIES

**Number of RV Sites:** 250. **Number of Tent-Only Sites:** 0. **Hookups:** Water, electric (20, 30, 50 amps), sewer. **Each Site:** Picnic table, fireplace. **Dump Station:** Yes. **Laundry:** Yes. **Pay Phone:** Yes. **Rest Rooms and Showers:** Yes. **Fuel:** No. **Propane:** Yes. **Internal Roads:** Gravel, in good condition. **RV Service:** Yes. **Market:** 5 mi. west. **Restaurant:** Yes. **General Store:** Yes. **Vending:** Yes. **Swimming Pool:** No. **Playground:** Yes. **Other:** Cyber cafe, marina, golf (championship course). **Activities:** Lake swimming, golf, tennis, archery, boating (rentals available), boat cruises aboard the Point Sebago Princess, fishing (licenses available), waterskiing (lessons available), mini-golf, basketball, ballfield, shuffleboard, children's program, planned activities. **Nearby Attractions:** Golf, mini-golf, seaplane rides, boat cruises, Songo River Queen paddleboat, Douglas Mountain hiking, Sebago Lake State Park, outlet shopping (North Conway, N.H.). **Additional Information:** Naples Business Assoc., (207) 693-3285.

## RESTRICTIONS

**Pets:** Only in one's own unit (not in rentals) & in specific areas. **Fires:** In fireplaces only. **Alcoholic Beverages:** Yes. **Vehicle Maximum Length:** 48 ft. **Other:** 7-day min. stay in peak season (third week of June through Labor Day.).

## TO GET THERE

From Maine Turnpike, take exit 8; travel 22 mi. on Rte. 302 to Point Sebago Rd.; proceed left to resort.

## CASCO/NAPLES

### Sebago Lake State Park

11 Park Access Rd., Casco 04015. T: (207) 693-6321 or (800) 332-1501 (reservations or ME number) or (207) 287-3824 (reservations or out of state); F: (207) 287-6170; www.state.me.us/doc/prkslands/reserve/htm.

🚐 ★★★          ⛺ ★★★

Beauty: ★★★★★          Site Privacy: ★★
Spaciousness: ★★★          Quiet: ★★
Security: ★★★          Cleanliness: ★★★★
Insect Control: ★★★★          Facilities: ★★★★

One of Maine's most beloved recreation areas, Sebago Lake State Park offers campers the opportunity to sleep along the sandy shores of Maine's deepest and second-largest lake. It's a real beauty spot, featuring woodlands of tall pine and oak, bogs and ponds. Weekends in summer book up really early, but you can often luck out with a great lakeside spot during the week (we did). Campsites are set in three sections: Naples Beach, Witch Cove Beach, and a hike-in tenting area near the amphitheater (offering more privacy than the other areas, if you don't mind carrying your gear from a nearby parking lot.) Sites 31M, non-reservable, and 30L, on Naples Beach, are awesome. Lakefront sites on Witch Cove Beach include 138M, 149L, 163M, and 164M (the letters refer to site size, small, medium, large or extra-large.) If you choose to tent at one of these, you probably won't enjoy the quietest night of your life, in spite of the park's supposed 'quiet hours.' If you're in an RV, you won't notice. And you'll no doubt forgive all when you step into the ripply-sand-bottomed lake for that morning swim.

## BASICS

**Operated By:** Maine Dept. of Conservation, Bureau of Parks & Lands. **Open:** May 1–Oct. 15. **Site Assignment:** In spring & fall, camping is on a first-come, first-served basis. For summer stays, reservations open on the first business day in Jan. From June 15 to the night before Labor Day, sites may be reserved for a min. of 2 nights & up to 2 weeks. (Note: This park is heavily-visited. For full details on how to best secure a site in season, see website or write to: Dept. of Conservation, Attn: Reservations, 22 SHS, Aug.a, ME 04333.) Full payment is charged to credit card when reservation is processed. Refund with $15 cancellation fee. About 40 sites are non-reservable, & available on a first-come, first-served basis. **Registration:** At office. **Fee:** $13 for Maine residents; $17 for non-residents; $2 extra charge if you reserve in advance. V, MC. **Parking:** At site.

## FACILITIES

**Number of RV Sites:** 250. **Number of Tent-Only Sites:** 0. **Hookups:** None. **Each Site:** Picnic table, fireplace. **Dump Station:** Yes. **Laundry:** No. **Pay Phone:** Yes. **Rest Rooms and Showers:** Yes. **Fuel:** No. **Propane:** No. **Internal Roads:** Gravel, in good condition. **RV Service:** No. **Market:** 5 mi. north. **Restaurant:** 5 mi. north. **General Store:** No. **Vending:** No. **Swimming Pool:** No. **Playground:** Yes. **Other:** Boat launch. **Activities:** Hiking, lake swimming, ball field, volleyball, interpretive programs. **Nearby Attractions:** Golf, mini-golf, seaplane rides, boat cruises, Songo River Queen paddleboat, Douglas Mountain hiking, outlet shopping (N. Conway, N.H.). **Additional Information:** Greater Windham Chamber of Commerce, (207) 892-8265; www.windhamchamber.sebagolake.org.

## RESTRICTIONS

**Pets:** No. **Fires:** In fire rings only. **Alcoholic Beverages:** No. **Vehicle Maximum Length:** 35

ft. **Other:** 2-week max. stay between last week in June & Labor Day.

## TO GET THERE

From junction of Rtes. 302 East and 11/114, go 4 mi. south on Rte. 302 E, then 2.5 mi. west to campground entrance.

## DAMARISCOTTA

### Lake Pemaquid Camping

P.O. Box 967, Damariscotta 04543. T: (207) 563-5202; lincoln.midcoast.com/~lakepem.

🚐 ★★★　　　　Å ★

| | |
|---|---|
| Beauty: ★★ | Site Privacy: ★ |
| Spaciousness: ★ | Quiet: ★ |
| Security: ★★★★★ | Cleanliness: ★★★ |
| Insect Control: ★★★★★ | Facilities: ★★★ |

A little bit of privacy, a lot of amusements—that's the best way to describe this very popular family campground on Maine's mid-coast, about 50 miles north of Portland. This sprawling place, set on seven-mile Lake Pemaquid, isn't the most manicured campground you'll ever see; piles of dead autumn leaves are still laying around in mid-July. But the families who show up to ride Chucky's Choo-Choo train, swim in the pool, and paddle around in pedal boats don't seem to mind. How often do you see a skate board area at a campground, and outdoor hot tubs? Rustic-style facilities include a restaurant that serves shore dinners. Campsites are wooded with pine, oak, and birch. There's about a mile of lakeside camping. Some sites have boat docks. We'd skip these, though—too crowded—and head for the more peaceful spots along Goose Cove (sites 16 through 18 are nice) and 250 through 253 (not on the water, but pleasant.) You might need a vacation after a visit here, but you're sure to have a good time.

## BASICS

**Operated By:** Rebecca Bickmore & Clayton Howard. **Open:** Memorial Day–Columbus Day. **Site Assignment:** Reservations recommended. Deposit of payment in full required for stays of less than 7 days. For longer stays, 50% deposit due. Refund for cancellations w/ 2-week notice, minus $10 service charge. **Registration:** At

office. **Fee:** $20–$37 based on 5 people. V, MC, AE, Novus, debit cards. **Parking:** At sites or parking lots only.

## FACILITIES

**Number of RV Sites:** 290. **Number of Tent-Only Sites:** 0. **Hookups:** Water, electric (20, 30, 50 amps), sewer, modem access. **Each Site:** Picnic table, fire ring. **Dump Station:** Yes. **Laundry:** Yes. **Pay Phone:** Yes. **Rest Rooms and Showers:** Yes, coin-op. **Fuel:** No. **Propane:** Yes. **Internal Roads:** Gravel, in fair condition. **RV Service:** No. **Market:** 5 mi. south. **Restaurant:** Yes. **General Store:** Yes. **Vending:** Yes. **Swimming Pool:** Yes. **Playground:** Yes. **Other:** Boat ramp & slips, rec hall, hot tubs, skate board park, kiddie train ride. **Activities:** Boating (rentals available), fishing (licenses available), tennis, basketball, volleyball, lake swimming, planned activities. **Nearby Attractions:** Ocean beaches, Maine windjammer fleet, Boothbay Railway train rides, golf. **Additional Information:** Damariscotta Region Chamber of Commerce, (207) 563-8340; Damariscotta Region Information Bureau, (207) 563-3176.

## RESTRICTIONS

**Pets:** Must be leashed, quiet, & cleaned up after. Must not be left unattended. Not allowed on beach or in pool area. **Fires:** In fireplaces. **Alcoholic Beverages:** At sites only. **Vehicle Maximum Length:** None. **Other:** Lakeside sites available for Saturday to Saturday only during July & Aug. 3-night min. on holidays.

## TO GET THERE

Take Maine Turnpike to exit 9, Falmouth/Rte. 1. Follow Rte. 95 to Brunswick, then take Rte. 1 to Bus. Rte. 1. Exit at Damariscotta. Head north from Damariscotta on Bus. Rte. 1 to Biscay Rd. (Turn right after McDonald's.) Follow signs to campground.

## DOVER-FOXCROFT

### Peaks-Kenny State Park

Rte. 1, P.O. Box 10, Dover-Foxcroft 04426. T: (207) 564-2003; www.state.me.us/doc/parks.htm.

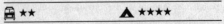

🚐 ★★　　　　　Å ★★★★

Beauty: ★★★
Site Privacy: ★★★★
Spaciousness: ★★★★
Quiet: ★★★★
Security: ★★★★
Cleanliness: ★★★★
Insect Control: ★★★
Facilities: ★★★

Set right in the heart of the state, about 45 miles northwest of Bangor, maybe 30 miles southeast of Greenville, this state park offers a pleasant day-use beach and picnic area, plus canoe rentals and hiking trails. No wonder it's so popular with families. A porkchop-shaped camping area is set along the south cove of 12-mile Sebec Lake. Trivia note: Benign as the lake looks, it reaches depths up to 160 feet, and divers have discovered shipwrecks here. A grassy slope leads to a nice, wide swimming area, sort of pebbly-bottomed. Most campers can't resist renting a canoe and paddling 'round the coastline. The campground is nicely forested,with big boulders providing rustic seating at some sites. The sites farthest from the beach are but a 10-minute walk to the shore, while the beachside sites aren't quite on the water, but have walking paths to the beach. Some of the choicest include sites 22S, 24S, 56X, and 54X (the letters referring to the size of the site; 'S' as in small, 'X' as in extra-large.) With swimming, canoeing, and nine miles of hiking trails, there's plenty to do here, and there's always the possibility of seeing a moose (though deer are more likely!)

### Basics

**Operated By:** Maine Dept. of Conservation, Bureau of Parks & Lands. **Open:** May 15–Sept. 30. **Site Assignment:** In spring & fall, camping is on a first-come, first-served basis. For summer stays, reservations open on the first business day in Jan. From June 15 to the night before Labor Day, sites may be reserved for a min. of 2 nights & up to 2 weeks. Full payment is charged to credit card when reservation is processed. Refund with $15 cancellation fee. 14 sites are non-reservable, & available on a first-come, first-served basis. Call the reservations line to cancel a reservation more than 3 days in advance. If cancelling less than 3 days in advance, call the park directly. **Registration:** At office. **Fee:** $13, Maine residents; $17, non-residents plus $2 fee if reserving in advance. V, MC. **Parking:** At site.

### Facilities

**Number of RV Sites:** 56. **Number of Tent-Only Sites:** 0. **Hookups:** None. **Each Site:** Picnic table, fire ring. **Dump Station:** Yes. **Laundry:** No. **Pay Phone:** Yes. **Rest Rooms and Showers:** Yes, coin-op. **Fuel:** No. **Propane:** No. **Internal Roads:** Gravel, in good condition. **RV Service:** No. **Market:** 8 mi. south. **Restaurant:** 8 mi. south. **General Store:** No. **Vending:** No. **Swimming Pool:** No. **Playground:** Yes. **Other:** Guarded sand beach. **Activities:** Lake swimming (lifeguards), canoeing (rentals available), hiking trails. **Nearby Attractions:** Blacksmith Shop Museum. **Additional Information:** Southern Piscataquis County Chamber of Commerce, (207) 564-7533.

### Restrictions

**Pets:** Must be leashed, quiet, & cleaned up after. Must not be left unattended. Not allowed on beach. **Fires:** In fire rings only. **Alcoholic Beverages:** No. **Vehicle Maximum Length:** 45 ft. **Other:** 2-week max. stay between last week in June & Labor Day.

### To Get There

From Dover-Foxcroft, go 6 mi. north on Rte. 153 (Greeley Landing Rd.), left at State Park Rd.

## EAST ORLAND

## Balsam Cove

P.O. Box C, Back Ridge Rd., East ORland 04431. T: (207) 469-7771 (800) 469-7771 (reservations); F: (207) 469-0065; www.holidayguide.com/campusa/maine/balsam-cove; c27young@aol.com.

RV ★★★ Tent ★★★

Beauty: ★★★
Site Privacy: ★★★
Spaciousness: ★★★
Quiet: ★★★★
Security: ★★★★
Cleanliness: ★★★
Insect Control: ★★★
Facilities: ★★★

This modest campground, located midway between Bucksport and Ellsworth, (within an hour's drive to Acadia National Park) offers relaxed lakeside camping. Families enjoy the sandy beach area and the warm, shallow waters.

There are boats to rent for paddling and fishing and, at night, a campground bonfire for roasting marshmallows. The long drive into the campground, a mile off busy Rte. 1, helps keep the atmosphere subdued and quiet. Sites are a bit helter-skelter placed in rows and loops throughout the property. There are larger pull-through sites near the front of the campground and a handful of beachfront and water view sites. Families may like sites 14-19 across from the swimming area and playground. One of two campgrounds in the area on pristine Toddy Pond (also see Whispering Pines), Balsam Cove offers a few more facilities (laundry, general store) but less rustic charm.

## BASICS

**Operated By:** Sharon & Charlie Young. **Open:** Memorial Day–Sept. **Site Assignment:** Reservations suggested in Jul.–Aug. 50 percent deposit required, 14-day cancellation policy with $10 service fee; MC, V, D, checks. **Registration:** At office. **Fee:** Full hookups, $22; waterfront (20 amp), $22; waterfront (no hookups), $19; wooded (30 amp), $20; wooded (20 amp), $19; wooded (no hookups), $17, based on 2 adults & 2 children under 18. **Parking:** At site.

## FACILITIES

**Number of RV Sites:** 56. **Number of Tent-Only Sites:** 4. **Hookups:** Water, electric (30 amps). **Each Site:** Picnic table, fire ring. **Dump Station:** Yes. **Laundry:** Yes. **Pay Phone:** Yes. **Rest Rooms and Showers:** Yes. **Fuel:** No. **Propane:** No. **Internal Roads:** Gravel (good). **RV Service:** No. **Market:** Bucksport (6 mi). **Restaurant:** No. **General Store:** Yes. **Vending:** Yes. **Swimming Pool:** No. **Playground:** Yes. **Other:** Lake frontage, beach, rowboat, canoe & paddleboat rentals, docks, boat ramp, rec room, group tent area, cabin rentals. **Activities:** Swimming, boating, fishing, basketball, horseshoes. **Nearby Attractions:** Deer Isle Peninsula, Bar Harbor, Acadia National Park. **Additional Information:** Bucksport Bay Area Chamber of Commerce, P.O. Box 1880, 263 Main St., Bucksport, ME 04416-1880 (207) 469-6818 & Acadia Information Center, P.O. Box 139, Mount Desert, ME 04660 (207) 667-8550 or (800) 358-8550, www.acadiainfo.com.

## RESTRICTIONS

**Pets:** Must be on a leash, never left unattended. No pets allowed on waterfront sites. 1 pet per site; some breeds not allowed. **Fires:** In grills, stoves, & fire rings only. **Alcoholic Beverages:** At site only. **Vehicle Maximum Length:** 35 ft.

## TO GET THERE

From junction Rtes. 1 and 15 (in East Orland), go north 1.7 mi. on Rte. 1, then south 1.5 mi. on Back Ridge Rd.; campground is 1 mi. east on entrance road.

## EAST ORLAND

## Whispering Pines

US Rte. 1, Gen. Del., East Orland 04431. T: (207) 469-3443; www.campmaine.com/whispering pines; wpines04431@aol.com.

🚐 ★★★                     ⛺ ★★★

| | |
|---|---|
| Beauty: ★★★★ | Site Privacy: ★★★★ |
| Spaciousness: ★★★★ | Quiet: ★★★★★ |
| Security: ★★★★ | Cleanliness: ★★★ |
| Insect Control: ★★★ | Facilities: ★★ |

This small lakeside campground, within commuting distance to Deer Isle Peninsula to the south and Acadia National Park to the north, oozes old-fashioned charm. A stay here is akin to visiting family and friends at their summer cottage and owners Dwight and Sandy Gates do everything they can to make you feel at home. The rustic, woodsy setting, along the shores of Toddy Pond, is scenic and tranquil: birds sing in the pines; loons call at dusk; beavers and otters frolic in the water. "Pond" is a misnomer; it runs 9.7 miles long and 130 feet deep. Relaxing is top activity here, but there's swimming and boating and the fishing, for landlocked salmon, lake trout and bass, is good. ("We're not an entertainment center," owner Sandy readily admits.) There is a handful of seasonal renters, an older clientele who come for the natural setting and peace and quiet. But there are plenty of sites to rent on a nightly basis. Most sites are clustered in the woods but there are a few on the water. Roomy sites B4 and B5, next to the beach, are most popular and are often booked a year in advance.

## BASICS

**Operated By:** Dwight & Sandy Gates. **Open:** Memorial Day–Sept. **Site Assignment:** Reservations suggested. $25 deposit, 3-day cancellation policy; no credit cards, checks accepted. **Registration:** At office. **Fee:** $23 for 2 adults; $1 each child; $1 for electricity; $1 for sewer; $3 extra adult. **Parking:** At site.

## FACILITIES

**Number of RV Sites:** 45. **Number of Tent-Only Sites:** 5. **Hookups:** Water, electric, sewer (20 amps). **Each Site:** Picnic table, fire ring. **Dump Station:** Yes. **Laundry:** No. **Pay Phone:** No. **Rest Rooms and Showers:** Yes. **Fuel:** No. **Propane:** No. **Internal Roads:** Gravel, dirt (fair). **RV Service:** No. **Market:** Bucksport (6 mi). **Restaurant:** No. **General Store:** No. **Vending:** No. **Swimming Pool:** No. **Playground:** Yes. **Other:** Lake frontage, beach, dock, picnic area, game room, canoe, rowboats & bicycles to use (free). **Activities:** Swimming, fishing, boating, volleyball, horseshoes. **Nearby Attractions:** Deer Isle Peninsula, Bar Harbor, Acadia National Park. **Additional Information:** Bucksport Bay Area Chamber of Commerce, P.O. Box 1880, 263 Main St., Bucksport, ME 04416-1880 (207) 469-6818 & Acadia Information Center, P.O. Box 139, Mount Desert, ME 04660 (207) 667-8550 or (800) 358-8550, www.acadiainfo.com.

## RESTRICTIONS

**Pets:** Must be on a leash, never left unattended. **Fires:** In grills, stoves, & fire rings only. **Alcoholic Beverages:** At site only. **Vehicle Maximum Length:** None.

## TO GET THERE

From junction Rtes. 1 and 15 (in East Orland), go north 2 mi. on Rte. 1; campground is on the right.

## ELLSWORTH

### Branch Lake Camping Area

180 Hansons Landing Rd., Ellsworth 04605. T: (207) 667-5174; www.campmaine.com.

🚐 ★★★          ⛺ ★★★

Beauty: ★★★          Site Privacy: ★★★
Spaciousness: ★★★          Quiet: ★★★

Security: ★★★          Cleanliness: ★★★
Insect Control: ★★★          Facilities: ★★★

This small lakeside campground is located halfway between Ellsworth and Bangor and a short drive to Bar Harbor and Acadia National Park. Set on the shores of 10-mile-long, spring-fed Branch Lake, the campground is a quiet getaway with pretty views of the crystal clear lake dotted with rocky, pine covered islands. Bring your boat (there's dock space if you reserve early) or rent a canoe from the campground. The campground's 175 feet of lake frontage includes a swimming beach and fishing pier. The sites are set randomly throughout the campground, tucked here and there under the trees and around scattered boulders; larger sites are angled in rows, furthest away from the beach area. Tenters may be frustrated. The separate tent area is tiny and has a view of the cluster of RV sites.

## BASICS

**Operated By:** Dick & Brenda Graves. **Open:** May–Sept. **Site Assignment:** Reservations suggested, 1 night deposit, 7-day cancellation policy, 2-night min. stay in Jul.–Aug.; MC, V, checks accepted. **Registration:** At office. **Fee:** Full hookups, $25; water & electric, $22, no hookups, $18, based on 2 adults & 3 children under 18. **Parking:** At site.

## FACILITIES

**Number of RV Sites:** 46. **Number of Tent-Only Sites:** 4. **Hookups:** Water, electric, sewer (30 amps). **Each Site:** Picnic table, fire ring. **Dump Station:** Yes. **Laundry:** No. **Pay Phone:** Yes. **Rest Rooms and Showers:** Yes (coin-op). **Fuel:** No. **Propane:** No. **Internal Roads:** Gravel, dirt (fair). **RV Service:** No. **Market:** Ellsworth (8 mi). **Restaurant:** No. **General Store:** Yes. **Vending:** Yes. **Swimming Pool:** No. **Playground:** Yes. **Other:** Lake frontage, beach, boat launch, boat dock, boat & canoe rentals. **Activities:** Swimming, boating, fishing, horseshoes, potluck dinners. **Nearby Attractions:** Bangor, Bar Harbor, Acadia National Park. **Additional Information:** Ellsworth Area Chamber of Commerce, P.O. Box 267, Ellsworth, ME 04605 (207) 667-5584 & Acadia Information Center, P.O. Box 139, Mount Desert, ME 04660 (207) 667-8550 or (800) 358-8550, www.acadiainfo.com.

## RESTRICTIONS

**Pets:** Must be on a leash, never left unattended. 2 dogs per site; some breeds not allowed. **Fires:** In grills, stoves, & fire rings only. **Alcoholic Beverages:** At site only. **Vehicle Maximum Length:** None.

## TO GET THERE

From junction Rte. 1 and 1A (in Ellsworth), go northwest 10 mi. on Rte. 1A, then southwest (left) 0.5 mi. on Winkumpaugh Rd., then south 1 mi. on Hanson Landing Rd.; campground is on the left.

## ELLSWORTH

### Lamoine State Park

RR 2 Box 194, Ellsworth 04605. T: (207) 667-4778;
www.state.me.us/doc/prkslnds/lamoine.htm.

🚐 ★★★          ▲ ★★★★

Beauty: ★★★★          Site Privacy: ★★★
Spaciousness: ★★★★          Quiet: ★★★★
Security: ★★★          Cleanliness: ★★★★
Insect Control: ★★★          Facilities: ★★★

The view of the ocean, the cool ocean breezes (even on the muggiest summer afternoons), the potent scents of evergreen forest blended with the salty tang of the ocean, and the aroma of woodsmoke drifting as the day draws to an end all help to make Lamoine State Park an excellent campground selection. The whole gestalt here is that of being on a windswept, oceanside bluff—which you are. The camping sites, like the park itself, run the gamut from sunny, breezy, spacious, and open and to densely forested, isolated, and tiny. Either way, you can't lose. There's a short path down to the water right across from site 49; and there's also the one-mile Loop Trail for those in need of a little exercise. Take a moment after you've set up your campsite to sit back, draw in a deep breath, and enjoy the sights, sounds, and scents of this oceanside campground.

## BASICS

**Operated By:** Maine Dept. of Conservation. **Open:** Mid-May–mid-Oct. **Site Assignment:** Reservations or first come first served. **Regis-**tration: At ranger station. **Fee:** $13–$17; additional $2 per night for reservations. **Parking:** At site.

## FACILITIES

**Number of RV Sites:** 61. **Number of Tent-Only Sites:** 0. **Hookups:** None. **Each Site:** Fire ring, picnic table. **Dump Station:** No. **Laundry:** No. **Pay Phone:** No. **Rest Rooms and Showers:** Yes. **Fuel:** No. **Propane:** No. **Internal Roads:** Gravel. **RV Service:** No. **Market:** No. **Restaurant:** No. **General Store:** No. **Vending:** No. **Swimming Pool:** No. **Playground:** Yes. **Other:** Boat launch. **Activities:** Boating, swimming, saltwater fishing. **Nearby Attractions:** Arcadia National Park, area lighthouses. **Additional Information:** (207) 941-4014.

## RESTRICTIONS

**Pets:** On leash. **Fires:** In fire ring. **Alcoholic Beverages:** At site. **Vehicle Maximum Length:** 30 ft. **Other:** Max. 6 people per party, 14-night max. stay during the summer.

## TO GET THERE

The campground is on ME Rte. 184, 8 mi. southeast from Ellsworth.

## ELLSWORTH

### Patten Pond Camping Resort

1470 Bucksport Rd., Ellsworth 04605. T: (207) 667-7600 or (877) 667-7376;
www.pattenpond.com.

🚐 ★★★★★          ▲ ★★★

Beauty: ★★★★          Site Privacy: ★★★
Spaciousness: ★★★          Quiet: ★★★
Security: ★★★★          Cleanliness: ★★★★★
Insect Control: ★★★★          Facilities: ★★★★★

This lively, modern camping resort, a half-hour from Bar Harbor and Acadia National Park, offers an array of activities and top-notch facilities. It's located on pretty Patten Pond, a crystal clear freshwater lake, dotted with rocky islands and flanked by pine tree forests. There's a sandy stretch of beach, a favorite hangout at the campground, with a fishing pier, boat dock, and viewing/sunning deck. When campers are not on the lake, they're buzzing about the campground, taking part in a host of activities: live entertainment, movies, kid's programs, Sunday morning church services, lobster bakes, and more.Most campers use the resort as a base to explore the area, near enough to major attractions but far enough from the summer traffic and commotion of the Bar Harbor area. Sites are uniform throughout the campground, most with three-way hookups, set side-by-side in rows. (No sites are on the water.) There's a separate tenting area that backs up to sparse woods.

## BASICS

**Operated By:** Pat Stanley. **Open:** May–Oct. **Site Assignment:** Reservations accepted year-round, suggested in Jul.–Aug. All sites require a 2 night min. reservation, 3-night min. on holiday weekends, $50 deposit required for 3 nights, $75 for 4–7 nights, $100 for 8 nights or more, 14-day cancellation policy with $10 service charge. Holidays are paid in full & non-refundable; MC, V, D, checks accepted for reservations; no checks upon arrival. **Registration:** At office. **Fee:** Full hookups (best, 50 amp), $37 peak, $29 early & late summer; full hookups (50 amp), $35–$28; full hookups (best, 30 amp), $32–$26; full hookup (30 amp), $29–$24; water & electric, $26–$20; best tent, $20–$17; tent, $18–$15, based on 2 adults & 2 children under 18. **Parking:** At site.

## FACILITIES

**Number of RV Sites:** 113. **Number of Tent-Only Sites:** 37. **Hookups:** Water, electric, sewer (30, 50 amps), modem. **Each Site:** Picnic table, fire ring. **Dump Station:** Yes. **Laundry:** Yes. **Pay Phone:** Yes. **Rest Rooms and Showers:** Yes. **Fuel:** No. **Propane:** Yes. **Internal Roads:** Gravel, dirt (good). **RV Service:** Yes. **Market:** Ellsworth (9 mi). **Restaurant:** No. **General Store:** Yes. **Vending:** No. **Swimming Pool:** No. **Playground:** Yes. **Other:** Lake frontage, beach, fishing pier, dock, paddleboat, sailboat, kayak & canoe rentals, entertainment pavilion, cabin, cottage & apartment rentals, gift store, game room, modem center, car rentals on site. **Activities:** Swimming, boating, fishing, basketball, volleyball, planned activities, including live entertainment, children's programs, lobster bakes. **Nearby Attractions:** Bar Harbor, Acadia National Park. **Additional**

**Information:** Ellsworth Area Chamber of Commerce, P.O. Box 267, Ellsworth, ME 04605 (207) 667-5584 & Acadia Information Center, P.O. Box 139, Mount Desert, ME 04660 (207) 667-8550 or (800) 358-8550, www.acadiainfo.com.

## RESTRICTIONS

**Pets:** Must be on a leash, never left unattended. **Fires:** In grills, stoves, & fire rings only. **Alcoholic Beverages:** At site only. **Vehicle Maximum Length:** None.

## TO GET THERE

From junction Rtes. 1 and 1A (in Ellsworth), go southwest 7.5 mi. on Rte. 1; campground is on the left.

## EUSTIS

## Cathedral Pines

P.O. Box 146, Eustis 04936. T: (207) 246-3491.

| 🚐 ★★★★★ | 🏕 ★★★★★ |
|---|---|
| Beauty: ★★★★★ | Site Privacy: ★★★★★ |
| Spaciousness: ★★★★★ | Quiet: ★★★★ |
| Security: ★★★★ | Cleanliness: ★★★★ |
| Insect Control: ★★★★ | Facilities: ★★★ |

Northern California has its redwoods; here in Eustis, Maine, the cathedral pines are famous for their lofty beauty. Happily, campers can enjoy this enchanted setting. Located in the rural Western corner of the state, just 26 miles south of the Canadian border, Cathedral Pines is a non-profit campground, and one of the most scenic in all of New England. Funds go to the towns of Stratton and Eustis, who operate the park. The tall, virgin stand of Norway (red) pines is set on the shores of Flagstaff Lake, where there's a private beach for campers, a public beach, and a picnic area. This site was one of Benedict Arnold's stops during his ill-fated march to Quebec City in 1775. The sand and gravel sites are canopied by the gorgeous pines, with buffer provided by low-growing shrubbery. Campsites are set in loops, including a separate area for tents (no water and electric); tent site 69, on the lake, is stunning. Among the water/electric sites, sites 13, 15, 16, 17, and 18 are nice, big, and lakeside. Three-way hookup sites are situated near the campground's entrance. All sites are widely-spaced, spacious, and private, not to mention jaw-droppingly beautiful. Don't miss this one.

### BASICS

**Operated By:** Stratton-Eustis Development Corp. **Open:** May 15–Oct. 1. **Site Assignment:** Reservations recommended. No reservations accepted for less than a 2-night stay. Must pay in full within 10 days of making reservation. No refunds for cancellation; credit for future stay only. **Registration:** At office. **Fee:** $15–$20 for 4 people. V, MC. **Parking:** At site.

### FACILITIES

**Number of RV Sites:** 115. **Number of Tent-Only Sites:** 0. **Hookups:** Water, electric (30 amps), sewer. **Each Site:** Picnic table, fireplace. **Dump Station:** Yes. **Laundry:** Yes. **Pay Phone:** Yes. **Rest Rooms and Showers:** Yes. **Fuel:** No. **Propane:** No. **Internal Roads:** Paved, in good condition. **RV Service:** No. **Market:** 4 mi. south. **Restaurant:** 4 mi. south. **General Store:** Yes. **Vending:** Yes. **Swimming Pool:** No. **Playground:** Yes. **Other:** Boat ramp, rec hall. **Activities:** Lake swimming, fishing (need license), hiking on Appalachian Trail, bicycling, boating (rentals available). **Nearby Attractions:** Moosewatching, Arnold Trail (follows Benedict Arnold's route to Quebec City), Dead River Historical Society Museum, golf, Bigelow Mountain. **Additional Information:** Flagstaff Area Business Assoc., (207) 246-4221; www.eustismaine.com.

### RESTRICTIONS

**Pets:** Must be leashed, quiet, & cleaned up after. Must not be left unattended. Not allowed in buildings or beaches. $10 refundable deposit required. **Fires:** In fireplaces only. **Alcoholic Beverages:** Yes. **Vehicle Maximum Length:** 40 ft. **Other:** 3-night min. stay on holidays, payable in advance.

### TO GET THERE

From Maine Turnpike, take exit 12 (Auburn) to Rte. 4 north. Connect w/Rte. 27 north in Farmington; follow to Eustis. Campground is on the right. (Total mileage from turnpike is 90 mi.)

## EUSTIS

## Natanis Point Campground

HC73 P.O. Box 270, Eustis 04936. T: (207) 297-2694 or (207) 645-5207 (winter); www.camp-maine.com/natanispointcampground

or

www.geocites.com/yosemite/cabin/3285/index.html.

🚐 ★★★　　　▲ ★★

Beauty: ★★★★　　　Site Privacy: ★★★★
Spaciousness: ★★★　　Quiet: ★★★★
Security: ★★★　　　　Cleanliness: ★★★★
Insect Control: ★★★　　Facilities: ★★★

We were all set to overlook this tiny, rustic campground, just six miles south of the Canadian border. But, we couldn't, once we realized one could camp here, on the Chain of Ponds, and wake up to gorgeous views of deep-blue water, flanked by pine-sloped mountains. Wooded campsites are set on two loops, overlooking Round Pond and Natanis Pond. We recommend the Natanis Pond side for best views, especially site 6. Sites 3 through 9 are fabulous; you couldn't be closer to the water unless you slept on your boat. Speaking of which, you can park your boat right alongside your tent or RV, and roll it in when you're ready. Sites 32 through 44 are farthest from the water. (Look for the Natanis Memorial just behind site 9; read about the legend of Natanis, a Native American female trapper, in the campground office.) The owners say this campground is at its best in fall, when the foliage season kicks in; however, the cold comes early here, and they drain the water pipes and close the bathhouse in early Oct. Rates drop to $10 per night.

### BASICS

**Operated By:** Ken & Sharon Thomas. **Open:** May 15–Oct. 15. **Site Assignment:** Reservations recommended for weekends. 50% deposit required. Refund for cancellation if made 1 week prior to arrival date. **Registration:** At office. **Fee:** $15 per night for 1 to 4 people. V, MC. **Parking:** At site.

## FACILITIES

**Number of RV Sites:** 63. **Number of Tent-Only Sites:** 0. **Hookups:** Water. **Each Site:** Picnic table, fire ring. **Dump Station:** Yes. **Laundry:** No. **Pay Phone:** Yes. **Rest Rooms and Showers:** Yes. **Fuel:** No. **Propane:** No. **Internal Roads:** Gravel, in good condition. **RV Service:** No. **Market:** 5 mi. north. **Restaurant:** 5 mi. north. **General Store:** Yes. **Vending:** No. **Swimming Pool:** No. **Playground:** Yes. **Other:** Supper building (rec hall). **Activities:** Fishing (license required), pond swimming, boating (kayak & canoe rentals available), volleyball, ATV trails, planned activities. **Nearby Attractions:** Arnold Trail (follows Benedict Arnold's route to Quebec City), Dead River Historical Society Museum, Flagstaff Lake, golf, Bigelow Mountain. **Additional Information:** Flagstaff Area Business Assoc., (207) 246-4221; www.eustismaine.com.

## RESTRICTIONS

**Pets:** Must be leashed, quiet, & cleaned up after. Must not be left unattended. **Fires:** In fire rings ony. **Alcoholic Beverages:** At sites only. **Vehicle Maximum Length:** 35 ft.

## TO GET THERE

From Maine Turnpike, take exit 12 (Auburn) to Rte. 4 north. Connect w/Rte. 27 North in Farmington; follow Rte. 27 north to Eustis. Stay on Rte. 27 for 17 mi., heading north. Campground is on the left.

## FREEPORT

### Cedar Haven

39 Baker Rd., Freeport 04032. T: (207) 865-6254 (800) 454-3403 (reservations); www.camp-maine.com/cedarhaven; campcedarhaven@yahoo.com.

| 🚐 ★★★ | 🔺 ★★★ |
|---|---|
| Beauty: ★★★ | Site Privacy: ★★★ |
| Spaciousness: ★★★ | Quiet: ★★★ |
| Security: ★★★ | Cleanliness: ★★★ |
| Insect Control: ★★★ | Facilities: ★★★ |

This woodsy campground is just two miles from touristy downtown Freeport, but campers feel worlds away. The modest, family-oriented property has a large sports field, a small (0.25-acre) spring-fed swimming pond (usually full of tiny tots at the end of long summer's day) and roomy sites. Tenters will especially enjoy the shaded, private, hillside sites, offering a natural-setting getaway from the busy Freeport area. (Site 38 set back in the woods is a favorite.) Big rig drivers will find four large-size, full hookup sites and extra wide roads for convenience. Most campers spend the day exploring the area (and outlet shopping) and breathe a heavy sigh of relief by the time they reach their site. Nothing fancy here—just a little peace and quiet.

## BASICS

**Operated By:** Private operator. **Open:** May–Oct. **Site Assignment:** Reservations suggested; hold w/ credit card during peak season; no shows charged 1-night fee; MC, V, D; no checks. **Registration:** At office. **Fee:** Full hookup, $30; water & electric, $24; no hookups, $18, based on 2 adults & 2 children under 18. **Parking:** At site.

## FACILITIES

**Number of RV Sites:** 48. **Number of Tent-Only Sites:** 10. **Hookups:** Water, electric, sewer (30 amps), cable TV. **Each Site:** Picnic table, fire ring, trash barrel. **Dump Station:** Yes. **Laundry:** Yes. **Pay Phone:** Yes. **Rest Rooms and Showers:** Yes (coin-op). **Fuel:** No. **Propane:** Yes. **Internal Roads:** Gravel (good). **RV Service:** No. **Market:** Freeport (2 mi). **Restaurant:** No. **General Store:** Yes. **Vending:** No. **Swimming Pool:** No. **Playground:** Yes. **Other:** Sports field, game room, mini-golf, spring-fed pond, beach, cabin rental, group area. **Activities:** Swimming, horseshoes, mini-golf, volleyball, basketball. **Nearby Attractions:** Freeport, outlet shopping, midcoast parks & beaches. **Additional Information:** Freeport Merchants Assoc., 23 Depot St., Freeport, ME 04032-0452, (207) 865-1212 (800) 865-0881, www.freeportusa.com.

## RESTRICTIONS

**Pets:** Must be on a leash, never left unattended. **Fires:** In grills, stoves, & fire rings only. **Alcoholic Beverages:** At site only. **Vehicle Maximum Length:** None.

## TO GET THERE

From I-95, exit 20, go, bear right on Rte.125/
136 for 0.5 mi, then turn right on Rte. 125 for
0.5 mi, then right on Baker Rd.; campground is
on the left.

## FREEPORT

### Desert Dunes of Maine Campground

95 Desert Rd., Freeport 04032. T: (207) 865-
6962; F: (207) 865-1678;
www.desertofmaine.com;
info@desertofmaine.com.

🚐 ★★★          ⛺ ★★★

| | |
|---|---|
| Beauty: ★★★ | Site Privacy: ★★★ |
| Spaciousness: ★★★ | Quiet: ★★★ |
| Security: ★★★ | Cleanliness: ★★★ |
| Insect Control: ★★★ | Facilities: ★★★ |

This is the only campground we know of in New
England that sits next to—and on top of— a
desert. The owners of the campground also own
the adjacent Desert of Maine attraction, a
unique natural phenomenon, drawing close to
50,000 visitors each year. Guided safari and
walking tours take visitors across vast sandy
dunes. There's a museum, sand art classes and
gemstone hunts for children. Campers have free
access to the attraction and most take advantage
of it. At the campground, sites are scattered in
the trees or up on hills. There's a handful of very
nice tent-only sites in the woods with plenty of
room and privacy. For extra seclusion, book site
T8, the honeymoon site, deep in the woods, set
apart from the others. There are also a number of
spacious wooded pull-through sites. Though the
campground is relatively small, just 50 sites
spread on 10 acres, it often feels busy. Not only
do tourists funnel through the office/gift store in
route to the attraction but the front of the campground, including the picnic area, is often taken
over by buses of day visitors.

## BASICS

**Operated By:** Sid & Carolyn Dobson. **Open:**
May–mid-Oct. **Site Assignment:** Reservations
suggested, 1-night deposit, 30-day cancellation
policy with $5 service charge; MC, V, D, AE, no
checks. **Registration:** At office. **Fee:** Full
hookups, $32; water & electric, $28; no hookups,
$20, based on 2 people per site, additional per-
son in RV, $5; additional person in tent, $7; children ages 3-12, $2; ages 13-16, $3. **Parking:** At
site.

## FACILITIES

**Number of RV Sites:** 40. **Number of Tent-
Only Sites:** 10. **Hookups:** Water, electric, sewer
(20, 30 amps), modem. **Each Site:** Picnic table,
fire ring. **Dump Station:** Yes. **Laundry:** Yes. **Pay
Phone:** No. **Rest Rooms and Showers:** Yes
(coin-op). **Fuel:** No. **Propane:** Yes. **Internal
Roads:** Gravel, dirt (good). **RV Service:** No.
**Market:** Freeport (6 mi). **Restaurant:** No. **General Store:** Yes. **Vending:** No. **Swimming Pool:**
Yes. **Playground:** No. **Other:** Free access to
Desert of Maine & discount on tours, group
area, picnic area, nature trails. **Activities:** Swimming, horseshoes. **Nearby Attractions:** Desert
of Maine, Freeport, mid-coast parks & beaches.
**Additional Information:** Freeport Merchants
Assoc., 23 Depot St. , Freeport, ME 04032-0452;
(207) 865-1212 (800) 865-0881;
www.freeportusa.com.

## RESTRICTIONS

**Pets:** Must be on a leash, never left unattended.
**Fires:** In grills, stoves, & fire rings only. **Alcoholic
Beverages:** At site only. **Vehicle Maximum
Length:** None.

## TO GET THERE

From I-95, exit 19, go west 2 mi. on Desert
Rd.; campground is on the left.

## FREEPORT

### Flying Point Campground

10 Lower Flying Point Rd., Freeport 04032. T:
(207) 865-4569 (800) 798-4569 (reservations).

🚐 ★★★          ⛺ ★★★

| | |
|---|---|
| Beauty: ★★★★ | Site Privacy: ★★★ |
| Spaciousness: ★★★ | Quiet: ★★★ |
| Security: ★★★ | Cleanliness: ★★★ |
| Insect Control: ★★★ | Facilities: ★★ |

This oceanfront campground, owned by a native
and life-long resident of Freeport, overlooks sce-

nic Casco Bay and Maquoit Bay. It boasts 1,200 feet of ocean frontage, with sandy beaches and sweeping views. Couples and families who can forego full hookups, heated pools and planned activities with love this place. Oceanfront sites (nearly half of the sites have ocean frontage) are set in a semi-circle, wrapped around a cove. Other sites are set in a row atop a bluff overlooking the water. There's a wide grassy lawn area in front of the sites that adds to the open, expansive feel of this campground. Water views are everywhere! If you can tear yourself away, downtown Freeport with outlet shopping, restaurants, theater, and more is just a few minutes away.

## BASICS

**Operated By:** Hilda Coskery. **Open:** May–Oct. 15. **Site Assignment:** Reservations suggested, 1-night deposit, 1-week cancellation policy; MC, V, no checks. **Registration:** At office. **Fee:** Water & electric, $23; no hookups, $17, based on 2 adults & 2 children under 18. **Parking:** At site.

## FACILITIES

**Number of RV Sites:** 30. **Number of Tent-Only Sites:** 8. **Hookups:** Water, electric (30 amps). **Each Site:** Picnic table, fire ring. **Dump Station:** Yes. **Laundry:** Yes. **Pay Phone:** Yes. **Rest Rooms and Showers:** Yes (coin-op). **Fuel:** No. **Propane:** No. **Internal Roads:** Gravel (good). **RV Service:** No. **Market:** Freeport (3cmi). **Restaurant:** No. **General Store:** No. **Vending:** Yes. **Swimming Pool:** No. **Playground:** No. **Other:** Ocean frontage, beach. **Activities:** Swimming, beachcombing, fishing, volleyball, badminton, horseshoes. **Nearby Attractions:** Freeport, mid-coast parks & beaches. **Additional Information:** Freeport Merchants Assoc., 23 Depot St., Freeport, ME 04032-0452; (207) 865-1212 (800) 865-0881; www.freeportusa.com.

## RESTRICTIONS

**Pets:** Must be on a leash, never left unattended. **Fires:** In grills, stoves, & fire rings only. **Alcoholic Beverages:** At site only. **Vehicle Maximum Length:** None. **Other:** Mini-bikes & motorcycles not allowed.

## TO GET THERE

From I-95, exit 29, go north 1 mi. on Rte. 1, then east (right) 3.75 mi. on Bow St. /Lower Flying Point Rd.; campground is on the left.

## GEORGETOWN
## Camp Seguin

Reid State Park Rd., Georgetown 04548. T: (207) 371-2777; campseguin.com.

🚐 ★★★               ⛺ ★★★

Beauty: ★★★★          Site Privacy: ★★
Spaciousness: ★★       Quiet: ★★★
Security: ★★★          Cleanliness: ★★★
Insect Control: ★★      Facilities: ★

What a great surprise! We went to sleep to the sound of the waves crashing over the rocks—pretty sweet. This testimonial comes from a wilderness camper, who stumbled upon this place en route to oceanside Reid State Park, just a quarter-mile up the street. Alas, the state park doesn't offer camping, but Camp Seguin fills the need, with a wonderful location on the rocky shoreline of Sheepscot Bay in mid-coast Maine. It's about an hour from Portland, Boothbay, and Augusta. Campsites are arrayed in a loop, with some right on the water. Many of the tent sites have platforms, a great idea on this rocky spot. Site 17, in the corner and alongside the bay, is semi-secluded, and beautiful. Among the water-and-electric sites, set inland a bit, sites 27 and 28 are the choicest, and most private. Site 29 is the worst; too close to the campground entrance. Facilities are clean but rustic. No matter; most campers spend the day at glorious Reid State Park, with its mile-and-a-half of sandy beaches, ocean swimming and lagoon. The park charges $2.50 per person, but, for a refundable $40 deposit, the campground will give you a pass, so you can use the state park for free. (Tip: Bring lots of bug spray; they're fierce around here.)

## BASICS

**Operated By:** Betsy & Craig Lane. **Open:** Mid-June-Labor Day. **Site Assignment:** Reservations recommended, 2-night min. stay for reservatons. Walk-ins OK for 1-night stay if space is available. For 2-night stay, payment in full required for deposit; for stays of 1 week or more, 50% of fee due as deposit. Refunds for cancellations w/ 7-day notice, minus $10 fee. **Registration:** At office. **Fee:** $23–$26 for 2 adults & up to 3 children. V, MC, D. **Parking:** At site.

## FACILITIES

**Number of RV Sites:** 17. **Number of Tent-Only Sites:** 14. **Hookups:** Water, electric (20 amps). **Each Site:** Picnic table, fire ring. **Dump Station:** Yes. **Laundry:** No. **Pay Phone:** Yes. **Rest Rooms and Showers:** Yes, coin-op. **Fuel:** No. **Propane:** No. **Internal Roads:** Gravel, in good to fair condition. **RV Service:** No. **Market:** 14 mi. south. **Restaurant:** 3 mi. east. **General Store:** Yes. **Vending:** No. **Swimming Pool:** No. **Playground:** Yes. **Other:** Rec hall. **Activities:** Fishing. **Nearby Attractions:** Reid State Park, Popham Beach State Park, Morse Mountain Sanctuary, Maine Maritime Museum, Bowdoin College Museum of Art, Peary-MacMillan Arctic Museum, deep-sea fishing. **Additional Information:** Chamber of Commerce of the Bath-Brunswick Region, (207) 725-8797 or (207) 443-9751; www.midcoastmaine.com.

## RESTRICTIONS

**Pets:** Must be leashed, quiet, & cleaned up after. Must not be left unattended. **Fires:** In fire rings only. **Alcoholic Beverages:** Yes. **Vehicle Maximum Length:** 27 ft. **Other:** Ask on arrival.

## TO GET THERE

From Rte. 1 in Bath, turn right on Rte. 127 south, immediately after crossing Carleton Bridge. Go 12 mi. south, then turn right on Seguinland Rd. (Reid St. Park Rd.) Campground entrance is on the left.

## GREENVILLE

### Casey's Spencer Bay Camps

P.O. Box 1190, Greenville 04441. T: (207) 695-2801; www.spencerbaycamps.com; casey@caseyspencerbaycamps.com.

🚐 ★★                          ⛺ ★★

Beauty: ★★                  Site Privacy: ★★★
Spaciousness: ★★★★      Quiet: ★★★
Security: ★★★              Cleanliness: ★★
Insect Control: ★★★      Facilities: ★

Want to enjoy the natural splendor of Moosehead Lake, but still have access to full hookups, and on-site motorboat (or canoe) rentals? This campground/cabin operation offers the Maine Sporting Camp Experience in all its rustic glory. So, if a bit of peeling linoleum in the shower house, and a junky-looking storage area don't offend your sensibilities, you'll be quite content here. The spot itself is quite lovely; you reach it via a six-mile gravel road lined with white birch. The drive will put you in the "getting away from it all" frame of mind, especially if you've encountered any moose along the way. Outside of the eyesore of a storage area—smack dab in the middle of things, sad to say—the campsites aren't bad at all. Set around a grassy field housing boat trailers, campsites are fairly wide—mostly 40 feet—with good buffer between sites. Cabins are set around Stevens Point. Some campsites are on the bayside (Spencer Bay), some face Moosehead Lake. Best RV sites are 16, 25, and 7 (awesome), on the bay side; best sites for tents are numbers 5 and 25 (high and dry when it rains.)

## BASICS

**Operated By:** Casey & Sarah LaCasce. **Open:** May 15–Oct. 15. **Site Assignment:** Reservations recommended. 50% deposit required. Refunds w/ 30-day notice of cancellation. **Registration:** At office. **Fee:** $18–$22 for 2 adults & their children under age 13. (Age 13 years & older, $4 extra per day.) V, MC. **Parking:** At site.

## FACILITIES

**Number of RV Sites:** 50. **Number of Tent-Only Sites:** 0. **Hookups:** Water, electric (20 amps), sewer. **Each Site:** Picnic table, fire ring. **Dump Station:** Yes. **Laundry:** No. **Pay Phone:** No. **Rest Rooms and Showers:** Yes, coin-op. **Fuel:** No. **Propane:** No. **Internal Roads:** Gravel, in good condition. **RV Service:** No. **Market:** 18.5 mi. south, in Greenville. **Restaurant:** 18.5 mi. south, in Greenville. **General Store:** Yes. **Vending:** No. **Swimming Pool:** No. **Playground:** No. **Other:** Boat ramp. **Activities:** Lake swimming, fishing (need license), boating (rentals available), hiking trail. **Nearby Attractions:** S.S. Katahdin steamboat cruises, Moosehead Marine Museum, Eveleth-Crafts-Sheridan Historical House, Lily whitewater rafting, boating, fishing, moosewatching at Lazy Tom Bog, Big Squaw

Mountain (chairlift & hiking). **Additional Information:** Moosehead Lake Region Chamber of Commerce, (207) 723-4443.

## RESTRICTIONS

**Pets:** Must be leashed, quiet, & cleaned up after. Must not be left unattended. $4 per day per pet. **Fires:** In fire rings only. **Alcoholic Beverages:** Yes. **Vehicle Maximum Length:** None. **Other:** Electricity limited to a few hours in the morning & a few hours at night.

## TO GET THERE

From Greenville, drive up Kokadjo Rd. 12 mi. north; watch for sign at left marking camp. Turn left. Last 6.5 mi. are a dirt road into camp (watch out for moose.)

## GREENVILLE
## Lily Bay State Park

HC 76 P.O. Box 425, Greenville 04441. T: (207) 695-2700 or (207) 941-4014 (off-season) or (800) 332-1501 (reservations or in ME) or (207) 287-3824 (reservations or outside ME); F: (207) 287-6170; www.state.me.us/doc/prkslands/reser.

 ★★★★　　　▲ ★★★

Beauty: ★★★★★　　Site Privacy: ★★★★★
Spaciousness: ★★★★★　　Quiet: ★★★★
Security: ★★★　　Cleanliness: ★★★
Insect Control: ★★　　Facilities: ★

I've waited my whole career for this, says Lily Bay State Park general manager Andy Haskell, spreading his arms to encompass his surroundings. It's easy to see why he's got a big grin on his face. Haskell's realm is a spectacular natural area set on the eastern shore of Moosehead Lake, the largest lake in New England. From the lake, campers look out toward mountain vistas all around, including Mt. Kineo, which seems to spring from the lake itself, rising 800 feet above the water. Campsites are set in two loops, both on the lake. There's Dunn Point, good for families because it's a close walk to the beach and playground, and Rowell Cove, which offers several walk-in tent sites. Plus, at Rowell Cove, tent sites are set closer to the water. Among the choic-

est sites at Rowell Cove are 20L and 21L, directly on the lake and roomy enough for 30 foot campers. Lake view sites at Dunn Point are those numbered 210, 211, 213, 214, and 215, and 218, 220, 221, and 222. You'll hear the haunting cry of loons at night. If you've brought a kayak or canoe, paddle out to Sugar Island (open to the public.) You knew there had to be a downside, and it's this: No showers and no flush toilets, though the park has an arrangement with Moosehead Family Campground in Greenville, where campers can use the coin-op showers. But if you can handle wilderness camping, it doesn't get better than Lily Bays

## BASICS

**Operated By:** Maine Dept. of Conservation, Bureau of Parks & Lands. **Open:** May 1–Oct. 15. **Site Assignment:** In spring & fall, camping is on a first-come, first-served basis. For summer stays, reservations open on the first business day in Jan. From June 15 to the night before Labor Day, sites may be reserved for a min. of 2 nights & up to 2 weeks. Full payment is charged to credit card when reservation is processed. Refund with $15 cancellation fee. 17 sites are non-reservable, & available on a first-come, first-served basis. Call the reservations line to cancel a reservation more than 3 days in advance. If cancelling less than 3 days in advance, call the park directly. **Registration:** At office. **Fee:** $12, Maine residents; $16, non-residents plus $2 fee if you reserve in advance. V, MC. **Parking:** At site.

## FACILITIES

**Number of RV Sites:** 91. **Number of Tent-Only Sites:** 0. **Hookups:** None. **Each Site:** Picnic table, fireplace. **Dump Station:** Yes. **Laundry:** No. **Pay Phone:** Yes. **Rest Rooms and Showers:** Yes (non-flush), no. **Fuel:** No. **Propane:** No. **Internal Roads:** Gravel, in good condition. **RV Service:** No. **Market:** 9 mi. southwest, in Greenville. **Restaurant:** 9 mi. southwest, in Greenville. **General Store:** No. **Vending:** Yes. **Swimming Pool:** No. **Playground:** Yes. **Other:** Boat ramps, boat docks. **Activities:** Lake swimming, shoreline hiking trail w/ interpretive signage, volleyball, boating, picnicking. **Nearby Attractions:** Moosehead Lake, S.S. Katahdin steamboat cruises, Moosehead Marine Museum, Eveleth-Crafts-Sheridan Historical House, Lily whitewater rafting, boating, fishing, moosewatching at Lazy Tom Bog. **Additional Information:** Moosehead Lake Region Chamber of Commerce, (207) 723-4443.

## RESTRICTIONS

**Pets:** Must be leashed, quiet, & cleaned up after. Must have rabies vaccination certificate. Not allowed on beach. **Fires:** In fireplaces only. **Alcoholic Beverages:** No. **Vehicle Maximum Length:** 35 ft. **Other:** 2-week max. stay between last week in June & Labor Day.

## TO GET THERE

From Greenville, go 9 mi. northeast on Lily Bay Rd. (also called Kodjako Rd. Campground is on the left.

## HERMON

## Pleasant Hill Campground

45 Mansell Rd., Hermon 04401. T: (207) 848-5127; www.mint.net/pleasanthill; pleasant@mint.net.

🚐 ★★★          ▲ ★★★

| | |
|---|---|
| Beauty: ★★★ | Site Privacy: ★★★ |
| Spaciousness: ★★★ | Quiet: ★★★ |
| Security: ★★★ | Cleanliness: ★★★ |
| Insect Control: ★★★ | Facilities: ★★★ |

The name says it all: friendly and pleasant, this rural campground, just outside of Bangor, attracts a wide variety of clientele, from family campers who return year after year for a weekend away to off-the-road travelers in and out in a day. It's situated just a few miles off the main interstate, an hour or so from Acadia National Park and en route to the Canadian Maritime Provinces, making it a favorite stopover for tourists needing a place to lay their heads for the night. Campers find a helpful staff, clean, maintained grounds and a choice of sunny or shaded sites. Pull-through, full hookups are set side-by-side off the main campground road; water and electric sites and tent sites are set in loops nestled in woods or in open, sunny fields. Families will find enough to keep little ones entertained for an evening or two: besides the swimming pool, there's a stocked fishing pond, modest mini-golf course, and game room on site.

## BASICS

**Operated By:** Montford family. **Open:** May–Oct. **Site Assignment:** First come, first served; call for reservations to reserve a specific site only. 1-night deposit, 2 week cancellation policy w/ a $7 service fee; MC, V, D, checks. **Registration:** At office. **Fee:** Full hookups, $30.50 (50 amp), $26 (30 amp); water & electirc, $23; water only (tent), $17. **Parking:** At site.

## FACILITIES

**Number of RV Sites:** 84. **Number of Tent-Only Sites:** 21. **Hookups:** Water, electric, sewer (30, 50 amps). **Each Site:** Picnic table, fire ring. **Dump Station:** Yes. **Laundry:** Yes. **Pay Phone:** Yes. **Rest Rooms and Showers:** Yes. **Fuel:** No. **Propane:** Yes. **Internal Roads:** Gravel, dirt (good). **RV Service:** No. **Market:** Bangor (5 mi). **Restaurant:** No. **General Store:** Yes. **Vending:** No. **Swimming Pool:** Yes. **Playground:** Yes. **Other:** Rec hall, mini golf, stocked fishing pond, adult reading lounge, pavilion. **Activities:** Swimming, fishing, horseshoes, volleyball, mini-golf, basketball. **Nearby Attractions:** Bangor, Bar Harbor, Acadia National Park, Maine coast. **Additional Information:** Bangor Regional Chamber of Commerce, 519 Maine St. , P.O. Box 1443, Bangor, ME 04402 (207) 947-0307, www.bangor-region.com.

## RESTRICTIONS

**Pets:** Must be on a leash, never left unattended. **Fires:** In grills, stoves, & fire rings only. **Alcoholic Beverages:** At site only. **Vehicle Maximum Length:** None.

## TO GET THERE

From I-95, exit 45, go 5 mi. west on Rte. 222 (Union St. ); campground is on the left.

## JACKMAN

## Moose River Campground

P.O. Box 98, Jackman 04945. T: (207) 668-3341; www.mooserivercampground.com; mooservr@ctel.net.

🚐 ★★★          ⛺ ★★

Beauty: ★★★          Site Privacy: ★★
Spaciousness: ★★          Quiet: ★★★★
Security: ★★          Cleanliness: ★★★
Insect Control: ★★★          Facilities: ★★

Nudging the Canadian border in Maine's Moose River Valley, the town of Jackman is a four-season recreational hotspot. In summer, the area draws hikers, rock-climbers, fat-tire bicyclists and whitewater rafting enthusiasts. But, since it's so far north, the crowds never equal the numbers of those at, say, Camden. It's not surprising that Jackman is home to about a half-dozen campgrounds. This one is the nicest, and most family-friendly. ("This campground rocks!" a camper-kid told us—we didn't ask—as we toured the property.) Located in a residential area near Old Mill Dam, the campground is wooded with tall pines and white birch, with campsites set in loops alongside a pond. There's a smaller, stocked fishing pond for kids, with nice grassy banks and benches. A swimming pool and a well-designed play structure add to the family-pleasing amenities. With canoe rentals besides, your bunch will find plenty to do. Sites 12 through 18, at waterside, have no hookups; sites 20 and 21, overlooking a small island, are good sites with electric hookups. Most-secluded site—nice here, since there are so many kids running around—is site 7. A few seasonal sites are grouped together in an inner loop. Rest rooms are no-frills, very basic. This is a good choice for those who want some comforts with their wilderness experience.

### BASICS

**Operated By:** Brian & Cheryl Cousineau. **Open:** May 15–Nov. 1. **Site Assignment:** Reservations accepted. Deposit of 1 nights' fee required. Must give 72-hour notice of cancella-tion for refund. **Registration:** At office. **Fee:** $14–$19 for 2 adults & 2 children under age 16. V, MC. **Parking:** At site or designated lot.

### FACILITIES

**Number of RV Sites:** 55. **Number of Tent-Only Sites:** 0. **Hookups:** Water, electric (30 amps), sewer, cable TV. **Each Site:** Picnic table, fireplace w/ grill top. **Dump Station:** Yes. **Laundry:** Yes. **Pay Phone:** Yes. **Rest Rooms and Showers:** Yes. **Fuel:** No. **Propane:** No. **Internal Roads:** Gravel, in good condition. **RV Service:** No. **Market:** 2.5 mi. south. **Restaurant:** 2.5 mi. south. **General Store:** Yes. **Vending:** Yes. **Swimming Pool:** Yes. **Playground:** Yes. **Other:** Rec room, boat dock. **Activities:** Fishing (licenses available in town), stocked pond for kid's fishing, boating (rentals available), volleyball, horseshoes, swimming. **Nearby Attractions:** Fishing, hiking, moosewatching. **Additional Information:** Jackman-Moose River Region Chamber of Commerce, (207) 668-417`.

### RESTRICTIONS

**Pets:** Must be leashed, quiet, & cleaned up after. Must not be left unattended. **Fires:** In fireplaces only. **Alcoholic Beverages:** At sites only. **Vehicle Maximum Length:** None. **Other:** 3-night min. stay during holiday weekends.

### TO GET THERE

From junction of Rtes. 6/15 and 201, go 2 mi. north on Rte. 201/6, then 1.5 mi. east on Heald Stream Rd. Campground entrance is on the right.

## LEEDS

## Riverbend Campground

R.R.2, P.O. Box 505, Leeds 04263. T: (207) 524-5711; www.megalink.net/~riverbend; riverbend@megalink.net.

🚐 ★★★          ⛺ ★★

Beauty: ★★★          Site Privacy: ★★
Spaciousness: ★★★          Quiet: ★★★
Security: ★★★          Cleanliness: ★★★
Insect Control: ★★★          Facilities: ★★★

Like to bass fish? Crazy for paddling? This might be the campground of your dreams. Set in rural

Maine, just west of Augusta, Riverbend is the home of Androscoggin Bass Masters, plus, L.L. Bean uses the campground as a base for its Discovery School canoe and kayak trips. Even without those endorsements, it won't take an outdoors-enthusiast long to discover that the campground boasts easy access to six miles of the Dead River, leading to 3,800-acre Androscoggin Lake, one mile up. The owners are happy to sell you a fishing license and bait, rent you a vessel (canoe or motorboat), and share the best places to haul in the biggest bass. Plus-size RVs occupy a grassy rolling field near the swimming pool (sites 53 and 54, and 57 through 59 are nice), while tents and self-contained units (water, no electric) hug the riverbank. Among these, site 80 is nice and private, overlooking the river. Tenters might find the space a bit wide-open, but if you plan to spend most of the day explore the waterways, who cares?

## BASICS

**Operated By:** Tom & Elaine Gomolka. **Open:** May 1–Sept.30. **Site Assignment:** Reservations recommended. Deposit of 25% required for 2-day stay; full payment required for 1-night stay & holiday weekends. Refund for cancellations w/ 30-day notice, minus $10 fee. **Registration:** At office. **Fee:** $19.50–$23 for a family of 2 adults & up to 4 children age 18 & under. V, MC, D. **Parking:** At site.

## FACILITIES

**Number of RV Sites:** 80. **Number of Tent-Only Sites:** 0. **Hookups:** Water, electric (20, 30 amps). **Each Site:** Picnic table, fire ring. **Dump Station:** Yes. **Laundry:** No. **Pay Phone:** Yes. **Rest Rooms and Showers:** Yes, coin-op. **Fuel:** No. **Propane:** Yes. **Internal Roads:** Gravel, in good condition. **RV Service:** No. **Market:** 11 mi. east, in Winthrop. **Restaurant:** 6 mi. east. **General Store:** Yes. **Vending:** Yes. **Swimming Pool:** Yes. **Playground:** Yes. **Other:** Game room. **Activities:** Fishing (licenses available), boating (rentals available), swimming, planned activities. **Nearby Attractions:** Norlands Living History Museum, Maine State Capitol & Museum, Fort Western, Monmouth Summer Theater. **Additional Information:** Androscoggin Chamber of Commerce, (207) 783-2249; www.androscoggincounty.com.

## RESTRICTIONS

**Pets:** Must be leashed, quiet, & cleaned up after. Must not be left unattended. **Fires:** In fire rings only. **Alcoholic Beverages:** At sites only. **Vehicle Maximum Length:** None. **Other:** No visitors allowed after 8:00 p.m.

## TO GET THERE

Take Maine Turnpike north to exit 12 (Auburn), then take Rte. 202 east to Rte. 106 north; follow for 7.5 mi. to campground.

## LOVELL

### Kezar Lake Camping Area

R.R. 1, P.O. Box 246, Lovell 04051. T: (207) 925-1631 or (888) 925-1631 (reservations); www.kezarlakecamping.com.

| 🚐 ★★★ | 🅰 ★★ |
|---|---|
| Beauty: ★★★ | Site Privacy: ★★ |
| Spaciousness: ★★ | Quiet: ★★ |
| Security: ★★★★★ | Cleanliness: ★★★ |
| Insect Control: ★★★ | Facilities: ★★ |

National Geographic named Kezar Lake one of the 10 most beautiful lakes in the world; a British journalist upped that, calling it one of the five loveliest lakes. For whatever that's worth, this is a peachy spot, with azure water, tawny sand, and a backdrop of piney green. Located in Maine's Western Lakes region, this campground sits right on the shoreline, with 400 feet of sandy beach and a variety of wooded campsites. The grass-and-gravel sites, mostly back-in, are a bit packed in, but, nobody spends much time at camp 'til nightfall, when the last child has been coaxed off the beach, the last canoe dragged in for the night. For keeping an eye on the little ones at play, waterfront sites DW3 and 4 and W3 through 7 are good choices. Sites W8 and W9 are winners, too, set back from the beach, but overlooking the lake. We like site L40 because it's backed up into the woods and a tad apart from the rest. Nicest tent sites are T2 and T3, near the marsh (you did pack that insect repellent, no?) Some new sites are being added, near the road and away from the beach; ask about construction activity when you book, if that concerns you.

### BASICS

**Operated By:** Pierce family. **Open:** May 15–Columbus Day. **Site Assignment:** Reservations recommended. May reserve while on site this year for next year. 50% deposit required. Refunds for cancellations if received more than 1 month before arrival, minus $20 service charge. If you book more than 1 month in advance, you must reserve for a full week. **Registration:** At office. **Fee:** $18–$35 for 2 adults & unmarried, dependent children under age 18. V, MC, D, AE. **Parking:** At site or storage area.

### FACILITIES

**Number of RV Sites:** 118. **Number of Tent-Only Sites:** 0. **Hookups:** Water, electric (20, 30 amps). **Each Site:** Picnic table, fireplace. **Dump Station:** Yes. **Laundry:** Yes. **Pay Phone:** Yes. **Rest Rooms and Showers:** Yes, coin-op. **Fuel:** No. **Propane:** Yes. **Internal Roads:** Gravel, in good condition. **RV Service:** No. **Market:** 13 mi. south, in Fryeburg. **Restaurant:** 25 mi. west, in N. Conway, N.H. **General Store:** Yes. **Vending:** Yes. **Swimming Pool:** No. **Playground:** Yes. **Other:** Rec hall, boat ramp. **Activities:** Fishing (license required), boating (rentals available), swimming, volleyball, basketball, planned activities. **Nearby Attractions:** Mt. Sabattus (hiking), outlet shopping (North Conway, N.H.). **Additional Information:** Bridgton Lakes Region Chamber of Commerce, (207) 647-3472.

### RESTRICTIONS

**Pets:** Must be leashed, quiet, & cleaned up after. Must not be left unattended. Not allowed on beach or in public areas. $2 charge per day. **Fires:** In fireplaces only. **Alcoholic Beverages:** At sites only. **Vehicle Maximum Length:** None. **Other:** 3-night min. stay for holidays.

### TO GET THERE

From Maine Turnpike, take exit 8, then Rte. 302 through Bridgton. From junction of Rte. 93, continue on Rte. 302 for 4.3 mi. Turn right on Knight's Hill Rd. to Lovell. Go north for 2.5 mi., then turn left at campground sign. Entrance is 3 mi. on the right.

## MEDWAY

## Katahdin Shadows

P.O. Box 606J, Rte. 157, Medway 04460. T: (207) 746-9349 (800) 794-5267; www.katahdin shadows.com; katshadcamp@midmaine.com.

🚐 ★★★★                    ⛺ ★★★★★

| | |
|---|---|
| Beauty: ★★★★★ | Site Privacy: ★★★★ |
| Spaciousness: ★★★★ | Quiet: ★★★★ |
| Security: ★★★★ | Cleanliness: ★★★★ |
| Insect Control: ★★★ | Facilities: ★★★★ |

We love this plush oasis nestled in the vast northern Maine woods, just outside of Baxter State Park. Outdoor enthusiasts have miles of hiking trails, canoeing, whitewater rafting, and some of the best fishing in Maine right outside their doorsteps. The ultra-friendly campground owners provide plenty of tips and information, and will set campers up with outdoor adventure guide and shuttle service. Guided fishing trips take off directly from the campground. Most campers come to play in the great outdoors but save plenty of time for relaxing around the campground. There are lots of nice facilities, here: swimming pool, lounges, sports fields, function hall, and more. On summer weekends, kids can join in a number of planned activities. Tenters looking for quiet and solitude will appreciate "the jungle," a separate, secluded area with plenty of privacy. RVers will like sites 51-56, with full hookups, easy access, and lots of shade. The campground also rents hutniks (8x8 wooded shelters with roll-down doors) and cabins. Added bonus: the campground stays open year-round with miles of cross-country, snowshoe, and snowmobile trails accessible from the property.

### BASICS

**Operated By:** David & Theresa Violette. **Open:** Year-round. **Site Assignment:** Reservations suggested Jul.–Aug.; 1-night deposit, 24-hour cancellation policy; MC, V, checks. **Registration:** At office. **Fee:** Full hookups, $21; water & electric, $19; no hookups, $17, based on 2 adults & 2 children. **Parking:** At site.

### FACILITIES

**Number of RV Sites:** 97. **Number of Tent-Only Sites:** 21. **Hookups:** Water, electric, sewer (30, 50 amps). **Each Site:** Picnic table, fire ring. **Dump Station:** Yes. **Laundry:** Yes. **Pay Phone:** Yes. **Rest Rooms and Showers:** Yes. **Fuel:** No. **Propane:** No. **Internal Roads:** Gravel, dirt (good). **RV Service:** No. **Market:** Medway (within walking distance). **Restaurant:** No. **General Store:** Yes. **Vending:** Yes. **Swimming Pool:** Yes. **Playground:** Yes. **Other:** Game room, sports fields, adult lounge, function hall, guided fishing trips, boat rentals, planned activities, guide & shuttle service to whitewater rafting, kayaking & canoeing. **Activities:** Swimming, boating, fishing, hiking, whitewater rafting, guided excursions. **Nearby Attractions:** Baxter State Park, Penobscot River, Gulf Hagas, Allagash River, Mattawamkeag Wilderness Park. **Additional Information:** Katahdin Area Chamber of Commerce, 1029 Central St., Millinocket, Maine 04462 (207) 723-4443, www.katahdinmaine.com.

### RESTRICTIONS

**Pets:** Must be on a leash; never left unattended. **Fires:** In grills, campstoves, & fire rings only. **Alcoholic Beverages:** At site only. **Vehicle Maximum Length:** None.

### TO GET THERE

From I-95, exit 56, go 1.7 mi. west on Rte. 157; campground is on the right.

## MT. DESERT ISLAND

### Somes Sound View Campground

86 Hall Quarry Rd., Mt. Desert Island 04660. T: (207) 244-3890; www.mtdesertisland.com.

| 🚐 ★★ | ▲ ★★★ |
|---|---|
| Beauty: ★★★★ | Site Privacy: ★★★ |
| Spaciousness: ★★★ | Quiet: ★★★★ |
| Security: ★★★ | Cleanliness: ★★★ |
| Insect Control: ★★★ | Facilities: ★★ |

This small, quirky campground sits on a rocky saltwater shore and offers tenters and small trailer campers fine views of the ocean and Somes Sound. There's a dock and small beach on the shoreline, and canoe and sailboat rentals

from the office, but don't expect much else in the way of services and conveniences. The boulder-strewn, rustic campground is best for those who like their pleasures simple and natural: the sound of the waves, the smell of the ocean, the wind in the trees. The sites vary in size and appeal. Some sites are quite tiny and close to the road; others sit up on flat rock and slabs of granite. Sites 36 and 37 are waterfront with great views but sit almost smack dab in the middle of the road or the public gravel beach, and waterfront sites 30 and 31 barely have enough room for a pup tent. There are also sites looping around an old historic quarry pond, but we find the chainlink fence around quarry unappealing. The best sites are actually off the water where you'll have more room and privacy. We like site 19 and 20 set back in the woods or site 8 set up high on a sunny slab of granite.

### BASICS

**Operated By:** Rudolf & Marilyn Musetti & Rick & Mimi. Mooers. **Open:** Memorial Day–Oct. 15. **Site Assignment:** Reservations suggested in Jul.–Aug., $20 non-refundable deposit. Cash only. **Registration:** At office. **Fee:** Waterfront, $21; wooded, $18; $3 extra for electric hookups. Waterfront sites are tent-only. **Parking:** At site; 1 walk-in site.

### FACILITIES

**Number of RV Sites:** 11. **Number of Tent-Only Sites:** 71. **Hookups:** Water, electric (20, 30 amps). **Each Site:** Picnic table, fire ring. **Dump Station:** Yes. **Laundry:** No. **Pay Phone:** Yes. **Rest Rooms and Showers:** Yes (coin-op). **Fuel:** No. **Propane:** No. **Internal Roads:** Gravel (good). **RV Service:** No. **Market:** Somesville (4mi). **Restaurant:** No. **General Store:** No. **Vending:** Yes. **Swimming Pool:** No. **Playground:** No. **Other:** Boat dock, ocean frontage, sailboat & canoe rentals. **Activities:** Swimming, fishing, boating. **Nearby Attractions:** Bar Harbor, Acadia National Park. **Additional Information:** Acadia National Park, P.O. Box 177, Bar Harbor, ME 04609 (207) 288-3338, www.nps/gov/acad. Also, Acadia Information Center, P.O. Box 139, Mount Desert, ME 04660 (207) 667-8550 (800) 358-8550, www.acadiainfo.com & Bar Harbor Chamber of Commerce, Bar Harbor Chamber of Commerce, 93 Cottage St., Bar Harbor, ME 04609 (207) 288-5103, www.barharborinfo.com.

### RESTRICTIONS

**Pets:** Must be on a leash, never left unattended. **Fires:** In grills, stoves, & fire rings only. **Alcoholic Beverages:** At site only. **Vehicle Maximum Length:** None.

### TO GET THERE

From junction Rtes. 198 and 102, in Somesville, go south 2.1 mi. on Rte. 102, then east (left) 1 mi. on Hall Quarry Rd., campground is on the left.

## NAPLES

### Bay of Naples Family Camping

Rte. 11/114, P.O. Box 240M, Naples 04055. T: (207) 693-6429 or (800) 348-9750 (reservations or outside of ME); www.bayofnaples.com.

🚐 ★★★　　　　　　Ａ ★★

| | |
|---|---|
| Beauty: ★★ | Site Privacy: ★★ |
| Spaciousness: ★★★ | Quiet: ★★★ |
| Security: ★★★★ | Cleanliness: ★★★ |
| Insect Control: ★★★★★ | Facilities: ★ |

We'll forgive this campground's rather ramshackle facilities—off-putting as they are—because it's set in such a pretty area. It is located in the Sebago Lake region of southwestern Maine, on the Bay of Naples, set amidst a stand of tall pines. Given the height of the trees, they don't provide much buffer between sites, but the gravel spaces are nicely carpeted with pine needles. Good sites include W6, near the beach, and, for tenters, site 40, offering good tree coverage. The roped-off swimming area here is very large, with two rafts; the Songo River Queen paddleboat cruises right past the beach. The bay accesses the 45-mile Sebago Lake-Long Lake chain of waterways, great for boating. Another plus, for some: the campground adjoins a public golf course. Fishing is another option, but beware the fishing pier if you have mobility issues—it's located down a long, bumpy hill. The attractions of downtown Naples, including an amusement area, and the paddleboat cruise dock, are located nearby, making this a good base for active families.

### BASICS

**Operated By:** James Ruhlin. **Open:** Memorial Day–Columbus Day. **Site Assignment:** Reservations recommended. Deposit of 3 nights' fee required. 3-night min. required for reservations; otherwise, walk-ins accepted. Refunds for cancellation if made within 30 days. **Registration:** At office. **Fee:** $22–$28 for 2 adults & 2 children under age 18. V, MC (accepted for 3 or more nights' stay only). **Parking:** At site.

### FACILITIES

**Number of RV Sites:** 150. **Number of Tent-Only Sites:** 0. **Hookups:** Water, electric (30 amps), sewer. **Each Site:** Picnic table, fireplace. **Dump Station:** Yes. **Laundry:** Yes. **Pay Phone:** Yes. **Rest Rooms and Showers:** Yes, coin-op. **Fuel:** No. **Propane:** Yes. **Internal Roads:** Gravel, in good condition. **RV Service:** No. **Market:** 1 mi. north on Rte. 302. **Restaurant:** 1 mi. north on Rte. 302. **General Store:** No. **Vending:** No. **Swimming Pool:** No. **Playground:** Yes. **Other:** Rec room, dock w/ boat slips. **Activities:** Swimming, boating (rentals available), fishing (license required). **Nearby Attractions:** Golf, mini-golf, seaplane rides, boat cruises, Songo River Queen paddleboat, Douglas Mountain hiking, Sebago Lake State Park, outlet shopping (N. Conway, N.H.). **Additional Information:** Naples Business Assoc., (207) 693-3285.

### RESTRICTIONS

**Pets:** No. **Fires:** In fireplaces only. **Alcoholic Beverages:** Yes. **Vehicle Maximum Length:** None. **Other:** No groups; families & couples only.

### TO GET THERE

Take Maine Turnpike north to exit 8, then Rte. 302 for 26 mi. to Naples. Turn left onto Rte. 11/114 for 1 mi. Bay of Naples Campground adjoins golf course.

## NAPLES

### Four Seasons Family Camping

P.O. Box 927, Rte. 302, Naples 04055. T: (207) 693-6797.

🚐 ★★★          ⛺ ★

Beauty: ★★★
Spaciousness: ★★
Security: ★★★★★
Insect Control: ★★

Site Privacy: ★★
Quiet: ★★★
Cleanliness: ★★★★
Facilities: ★★★

Located on 14-mile Long Lake in the Sebago Lake region of southwest Maine, this family campground is set on rolling woodland, alongside a good-sized sandy beach. Some guests bring their boats along, and use the ramp and boat docks. Some waterfront sites have their own docks. Other campers are happy to rent a rowboat, canoe, sailboat or paddleboat. This isn't the best place for tenting in the area, since tent sites sit right alongside a large field, quite exposed, but RVers should be especially happy with site 16A, good-sized, with a water view, and 25, near the beach but tucked into a corner for privacy. Nice features include bike racks and lots of electrical outlets in the ladies' room. Most families (and they stress the family aspect here) come for a week, not a weekend, giving the place a rather lived-in look. Campers here aren't looking for pristine surroundings, however, just a nice, safe place to play outside and enjoy the obvious charms of the Chain of Lakes area.

#### BASICS

**Operated By:** Van Der Zee family. **Open:** Mid-May–mid-Oct. **Site Assignment:** Reservations recommended. Deposit of $100 for 1-week stay or full payment in advance for weekend stay or part of week. 14-day notice required for refunds due to cancellation. **Registration:** At office. **Fee:** $22–$37 per family. Includes 2 adults & their unmarried children. V, MC, D. **Parking:** At site.

#### FACILITIES

**Number of RV Sites:** 115. **Number of Tent-Only Sites:** 0. **Hookups:** Water, electric (20, 30 amps). **Each Site:** Picnic table, fire ring. **Dump Station:** Yes. **Laundry:** No. **Pay Phone:** Yes.

**Rest Rooms and Showers:** Yes, coin-op. **Fuel:** No. **Propane:** No. **Internal Roads:** Gravel, in good condition. **RV Service:** No. **Market:** 3 mi. south & 5 mi. north. **Restaurant:** 3 mi. south & 5 mi. north. **General Store:** Yes. **Vending:** Yes. **Swimming Pool:** Yes. **Playground:** Yes. **Other:** Boat ramp, rec hall. **Activities:** Lake swimming, boating, fishing (license required), volleyball. **Nearby Attractions:** Golf, mini-golf, seaplane rides, boat cruises, Songo River Queen paddleboat, Douglas Mountain hiking, Sebago Lake State Park, outlet shopping (N. Conway, N.H.). **Additional Information:** Greater Windham Chamber of Commerce, (207) 892-8265; www.windhamchamber.sebagolake.org.

#### RESTRICTIONS

**Pets:** Must be leashed, quiet & cleaned up after. No pets in rental units. **Fires:** In fire rings only. **Alcoholic Beverages:** Yes. **Vehicle Maximum Length:** None. **Other:** 3-night min. stay required on holiday weekends.

#### TO GET THERE

Take exit 8 off Maine Turnpike, then Rte. 302W to Naples. Continue 3 mi. to campground sign, on the right.

## NEW HARBOR

### Sherwood Forest Campsite

Pemaquid Beach, P.O. Box 189, New Harbor 04554. T: (800) 274-1593.

🚐 ★★★          ⛺ ★★★

Beauty: ★★★
Spaciousness: ★★★
Security: ★★★
Insect Control: ★★★

Site Privacy: ★★★
Quiet: ★★★★
Cleanliness: ★★★★
Facilities: ★★★

In the party mood? Keep going. "Go to Lake Pemaquid Campground!" owner Marilyn Stooky advises. "You won't be happy here." This wooded campground, about a half-hour's drive from Boothbay Harbor on Maine's mid-coast, is located in the Pemaquid Beach area, but sits inland from the ocean. If you prefer 'quiet and woodsy' to 'crowded and beachy', you 'll be quite content here. This campground has been in the same family for 23 years, with a younger generation poised to take over. Sites are grassy, and set in a loop that starts just beyond the pool, store, and pavilion area, which is bordered by four cabins. Sites are heavily wooded and nicely buffered for privacy; sunlight filters through the dense canopy of foliage on bright summer days. Sites 15E and F, facing a small pond, are pretty, but stay away from 15H, alongside a big brush pile when we visited. Site 15D2 is nestled in woodlands and very private. Sites 9A and 9B sit in a wooded glen, nicely situated. Among the tent sites, the owner recommends sites B, C, and D, set on a cul-de-sac; we like nicely-shaded site 43, which backs into the woods. Outbuildings are fairly rustic, but changes may come as the kids take over.

## BASICS

**Operated By:** Gary & Marilyn Stooky. **Open:** May 1–Oct. 1. **Site Assignment:** Reservations recommended. $25 deposit required. Refunds for cancellations w/ 1-week notice, minus $5 fee. **Registration:** At office. **Fee:** $18–$24 for 2 adults & 2 children. No credit cards. **Parking:** At site.

## FACILITIES

**Number of RV Sites:** 49. **Number of Tent-Only Sites:** 13. **Hookups:** Water, electric (15, 20, 30 amps). **Each Site:** Picnic table, fire ring. **Dump Station:** Yes. **Laundry:** Yes. **Pay Phone:** Yes. **Rest Rooms and Showers:** Yes, coin-op. **Fuel:** No. **Propane:** No. **Internal Roads:** Gravel, in good condition. **RV Service:** No. **Market:** 1 mi. east. **Restaurant:** 1 mi. east. **General Store:** Yes. **Vending:** Yes. **Swimming Pool:** Yes. **Playground:** Yes. **Activities:** Swimming, basketball, boating (may add rentals; pending). **Nearby Attractions:** Pemaquid Point Lighthouse, Boothbay Railway Village, Maine Resources Aquarium, Boothbay Harbor restaurants, shops & galleries, deep-sea fishing, whale-watching cruises, golf. **Additional Information:** Boothbay Harbor Region Chamber of Commerce, (207) 633-2353 or (800) 266-8422.

## RESTRICTIONS

**Pets:** Must be leashed, quiet, & cleaned up after. Must not be left unattended. $1 charge per dog, per day. **Fires:** In fireplaces only. **Alcoholic Beverages:** Yes. **Vehicle Maximum Length:** None.

**Other:** 3-day min. stays on July 4th weekend, Old Bristol Days (in Aug., call to confirm dates), & Labor Day.

## TO GET THERE

From Bus. Rte. 1 and Rte. 130 in Damariscotta, go 12 mi. south on Rte. 130, then 0.75 mi. west on Snowball Hill Rd., then 800 ft. south on Pemaquid Tr. Entrance is on the left.

# NORTH MONMOUTH

## Beaver Brook Campground

R.R. 1, P.O. Box 1835, North Monmouth 04265. T: (207) 933-2108 or (207) 622-5231 (off-season); F: (207) 933-3826; www.beaver-brook.com.

| 🚐 ★★★ | 🅰 ★★★ |
|---|---|
| Beauty: ★★ | Site Privacy: ★★ |
| Spaciousness: ★★ | Quiet: ★★ |
| Security: ★★★★★ | Cleanliness: ★★★ |
| Insect Control: ★★ | Facilities: ★★ |

Located just 15 miles west of Augusta in south-central Maine, this campground offers a lakeside escape with plenty of action. Woodsy and terraced, this 150-acre property sits on the shore of Androscoggin Lake. They rent all kinds of boats—motorboats, canoes, kayaks, paddleboats—and sell fishing gear and non-resident licenses, all the better to try your luck against small- and large-mouth bass. You might even spot wildlife here; we saw a great blue heron perched on a boulder near the (tiny) beach. Planned activities include goofy stuff like a "Wild & Wacky 'Survivor' Weekend." Among the campsites are 50 seasonals. There's not much buffer between campsites. We'd skip the crowded waterfront camping area, and head out back to the Hemlock Ln.Loop, wooded, quieter, state parkish. Sites 354 through 360 (even numbers) are fairly spacious in this bunch. If you can't resist the waterfront, try sits 216 through 221. For total seclusion, though, you can't beat sites 339, 340, and 341, off in the woods by themselves. One complaint: charging campers $5 each time they launch their boat from the ramp is pretty niggling.

## BASICS

**Operated By:** Dick & Jean Parent. **Open:** May 1–Columbus Day. **Site Assignment:** Reservations recommended. Reservation request form available online. 50% of fee due w/ reservation. Must pre-pay in full for holiday weekend stays. Refunds for cancellations if received 14 days prior to arrival date, minus service charge. No refunds for holiday weekend cancellations. **Registration:** At office. **Fee:** $18–$24 for 2 adults & up to 4 children under age 18. V, MC (No checks.). **Parking:** At site.

## FACILITIES

**Number of RV Sites:** 191. **Number of Tent-Only Sites:** 0. **Hookups:** Water, electric (20, 30 amps). **Each Site:** Picnic table, fire ring. **Dump Station:** Yes. **Laundry:** Yes. **Pay Phone:** Yes. **Rest Rooms and Showers:** Yes. **Fuel:** No. **Propane:** Yes. **Internal Roads:** Gravel, in fair condition. **RV Service:** No. **Market:** 5 mi. north. **Restaurant:** Yes. **General Store:** Yes. **Vending:** Yes. **Swimming Pool:** Yes. **Playground:** Yes. **Other:** Rec hall, boat launch. **Activities:** Boating (rentals available), swimming, fishing (licenses available), volleyball, horseshoes, planned activities. **Nearby Attractions:** Maine State Capitol & Museum, Fort Western, Monmouth Summer Theater. **Additional Information:** Kennebec Valley Chamber of Commerce, (207) 623-4559.

## RESTRICTIONS

**Pets:** Must be leashed, quiet, & cleaned up after. Must not be left unattended. **Fires:** In fire rings only. **Alcoholic Beverages:** Yes. **Vehicle Maximum Length:** None. **Other:** 2-week min. stay on weekends in July & Aug. From late June to mid-Aug., prime sites (numbers 100s & 200s) are rented on a Saturday to Saturday basis. 3-night min. on holiday weekends.

## TO GET THERE

Take Maine Turnpike to exit 12 (Auburn.) Follow Rte. 202 east 19.5 mi. to Beaver Brook sign. Turn left onto Back St.; follow to end. Turn left on Wilson Pond Rd., follow to end. Look for campground sign.

# OLD ORCHARD BEACH

## Hid 'n Pines

P.O. Box 647, 8 Cascade Rd., Old Orchard Beach 04064. T: (207) 934-2352; www.mainerec.com/hidnpines; hidnpines@cybertours.com.

🚐 ★★★              ⛺ ★★★

Beauty: ★★              Site Privacy: ★★★
Spaciousness: ★★★       Quiet: ★★
Security: ★★★★★         Cleanliness: ★★★
Insect Control: ★★★     Facilities: ★★★

This campground, just minutes from Old Orchard Beach (some folks walk the distance and avoid the parking problems and traffic congestion downtown), really packs 'em in. This large, 250+ site property, bustles with summer vacationers, who head to the beach during the day and crowd into the campground at night. Expect it to be crawling with families, a bit noisy, and congested. Sites are on the smallish side, tucked under pine trees, side-by-side, flanking each side of the campground roads. But there are conveniences: clean bathrooms with free hot showers (nice after a day in the salt-tinged air and ocean waters); heated swimming pool, and a nearby strip mall (you can walk to it) with an ice cream shop and groceries.

## BASICS

**Operated By:** Lori Owen. **Open:** Mid-May–Columbus Day. **Site Assignment:** Reservations suggested, $30 deposit, 7-day cancellation notice with $3 service charge; MC, V, no checks. **Registration:** At office. **Fee:** Full hookups, $30.50; water & electric, $27.50; no hookups, $24.50, based on family of 3; additional adults, $5; additional children, ages 3-21, $3. **Parking:** At site, 1 car per site.

## FACILITIES

**Number of RV Sites:** 200. **Number of Tent-Only Sites:** 50. **Hookups:** Water, electric, sewer (20, 30 amps). **Each Site:** Picnic table, fire ring. **Dump Station:** Yes. **Laundry:** Yes. **Pay Phone:** Yes. **Rest Rooms and Showers:** Yes. **Fuel:** No. **Propane:** Yes. **Internal Roads:** Paved, gravel (good). **RV Service:** No. **Market:** Old Orchard Beach (500 ft.). **Restaurant:** No. **General Store:** No. **Vending:** Yes. **Swimming Pool:** Yes. **Playground:** Yes. **Other:** Game room. **Activities:** Swimming, basketball. **Nearby Attractions:** Old Orchard Beach, southern coast parks & beaches, Portland. **Additional Information:** Old Orchard Beach Chamber of Commerce, First St., Old Orchard Beach, ME 04064 (207) 934-2500 (800) 365-9386; www.oldorchardbeachmaine.com.

### RESTRICTIONS

**Pets:** Must be on a leash, never left unattended. Only 1 pet allowed per site. **Fires:** In grills, stoves, & fire rings only. **Alcoholic Beverages:** At site only. **Vehicle Maximum Length:** None. **Other:** No motocycles allowed.

### TO GET THERE

From junction, Maine Turnpike and I-195, exit 5, go east 2 mi. on I-195, then east 2 mi. on Rte. 5, then northwest 0.5 mi. on Rte. 98; campground is on the right.

## OLD ORCHARD BEACH

## Old Orchard Beach Campground

27 Ocean Park Rd., Old Orchard Beach 04064. T: (207) 934-4477; www.gocamping.com; relax@gocamping.com.

🚐 ★★★                      ⛺ ★★★★

Beauty: ★★★                 Site Privacy: ★★★
Spaciousness: ★★★           Quiet: ★★★
Security: ★★★★★             Cleanliness: ★★★
Insect Control: ★★★         Facilities: ★★★

Location, just off the highway and minutes from Old Orchard Beach, makes this campground popular with travelers exploring the southern coast of Maine. Families come for weekends and week-long stays, to vacation at popular Old Orchard Beach. The price is right (particularly when compared to some beach area resorts) and there's the added convenience of the campground shuttle bus. Campers can avoid parking fees and traffic hassles. The campground has modest facilities: clean rest rooms and free show-

ers, two pools, and a kid-friendly arcade room. Most hookup sites are set side-by-side in rows, flanked by woods for shade and privacy. There's a large wooded wilderness area for open tenting (no numbered sites) set in a dense forest apart from the others. Be forewarned: This area is sometimes a magnet for partying groups.

### BASICS

**Operated By:** Daigle family. **Open:** May–Columbus Day. **Site Assignment:** Reservations suggested, $25 deposit, 14 day cancellation policy with $10 service charge, 3-night min. stay for holiday weekends; MC, V, D; checks accepted as deposits but not upon arrival. **Registration:** At office. **Fee:** Full hookups, $32; water & electric, $29; no hookups, $25, based on family of 2; additional adults, $7; additional children, ages 3-17, $5. **Parking:** At site.

### FACILITIES

**Number of RV Sites:** 150. **Number of Tent-Only Sites:** 150. **Hookups:** Water, electric, sewer (20, 30 amps). **Each Site:** Picnic table, fire ring. **Dump Station:** Yes. **Laundry:** Yes. **Pay Phone:** Yes. **Rest Rooms and Showers:** Yes. **Fuel:** No. **Propane:** Yes. **Internal Roads:** Gravel, dirt (good). **RV Service:** No. **Market:** Saco (5 mi). **Restaurant:** No. **General Store:** Yes. **Vending:** No. **Swimming Pool:** Yes. **Playground:** Yes. **Other:** Rec hall, bus shuttles to the beach. **Activities:** Swimming, basketball, horseshoes, volleyball. **Nearby Attractions:** Old Orchard Beach, southern coastal parks & beaches, Portland. **Additional Information:** Old Orchard Beach Chamber of Commerce, First St., Old Orchard Beach, ME 04064 (207) 934-2500 (800) 365-9386; www.oldorchardbeachmaine.com.

### RESTRICTIONS

**Pets:** Must be on a leash, never left unattended. Only adults can walk dogs in campground. **Fires:** In grills, stoves, & fire rings only. **Alcoholic Beverages:** At site only. **Vehicle Maximum Length:** None.

### TO GET THERE

From junction Maine Turnpike and I-195, exit 5, go 2 mi. east on I-195, then east 1,500 feet on Rte. 5; campground is on the right.

## OLD ORCHARD BEACH

### Paradise Park

P.O. Box 4, Upper Main St., Adelaine Rd., Old Orchard Beach 04064. T: (207) 934-4633; F: (207) 934-8510; www.paradisepark.com.

🚐 ★★                    ▲ ★★

Beauty: ★★                Site Privacy: ★★
Spaciousness: ★★          Quiet: ★★
Security: ★★★             Cleanliness: ★★★
Insect Control: ★★★       Facilities: ★★★

The best thing about this busy and often crowded campground is its proximity to popular Old Orchard Beach. Campers are within walking distance to the pier, shopping, amusements, and one of Maine's longest, white sand beaches. If you like the hustle and bustle of tourist-laden, honky-tonk Old Orchard Beach, you're likely to feel right at home at Paradise Park. You'll have close quarters at this campground. Sites are squished together, often close to the road; vehicles are helter-skelter, parked wherever they'll fit. There are a handful of sites ringed around a five-acre bass pond (there are paddleboat races and fishing tournaments for the kids); other sites are clustered in the woods—all tight spaces. If you like friendly folks and a bit of commune living, you'll have fun here. Nice touch: we like the two hot tubs.

### BASICS

**Operated By:** Halle family. **Open:** May 15–Oct. 15. **Site Assignment:** Reservations suggested, $50 deposit, 10-day cancellation policy; MC, V, D, no checks. **Registration:** At office. **Fee:** Full hookups, $32, water & electric, $29; no hookups, $26; waterfront sites, $3 extra, based on 2 people; additional adults, $5; additional children, ages 4-21, $3. **Parking:** At site.

### FACILITIES

**Number of RV Sites:** 162. **Number of Tent-Only Sites:** 15. **Hookups:** Water, electric, sewer (20, 30 amps), cable TV, modem. **Each Site:** Picnic table, fire ring. **Dump Station:** Yes. **Laundry:** Yes. **Pay Phone:** Yes. **Rest Rooms and Showers:** Yes. **Fuel:** No. **Propane:** No. **Internal Roads:** Paved (good). **RV Service:** No. **Market:** Old Orchard Beach (0.5 mi). **Restaurant:** No. **General Store:** Yes. **Vending:** No. **Swimming Pool:** Yes. **Playground:** Yes. **Other:** Pond, paddleboat rentals, hot tubs, game room, rec hall. **Activities:** Swimming, fishing, shuffleboard, basketball, volleyball, horseshoes, planned activities on Saturdays during summer. **Nearby Attractions:** Old Orchard Beach, southern coast parks & beaches, Portland. **Additional Information:** Old Orchard Beach Chamber of Commerce, First St., Old Orchard Beach, ME 04064 (207) 934-2500 (800) 365-9386; www.oldorchardbeachmaine.com.

### RESTRICTIONS

**Pets:** Must be on a leash, never left unattended. **Fires:** In grills, stoves, & fire rings only. **Alcoholic Beverages:** At site only. **Vehicle Maximum Length:** None. **Other:** Families & couples only, no singles.

### TO GET THERE

From junction Maine Turnpike and I-195, go east 2 mi. on I-195, then north 2 mi. on Rte. 5, then 0.2 mi. west on Adelaine Rd.; campground is at the end of the street.

## OLD ORCHARD BEACH

### Powder Horn Family Camping Resort

P.O. Box 366, Old Orchard Beach 04064. T: (207) 934-4733 (800) 934-7038 (reservations); www.mainecampgrounds.com; phorn36504@aol.com.

🚐 ★★★★                  ▲ ★★★

Beauty: ★★★              Site Privacy: ★★★
Spaciousness: ★★★        Quiet: ★★
Security: ★★★★★          Cleanliness: ★★★★★
Insect Control: ★★★      Facilities: ★★★★★

This giant-size resort in southern Maine is a popular summer vacation destination for New England campers. If you're looking to get away from it all, this is not the place to go. Powder Horn is chockful of nonstop activities and crowds of vacationing families. It's located just minutes from rolicking Old Orchard Beach (the campground offers shuttle bus service to the beach and downtown area), but the pace doesn't slow or calm down much at the campground. The three-pool complex, adjacent to the sports fields and mini golf course, is a hub of activity, especially late afternoon and evening when campers return for the day. There are almost 500 sites, so there's plenty of choice. A number of sites are set in open meadows, with full and partial sun throughout the day. Others, including an open tent-only area, are tucked in oak and pine groves toward the back of the campground, away from the busy front recreation/office area.

## BASICS

**Operated By:** David & Glenna Ahearn. **Open:** Memorial Day–Columbus Day. **Site Assignment:** Reservations suggested, $50 deposit, 7-day cancellation policy with $10 service charge; MC, V, D, no checks. **Registration:** At office. **Fee:** Full hookups (50 amp & cable), $41.50; full hookups (30 amp), $38.50; water & electric, 33.50; no hookups, $28.50, based on 2 people; additional adults, $7; additional children, ages 3-21, $3. **Parking:** At site, 1 vehicle per site; extra vehicles, $3.

## FACILITIES

**Number of RV Sites:** 442. **Number of Tent-Only Sites:** 56. **Hookups:** Water, electric (20, 30, 50 amps), sewer, cable TV, modem. **Each Site:** Picnic table, fire ring. **Dump Station:** Yes. **Laundry:** Yes. **Pay Phone:** Yes. **Rest Rooms and Showers:** Yes. **Fuel:** No. **Propane:** Yes. **Internal Roads:** Paved (good). **RV Service:** No. **Market:** full service store on the premises. **Restaurant:** Yes. **General Store:** Yes. **Vending:** No. **Swimming Pool:** Yes. **Playground:** Yes. **Other:** Game room, shuttle bus to beach, hot tubs, adult lounge, rec room, 18-hole mini-golf course.
**Activities:** Swimming, horseshoes, shuffleboard, basketball, mini-golf, planned activities, including children's programs, arts & crafts, contests, live entertainment, dances, socials, & more. **Nearby Attractions:** Old Orchard Beach, southern coast parks & beaches, Portland. **Additional Information:** Old Orchard Beach Chamber of Commerce, First St., Old Orchard Beach, ME 04064 (207) 934-2500 (800) 365-9386; www.oldorchardbeachmaine.com.

## RESTRICTIONS

**Pets:** Must be on a leash, never left unattended. **Fires:** In grills, stoves, & fire rings only. **Alcoholic Beverages:** At site only. **Vehicle Maximum Length:** None.

## TO GET THERE

From junction Maine Turnpike and I-195, exit 5, go east 1.2 mi. on I-195, then north 3 mi. on Rte. 1, then east 2 mi. on Rte. 98; campground is on the left.

## OLD ORCHARD BEACH

### Wild Acres

179 Saco Ave., Old Orchard Beach 04064. T: (207) 934-2535; F: (207) 934-1947; www.mainecamping.com; wildacres@cybertours.com.

| 🚐 ★★★★ | 🏕 ★★★★ |
|---|---|
| Beauty: ★★★ | Site Privacy: ★★★ |
| Spaciousness: ★★★ | Quiet: ★★ |
| Security: ★★★★ | Cleanliness: ★★★★ |
| Insect Control: ★★★ | Facilities: ★★★★ |

This is one of southern Maine's bustling mega camping resorts, with more than 500 sites, crowds, and activities galore. Wild Acres is the closest campground to Old Orchard Beach and offers direct ocean access for walking, swimming, and sunbathing. On the property, you'll find more activities than you could possibly do in a weekend, or perhaps, even a week. There are three swimming pools (two adult and one kiddie pool), three hot tubs, an 18-hole mini-golf course, and weekend entertainment. The adult lounge features pool tables, big screen TV and a fieldstone fireplace. Kids have their own rec hall. The landscaping throughout the campground has received special attention (we like the small ponds and fountains scattered throughout the property), and the owner has left several undeveloped areas, adding to the natural ambiance of the resort. Sites are good-sized, shaded or in the open. Pull-through, full hookup sites are set side-by-side near the front of the resort. The tent-only section is nestled in the back of the property, closest to the ocean walk access, with its own nearby pool and playground area.

## BASICS

**Operated By:** Rick Ahearn. **Open:** Memorial Day–Columbus Day. **Site Assignment:** Reservations suggested, $50 credit card deposit, 7-day cancellation policy w/ a $10 service charge. No min. stay Memorial Day weekend, 3-day min. stay on July 4th & Labor Day; MC, V, D, no checks. **Registration:** At office. **Fee:** Full hookups, $38.50; water & electric, $33.50; no hookups, $28.50, based on 2 people, additional adults, $7; children ages 3-21, $3. **Parking:** At site.

## FACILITIES

**Number of RV Sites:** 455. **Number of Tent-Only Sites:** 45. **Hookups:** Water, electric, sewer (30, 50 amps), cable TV, modem. **Each Site:** Picnic table, fire ring. **Dump Station:** Yes. **Laundry:** Yes. **Pay Phone:** Yes. **Rest Rooms and Showers:** Yes. **Fuel:** No. **Propane:** No. **Internal Roads:** Gravel, dirt (good). **RV Service:** No. **Market:** Saco (2 mi). **Restaurant:** No. **General Store:** Yes. **Vending:** Yes. **Swimming Pool:** Yes. **Playground:** Yes. **Other:** Hot tubs, rec hall, adult lounge, nature trails, stocked fishing pond, 18-hole mini-golf course, entertainment pavilion, access to ocean & beach, tennis courts. **Activities:** Swimming, fishing, beachcombing, tennis, mini-golf, horseshoes, shuffleboard, volleyball. **Nearby Attractions:** Old Orchard Beach, Portland, southern coastal parks & beaches. **Additional Information:** Old Orchard Beach Chamber of Commerce, First St., Old Orchard Beach, ME 04064 (207) 934-2500 (800) 365-9386; www.oldorchardbeachmaine.com.

## RESTRICTIONS

**Pets:** Must be on a leash, never left unattended. Some breeds not allowed. **Fires:** In grills, stoves, & fire rings only. **Alcoholic Beverages:** At site only. **Vehicle Maximum Length:** None. **Other:** Skateboards, scooters, & rollerblades not allowed.

## TO GET THERE

From Maine Turnpike and I-195, exit 5, go east 2 mi. on I-195, then east 1.5 mi. on Rte. 5; campground is on the right.

# OQUOSSOC

## Cupsuptic Campground

P.O. Box 326, Rte. 16, Oquossoc 04964. T: (207) 864-5249; www.cupsupticcampground.com; cupsuptic@megalink.net.

🚐 ★★★          ▲ ★★

Beauty: ★★★          Site Privacy: ★★★
Spaciousness: ★★          Quiet: ★★★★
Security: ★★★          Cleanliness: ★★
Insect Control: ★★          Facilities: ★★★

This pleasant, small campground is set in a pine grove on pristine Cupsuptic Lake, just north of Rangeley. A few campsites sit along a sandy beach on the lakeshore, a few others face Toothaker Brook. Twelve sites are set in the woods. If you really like privacy, and you're tenting, rent out an entire island. Some of the choicest spots include DS, V, IV, III, 48, and 50, on the beach, but nicely buffered for privacy. Sites 51 and 52, across Loon Ln.but near the beach, are huge, and great for RVs. Site 23, at the other end of the beach, is an awesome tent site. The rest of that bunch, sites 13 through 29, are fairly open, though. Newly-renovated modern rest rooms, too; just what we like to see. (Look for the flower "bed.") This is a great place to kick back and enjoy the outdoors with little fuss. All you really need is a boat—they'll rent you one—and some fishing gear (look to hook trout or salmon.) Take a day trip to Rangeley Lake, or cruise Rte. 16, a famous moose hang-out. Best time to spot these gangly, cartoony beasts: spring and summer.

## BASICS

**Operated By:** Barbara & Danny Gallant. **Open:** May 1–Dec. 1. **Site Assignment:** Reservations recommended (may reserve online.) Deposit of 1- to 2-night fee, depending on length of stay. Refund for cancellation if received within 3 weeks of scheduled arrival, minus $10 fee. **Registration:** At office. **Fee:** $17–$22 for 2 adults & their children under age 18. Wilderness sites, $12. Island sites, $17. No credit cards. **Parking:** At sites or as designated.

## FACILITIES

**Number of RV Sites:** 55. **Number of Tent-Only Sites:** 0. **Hookups:** Water, electric (15, 30 amps). **Each Site:** Picnic table, fire pit. **Dump Station:** Yes. **Laundry:** No. **Pay Phone:** Yes. **Rest Rooms and Showers:** Yes, coin-op. **Fuel:** No. **Propane:** No. **Internal Roads:** Gravel, in good condition. **RV Service:** No. **Market:** 5 mi. east. **Restaurant:** 5 mi. east. **General Store:** Yes. **Vending:** No. **Swimming Pool:** No. **Playground:** Yes. **Other:** Rec hall. **Activities:** Fishing (licenses available), lake swimming, horseshoes, basketball, boating (rentals available), planned activities. **Nearby Attractions:** Rangeley Lake State Park, Wilhelm Reich Museum, moose-watching, golf, scenic flights. **Additional Information:** Rangeley Lakes Region Chamber of Commerce, (207) 864-5364 or (800) MT-LAKES.

## RESTRICTIONS

**Pets:** Must be leashed, quiet, & cleaned up after. Must not be left unattended. Not allowed on beach. Use pet walk area. **Fires:** In fire pits only. **Alcoholic Beverages:** Yes. **Vehicle Maximum Length:** 40 ft. **Other:** Ask on arrival.

## TO GET THERE

From junction of Rtes. 16 and 4, go 4.5 mi. northwest on Rte. 16. Campground entrance is on the left.

## OQUOSSOC

### Black Brook Cove Campground

P.O. Box 319, Oquossoc 04964. T: (207) 486-3828; www.blackbrookcove.com.

🚐 ★★★          ▲ ★★

Beauty: ★★★          Site Privacy: ★★★
Spaciousness: ★★          Quiet: ★★★★
Security: ★★★          Cleanliness: ★★
Insect Control: ★★          Facilities: ★

If your fantasy includes venturing in Maine's backcountry with your own secret weapon, a registered Maine guide, this is your place. Campground owner Jeff LaRochelle is a Maine guide who leads moose- and bear-hunting trips (in season) and fishing expeditions, including fly-in trips

to backcountry ponds via seaplane. Even if you don't choose a walk on the wild side, this intimate campground offers a pleasant outdoors experience. It's set on a cove at the southeast end of Aziscohos Lake (stocked with landlocked salmon and brook trout) in Maine's western mountains. Grass and gravel campsites are scattered around the property, including some seasonal sites. Only a few sites are set along the waterfront, including site 25 (by itself, and very private), and sites 21 A and B. Not so close to the beach, but very private, area tent sites 10 and 11, backed into the woods. RV sites 26, 27, and 28 are close to the beach and the boat launch. Got the urge to escape? Sixteen remote sites, reachable by boat only, are available on 20-acre Beaver Island. This is the kind of place that's decorated with snapshots of people posing with really big fish.

## BASICS

**Operated By:** Janet & Jeff LaRochelle. **Open:** Apr. 15–Nov. 30. **Site Assignment:** Reservations recommended. Full payment required. Refund for cancellation w/ 30-day notice. **Registration:** At office. **Fee:** $15 for 2 adults & their children under age 18. V, MC. **Parking:** At site.

## FACILITIES

**Number of RV Sites:** 70. **Number of Tent-Only Sites:** 0. **Hookups:** Water, electric (20 amps). **Each Site:** Picnic table, fire ring. **Dump Station:** Yes. **Laundry:** Yes. **Pay Phone:** No. **Rest Rooms and Showers:** Yes, coin-op. **Fuel:** No. **Propane:** Yes. **Internal Roads:** Gravel, in good condition. **RV Service:** No. **Market:** 20 mi. east. **Restaurant:** 20 mi. east. **General Store:** Yes. **Vending:** No. **Swimming Pool:** No. **Playground:** Yes. **Other:** Boat ramp. **Activities:** Boating (rentals available), hiking, guiding hunting & fishing. **Nearby Attractions:** Rangeley Lake State Park, Wilhelm Reich Museum, moose-watching, golf, scenic flights, Appalachian Trail hiking. **Additional Information:** Rangeley Lakes Region Chamber of Commerce, (207) 864-5364 or (800) MT-LAKES.

## RESTRICTIONS

**Pets:** Must be leashed, quiet, & cleaned up after. Must not be left unattended. Not allowed in buildings. **Fires:** In fire rings only. **Alcoholic Beverages:** Yes. **Vehicle Maximum Length:** 45 ft. **Other:** Mandatory recycling.

## To Get There

From southern Maine, take Rte. 95 north to exit 11 (Gray.) Take Rte. 26 north to Errol, N.H. Take right onto Rte. 16 north; follow for 18-20 mi. and take left onto Lincoln Pond Rd. Campground is on the right.

## ORLAND

### Shady Oaks

32 Leaches Point, Orland 04472. T: (207) 469-7739; www.shadyoakscampground.com; cuatsorvpk@aol.com.

🚐 ★★★            ▲ ★★

| | |
|---|---|
| Beauty: ★★ | Site Privacy: ★★ |
| Spaciousness: ★★★ | Quiet: ★★★ |
| Security: ★★★★★ | Cleanliness: ★★★★ |
| Insect Control: ★★★ | Facilities: ★★★ |

Shady Oaks caters to a mature crowd, mostly retirees, who return year after year. It also draws tourists traveling in the area to see the Maine coastline and en route to and from Acadia National Park. Families with young children do okay here; there's a swimming pool, train rides, and kid's crafts. But if you have preteens or teens, forget about it—they'll most likely be miserable. Most sites are too small for our comfort, set out in the open with little privacy. Most campers here don't seem to mind the cramped, open quarters; they're a friendly bunch eager to meet their neighbors and join in on nightly socials, potluck dinners and pancake breakfasts. The cabins (at a reasonable $30 a night) are a bargain.

## Basics

**Operated By:** Joyce & Don Nelson. **Open:** May–Sept. **Site Assignment:** Reservations suggested in Jul.–Aug.; credit card will hold reservation, no cancellation policy; MC, V, checks. **Registration:** At office. **Fee:** Full hookups, $21; water & electric, $20 based on 2 people per site; additional people, $2. **Parking:** At site, 2 vehicles per site.

## Facilities

**Number of RV Sites:** 55. **Number of Tent-Only Sites:** 0. **Hookups:** Water, electric, sewer (30, 50 amps). **Each Site:** Picnic table, fire ring. **Dump Station:** Yes. **Laundry:** Yes. **Pay Phone:** Yes. **Rest Rooms and Showers:** Yes. **Fuel:** No. **Propane:** Yes. **Internal Roads:** Gravel (good). **RV Service:** Yes. **Market:** Bucksport (1 mi). **Restaurant:** No. **General Store:** Yes. **Vending:** Yes. **Swimming Pool:** Yes. **Playground:** Yes. **Other:** Rec hall, cabin rentals, nature trails. **Activities:** Swimming, trail walking/hiking, horseshoes, planned activities, including potluck suppers, bingo, socials, arts & crafts, & more. **Nearby Attractions:** Bucksport/Searsport, Deer Isle Peninsula, Bar Harbor, Acadia National Park. **Additional Information:** Bucksport Bay Area Chamber of Commerce, P.O. Box 1880, 263 Main St. , Bucksport, ME 04416-1880 (207) 469-6818 & Acadia Information Center, P.O. Box 139, Mount Desert, ME 04660 (207) 667-8550 or (800) 358-8550, www.acadiainfo.com.

## Restrictions

**Pets:** No dogs allowed. **Fires:** In grills, stoves, & fire rings only. **Alcoholic Beverages:** At site only. **Vehicle Maximum Length:** None.

## To Get There

From junction Rtes.1 and 15 (in Bucksport), go north 1.6 mi. on Rte. 1, then south 0.2 mi. on Leaches Point Rd. (at intersection of Rte. 1, 175 and Leaches Point Rd.); campground is on the left.

## ORR'S ISLAND

### Orr's Island Campground

45 Bond Point Rd., Orr's Island 04066. T: (207) 833-5595; www.orrsisland.com; camping@orrsisland.com.

🚐 ★★★★            ▲ ★★★★

| | |
|---|---|
| Beauty: ★★★★★ | Site Privacy: ★★★★ |
| Spaciousness: ★★★★★ | Quiet: ★★★★★ |
| Security: ★★★★★ | Cleanliness: ★★★★ |
| Insect Control: ★★★ | Facilities: ★★★ |

Orr's Island is quite far out into Casco Bay, but the drive out from Brunswick and over Great

Island will melt away any stress. Once you've set up your campsite, take a moment to walk around and drink in the views of Muscongus Bay, Harpswell Cove, and Reed Cove. Close your eyes and feel the breezes and the sunlight washing over you. The open camping sites up on North Bluff offer a view of Harpswell Sound and many feature small stands of trees separating them from their neighbors. Plus, from North and South Bluff, you'll have access to the shore for beachcombing, hanging out on the rocks, or swimming if you're cast of sturdy Scandinavian stock. The Cove Rd. lettered sites are perfectly situated for tents and kayaks—what a stellar combination. After a night spent in one of these sites, you'll have that pleasant ache in your lungs from the fresh salt air.

## BASICS

**Operated By:** The Bond Family. **Open:** Memorial Day–mid-Sept. **Site Assignment:** Reservations or first come first served; 2 night min. for advance reservations. **Registration:** At office. **Fee:** $19–$30. **Parking:** At site.

## FACILITIES

**Number of RV Sites:** 70. **Number of Tent-Only Sites:** 0. **Hookups:** Water, electric, sewer. **Each Site:** Fire ring, picnic table. **Dump Station:** Yes. **Laundry:** Yes. **Pay Phone:** Yes. **Rest Rooms and Showers:** Yes. **Fuel:** No. **Propane:** No. **Internal Roads:** Gravel. **RV Service:** No. **Market:** 0.5 mi. north on Rte. 24. **Restaurant:** No. **General Store:** Ice, soft drinks, camping supplies. **Vending:** No. **Swimming Pool:** No. **Playground:** Yes. **Other:** Recreationsl equipment can be borrowed. **Activities:** Swimming, boating, canoe rental, wild berry picking, bird-watching, games & books. **Nearby Attractions:** L. L. Bean, Boothbay Harbor, movie theater, Reid Sate Park, Popham Beach, Eagle Island. **Additional Information:** Boothbay Harbor Region Chamber of Commerce, (207) 633-2353 or (800) 266-8422.

## RESTRICTIONS

**Pets:** On leash. **Fires:** In fire ring. **Alcoholic Beverages:** Yes. **Vehicle Maximum Length:** 40 ft. **Other:** Advance reservations require a 2-night stay.

## TO GET THERE

Take Exit 22 off of Rte. 95. This will put you on Rte. #1 between Brunswick and Bath. From Rte. 1 take the Cooks Corner exit for Orr's and Bailey Island. Take Rte. 24 (straight ahead at the traffic light). Follow Rte. 24 the rest of the way. Crossing the first bridge puts you on Great Island. Crossing the second bridge puts you on Orr's Island. Turn right on to Bond Point Rd. (our entrance). A large white ship's wheel (our logo) will be at the turn onto Bond Point Rd. We are approximately 2 mi. from the Orr's Island Bridge, or a total of 11 mi. from Cooks Corner.

## OXFORD

## Two Lakes Camping Area

P.O. Box 206, Oxford 04270. T: (207) 539-4851; F: (207) 539-4001; www.campmaine.com; twolakes@megalink.net.

🚐 ★★                        ▲ ★★

| | |
|---|---|
| Beauty: ★★ | Site Privacy: ★★ |
| Spaciousness: ★★★★ | Quiet: ★★ |
| Security: ★★★ | Cleanliness: ★★★★ |
| Insect Control: ★★★ | Facilities: ★★ |

Located in the Western lakes region of southwest Maine, about 35 miles north of Portland, this terraced campground is set on Hogan and Whitney lakes. The 600-foot sandy beach and lake swimming (on Hogan Lake) help make up for the fact that this campground has a somewhat cluttery feel. It's pleasant and wooded, though, with some sites that are fenced in for privacy. Campsites are set on loop roads off Lake View Dr., with seasonal sites lined up along Chipmonk Ln. (that's how they spell it.) Although most people clamor for sites near the lake, the nicest spots, in our view, are on a quiet dead-end road off Moose Run, numbered 103 to 116. These boast some good tree cover between sites, and promise more peace than the busy area near the beach, game room, and boat launch at the other end of the campground. Nice feature: there's a beach for pets, away from the 'people beach.'

## BASICS

**Operated By:** Barbara & Dick Varney. **Open:** May 1–Oct. 1. **Site Assignment:** Reservations recommended. 50% deposit required. No refunds for cancellation, but may get credit for future camping. **Registration:** At office. **Fee:** $20–$31 for 2 adults & up to 3 children. V, MC, D. **Parking:** At site.

## FACILITIES

**Number of RV Sites:** 107. **Number of Tent-Only Sites:** 13. **Hookups:** Water, electric (30 amps), sewer. **Each Site:** Picnic table, fire ring. **Dump Station:** Yes. **Laundry:** Yes. **Pay Phone:** Yes. **Rest Rooms and Showers:** Yes, coin-op. **Fuel:** No. **Propane:** No. **Internal Roads:** Gravel, in good condition. **RV Service:** No. **Market:** 6 mi. north. **Restaurant:** 8 mi. north, on Rte. 26. **General Store:** Yes. **Vending:** Yes. **Swimming Pool:** No. **Playground:** Yes. **Other:** Boat dock, rec hall. **Activities:** Boating (rentals available), fishing (licenses available), volleyball, basketball, horseshoes, mini-golf, planned activities. **Nearby Attractions:** Oxford Plains Speedway. **Additional Information:** Oxford Hills Chamber of Commerce, (207) 743-228.

## RESTRICTIONS

**Pets:** Must be leashed, quiet, & cleaned up after. Must not be left unattended. No aggressive breeds (ie. Rottweilers, Dobermans, Huskies, Shepherds.). **Fires:** In fireplaces only. **Alcoholic Beverages:** At sites only. **Vehicle Maximum Length:** None. **Other:** 2-day min. stay for reservations. For 1-night stay, call same day to check on availability for walk-ins.

## TO GET THERE

From Maine Turnpike, take exit 11 (Gray.) From Gray, take Rte. 26 21 mi. north to Oxford. As you descend hill, slow your speed; campground sign is on the left. Follow road 1 mi. in to lake and lodge.

## PALMYRA

### Palmyra Golf and RV Resort

147 Lang Hill Rd., Palmyra 04965. T: (207) 938-5677; F: (207) 938-5130; www.palmyra-me.com; palmyra@www.palmyra-me.com.

🚐 ★★★★★     ⛺ ★★

| | |
|---|---|
| Beauty: ★★★ | Site Privacy: ★★★ |
| Spaciousness: ★★★ | Quiet: ★★★ |
| Security: ★★★★ | Cleanliness: ★★★★★ |
| Insect Control: ★★★★ | Facilities: ★★★★★ |

If you like to golf, you're going to love this campground in central Maine, with its own 18-hole, 72 par course, pro shop and clubhouse on the premises. Located off the interstate, just south of Bangor, this campground caters to large motor home and RV travelers who enjoy a pampered camping experience. Local golfers use the public course but campers get a discount. There's a driving range and pitch and putt center, too. You'll have a choice of roomy, bigger-than-average open sites, all set in rows off the campground's long, one-way streets. There's also a separate loop of shaded sites behind the office and recreation area. There's plenty of room to spread out in this campground, and the hilly, terraced terrain and views of the golf course add to its expansiveness and beauty.

## BASICS

**Operated By:** Cayer family. **Open:** May 15–Oct. 15. **Site Assignment:** Reservations suggested, no deposit required (if you don't show by 6:30 p.m. of scheduled day of arrival, they rent space) MC, V, D. **Registration:** At office. **Fee:** Full hookups, $24; water & electric, $23 (50 amp); $21.50 (30 amp). **Parking:** At site.

## FACILITIES

**Number of RV Sites:** 143. **Number of Tent-Only Sites:** 4. **Hookups:** Water, electric, sewer (30, 50 amps), modem. **Each Site:** Picnic table, fire ring, light. **Dump Station:** Yes. **Laundry:** Yes. **Pay Phone:** Yes. **Rest Rooms and Showers:** Yes. **Fuel:** No. **Propane:** No. **Internal Roads:** Paved, gravel (good). **RV Service:** No. **Market:** Palmyra (2 mi). **Restaurant:** Yes. **General Store:** Yes.

**Vending:** No. **Swimming Pool:** Yes. **Playground:** No. **Other:** 18 hole golf course, pro shop, clubhouse, driving range, function hall, group area. **Activities:** Golf, swimming, horseshoes, volleyball, shuffleboard. **Nearby Attractions:** Bangor, Augusta. **Additional Information:** Bangor Regional Chamber of Commerce, 519 Maine St., P.O. Box 1443, Bangor, ME 04402 (207) 947-0307, www.bangorregion.com.

## RESTRICTIONS

**Pets:** Must be on a leash, never left unattended. **Fires:** In grills, stoves, & fire rings only. **Alcoholic Beverages:** At site only. **Vehicle Maximum Length:** None.

## TO GET THERE

From I-95, exit 39, go west 3 mi. on Rte. 2; campground is on the right.

## PERU

### Honey Run Beach & Campground

456 East Shore Rd., Peru 04290. T: (207) 562-4913; www.honeyruncampground.com; drjeff@mindspring.com.

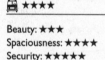 

Beauty: ★★★
Spaciousness: ★★★★
Security: ★★★★★
Insect Control: ★★★

Site Privacy: ★★
Quiet: ★★★★
Cleanliness: ★★★★★
Facilities: ★★★

Located in a small lakeside community just east of Rumford, Honey Run Beach & Campground is getting a real sprucing up, thanks to new ownership. Formerly more geared to seasonal campers, Honey Run is being reinvented as a vacation destination. Just a handful of sites are seasonal now. A new pavilion is in place for groups and the family reunion set. Campsites (suitable for big rigs) dot a big, grassy field surrounded by woods. Woodsy sites ring the perimeter of the property, and there are even a few primitive tent sites "up the mountain," as owner Jeff Lennox puts it. OK, so it's not really a mountain, but a climb up the hill would make a dandy work-out and leg-stretch for the road-weary RVer! Another good selling point here: a short but wide, private sandy beach on sparkling Worthley Pond, located across the street. There's enough space for a few sun-bathers, plus some picnic tables and rental canoes and kayaks; good for taking a peek at the houses surrounding the pond and playing the "Would you ever want to move here?" game.

## BASICS

**Operated By:** Jeff Lennox. **Open:** Memorial Day–Labor Day. **Site Assignment:** Reservations suggested. Deposit of first night's fee required. Refund for cancellations w/ 14-day notice. **Registration:** At office. **Fee:** $15–$25. No credit cards. **Parking:** At site.

## FACILITIES

**Number of RV Sites:** 72. **Number of Tent-Only Sites:** 0. **Hookups:** Water, electric (30, 50 amps), sewer. **Each Site:** Picnic table, fire ring. **Dump Station:** Yes. **Laundry:** Yes. **Pay Phone:** Yes. **Rest Rooms and Showers:** Yes. **Fuel:** No. **Propane:** No. **Internal Roads:** Gravel, in good condition. **RV Service:** No. **Market:** 12 mi. north. **Restaurant:** 12 mi. north. **General Store:** Yes. **Vending:** Yes. **Swimming Pool:** No. **Playground:** Yes. **Other:** Rec hall w/ pavilion. **Activities:** Lake swimming, hiking (on hillside trails behind campground), boating (canoe & kayak rentals available). **Nearby Attractions:** Norland's Living History Museum, Appalachian Trail hiking, Black Mountain, Pennacook Falls, Santa's Village, Mt. Blue State Park. **Additional Information:** River Valley Chamber of Commerce, (207) 364-3241.

## RESTRICTIONS

**Pets:** Must be leashed, quiet, & cleaned up after. Must not be left unattended. **Fires:** In fire rings only. **Alcoholic Beverages:** At sites only. **Vehicle Maximum Length:** None. **Other:** Ask on arrival.

## TO GET THERE

Take Maine Turnpike to exit 12 (Auburn.) Follow Rte. 4 north to Rte. 108 west. Follow Rte. 108 for 11 mi., then turn left at Worthley Pond and campground sign. Campground is 3.5 mi. in.

## PHIPPSBURG

### Meadowbrook Camping

33 Meadowbrook Rd., Phippsburg 04562. T: (207) 443-4967 or (800) 370-CAMP; F: (207) 386-0335; www.meadowbrookme.com; mbcamp@gwi.net.

🚐 ★★★★          ⛺ ★★★

| | |
|---|---|
| Beauty: ★★ | Site Privacy: ★★ |
| Spaciousness: ★★ | Quiet: ★★★ |
| Security: ★★★ | Cleanliness: ★★★★★ |
| Insect Control: ★★★ | Facilities: ★★★ |

This mid-coast campground, located just five miles south of Bath, is wildly popular with RVers, who don't seem to care that the ocean is nowhere in sight. Matter of fact, one of Maine's nicest stretches of sand, Popham Beach State Park, is but a 10-mile drive away, and if you can't wait to swim, there's always the campground's heated pool, surely warmer than the North Atlantic! (About that pool, we think some umbrellas would be a nice touch.) And should you want a shore dinner, you don't have to leave; they sell lobsters, clams, and corn, daily, and will cook it up for you for no extra charge. Campsites, set in loops, are gravel, of varying size. The largest RV sites are in an open, grassy area near the (funky) rec hall and pool area; head farther back into the property, and sites are wooded, nudging toward cliffs and a beaver pond. Sites 77 through 82 overlook a marsh; stay away from 82 if you're tenting, though, since it's on a downhill slope that would be a real mess in the rain. Site 35 is great, with a long approach to a woodsy spot on a hill; site 33 offers great cliffside views, as well, edging a wooded area. Among the tent sites, we'd go for site 73, near the nature trail, built on a platform.

### BASICS

**Operated By:** TLM Enterprises. **Open:** May 1–Oct. 1. **Site Assignment:** Reservations recommended. For less than 1-week stay, full fee required for deposit. For stays of more than 1 week, 10% deposit required. Refunds for cancellations within 7 days, minus $10 service fee. **Reg-**istration: At office. **Fee:** $20–$26 per family. V, MC, D, AE. **Parking:** At site.

### FACILITIES

**Number of RV Sites:** 90. **Number of Tent-Only Sites:** 10. **Hookups:** Water, electric (15, 20, 30, 50 amps). **Each Site:** Picnic table, fireplace. **Dump Station:** Yes. **Laundry:** Yes. **Pay Phone:** Yes. **Rest Rooms and Showers:** Yes. **Fuel:** No. **Propane:** Yes. **Internal Roads:** Gravel, in good to fair condition. **RV Service:** No. **Market:** 5 mi. north. **Restaurant:** 5 mi. north. **General Store:** Yes. **Vending:** No. **Swimming Pool:** Yes. **Playground:** Yes. **Other:** Rec hall, mini-golf. **Activities:** Swimming, mini-golf, mile-long nature trail, basketball, shuffleboard, horseshoes. **Nearby Attractions:** Popham Beach State Park, Morse Mountain Sanctuary, Maine Maritime Museum, Bowdoin College Museum of Art, Peary-MacMillan Arctic Museum, deep-sea fishing. **Additional Information:** Chamber of Commerce of the Bath-Brunswick Region, (207) 725-8797 or (207) 443-9751; www.midcoastmaine.com.

### RESTRICTIONS

**Pets:** Must be leashed, quiet, & cleaned up after. Must not be left unattended. **Fires:** In fireplaces only. **Alcoholic Beverages:** At sites only. **Vehicle Maximum Length:** None. **Other:** 1 vehicle per site.

### TO GET THERE

From Rte. 1 in Bath, take Popham Beach exit, Rte. 209. Follow for 2.5 mi., heading south, to Winnegance Store, then turn right and go 3 mi. to campground. Entrance is on right.

## POLAND SPRING

### Poland Spring Campground

P.O. Box 409, Poland Spring 04274. T: (207) 998-2151; www.polandspringcamp.com; info@polandspringcamp.com.

🚐 ★★★          ⛺ ★★

| | |
|---|---|
| Beauty: ★★★ | Site Privacy: ★★★ |
| Spaciousness: ★★★ | Quiet: ★★★★ |
| Security: ★★★★ | Cleanliness: ★★★★★ |
| Insect Control: ★★★ | Facilities: ★★★ |

The nicest feature of this Western Lakes-area campground: it sits on a pretty, forested pond, dotted with islands. Three-mile-long Lower Range Pond, sandy-bottomed, provides a great swimming hole for campers here. While there isn't much of a beach, the buoyed swimming area is plenty big. Bonus: If you don't like lake swimming, there's a pool. The campground itself is shaded with pines and mixed hardwoods, and campsites are level and woodsy. This campground is better-tended, and the campsites more prepared, than what you'll find at neighboring Two Lakes Camping Area (see listing.) The friendly owners take care of the details that make all the difference: plenty of trash barrels, an inviting picnic grove overlooking the pond, and a nice booklet for campers, chock-full of information about the local area, dining, shopping, and attractions. Campsites are set on spokelike roads, surrounding the activity pod of rec hall, office, store, rest rooms, laundry, game room, and so on. It's quiet, child-friendly, and appealing.

## BASICS

**Operated By:** David & Tami. Wight. **Open:** May 1–Columbus Day. **Site Assignment:** Reservations recommended. $30 deposit required for weekend stay; $40 for week-long stay. Refunds for cancellation w/ 7-day notice, minus $5 fee. **Registration:** At office. **Fee:** $19–$25 for 2 adults & up to 3 children. V, MC, D, debit cards. **Parking:** At site.

## FACILITIES

**Number of RV Sites:** 121. **Number of Tent-Only Sites:** 11. **Hookups:** Water, electric (20, 30 amps), sewer, modem. **Each Site:** Picnic table, fire ring. **Dump Station:** Yes. **Laundry:** Yes. **Pay Phone:** Yes. **Rest Rooms and Showers:** Yes, coin-op. **Fuel:** No. **Propane:** Yes. **Internal Roads:** Gravel, in good condition. **RV Service:** No. **Market:** 5 mi. north. **Restaurant:** 1 mi. north; 8 mi. south. **General Store:** Yes. **Vending:** Yes. **Swimming Pool:** Yes. **Playground:** Yes. **Other:** Game room, adult rec room, boat dock. **Activities:** Fishing (licenses available), lake swimming, boating (rentals available), volleyball, planned activities. **Nearby Attractions:** Sabbathday Lake shaker village, Maine Wildlife Park, tour-

maline gem mines, golf, hiking at Range Pond State Park. **Additional Information:** Androscoggin County Chamber of Commerce, (207) 783-2249; www.androscoggincounty.com.

## RESTRICTIONS

**Pets:** Must be leashed, quiet, & cleaned up after. Must not be left unattended. Not allowed in pool, lake, & public areas. **Fires:** In fireplaces only. **Alcoholic Beverages:** Yes. **Vehicle Maximum Length:** 40 ft. **Other:** 2-night min. stay on weekends in July & Aug.; 3-night min. on holidays.

## TO GET THERE

From the Maine Turnpike, take exit 11 (Gray.) Follow Rte. 26 north for 12 mi. Turn right on Connor Ln. Entrance is at end of road, 0.5 mi.

## RANGELEY

### Rangeley Lake State Park

HC 32 P.O. Box 5000, Rangeley 04970. T: (207) 864-3858 or (207) 624-6080 (off-season); www.state.me.us/doc/parks.htm.

| 🚐 ★★★★ | ▲ ★★★★★ |
|---|---|
| Beauty: ★★★★ | Site Privacy: ★★★★ |
| Spaciousness: ★★★★ | Quiet: ★★★★ |
| Security: ★★★★★ | Cleanliness: ★★★★ |
| Insect Control: ★★ | Facilities: ★★★ |

Set in Maine's western mountains region, an area famous for rugged beauty and great fishing, this state park draws nature-loving campers from New England and beyond. The town of Rangeley has several boat rental outfits; bring your boat to the campground and you can launch it for free. Don't forget the fishing license. You'll want to have a go at the trout and land-locked salmon in this icy-cold lake. Should you wish to brave the waters yourself, there's a grassy hill with granite stairs that lead to a marked off, somewhat pebbly swimming area. Campsites are set in a loop on the lakeside, at the opposite end of the park from the day-use area, beach, and boat launch. Well-spaced, offering plenty of privacy, sites are heavily wooded with spruce and fir. Some campsites have footpaths through the trees that lead to the lake. Most desirable sites (closest to the water) are 11M through 21L, even numbers. Letters refer to size of site; 's' is small, 'm' is medium, and so on. Site 42X (as in extra-large) is very private, set off by itself way back in the woods. Besides all the natural beauty you could wish for, this campground boasts another winning attribute, not to be taken lightly in a state park: great showers!

## BASICS

**Operated By:** Maine Dept. of Conservation, Bureau of Parks & Lands. **Open:** May 15–Sept. 30. **Site Assignment:** In spring & fall, camping is on a first-come, first-served basis. For summer stays, reservations open on the first business day in Jan. From June 15 to the night before Labor Day, sites may be reserved for a min. of 2 nights & up to 2 weeks. Full payment is charged to credit card when reservation is processed. Refund with $15 cancellation fee. 10 sites are non-reservable, & available on a first-come, first-served basis. Call the reservations line to cancel a reservation more than 3 days in advance. If cancelling less than 3 days in advance, call the park directly. **Registration:** At office. **Fee:** $13, Maine residents; $17, non-residents, plus $2 fee if reserving in advance. V, MC. **Parking:** At sites & designated lots only.

## FACILITIES

**Number of RV Sites:** 50. **Number of Tent-Only Sites:** 0. **Hookups:** None. **Each Site:** Yes. **Dump Station:** No. **Laundry:** No. **Pay Phone:** Yes. **Rest Rooms and Showers:** Yes. **Fuel:** No. **Propane:** No. **Internal Roads:** Gravel & paved, in good condition. **RV Service:** No. **Market:** 7 mi. northwest. **Restaurant:** 7 mi. northwest. **General Store:** No. **Vending:** No. **Swimming Pool:** No. **Playground:** Yes. **Other:** Boat ramps & slips. **Activities:** Lake swimming, boating, fishing (need license; available in town), ball field, volleyball, horseshoes, hiking, picnicking. **Nearby Attractions:** Wilhelm Reich Museum, moose-watching, golf, scenic flights, Appalachian Trail hiking. **Additional Information:** Rangeley Lakes Region Chamber of Commerce, (207) 864-5364 or (800) MT-LAKES.

## RESTRICTIONS

**Pets:** Must be leashed, quiet, & cleaned up after. Must not be left unattended. **Fires:** In fireplaces only. **Alcoholic Beverages:** No. **Vehicle Maximum Length:** 40 ft. **Other:** 2-week max. stay between last week in June & Labor Day.

## TO GET THERE

From junction of Rtes. 16 and 4, go 4 mi. south on Rte. 4, then 5 mi. west on S. Shore Dr., then 1 mi. north to campground.

# RAYMOND

## Kokatosi Campground

635 Webbs Mills Rd., Raymond 04071. T: (207) 627-4642 or (800) 9-CAMPIN (outside ME); www.maine.com/kokatosi; kokatosi@maine.com.

🚐 ★★★                    ⛺ ★★★

| | |
|---|---|
| Beauty: ★★★ | Site Privacy: ★ |
| Spaciousness: ★★ | Quiet: ★★★ |
| Security: ★★★★★ | Cleanliness: ★★★★ |
| Insect Control: ★★ | Facilities: ★★★ |

Whether you're looking for a ride on an antique "Hooterville" fire engine or prefer a freshwater cruise on an eight-seater "Patio Boat," Kokatosi's the place. Located in the Western Lakes region of southwest Maine, on five-mile-long Crescent Lake, this campground offers a "summer camp for families" experience. In fact, this lake-dotted, woodsy area is chock-a-block with summer camps. Most campers can't resist paddling or motoring to Tenney River, a mile-and-a-half away, then on to Panther Pond. The fishing is said to be pretty good, too. The campground offers a rather communal experience; you're bound to get to know your neighbors, since sites don't have much buffer between them (only boulders, in some cases.) About 50 percent of the sites are seasonal, but the transient sites are closest to the beach. RV sites 25, 26, and 28 overlook the lake. Some of the tent sites have platforms and canopies, providing a tree-house effect perched over the lake. Sites 4 through 7 and 11 are among them. A nicely-done rec hall is the scene for country bands and potluck suppers.

## BASICS

**Operated By:** Terri & Neil Southwick. **Open:** May 15–Columbus Day. **Site Assignment:** Resevations recommended. 50% deposit required.

Must pay in full for holiday weekends. Refund w/ cancellation w/ 30-day notice, minus $10 fee. No refunds for holiday weekend reservations. **Registration:** At office. **Fee:** $32–$38 for 2 adults & 2 children under age 18. V, MC. **Parking:** At sites & designated lot (tenters).

## FACILITIES

**Number of RV Sites:** 145. **Number of Tent-Only Sites:** 17. **Hookups:** Water, electric (20, 30 amps), sewer. **Each Site:** Picnic table, fire ring. **Dump Station:** Yes. **Laundry:** Yes. **Pay Phone:** Yes. **Rest Rooms and Showers:** Yes. **Fuel:** No. **Propane:** Yes. **Internal Roads:** Gravel, in good condition. **RV Service:** No. **Market:** 10 mi. east. **Restaurant:** 10 mi. east. **General Store:** Yes. **Vending:** Yes. **Swimming Pool:** No. **Playground:** Yes. **Other:** Rec hall, boat dock. **Activities:** Lake swimming, fishing (license required), boating (rentals available, including 14 ft. motorboats), volleyball, bocces, horseshoes, planned activities. **Nearby Attractions:** Golf, mini-golf, seaplane rides, boat cruises, Songo River Queen paddleboat, Douglas Mountain hiking, Sebago Lake State Park, outlet shopping (N. Conway, N.H.). **Additional Information:** Gray Business Assoc., (207) 657-7000.

## RESTRICTIONS

**Pets:** Must be leashed, quiet, & cleaned up after. Not allowed on beach or in buildings. **Fires:** In fireplaces only. **Alcoholic Beverages:** Yes. **Vehicle Maximum Length:** None. **Other:** 2-day min. stay required; 3-day min. on holidays.

## TO GET THERE

From junction of Rtes. 302 and 85, go 6 mi. northeast on Rte. 85. Campground entrance is on the right.

# RICHMOND

## Augusta/Gardiner KOA

Rte. 1, Box 2410, Richmond 04357. T: (207) 582-5086 (800) 562-1496 (reservations); www.agkoa.homestead.com; augustakoa@hotmail.com.

 ★★★　　　　 ★★★

Beauty: ★★　　　　Site Privacy: ★★★
Spaciousness: ★★★　　Quiet: ★★★
Security: ★★★　　　Cleanliness: ★★★
Insect Control: ★★★　Facilities: ★★★

This centrally-located franchise campground is just off the interstate and a welcome sight for weary travelers. The rural setting offers many shady sites, clean facilities, and a few extras: heated swimming, lake access, rec room and laundry. The lake access is about a quarter-mile walk down the road, where the campground has a dock and launch. A bit inconvenient but good for campers who like to fish (smallmouth bass, perch, pickerel and catfish are abundant.) Campers can bring their boats or rent rowboats and canoes at the office. About 50 percent of the campers are walk-ins, stopping for the night en route to sights and attractions around the state. Most sites are gravel and there are several pull-throughs. Though the facilities are well-maintained, we find the landscaping and general appearance of the individual sites a bit shabby and overgrown.

## BASICS

**Operated By:** Al & Lou Maenz. **Open:** Mid-May–mid-Oct. **Site Assignment:** Reservations usually not needed; 1 night deposit; 24-hour cancellation policy; MC, V, D, checks. **Registration:** At office. **Fee:** Full hookups, $27.75; water & electric, $25.75; no hookups, $19.75, based on 2 adults, additional child, ages 5–17, $3; additional adult, $4; ages 5 & under, free. **Parking:** At site.

## FACILITIES

**Number of RV Sites:** 66. **Number of Tent-Only Sites:** 11. **Hookups:** Water, electric, sewer (30, 50 amps). **Each Site:** Picnic table, fire ring. **Dump Station:** Yes. **Laundry:** Yes. **Pay Phone:** Yes. **Rest Rooms and Showers:** Yes. **Fuel:** No. **Propane:** Yes. **Internal Roads:** Gravel (good). **RV Service:** No. **Market:** Gardiner (7 mi). **Restaurant:** No. **General Store:** Yes. **Vending:** No. **Swimming Pool:** Yes. **Playground:** Yes. **Other:** Lake frontage, dock, canoe & rowboat rentals, cabin rentals, pavilion, game room. **Activities:** Swimming, fishing, boating, volleyball, badminton, basketball, horseshoes. **Nearby Attractions:** mid-coast parks & beaches, western lakes & mountains. **Additional Information:** Kennebec Valley Chamber of Commerce, P.O. Box 676, Augusta, ME 04332-0676 (207) 623-4559, www.info@augustamaine.com.

### RESTRICTIONS

**Pets:** Must be on a leash, never left unattended. **Fires:** In grills, stoves, & fire rings only. **Alcoholic Beverages:** At site only. **Vehicle Maximum Length:** None.

### TO GET THERE

From I-95, exit 27, go south (toward Richmond) 2.25 mi. on Rte. 201; campground is on the right.

## ROCKPORT

### Camden Rockport Camping

P.O. Box 639, Rte. 40, Rockport 04856. T: (207) 236-2498 or (888) 842-0592.

🚐 ★★★           ⛺ ★★

Beauty: ★★★              Site Privacy: ★★★
Spaciousness: ★★★         Quiet: ★★★★★
Security: ★★★             Cleanliness: ★★★★★
Insect Control: ★★★       Facilities: ★★★

We know where to get the freshest, best, and cheapest lobster around! they whisper conspiratorially at Camden Rockport Camping, and if that's not a selling point, we don't know what is. This quiet, peaceful family campground is located near the bustling seaport towns of Camden and Rockport (thus the name) in mid-coast Maine. You'd never know you were a hop and a skip from tourist-filled streets, shops, and galleries, though. This campground is the quietest one around (quieter than nearby Megunticook By the Sea), since it's off the beaten track—Rte. 1—a bit. The new owners are planning renovations, so we can't offer a complete review. But what probably won't change are the grassy, back-in campsites, with good shade trees dotting the big rig area. Even the tent sites are grassy. They're not super-level, though. Ask for tent site 14, very private and wooded with white birch. The campground is neat as a pin, and boasts nice touches

like fresh flowers in the rest room and a rec hall with a kitchen and book exchange.

### BASICS

**Operated By:** John & Lori Alexander. **Open:** May 1–Nov. 1. **Site Assignment:** Reservations recommended, especially for July & Aug. Deposit of first nights' fee required. Refund for cancellation w/ 7-day notice, minus $15 fee. **Registration:** At office. **Fee:** $25–$32 for 2 adults & 2 children under age 18. No credit cards. **Parking:** At site.

### FACILITIES

**Number of RV Sites:** 40. **Number of Tent-Only Sites:** 17. **Hookups:** Water, electric (30, 50 amps), sewer, cable TV. **Each Site:** Picnic table, fire ring. **Dump Station:** Yes. **Laundry:** Yes. **Pay Phone:** Yes. **Rest Rooms and Showers:** Yes. **Fuel:** No. **Propane:** Yes. **Internal Roads:** Gravel, in good condition. **RV Service:** No. **Market:** 3 mi.east. **Restaurant:** 3 mi. east. **General Store:** Yes. **Vending:** Yes. **Swimming Pool:** No (new owners are renovating & may add one; call to inquire). **Playground:** Yes. **Other:** Rec hall (under renovation). **Activities:** Basketball, ball field, horseshoes, volleyball. **Nearby Attractions:** Camden galleries, museums & shops), windjammer fleet, Penobscot Bay cruises, Conway Homestead & Mary Cramer Museum (28th century restored farmhouse & gardens), Camden Hills State Park, Merryspring Park, Owl's Head Transportation Museum, golf, ocean swimming. **Additional Information:** Rockport-Camden-Lincolnville Chamber of Commerce, (207) 236-4404; (800) 223-5459.

### RESTRICTIONS

**Pets:** Must be leashed, quiet, & cleaned up after. Must not be left unattended. **Fires:** In fire rings only. **Alcoholic Beverages:** At sites only. **Vehicle Maximum Length:** None. **Other:** No electric heaters. 2-night min. stay on weekends in July & Aug.; 3-night min. stay during Maine Lobster Festival (early Aug.).

### TO GET THERE

From junction of Rtes. 1 and 90, go 2 mi. southwest on Rte. 90. Campground entrance is on the left.

## ROCKPORT

### Megunticook Campground by the Sea

Rte. 1, P.O. Box 375, Rockport 04856. T: (207) 594-2428 or (800) 884-2428; F: (207) 594-0549; www.campgroundbythesea.com.

🚐 ★★★★      ▲ ★★★

| | |
|---|---|
| Beauty: ★★★★★ | Site Privacy: ★★★ |
| Spaciousness: ★★ | Quiet: ★★★ |
| Security: ★★★ | Cleanliness: ★★★★★ |
| Insect Control: ★★★ | Facilities: ★★★★★ |

As you're enjoying a lobster bake on the oceanfront deck, watching a Maine windjammer schooner sail past on Penobscot Bay, one question might cross your mind: "This is camping?" Oh, yeah, this is camping at Megunticook, a camping resort on mid-coast Maine, just three miles south of Camden. Want freshly-brewed Green Mountain coffee, or pizza delivered to your site? Perhaps a harbor tour on a Downeast cruiser? No problem. Other nice touches include a pool area with a picket fence surrounding it, not that ugly chain-link stuff. A waterfront deck is graced with a tumble of gardens and seating, the perfect place to watch the world—or local lobstermen—go by. Admire Indian Island lighthouse in the distance. A row of rental cabins sits close to busy Rte. 1; we'd head back as far as possible, away from the road and toward the ocean. RV sites 46 through 49, near Vernah Brook, fill the bill. Tent sites are set 'way back, toward the water, nicely level with good surfacing for drainage. Tent site 81 is huge, while site 87 boasts the most privacy, and is closest to the water. This is a classic Maine beauty spot.

## BASICS

**Operated By:** Megunticook Campground By the Sea. **Open:** May 15–Oct. 15. **Site Assignment:** Reservations recommended, Jul.-Oct. Deposit of 1 nights' fee required. Refunds for cancellation w/ 7-day notice, minus $15 fee. **Reg-**istration: At office. **Fee:** $26–$35 for 2 adults & 2 children. V, MC, D. **Parking:** At site.

## FACILITIES

**Number of RV Sites:** 66. **Number of Tent-Only Sites:** 20. **Hookups:** Water, electric (20, 30, 50 amps), sewer, cable TV, phone. **Each Site:** Picnic table, fire ring. **Dump Station:** Yes. **Laundry:** Yes. **Pay Phone:** Yes. **Rest Rooms and Showers:** Yes. **Fuel:** No. **Propane:** No. **Internal Roads:** Gravel, in good condition. **RV Service:** No. **Market:** 2.5 mi. north. **Restaurant:** 3 mi. north. **General Store:** Yes. **Vending:** Yes. **Swimming Pool:** Yes. **Playground:** Yes. **Other:** Game room. **Activities:** Biking (rentals available), kayaking (rentals available), boat cruises on "Loriander," swimming, ball field, croquet, horseshoes, badminton. **Nearby Attractions:** Camden galleries, museums & shops), windjammer fleet, Penobscot Bay cruises, Conway Homestead & Mary Cramer Museum (28th century restored farmhouse & gardens), Camden Hills State Park, Merryspring Park, Owl's Head Transportation Museum, golf. **Additional Information:** Rockport-Camden-Lincolnville Chamber of Commerce, (207) 236-4404; (800) 223-5459.

## RESTRICTIONS

**Pets:** Must be leashed, quiet, & cleaned up after. Must not be left unattended. **Fires:** In fireplaces only. **Alcoholic Beverages:** At sites only. **Vehicle Maximum Length:** None. **Other:** 2-night min. stay required on weekends in July & Aug. 3-night min. stay required on holiday weekends & Aug. 1-5 (Maine Lobster Festival.).

## TO GET THERE

From junction of Rtes. 1 and 90 in Rockport, go 2 mi. south on Rte. 1. Campground is on the left.

## SACO

### Saco/Portland South KOA

814A Portland Rd., Saco 04072. T: (207) 282-0502 (800) 468-6567; www.koa.com.

🚐 ★★★★★          ⛺ ★★★★

Beauty: ★★★               Site Privacy: ★★★
Spaciousness: ★★★         Quiet: ★★★★
Security: ★★★★★           Cleanliness: ★★★★★
Insect Control: ★★★       Facilities: ★★★★

This woodsy campground is just two miles from Old Orchard Beach and many of southern Maine's best parks and attractions, and offers a natural, quiet escape from the summer masses. Ultra clean facilities, a family-friendly atmosphere, and lots of added conveniences make this property a favorite with locals and out-of-town travelers alike. Most sites are tucked in a shady, cool virgin forest; tent sites are nestled under old growth pine trees. Recreation fields, pool, office and pavilion areas are clustered in front. We like the porch off the office cabin, with rockers and benches overlooking the pool and playground. The campground also offers discounted tickets to area attractions. Before heading out for the day, feast on a wild blueberry pancake breakfast, offered each day at the campground. Spaghetti dinners and assorted desserts are available in the evening.

### BASICS

**Operated By:** Sylvia & Frank Kelly. **Open:** May–Oct. **Site Assignment:** Reservations suggested, $25 deposit, 24-hour cancellation policy; MC, V, no checks. **Registration:** At office. **Fee:** Full hookups, $34; water & electric, $32; premium tent (w/ water & electric), $30.50; no hookups, $28.50. **Parking:** At site.

### FACILITIES

**Number of RV Sites:** 96. **Number of Tent-Only Sites:** 22. **Hookups:** Water, electric, sewer (20, 30 amps). **Each Site:** Picnic table, fire ring. **Dump Station:** Yes. **Laundry:** Yes. **Pay Phone:** Yes. **Rest Rooms and Showers:** Yes. **Fuel:** No. **Propane:** Yes. **Internal Roads:** Gravel, dirt (good). **RV Service:** No. **Market:** Old Orchard Beach (2 mi). **Restaurant:** No. **General Store:** Yes. **Vending:** No. **Swimming Pool:** Yes. **Playground:** Yes. **Other:** Pavilion, game room, cabin rentals, discount tickets to area attractions. **Activities:** Swimming, basketball, volleyball, horseshoes. **Nearby Attractions:** Old Orchard Beach, southern coast parks & beaches, Portland. **Additional Information:** Old Orchard Beach Chamber of Commerce, First St. , Old Orchard Beach, ME 04064 (207) 934-2500 (800) 365-9386; www.oldorchardbeachmaine.com.

### RESTRICTIONS

**Pets:** Must be on a leash, never left unattended. **Fires:** In grills, stoves, & fire rings only. **Alcoholic Beverages:** At site only. **Vehicle Maximum Length:** None.

### TO GET THERE

From junction I-95 and I-195, exit 5, go 1.2 mi. east on I-195, then north 1.5 mi. on Rte. 1 (exit 2B); campground is on the left.

## SACO

### Silver Springs

705 Portland Rd., Saco 04072. T: (207) 283-3880; www.silver-springs.com; silver-springs@cyber-tours.com.

🚐 ★★★          ⛺ ★★

Beauty: ★★                Site Privacy: ★★★
Spaciousness: ★★★         Quiet: ★★★
Security: ★★★★★           Cleanliness: ★★★
Insect Control: ★★★       Facilities: ★★★

Campers looking to get away from the hustle and bustle of Old Orchard Beach and the surrounding area, will find a quiet oasis at Silver Springs campground. The modest facility, less than two miles from Old Orchard Beach, is one of Maine's newest campgrounds. (Though the site, dubbed Goosefare Hill, and the large home on the property has been around for more than 170 years.) Sites are set side-by-side with a choice of shaded or wooded spaces. You won't find anything extraordinary or fancy at Silver Springs, just a pleasant, economical base to call home while you explore, and an alternative to some of the gigantic, mega camping resorts in the area.

## BASICS

**Operated By:** Michael & Jeanne Glaude. **Open:** May–Columbus Day. **Site Assignment:** Reservations required, 1-night deposit, 10-day cancellation policy w/ a $10 service charge, 3-day min. stay on holidays; MC, V, D, no checks. **Registration:** At office. **Fee:** Full hookups, $34; water & electric, $30; no hookups, $23, based on 2 adults & 2 children under 17. **Parking:** At site.

## FACILITIES

**Number of RV Sites:** 101. **Number of Tent-Only Sites:** 20. **Hookups:** Water, electric, sewer (30, 50 amps), cable TV. **Each Site:** Picnic table, fire ring. **Dump Station:** Yes. **Laundry:** Yes. **Pay Phone:** Yes. **Rest Rooms and Showers:** Yes (coin-op). **Fuel:** No. **Propane:** Yes. **Internal Roads:** Gravel, dirt (good). **RV Service:** No. **Market:** Old Orchard Beach (1.5 mi). **Restaurant:** No. **General Store:** Yes. **Vending:** Yes. **Swimming Pool:** Yes. **Playground:** Yes. **Other:** Game room, on-site motel, cottage rentals. **Activities:** Swimming, horseshoes, basketball, shuffleboard, volleyball. **Nearby Attractions:** Old Orchard Beach, southern coast parks & beaches, Portland. **Additional Information:** Old Orchard Beach Chamber of Commerce, First St. , Old Orchard Beach, ME 04064 (207) 934-2500 (800) 365-9386; www.oldorchardbeachmaine.com.

## RESTRICTIONS

**Pets:** Must be on a leash, never left unattended. Only 2 pets allowed per site. **Fires:** In grills, stoves, & fire rings only. **Alcoholic Beverages:** At site only. **Vehicle Maximum Length:** None.

## TO GET THERE

From junction Maine Turnpike and I-195, exit 5, go east 1.2 mi. on I-195, then north 0.5 mi. on Rte. 1 (exit 2B); campground is on the right.

## SCARBOROUGH

### Bayley's

275 Pine Point Rd., Scarborough 04074. T: (207) 883-6043; www.bayleys-camping.com; info@bayleys-camping.com.

 ★★★★★         ★★★★

| | | |
|---|---|---|
| Beauty: ★★★ | Site Privacy: ★★★ |
| Spaciousness: ★★★ | Quiet: ★ |
| Security: ★★★★★ | Cleanliness: ★★★★ |
| Insect Control: ★★★ | Facilities: ★★★★★ |

This mega-resort campground in southern coastal Maine is one of the largest in New England. It's a sprawling family resort, spread over 200 acres, with activities to keep everyone entertained. There's professional entertainment four nights a week: bands play, comedians joke, jugglers juggle. there are three swimming pools, three ponds, a full-service restaurant (lobsters anyone?), mini golf, sports fields, and nonstop planned activities morning to night. If that's not enough, campers can hop on the free double decker bus and head to Old Orchard Beach, only a few minutes away. This is probably the best bargain in southern coastal Maine. With 500+ sites, you'll have plenty to choose from. If you're driving a large motor home, the A and C sites are best—shaded, level and easy to pull in and out. They're close to the front office, pool, theater, and restaurant. If you want more privacy, try the V section. If you're a tenter, who prefers to get away from the action, there's a wilderness area in the back of the property. Nature trails, fishing ponds, mini gold, sports fields, and another pool are back even further, and make up one of Maine's largest outdoor activity centers.

## BASICS

**Operated By:** Fred & Kathleen Bayley. **Open:** May–Oct. 15. **Site Assignment:** Reservations suggested, stays of 4 days or less must be paid in full; $150 deposit for longer stays, 30 day cancellation policy w/ a $25 service charge. 3-nigh min. stays over Memorial Day & Labor Day weekends, 4-night min. over July 4th holiday; MC, V, no checks. **Registration:** At office. **Fee:** Full hookups (w/ cable TV & AC), $46; full hookups (without AC), $41; water, electric & cable TV (Bayley's Best), $41; water, electric, cable TV, $39, no hookups, $34; 50 amp service is additional $3. **Parking:** At site, 1 vehicle per site (additional vehicle, $5/day).

## FACILITIES

**Number of RV Sites:** 450. **Number of Tent-Only Sites:** 150. **Hookups:** Water, electric, sewer (30, 50 amps), cable TV, modem. **Each**

**Site:** Picnic table, fire ring. **Dump Station:** Yes. **Laundry:** Yes. **Pay Phone:** Yes. **Rest Rooms and Showers:** Yes. **Fuel:** No. **Propane:** Yes. **Internal Roads:** Gravel (good). **RV Service:** No. **Market:** Old Orchard Beach (2 mi). **Restaurant:** Yes. **General Store:** Yes. **Vending:** Yes. **Swimming Pool:** Yes. **Playground:** Yes. **Other:** 3 ponds (2 stocked fishing ponds), boat dock, hot tubs, mini golf course, boat rentals, outdoor theater, nature trails, bike rentals, complimentary beach bus, trailer rentals, game room, rec hall, sports fields. **Activities:** Swimming, boating, fishing, mini-golf, basketball, volleyball, horseshoes, live entertainment, planned activities, including children's games, fishing derbies, contests, dinners, movies, & more. **Nearby Attractions:** Old Orchard Beach, Portland, southern coastal parks & beaches. **Additional Information:** Old Orchard Beach Chamber of Commerce, First St., Old Orchard Beach, ME 04064 (207) 934-2500 (800) 365-9386; www.oldorchardbeachmaine.com.

## RESTRICTIONS

**Pets:** Must be on a leash, never left unattended. Pets not allowed in activity areas; only adults may walk pets in the campground. **Fires:** In grills, stoves, & fire rings only. **Alcoholic Beverages:** At site. **Vehicle Maximum Length:** None. **Other:** No children allowed in hot tubs.

## TO GET THERE

From Maine Turnpike (exit 5) and I-195, go east 1.2 mi. on I-195, then north 5 mi. on Rte.1, then east (right) 3 mi. on Rte. 9 (Pine Point Rd.); campground is on right.

## SCARBOROUGH

### Wassamki Springs

56 Saco St., Scarborough 04074. T: (207) 839-4276; F: (207) 839-2936; www.wassamkisprings.com; wassamkisprings@aol.com.

🚐 ★★★★                    ▲ ★★★

| | |
|---|---|
| Beauty: ★★★★ | Site Privacy: ★★★ |
| Spaciousness: ★★★ | Quiet: ★★★ |
| Security: ★★★ | Cleanliness: ★★★★ |
| Insect Control: ★★★ | Facilities: ★★★★ |

Vacationing families and Maine's summer tourists clamor to this Portland area, activity-based campground. We like that the campground is only a few minutes from Maine's largest city (with restaurants, galleries and historic sites) with quick access to southern coastal beaches, cruises, and attractions. But, if you stay here, you don't have to be in the hub of it all. The property flanks a 30 acre private lake and campers have their own mile-long sandy beach and warm, crystal clear swimming waters. There are boat rentals, family hayrides, group bonfires, and planned activities to keep things entertaining. There's also a trout-stocked fishing pond popular with kids and parents, alike. Facilities are clean and modern and campers have a choice of sites: lakefront, shaded or open (though a little over half of the campground is taken by seasonal renters.) Tent-only sites are few (9) and tucked back away from the lake.

## BASICS

**Operated By:** Hillock family. **Open:** May–Columbus Day. **Site Assignment:** Reservations suggested in Jul.–Aug.; $10 per day deposit, holiday weekends paid in full, 2-week cancellation policy, no refunds for holiday weekends; MC, V, D; checks accepted for deposit but not upon arrival. **Registration:** At office. **Fee:** Full hookups (50 amp), $31; full hookups, $29; water & electric, $27; no hookups, $24, base on 2 adults & up to 4 children. **Parking:** At site.

## FACILITIES

**Number of RV Sites:** 151. **Number of Tent-Only Sites:** 9. **Hookups:** Water, electric, sewer (30, 50 amps), phone, modem. **Each Site:** Picnic table, fire ring. **Dump Station:** Yes. **Laundry:** Yes. **Pay Phone:** Yes. **Rest Rooms and Showers:** Yes. **Fuel:** No. **Propane:** Yes. **Internal Roads:** Gravel, dirt (good). **RV Service:** No. **Market:** Scarborough (0.5 mi). **Restaurant:** Yes. **General Store:** Yes. **Vending:** Yes. **Swimming Pool:** No. **Playground:** Yes. **Other:** Lake frontage, beach, boat rentals, stocked fishing pond, pavilion, game room, sports fields, planned activities. **Activities:** Swimming, boating, fishing, volleyball, horseshoes, basketball, softball. **Nearby Attractions:** Portland, Casco Bay, coastal beaches, Freeport. **Additional Information:** Greater Portland Area

Chamber of Commerce, 60 Pearl St., Portland, ME 04101 (207) 772-2811, www.portlandregion.com.

## RESTRICTIONS

**Pets:** Must be on a leash; never left unattended. **Fires:** In grills, campstoves, & fire rings only. **Alcoholic Beverages:** At site only. **Vehicle Maximum Length:** None.

## TO GET THERE

From I-95 and exit 7A, go 4 mi. west on Rte. 22, then 0.2 mi. east on Saco St.; campground is on the left

# SEARSPORT

## Searsport Shores Camping Resort

216 W. Main St., Searsport 04974. T: (207) 548-6059; www.campocean.com; camping@ime.net.

🚐 ★★★★★                    ⛺ ★★★★★

Beauty: ★★★★★          Site Privacy: ★★★★
Spaciousness: ★★★★     Quiet: ★★★★
Security: ★★★★             Cleanliness: ★★★★★
Insect Control: ★★★★     Facilities: ★★★★★

This midcoastal Maine campground, boasting 1,200 feet of scenic ocean shoreline, is one of the top in New England. The views of rocky coastline, picturesque coves, Sears Island (the largest uninhabited, undeveloped island in the state) and open ocean are spectacular. Campers have a long stretch of private beaches to enjoy, ranging from rocky tidepools to water smoothed pebbles to soft sand. Keep meandering and you'll run into Moose Lake State Park, just down the coast, within walking distance from the campground. The grounds include ocean viewing decks and sitting areas, arbors and trellis, and artistic wood carvings. Facilities are top-notch, including new rest rooms and showers, a large rec hall with a library lending area, an array of musical instruments, and an indoor play area for young children. There are hiking and biking trails, kayak and canoe rentals, and a list of planned activities, including old-fashioned lobster bakes on the beach, guided nature walks, children's programs, and more. Sites are spacious and include a sepa-

rate, large adult-only tenting area overlooking the ocean, affectionately dubbed the "honeymoon suite."

## BASICS

**Operated By:** Rosalie & Zaban Koltookian. **Open:** May 15–Oct. 15. **Site Assignment:** Reservations suggested Jul.–Aug. 50 percent deposit for stays less than 1 week, $100 deposit for stays of 1 week or more, 10-day cancellation policy with $15 service fee; sites must be paid in full for holiday weekend reservations & are nonrefundable; MC, V, D, checks. **Registration:** At office. **Fee:** Water & electric (premium), $38; water & electric (oceanview), $35; no hookups (premium ocean), $28 (ocean tent), $21. **Parking:** At site.

## FACILITIES

**Number of RV Sites:** 70. **Number of Tent-Only Sites:** 30. **Hookups:** Water, electric (30 amps). **Each Site:** Picnic table, fire ring. **Dump Station:** Yes. **Laundry:** Yes. **Pay Phone:** Yes. **Rest Rooms and Showers:** Yes. **Fuel:** No. **Propane:** Yes. **Internal Roads:** Gravel (good). **RV Service:** No. **Market:** Searsport (1mi). **Restaurant:** No. **General Store:** Yes. **Vending:** Yes. **Swimming Pool:** No. **Playground:** Yes. **Other:** Ocean frontage, beaches, rec hall, library, patios, ocean viewing sitting areas, group area, biking & walking trails, canoe & kayak rentals, guided kayak lessons & tours, guided tours of Acadia National Park, intrepretive walks on the beach, indoor play center, sports field, cabin rentals. **Activities:** Swimming, fishing, boating, beachcombing, nature walks, baseball, volleyball, horseshoes, basketball, guided tours, planned activities, including potluck suppres, lobster bakes, live entertainment, craft classes, treasure hunts, & more. **Nearby Attractions:** Bucksport, Searsport, Maine coastal beaches, Deer Isle Peninsula, Bar Harbor, Acadia National Park. **Additional Information:** Searsport Economic Development Committee, Reservoir St., Searsport, ME 04974 (207) 54807255, www.searsportme.com & Acadia Information Center, P.O. Box 139, Mount Desert, ME 04660 (207) 667-8550 or (800) 358-8550, www.acadiainfo.com.

**Pets:** Must be on a leash, never left unattended. 1 pet per site only. **Fires:** In grills, stoves, & fire rings only. **Alcoholic Beverages:** At site only. **Vehicle Maximum Length:** 75 ft.

**TO GET THERE**

From junction Rtes. 1 and 3 (in Belfast), go north 5 mi. on Rte. 1; campground is on the right.

## SMALL POINT
### Hermit Island

6 Hermit Island Rd., Phippsburg 04562. T: (207) 443-2101; www.hermitisland.com; info@hermitisland.com.

🚐 ★                                    ▲ ★★★

Beauty: ★★★★            Site Privacy: ★★★
Spaciousness: ★★         Quiet: ★★
Security: ★★★★          Cleanliness: ★★★
Insect Control: ★★★      Facilities: ★★★

This campground isn't for everyone, but, wow, what a spot. Set on a sandy spit of land in the open Atlantic, bounded by Maine's famously rocky shore, its delicate geography make it suitable for tents, small-to-medium tent trailers, and small pickup trailers only. Here, you can camp amidst sand dunes, with panoramic views of surf and sky, or nestled among groves of young birch or tall spruce. Waterfront sites include some prime spots on Casco Bay, and lower-priced sites on The Branch, an inlet near Small Point Harbor. The farther inland you go, the more breathing room around the campsites (lower prices, too.) Sites at Osprey Point, on the ocean side, perch on hillside dunes; sites 2 and 3 of this bunch offer the most privacy. Branch sites 4 through 12 are really nice, as well. Close to Osprey Point, but inland, value sites 8,10, and 11, at Cross Island and Luff Ln., are woodsy, and a short walk to the beach. Without many frills, save sun, sand, and surf, this campground caters to a young demographic. Kids are everywhere, especially around the store and Kelp Shed, where boat rentals and fishing arrangements are made.

**BASICS**

**Operated By:** Nicholas Sewall. **Open:** Mid-May–Columbus Day. **Site Assignment:** Reservations recommended from June 15 to Labor Day. Reservations for a weeks' stay or longer are accepted the first business day in Jan. Full fee payable within 30 days of booking. Reservations for less than 1 week are accepted starting Mar. 1; full payment required. Refund for cancellations made w/ at least 72-hour notice, minus 1-day fee. **Registration:** At office. **Fee:** $27–$38 for 2 adults & their children or 4 adults, no children. No credit cards. **Parking:** At sites. 1 car per site only.

**FACILITIES**

**Number of RV Sites:** 275. **Number of Tent-Only Sites:** 0. **Hookups:** None. **Each Site:** None. **Dump Station:** No. **Laundry:** Dryers only. **Pay Phone:** Yes. **Rest Rooms and Showers:** Yes. **Fuel:** No. **Propane:** No. **Internal Roads:** Gravel, in good condition. **RV Service:** No. **Market:** 16 mi. north, in Bath. **Restaurant:** 16 mi. north, in Bath. **General Store:** Yes. **Vending:** No. **Swimming Pool:** No. **Playground:** No. **Other:** Rec hall, boat ramp. **Activities:** Ocean swimming, boating (rentals available), saltwater fishing, hiking. **Nearby Attractions:** Popham Beach State Park, Morse Mountain Sanctuary, Maine Maritime Museum, Bowdoin College Museum of Art, Peary-MacMillan Arctic Museum, deep-sea fishing. **Additional Information:** Chamber of Commerce of the Bath-Brunswick Region, (207) 725-8797 or (207) 443-9751; www.midcoastmaine.com.

**RESTRICTIONS**

**Pets:** Must be leashed, quiet, & cleaned up after. Must not be left unattended. **Fires:** In fire rings only. **Alcoholic Beverages:** At sites only. **Vehicle Maximum Length:** 25 ft. **Other:** Visitor's are not allowed in the campground.

**TO GET THERE**

From I-95 in Brunswick, take Rte. 1 to Bath, then Rtes. 209 and 216 south to Hermit Island. Campground entrance is on the right.

## SOMESVILLE

## Mt. Desert Campground

Rte. 198 (Somesville), Mount Desert 04660. T: (207) 244-3710; mdcg@midmaine.com.

🚐 ★★                          ▲ ★★★★★

Beauty: ★★★★★              Site Privacy: ★★★★★
Spaciousness: ★★★★★        Quiet: ★★★★
Security: ★★★               Cleanliness: ★★★★★
Insect Control: ★★★         Facilities: ★★

This is traditional camping at its best: quiet, wooded sites on the saltwater shore of scenic Somes Sound on Mount Desert Island. You're in the heart of the island, only 5 miles from with Bar Harbor, Northeast Harbor and Southwest Harbor. The pristine property, nestled in a pine wood forest and perched on a knoll overlooking the water, is a favorite with tenters and small tent trailer campers. (There are only basic water and electric hookups; RVs more than 20 feet long are not allowed.) There's kayaking and canoeing from the campground, salt water fishing and swimming, and guided bird walks and beach strolls in the summer. Pick up a fresh brewed cup of coffee at the Gathering Place in the morning and go back in the afternoon for their home-made ice cream. Sites offer plenty of room and privacy (many tent sites have platforms) but reserve early: many families have been coming here for 25 to 30 years, returning year after year for summer vacation.

### BASICS

**Operated By:** Craighead family. **Open:** Mid-June–mid-Sept. **Site Assignment:** Reservations suggested in Jul.–Aug. During Jul.–Aug., water-front/waterview sites require 1-week stay (Sat-urday–Saturday), off water sites require 3 night stay. $40 deposit for reservation for less than a week, $60 deposit for each week reserved. Deposits are non-refundable; MC, V, checks. **Registration:** At office. **Fee:** Waterfront, $32; water-view, $29; off-water platform, $26; off-water ground, $24, based on 2 adults & 2 children under 18. **Parking:** At site, 1 vehicle per site.

### FACILITIES

**Number of RV Sites:** 50. **Number of Tent-Only Sites:** 100. **Hookups:** Water, electric (15 amps). **Each Site:** Picnic table, fire ring. **Dump Station:** No. **Laundry:** No. **Pay Phone:** Yes. **Rest Rooms and Showers:** Yes (coin-op). **Fuel:** No. **Propane:** No. **Internal Roads:** Paved, gravel (good). **RV Service:** No. **Market:** Somesville (5mi). **Restaurant:** No. **General Store:** Yes. **Vending:** Yes. **Swimming Pool:** No. **Play-ground:** No. **Other:** Saltwater frontage, beach, boat launch, dock, canoe & kayak rentals. **Activi-ties:** Swimming, boating, fishing, guided bird watch & wildlife viewing programs. **Nearby Attractions:** Bar Harbor, Acadia National Park. **Additional Information:** Acadia National Park, P.O. Box 177, Bar Harbor, ME 04609 (207) 288-3338, www.nps/gov/acad. Also, Acadia Informa-tion Center, P.O. Box 139, Mount Desert, ME 04660 (207) 667-8550 (800) 358-8550, www.acadiainfo.com & Bar Harbor Chamber of Commerce, 93 Cottage St., Bar Harbor, ME 04609 (207) 288-5103, www.barharborinfo.com.

### RESTRICTIONS

**Pets:** No pets allowed in July-Aug. & holiday weekends. **Fires:** In grills, stoves, & fire rings only. **Alcoholic Beverages:** At site only. **Vehicle Maximum Length:** 20 ft. **Other:** 1 tent only on each site (a family w/ an extra tent for chidlren or screenhouse is permissible).

### TO GET THERE

From junction Rtes. 233 and 198, go 0.5 mi. on Rte. 198.

## SOUTHPORT

## Gray Homestead Campground

21 Homestead Rd., Southport 04576. T: (207) 633-4612; graysoceancamping.com; grays@gwi.net.

🚐 ★★★★                        ▲ ★★★★

Beauty: ★★★★               Site Privacy: ★★
Spaciousness: ★★★          Quiet: ★★★
Security: ★★★               Cleanliness: ★★★★
Insect Control: ★★★         Facilities: ★★

Finally, a Boothbay-area campground with ocean views! Gray Homestead was once a boarding house for the wealthy; now, the property—still owned by the Gray family— includes a cottage, two apartments, and a small, wooded campground. "People either love it or hate it," says Rachel, a campground employee. "There's nothing to do here, just nature." Big, beautiful nature, as in the Atlantic Ocean. Sounds good to us. There are kayaks, for poking around the peninsula, and owner Steve has a lobster boat. He'll catch lobsters for campers, and they'll cook 'em for you, or they'll lend you a big pot so you can do it yourself. While the campground offers awesome ocean views, and all campsites are a brief walk to the shore, sites tend to be small (and wet, when we visited), better for smaller RVs and pop-ups than tent camping. Site 17C, overlooking the water, is woodsy, with wonderful views. Oceanfront sites go first, naturally. Sites 9A and 9B are pretty, and set back in the woods, while sites 29A through C are nicely secluded for tenters. Sites 23 and 24 (water and electric) are good choices for RVers. Campers are drawn to the rocky point— great for fishing or just basking in the sun.

## BASICS

**Operated By:** Steve & Suzanne Gray. **Open:** May 1–Columbus Day. **Site Assignment:** Reservations recommended. 50% deposit required. No refunds for cancellation, but will issue credit for future stay. **Registration:** At office. **Fee:** $19–$27 per campsite. No credit cards. **Parking:** At site.

## FACILITIES

**Number of RV Sites:** 40. **Number of Tent-Only Sites:** 0. **Hookups:** Water, electric (20, 30 amps). **Each Site:** Picnic table, fire ring. **Dump Station:** Yes. **Laundry:** Yes. **Pay Phone:** Yes. **Rest Rooms and Showers:** Yes, coin-op. **Fuel:** No. **Propane:** No. **Internal Roads:** Gravel, in good condition. **RV Service:** No. **Market:** 4.5 mi. north. **Restaurant:** 2 mi. north. **General Store:** No. **Vending:** Yes. **Swimming Pool:** No. **Playground:** Yes (swings). **Activities:** Boating (kayak rentals), fishing. **Nearby Attractions:** Boothbay Railway Village, Maine Resources Aquarium, Boothbay Harbor restaurants, shops & galleries, deep-sea fishing, whale-watching cruises, golf. **Additional Information:** Boothbay Harbor

Region Chamber of Commerce, (207) 633-2353 or (800) 266-8422.

## RESTRICTIONS

**Pets:** Must be leashed, quiet, & cleaned up after. Must not be left unattended. **Fires:** In fire rings only. **Alcoholic Beverages:** At sites only. **Vehicle Maximum Length:** 40 ft. **Other:** 3-day min. stay on holidays.

## TO GET THERE

From Maine Turnpike, take exit 9 to Coastal Rte. 1, then take exit 22 for Brunswick/Bath. Follow Rte. 1 through Bath and Wiscasset to Rte. 27 south. Follow Rte. 27 to Boothbay Harbor; stay on Rte. 27 through Boothbay to Southport. At second bridge, take a left onto Rte. 238. Campground is 2 mi. on left.

## SOUTHWEST HARBOR

## Smuggler's Den Campground

P.O. Box 787, Rte. 102, Southwest Harbor 04679. T: (207) 244-3944; F: (207) 244-4072; www.smugglersden.com; smugglersden@acadia.net.

🚐 ★★★　　　　　　▲ ★★★★

| | |
|---|---|
| Beauty: ★★★ | Site Privacy: ★★★ |
| Spaciousness: ★★★★ | Quiet: ★★★★ |
| Security: ★★★★ | Cleanliness: ★★★★ |
| Insect Control: ★★★ | Facilities: ★★★ |

We like the fact that once we park our car at this campground we never have to get in it again until we leave to go home. There are several hiking trails accessible from the campground, including trails to Long Pond and Echo Lake (one of the best places to swim in the area!) You can walk into lovely Southwest Harbor, if you like, where you'll find supplies, restaurants, galleries, shops, and more. Live lobsters are for sale at the campground store! It's a great base to explore the quiet side of Mount Desert Island and Acadia National Park. We like the airy, sunny sites with views across open fields and mountains in distance. There's a separate group camping area, nestled in the trees, with plenty of elbow room and privacy.

## BASICS

**Operated By:** Damaris Smith. **Open:** Memorial Day–Columbus Day. **Site Assignment:** Reservations suggested in Jul.–Aug., accepted for 2 nights or longer, 50% deposit required, 14-day cancellation policy with $15 service charge; MC, V & checks. **Registration:** At office. **Fee:** Full hookups, $31.50; water & electric, $27.50; no hookups, $23.50, based on 4 people per site, over 6 years old. **Parking:** At site.

## FACILITIES

**Number of RV Sites:** 70. **Number of Tent-Only Sites:** 30. **Hookups:** Water, electric, sewer (20, 30 amps). **Each Site:** Picnic table, fire ring. **Dump Station:** Yes. **Laundry:** Yes. **Pay Phone:** Yes. **Rest Rooms and Showers:** Yes. **Fuel:** No. **Propane:** Yes. **Internal Roads:** Gravel, dirt (good). **RV Service:** No. **Market:** Southwest Harbor (0.5 mi). **Restaurant:** No. **General Store:** Yes. **Vending:** Yes. **Swimming Pool:** Yes. **Playground:** Yes. **Other:** Hiking trails, sports field, cabin rentals, group camping area. **Activities:** Swimming, hiking, horseshoes. **Nearby Attractions:** Bar Harbor, Acadia National Park. **Additional Information:** Acadia National Park, P.O. Box 177, Bar Harbor, ME 04609 (207) 288-3338, www.nps/gov/acad. Also, Acadia Information Center, P.O. Box 139, Mount Desert, ME 04660 (207) 667-8550 (800) 358-8550, www.acadiainfo.com & Bar Harbor Chamber of Commerce, 93 Cottage St., Bar Harbor, ME 04609 (207) 288-5103, www.barharborinfo.com.

## RESTRICTIONS

**Pets:** On a leash, never left unattended. **Fires:** In grills, stoves, & fire rings only. **Alcoholic Beverages:** At site only. **Vehicle Maximum Length:** None.

## TO GET THERE

From junction Rtes. 3, 198 and 102, go south 9.5 mi. on Rte. 102; campground is on right.

## SOUTHWEST HARBOR

## White Birches Campground

195 Seal Cove Rd., Southwest Harbor 04679. T: (207) 244-3797 or (888) 716-0727; www.mainecamper.com; whitebirches@downeast.net.

🚐 ★★★          ⛺ ★★★

| | |
|---|---|
| Beauty: ★★★ | Site Privacy: ★★★ |
| Spaciousness: ★★★★ | Quiet: ★★★ |
| Security: ★★★ | Cleanliness: ★★★ |
| Insect Control: ★★★ | Facilities: ★★★ |

This modest, no frills campground sits on the doorstep of Acadia National Park, 20 minutes from Bar Harbor and only minutes from Echo Lake, Southwest Harbor and other major sights and attractions. Hiking, biking, kayaking, and swimming are nearby. Most campers use it as a quiet—and economical— base to explore the area. The campground is best for tenters and small pop-up trailer campers who like privacy and elbow room and won't miss the planned activities and evening entertainment offered at other area campgrounds. The campground is divided by Seal Cove Rd. with sites on both sides. Each area offers wooded sites, tucked under pine trees. We like the extra room and privacy of the "b" loop sites, on the opposite side of the street from the office, pool, and play area. Sites 9B-11B are especially nice. But, these sites are also across the street from the campground's only rest rooms and showers, an inconvenient distance away.

## BASICS

**Operated By:** Ronald, Jaylene, Melody, & Colton Sanborn. **Open:** May 15–Oct. 15. **Site Assignment:** Reservations accepted year-round, suggested in Jul.–Aug. 1-night non-refundable deposit required for reservation; MC, V & checks. **Registration:** At office. **Fee:** Water & electric, $24; no hookups, $20, based on 2 adults & 2 children under 16. **Parking:** At site, 1 vehicle per site.

## FACILITIES

**Number of RV Sites:** 15. **Number of Tent-Only Sites:** 45. **Hookups:** Water, electric (20, 30 amps). **Each Site:** Picnic table, fire ring. **Dump Station:** Yes. **Laundry:** Yes. **Pay Phone:** Yes. **Rest Rooms and Showers:** Yes. **Fuel:** No. **Propane:** No. **Internal Roads:** Gravel, dirt (good). **RV Service:** No. **Market:** Southwest Harbor (1.5 mi). **Restaurant:** No. **General Store:** Yes. **Vending:** Yes. **Swimming Pool:** Yes. **Playground:** Yes. **Other:** Cabin rentals. **Activities:** Swimming, tetherball, basketball. **Nearby Attractions:** Bar Harbor, Acadia National Park. **Additional Information:** Acadia National Park, P.O. Box 177, Bar Harbor, ME 04609 (207) 288-3338, www.nps/gov/acad. Also, Acadia Information Center, P.O. Box 139, Mount Desert, ME, 04660 (207) 667-8550, (800) 358-8550, www.acadiainfo.com & Bar Harbor Chamber of Commerce, 93 Cottage St. , Bar Harbor, ME 04609 (207) 288-5103, www.barharborinfo.com.

## RESTRICTIONS

**Pets:** Must be on a leash, never left unattended. **Fires:** In grills, stoves, & fire rings only. **Alcoholic Beverages:** At site only. **Vehicle Maximum Length:** 35 ft.

## TO GET THERE

From junction Rtes. 3 and 102/198, go east 10.5 mi. on Rte. 102 (toward Southwest Harbor), then south (right) 1.2 mi. on Seal Cove Rd.; the campground is on the left.

## STANDISH

## Family and Friends Campground

140 Richville Rd., Standish 04084. T: (207) 642-2200; www.familynfriends.com; info@familynfriends.com.

🚐 ★★★          ▲ ★★

| | |
|---|---|
| Beauty: ★★★ | Site Privacy: ★★★ |
| Spaciousness: ★★★ | Quiet: ★★ |
| Security: ★★★★★ | Cleanliness: ★★★ |
| Insect Control: ★★ | Facilities: ★★★★ |

This campground, set in the Sebago Lake area of southwestern Maine, is not on the water, unless you count their swimming pool. But the Sebago-Long Lake chain of lakes, a 42-mile waterway, is just a short hop away. A public boat launch and small beach are less than a mile away. Mean-while, the campground offers plenty of distractions, from bean-hole dinners (a Maine tradition) to karaoke. A nice log-hewn rec hall, with a fireplace and mounted trophy heads, is a base for activities. They even have hot tubs. The campground is nicely shaded with hemlocks and hardwoods, offering plenty of piney buffer between sites. Little touches provide a pleasant ambience here, such as the stone-banked pond with water fountain, the umbrellaed lounge chairs around the pool, and chipmunk feeders (so, presumably, the critters will leave your goodies alone.) Campsites, which include about 20-some seasonal spots, are set in loops. Tent sites 8, 9, and 10 are nicely backed up into the woods, while RV sites 44 and 46 are very private. Steer clear of sites 12, 15, and 16; too close to the road.

## BASICS

**Operated By:** Joanne & Jim Lavalle. **Open:** Apr. 1–Nov. 1. **Site Assignment:** Reservations recommended. $25 deposit required. Refunds for cancellations w/ 15-day notice. **Registration:** At office. **Fee:** $25 per night for 2 adults & unmarried children under age 18. V, MC, D, AE. **Parking:** At site.

## FACILITIES

**Number of RV Sites:** 65. **Number of Tent-Only Sites:** 0. **Hookups:** Water, electric (30 amps), sewer. **Each Site:** Picnic table, fireplace. **Dump Station:** Yes. **Laundry:** No. **Pay Phone:** Yes. **Rest Rooms and Showers:** Yes. **Fuel:** No. **Propane:** No. **Internal Roads:** Gravel, in good condition. **RV Service:** No. **Market:** 3 mi. north. **Restaurant:** 5 mi. south. **General Store:** Yes. **Vending:** Yes. **Swimming Pool:** Yes. **Playground:** Yes. **Other:** Rec hall, arcade, hot tubs. **Activities:** Swimming, horseshoes, basketball, planned activities. **Nearby Attractions:** Boating (public boat launch is 0.6 mi. away), lake swimming, fishing, Songo River Queen paddlewheeler cruise, Sebago Lake State Park. **Additional Information:** Bridgton Lakes Region Chamber of Commerce, (207) 647-3472.

## RESTRICTIONS

**Pets:** Must be leashed, quiet, & cleaned up after. Must not be left unattended. Not allowed in buildings, lodge, or pool area. **Fires:** In fireplaces only. **Alcoholic Beverages:** Yes. **Vehicle Maximum Length:** 40 ft. **Other:** 3-night min. on holiday weekends.

## To Get There

From Maine Turnpike, take exit 7 (mi. 42); follow Rte. 114 northwest through Gorham to intersection of Rte. 35 in Sebago Lake Village. Continue straight on Rte. 114 for 0.75 mi. to campground, on the left.

# STEEP FALLS
## Acres of Wildlife

Rte. 113/11, P.O. Box 2, Steep Falls 04085. T: (207) 675- CAMP; www.acresofwildlife.com.

🚐 ★★★★          ▲ ★★★★

Beauty: ★★★★            Site Privacy: ★★★
Spaciousness: ★★★★      Quiet: ★★★
Security: ★★★★★         Cleanliness: ★★★
Insect Control: ★★★      Facilities: ★★★★

The long gravel approach to this campground might scare some campers off. To others, it's a sign that they're getting away from it all. Indeed, this southwestern Maine campground, a half-hour from Portland, is its own world of family fun. In summer, the activity schedule is virtually non-stop (we like the water balloon slingshot contest); meanwhile, down at Rainbow Lake, there's swimming, tubing, boating, and fishing, and mini-golf up by the playground and ball field, and a mammoth arcade. Hard to believe this place was once a turkey farm. In that spirit, they still bake turkey pies, but you're more like to see a moose than a turkey lurking around these acres. The fresh baked goods (mostly made here) are a big draw. Savvy muffin-mavens order their breakfast goodies the night before. Campsites (gravel) are clustered around the lake, with a couple rows of seasonal sites set back into the woods. Some tent sites are located in a woodsy wilderness area, as well. We like two-way hookup sites W5 through 8, on the lake, and 61A (if you miss out on the lakeside sites.) Water-only sites B6 through B22 (even numbers) are also lakeside, and really nice.

## Basics

**Operated By:** Baptista family. **Open:** May 1–Columbus Day. **Site Assignment:** Reservations recommended. For less than 1 week stays in summer season, reserve 30 days in advance. 50% deposit required w/ reservation; refunds for cancellations w/ 30-day notice, minus $10 service charge. **Registration:** At office. **Fee:** $24–$38 for 2 adults & up to 3 children under age 18. V, MC, D, AE. **Parking:** At site (2 cars allowed) or designated lot.

## Facilities

**Number of RV Sites:** 200. **Number of Tent-Only Sites:** 0. **Hookups:** Water, electric (30, 50 amps), sewer, cable TV. **Each Site:** Picnic table, fireplace. **Dump Station:** Yes. **Laundry:** Yes. **Pay Phone:** Yes. **Rest Rooms and Showers:** Yes. **Fuel:** No. **Propane:** Yes. **Internal Roads:** Gravel, in good condition. **RV Service:** No. **Market:** 1 mi. east, in Standish. **Restaurant:** Yes. **General Store:** Yes. **Vending:** Yes. **Swimming Pool:** No. **Playground:** Yes. **Other:** Mini-golf, pub, restaurant, rec hall. **Activities:** Fishing (no license required), lake swimming, boating (rentals available), vollyeball, basketball, ball field, bocce, planned activities. **Nearby Attractions:** Songo River Queen paddlewheeler cruise, Sebago Lake State Park, hiking at Douglas Hill, Willbrook Antique Museum, Jones Gallery Glass Museum, Portland. **Additional Information:** Bridgton Lakes Region Chamber of Commerce, (207) 647-3472.

## Restrictions

**Pets:** Must be leashed, quiet, & cleaned up after. Must not be left unattended. Charge is $5 per night in season. **Fires:** In fireplaces only. **Alcoholic Beverages:** Yes. **Vehicle Maximum Length:** None. **Other:** 3-night min. stay during holiday weekends.

## To Get There

From Maine Turnpike, take exit 7A, go left, and follow signs to Rte. 22/114 North (Gorham) on your left. In Gorham, take Rte. 25W on your left, to Rte. 113, on the right. Go 6 mi. on Rte. 113 to campground entrance, then 3 mi. on gravel entrance road.

## SURRY

### The Gatherings Family Campground

RR 1, Box 4069, Surry 04684. T: (207) 667-8826.

🚐 ★★                          ⛺ ★★★★

Beauty: ★★★★              Site Privacy: ★★★★
Spaciousness: ★★★★        Quiet: ★★★
Security: ★★★              Cleanliness: ★★★
Insect Control: ★★★        Facilities: ★★

This scenic campground on Union River Bay offers a fabulous slice of Maine's rocky, undeveloped coastline and is best for campers who crave a natural, seaside setting. The campground sites are a bit rustic geared more for campers with tents, small trailers and pop-ups as opposed to larger RVs. You'll get a whiff of the ocean and feel the sea breezes the moment you walk up to the old-fashioned camp quarters. Inside, there's a woodstove for cool Maine nights and a small diner-style restaurant. Outside, there's a wonderful boulder-strewn and pebble oceanside beach and two freshwater fishing ponds. There are a number of fine oceanfront sites with unbeatable views; other sites circle the ponds or loop around the center of the camground in between the ponds and ocean. Rest rooms and shower facilities are clean but dated and the grounds are natural not landscaped but, did we mention the views?

### BASICS

**Operated By:** Rob Salois. **Open:** May 15–Oct. 15. **Site Assignment:** Reservations suggested, 3-night min. stay on waterfront sites, one-half of fee required for deposit, 14-day cancellation policy with $15 service charge; MC, V & checks. **Registration:** At office. **Fee:** Full hookup, $35; waterfront, $45 (30 amp), $42 (20 amp); off oceanfront, $30; no hookups $15–$17. **Parking:** At site.

### FACILITIES

**Number of RV Sites:** 100. **Number of Tent-Only Sites:** 11. **Hookups:** Water, electric, sewer (20, 30 amps). **Each Site:** Picnic table, fire ring. **Dump Station:** Yes. **Laundry:** Yes. **Pay Phone:** Yes. **Rest Rooms and Showers:** Yes (coin-op). **Fuel:** No. **Propane:** No. **Internal Roads:** Gravel, dirt (fair). **RV Service:** No. **Market:** Ellsworth (5 mi). **Restaurant:** Yes. **General Store:** Yes. **Vending:** Yes. **Swimming Pool:** No. **Playground:** Yes. **Other:** Ocean frontage, beach, cabin & cottage rentals, 2 fishing ponds. **Activities:** Swimming, fishing, horseshoes. **Nearby Attractions:** mid-coast Maine, Bar Harbor, Acadia National Park. **Additional Information:** Ellsworth Area Chamber of Commerce, P.O. Box 267, Ellsworth, ME 04605 (207) 667-5584 or Acadia Information Center, P.O. Box 139, Mount Desert, ME 04660 (207) 667-8550 or (800) 358-8550, www.acadiainfo.com.

### RESTRICTIONS

**Pets:** Must be on a leash, never left unattended. **Fires:** In grills, stoves, & fire rings only. **Alcoholic Beverages:** At site only. **Vehicle Maximum Length:** 36 ft.

### TO GET THERE

From junction Rtes. 1 and 1A, go southwest 0.5 mi. to Rte. 172, then southwest 4 mi.; campground is on the left.

## THOMASTON

### Saltwater Farm Campground

P.O. Box 165, Thomaston 04861. T: (207) 354-6735; www.midcoast.com/~sfc; sfc@midcoast.com.

🚐 ★★★                         ⛺ ★★

Beauty: ★★★               Site Privacy: ★★
Spaciousness: ★★           Quiet: ★★★★
Security: ★★★              Cleanliness: ★★★★★
Insect Control: ★★★        Facilities: ★★★

Located in mid-coast Maine, 50 miles east of Brunswick, this small, quiet campground is set on a 35-acre meadow overlooking the St. George River. The bustling Camden-Rockport area is nearby, but this spot is anti-bustle. The main activity here is dropping a line in the river (fishing is said to be terrific) or watching the sun rise over the water. Campsites are open and grassy, with great views of the river. If you've brought a canoe or kayak, launch it here and explore the waterway. A few sites are set along the perimeter of the wooded perimeter of the property, including some tent sites and full hookup spots. There's one huge (unnumbered) riverfront tent site that gets snapped up first; ask for it, they'll know what you mean. Full hookup sites 32 through 35 sit atop the hill, with water views. A few seasonal sites are included in the mix. Things might change, because they're adding some sites. But we're guessing the ambience of the place will remain peaceful and inviting.

## BASICS

**Operated By:** Bruce & Linda Jennings. **Open:** May 15–Oct. 15. **Site Assignment:** Reservations recommended, especially during July & Aug. Deposit of 1 nights' fee required. Refund w/ cancellations within 7 days, minus $5 fee. **Registration:** At office. **Fee:** $20–$28 for 2 adults & up to 3 children. V, MC, D. **Parking:** At site or as directed.

## FACILITIES

**Number of RV Sites:** 33. **Number of Tent-Only Sites:** 7. **Hookups:** Water, electric (50 amps), sewer. **Each Site:** Picnic table, fire ring. **Dump Station:** Yes. **Laundry:** Yes. **Pay Phone:** Yes. **Rest Rooms and Showers:** Yes, coin-op. **Fuel:** No. **Propane:** No. **Internal Roads:** Gravel, in good condition. **RV Service:** No. **Market:** 1.5 mi. west. **Restaurant:** 1.5 mi. west. **General Store:** Yes. **Vending:** Yes. **Swimming Pool:** Yes. **Playground:** Yes. **Other:** 2-hole pitch & putt. **Activities:** Fishing along tidal shore. **Nearby Attractions:** Owl's Head Transportation Museum, Farnsworth Museum & Wyeth Center, Maine Lighthouse Museum, boat cruises, golf. **Additional Information:** Rockland/Thomaston Area Chamber of Commerce, (207) 596-0376; (800) 562-2529.

## RESTRICTIONS

**Pets:** Must be leashed, quiet, & cleaned up after. Must not be left unattended. **Fires:** In fire rings. **Alcoholic Beverages:** Yes. **Vehicle Maximum Length:** None. **Other:** 3-night min. during Maine Lobster Festival (first week in Aug.).

## TO GET THERE

Follow I-95 to Maine Turnpike. Exit I-95 at Brunswick, exit 22. Follow Rte. 1 north to Thomaston. Turn right onto Wadsworth St. at the Prison Store. Campground is 1.5 mi. ahead, on left.

# TRENTON

## Narrows Too

Rte. 3, 1150 Bar Harbor Rd., Trenton 04605. T: (207) 667-4300; www.narrowstoo.com.

🚐 ★★★★★          ⛺ ★★★★

Beauty: ★★★★          Site Privacy: ★★★
Spaciousness: ★★★          Quiet: ★★★
Security: ★★★          Cleanliness: ★★★★★
Insect Control: ★★★          Facilities: ★★★★★

In an area blessed with a multitude of fine campgrounds, this oceanfront property remains a standout, especially for campers who like a lot of activities and facilities on site. It has a busy, bustling atmosphere full of families, young couples, and retirees on vacation, here to explore Acadia National Park and the surrounding area. There's plenty to do at the campground: magic shows and movies in the evenings, mini-golf, swimming, and more; most activities and sports fields are clustered in the front of the campground. Head toward the back of the site and you'll have splendid views of the ocean. Days are typically quiet when most campers leave to visit area attractions (there's a free shuttle bus service from the campground to downtown Bar Harbor) but by late afternoon the campground is a hive of activity. You'll have a choice of sites, most are sunny and open, and many have expansive ocean views. There is a cluster of cabins and shaded sites in the woods that offer more privacy (sites 203–206 are favorites), and a separate tenting circle. As expected, most popular sites are on the ocean (sites 311–314 are particularly nice.)

## BASICS

**Operated By:** Pat Stanley. **Open:** Memorial Day–Columbus Day. **Site Assignment:** Reservations accepted year–round, recommended in Jul.–Aug. All sites require a 2 night min. reservation w/ a 3-night min. on holiday weekends; holidays are paid in full & non-refundable. Oceanfront sites are a 3-night min. stay in July & Aug. There are no sewer sites on the ocean. $50 deposit for 2 nights, $100 for 3 nights, $150 for 4–7 nights, $200 for 8 or more nights. 30-day cancellation policy minus a $10 service charge;

MC, V, D & checks for reservations; no checks upon arrival. **Registration:** At office. **Fee:** Full hookups, $30 (early & late summer) $45 (peak season); water & electric, $35–$50 (best ocean); $30–$45 (ocean); $23–$35 (narrows best); $22–$32 (narrows choice) & $21–$30 (water/electric); no hookups, $18–$21. **Parking:** At site.

## FACILITIES

**Number of RV Sites:** 120. **Number of Tent-Only Sites:** 12. **Hookups:** Water, electric, sewer (20, 30, 50 amps), cable TV, modem. **Each Site:** Picnic table, fire ring. **Dump Station:** Yes. **Laundry:** Yes. **Pay Phone:** Yes. **Rest Rooms and Showers:** Yes. **Fuel:** No. **Propane:** Yes. **Internal Roads:** Gravel, dirt (good). **RV Service:** No. **Market:** Trenton (1.5 mi). **Restaurant:** No. **General Store:** Yes. **Vending:** No. **Swimming Pool:** Yes. **Playground:** Yes. **Other:** Ocean frontage, rec room, entertainment center, exercise room, reading room, mini golf, free shuttle bus service to Bar Harbor, cabin rentals. **Activities:** Swimming, volleyball, basketball, horseshoes, mini golf, live entertainment & planned activities, including children's programs, arts & crafts, movies, & more. **Nearby Attractions:** Bar Harbor, Acadia National Park. **Additional Information:** Acadia National Park, P.O. Box 177, Bar Harbor, ME 04609 (207) 288-3338, www.nps/gov/acad. Also, Acadia Information Center, P.O. Box 139, Mount Desert, ME, 04660 (207) 667-8550 (800) 358-8550, www.acadiainfo.com & Bar Harbor Chamber of Commerce, 93 Cottage St., Bar Harbor, ME 04609 (207) 288-5103, www.barharborinfo.com.

## RESTRICTIONS

**Pets:** Must be on a leash, never left unattended. **Fires:** In grills, stoves, & fire rings only. **Alcoholic Beverages:** At site only. **Vehicle Maximum Length:** None.

## TO GET THERE

From junction Rtes. 230 and 3, go east 200 feet on Rte. 3; campground is on the left.

# TRENTON

## Timberland Acres

57 Bar Harbor Rd., Trenton 04605. T: (207) 667-3600 or (207) 667-5663.

🚐 ★★★          ⛺ ★★

Beauty: ★★                Site Privacy: ★★
Spaciousness: ★★          Quiet: ★★★
Security: ★★★             Cleanliness: ★★★★
Insect Control: ★★★       Facilities: ★★

This large RV park is just outside Bar Harbor and Acadia National Park (15 miles away) and caters to an older, retiree crowd that prefers to stay away from the hustle and bustle surrounding the park. It also draws off-the-road travelers en route to and from the popular vacation area. All sites are uniform and fairly nondescript, set side-by-side in rows. The front sites are blessed with a few trees but most have been snatched up by seasonal renters (there are about 50-60 seasonals at the campground.) The rest of the sites are further back in the campground, a bit cramped for our tastes, and in the open (bring those awnings for shade!) But, there are plenty of convenient pull-throughs, ultra clean facilities, and level, easy hookup sites throughout the campground. On summer weekends, campers can join in planned activities, including arts and crafts projects, bingo tournaments, and socials.

## BASICS

**Operated By:** Jim & Elizabeth Awalt. **Open:** May 15–Oct. 15. **Site Assignment:** Reservations suggested in Jul.–Aug., 1-night deposit, 2-week cancellation policy; MC, V & checks. **Registration:** At office. **Fee:** Full hookups, $28 (50 amp), $26 (30 amp); water & electric, $25 (50 amp), $23 (30 amp); no hookups, $20, based on family of 4. **Parking:** At site.

## FACILITIES

**Number of RV Sites:** 210. **Number of Tent-Only Sites:** 12. **Hookups:** Water, electric, sewer (30, 50 amps). **Each Site:** Picnic table, fire ring. **Dump Station:** Yes. **Laundry:** Yes. **Pay Phone:** Yes. **Rest Rooms and Showers:** Yes (coin-op). **Fuel:** No. **Propane:** Yes. **Internal Roads:** paved.

**RV Service:** Yes. **Market:** Ellsworth (2 mi). **Restaurant:** No. **General Store:** Yes. **Vending:** Yes. **Swimming Pool:** Yes. **Playground:** Yes. **Other:** Rec room, pavilion, group area. **Activities:** Swimming, horseshoes, shuffleboard, basketball, volleyball, planned activities, including arts & crafts, bingo, socials, & more. **Nearby Attractions:** Bar Harbor, Acadia National Park. **Additional Information:** Ellsworth Area Chamber of Commerce, P.O. Box 267, Ellsworth, ME 04605 (207) 667-5584 & Acadia Information Center, P.O. Box 139, Mount Desert, ME 04660 (207) 667-8550 or (800) 358-8550, www.acadiainfo.com.

## RESTRICTIONS

**Pets:** Must be on a leash, never left unattended. **Fires:** In grills, stoves, & fire rings only. **Alcoholic Beverages:** At site only. **Vehicle Maximum Length:** None.

## TO GET THERE

From junction Rtes. 1 and 3 (in Ellsworth), go east 2 mi. on Rte. 3; campground is on the right.

## WATERFORD

## Papoose Pond Resort & Campground

100 Norway Rd., Rte. 118, Waterford 04088. T: (207) 583-4470; www.papoosepondresort.com; thepond@papoosepondresort.com.

🚐 ★★★★★          ▲ ★★

Beauty: ★★★             Site Privacy: ★★★
Spaciousness: ★★★★      Quiet: ★★
Security: ★★★★          Cleanliness: ★★★★
Insect Control: ★★★      Facilities: ★★★★

The sign at the bathhouse says it all: "Do not use bathhouse sinks for water balloons"! This is definitely a family scene, with a rousing schedule of canoe trips, hayrides, and nightly entertainment. "We're like Beaver Cleaver-ville," says owner Bill Strauss. Set on an 80-acre pond in Western Maine, complete with antique carousel, this place evokes a wholesome, early-60s feel. The only thing lacking: Moms with buoffant hairdos. Three generations of families have been coming here, to splash in the pond, take out the paddleboats, and roast marshmallows around the campfire. The prime lakeside spots are taken by rental cabins, although BS (beachside) sites 14 through 16, with electric and water, are pretty sweet. Forget the other end of the beach, though; BS sites 4 through 8, plus two on the end, are fairly exposed. Surprise: there's a whole section of campsites across the street, and nestled into the woods. For the sake of peace, quiet, and privacy, we'd opt for any of these, especially sites HB 14 through 16 (they're huge) and HBHM 1 through 11 (ultra-private.) This is definitely a destination campground, great fun for kids.

## BASICS

**Operated By:** Strauss family. **Open:** Mid-May–Columbus Day. **Site Assignment:** Reservations recommended. Reservations open 1 year in advance. 50% deposit due for reservations; payment in full due if staying less than 1 week. Refunds for cancellation w/ 30-day notice, minus $15 service fee. $5 service fee charged for each reservation change. **Registration:** At office. **Fee:** $25–$56 for 2 adults & up to 4 children. V, MC. **Parking:** At site.

## FACILITIES

**Number of RV Sites:** 225. **Number of Tent-Only Sites:** 0. **Hookups:** Water, electric (20, 30 amps), sewer, modem. **Each Site:** Picnic table, fireplace. **Dump Station:** Yes. **Laundry:** Yes. **Pay Phone:** Yes. **Rest Rooms and Showers:** Yes. **Fuel:** No. **Propane:** No. **Internal Roads:** Gravel, in good condition. **RV Service:** No. **Market:** 15 mi. south, in Norway. **Restaurant:** Yes. **General Store:** Yes. **Vending:** Yes. **Swimming Pool:** No. **Playground:** Yes. **Other:** Rec hall, game room, mini-golf, carousel. **Activities:** Mini-golf, lake swimming, tennis, boating (rentals available), fishing, basketball, volleyball, shuffleboard, horseshoes, carousel rides, planned daily activities. **Nearby Attractions:** Mt. Sabattus (hiking), outlet shopping (North Conway, N.H.). **Additional Information:** Bridgton Lakes Region Chamber of Commerce, (207) 647-3472.

## RESTRICTIONS

**Pets:** Must be leashed, quiet, & cleaned up after. Must be under control at all times. Not allowed on beach. **Fires:** In fire rings only. **Alcoholic Beverages:** At sites only. **Vehicle Maximum Length:** None. **Other:** 3-night min. on Memorial Day & Labor Day weekends.

## TO GET THERE

From Maine Turnpike, take exit 11 (Gray.) From Gray, take Rte. 26 north to Norway, then Rte. 118 for 10 mi. west to campground.

## WELD

## Mount Blue State Park

R.R. 1, P.O. Box 610, Weld 04285. T: (207) 585-2347 or (207) 585-2261 (off-season); www.state.me.us/doc/parks.htm.

🚐 ★★★          ▲ ★★★

Beauty: ★★★          Site Privacy: ★★★
Spaciousness: ★★★     Quiet: ★★★★
Security: ★★★★        Cleanliness: ★★★★
Insect Control: ★★★    Facilities: ★★★★

Gold-panning on the Swift River? Moonlight owl walks? Intriguing ranger-led programs like these are just part of the appeal at this state park, located in mountainous western Maine. The park is split into two areas: a beach and camping area on Lake Webb, and, 14 miles away, 3167-foot Mt. Blue, reachable via hiking trails. If you like to hike, this is your kind of place, with a variety of hikes for all abilities (ask rangers for suggestions.) Campsites are set in three loops, with trails leading to the narrow, sandy beach and big, roped-off swim area. If you're tenting, inquire about a level one, like site 70L; some are pretty bumpy here. Most sites are set far back from the road. Some, like site 22L, even boast their own furnishings—nice, flat boulders that make perfect chairs. Lots of fallen logs are left to nature to deal with here, but campsites are mostly cleared. Site 104X (as in extra-large) has a nice approach, and is great for big rigs. Friday and Saturday evening ranger programs in the amphitheater are worth attending. There's only one shower room at this park, but at least it has plenty of showers.

## BASICS

**Operated By:** Maine Dept. of Conservation, Bureau of Parks & Lands. **Open:** May 15–Oct. 1. **Site Assignment:** In spring & fall, camping is on a first-come, first-served basis. For summer stays, reservations open on the first business day in Jan. From June 15 to the night before Labor Day, sites may be reserved for a min. of 2 nights & up to 2 weeks. Full payment is charged to credit card when reservation is processed. Refund with $15 cancellation fee. 26 sites are non-reservable, & available on a first-come, first-served basis. Call the reservations line to cancel a reservation more than 3 days in advance. If cancelling less than 3 days in advance, call the park directly. **Registration:** At office. **Fee:** $13, Maine residents; $17, non-residents; plus $2 fee if reserving in advance. V, MC. **Parking:** At sites or assigned lots.

## FACILITIES

**Number of RV Sites:** 136. **Number of Tent-Only Sites:** 0. **Hookups:** None. **Each Site:** Picnic table, fireplace. **Dump Station:** Yes. **Laundry:** No. **Pay Phone:** Yes. **Rest Rooms and Showers:** Yes. **Fuel:** No. **Propane:** Yes. **Internal Roads:** Gravel, in good condition. **RV Service:** No. **Market:** 14 mi. southeast. **Restaurant:** 14 mi. southeast. **General Store:** Yes. **Vending:** Yes. **Swimming Pool:** No. **Playground:** Yes. **Other:** Boat ramp, amphitheater, nature center. **Activities:** Bicycling, mountain biking, hiking (multi-use trail & nature trail), boating (rentals available), volleyball, basketball, moosewatching, interpretive programs. **Nearby Attractions:** Mt. Blue (14 mi.), other day hikes. **Additional Information:** Greater Farmington Chamber of Commerce, (207) 778-4215.

## RESTRICTIONS

**Pets:** Must be leashed, quiet, & cleaned up after. Must not be left unattended. Not allowed on beach. **Fires:** In fire rings only. **Alcoholic Beverages:** No. **Vehicle Maximum Length:** 38 ft. **Other:** 2-week max. stay between last week in June & Labor Day.

## TO GET THERE

From junction of Rtes. 156 and 142, go 2.75 mi. north on 156, then 4 mi. west on Shore Rd., then 1 mi. south to campground.

# WELLS

## Sea Breeze

2073 Post Rd., Wells 04090. T: (207) 646-4301
(888) 792-2177; F: (207) 646-4803.

🚐 ★★★          ⛺ ★★

Beauty: ★★              Site Privacy: ★★
Spaciousness: ★★        Quiet: ★★★
Security: ★★★★          Cleanliness: ★★★★
Insect Control: ★★★     Facilities: ★★

There's not much happening at this tranquil campground in southern Maine, just a few miles from downtown Wells. If you have active preteens and teens in your bunch, they'll probably be bored—with a capital B (though the campground is on the Wells Trolley line and they can easily head into town.) The campground draws an older, mature crowd, who appreciate the relative peace and quiet and don't crave a lot of activities. There's a full-service market, deli and hot food counter as you enter the property, and two pools—one for the motel and cottages and one for the campground. Sites are basic, set side-by-side in rows off the main road. Trees flank the property, but most sites are in the open. Tenters are placed on multi-purpose sites among the RVs.

### BASICS

**Operated By:** Phil & Chun Tumminia. **Open:** Mid-May–mid-Oct. **Site Assignment:** Reservations suggested, 1 night deposit, 14 day cancellation policy, no deposit refunds on holiday & no vacancy nights, 3-night min. stay on holiday weekends; MC, V, D, no checks. **Registration:** At office. **Fee:** Full hookups, $34 (weekday), $38 (weekend); no hookups, $25–$28, based on 4 people per site. **Parking:** At site.

### FACILITIES

**Number of RV Sites:** 57. **Number of Tent-Only Sites:** 0. **Hookups:** Water, electric, sewer (30, 50 amps), cable TV. **Each Site:** Picnic table, fire ring. **Dump Station:** Yes. **Laundry:** Yes. **Pay Phone:** Yes. **Rest Rooms and Showers:** Yes. **Fuel:** No. **Propane:** Yes. **Internal Roads:** Gravel, dirt (good). **RV Service:** No. **Market:** Wells (1.5 mi). **Restaurant:** Yes. **General Store:** Yes. **Vend-**ing: Yes. **Swimming Pool:** Yes. **Playground:** Yes. **Other:** Motel & cottage rentals. **Activities:** Swimming. **Nearby Attractions:** Old Orchard Beach, Wells Harbor, Ogunquit, Kennebunkport, southern coast parks & beaches, Portland. **Additional Information:** Wells Chamber of Commerce, 136 Post Rd., Rte. 1, Wells, ME 04090 (207) 646-2451; www.wellschamber.org.

### RESTRICTIONS

**Pets:** Must be on a leash, never left unattended. **Fires:** In grills, stoves, & fire rings only. **Alcoholic Beverages:** At site only. **Vehicle Maximum Length:** None.

### TO GET THERE

From junction Maine Turnpike and Rte. 109, exit 2, go east 1.5 mi. on Rte. 109, then north 1.3 mi. on Rte. 1; campground is on the right.

# WELLS

## Sea-Vu Campground

Rte. 1, P.O. Box 67, Wells 04090. T: (207) 646-7732; www.sea-vucampground.com; sea-vu@cybertours.com.

🚐 ★★★          ⛺ ★★★

Beauty: ★★★             Site Privacy: ★★★
Spaciousness: ★★★       Quiet: ★★★
Security: ★★★★★         Cleanliness: ★★★★
Insect Control: ★★★     Facilities: ★★★

This southern coast campground, with quick and easy access to area parks, beaches, and attractions, boasts picturesque views of the Atlantic Ocean and Wells Harbor. Up front, there's a small fitness area where early morning classes are held throughout the summer. Several rows of seasonal renters stretch from the front office area toward the water. Most sites don't have much of a view but there is a nice seating area overlooking the wide expanse of tidal marshes, inlets, and open ocean. The handful of tent-only sites have ocean views, nestled in a grassy, shaded area in the back. Most campers don't demand much from their stay at Sea-Vu: a clean, friendly place to set up home away from home so they can explore the region. Sea-Vu delivers that.

## BASICS

**Operated By:** Dave & Elaine Talevi. **Open:**
May–Oct. 15. **Site Assignment:** Reservations
suggested, full deposit for 3 nights or less, one-
half deposit for 4 nights or more, 14-day cancellation policy; no refunds given for holiday
reservations; MC, V, no checks. **Registration:** At
office. **Fee:** Full hookups, $41; no hookups
(water nearby), $32, based on 2 people, addi-
tional people, $4. **Parking:** At site.

## FACILITIES

**Number of RV Sites:** 262. **Number of Tent-
Only Sites:** 8. **Hookups:** Water, electric, sewer
(30, 50 amps), cable TV. **Each Site:** Picnic
table, fire ring. **Dump Station:** Yes. **Laundry:** Yes.
**Pay Phone:** Yes. **Rest Rooms and Showers:** Yes
(coin-op). **Fuel:** No. **Propane:** Yes. **Internal
Roads:** Paved, gravel (good). **RV Service:** Yes.
**Market:** Wells (1 mi). **Restaurant:** Yes. **General
Store:** Yes. **Vending:** Yes. **Swimming Pool:** Yes.
**Playground:** Yes. **Other:** Game room, fitness
center, 18-hole mini-golf course, sports field.
**Activities:** Swimming, mini-golf, basketball, volleyball, horseshoes. **Nearby Attractions:** Old
Orchard Beach, Wells Harbor, Ogunquit, Kennebunkport, southern coast parks & beaches, Portland. **Additional Information:** Wells Chamber
of Commerce, 136 Post Rd., Rte. 1, Wells, ME
04090 (207) 646-2451; www.wellschamber.org.

## RESTRICTIONS

**Pets:** Must be on a leash, never left unattended.
**Fires:** In grills, stoves, & fire rings only. **Alcoholic
Beverages:** At site only. **Vehicle Maximum
Length:** None.

## TO GET THERE

From junction Maine Turnpike and Rte. 109,
exit 2, go east 1.5 mi. on Rte. 109, then north
0.4 mi. on Rte. 1; campground is on the right.

## WELLS

### Wells Beach Resort Campground

1000 Post Rd., Wells 04090. T: (207) 646-7570
(800) 640-2267 (reservations); www.wells-
beach.com.

 ★★★★           ★★★

Beauty: ★★          Site Privacy: ★★★
Spaciousness: ★★★     Quiet: ★★
Security: ★★★         Cleanliness: ★★★★
Insect Control: ★★★    Facilities: ★★★★

This is one of the nicest campgrounds in the
popular Wells Beach area, boasting super clean
facilities, modern hookups and level sites, and
plenty of amenities for kids and grownups
alike— all this in the heart of Maine's southern
coastal resort area. What you don't find at the
campground, is within easy walking distance:
fast food franchises, local restaurants, movie theaters, factory outlet shops, beaches, and more.
We like the poolside laundry with an outdoor
sitting area and the small fitness room for early
morning workouts. There's a choice of open and
shaded sites; tent sites come with water, electric
and cable TV and are set in the back, flanked by
trees. Don't expect much privacy or quiet; it's a
busy, activity-oriented place, swarming with
southern coastal Maine tourists and vacationing
families.

## BASICS

**Operated By:** Griffin family. **Open:** May
15–Oct. 15. **Site Assignment:** Reservations suggested, $80 deposit for stays of 3 days or less,
$150 deposit for 4 days or more, in full for holi-
day stays, 14-day cancellation policy w/ a $10
service charge; MC, V, D, no checks. **Registration:** At office. **Fee:** Full hookups (50 amp), $46;
(20, 30) amp, $41; water, electric & cable, $38.50,
summer weekends may be higher, based on 2
people; additional person, ages 4 & older, $6.
**Parking:** At site, 1 vehicle per site.

## FACILITIES

**Number of RV Sites:** 200. **Number of Tent-
Only Sites:** 12. **Hookups:** Water, electric, sewer
(20, 30, 50 amps), cable TV, modem. **Each Site:**
Picnic table, fire ring. **Dump Station:** Yes. **Laundry:** Yes. **Pay Phone:** Yes. **Rest Rooms and
Showers:** Yes. **Fuel:** No. **Propane:** No. **Internal
Roads:** Gravel, dirt (good). **RV Service:** No.
**Market:** Wells (0.5 mi). **Restaurant:** No. **General Store:** Yes. **Vending:** Yes. **Swimming Pool:**
Yes. **Playground:** Yes. **Other:** Fitness center, rec
hall, sports fields., 18-hole mini-golf course, pavilion, Wells Trolley Car stop. **Activities:** Swimming, bocce ball, mini-golf, volleyball, basketball,

horseshoes. **Nearby Attractions:** Old Orchard Beach, Wells Harbor, Ogunquit, Kennebunkport, southern coast parks & beaches, Portland. **Additional Information:** Wells Chamber of Commerce, 136 Post Rd., Rte. 1, Wells, ME 04090 (207) 646-2451; www.wellschamber.org.

## RESTRICTIONS

**Pets:** Must be on a leash, never left unattended. Pets are not allowed on tent sites. **Fires:** In grills, stoves, & fire rings only. **Alcoholic Beverages:** At site only. **Vehicle Maximum Length:** None.

## To Get There

From junction Maine Turnpike and Rte. 109 (exit 2), go east 1.5 mi. on Rte. 109, then south 1.4 mi. on Rte. 1; campground is on the right.

## WISCASSET

### Chewonki Campgrounds

P.O. Box 261, Wiscasset 04578. T: (207) 882-7426.

| 🚐 ★★★★ | ⛺ ★★★★ |
|---|---|
| Beauty: ★★★★★ | Site Privacy: ★★ |
| Spaciousness: ★★★★ | Quiet: ★★ |
| Security: ★★★ | Cleanliness: ★★★★ |
| Insect Control: ★★ | Facilities: ★★★★ |

Wiscasset calls itself "Maine's Prettiest Village." If you'd like to check out the veracity of that statement, or simply want a pleasant, centralized base for exploring mid-coast Maine, consider this inviting campground. Run by the Brackett family for 25 years, and currently managed by sisters Ann and Pamela, Chewonki Campgrounds overlooks a saltwater inlet of Montsweag Bay. It's a really pretty spot, with rolling hillsides leading to saltmarsh and sea. Watery nooks and crannies beckon paddlers. (When we visited, a large group of kayakers were tent-camping here.) The grassy sites are spacious, with mature trees providing a measure of privacy for some. Sites 10, 10A, and 10B (no hookups) are right on the water, but the best views, we think, are from sites 13 through 16 (water and electricity), overlooking the saltmarsh. Flower plantings add to the sense that this campground is well cared-for; plus, everything from the saltwater-filtered pool area to the rest rooms are super-clean. A downside here: there's a small airport nearby, so you're bound to hear aircraft overhead during the day. By night, they stop flying, so it's peaceful. One look at the star-filled sky, and you'll feel far from the urban hustle and bustle.

## BASICS

**Operated By:** Pamela D. Brackett & Ann Brackett Beck. **Open:** Mid-May–mid-Oct. **Site Assignment:** Reservations recommended. 1-month advance booking in July & Aug. recommended. $25 deposit for stays of 3 days or less; $50 deposit for stays of 4 or more days. Refunds for cancellation w/ 2-week notice, minus $10 service fee. **Registration:** At office. **Fee:** $25–$35 for 2 adults & their unmarried children under 21 years of age. V, MC. **Parking:** At site.

## FACILITIES

**Number of RV Sites:** 47. **Number of Tent-Only Sites:** 0. **Hookups:** Water, electric (20, 30 amps), sewer. **Each Site:** Picnic table, fire ring. **Dump Station:** Yes. **Laundry:** No. **Pay Phone:** Yes. **Rest Rooms and Showers:** Yes, coin-op. **Fuel:** No. **Propane:** No. **Internal Roads:** Gravel, in good condition. **RV Service:** No. **Market:** 2 mi. north. **Restaurant:** 1.5 mi. south. **General Store:** Yes. **Vending:** No. **Swimming Pool:** Yes. **Playground:** Yes. **Other:** Rec hall, tennis courts, boat ramp (for small craft). **Activities:** Boating (canoe & kayak rentals), swimming, volleyball, croquet, nature walk, one-hole golf course. **Nearby Attractions:** Historic village of Wiscasset, Pemaquid Point lighthouse, art museums, Old Jail, boat cruises, deep-sea fishing, antique shops, flea markets. **Additional Information:** Wiscasset Regional Business Assoc., (207) 882-4600; www.wiscassetmaine.com.

## RESTRICTIONS

**Pets:** Must be leashed, quiet, & cleaned up after. Must not be left unattended. **Fires:** In fire rings only. **Alcoholic Beverages:** At sites only. **Vehicle Maximum Length:** None. **Other:** 3-day min. stay on holidays.

## To Get There

From Maine Turnpike, take exit 9, Rte. 95 and Rte. 1 to Bath. Follow 7 mi. to Rte. 144, then turn right. Follow signs to campground, 1.5 mi. on right.

## YORK HARBOR

### Libby's Oceanside Camp

Rte. 1A, P.O. Box 40, York Harbor 03911. T: (207) 363-4171; F: (207) 363-5375; www.libbysoceancamping.com.

🚐 ★★★★            ⛺ ★★

Beauty: ★★★★         Site Privacy: ★★
Spaciousness: ★★       Quiet: ★★★
Security: ★★★         Cleanliness: ★★★★★
Insect Control: ★★★★   Facilities: ★★★

Never mind that the sites are a bit tight and that you won't have much privacy: this campground has one of the finest pieces of real estate on the southern coast. Just down the road are multi-million dollar houses; their owners don't have any better views than campers at Libby's. The campground boasts 1,100 feet of ocean frontage, with unsurpassed views of beaches, harbors, coves, and open ocean. On clear days, you can see Nubble Lighthouse, one of the most photographed sights in Maine. There are 45 oceanfront sites. Many are taken by seasonal renters but the owners have been freeing up more and more each year for the transient crowd. There's access to a rocky beach on one end of the campground, a great place for tidepooling at low tide. At high tide, locals come down with their fishing rods. When we were there, they were casting for stripers from the beach. When you've had enough of "roughing it," head to upscale York Harbor or nearby Ogunquit for gallery hopping and gourmet meals.

### BASICS

**Operated By:** Davidson family. **Open:** May 15–Oct. 15. **Site Assignment:** Reservations accepted for 1 week stays only, Sunday–Sunday; shorter stays are first come, first served. $100 deposit for each week reserved, 14-day cancellation policy; MC, V, D, no checks. **Registration:** At office. **Fee:** Oceanfront sites, $52; all other sites, $42; 50 amp, $2; cable TV, $1.50, based on 2 adults & 2 children under 16, or 3 adults (all sites include sewer, water & 30 amp electric). **Parking:** At site.

### FACILITIES

**Number of RV Sites:** 85. **Number of Tent-Only Sites:** 10. **Hookups:** Water, sewer, electric (20, 30, 50 amps), cable TV. **Each Site:** Picnic table. **Dump Station:** No. **Laundry:** No. **Pay Phone:** Yes. **Rest Rooms and Showers:** Yes. **Fuel:** No. **Propane:** No. **Internal Roads:** Gravel, dirt (good). **RV Service:** No. **Market:** York Harbor (1 mi). **Restaurant:** No. **General Store:** No. **Vending:** Yes. **Swimming Pool:** No. **Playground:** No. **Other:** Hot tub, ocean frontage, beach, activity room. **Activities:** Swimming, saltwater fishing, beachcombing, tidepooling. **Nearby Attractions:** Yok Harbor, York beaches, southern coast parks & beaches, Portsmouth. **Additional Information:** Yorks Chamber of Commerce, One Stonewall Ln., York, ME 03909 (207) 363-4422 (800) 639-2442; www.yorkme.org.

### RESTRICTIONS

**Pets:** Must be on a leash, never left unattended. No pets allowed on the beach; only 2 pets allowed per site. **Fires:** In grills, stoves, & fire rings only. **Alcoholic Beverages:** At site only. **Vehicle Maximum Length:** None.

### TO GET THERE

From I-95, exit 4, go east 0.3 mi. on connector road, then south 0.3 mi. on Rte. 1, then north 3 mi. on Rte. 1A; campground is on the right.

# Massachusetts

What's really special about camping in Massachusetts? No matter where you choose to settle in for the night, you're never too far from great places to sight-see, museum-hop, and soak up the city scene. It takes less than four hours to drive the width of the state—unless you're amazingly unlucky in traffic—so you could wake up in a woodsy rural campground in the **Berkshire Hills** and arrive in **Boston** in time for lunch. Tip: We'd ditch the rig first, and take the car into the city—all the better to navigate those cow paths-turned-cobblestone streets! Happily, there are several campgrounds within a 30-mile radius of the city. Some offer bus tours of Boston, while others are located near the commuter rail line, should you choose not to brave city traffic.

While Massachusetts may not have a huge number of commercial campgrounds, those that do exist are generally clean and well-kept. Also, they tend to be clustered near desirable places to visit. Example: Cape Ann Camp Site, in **Gloucester,** overlooks the salt marshes of the North Shore and is a bike ride away from a lovely ocean beach; close by are fishing villages and art colonies, whale watch tours and sunset boat cruises. All in all, it's a dandy place to enjoy some seaside ambience. **Cape Cod** is home to numerous campgrounds, some chock-full of amenities, others all swaying sea oats and salt air. Even tony **Martha's Vineyard** (shh!) is home to a campground. Besides being surrounded by some of the most dazzling scenery in New England, campers on the Cape and Islands are enjoying it all at a bargain (a word not heard frequently in these parts!)

Fact is, some of the most prime real estate in Massachusetts is open to campers. Twenty-eight state parks offer camping, and the settings are truly spectacular. Settle in for the night behind a sand dune at **Horseneck Beach State Reservation,** just steps away from **Buzzard's Bay.** Farther north, **Salisbury Beach** offers nearly 500 campsites, hugging the Atlantic Coast. These are wildly popular, so reserve early; reserve a site at any state campground by calling the same toll-free number. For a totally different experience, check out the hidden gems in the Western part of the state, the arts-and-theater mecca known as the Berkshires. Besides all the culture you could ask for, this region offers wonderful hiking and paddling, and glorious state parks. Deeply wooded, dotted with sapphire ponds, these campgrounds are a great choice for tent campers or RVers with self-contained units, who consider a pristine natural setting to be the ultimate amenity.

The camping season in Massachusetts generally runs from Memorial Day to Columbus Day.

*The following facilities accept payment in checks or cash only:*

Coastal Acres Campground, Provincetown

Dune's Edge Campground, Provincetown

Historic Valley Campground, N. Adams

The Old Holbrook Place, Sutton

# Campground Profiles

## BELLINGHAM

### Circle CG Farm

131 North Main St., Bellingham 02019. T: (508) 966-1136; www.hometown.aol.com/cgfrmcamp; cgfrm camp@aol.com.

 ★★★     ★

Beauty: ★★                  Site Privacy: ★★
Spaciousness: ★★★       Quiet: ★★★
Security: ★★★★★         Cleanliness: ★★★★★
Insect Control: ★★★       Facilities: ★★★

This Western-themed campground is situated smack-dab in the "golden triangle" of Boston, Providence, and Worcester. Depending on your luck with traffic, it's 35 or 45 minutes from Boston, and 45 minutes from Providence, Rhode Island. But you might feel like you're in the heart of the Smokies, what with the Opry Hall (a funky rec hall with a fake jail), horse corral, and rest rooms designated "Cowboys" and "Cowgirls." Despite the petting animals—horses, a burro, goats—this isn't a particularly child-friendly place. There's no playground and, as a long-time camper put it, "Just not much for kids here." One of the pools is designated for seniors only, while an adult game area is marked for ages 15 and up. The presence of a beauty parlor and guided bus tours provide more evidence that this place is geared to grown-ups. Campsites are arrayed in a series of loops around an open, grassy field; side loops are wooded. Tall pines don't provide much buffer between sites, though. Nicely shaded RV sites (21S through 24S) are set along Six Gun Rd.; on the frog pond, site 91 is a winner. Tents are set along TeePee Ln., a low-lying area that could get very muddy.

### BASICS

**Operated By:** Rob & Linda Daley. **Open:** All year. **Site Assignment:** Reservations suggested. Site preference noted, but not guaranteed. One night's fee required for deposit, check or credit card OK. Refunds issued for cancellation if received one week prior to scheduled arrival date, minus $5 service charge. **Registration:** At office. **Fee:** $31–$33; rate based on two people. Additional person, $5; children under age 1 free. V, MC. **Parking:** At site.

### FACILITIES

**Number of RV Sites:** 138. **Number of Tent-Only Sites:** 20. **Hookups:** Water, electric (20, 30, 50 amps), sewer. **Each Site:** Picnic table, fireplace or grill. **Dump Station:** Yes. **Laundry:** Yes. **Pay Phone:** Yes. **Rest Rooms and Showers:** Yes. **Fuel:** No. **Propane:** Yes. **Internal Roads:** Paved, in good condition. **RV Service:** No. **Market:** 1 mi. north. **Restaurant:** 1 mi. north. **General Store:** Yes. **Vending:** No. **Swimming Pool:** Yes (2). **Playground:** No. **Other:** Mini-golf, beauty parlor, exercise room, rec room. **Activities:** Guided tours to Boston & Cape Cod, planned activities, fishing, swimming, horseshoes, shuffle-board, bocce, petting farm. **Nearby Attractions:** Old Sturbridge Village living history museum, New England Science Center, Ecotarium, Worcester Art Museum, outlet shopping. **Additional Information:** Central Massachusetts Tourist Council, (508) 755-7400; www.worcester.org.

### RESTRICTIONS

**Pets:** Must be leashed & cleaned up after. Must not be left unattended. Not allowed in or around buildings or pools. **Fires:** In steel rings, 6 p.m.–11:30 p.m. only. **Alcoholic Beverages:** Yes. **Vehicle Maximum Length:** 45 ft. **Other:** Three day min. stay on holiday weekends.

## To Get There

Take I-95 to Rte. 495 North to exit 18 (Rte. 126), heading south. Bear left at the light, where Rte. 126 splits. Follow Rte. 126 south 1 mi. to the campground entrance on the left.

## BOURNE

### Bay View Campgrounds

260 MacArthur Blvd., Rte. 28, Bourne 02532. T: (508) 759-7610; www.bayviewcampground.com.

 ★★★★           ★★

| | |
|---|---|
| Beauty: ★★★★ | Site Privacy: ★★★ |
| Spaciousness: ★★★★ | Quiet: ★★ |
| Security: ★★★★ | Cleanliness: ★★★★★ |
| Insect Control: ★★★ | Facilities: ★★★★★ |

Located on the Upper Cape, just beyond the Bourne Bridge (one of two bridges that connect Cape Cod to the mainland), Bay View is about 60 percent seasonal. Don't let that put you off, though. This is a great spot for RV campers (tenters might find its location near the busy roadway a bit noisy) who want to enjoy the Cape Cod experience without driving the length of the Cape. They also sell tickets here for ferry boats to Martha's Vineyard and Nantucket, a nice convenience. Campsites are level, spacious, and semi-shaded; sites 155 through 160 are especially pleasant, and backed by woods. Number 59 is another good choice, big and level. We'd skip site 169, an elevated site with views of other RV's roofs. There's plenty to do here, from daily planned activities to a really elaborate, state-of-the-art arcade. Nice touches make a difference, including vanity lights around mirrors and a baby changing table in the ladies' room, and good signage and trash bag dispensers throughout the campground. One quibble: the $10 per person guest fee is pretty pricey. Chalk it up to the desirability of the Cape.

## BASICS

**Operated By:** Bay View Campground Inc. **Open:** May 1–Oct. 15. **Site Assignment:** Reservations recommended. Call to reserve after Jan. 10; secure reservation with a non-refundable deposit on Visa or Mastercard. If stay is less than one week, a deposit of one night's fee is required. Otherwise, deposit is generally one night's fee per week of stay. Full balance is required upon arrival in cash, traveler's checks or credit card. **Registration:** At office. **Fee:** $29–$35. Rate based on two adults. Additional children under age 18, $2–$3; additional adult, $8–$10. V, MC. **Parking:** At site.

## FACILITIES

**Number of RV Sites:** 425. **Number of Tent-Only Sites:** 0. **Hookups:** Water, electric (20, 30 amps), sewer, cable TV, modem (in office). **Each Site:** Picnic table, fireplace. **Dump Station:** Yes. **Laundry:** Yes. **Pay Phone:** Yes. **Rest Rooms and Showers:** Yes, coin-op. **Fuel:** No. **Propane:** Yes. **Internal Roads:** Paved, in good condition. **RV Service:** No. **Market:** 3 mi. north. **Restaurant:** Yes. **General Store:** Yes (snack bar). **Vending:** Yes. **Swimming Pool:** Yes (2–3). **Playground:** Yes. **Other:** Rec hall, tennis courts. **Activities:** Swimming, tennis, volleyball, basketball, shuffleboard, horseshoes, ball field, planned activities. **Nearby Attractions:** Cape Cod beaches, boating, fishing, antique shops, golf, scenic bike paths, ferries to Martha's Vineyard & Nantucket. **Additional Information:** Cape Cod Chamber of Commerce, (888) 33-CAPECOD or (508) 362-3225; www.capecodchamber.org.

## RESTRICTIONS

**Pets:** Must be leashed, quiet, & cleaned up after. Current rabies certificate required upon request. **Fires:** At sites only. **Alcoholic Beverages:** Yes. **Vehicle Maximum Length:** 40 ft. **Other:** Two-night min. stay required on weekends between Memorial Day & Labor Day. Three-night min. stay on holidays. Seven-night min. on July 4th week.

## To Get There

Take I-195 or I-495 to Rte. 25, go over Bourne Bridge and continue 1 mi. on Rte. 28 south. Campground entrance is on the right.

## BREWSTER

### Nickerson State Park

3488 Main St., Rte. 6A, Brewster 02631. T: (508) 896-3491; www.state.ma.us/dem/parks/nick.htm.

🚐 ★★      ▲ ★★★★

Beauty: ★★★★★    Site Privacy: ★★★
Spaciousness: ★★★★    Quiet: ★★★★
Security: ★★★★    Cleanliness: ★★★
Insect Control: ★★★★    Facilities: ★★★

Self-sufficient, energetic types will adore this state park, located in the mid-Cape area of Cape Cod. You won't find hookups, but you will find acres of piney woods, more reminiscent of the Berkshires than the Cape. The woodsy landscape is dotted with eight freshwater kettle ponds, formed when glaciers retreated from the Cape more than 10,000 years ago. Ponds are stocked with land-locked trout and salmon; marked bike trails connect with 25-mile Cape Cod Rail Trail (rail trail users can park for free). Deep-blue Flax Pond, with a sandy beach, is great for swimming and boating. Hiking trails lead to the beach. For the winter tenting crowd, the park offers yurts (available all year). Campsites are grouped in seven areas. Area 4 is heavily used, since it's close to the beach; sites 41 through 51 (odd numbers) are pretty, and backed by pines. Area 3 is hilly, and not as desirable as Area 2, which boasts wooded water views (especially sites 112 through 120). You'd think the farthest-back camping areas, 6, 6X, and 7 would be quietest, but you'd be wrong; that tends to be Party Central in summer.

### BASICS

**Operated By:** Massachusetts State Parks & Forests. **Open:** All year. **Site Assignment:** Reservations recommended. Reserve up to six months in advance by calling ReserveAmerica at (877) 1-CAMP-MA or online at www.reservamerica.com. 20% of sites are non-reservable, & available for walk-in campers. To change arrival or departure date, or site type, call at least three dayas prior to arrival date. $10 cancellation/transfer fee. No refunds for amounts less than $5. **Registration:** At headquarters. **Fee:** $5–$30, V, MC. **Parking:** At sites or designated parking lots.

### FACILITIES

**Number of RV Sites:** 420. **Number of Tent-Only Sites:** 0. **Hookups:** None. **Each Site:** Picnic table, fireplace. **Dump Station:** Yes. **Laundry:** No. **Pay Phone:** Yes. **Rest Rooms and Showers:** Yes. **Fuel:** No. **Propane:** No. **Internal Roads:** Paved, in good condition. **RV Service:** No. **Market:** 5 mi. east. **Restaurant:** Yes (snack bar). **General Store:** Yes. **Vending:** No. **Swimming Pool:** No. **Playground:** Yes. **Other:** Nature center, amphitheater, boat rentals, bike rentals. **Activities:** Pond swimming, fishing (catch & release) in Higgins Pond, bicycling, boating, hiking. **Nearby Attractions:** Golf, biking (Cape Cod Rail Trail), ocean swimming, pond swimming, boating, tennis, antiquing. **Additional Information:** Cape Cod Chamber of Commerce, (508) 862-0700 or (888) 33-CAPECOD; www.capecodchamber.org.

### RESTRICTIONS

**Pets:** Must be leashed & cleaned up after. Must not be left unattended. Proof of rabies vaccination required. Not allowed on Flax Pond swimming beach. **Fires:** In fire rings only. **Alcoholic Beverages:** Not permitted. **Vehicle Maximum Length:** 35 ft. **Other:** Must renew by 8 p.m. the night prior to your scheduled check-out. Maximum stay is 14 cumulative days between Memorial Day & Labor Day.

### TO GET THERE

Take Rte. 6 east to Exit 12. Go left off the ramp. Park is approximately 1 mi. ahead on the left.

## BREWSTER

### Shady Knoll Campground

1708 Rte. 6A, Brewster 02631. T: (508) 896-3002; www.capecamping.com.

🚐 ★★      ▲ ★★

Beauty: ★★    Site Privacy: ★★
Spaciousness: ★★    Quiet: ★★★
Security: ★★★★    Cleanliness: ★★★★
Insect Control: ★★★★    Facilities: ★★★★

Location, location, location. This low-key family campground is in mid-Cape, central to Cape Cod attractions, including bay swimming (just a mile away) and the Cape Cod Rail Trail for biking. It has a wholesome feel (maybe because of all the rosy-cheeked cyclists who converge here in summer.) A nice-looking lodge houses the camp store, game room, and small lounge with a fireplace and TV, where they show movies every night during the summer. The (free) showers and bathrooms are roomy and modern. And what's not to like about a place that sells Hawaiian shirts in the campstore? Campsites are mostly shaded, on gravel. Seasonal sites are set apart. Tent sites are clustered in a corner, and fairly exposed. Most appealing tent sites are sites 93 and 94, with plenty of space and no neighbors nearby. RV sites 67 and 68 are level and wooded, while site 82 is set apart by itself for maximum privacy. We'd skip sites 51 through 52, exposed to a busy thoroughfare. Perhaps not as pretty a place as nearby Sweetwater Forest (see listing), but not bad, either.

## BASICS

**Operated By:** Dave & Donna Nussdorfer. **Open:** May 15–Oct. 15. **Site Assignment:** Reservations recommended. 50% deposit required for stays of 5 days or more; all other reservations must be prepaid. No refunds without 14 days' notice. $10 service charge applies to cancellations. Checks OK for advance reservations. **Registration:** At office. **Fee:** $30–$37 for two people; extra unmarried child age 6-18, $2 per night; extra adult, $7.50; age 5 & under free. V, MC, D. **Parking:** At site.

## FACILITIES

**Number of RV Sites:** 100. **Number of Tent-Only Sites:** 0. **Hookups:** Water, electric (30 amps), sewer. **Each Site:** Picnic table, fireplace. **Dump Station:** Yes. **Laundry:** Yes. **Pay Phone:** Yes. **Rest Rooms and Showers:** Yes. **Fuel:** No. **Propane:** Yes. **Internal Roads:** Gravel, in good condition. **RV Service:** No. **Market:** Just outside campground entrance. **Restaurant:** 1 mi. east on Rte. 6A. **General Store:** Yes. **Vending:** No. **Swimming Pool:** No. **Playground:** Yes. **Other:** Rec room. **Activities:** Bicycling, ball field, nightly movies. **Nearby Attractions:** Golf, biking (Cape Cod Rail Trail), ocean swimming, pond swimming, boating, tennis, antiquing. **Additional Information:** Cape Cod Chamber of Commerce, (508)

862-0700 or (888) 33-CAPECOD; www.capecod-chamber.org.

## RESTRICTIONS

**Pets:** Must be leashed & cleaned up after. Must be taken w/you when you leave the campground. Use pet walk located in storage area. Dogs not permitted on beaches. **Fires:** In fireplaces only. **Alcoholic Beverages:** Yes. **Vehicle Maximum Length:** 32 ft. **Other:** Some weekends in July & Aug. may require three-night min. reservation. July 4th week requires four nights.

## TO GET THERE

From Sagamore Bridge, follow Rte. 6 to Exit 11. Turn right onto Rte. 137 towards Brewster. Follow Rte. 137 to the end. Campground is directly across Rte. 6A.

## BREWSTER

### Sweetwater Forest

676 Rte. 124, P.O. Box 1797, Brewster 02631. T: (508) 896-3773; F: (508) 896-2013; www.sweetwaterforest.com; sweeth2orv@aol.com.

| 🚐 ★★★ | 🅰 ★★★★ |
|---|---|
| Beauty: ★★★★ | Site Privacy: ★★★ |
| Spaciousness: ★★★★ | Quiet: ★★★★ |
| Security: ★★★★ | Cleanliness: ★★★ |
| Insect Control: ★★★ | Facilities: ★★★ |

Conveniently located in a desirable area of the mid-Cape (Cape Cod), this is the most inviting private campground around. (Brewster is also home to terrific Nickerson State Park.) It has a pleasant feel; campers are greeted with tumbles of blue hydrangea and well-tended plantings, and a winding entrance road skirting oak trees and lofty pines. Set amidst 60 acres of woodland, the property includes Snow's Pond, with a fishing dock and small swimming area. For cyclists, the best feature here may well be the bike path connecting with the Cape Cod Rail Trail, a paved, 25-mile bike path. Rental rowboats and canoes add to the recreation possibilities. Families will have a good time here. Seasonal sites are grouped together to the left of the entrance. Among the rest, sites C6 through 10 (electric and water) are big, level, and wooded, while site C28B is so big, you could put a house on it. Some tent sites are set alongside a retired cranberry bog. Sites B13 through 16 are close to a rest room, and a short walk to the pond.

## BASICS

**Operated By:** Jim Rylander. **Open:** All year. **Site Assignment:** Reservations recommended; can reserve one year in advance & on-line. $30 deposit required. $15 refund if cancellation occurs two weeks in advance of scheduled arrival. **Registration:** At office. **Fee:** $18–$25 for two adults, plus unmarried children under age 18. V, MC, D. **Parking:** At site.

## FACILITIES

**Number of RV Sites:** 250. **Number of Tent-Only Sites:** 0. **Hookups:** Water, electric (30 amps), sewer, cable TV. **Each Site:** Picnic table, fireplace. **Dump Station:** Yes. **Laundry:** No. **Pay Phone:** Yes. **Rest Rooms and Showers:** Yes. **Fuel:** No. **Propane:** Yes. **Internal Roads:** Gravel, in good condition. **RV Service:** Yes. **Market:** 3 mi. east. **Restaurant:** 5 mi. east. **General Store:** Yes. **Vending:** Yes. **Swimming Pool:** No. **Playground:** Yes. **Other:** Rec lodge, mini-golf. **Activities:** Boating (rowboat & canoe rentals), hiking, basketball, biking (access to Cape Cod Rail Trail), horseshoes, fishing, planned activities. **Nearby Attractions:** Ocean beaches, freshwater swimming, boating, golf, antiques, Cape Cod Museum of Natural History, charter boat fishing trips, whale-watching cruises. **Additional Information:** Cape Cod Chamber of Commerce, (508) 862-0700 or (888) 33-CAPECOD; www.capecodchamber.org.

## RESTRICTIONS

**Pets:** Must be leashed. Must not be left unattended. Proof of rabies vaccination required. Dog boarding service available. **Fires:** In fireplaces only. **Alcoholic Beverages:** Yes. **Vehicle Maximum Length:** None. **Other:** Two-night min.; three-night min. on holidays.

## TO GET THERE

From Sagamore Bridge, enter Rte. 6. Follow Rte. 6 to Exit 10, Rte. 124. Turn left off ramp, heading north toward Brewster on Rte. 124. Follow Rte. 124 for 2.8 mi. Look for the sign on the left to the campground entrance.

## BRIMFIELD

## Quinebaug Cove Campsite

49 East Brimfield-Holland Rd., Brimfield 01010. T: (413) 245-9525; www.quinebaugcove.com.

🚐 ★★★                    ⛺ ★★

| | |
|---|---|
| Beauty: ★★ | Site Privacy: ★★ |
| Spaciousness: ★★★ | Quiet: ★★★ |
| Security: ★★★ | Cleanliness: ★★★ |
| Insect Control: ★★★ | Facilities: ★★★ |

When someone asks, "Are they biting?" at a campground, they're usually referring to mosquitoes. Not here. At Quinebaug Cove Campsite, avid anglers fish for trout, bass, pickerel, Northern Pike, and perch. (Fishing licenses are available at a nearby Wal-Mart; bait, they'll sell you right here.) The campground, about 10 miles west of Sturbridge, abuts the Brimfield Reservoir and Long Pond. Besides fishing, there's a five-mile canoe trail and a small sandy beach with a swimming area. About 95 percent of the campers here are families. Quinebaug Cove is a privately-owned co-op, or camping club, although one need not be a member to camp here. Set on a series of loop roads, some of the campsites are open, others are shaded. The nicest sites, as you'd expect, are on the waterfront. Sites 908 to 916B (even numbers), with water and electric, are near the beach, as are tent sites 216 to 224. Getting around the campground can be tricky; signage is poor. Tent sites are grouped together, on the lower part of the campground, convenient to the snack bar, rec hall, and pool area. Located in a rural area, the campground offers a quiet setting, except (we're guessing) during July 4th week, when a biker's group shows up for their annual camp-out.

## BASICS

**Operated By:** Board of Directors. **Open:** All year. **Site Assignment:** Reserve by phone or on web site. Reservations accepted after Jan. 2. Two-night min. on summer weekends; three-night min. on holiday weekends. No refunds for cancellation of campsite with less than seven days' notice. Cancellation fee, $10, V, MC, D. **Registration:** At office. **Fee:** $26–$32. Rates based on two people per night. Extra adult, $6. Extra child (age 3–18), $3. **Parking:** At site or in visitor parking lot.

## FACILITIES

**Number of RV Sites:** 114. **Number of Tent-Only Sites:** 11. **Hookups:** Water, electric (20, 30 amps), sewer. **Each Site:** Picnic table, fireplace. **Dump Station:** Yes. **Laundry:** Yes. **Pay Phone:** Yes. **Rest Rooms and Showers:** Yes. **Fuel:** No. **Propane:** Yes. **Internal Roads:** Paved & gravel, in fair condition. **RV Service:** No. **Market:** 5 mi. west in Palmer. **Restaurant:** Yes. **General Store:** Yes. **Vending:** Yes. **Swimming Pool:** Yes. **Playground:** Yes. **Other:** Basketball court, rec hall, boat ramp. **Activities:** Boating (rental canoes & rowboats), swimming (freshwater pond & pool), volleyball, basketball, bocce, shuffleboard, basketball, hayrides, lake fishing, planned activities. **Nearby Attractions:** Old Sturbridge Village living history museum, Six Flags New England theme park, Brimfield Antique Flea Market. **Additional Information:** www.quinebaugcove.com.

## RESTRICTIONS

**Pets:** Must be quiet & leashed at all times. Do not leave pets unattended. Clean up after pets. Must have proof of rabies vaccination. No more than 2 pets per site. **Fires:** In fireplaces only. **Alcoholic Beverages:** Yes. **Vehicle Maximum Length:** 35 ft. **Other:** No electric heaters. No admittance to campground after 9 p.m. Maximum 2 cars & 8 people per site.

## TO GET THERE

From the junction of I-84 and Rte. 20, go 3.5 mi. west on Rte. 20, then 0.25 mi. south on Brimfield Rd. Campground entrance is on the left.

## BROOKFIELD

### Lakeside Resort

13 Hobbs Ave., Brookfield 01506. T: (508) 867-2737 or (800) 320-CAMP; www.camplakeside.com.

| 🚐 ★★★ | 🏕 ★★ |
|---|---|
| Beauty: ★★ | Site Privacy: ★ |
| Spaciousness: ★★ | Quiet: ★★★ |
| Security: ★★★★ | Cleanliness: ★★ |
| Insect Control: ★★★ | Facilities: ★★ |

Located just north of Sturbridge in the village of Brookfield, this campground is set on a 540-acre lake. If you agree with the sentiment, "You're not really camping unless you've got your laptop and cable TV," (said by one of the campground's owners, only partially in jest), you'll be very content here. A wilderness escape, it's not. A couple of drawbacks: Grounds and facilities could benefit from some sprucing up, plus the much-ballyhooed lake is actually across the street, reachable via footpath through a gate. Private homes are set right beside the campground's waterfront clubhouse. Campsites are mostly grassy and level (some are pull-thru.) Look for shaded sites on the perimeter of the property. About one-third are seasonal. Sites beginning with letter 'J' are the most remote, but skip J17 and 18 (near the main entrance.) Most campsites are about 40 feet wide, but packed closely together, making this place a better bet for RVs than for tents. Weekend and holiday activities—scavenger hunts and crafts for the kids, and cook-outs, live music, dances, family movies—enhance the resort-like atmosphere.

## BASICS

**Operated By:** Lakeside Condominiums. **Open:** Apr. 15–Oct. 15. Limited winter camping available by registration. **Site Assignment:** Reservations recommended. Deposit required. **Registration:** At check-in/guest services building. **Fee:** $25-$28 for two persons. Extra fee may be charged on holidays. V, MC, D, AMEX. **Parking:** At site.

## FACILITIES

**Number of RV Sites:** 120. **Number of Tent-Only Sites:** 0. **Hookups:** Water, electric (20, 30, 50 amps), sewer, cable TV, modem. **Each Site:** Picnic table, fireplace. **Dump Station:** Yes. **Laundry:** Yes. **Pay Phone:** Yes. **Rest Rooms and Showers:** Yes, coin op. **Fuel:** No. **Propane:** Yes. **Internal Roads:** Gravel, good condition. **RV Service:** No. **Market:** 1 mi. north. **Restaurant:** 1 mi. north. **General Store:** Yes. **Vending:** Yes. **Swimming Pool:** Yes. **Playground:** Yes. **Other:** Rec hall, club house, boat moorings. **Activities:** Boating (paddle boat & canoe rentals), swimming, fishing, basketball, shuffleboard, volleyball, arcade games, planned activities. **Nearby Attractions:** Old Sturbridge Village living history museum, Brimfield Antique Flea Markets, golf. **Additional Information:** www.camplakeside.com.

### RESTRICTIONS

**Pets:** Must be quiet, & on leash only. Must not be left unattended. Must be cleaned up after. Do not walk pets in or around recreational facilities. **Fires:** Fireplaces only. **Alcoholic Beverages:** Sites only. **Vehicle Maximum Length:** None. **Other:** Reservations are not assured until confirmation & deposit are received.

### TO GET THERE

From junction of I-84 and Rte. 20, head east 2 mi. to Rte. 49. Go north to Rte. 9, then head west 3.9 mi. to Quaboag St. Take left 0.8 mi. to Hobbs Ave. Campground entrance is on the right.

## CHARLEMONT

### Country Aire Campground

P.O. Box 289, Charlemont 01339. T: (413) 625-2996; www.country-aire-com; dfinn@valinet.com.

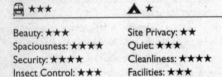

Beauty: ★★★
Spaciousness: ★★★★
Security: ★★★★
Insect Control: ★★★

Site Privacy: ★★
Quiet: ★★★
Cleanliness: ★★★★
Facilities: ★★★

Located in the scenic, outdoorsy Berkshire Hills ("The Berkshires") in Western Massachusetts, Country Aire Campground is a pleasant, if slightly quirky, home away from home. The campground is set behind a motel and golf course, on a wide, grassy meadow bordered by trees. The Berkshire Hills provide a colorful backdrop in autumn. The Deerfield River is right across the street, a favorite destination for fly-fishing, paddling, and rafting. Seasonal sites (numerous) are at the rear and perimeter of the property, while transients are grouped toward the front. Sites are grassy, with a few pull-thrus. The tenting area is located in a separate, nicely shaded spot, not far from the pool. If you want to be away from the crowd, ask for RV sites 27 to 30, or one of the two tent sites to the left (not right) of the property, near the hiking trail. But you'll end up hanging with fellow campers at the rec hall, where you can order a treat at the snack bar, shoot some pool, or catch up on the latest news. Try one of Country Aire's own private-label vanilla sodas or sign up for the Halloween-in-August party, when little gremlins go trick-or-treating at RVs. (See what we mean by quirky?)

### BASICS

**Operated By:** Doug & Nancy Finn. **Open:** May 1–Dec. 1. **Site Assignment:** Reservations recommended. Deposit of one nights' stay required. Refund w/cancellation if within 7 days of scheduled stay, minus $5 service charge. **Registration:** At office. **Fee:** $20–$25 for two adults/two children. Extra adult, $6; extra child, $3. V, MC. **Parking:** At sites & designated areas.

### FACILITIES

**Number of RV Sites:** 95. **Number of Tent-Only Sites:** 10. **Hookups:** Water, electric (20, 30, 50 amps), sewer, modem. **Each Site:** Picnic table, fire ring. **Dump Station:** Yes. **Laundry:** Yes. **Pay Phone:** Yes. **Rest Rooms and Showers:** Yes, coin-op. **Fuel:** No. **Propane:** Yes. **Internal Roads:** Gravel, good condition. **RV Service:** No. **Market:** 2 mi. west, in Charlemont. **Restaurant:** Yes. **General Store:** Yes. **Vending:** No. **Swimming Pool:** Yes. **Playground:** Yes. **Other:** Game room, picnic pavilion. **Activities:** Basketball, horseshoes, pool table, planned activities. **Nearby Attractions:** Bridge of Flowers, antiques, whitewater rafting & kayaking (Zoar Outdoors). **Additional Information:** Berkshire Hills Visitors Bureau, (413) 443-9186 or (800) 237-5747; www.berkshires.org.

### RESTRICTIONS

**Pets:** Must be leashed, quiet, & cleaned up after. **Fires:** In fire rings only. **Alcoholic Beverages:** Yes. **Vehicle Maximum Length:** None. **Other:** Children under 16 must be accompanied by an adult while using the pool.

### TO GET THERE

From I-91, take exit 26, Rte. 2 west, for 13 mi. Campground is on the right, directly behind the Oxbow Motel & Restaurant.

## CHARLEMONT

### Mohawk Trail State Forest

P.O. Box 7, Rte. 2, Charlemont 01339. T: (413) 339-5504;
www.state.ma.us/dem/parks/mhwk.htm.

🚐 ★★  ⛺ ★★★★

| | |
|---|---|
| Beauty: ★★★★ | Site Privacy: ★★ |
| Spaciousness: ★★★ | Quiet: ★★ |
| Security: ★★★ | Cleanliness: ★★★ |
| Insect Control: ★★ | Facilities: ★★★ |

This rustic area, set in the Berkshire Hills in Western Massachusetts, is Bear Country. They've had bear sightings here, so it's wise to heed the advice on the bear flyer you get when you enter the park. The best campsites here are set on the banks of the Cold River. Snag one of these, and you can listen to the rushing water as you drift off to sleep (provided bear nightmares don't keep you awake). The sites are on gravel, and they are close together but buffered by trees. Campsites are set on two loops running alongside the river, with a little string of non-reservable sites at the end of the road. Of the non-reservable sites, numbers 15 through 22 are nice, and close to the river, while 18 and 41 are both good, roomy options for an RV. Sites 46 and 47 are dandy for tenters, with the advantage of an end-of-the-road location. The farther you head back from the river, though, the farther you get from Rte. 2 and the hum of traffic. Reserve a site numbered 23 through 35 if quiet, not water views, are your priority. The showers—just one set serves all, alas—are located near site 24. This is primarily a family camping area, but whitewater paddlers take over when the dam is released. Be sure to grab a trail map when you enter the park; this is a superb area for hiking, with good views from Totem Trail overlook.

### BASICS

**Operated By:** Massachusetts Forest & Park Service. **Open:** Mid-Apr.–mid-Oct. **Site Assignment:** Reservations recommended. Reserve up to six months in advance by calling ReserveAmerica at (877) 1-CAMP MA or on-line at www.reservamerica.com. Ten sites non-reservable, set aside for walk-ins on a first-come, first-served basis. To change arrival or departure date, or site type, call at least three days prior to arrival date. $10 cancellation/transfer fee. No refunds for amounts less than $5. **Registration:** At office. **Fee:** Massachusetts residents, $10; non-residents, $12. V, MC. **Parking:** At site.

### FACILITIES

**Number of RV Sites:** 56. **Number of Tent-Only Sites:** 0. **Hookups:** None. **Each Site:** Picnic table, fireplace. **Dump Station:** No. **Laundry:** No. **Pay Phone:** Yes. **Rest Rooms and Showers:** Yes. **Fuel:** No. **Propane:** No. **Internal Roads:** Gravel, in good condition. **RV Service:** No. **Market:** 4 mi. east, in Charlemont. **Restaurant:** 20–24 mi. east or west, in Greenfield or North Adams. **General Store:** No. **Vending:** Yes. **Swimming Pool:** Yes. **Playground:** No. **Activities:** Canoeing, picnicking, hiking, fishing, swimming, interpretive programs. **Nearby Attractions:** Mass MOCA (Museum of Contemporary Art), Clark Art Museum, Natural Bridge, Bridge of Flowers. **Additional Information:** Berkshire Hills Visitors Bureau, (413) 443-9186 or (800) 237-5747; www.berkshires.org.

### RESTRICTIONS

**Pets:** Must be leashed & cleaned up after. Must not be left unattended. Proof of rabies vaccination required. **Fires:** In fireplaces only. **Alcoholic Beverages:** No. **Vehicle Maximum Length:** 35 ft. **Other:** Maximum stay is 14 cumulative days between Memorial Day & Labor Day.

### TO GET THERE

From I-91, take Exit 26 (Rte. 2) west to Charlemont. Campground is 4 mi. west of Charlemont Center; entrance is on the right.

## CHESTER

### Walker Island Camping

No. 27 Rte. 20, Chester 01011. T: (413) 354-2295; shawn1221@aol.com.

🚐 ★★★★  ⛺ ★★

| | |
|---|---|
| Beauty: ★★★ | Site Privacy: ★★ |
| Spaciousness: ★★★ | Quiet: ★★★ |
| Security: ★★ | Cleanliness: ★★★ |
| Insect Control: ★★ | Facilities: ★★ |

This family-friendly campground is located in the Berkshire Hills region of Western Massachusetts. Dead-center in the place is, of all things, a small island, home to a mini golf course, a small beach, a slightly worse-for-wear kiddie playground, and a sports court for bocce, horseshoes, and shuffleboard. Trout-stocked Walker Brook flows around the island, and offers its own recreation possibilities, including fishing and tubing. The brook, abundant trees, and rocky ledges lend a serene aspect to an otherwise rather cluttery place. Campsites are set on three levels, becoming more "wild" the higher you go. On the upper level, campsites are tucked into ledges, offering plenty of seclusion. (Warning: the rest rooms are the non-flush type up there.) Site 68 is a super tent site if you like privacy, while RV sites 49 through 54, near the back entrance, are among the most inviting. There's a lot going on, plus kids everywhere, making this a very different scene than you'll encounter at one of the numerous state park camping areas in the region. Still, it's homey and easy-going.

## BASICS

**Operated By:** Shawn Myrick. **Open:** May 1–Oct. 31. **Site Assignment:** Reservations recommended. Deposit equal to one night's stay due w/ reservation. Deposits are refundable w/ min. of one week's notice. **Registration:** At office. **Fee:** $22–$27 for two people per night; extra adult is $5; extra child is $3. V, MC. **Parking:** At site.

## FACILITIES

**Number of RV Sites:** 70. **Number of Tent-Only Sites:** 15. **Hookups:** Water, electric (30 amps), sewer, cable TV. **Each Site:** Picnic table, fire ring. **Dump Station:** Yes. **Laundry:** Yes. **Pay Phone:** Yes. **Rest Rooms and Showers:** Yes. **Fuel:** No. **Propane:** Yes. **Internal Roads:** Gravel, in good conditon. **RV Service:** No. **Market:** 25 mi. east or west. **Restaurant:** 3 mi. east. **General Store:** No. **Vending:** No. **Swimming Pool:** Yes. **Playground:** Yes. **Other:** Rec hall, game room, mini golf. **Activities:** Swimming, mini golf, tubing, shuffleboard, hiking, fishing, planned activities. **Nearby Attractions:** Norman Rockwell Museum, Tanglewood (music), Jacob's Pillow (dance), Six Flags New England theme park, waterfalls, summer theater, Chesterfield Gorge, golf, horseback riding, boating. **Additional Infor-**

**mation:** Berkshire Hills Visitors Bureau, (413) 443-9186 or (800) 237-5747; www.berkshires.org.

## RESTRICTIONS

**Pets:** Must be leashed, quiet, & cleaned up after. Must not be left unattended. **Fires:** Fireplaces only. **Alcoholic Beverages:** Yes. **Vehicle Maximum Length:** 40 ft. **Other:** Quiet hours are from 10:00 p.m. until 7:00 a.m.

## TO GET THERE

From I-90 (Massachusetts Turnpike), take Exit 3, turn right and proceed for 2 mi. Turn right onto Rte. 20, heading west. Follow Rte. 20 for 17 mi. to Chester. Campground entrance is on the right.

## CLARKSBURG

## Clarksburg State Park

Middle Rd., Clarksburg 01247. T: (413) 664-8345; www.state.ma.us/dem/parks/clsp.htm.

| 🚐 ★★ | 🏕 ★★★★★ |
|---|---|
| Beauty: ★★★★★ | Site Privacy: ★★★★ |
| Spaciousness: ★★★ | Quiet: ★★★ |
| Security: ★★ | Cleanliness: ★★★★ |
| Insect Control: ★★ | Facilities: ★★★ |

Set in the far northwest corner of the state, nudging the Vermont border, this densely-forested camping area is beautiful, with secluded, well-spaced campsites. The good looks even extend to the rest rooms, which are nicely landscaped (with usable mirrors, a rarity at state parks) thanks to a recent park beautification program. One of the nicest features here is sparkling Mauserts Pond, a day-use area for swimming, fishing, and picnicking. Campsites are arrayed in a loop near the south end of the pond, but not directly on the waterfront. A scenic hiking trail skirts the pond, great for wildlife watching. The most enticing feature of this park may well be its proximity to the Appalachian Trail. Hikers come here when they want to trek the A.T. and Mt. Greylock (the highest point in the state), the park supervisor tells us. They prefer to camp here rather than at primitive Mt. Greylock so they can take advantage of creature comforts, like hot showers and running water. Only four sites are big enough for 36-footers, so plan ahead. Sites boasting excellent water views include 2, 4, 6, 8, 24, and 25.

## BASICS

**Operated By:** Massachusetts State Forests & Parks. **Open:** Memorial Day–Labor Day (perhaps later; call ahead). **Site Assignment:** Reservations may be made up to six months in advance by calling ReserveAmerica at (877) 1 CAMP-MA or online at www.reserveamerica.com. Ten sites are held for walk-ins on a first-come, first-served basis. To change arrival or departure date, or site type, call at least three days prior to arrival date. $10 cancellation/transfer fee. No refunds for amounts less than $5. **Registration:** At office. **Fee:** Massachusetts residents, $10; non-residents, $12. V, MC. **Parking:** At site.

## FACILITIES

**Number of RV Sites:** 44. **Number of Tent-Only Sites:** 0. **Hookups:** None. **Each Site:** Picnic table, fireplace. **Dump Station:** No. **Laundry:** No. **Pay Phone:** Yes. **Rest Rooms and Showers:** Yes. **Fuel:** No. **Propane:** No. **Internal Roads:** Paved, in good condition. **RV Service:** No. **Market:** 3 mi. south, in North Adams. **Restaurant:** 3 mi. south, in North Adams. **General Store:** No. **Vending:** No. **Swimming Pool:** No. **Playground:** No. **Other:** Pavilion. **Activities:** Swimming, fishing, picnicking, hiking. **Nearby Attractions:** Mass MOCA (contemporary art museum), Appalachian Trail. **Additional Information:** Berkshire Hills Visitors Bureau, (413) 443-9186 or (800) 237-5747; www. berkshires.org.

## RESTRICTIONS

**Pets:** Must be leashed & cleaned up after. Must not be left unattended. Proof of rabies vaccination required. **Fires:** Fireplaces only. **Alcoholic Beverages:** No. **Vehicle Maximum Length:** 36 ft. **Other:** Maximum stay of 14 cumulative days between Memorial Day & Labor Day.

## TO GET THERE

Follow Rte. 8 north to Middle Rd. in Clarksburg; follow signs.

## DENNISPORT

## Campers Haven RV Resort

184 Old Wharf Rd., Dennisport 02639. T: (508) 398-2811; F: (508) 398-3661; www.campershaven.com; camphvn@capecod.net.

🚐 ★★★                    ⛺ n/a

Beauty: ★★                Site Privacy: ★★
Spaciousness: ★★          Quiet: ★★
Security: ★★★★★           Cleanliness: ★★★★
Insect Control: ★★★       Facilities: ★★

This mid-Cape campground, located on the beach road in Dennisport, has bragging rights to a major amenity: a private sandy beach on Nantucket Sound, right across the street from the campground. Never mind that it's a little, fenced-off thing—it's a beach, with a nice swath of swimmable water which, they say, averages a toasty 80 degrees in the summer. Beyond that, the campground offers open, grassy sites for RVs (no tenting), mostly back-in. Many sites are seasonal. Nice touch: If you're in a class A or class C motor home with no car in tow, they'll shuttle you to local restaurants and ferries. A plethora of planned activities, like sing-alongs and ice cream socials, plus an on-site snack bar, make this a destination park. But, all the attractions of Hyannis, the Cape's biggest town, are just 12 miles away. For all that, it plays to an older crowd. We'd suggest another Cape campground if you have kids in tow.

## BASICS

**Operated By:** Paul & Elaine Peterson. **Open:** May 1–Columbus Day. **Site Assignment:** Reservations recommended. 50% deposit required. Reservations of two nights or less & holidays require payment in full in advance. Deposits for cancellations are refundable, minus a $15 service fee, w/ two weeks' notice. **Registration:** At office. **Fee:** $35–$42 per night for two adults & two children. July 4th & Labor Day weekend, $47 per night, three-night min. V, MC, AE. **Parking:** At sites or by permission only (w/extra charge.).

## FACILITIES

**Number of RV Sites:** 262. **Number of Tent-Only Sites:** 0. **Hookups:** Water, electric (30, 50 amps), sewer, cable TV. **Each Site:** None. **Dump Station:** Yes. **Laundry:** Yes. **Pay Phone:** Yes. **Rest Rooms and Showers:** Yes. **Fuel:** No. **Propane:** No. **Internal Roads:** Paved, in good condition. **RV Service:** No. **Market:** 3 mi. west. **Restaurant:** Yes. **General Store:** Yes. **Vending:** No. **Swimming Pool:** No. **Playground:** Yes. **Other:** Rec hall (pavilion), mini-golf, adult clubhouse w/exercise equipment & hot tub. **Activities:** Swimming (private ocean beach), horseshoes, mini-golf, basketball, shuffleboard, bocce, planned activities. **Nearby Attractions:** JFK Hyannis Museum, Cape Cod Rail Trail, golf, fishing, ferries to islands. **Additional Information:** Cape Cod Chamber of Commerce, (508) 862-0700 or (888) 33-CAPECOD; www.cape chamber.org.

### RESTRICTIONS

**Pets:** No dogs allowed June 25 to Labor Day. Limit one dog per site when allowed. No outdoor cats. **Fires:** No campfires. **Alcoholic Beverages:** Yes. **Vehicle Maximum Length:** 40 ft. **Other:** No smoking in any of the buildings.

### TO GET THERE

Take Rte. 6 to Exit 8. Turn right onto Rte. 134 and go to the end. Turn left onto Lower County Rd. and go 0.5 mi. to Old Wharf Rd. (Look closely; signs are on stone road posts and devilishly hard to read.) Turn right and go 1 mi. to campground, on left.

## EAST FALMOUTH

### Cape Cod Campresort

176 Thomas Landers Rd., East Falmouth 02536. T: (508) 548-1458; www.resortcamplands.com.

| 🚐 ★★★ | 🏕 ★★★ |
|---|---|
| Beauty: ★★★ | Site Privacy: ★★ |
| Spaciousness: ★★★ | Quiet: ★★★ |
| Security: ★★★★★ | Cleanliness: ★★★ |
| Insect Control: ★★ | Facilities: ★★★ |

This campground is actually three entities: a camping club, a camping co-op with some transient and seasonal sites, and the Cape Cod Campresort, with sites available specifically for transient use. Everybody shares the amenities, including a swimming pool, kiddie pool, and clubhouse; otherwise, everybody sticks to their area (marked by signage.) There's a small beach, with a swimming area, on Round Pond. It's a nice-looking place, with campsites nestled in cool pines. Sites are grassy and back-in, carpeted with pine needles. The tenting area is off to one side, just to the right of the office, with tents clustered in a pine grove off a skinny gravel road. Tent site E is especially nice. Among the RV sites, 98 and 99 are very private and set off the road. Site 76 is a winner, too, backed up into the woods. There's not much buffer between campsites. Another quibble: where are the umbrellas alongside the well-used pool area? Compared to nearby Sippewissett Campground (see listing), this one offers more activities for families and a bit more breathing room.

### BASICS

**Operated By:** Cape Cod Campresort. **Open:** Apr. 15–Oct. 15. **Site Assignment:** Reservations recommended. 30% deposit required. No refunds for cancellations occuring 7 days or less prior to scheduled arrival date. **Registration:** At office. **Fee:** $28–$34 based on two people. Extra adult, $6 per night; extra child under age 15, $3 per night. V, MC. **Parking:** At sites & designated parking lots only.

### FACILITIES

**Number of RV Sites:** 200. **Number of Tent-Only Sites:** 0. **Hookups:** Water, electric (30, 50 amps), sewer. **Each Site:** Picnic table, fireplace. **Dump Station:** Yes. **Laundry:** No. **Pay Phone:** Yes. **Rest Rooms and Showers:** Yes. **Fuel:** No. **Propane:** No. **Internal Roads:** Gravel, in good condition. **RV Service:** No. **Market:** 2 mi. east. **Restaurant:** 5 mi. east. **General Store:** Yes. **Vending:** Yes. **Swimming Pool:** Yes. **Playground:** Yes. **Other:** Rec hall. **Activities:** Ball field, swimming, horseshoes, boating (boat rentals). **Nearby Attractions:** Ferries to Martha's Vineyard, Woods Hole aquarium, ocean beaches, Nobska Lighthouse, golf. **Additional Information:** Cape Cod Chamber of Commerce, (508) 862-0700 or (888) 33-CAPECOD; www.capecodchamber.org.

### RESTRICTIONS

**Pets:** Must be leashed, quiet, & cleaned up after. Proof of rabies vaccination required. $3 charge per day. **Fires:** In fire rings only. **Alcoholic Beverages:** Yes. **Vehicle Maximum Length:** None. Over 30 ft. incurs extra charge of $1 per ft. per night. **Other:** All visitors must register upon entering the park.

## TO GET THERE

From Bourne Bridge, take Rte. 28S (second turn off rotary) to next rotary; continue on 28S, then take second exit to Thomas Landers Rd. Take left off ramp. Campground is exactly 2.7 mi. on the right.

## EASTHAM

### Atlantic Oaks

3700 Rte. 6, Eastham 02642. T: (508) 255-1437 or (800) 332-2267; F: (508) 247-8216; www.capecamp ing.com.

🚐 ★★★            ▲ ★

| | |
|---|---|
| Beauty: ★★ | Site Privacy: ★★ |
| Spaciousness: ★★ | Quiet: ★★★ |
| Security: ★★★★★ | Cleanliness: ★★★★ |
| Insect Control: ★★★★ | Facilities: ★★ |

Atlantic Oaks, owned by the same family who operates Shady Knoll in Brewster, is located in the town of Eastham on Cape Cod. Eastham is known for its working windmill (visible from Rte. 6), First Encounter Beach (where the pilgrims met the native Wampanoags), and Cape Cod National Seashore's Salt Pond Visitor Center, just one half-mile from the campground. If you're traveling in a big rig, and want to be near the seashore, this one fills the bill. The Cape Cod Rail Trail bike path runs just behind the property. Alas, a motel with a pool and tennis courts is also adjacent to the property; not good if you're traveling with kids, who might be tempted to trespass! Campsites are semi-shaded, on gravel; many are pull-thrus. There's not much buffer between sites, though. The prettiest sites back up against the woods and bike trail. These include sites C8, B8, A8, and P4. The T area, off Pine St. , is best for tents. All the basics are covered here. While there's not a lot of atmosphere, the location is great.

## BASICS

**Operated By:** Dave & Donna Nussdorfer. **Open:** May 1–Nov. 1. **Site Assignment:** Reservations recommended. 50% deposit required for stays of 5 days or more; all other reservations must be prepaid. No refunds without 14 days' notice. $10 service charge applies to cancellations. Checks OK for advance reservations. Reservations recommended. **Registration:** At office. **Fee:** $30–$42 for two people. Extra unmarried child age 6-18, $2 per night; extra child age 5 & under, free. Extra adult, $7.50 per night. V, MC, D. **Parking:** At site.

## FACILITIES

**Number of RV Sites:** 100. **Number of Tent-Only Sites:** 0. **Hookups:** Water, electric (30 amps), sewer, cable TV. **Each Site:** Picnic table. **Dump Station:** Yes. **Laundry:** Yes. **Pay Phone:** Yes. **Rest Rooms and Showers:** Yes. **Fuel:** No. **Propane:** Yes. **Internal Roads:** Gravel, in good condition. **RV Service:** No. **Market:** 4.5 mi. north. **Restaurant:** 0.25 mi. west. **General Store:** Yes. **Vending:** No. **Swimming Pool:** No. **Playground:** Yes. **Other:** Rec room. **Activities:** Horseshoes, bicycling, nightly movies (summer). **Nearby Attractions:** Cape Cod National Seashore Visitor Center, ocean beaches, Cape Cod Rail Trail. **Additional Information:** Cape Cod Chamber of Commerce, (508) 862-0700 or (888) 33-CAPECOD; www.capecodchamber.org.

## RESTRICTIONS

**Pets:** Must be leashed & cleaned up after. Must not be left unattended. **Fires:** No open fires. Charcoal grills & campstoves may be used w/caution. **Alcoholic Beverages:** Yes. **Vehicle Maximum Length:** None. **Other:** Minimum stay required for all weekends in July & Aug.

## TO GET THERE

From Sagamore Bridge, follow Rte. 6 past the Orleans rotary. Atlantic Oaks is 4 mi. east past rotary, on the left.

## ERVING

## Erving State Forest

200 East Main St., Erving 01344. T: (978) 544-3939 or (978) 544-7745;
www.state.ma.us/dem/parks/ ervf.htm.

🚐 ★★                     ▲ ★★★

| | |
|---|---|
| Beauty: ★★★★ | Site Privacy: ★★ |
| Spaciousness: ★★ | Quiet: ★★★ |
| Security: ★★★ | Cleanliness: ★★★★ |
| Insect Control: ★★ | Facilities: ★★ |

Great find: a camping area that stays open into Oct., for the leaf-peeping crowd. The Mohawk Trail is great route for fall color tours, so this campground couldn't be handier. Right off Rte. 2, it's got a great approach: a winding, tree-lined road bordered with lush ferns. Gravel sites are set on both sides of Camp Rd., backed by forest. The centerpiece of the state park is pretty Laurel Lake, stocked with brook trout. There are a few private cottages on the waterfront, but no campsites; campers stay at sites on the other side of the main road, and walk a short distance to picnic areas along the shore. There's a nice beach for campers, and a big buoyed swimming area, complete with lifeguards (sometimes!) Campsites here are not as nice as the surrounding area, but they're adequate, mostly measuring 30 by 30 feet, with mature trees as a buffer between them. Sites 11 and 12 offer a good amount of privacy, since they're spaced far apart. A nice feature here: engaging interpretive programs, such as "Serpent Session" (local snakes) and "Beginnng Birding." A not-so-nice feature: No showers—that's why this park charges only $5 or $6 per night. This may change, however. It is rumored that showers will be coming, if the budget allows. Stay tuned.

### BASICS

**Operated By:** Massachusetts State Forests & Parks. **Open:** May–Oct. **Site Assignment:** Reservations may be made up to six months in advance by calling ReserveAmerica at (877) 1 CAMP-MA or online at www.reserveamerica.com. Ten sites are held for walk-ins on a first-come, first-served basis. To change arrival or departure date, or site type, call at least three days prior to arrival date. $10 cancellation/transfer fee. No refunds for amounts less than $5. **Registration:** At office. **Fee:** Massachusetts residents, $5; non-residents, $6. V, MC. **Parking:** At site.

### FACILITIES

**Number of RV Sites:** 29. **Number of Tent-Only Sites:** 0. **Hookups:** None. **Each Site:** Picnic table, fireplace. **Dump Station:** No. **Laundry:** No. **Pay Phone:** Yes. **Rest Rooms and Showers:** Yes (non-flush), no showers. **Fuel:** No. **Propane:** No. **Internal Roads:** Paved, in good condition. **RV Service:** No. **Market:** 5 mi. east or west. **Restaurant:** 5 mi. east or west. **General Store:** No. **Vending:** No. **Swimming Pool:** No. **Playground:** No. **Other:** Boat ramp, nature center. **Activities:** Swimming, hiking, boating, fishing (need MA license, available at Wal-Mart in Orange), interpretive programs. **Nearby Attractions:** Mohawk Trail scenic drive, Bridge of Flowers (Shelburne), Historic Deerfield. **Additional Information:** Mohawk Trail Assocation, (413) 743-8127; www.mohawktrail.com.

### RESTRICTIONS

**Pets:** Must be leashed & cleaned up after. Must not be left unattended. Proof of rabies vaccination required. **Fires:** In fireplaces only. **Alcoholic Beverages:** No. **Vehicle Maximum Length:** 30 ft. **Other:** Maximum stay is 14 cumulative days between Memorial Day & Labor Day.

### TO GET THERE

Take Rte. 2 west to Erving Center. Take immediate left on Church St., exit right, and follow signs.

## FALMOUTH

## Sippewissett Campground and Cabins

836 Palmer Ave., Falmouth 02540. T: (508) 548-2542 or (800) 957-CAMP; www.sippewissett.com; camp capecod@aol.com.

🚐 ★★★                     ▲ ★★★★

| | |
|---|---|
| Beauty: ★★★★ | Site Privacy: ★★ |
| Spaciousness: ★★ | Quiet: ★★★ |
| Security: ★★★★★ | Cleanliness: ★★★ |
| Insect Control: ★★★ | Facilities: ★★★ |

You know you're on Cape Cod when your campground will lend you a lobster pot and lobster crackers, and give you an impromptu lesson on how to boil 'em! It happens here, where the main drawing card (aside from lobster lessons) is close proximity to salt water beaches (one mile away) and ferry boats to Martha's Vineyard. They'll shuttle you to the beach, and ferry dock, for free. They'll also sell you tickets for the ferry. Same price, but less waiting in line at the boat docks. This is the closest campground to the ferry and Wood's Hole. Trivia note: Falmouth is the home of "America the Beautiful" author Katherine Lee Bates. The campground is a quiet, family place, and it feels a bit crowded, except outside the main clusters of campsites. Sites numbered 60 through 64 are most popular, but we prefer the more woodsy and spacious sites 122 through 125. Sites 99 through 103 are pretty, too.

## BASICS

**Operated By:** Tessier family. **Open:** May 15–Oct. 15. **Site Assignment:** Reservations recommended. 50% deposit required. Balance is due 30 days prior to arrival date. Checks OK. Full refunds for cancellations made 20 days prior to scheduled arrival date. No refunds for less than 20 day notice. **Registration:** At office. **Fee:** $30–$32 for two people; same rate for families, w/one or two parents & children under age 21. V, MC. **Parking:** At site.

## FACILITIES

**Number of RV Sites:** 120. **Number of Tent-Only Sites:** 0. **Hookups:** Water, electric (20 amps). **Each Site:** Picnic table, fire ring. **Dump Station:** Yes. **Laundry:** Yes. **Pay Phone:** Yes. **Rest Rooms and Showers:** Yes. **Fuel:** No. **Propane:** No. **Internal Roads:** Gravel, in fair condition. **RV Service:** No. **Market:** 2 mi. south. **Restaurant:** 2 mi. south. **General Store:** Yes. **Vending:** Yes. **Swimming Pool:** No. **Playground:** Yes. **Other:** Rec room. **Activities:** Volleyball. **Nearby Attractions:** Ocean beaches (free shuttles), ferry to Martha's Vineyard, golf, Nobska Lighthouse, Woods Hole aquarium. **Additional Information:** Cape Cod Chamber of Commerce, (508) 862-0700 or (888) 33-CAPECOD; www.capecodchamber.org.

## RESTRICTIONS

**Pets:** No dogs. **Fires:** In fire rings only. **Alcoholic Beverages:** Yes. **Vehicle Maximum Length:** 30 ft. **Other:** No animals in cabins.

## TO GET THERE

From junction of Rte. 6 and Rte. 28, head south 12.5 mi. on Rte. 28 to Sippewissett exit (Palmer Ave.). Exit right and make immediate left at blinking yellow light. Go 0.5 mi. to campground entrance, on the right.

# FOXBORO

# Normandy Farms Family Camping Resort

72 West St., Foxboro 02035. T: (508) 543-7600; F: (508) 543-7667; www.normandyfarms.com; camp@normandyfarms.com.

| 🚐 ★★★★★ | 🔺 ★★★ |
|---|---|
| Beauty: ★★★★★ | Site Privacy: ★★★ |
| Spaciousness: ★★★★ | Quiet: ★★★★★ |
| Security: ★★★★ | Cleanliness: ★★★★ |
| Insect Control: ★★★★★ | Facilities: ★★★★★ |

Wow. The facilities at this four-season camping resort are really something. The timber-beamed rec center is reminiscent of a ski lodge, complete with an 18-plus adult loft and arcade. The lodge overlooks a lovely pool area with two pools. Elsewhere, there's yet another pool and two hot tubs. Campsites are, mostly, located in an open, grassy field, beautifully landscaped and surrounded by woods. The nicest full hookup sites, backing up into the woods, are 801 through 807, 901 through 908, and 1001 through 1008. Test sites are shaded, and set around the perimeter of the park. Best tent sites are T1 through T10, located near the fishing pond. Anywhere, though, there's not much privacy for tenters. This place speaks more to the RVer who's looking for some frills, not a wilderness-seeking tenter. There are lots of daily activities going on in the summer, and during holiday weekends all year, from an Elvis Tribute to ice cream socials. Most of these are free. (Free swim lessons and free water aerobics classes are a nice touch.) The campground runs guided bus trips to the Cape and Boston (30 miles south), very popular with campers.

## BASICS

**Operated By:** Daniels family. **Open:** All year. **Site Assignment:** Reservations recommended. May be made by phone, mail, email, or on-line. Reservations line opens Mar. 15 for bookings for the following year. For holidays, book one year in advance; for summer weekends, book at least one month in advance. Two-day min. stay required on weekends; three-to-four day stay required on holiday weekends. Deposit is required within three weeks of reservation; secure w/cash, traveler's checks, checks, or credit cards. Refunds for cancellation received one week prior to scheduled arrival date. **Registration:** At office. **Fee:** $32–$48 (late May to Labor Day). V, MC, D. **Parking:** At sites & designated lots only.

## FACILITIES

**Number of RV Sites:** 400. **Number of Tent-Only Sites:** 23. **Hookups:** Water, electric (20, 30, 50 amps), sewer. **Each Site:** Picnic table, fire ring. **Dump Station:** Yes. **Laundry:** Yes. **Pay Phone:** Yes. **Rest Rooms and Showers:** Yes. **Fuel:** No. **Propane:** Yes. **Internal Roads:** Paved, in good condition. **RV Service:** Yes. **Market:** 6 mi. east, in Mansfield. **Restaurant:** Yes. **General Store:** Yes. **Vending:** Yes. **Swimming Pool:** Yes (3). **Playground:** Yes. **Other:** Hot tubs, rec lodge, 18-hole frisbee golf course. **Activities:** Guided tours to Boston, Plymouth, & Cape Cod, swimming, fishing, volleyball, basketball, soccer field, horseshoes, basketball, planned activities. **Nearby Attractions:** Tweeter Center for the Performing Arts (concerts), CMGI Stadium (football), Edaville Railroad, Plimoth Plantation, Cranberry World Visitors Center, Pilgrim Hall Museum. **Additional Information:** Plymouth County CVB, (508) 747-0100 or (800) 231-1620; www.plymouth-1620.com.

## RESTRICTIONS

**Pets:** Must be leashed & cleaned up after. May not be left unattended. **Fires:** In fire rings only. **Alcoholic Beverages:** Yes. **Vehicle Maximum Length:** 45 ft. **Other:** Visitors must pay a fee & are not allowed to bring their pets in.

## TO GET THERE

From Boston, take I-93 south to Exit 1, then I-95 south to Exit 9. Take Rte. 1 south for 6.7 mi. to Thurston St. Turn left onto Thurston. Campground is 1.4 mi. on the right.

## GLOUCESTER

### Cape Ann Camp Site

80 Atlantic St., Gloucester 01930. T: (978) 283-8683; F: (978) 283-5976; ww.capeann.com/campsite.

🚐 ★★★★          ⛺ ★★★

| | |
|---|---|
| Beauty: ★★★★★ | Site Privacy: ★★★★ |
| Spaciousness: ★★★★ | Quiet: ★★★★ |
| Security: ★★★ | Cleanliness: ★★★ |
| Insect Control: ★★ | Facilities: ★★★ |

Located about an hour's drive north of Boston, this coastal campground overlooks the Jones River salt marsh and the briny bays of the Atlantic Ocean. Salt air, sand dunes, and sea oats beckon at Wingaersheek Beach, a mile away. The lower area of the campground is reserved for sizable RVs; beyond that, a series of loop roads winds up a hill through a woodsy, boulder-studded camping area. Designated areas are set aside for tent campers. Secluded site 330 is a superb choice for tenters, offering the ultimate room-with-a-view: a footpath leads to a rocky ledge with sweeping views of the river, estuaries, and East Gloucester shoreline. For smaller RVs, the electricity-only sites 215E to 217E are pleasant and out-of-the-way. Don't expect much in the way of amenities here; it's just the basics. But the campground's natural beauty, and its superb location, makes up for the lack of frills. During the day, everyone heads out to the beach, or to take in the sights on Cape Ann. Among the options: Gloucester's Rocky Neck, the oldest artists' colony in America, and the arts-flavored town of Rockport—home of the most-painted, most-photographed, fishing shack anywhere, Motif #1

## .BASICS

**Operated By:** Matz family. **Open:** May 1–Nov. 1. **Site Assignment:** Reservations recommended. Reserve by phone beginning in Apr. $30 deposit due w/ reservation. Personal checks accepted for deposit only. **Registration:** At office. **Fee:** $20–$28 per day, per car, up to 2 people. Additional person, $1-$6 per day. V, MC. **Parking:** At sites only. 1 vehicle per site.

## FACILITIES

**Number of RV Sites:** 125. **Number of Tent-Only Sites:** 125. **Hookups:** Water, electric (30, 50 amps), sewer. **Each Site:** Picnic table, fireplace. **Dump Station:** Yes. **Laundry:** No. **Pay Phone:** Yes. **Rest Rooms and Showers:** Yes, coin op. **Fuel:** No. **Propane:** No. **Internal Roads:** Paved & gravel, good conditon. **RV Service:** No. **Market:** 0.5 mi. west. **Restaurant:** 2 mi. south off Rte. 128. **General Store:** Yes. **Vending:** No. **Swimming Pool:** No. **Playground:** No. **Other:** Metered showers, modem in a central location. **Activities:** Swimming at ocean beach, saltwater fishing (no license needed), bike riding. **Nearby Attractions:** Wingaersheek Beach (1 mi. east; discounted parking permit available at campground office), Hammond Castle Museum, whale-watching boat trips, antiquing, Bearskin Neck artists' colony. **Additional Information:** North of Boston CVB, (978) 977-7760 or (800) 742-5306; www.northofboston.org.

## RESTRICTIONS

**Pets:** Must be leashed, quiet, & cleaned up after. Must have rabies vaccination certificate. **Fires:** In fireplaces only. **Alcoholic Beverages:** At sites only. **Vehicle Maximum Length:** 45 ft. **Other:** 3-night min. stay for Fri. arrivals, from June 15 through Labor Day. 2-night min. stay for Sat. arrivals during same time period. May require 4-day min. on July 4th & Labor Day weekends. Walk-ins OK if space is available.

## TO GET THERE

Take Rte. 129 North to Exit 13. Go northeast on Concord St. for 0.7 mi., then turn right onto Atlantic St. Campground is located 0.5 mi. east; entrance is on the left.

## GRANVILLE

# Prospect Mountain Campground

P.O. Box 323, 1349 Main Rd., Granville 01034. T: (413) 357-6494; F: (413) 357-6373; www.prospectmtncampground.com; info@prospect mtncampground.com.

| 🚐 ★★★ | 🏕 ★★★ |
|---|---|
| Beauty: ★★★ | Site Privacy: ★★★★ |
| Spaciousness: ★★★★ | Quiet: ★★★★★ |
| Security: ★★★ | Cleanliness: ★★★★ |
| Insect Control: ★★ | Facilities: ★★★★ |

Located in the rural town of Granville, southwest of Springfield and nudging the Connecticut border, this is a handy base camp for area attractions. Six Flags New England, the region's largest theme park, is a half-hour drive east, and the campground offers good discounts on admission tickets. ($14 off adult ticket prices, at press time.) Sodom Mountain Campground, in Southwick (see listing), is closer, and they, too, offer steeply-discounted tickets to Six Flags. The trade-off here: impeccably-maintained facilities, with nice touches like tent platforms, a nice kiddie playscape, private, bug-free (!) showers, and umbrellaed tables around the swimming pool. Instead of mountain hiking, a la Sodom Mountain, this campground has walking trails, and really gets into the theme stuff, with pig roasts and "Survivor" weekends. The campground boasts a nice spot, at a 1300-foot elevation, with lots of trees and two fishing ponds. The gravel sites are set in loops, with tent sites set at the far end of the property. Tent site T15, on Gaintner Pond, is nice, while the water-and-electric sites along Peter's Pond, especially sites 64 and 65, are inviting.

## BASICS

**Operated By:** Ann Schlosser. **Open:** May 1–Oct. 15. **Site Assignment:** Reservations recommended. 50% deposit required on credit card. No-shows will be charged. Refunds for cancellations w/ two weeks' notice. **Registration:** At office. **Fee:** $24–$28 for two adults & two children. V, MC, AE, D. **Parking:** At site.

## FACILITIES

**Number of RV Sites:** 200. **Number of Tent-Only Sites:** 0. **Hookups:** Water, electric (30, 50 amps), sewer. **Each Site:** Picnic table, fire ring. **Dump Station:** Yes. **Laundry:** Yes. **Pay Phone:** Yes. **Rest Rooms and Showers:** Yes. **Fuel:** No. **Propane:** Yes. **Internal Roads:** Gravel, in good condition. **RV Service:** No. **Market:** 11 mi. east, in Southwick. **Restaurant:** 11 mi. east, in Southwick. **General Store:** Yes. **Vending:** Yes. **Swimming Pool:** Yes. **Playground:** Yes. **Other:** Rec hall. **Activities:** Swimming, volleyball, basketball, nature trail, paddleboats, planned activities, themed weekends. **Nearby Attractions:** Six Flags New England theme park, Basketball Hall of Fame, Southwick Motocrosse 338, Big E (Eastern States Exposition) fair, late Sept. **Additional Information:** Greater Springfield CVB, (413) 755-1343; www.valleyvisitor.com.

## RESTRICTIONS

**Pets:** Must be leashed, quiet, & cleaned up after. Must not be left unattended. Not allowed in cabins or rental trailers. **Fires:** In fire rings only. **Alcoholic Beverages:** At sites only. **Vehicle Maximum Length:** 40 ft. **Other:** Three-night min. stay required on holidays.

## TO GET THERE

Take I-90 (Massachusetts Turnpike) to Exit 3, Westfield. Turn right onto Rtes. 10 and 202, follow into Southwick Center. In town, take a right at second light onto Rte. 57 west. Follow Rte. 57 into center of Granville (6.5 mi.) Continue on 57W for another 4.1 mi. Campground is directly off Rte. 57, on the left.

## HINGHAM

### Wompatuck State Park

Union St., Hingham 02043. T: (781) 749-7160; www.state.ma.us/dem/parks/womp.htm.

| 🚐 ★★★★ | ⛺ ★★★★ |
|---|---|
| Beauty: ★★★ | Site Privacy: ★★★★★ |
| Spaciousness: ★★★ | Quiet: ★★★★ |
| Security: ★★★★ | Cleanliness: ★ |
| Insect Control: ★★★★ | Facilities: ★★★ |

This is the closest campground to Boston where campers can enjoy a wilderness experience. Located on the South Shore of Massachusetts, about 19 miles from the city, Wompatuck State Park is a favorite of cycling enthusiasts. The park offers 10 miles of paved bike paths and another 30 miles or so of unpaved multiuse (bike, hike, horseback) trails, winding through lush forests and alongside freshwater ponds. Campsites are set in two areas, one with electric hookups (Camping Area 2), one without (Camping Area 1). Sites along the perimeter road, backed by woodlands, offer the most privacy, especially C-1 through C-14 (with electric hookups). Nearby, sites E-15, 17, and 19, are also nice, and near the rest rooms. In general, the sites in Camping Area 2 are set back farther from the road, more shaded, and more secluded than those in Area 1. Tent campers can use either one. A nice feature of this park is the abundance of fresh water, available at stone washbasins and water fountains scattered throughout the park. There's also collectible spring water, available at Mt. Blue Spring. (Avoid heavily-trafficked campsite X-9, nearest the hiking trail to the spring.) A not-so-nice feature: the rest rooms, where a recent visit revealed missing mirrors, overflowing waste cans and a lack of toilet paper.

## BASICS

**Operated By:** Massachusetts State Forests & Parks. **Open:** Mid-Apr.–mid-Oct. **Site Assignment:** Reservations recommended. Reserve up to six months in advance by calling ReserveAmerica at (877) 1-CAMP-MA or online at www.reservamerica .com. Sixty-five sites are non-reservable & held on a first-come, first-served basis. To change arrival or departure date, or site type, call at least three dayas prior to arrival date. $10 cancellation/transfer fee. No refunds for amounts less than $5. **Registration:** At office. **Fee:** Massachusetts residents, $10–$13; non-residents, $12–$15. V, MC. **Parking:** At site.

## FACILITIES

**Number of RV Sites:** 400. **Number of Tent-Only Sites:** 0. **Hookups:** Electric (20 amps). **Each Site:** Picnic table, fireplace w/ grill top. **Dump Station:** Yes. **Laundry:** No. **Pay Phone:** Yes. **Rest Rooms and Showers:** Yes. **Fuel:** No. **Propane:** No. **Internal Roads:** Paved, in good condition. **RV Service:** No. **Market:** 2.5 mi. north. **Restaurant:** 3.5 mi. north. **General

**Store:** No. **Vending:** Yes. **Swimming Pool:** No. **Playground:** No. **Other:** Boat ramp. **Activities:** Hiking, bicycling, mountain biking, interpretive programs. **Nearby Attractions:** Boston attractions, golf, South Shore Music Circus (outdoor concerts). **Additional Information:** Greater Boston CVB, (617) 536-4100 or (888) SEE-BOSTON; www.bostonusa.com.

## RESTRICTIONS

**Pets:** Must be leashed & cleaned up after. Must not be left unattended. Proof of rabies vaccination required. **Fires:** In fireplaces only. **Alcoholic Beverages:** No. **Vehicle Maximum Length:** 35 ft. **Other:** Two-night min. stay required between Memorial Day & Labor Day. Maximum stay is 14 cumulative days between Memorial Day & Labor Day. No swimming.

## TO GET THERE

Follow Rte. 35 to Exit 14; then take Rte. 228 north (left) into Hingham. Turn right on Free St. to campground entrance.

## LANESBOROUGH

### Hidden Valley Campground

15 Scott Rd., P.O. Box 700, Lanesborough 01237. T: (413) 447-9419 or (877) 392-2267; F: (413) 447-3775; www.campmass.com; hdnvaly@bcn.net.

| 🚐 ★★★ | ⛺ ★★★ |
|---|---|
| Beauty: ★★★ | Site Privacy: ★★★ |
| Spaciousness: ★★★ | Quiet: ★★★ |
| Security: ★★ | Cleanliness: ★★★★ |
| Insect Control: ★★★ | Facilities: ★★★★ |

This rural area of the western Berkshires is generously endowed with state parks, but not so rich with good commercial campgrounds. Hidden Valley, nestled at the base of Mt. Greylock, is a happy exception. This campground offers a bit of a natural look (arguably, too natural in spots, where fallen trees interfere with tenting sites), with plentiful trees and big boulders, along with some extras. These include live entertainment, and an inviting rec hall with a wide-screen TV, piano, and ping-pong table. The crowd is mostly seasonal, but 24 to 30 sites are available for tran-

sient guests. Unusual and welcoming touches include a full-length mirror and lots of hooks in the rest room; also, tent sites are marked off with logs, and raised on six inches of beach sand, a good move, since water seeps away when it rains. Nice tent sites include numbers 6 and 7, set back with dense tree cover. Numbers 29 and 48 are pretty, secluded RV sites. This campground offers a good blend of amenities and woodsy appeal.

## BASICS

**Operated By:** DiLego family. **Open:** May 1–Oct. 31 (may stay open all year; call to check). **Site Assignment:** Reservations recommended; may reserve on-line. Must pay in full when making reservation. A credit card will hold reservation, but no-shows will be charged. Checks accepted for payment if received at least 30 days prior to arrival. Refunds for cancellations made 21 days or more prior to arrival, minus $15 fee. **Registration:** At office. **Fee:** $23, RVs; $18, tents. Rates based on two adults & two children under the age of 18. V, MC, D. **Parking:** At site.

## FACILITIES

**Number of RV Sites:** 90. **Number of Tent-Only Sites:** 20. **Hookups:** Water, electric (20, 30 amps). **Each Site:** Picnic table, fireplace. **Dump Station:** Yes. **Laundry:** Yes. **Pay Phone:** Yes. **Rest Rooms and Showers:** Yes, coin-op. **Fuel:** No. **Propane:** Yes. **Internal Roads:** Gravel, in fair condition. **RV Service:** No. **Market:** Within 2 mi. south. **Restaurant:** Yes (snack bar). **General Store:** Yes. **Vending:** Yes. **Swimming Pool:** Yes. **Playground:** Yes. **Other:** Rec hall. **Activities:** Swimming, fishing (in private pond), horseshoes, planned activities. **Nearby Attractions:** Tanglewood, Hancock Shaker Village, Mt. Greylock, Norman Rockwell Museum, Mass MOCA (contemporary art), Clark Art Institute, Jacob's Pillow (dance), golf. **Additional Information:** Berkshire Hills Visitors Bureau, (413) 443-9186 or (800) 237-5747; www.berkshires.org.

## RESTRICTIONS

**Pets:** 1 pet per RV site. Pets not allowed at tent sites. **Fires:** In fireplaces only. **Alcoholic Beverages:** Yes. **Vehicle Maximum Length:** 38 ft. (5 sites available for big rigs). **Other:** Three-night min. stay on holiday weekends.

## TO GET THERE

From Williamstown (Rte. 2), take Rte. 7 south to Lanesborough, 9 mi. Go 3 mi. to the blue camper sign; make an extreme left-hand turn onto N. Main St. Follow for 0.7 mi., then bear left onto Scott Rd. Follow 0.3 mi. to campground.

## LEE

### October Mountain State Forest

317 Woodland Rd., Lee 01238. T: (413) 243-1778; www.state.ma.us/dem/parks/octm.htm.

| 🚐 ★★★ | 🏕 ★★★ |
|---|---|
| Beauty: ★★ | Site Privacy: ★★★ |
| Spaciousness: ★★★ | Quiet: ★★ |
| Security: ★★★ | Cleanliness: ★★★ |
| Insect Control: ★★ | Facilities: ★★★ |

Set on a sunny hillside in the center of Berkshire County, this campground is a good base for enjoying the area's numerous cultural attractions. Tanglewood Music Festival is just six miles away, so this campground offers visitors the chance to hear music under the stars, then return to the park to sleep under the stars (well, sort of!) October Mountain also boasts several miles of hiking paths, including a section of the famous Appalachian Trail. A favorite footpath leads to Schermerhorn Gorge; others lead to lakes and (minor) mountain summits. Trailer sites are set in a loop near the campground entrance. These are mostly open, level, and grassy, with just a bit of shade. Tent sites are grouped together on the second level of the camping area. Site 47 is very secluded, and close to the rest room, and site 40 is also a good, end-of-the-road spot. Stay clear of site 34, on the third level, where an old tank detracts from the beauty of the space. One downside of this park: off-road vehicles are allowed to use the multi-use trails. They're gone by evening, so this shouldn't disturb anyone's sleep. Also, a nearby power plant makes a humming noise. This is most audible near the entrance of the park and the trailer sites, and shouldn't bother tenters, who are sited farther back on the second and third levels of the park. (Trivia note: October Mountain is the largest state forest in Massachusetts.)

## BASICS

**Operated By:** Massachusetts State Forests & Parks. **Open:** Mid-May–mid-Oct. **Site Assignment:** Reservations may be made up to six months in advance by calling ReserveAmerica at (877) 1 CAMP-MA or online at www.reserveamerica.com. Ten sites are held for walk-ins on a first-come, first-served basis. To change arrival or departure date, or site type, call at least three days prior to arrival date. $10 cancellation/transfer fee. No refunds for amounts less than $5. **Registration:** At office. **Fee:** Massachusetts residents, $10; non-residents, $12 V, MC. **Parking:** At site.

## FACILITIES

**Number of RV Sites:** 50. **Number of Tent-Only Sites:** 0. **Hookups:** None. **Each Site:** Picnic table, fireplace. **Dump Station:** Yes. **Laundry:** No. **Pay Phone:** Yes. **Rest Rooms and Showers:** Yes. **Fuel:** No. **Propane:** No. **Internal Roads:** Paved, in good condition. **RV Service:** No. **Market:** 2 mi. east, in Lee. **Restaurant:** 2 mi. east, in Lee. **General Store:** No. **Vending:** No. **Swimming Pool:** No. **Playground:** No. **Other:** Boat ramp. **Activities:** Hiking, fishing, ATV riding. **Nearby Attractions:** Tanglewood, Jacob's Pillow (dance). **Additional Information:** Berkshire Hills Visitors Bureau, (413) 443-9186 or (800) 237-5747; www.berkshires.org.

## RESTRICTIONS

**Pets:** Must be leashed & cleaned up after. Must not be left unattended. Proof of rabies vaccination required. **Fires:** In fireplaces only. **Alcoholic Beverages:** No. **Vehicle Maximum Length:** 35 ft. **Other:** Pets are not allowed in buildings.

## TO GET THERE

From I-90 (Massachusetts Turnpike), take Exit 2, Rte. 20 west. Turn right on Center St., follow signs.

## LITTLETON

### Boston Northwest/Minuteman KOA

P.O. Box 2122, Littleton 01460. T: (978) 772-0042 or (800) 562-7606 (reservations); F: (978) 772-9332; www.minutemancampground.com; minuteman@ ma.ultranet.com.

|  🚐 ★★★★ |  🏕 ★★★★ |
|---|---|

Beauty: ★★★★★          Site Privacy: ★★★
Spaciousness: ★★★       Quiet: ★★★
Security: ★★★★          Cleanliness: ★★★★★
Insect Control: ★★★     Facilities: ★★★★

A scenic drive, it's not. As you head west on Rte. 2-A, a quarry-lined industrial corridor, you may well be wondering why you'd ever consider camping in such an unlikely area. Then, you spot the KOA sign, and pull into a road flanked by tall white pines. Trees never looked so good! And so it is at Boston Northwest/Minuteman KOA campground, about an hour's drive west of Boston. Not only do the trees provide shade for campsites, but they help muffle the sound of traffic. The heart of the campground is the familiar KOA A-frame with an office, convenience store (very complete, with everything from supplies to souvenirs to rental videos), laundry facility, and rest rooms. A pool and a rec hall are situated nearby. From there, five streets branch out, with a total of 100 campsites. This is definitely an RV camper's scene; just nine sites are designated for tenters, although 25 are multi-use. Seven cabins are sprinkled throughout the property. The park-like setting, plus the pool and (nice) playground make this a good choice for day-tripping families, especially those with the battle sites at Lexington and Concord on their itineraries.

## BASICS

**Operated By:** Ted & Maureen Nussdorfer.
**Open:** May 1–week after Columbus Day. **Site Assignment:** Reservations taken all year. Special requests should be made in advance; smaller units can typically book within a week of arrival date. **Registration:** At office. **Fee:** $24–$33 for two adults; extra adult, $5; extra child over age 5, $2. Discounted rates w/ KOA Value Card. V, MC, D. **Parking:** At site.

## FACILITIES

**Number of RV Sites:** 91. **Number of Tent-Only Sites:** 9. **Hookups:** Water, electric (20, 30, 50 amps), sewer. **Each Site:** Picnic table, fire ring. **Dump Station:** Yes. **Laundry:** Yes. **Pay Phone:** Yes. **Rest Rooms and Showers:** Yes. **Fuel:** No. **Propane:** Yes. **Internal Roads:** Paved & gravel, good condition. **RV Service:** No. **Market:** 4 mi. east. **Restaurant:** 1 mi. west. **General Store:**

Yes. **Vending:** No. **Swimming Pool:** Yes. **Playground:** Yes. **Other:** Rec hall. **Activities:** Volleyball, horseshoes, videos, planned activities. **Nearby Attractions:** Lexington & Concord historic sites, golf, mini-golf. **Additional Information:** Greater Merrimack Valley CVB, (978) 459-6150 or (800) 443-3332; www.lowell.org.

## RESTRICTIONS

**Pets:** Must be leashed, quiet & cleaned up after. Must not be left unattended. Use enclosed Dog Walk area. **Fires:** In fire rings only. **Alcoholic Beverages:** At sites only. **Vehicle Maximum Length:** 40 ft. **Other:** Maximum stay is 14 days.

## TO GET THERE

Take I-495 to Exit 30. Go west on Rte. 2A and Rte. 110 for 2.5 mi. Campground is on the left.

## MANSFIELD

### Canoe River Campgrounds

137 Mill St., Mansfield 02048. T: (508) 339-6462; F: (508) 339-5237.

🚐 ★★★                    ⛺ ★★★

Beauty: ★★               Site Privacy: ★
Spaciousness: ★★         Quiet: ★★★
Security: ★★★★★          Cleanliness: ★★★
Insect Control: ★★★      Facilities: ★★

Compared to nearby Normandy Farms campground, this one is a bargain. Located in southern Massachusetts, halfway between Boston and Cape Cod, Canoe River is geared to families. About half the sites are seasonal—you'll notice a wildly-decorated seasonal site just past the campground entrance. The presence of water makes all the difference here, providing a peaceful aspect to the rather closely-packed campsites. The campground is set on a river plateau, with a duck pond (lots of waterfowl), the larger Mill Pond (good for fishing and boating), and access to Canoe River. There's a bit of paddling on the river, but it's fairly overgrown. Sites are grass and gravel, with best tent sites on the river, at a dead end, numbers M4 and M5. Lakeside sites LS9 through 15 are also nice. RVers will like shady sites S5 through S12. This campground is casual, homey, and family-friendly. Ducklings toddle past plastic pink flamingoes. And the snack bar has blast-from-the-past prices—grilled cheese for under a buck, two eggs and toast for $2.15!

## BASICS

**Operated By:** Joe & Emma Gonsalves. **Open:** Apr. 15–Oct. 15. **Site Assignment:** Reservations recommended. Deposit of one night's stay required. Two-night min. stay in summer; three-night min. on holidays. Refunds for cancellation if made within 7 days of scheduled arrival date. **Registration:** At office. **Fee:** $19–$23. Checks, V, MC, D. **Parking:** At site.

## FACILITIES

**Number of RV Sites:** 70. **Number of Tent-Only Sites:** 50. **Hookups:** Water, electric (20, 30 amps), sewer (to come). **Each Site:** Picnic table, fire ring. **Dump Station:** Yes. **Laundry:** Yes. **Pay Phone:** Yes. **Rest Rooms and Showers:** Yes, coin-op. **Fuel:** No. **Propane:** Yes. **Internal Roads:** Gravel, in good condition. **RV Service:** No. **Market:** 3–4 mi., east or west. **Restaurant:** Yes. **General Store:** Yes. **Vending:** Yes. **Swimming Pool:** Yes (2). **Playground:** Yes. **Other:** Rec hall. **Activities:** Boating (rental canoes, rowboats, paddle-boats & kayaks), fishing, swimming, planned activities. **Nearby Attractions:** Tweeter Center for the Performing Arts (concerts), CMGI Stadium (football), Edaville Railroad, Plimoth Plantation, Cranberry World Visitors Center, Pilgrim Hall Museum. **Additional Information:** Plymouth County CVB, (508) 747-0100 or (800) 231-1620; www.plymouth-1620.com.

## RESTRICTIONS

**Pets:** Must be leashed, quiet, & cleaned up after. **Fires:** In fire rings only. **Alcoholic Beverages:** Yes. **Vehicle Maximum Length:** 45 ft. **Other:** Limited winter camping.

## TO GET THERE

From junction of I-495 and Rte. 123 (Exit 10), go 1 mi. east on Rte. 123, then turn left on Newland St. Go 2.25 mi. north to campground entrance, on left.

# MIDDLEBORO

## Boston South/Middleboro/Plymouth KOA

483 Plymouth St., P.O. Box 616, Middleboro 02346. T: (508) 947-6435 or (800) 562-3046 (reservations); www.koa.com; wrnken@ix.netcom.com.

| 🚐 ★★ | ▲ ★ |
|---|---|
| Beauty: ★★ | Site Privacy: ★★ |
| Spaciousness: ★★★★ | Quiet: ★ |
| Security: ★★★★★ | Cleanliness: ★★★★ |
| Insect Control: ★★★ | Facilities: ★★★ |

This urban campground is centrally located, about 15 miles west of Plymouth, 40 miles south of Boston, and about 25 miles northwest of Cape Cod. And there's nearby commuter rail service, from Middleboro to Boston, so you can see the city sights and avoid the awful drive in. That's the good news. The bad news is, this campground is set alongside busy Rte. 44, and not really woodsy enough to muffle the incessant sound of traffic. The least-desirable campsites are, naturally, those closest to the road, including sites numbered in the 100s (except 124 through 132 and 158 through 166, set farther back) and those in the 200s (except 226 through 239 and 258 through 271, same deal.) Sites numbered 500-plus are set back, and might be the best bet for RVers. Tent sites are, mercifully, located in the middle of the campground, which may help with the noise level; still, we wouldn't recommend tent camping here. On the plus side, the place is spanking clean in true KOA style, and the pool is nice, if fairly exposed beside the campground entrance.

## BASICS

**Operated By:** Nicholson family. **Open:** Mar. 1–Dec. 1. **Site Assignment:** Reservations recommended. Deposit of $22 required to guarantee deposit for campsites. Cancel by 4 p.m. the day before your arrival date for refund; exceptions may be in effect due to high demand during holidays or special events. **Registration:** At office. **Fee:** $25–$36. V, MC, D. **Parking:** At site.

## FACILITIES

**Number of RV Sites:** 276. **Number of Tent-Only Sites:** 0. **Hookups:** Water, electric (50 amps), sewer. **Each Site:** Picnic table, fire ring. **Dump Station:** Yes. **Laundry:** Yes. **Pay Phone:** Yes. **Rest Rooms and Showers:** Yes. **Fuel:** No. **Propane:** Yes. **Internal Roads:** Paved, in good condition. **RV Service:** No. **Market:** 3 mi. west on Rte. 44. **Restaurant:** 2.5 mi. west on Rte. 44. **General Store:** Yes. **Vending:** No. **Swimming Pool:** Yes. **Playground:** Yes. **Other:** Rec hall. **Activities:** Guided tours to Boston, Plymouth, & Cape Cod (June 1–Nov. 1), public transportation (commuter rail) to Boston, swimming, horseshoes, volleyball, basketball, bocce, planned activities. **Nearby Attractions:** Edaville Railroad, Tom Thumb Museum, Robbens Museum of Archeology, Eddy Homestead, Plimoth Plantation, Pilgrim Hall Museum, whalewatching, ocean beaches. **Additional Information:** Plymouth County CVB, (508) 747-0100 or (800) 231-1620; www.plymouth-1620.com.

## RESTRICTIONS

**Pets:** Leashed only. **Fires:** In fire rings only. **Alcoholic Beverages:** Yes. **Vehicle Maximum Length:** 45 ft. **Other:** No charge for use of modem data port.

## TO GET THERE

From I-495, take Exit 6 onto Rte. 44. Head east for 2.5 mi. Entrance is on the left

## MONSON

### Sunsetview Farm Camping Area

57 Town Farm Rd., Monson 01057. T: (413) 267-9269; F: (413) 267-3163; www.sunsetview.com; camp@sunsetview.com.

🚐 ★★★          ⛺ ★★

| | |
|---|---|
| Beauty: ★★★ | Site Privacy: ★ |
| Spaciousness: ★ | Quiet: ★★★★ |
| Security: ★★★★★ | Cleanliness: ★★★★ |
| Insect Control: ★★★ | Facilities: ★★★★ |

Formerly a dairy farm and apple orchard, Sunsetview has hosted campers for 31 years. Off the beaten path in rural Monson, the campground is located between Sturbridge and Springfield, about six miles from the Massachusetts Turnpike. All recreation facilities, including a softball field, swimming pool, pond, and volleyball pit, are located near the campground's gated entrance. The farther back you head, the more woodsy the campsite. The grassy sites near the beach are tightly packed and the least desirable, in our view. For privacy, the best bet for RVers are sites 20, 20A, and 22A. For tenters, grouped together here at the far end of the property, sites T16 and T11 are set apart from their neighbors; T11 has the advantage of being close to the rest room. Most sites are back-in, some are pull-thru, and many are seasonal. Summer weekends here are jampacked with activities; we like the Annual Trailer Rodeo (see which Dad can park the best!) This campground offers a country setting with close proximity to the urban areas of Springfield and Worcester (both, a half-hour away).

## BASICS

**Operated By:** Carpenter family. **Open:** Apr. 15–Oct. 15. **Site Assignment:** Reservations recommended. A deposit of one night's fee required to hold reservation. Holiday weekends must be paid in full one month prior to arrival. A $5 fee will be charged for all cancelled reservations. Walk-ins accepted for single night stay, if available. **Registration:** At office. $15 refundable deposit due for key to entrance gate. **Fee:** $22–$28. Extra fee for holiday weekends. Rates are for two persons; extra adult (age 18 & up) $2; extra child (age 6 & up), $1. MC, V, D. **Parking:** At site.

## FACILITIES

**Number of RV Sites:** 160. **Number of Tent-Only Sites:** 20. **Hookups:** Water, electric (30, 50 amps), sewer. **Each Site:** Picnic table, fire ring. **Dump Station:** Yes. **Laundry:** Yes. **Pay Phone:** Yes. **Rest Rooms and Showers:** Yes, coin op. **Fuel:** No. **Propane:** No. **Internal Roads:** Gravel, in good condition. **RV Service:** No. **Market:** In Palmer, 3 mi. north. **Restaurant:** Yes. **General Store:** Yes. **Vending:** No. **Swimming Pool:** Yes. **Playground:** Yes. **Other:** Game room. **Activities:** Basketball, volleyball, ball field, hiking trails, teen area, planned activities. **Nearby Attractions:** Six Flags New England theme park (discounted tickets available), Old Sturbridge Village living history museum, Basketball Hall of Fame. **Additional Information:** Greater Springfield CVB, (413) 787-1548 or (800) 723-1548; www.valleyvisitor.com.

## RESTRICTIONS

**Pets:** Must be leashed, quiet, & cleaned up after. Must not be left unattended. Rabies vaccine certificate required. **Fires:** In fire rings only. **Alcoholic Beverages:** At site. **Vehicle Maximum Length:** 45 ft. **Other:** Two night min. stay required in July & Aug.; three night min. on holiday weekends.

## TO GET THERE

From junction of I-90 (Massachusetts Turnpike) and Exit 8 (Rte. 32), head south. After entering Monson, take first left onto Fenton Farm Rd. Proceed 0.25 mi., then take a right onto Town Farm Rd. Follow road for 1.5 mi. Campground is on the left.

## NORTH ADAMS

### Historic Valley Campground

10 Main St., North Adams 01247. T: (413) 662-3198.

🚐 ★★★                          ▲ ★★★

| | |
|---|---|
| Beauty: ★★★ | Site Privacy: ★★★ |
| Spaciousness: ★★★ | Quiet: ★★★ |
| Security: ★★★ | Cleanliness: ★★ |
| Insect Control: ★★★ | Facilities: ★★★ |

This tidy little city-owned campground is tucked away at the end of a city street. If it weren't for the sign, you might not guess it existed. What a nice surprise: the campsites are ringed by woods and a lake, flanked by the lofty hillsides of the Berkshires. There are two beaches here, a municipal beach and a private beach for the camping crowd. Campers are mostly families, with about 30 seasonal sites in the mix. RV sites are back-in and gravel, buffered by trees. Happily, they've left lots of trees in place on the property. Sites 5 and 7 are nice and on the lakefront, while 50 through 52 and 65 through 67 are nicely bordered by woods. We'd skip sites 1 through 7;

they're too close to the busy beach pavilion. In general, the perimeter sites are most spacious here. Tenters who don't need electric can choose from among the wilderness sites. (Wilderness I is closest to the lake.) The crumbling fireplaces could use some help. All in all, a pleasant, if busy, camping destination.

## BASICS

**Operated By:** City of North Adams. **Open:** May 15–Oct. 15. **Site Assignment:** Reservations recommended; call year-round. All reservations require a full deposit. **Registration:** At office. **Fee:** $12 (wilderness)–$30 (lakefront) No credit cards. **Parking:** At site.

## FACILITIES

**Number of RV Sites:** 106. **Number of Tent-Only Sites:** 0. **Hookups:** Water, electric (20 amps). **Each Site:** Picnic table, fireplace. **Dump Station:** Yes. **Laundry:** Yes. **Pay Phone:** Yes. **Rest Rooms and Showers:** Yes. **Fuel:** No. **Propane:** No. **Internal Roads:** Gravel, in good condition. **RV Service:** No. **Market:** 2 mi. north. **Restaurant:** 0.5 mi. south, & 2 mi. south (at Adams/North Adams line). **General Store:** Yes. **Vending:** Yes. **Swimming Pool:** No. **Playground:** Yes. **Other:** Rec room, pavilion. **Activities:** Boating on Windsor Lake (rentals available), swimming, horseshoes, volleyball, hiking, ball field. **Nearby Attractions:** Mt. Greylock State Reservation (hiking), Natural Bridge State Park, Hancock Shaker Village, Mass MOCA (contemporary art), Clark Art Institute, Norman Rockwell Museum, summer theater, golf, whitewater canoeing, fishing, horseback riding, Tanglewood (music), Jacob's Pillow (dance). **Additional Information:** Berkshire Hills Visitors Bureau, (413) 443-9186 or (800) 237-5747; www.berkshires.org.

## RESTRICTIONS

**Pets:** Dogs & cats permitted; must be leashed at all times. Not allowed on beach, pavilion, or playgrounds. **Fires:** In fireplaces only. **Alcoholic Beverages:** No. **Vehicle Maximum Length:** 40 ft. **Other:** No motorcycles.

## TO GET THERE

Follow Rte. 2 (Mohawk Trail) to east side of North Adams. Turn onto East Main St. (look for Ed's Variety), go 0.25 mi. left onto Kemp Ave. Travel 1.5 mi. on Kemp to lake and campground entrance.

## NORTH ANDOVER
### Harold Parker State Forest

1951 Turnpike Rd., North Andover 01845. T: (978) 686-3391 or (877) 1 CAMP-MA; F: (978) 689-7504; www.state.ma.us/dem/parks/harp.htm.

 ★★                      ▲ ★★★★

Beauty: ★★★★            Site Privacy: ★★★★
Spaciousness: ★★★★      Quiet: ★★★★★
Security: ★★★            Cleanliness: ★★★
Insect Control: ★★       Facilities: ★★

About 25 miles north of Boston, Massachusetts, 3,500-acre Harold Parker State Forest offers a taste of the wilderness with easy access to big-city attractions. A drive into the forest reveals a mix of hardwoods and fragrant pine, studded with nine ponds. Ninety campsites are arrayed in a loop, just to the west of jalapeño-shaped Frye Pond. The most popular sites, for good reason, are those on the waterfront (63–87). If those are taken, site 15 is a good choice, located up a small hill and away from the road. We'd steer clear of sites 52, 54, and 56 if you need proximity to a rest room. Once settled in, you'll enjoy the rustic setting and woodsy hiking trails. (Ask for a trail map when you come in.) If you've brought a kayak or canoe, don't miss a sunset paddle on Frye Pond. The campground opens in mid-Apr., but Apr. tends to be muddy around here. Also beware of mid-May, black fly season. Given the lack of facilities, Harold Parker State Forest is best-suited for tent campers, or self-sufficient RVers looking for a back-to-nature escape. It makes a great base for campers who want to play tourist in bustling Boston and the North Shore, then return to the tranquility of woods and water.

### BASICS
**Operated By:** Massachusetts Division of Forests & Parks. **Open:** Mid-Apr.–mid-Oct. **Site Assignment:** Reserve up to 6 months in advance by calling (877) 1 CAMP-MA or on line at www.reserve

america.com. If you cancel or change dates or type of site, call (877) 422-6762 at least 3 days prior to arrival. $10 cancellation/transfer fee. Walk-ins welcome if space is available; best time to try is after 11 a.m. check-out period. **Registration:** At office. **Fee:** MA residents, $10; non-residents, $12. Accessible sites available. V, MC. **Parking:** At site.

### FACILITIES
**Number of RV Sites:** 90. **Number of Tent-Only Sites:** 0. **Hookups:** None. **Each Site:** Picnic table, fireplace, grills (to come). **Dump Station:** Yes. **Laundry:** No. **Pay Phone:** Yes. **Rest Rooms and Showers:** Yes. **Fuel:** No. **Propane:** No. **Internal Roads:** Paved, in good condition. **RV Service:** No. **Market:** 5 mi. east in Middleton. **Restaurant:** 5 mi. east in Middleton. **General Store:** No (firewood for sale at campground office). **Vending:** No. **Swimming Pool:** No. **Playground:** Planned. **Other:** Ball field, basketball court (planned), small beach. **Activities:** 25 mi. of multi-use trails (hiking, biking, bridle), fishing (license required), canoeing, pond swimming, hunting (limited; mostly in fall). **Nearby Attractions:** Witchcraft & maritime-related attractions in Salem, Peabody-Essex Museum, whale-watching boat trips out of Gloucester, Salem, and Newburyport, Lexington & Concord, Boston. **Additional Information:** North of Boston CVB, (978) 977-7760 or (800) 742-5306; www.northofboston.org.

### RESTRICTIONS
**Pets:** Must be leashed, quiet, & cleaned up after. Rabies vaccination certificate required. **Fires:** In fireplaces only. **Alcoholic Beverages:** No. **Vehicle Maximum Length:** None. **Other:** 14-day max. cumulative stay from Memorial Day through Labor Day.

### TO GET THERE
Take Rte. 495 to Exit 42E to Rte. 114W; follow signs to forest. Go right at camping sign, left at first stop sign. Pass residential area; go left onto Jenkins Rd. Camp office will be on your right.

## NORTH TRURO

### Horton's Camping Resort

71 Highland Rd., P.O. Box 308, North Truro 02652. T: (508) 487-1220 or (800) 252-7705 (reservations); www.HortonsCampingResort.com; camphrcr@capecod.net.

🚐 ★★★    ▲ ★★★

Beauty: ★★★          Site Privacy: ★★
Spaciousness: ★★★    Quiet: ★★★
Security: ★★★★        Cleanliness: ★★★★
Insect Control: ★★     Facilities: ★★

Of the three campgrounds in North Truro, this one feels the most inviting. Set on the Outer Cape of Cape Cod, just eight miles from both bustling Provincetown (to the east) and fishing town-turned-artist's-colony Wellfleet (to the west), this campground has an open, pastoral feel. Most sites are grassy, on gravel, and carpeted with pine needles. A section here called 'Wooded Area' is, naturally, woodsy (!), and it's the prettiest area of the property. An interesting feature here: an adult-only section, meant to be peaceful. The best of that bunch is very isolated site 203. Nearby are prime view sites, 173–176. Stand on the hill, and you may see a ribbon of blue ocean. (They claim other 'best view' sites as well, but these are the best!) No campfires allowed, but you can get a permit from the Truro Fire Dept. for a campfire on the beach. Speaking of which, Coast Guard Beach, on the National Seashore, is just a mile away. Walk it, and save money on a parking permit.

### BASICS

**Operated By:** Horton family. **Open:** Early May–mid-Oct. **Site Assignment:** Reservations recommended. Three-night min. stay required in season, w/$50 deposit per week for non-hookup sites & $75 per week for hookup sites. No personal checks within 30 days of arrival. No refunds without two-week notice of cancellation. $5 service charge applied to cancellations or alterations to reservation. **Registration:** At office. **Fee:** $19–$28 for one to two people. Extra adult, $8 per night; extra child age 2 to 16, $3. V, MC. **Parking:** At site.

### FACILITIES

**Number of RV Sites:** 200. **Number of Tent-Only Sites:** 0. **Hookups:** Water, electric (30 amps), sewer. **Each Site:** Picnic tables. **Dump Station:** Yes. **Laundry:** Yes. **Pay Phone:** Yes. **Rest Rooms and Showers:** Yes, coin-op. **Fuel:** No. **Propane:** No. **Internal Roads:** Gravel, in fair condition. **RV Service:** No. **Market:** 12 mi. west. **Restaurant:** 5 mi. west. **General Store:** Yes. **Vending:** No. **Swimming Pool:** No. **Playground:** Yes. **Other:** Volleyball court, winter storage available. **Activities:** Volleyball, horseshoes. **Nearby Attractions:** Cape Cod National Seashore, Cape Cod Light, ocean & bay swimming (1 mi.), golf, hiking, biking, antique shops, fishing, galleries. **Additional Information:** Cape Cod Chamber of Commerce, (508) 862-0700 or (888) 33-CAPECOD; www.capechamber.org.

### RESTRICTIONS

**Pets:** No dogs. **Fires:** No open fires. Campstoves, & charcoal grills OK. **Alcoholic Beverages:** Yes. **Vehicle Maximum Length:** 40 ft. **Other:** Children are not allowed at certain sites.

### TO GET THERE

From Sagamore Bridge, take Rte. 6 east to Orleans rotary (about 35 mi.). Continue on Rte. 6 to town of Truro, about 13 mi. Approximately 4.5 mi. past the Truro-Wellfleet town line, you'll see the Truro Central School on right. Turn right after school at blue and white 'camping' sign onto South Highland Rd. Campground entrance is 1 mi. on the right after the red bar (campground office and store.)

## NORTH TRURO

### North Truro Camping Area

46 Highland Rd., P.O. Box 365, North Truro 02652. T: (508) 487-1847; F: (508) 487-9576; www.ntca camping.com; email@ntcacamping.com.

🚐 ★★    ▲ ★★

Beauty: ★★          Site Privacy: ★★
Spaciousness: ★★★    Quiet: ★★★
Security: ★★★        Cleanliness: ★★★★
Insect Control: ★★     Facilities: ★★

Located just north of Truro, one of the most desirable (and sleepiest) towns on the Outer Cape, this hilly campground is dotted with skinny pines that rise out of the sandy soil at odd angles. These provide a nice, sun-dappled effect on bright summer days, but don't provide much privacy between campsites, which are pretty much wall-to-wall with RVs in season. There are no group sites here, but lots of families. Campsites are set in a grid, off a main road. Finding one's way around the one-way streets can be challenging. The most secluded tent sites are 268, 270, and 272, on the far left-hand corner of the property. Tent sites 242, 252, and 254, on the last row of campsites, are also nice, backing up into the woods. Look to the perimeters if you want some privacy. Site 144A (water only) is a good choice, as is 72C (complete hookup.) Tip: Bring your own hand towels for the rest rooms, or drip-dry. This is basically a cheap sleep—two campers can stay with complete hookups and cable TV for $26 a day—and it's close to Provincetown, but quieter.

## BASICS

**Operated By:** Edgar Francis. **Open:** Apr. 1–Dec. 31. **Site Assignment:** Reservations recommended. $50 deposit required. Balance due upon arrival. Refunds for cancellation w/ two weeks' notice, minus $5 fee. **Registration:** At office. **Fee:** $9 per person per day; $18 min. Electric (15 amp) & water, $5 per day; complete (30 amp electric), $8 per day. V, MC. **Parking:** At site.

## FACILITIES

**Number of RV Sites:** 300. **Number of Tent-Only Sites:** 0. **Hookups:** Water, electric (15, 30 amps), sewer, cable TV. **Each Site:** Picnic table. **Dump Station:** Yes. **Laundry:** Yes. **Pay Phone:** Yes. **Rest Rooms and Showers:** Yes, coin-op. **Fuel:** No. **Propane:** Yes. **Internal Roads:** Paved, in good condition. **RV Service:** No. **Market:** 12 mi. west. **Restaurant:** 1 mi. west. **General Store:** Yes. **Vending:** No. **Swimming Pool:** No. **Playground:** No. **Other:** Metered showers, data port. **Activities:** Golf, hiking, biking, beachcombing. **Nearby Attractions:** Cape Cod National Seashore, Cape Cod Light, ocean & bay swimming (1 mi.), golf, hiking, biking, antique shops,

fishing, galleries. **Additional Information:** Cape Cod Chamber of Commerce, (508) 862-0700 or (888) 33-CAPECOD; www.capechamber.org.

## RESTRICTIONS

**Pets:** Must be leashed. No dogs from June 16 to Labor Day. **Fires:** No open fires. Campstoves, & charcoal grills OK. **Alcoholic Beverages:** Yes. **Vehicle Maximum Length:** None. **Other:** All visitors must register upon entering the park.

## TO GET THERE

From Sagamore Bridge, take Rte. 6 east through Truro (about 48 mi.) After passing Truro, watch for sign marked Highland Rd. (Do not turn off at South Highland Rd.) Turn right on Highland Rd. Campground is 0.25 mi. left

# OAKHAM

## Pine Acres Family Camping Resort

203 Bechan Rd., Oakham 01068. T: (508) 882-9509; F: (508) 882-3302; www.pineacresresort.com.

| 🚐 ★★★★★ | 🛖 ★★★★★ |
|---|---|
| Beauty: ★★★★★ | Site Privacy: ★★★ |
| Spaciousness: ★★★ | Quiet: ★★★★ |
| Security: ★★★★★ | Cleanliness: ★★★★★ |
| Insect Control: ★★ | Facilities: ★★★★★ |

This wonderfully appealing campground is located almost dead-center in the state, 15 miles from Worcester and about 50 miles west of Boston. Amidst a small-town New England landscape, this campground is a destination in itself. Set on a pine-shrouded hillside above 70-acre Lake Dean, it's a mini resort-land, with everything from tennis and boating to gourmet coffee and live entertainment. (Even waterskiing, if you bring your own boat.) Operated for 41 years by the Packard family, this place sets the standard, combining natural beauty with loads of amenities and small touches that add up: a porta-potty by the beach, a dog walk, stone fire rings (not the rusty jobs that are all too prevalent.) Campsites are set on loop roads, off a center pod with a lodge, rec hall, store, and so on. About half are seasonal. Site 137, on a hill overlooking the lake, is a fine choice, while sites 78 and 79 face the beach. Ditto sites 89, 93, and 93A. Sites H10 and H11, near wilderness trails, are good for hikers, while site 105, among the tent sites, offers a wooded spot on a hill with lake views. We'd pass on the M sites; too close to the hub of activity. Tip: Don't forget the bug juice!

## BASICS

**Operated By:** Oakham Pine Acres, Inc. **Open:** All year. **Site Assignment:** Reservations recommended; three-week advance notice is good. Can reserve on-line. 50% deposit required. Holiday weekends require three-night min. stay & payment in full w/ reservation. Will try to honor specific site requests, but cannot guarantee site requests for stays of less than 1 week. Refund given for cancellations w/ 30 days' notice, minus $10 service fee. If cancelling less than 30 days but at least 7 days prior to arrival, payments will be used as credit for future stay. **Registration:** At office. **Fee:** $17–$42 per family, w/ up to three unmarried children under age 18. V, MC, D. **Parking:** At sites & designated lots only.

## FACILITIES

**Number of RV Sites:** 300. **Number of Tent-Only Sites:** 0. **Hookups:** Water, electric (20, 30, 50 amps), sewer, cable TV, modems. **Each Site:** Picnic table, fire ring. **Dump Station:** Yes. **Laundry:** Yes. **Pay Phone:** Yes. **Rest Rooms and Showers:** Yes, coin-op. **Fuel:** No. **Propane:** Yes. **Internal Roads:** Paved & gravel, in good condition. **RV Service:** Yes. **Market:** 3 mi. south on Rte. 148. **Restaurant:** Yes. **General Store:** Yes. **Vending:** Yes. **Swimming Pool:** No. **Playground:** Yes. **Other:** Boat ramp, rec hall, adult lounge, tennis court, mini-golf. **Activities:** Fishing (need MA license, available in Rutland), tennis, boating (rentals available), volleyball, horseshoes, ball field, hiking, planned activities. In winter, cross-country skiing, skating, snowmobiling, ice fishing. **Nearby Attractions:** Old Sturbridge Village living history museum, Worcester Art Museum, Worcester Centrum (events), New England Science Center, Quabbin Reservoir, Higgins Armory Museum, Brimfield Flea Markets, apple orchards, golf. **Additional Information:** Central Massachusetts Tourist Council, (508) 755-7400; www.worcester.org.

## RESTRICTIONS

**Pets:** Must be leashed, quiet, & cleaned up after. Must not be left unattended. **Fires:** In fire rings only. **Alcoholic Beverages:** Yes. **Vehicle Maximum Length:** 40 ft. **Other:** children must be supervised at all times.

## TO GET THERE

From Boston, take Massachusetts Turnpike (I-90) west to Exit 10 (Auburn), then Rte. 20W. Turn right onto Rte. 56N, go through Leicester, then left onto Rte. 122N, and left again onto Rte. 148S. Watch for campground signs on Rte. 148.

## PITTSFIELD

### Pittsfield State Forest

Cascade St., Pittsfield 01201. T: (413) 442-8992; www.state.ma.us/dem/paraks/pitt.htm.

| 🚍 ★★★ | 🅰 ★★★★ |
|---|---|
| Beauty: ★★★★★ | Site Privacy: ★★★ |
| Spaciousness: ★★★ | Quiet: ★★★★ |
| Security: ★★★★ | Cleanliness: ★★★ |
| Insect Control: ★★ | Facilities: ★★★ |

If you don't mind doing without some creature comforts (namely, flush toilets and showers), you'll appreciate the wonderful natural features at this pristine state park located at the far Western edge of the state (Berkshire County.) From late May into June, 65 acres of wild azaleas bloom into a sea of pink blossoms. Two camping areas are clustered nearby, surrounding Berry Pond, the highest natural water body in Massachusetts at 2,150 feet. Fishing enthusiasts have discovered the pond, while hikers enjoy the vista from the top of Berry Mountain, a great place for sunset-watching. Great tent sites in this area include site 7, with good pond views, and sites 9–12, which are roomy, flat, and wooded. The only toilet here is pit-style (non-flush). Follow the loop road, running alongside Parker Brook, and you'll reach the second set of campsites, grouped near a flush toilet. These are pretty and woodsy as well, but set a bit closer together than those at Berry Pond, with less buffer between sites. Site 18 is big, but not very secluded. Hiking trails wind through a variety of forest, and beckon visitors to escape into the woods.

## BASICS

**Operated By:** Massachusetts State Forests & Parks. **Open:** May–Oct. **Site Assignment:** Reservations may be made up to six months in advance by calling ReserveAmerica at (877) 1 CAMP-MA or online at www.reserveamerica.com. Some sites are held for walk-ins on a first-come, first-served basis. To change arrival or departure date, or site type, call at least three days prior to arrival date. $10 cancellation/transfer fee. No refunds for amounts less than $5. **Registration:** At office. **Fee:** Parker Brook area, $5; Berry Pond area, $4 (no flush toilets) V, MC. **Parking:** At site.

## FACILITIES

**Number of RV Sites:** 31. **Number of Tent-Only Sites:** 0. **Hookups:** None. **Each Site:** Picnic table, fireplace. **Dump Station:** No. **Laundry:** No. **Pay Phone:** Yes. **Rest Rooms and Showers:** Yes, no showers. **Fuel:** No. **Propane:** No. **Internal Roads:** Paved & gravel, good to fair condition. **RV Service:** No. **Market:** 5 mi. east. **Restaurant:** 5 mi. east. **General Store:** No. **Vending:** No. **Swimming Pool:** No. **Playground:** No. **Other:** Nature center. **Activities:** Hiking (including wheelchair-accessible trail), swimming (in Lulu Pond), bicycling, fishing, horseback riding, interpretive programs. **Nearby Attractions:** Tanglewood (music), Jacob's Pillow (dance), Mt. Greylock, Norman Rockwell Museum. **Additional Information:** Berkshire Hills Visitors Bureau, (413) 443-9186 or (800) 237-5747; www.berkshires.org.

## RESTRICTIONS

**Pets:** Must be leashed & cleaned up after. Must not be left unattended. Proof of rabies vaccination required. **Fires:** In fireplaces only. **Alcoholic Beverages:** No. **Vehicle Maximum Length:** 16 ft. **Other:** Paved trail ideal for those in a wheelchair.

## TO GET THERE

From the Massachusetts Turnpike (I-90), take Exit 2. At the junction of Rtes. 7 and 20, go west on Rte. 7. Take West St. to Cascade St. Follow signs.

## PLAINFIELD

## Peppermint Park Camping Resort

169 Grant St. , Plainfield 01070. T: (413) 634-5385; peppermintpark.net; pprc@bcn.net.

🚐 ★★★          ⛺ ★★

| | |
|---|---|
| Beauty: ★★ | Site Privacy: ★★★★ |
| Spaciousness: ★★★★★ | Quiet: ★★★★★ |
| Security: ★★★★★ | Cleanliness: ★★★ |
| Insect Control: ★★ | Facilities: ★★★ |

Set in the rural landscape of the Berkshire Hills in Western Massachusetts, Peppermint Park offers a low-key family getaway in summer, and a toasty haven for snowmobilers in winter months. (280 miles of trails are accessible here.) Leaf-peepers descend on the campground in Sep. and Oct. Buffered by trees and shrubs, campsites are mostly grassy and wooded, offering plenty of breathing room. Most sites are set back from the main activities area near the entrance of the campground, except for numbers 122 and 123 and 126–132, which are near the pool area. Campsites are arrayed in two main sections, plus a string of sites running along the perimeter of the property. Sites 27–31 are fairly private and nicely shady. Tent sites are clustered in two sections (with and without water), in close proximity to (pretty basic) rest rooms. Be sure to bring a tarp if you're tenting, and avoid rainy periods if possible; it can get pretty muddy here when it rains. Nice features include a book swap, and an appealing lounger with a stone fireplace. Located within just five miles of another campground, Shady Pines (see listing), Peppermint Park is the quieter of the two.

## BASICS

**Operated By:** David & Gale Bulissa. **Open:** All year. **Site Assignment:** Reservations recommended. 50% deposit required; for holidays, must pay in full to reserve. **Registration:** At office. **Fee:** $20–$24, based on two adults & two children. V, MC, D. **Parking:** At site.

## FACILITIES

**Number of RV Sites:** 125. **Number of Tent-Only Sites:** 75. **Hookups:** Water, electric (20, 30, 50 amps), sewer. **Each Site:** Picnic table, fire ring. **Dump Station:** Yes. **Laundry:** Yes. **Pay Phone:** Yes. **Rest Rooms and Showers:** Yes, coin-op. **Fuel:** No. **Propane:** Yes. **Internal Roads:** Gravel, in fair condition. **RV Service:** No. **Market:** In Adams, 20 mi. west. **Restaurant:** 5 mi. south, in Ashfield. **General Store:** Yes. **Vending:** Yes. **Swimming Pool:** Yes. **Playground:** Yes. **Other:** Pub, hot tub, rec hall. **Activities:** Swimming, horseshoes, hiking, planned activities. **Nearby Attractions:** Mohawk Trail scenic drive, Historic Deerfield, Yankee Candle Factory, Bridge of Flowers, Antique Car Museum, Mount Greylock. **Additional Information:** Berkshire Hills Visitors Bureau, (413) 443-9186 or (800) 237-5747; www.berkshires.org.

## RESTRICTIONS

**Pets:** Must be leashed & cleaned up after. Must not be left unattended. **Fires:** Fire rings only. **Alcoholic Beverages:** Yes. **Vehicle Maximum Length:** None. **Other:** A copy of current rabies certificate must be shown upon check-in for all pets.

## TO GET THERE

From I-91, take Exit 26 (Greenfield); follow Rte. 2 west to Rte. 112, then south to Rte. 116 north. Continue 6.5 mi. to Bow St. Follow Bow St. 0.75 mi. to campground; entrance is on right.

## PLYMOUTH

### Ellis Haven Camping Resort

531 Federal Furnace Rd., Plymouth 02360. T: (508) 746-0803; www.ellishaven.com.

🚐 ★★★          ▲ ★★

| | |
|---|---|
| Beauty: ★★ | Site Privacy: ★★ |
| Spaciousness: ★★ | Quiet: ★★ |
| Security: ★★★★★ | Cleanliness: ★★★★★ |
| Insect Control: ★★★★ | Facilities: ★★★ |

Got teens or pre-teens in your party? You'll win major "props" for bringing them here. Unusual features at this campground include a huge, state-of-the-art arcade, and a tournament-worthy baseball diamond. And that's just the beginning. Set on good-sized Ellis Pond, in a residential area of Plymouth, Ellis Haven offers a day-use picnic area and a private beach. The number of activities at this resort-flavored campground rivals nearby Pinewood Lodge, but this place loses points when it comes to esthetics. Why call a pond "Stupid Duck Pond"? Why all the garish metal signs, every three feet, that read the same thing ("No Fishing")? Why is yellow police tape festooned around Thousand Frog Pond? That said, the camping area isn't bad, with grassy sites amidst plenty of tree coverage. Head to the northwest area of the resort, where you'll get away from the seasonal and permanent-looking set ups (unless you have a fondness for lawn art!) Sites 105 and 106 are nice, overlooking the baseball diamond, but not so close you need beware of fly balls. Amazing to think that this lively place borders its complete opposite, Miles Standish State Forest.

## BASICS

**Operated By:** Carreau family. **Open:** May 1–Oct. 1. **Site Assignment:** Reservations recommended. Reservations for two to five nights must be made two weeks prior to arrival date. Four night min. stay required on holidays. Fifty percent deposit required. Payment due in full 30 days prior to arrival. Cancellations made w/15-day notice, full refund minus $10 service charge. Cancellations w/seven day notice, credit available. **Registration:** At office. **Fee:** $25–$38 based on two adults, two children. V, MC, D. **Parking:** At site.

## FACILITIES

**Number of RV Sites:** 450. **Number of Tent-Only Sites:** 50. **Hookups:** Water, electric (20, 30, 50 amps), sewer. **Each Site:** Picnic table, fireplace. **Dump Station:** Yes. **Laundry:** Yes. **Pay Phone:** Yes. **Rest Rooms and Showers:** Yes. **Fuel:** No. **Propane:** Yes. **Internal Roads:** Gravel, in good condition. **RV Service:** No. **Market:** 3 mi. north, in Plymouth. **Restaurant:** Yes. **General Store:** Yes. **Vending:** Yes. **Swimming Pool:** No. **Playground:** Yes. **Other:** Rec hall, arcade, rental boats, petting zoo. **Activities:** Swimming in Ellis Pond, catch-and-release fishing, paddle boats, baseball, basketball, volleyball, picnicking, arcade games. **Nearby Attractions:** Plimoth Plantation, whale-watching cruises, scenic harbor cruises, Mayflower II, Plymouth National Wax Museum,

Pilgrim Hall Museum, winery, Ocean Spray Cranberry World, tours, winery. **Additional Information:** Destination Plymouth, (800) USA-1620 or www.visit-ply mouth.com.

## RESTRICTIONS

**Pets:** One dog per family. **Fires:** In fireplaces only. **Alcoholic Beverages:** Yes. **Vehicle Maximum Length:** None. **Other:** No teen-aged guests over holiday weekends. Two-night min. stay required except during May & September. Three-night min. stay required on holiday weekends.

## To Get There

From Rte. 3 southbound, take exit 6B; turn right at bottom of ramp to Rte. 44W. At second light, take left. At next light, take right onto Federal Furnace Rd. Proceed 3.5 mi. Campground entrance is on the right.

## PLYMOUTH

### Pinewood Lodge

190 Pinewood Rd., Plymouth 02360. T: (508) 746-3548; www.pinewoodlodge.com.

| 🚐 ★★★★★ | ⛺ ★★★★★ |
|---|---|
| Beauty: ★★★ | Site Privacy: ★★ |
| Spaciousness: ★★★★ | Quiet: ★★★★ |
| Security: ★★★★ | Cleanliness: ★★★★★ |
| Insect Control: ★★★★★ | Facilities: ★★★★ |

The tasteful white wooden sign that welcomes guests to Pinewood Lodge is a harbinger of things to come. Run by the Saunders family since 1962 (now operated by the great-grandchildren), this campground is the nicest one in the Plymouth area. Families who stay here while exploring Plimoth Plantation, ten miles away, won't be disappointed. Set amidst the pines on Pinewood Lake, at the end of a dead-end road, the campground boasts 3,000 feet of lake frontage. A private beach is buoyed off for swimming; near the beach there's a playground and rental rowboats and canoes. With its bustling rec room (nice feature: a piano) and activities galore (air hockey tournaments, a pots-and-pans parade), Pinewood Lodge is a destination resort. In summer, that is; in fall, retirees replace kids on bikes and the mood

changes completely. Campsites are mostly wooded, carpeted with pine needles, and set fairly close together. Avoid the sites along the main road (beginning with letter D) and head to the East & West Park areas (beginning with letter S.) Nicest sites for tents is the small colony on the opposite side of the park, numbers 14 through 21. Fees are comparable to other area campgrounds, although they charge extra per child, but Pinewood Lodge offers more in the way of cleanliness, amenities, and attention to detail.

## BASICS

**Operated By:** Saunders family. **Open:** May 1–Nov. 1. **Site Assignment:** Reservations recommended. Deposit required equal to one night's stay. $50 deposit required for holiday stay. Deposits refunded w/two-week notice only. $5 service charge applies to cancelled or shortened stays. **Registration:** At office. **Fee:** $23–$33 in season; $20–$30, off-peak. Rates based on two people; extra children age 13-plus, $5; 12 & under, $2. V, MC. **Parking:** At sites & parking lots.

## FACILITIES

**Number of RV Sites:** 230. **Number of Tent-Only Sites:** 20. **Hookups:** Water, electric (20, 30, 50 amps), sewer. **Each Site:** Picnic table, ring. **Dump Station:** Yes. **Laundry:** Yes. **Pay Phone:** Yes. **Rest Rooms and Showers:** Yes, coin-op. **Fuel:** No. **Propane:** Yes. **Internal Roads:** Paved & gravel, in good condition. **RV Service:** Yes. **Market:** 5 mi. east, in Plymouth. **Restaurant:** Yes. **General Store:** Yes. **Vending:** No. **Swimming Pool:** No. **Playground:** Yes. **Other:** Rec hall. **Activities:** Fishing, swimming, boating (rentals available), canoeing, basketball, planned activities. **Nearby Attractions:** Plimoth Plantation, whale-watching cruises, scenic harbor cruises, Mayflower II, Plymouth National Wax Museum, Pilgrim Hall Museum, winery, Ocean Spray Cranberry World, tours, winery. **Additional Information:** Destination Plymouth, (800) USA-1620 or www.visit-plymouth.com.

## RESTRICTIONS

**Pets:** No. **Fires:** In fire rings only. **Alcoholic Beverages:** Yes. **Vehicle Maximum Length:** None. **Other:** Three-night min. stay required on holiday weekends; five-night min. on 4th of July.

## TO GET THERE

Take Rte. 3 south to Rte. 44, exit 6B. Take Rte.44 west 3 mi. to Pinewood Rd., turn left to campground entrance.

## PROVINCETOWN

### Coastal Acres Camping Court

West Vine St. Extension, P.O. Box 593, Provincetown 02657. T: (508) 487-1700; www.coastalacres.com.

🚐 ★★                    ▲ ★★★

Beauty: ★★                  Site Privacy: ★★
Spaciousness: ★★★★      Quiet: ★★★
Security: ★★                Cleanliness: ★★★
Insect Control: ★★★        Facilities: ★★

If you want to stay within walking distance of Provincetown, on the tip of Cape Cod, this is the place. This campground is set in a residential area in town, so all of P'town's street scene, restaurants, galleries, and charter boats are merely a stroll away. Beaches are close by, as well. Campsites are set in a grid, with the office, store, and rest rooms in the middle. RV sites are open and grassy; biggest sites are 1A through 8. Tent sites are fairly private, set in the pines, with plenty of buffer between sites. Nicest spots are along inland pond—these are lettered, not numbered. Campers are a mix of couples and families. If you want to leave the car behind and explore lively Provincetown and its dazzling beaches, you'll do well here. Bonus: the staff is happy to offer recommendations on restaurants, boat tours, and other attractions, and will happily assist you in making reservations.

## BASICS

**Operated By:** Richard Perry. **Open:** Apr. 1–Nov. 1. **Site Assignment:** Reservations recommended for peak season, Memorial Day to Labor Day. Three-night min. reservation, payable in advance. For one weeks' reservation, three-night deposit required; for two weeks or longer stay, one week deposit required. Refunds granted for cancellations w/one weeks' notice prior to scheduled arrival date, minus $7 service charge. No credit cards. **Registration:** At office. **Fee:** $24–$34 per day for two people; extra adult, $9 per night; extra child $6 per day. No charge for children under age 3. No credit cards. **Parking:** At site only.

## FACILITIES

**Number of RV Sites:** 114. **Number of Tent-Only Sites:** 0. **Hookups:** Water, electric (30 amps). **Each Site:** Picnic table. **Dump Station:** Yes. **Laundry:** No. **Pay Phone:** Yes. **Rest Rooms and Showers:** Yes, coin-op. **Fuel:** No. **Propane:** Yes. **Internal Roads:** Paved, in good condition. **RV Service:** No. **Market:** 1 mi. **Restaurant:** Several within walking distance. **General Store:** Yes. **Vending:** Yes. **Swimming Pool:** No. **Playground:** No. **Other:** Patios, private parking. **Activities:** Biking, horseback riding, boating. **Nearby Attractions:** Cape Cod National Seashore, Provincetown, Pilgrim Monument & Provincetown Museum, Provincetown Repertory Theater, whale watch cruises, charter boats, golf, tennis, hiking, bike trails. **Additional Information:** Cape Cod Chamber of Commerce, (508) 862-0700 or (888) 33-CAPECOD; www.capechamber.org.

## RESTRICTIONS

**Pets:** Must be leashed, quiet, & cleaned up after. **Fires:** No open fires. Campstoves, & charcoal grills OK. **Alcoholic Beverages:** Yes. **Vehicle Maximum Length:** None. **Other:** Minimum of a three night stay when making a reservation.

## TO GET THERE

Follow Rte. 6 east to end. Go left on Herring Cove (Rte. 6A), continue to Bradford St. Look for campground sign on the left of Bradford St., just before Seafood Connection. Turn left on West Vine, heading into campground.

## PROVINCETOWN

### Dunes' Edge Campground

386 Rte. 6, P.O. Box 875, Provincetown 02657. T: (508) 487-9815; F: (508) 487-5918; www.dunes-edge .com.

🚐 ★★                    ▲ ★★★

Beauty: ★★★              Site Privacy: ★★
Spaciousness: ★★          Quiet: ★★★★
Security: ★★★            Cleanliness: ★★★
Insect Control: ★★        Facilities: ★★

You'll know you're in Cape Cod when you arrive here; to enter the campground, you drive up a long hill flanked by a huge, sloping sand dune. Aptly-named Dunes' Edge sits in the shadow of Horse's Head, one of Provincetown's tallest hills. This campground sits at the edge of P'town, about a 15-minute walk, so it's more 'country' than 'city', unlike its nearest neighbor, Coastal Acres Camping Court (see listing.) In fact, the brown wood office building with neon-orange lettering reminded us of The Flintstones! It's a five-minute ride by car to two wonderful beaches, Herring Cove and Race Point (expect to pay a $7 parking fee.) Or, take the bike trail to the beach; that's a 20 minute ride or so, depending on your energy level. It's all nicely wooded, and more geared to tenters than RVers. Nice small touches: A full-length mirror, and lots of hooks, in the ladies' room. Campsites are set in a big loop, and a smaller loop with spokes. We'd skip sites 18, 20, 21, 28, and 30, set close to Ground Hog Hill and tightly packed to boot. Nicer tent sites, but harder to get to, are sites 36 through 39. On the other side of the campground, sites 65 and 65A are plenty spacious. Site 71 is a super hilltop spot.

## BASICS

**Operated By:** Miriam Collinson & Jim Buckingham. **Open:** May–late Sept. **Site Assignment:** Reservations accepted, & recommended by Jul., Aug., & holiday weekends (three-night min.) $30 deposit on reservations, payable by check. Two-week notice required for refunds due to cancellation, minus $5 service charge. **Registration:** At office. **Fee:** $25–$34 for two people; extra adult is $10 per night; extra child is $3. No credit cards. **Parking:** At site.

## FACILITIES

**Number of RV Sites:** 15. **Number of Tent-Only Sites:** 85. **Hookups:** Water, electric (20 amps). **Each Site:** Picnic table. **Dump Station:** Yes. **Laundry:** Yes. **Pay Phone:** Yes. **Rest Rooms and Showers:** Yes, coin-op. **Fuel:** No. **Propane:** No. **Internal Roads:** Paved, in good condition. **RV Service:** No. **Market:** 1 mi. north. **Restaurant:** 1 mi. north. **General Store:** Yes. **Vending:** Yes. **Swimming Pool:** No. **Playground:** No. **Other:** Modem in central area. **Activities:** Hiking, biking. **Nearby Attractions:** Cape Cod National Seashore, Provincetown, Pilgrim Monument & Provincetown Museum, Provincetown Repertory Theater, whale watch cruises, charter boats, golf, tennis, hiking, bike trails. **Additional Information:** Cape Cod Chamber of Commerce, (508) 862-0700 or (888) 33-CAPECOD; www.capechamber.org.

## RESTRICTIONS

**Pets:** Must be leashed, quiet, & cleaned up after. Must not be left unattended. One pet per site. **Fires:** No open fires. Charcoal grills or camp-stoves OK. **Alcoholic Beverages:** Yes. **Vehicle Maximum Length:** 32 ft. **Other:** Two-week max. & three-night min. stay.

## TO GET THERE

Follow Rte. 6 east to Provincetown. Turn right off Rte. 6 at the blue and white 'seasonal camping' sign, just beyond Mile Marker 116. Campground is on the right.

## ROCHESTER

## Outdoor World—Gateway to Cape Cod

90 Stevens Rd., Rochester 02770. T: (508) 763-5911 or (800) 588-2221 (reservations); F: (508) 763-2052; www.campoutdoorworld.com.

| 🚐 ★★★★ | 🅰 ★★ |
|---|---|
| Beauty: ★★★★ | Site Privacy: ★★★ |
| Spaciousness: ★★★ | Quiet: ★★★★ |
| Security: ★★★★★ | Cleanliness: ★★★★ |
| Insect Control: ★★★ | Facilities: ★★★★★ |

Located about 55 miles south of Boston and 20 miles from the Cape Cod Canal, this membership park is nestled in tall pines at the end of a dead-end road. This is big rig country—you might even see five-wheelers here—so tent campers are likely to feel dwarfed in these surroundings. But RVers will find plenty to like, from pull-thru sites to natural beauty to nice touches, like big umbrellas at poolside. And how often do you find tennis courts at a campground? There's a nice spot to get away from it all, too; a couple of picnic tables overlooking Leonard's Pond, at the end of Whitehorse Rd. (The rusted-out grills at several campsites are a downer, though.) Campsites are set in three sections, with 'A' and 'B' sections closest to the entrance and activities areas, and 'C' section set back, near the tennis courts, basketball court, playground, and, at the very end, the pond and overflow sites. Among the nicest, in our view, are sites A42 through A47, which back up into the woods but are an easy walk to the snack bar, pool, and other facilities. Tent sites are clustered just behind the 'A' section. With so much to do, families will be happy here, in this very resort-like property.

## BASICS

**Operated By:** Resorts USA. **Open:** Mid-Apr.–mid-Oct. **Site Assignment:** Outdoor World is a membership park. Call (800) 222-5557 for information on arranging a visit. or to reserve a campsite. **Registration:** At office. **Fee:** $25 per family. V, MC, D, Amex. **Parking:** At site.

## FACILITIES

**Number of RV Sites:** 180. **Number of Tent-Only Sites:** 8. **Hookups:** Water, electric (30, 50 amps), sewer. **Each Site:** Picnic table, fire ring, grill. **Dump Station:** No. **Laundry:** Yes. **Pay Phone:** Yes. **Rest Rooms and Showers:** Yes. **Fuel:** No. **Propane:** Yes. **Internal Roads:** Gravel, in good condition. **RV Service:** No. **Market:** 5 mi. east. **Restaurant:** Yes. **General Store:** Yes. **Vending:** Yes. **Swimming Pool:** Yes. **Playground:** Yes. **Other:** Game room, rec hall, tennis courts. **Activities:** Tennis, swimming, volleyball, softball, bocce, shuffleboard, horseshoes, canoeing, kayaking, planned activities. **Nearby Attractions:** Edaville Railroad, berry picking, golf, outlet shopping, Plymouth attractions. **Additional Information:** Bristol County CVB, (508) 997-1250 or (800) 288-6263; www.bristol-county.org.

## RESTRICTIONS

**Pets:** Must be leashed, quiet, & cleaned up after. Not permitted in buildings, pavilions, or pool & lake areas. Must not be left unattended. **Fires:** In fireplaces only. **Alcoholic Beverages:** Yes. Must be in a cup when carried off site. **Vehicle Maximum Length:** None. **Other:** Maximum 10 people per campsite (including visitors) at any time.

## TO GET THERE

Take I-495 south to junction of Rte. 58, exit 2. Turn right and go to traffic light where Rte. 58 becomes County Rd. Continue south on County Rd. 1.5 mi. to High St. Turn right on High St. and go another 1.5 mi. to Stevens Rd. Turn left onto Stevens Rd., follow signs 0.5 mi. to campground entrance.

## SAGAMORE

## Scusset Beach State Reservation Camping Area

140 Scusset Beach Rd., Buzzards Bay 02532. T: (508) 888-0859; www.state.ma.us/dem/parks/scus.htm.

| 🚐 ★★★ | 🏕 ★★★★ |
|---|---|
| Beauty: ★★★★ | Site Privacy: ★★★ |
| Spaciousness: ★★★★ | Quiet: ★★★★ |
| Security: ★★★★★ | Cleanliness: ★★★ |
| Insect Control: ★★★ | Facilities: ★★ |

Set on Cape Cod Bay on the Upper Cape, Scusset Beach State Reservation is the quietest camping place in the area. The public beach is reachable via a long, looping road; the camping area is set back from the shore, behind the bathhouse, snack bar, and parking lot. The grassy, back-in RV sites are fairly open; scattered low trees provide some buffer between sites, but not much shade. The worst RV sites are numbers 80 through 91, located on an open field right next to the beach parking lot. Anything set back (lower numbers) is much better. Tent sites are surprisingly secluded. While the tent sites (grouped together) are a stroll from the beach, they're tucked away down walking paths, roomy and very private. Each tent site is surrounded by trees. If you're an RVer, don't count on an evening 'round the fire, unless you've brought a campstove; only the tent sites have fireplaces. Only one rest room serves all. This place is low on the frills meter, unless you consider a Cape Cod beach the ultimate amenity.

## BASICS

**Operated By:** Massachusetts State Forests & Parks. **Open:** Apr.–Columbus Day. **Site Assignment:** Reservations recommended. Reserve up to six months in advance by calling ReserveAmerica at (877) 1-CAMP MA or online at www.reservamerica.com. To change arrival or departure date, or site type, call at least three dayas prior to arrival date. $10 cancellation/transfer fee. No refunds for amounts less than $5. **Registration:** At office. **Fee:** Massachusetts residents, $17; non-residents, $20. V, MC. **Parking:** At sites or parking lots only.

## FACILITIES

**Number of RV Sites:** 98. **Number of Tent-Only Sites:** 5. **Hookups:** Water, electric (20, 30 amps). **Each Site:** Picnic table (fireplaces at tent sites only). **Dump Station:** Yes. **Laundry:** No. **Pay Phone:** Yes. **Rest Rooms and Showers:** Yes. **Fuel:** No. **Propane:** No. **Internal Roads:** Paved, in good condition. **RV Service:** No. **Market:** 4-5 mi. west in Bourne. **Restaurant:** 2 mi. south. **General Store:** Yes. **Vending:** No. **Swimming Pool:** No. **Playground:** No. **Other:** Interpretive center, fishing pier. **Activities:** Swimming (in Cape Cod Bay), bicycling, volleyball, planned activities. **Nearby Attractions:** Boating, fishing, antique shops, golf, scenic bike paths, ferries to Martha's Vineyard & Nantucket. **Additional Information:** Cape Cod Chamber of Commerce, (888) 33-CAPECOD or (508) 362-3225; www.capecodchamber.org.

## RESTRICTIONS

**Pets:** Must be leashed, quiet, & cleaned up after. Current rabies vaccination certificate required. Posted areas are off-limits to pets. **Fires:** In fireplaces at tent sites only. **Alcoholic Beverages:** No. **Vehicle Maximum Length:** 35 ft. **Other:** Maximum stay is 14 cumulative days between Memorial Day & Labor Day.

## TO GET THERE

Follow Rte. 3 to Sagamore Bridge traffic circle, then follow signs to campground.

## SALEM

### Winter Island Park

50 Winter Island Rd., Salem 01970. T: (978) 745-9430; www.salemweb.com/winterisland; winter island@cove.com.

 ★★★           ★★

Beauty: ★★★★  Site Privacy: ★★
Spaciousness: ★  Quiet: ★★
Security: ★★★★  Cleanliness: ★★
Insect Control: ★★★  Facilities: ★★

Talk about a waterfront RV site: at Winter Island Park, you can pull your rig right up alongside the boat ramp and plug in. Any closer, and you'd better sprout a pair of pontoons. Managed by the city of Salem's Park and Recreation Dept., 20-acre Winter Island is a rare thing; a seaside park tucked away in an urban area. Some might call it a hidden gem; if so, it's a rather rough-cut sparkler. The rest rooms could use some attention, and the property has a rather ramshackle feel, with scattered out-buildings that reveal the history of the place. For more than 250 years, the island was a center for commercial fish preparation and boat building. A 1934 Federalist-style seaplane hangar is on the property, as are the ruins of Fort Pickering (1799), a colonial fortress. Interpretive signs offer historical details. Just behind the fort is the best tent site, #27, offering shade, seclusion, and close proximity to Waikiki Beach (so named by Coast Guardsmen), a nice crescent of tawny sand on the north end of the park. And how many campgrounds boast a lighthouse on their property? RV sites edge the bustling waterfront, and are also located on a grassy hill inland.

## BASICS

**Operated By:** City of Salem. **Open:** May 1–Nov. 1. **Site Assignment:** Reservation line opens on Feb. 1. Deposit of first night's fee required. Refunds issued for cancellation if made 7 days or more prior to arrival date. **Registration:** At office. **Fee:** Tents, $15; RVs, $25–$35. Checks, V, MC. **Parking:** At sites only or as directed.

## FACILITIES

**Number of RV Sites:** 34. **Number of Tent-Only Sites:** 25. **Hookups:** Water, electric (30, 50 amps). **Each Site:** Picnic table, grill. **Dump Station:** Yes. **Laundry:** No. **Pay Phone:** Yes. **Rest Rooms and Showers:** Yes. **Fuel:** No. **Propane:** No. **Internal Roads:** Gravel, good condition. **RV Service:** No. **Market:** 1 mi. north. **Restaurant:** 1 mi. north on Bridge St. **General Store:** Yes.

**Vending:** Yes. **Swimming Pool:** No. **Playground:** Yes. **Other:** Boat ramp. **Activities:** Ocean beach, swimming, boating, walking trail w/interpretive signage, volleyball, picnic shelter (planned). **Nearby Attractions:** Peabody Essex Museum, Salem Willows amusement park, Salem Witch Museum, Witch Dungeon Museum, House of Seven Gables, McIntyre Historic District self-guided walking tour, whale-watching boat cruises, Le Grand David magic show, scenic Marblehead Harbor. **Additional Information:** North of Boston CVB, (978) 977-7760 or (800) 742-5306; www.northofboston.org.

## RESTRICTIONS

**Pets:** Must be leashed & cleaned up after. Must show proof of rabies vaccination at check-in. Clean up after pets. Do not leave pets unattended. Pets prohibited on ocean, beach, & in rest rooms. **Fires:** In grills only. **Alcoholic Beverages:** No. **Vehicle Maximum Length:** None. **Other:** Big rigs welcome.

## TO GET THERE

From Rte. 128N, take Exit 25A and follow Rte. 114E into Salem. There will be a gas station on your left; go up on overpass and take your first right, then take a right back under the overpass onto Bridge St. Go straight around the rotary until you come to a blinking yellow light. Keep going straight onto island until you reach the first set of working lights. Take that right onto Webb St. Follow Webb all the way until you see a power plant on your right. After passing the power plant, take your first right onto Winter Island Rd. Road leads into park and entrance gate.

## SALISBURY

## Black Bear Family Campground

54 Main St., Salisbury 01952. T: (978) 462-3183; www.blackbearcamping.com; bbcamping@aol.com.

🚐 ★★★★                    ▲ ★★

Beauty: ★★★              Site Privacy: ★★★
Spaciousness: ★★          Quiet: ★★★★
Security: ★★★             Cleanliness: ★★★★
Insect Control: ★★★       Facilities: ★★★★

Despite the menacing appearance of the black bear sculpture at the entrance, the Chouinard family welcomes campers who like a few amenities with their outdoor experience. Although it is located near Salisbury Beach State Reservation, (see listing), this campground offers a completely different experience. The trappings at this suburban campground include two swimming pools, a nice playground area, and a '50s-style rec hall with a pool table and video games. The campground owners operate a pizza shop/bakery next door. The campground is located just south of the New Hampshire border, near the junctions of I-95 and Rte. 1, so it's a handy base for exploring Portsmouth, New Hampshire and Hampton Beach, and it's only three miles from Salisbury Beach. (Bonus: there's a free trolley to the beaches.) Some campsites are shaded, some are open, and some look to be fairly permanent. If your list of campground qualifications reads: 'quiet, family-friendly, and easily accessible to the highway,' Black Bear Family Campground will meet your needs squarely.

## BASICS

**Operated By:** Chouinard family. **Open:** May 15–Sept. 30. **Site Assignment:** Reservations accepted year-round. Reservations recommended for Jul. & Aug. For 7 nights or less, payment due in full or 1 weeks' deposit. Refunds only w/cancellation 2 weeks prior to arrival date. Walk-ins & weekenders are welcome & assigned on a space-available basis. (Limited number of sites available for less than 1 week.). **Registration:** At office. **Fee:** Tents, $25–$35. Rate is based on 2 people. Extra adult, $5; extra child under age 18, $1. V, MC. **Parking:** At site. Only 1 car per site.

## FACILITIES

**Number of RV Sites:** 225. **Number of Tent-Only Sites:** 25. **Hookups:** Water, electric (30, 50 amps), sewer, modem. **Each Site:** Picnic table, fire ring. **Dump Station:** Yes. **Laundry:** Yes. **Pay Phone:** Yes. **Rest Rooms and Showers:** Yes, coin op. **Fuel:** No. **Propane:** No. **Internal Roads:** Gravel, in good condition. **RV Service:** No. **Market:** 1 mi. north. **Restaurant:** Yes. **General Store:** No. **Vending:** No. **Swimming Pool:** Yes.

**Playground:** Yes. **Other:** Rec hall. **Activities:** Volleyball, basketball, horseshoes, shuffleboard, pool table, arcade games. **Nearby Attractions:** Ocean beaches, whale-watching cruises, Salisbury Beach amusement area, deep sea fishing charters, golf. **Additional Information:** North of Boston CVB, (978) 977-7760 or (800) 742-5306; www.northof boston.org.

## RESTRICTIONS

**Pets:** Small pets permitted if leashed at all times & cleaned up after. **Fires:** In fire rings only. **Alcoholic Beverages:** Sites only. **Vehicle Maximum Length:** None. **Other:** 2 week max. stay for tent campers.

## TO GET THERE

From I-95, take Exit 60. At first set of lights, take a left. Campground entrance is 200 feet on the left.

## SALISBURY

## Rusnik Campground

Rte. 1, Salisbury 01952. T: (978) 462-0551 (summer) or (978) 465-5295 (winter); www.gocampingamer ica.com/rusnik; www.rusnik.com; rusnik2001@ aol.com.

🚐 ★★★          ▲ ★★★

Beauty: ★★★            Site Privacy: ★★
Spaciousness: ★★★       Quiet: ★★★
Security: ★★★★★          Cleanliness: ★★★
Insect Control: ★★       Facilities: ★★★

Located about 40 miles north of Boston, near the border of New Hampshire, Rusnik Family Campground is one of a cluster of campsites near Salisbury Beach and the Atlantic Coast. Salisbury Beach is just three miles away; more upscale Hampton Beach (New Hampshire) is a four-mile jaunt. The inviting, tourist-friendly seaport towns of Portsmouth, New Hampshire and Newburyport, Massachusetts are a close hop away, beckoning vacationers with unique shops, good restaurants, and whale watch boat cruises. With all that going for it, this campground doesn't have to offer much in the way of amenities, although there's a swimming pool (in need of umbrellas for shade) and a pretty basic mini-golf course. Campsites are grouped around an open green.

About half are seasonal sites. All sites have water and electricity, and all are back-ins, with some shade and gravel. Site A2 is close to the pool, handy if you're camping with kids who'll use it a lot. Sites E37, 38, and 39 are quiet, and will hold RVs bigger than 40 feet. Site B11 is pretty and wooded. All in all, Rusnik Campground is a quiet and appealing base for sightseeing.

## BASICS

**Operated By:** Murray family. **Open:** May 15–Columbus Day. **Site Assignment:** Reservations recommended. Deposit for full amount required to secure reservation (checks OK); refund upon cancellation w/two weeks' notice. **Registration:** At office. **Fee:** $28 for two adults; additional adults, $5 per day; addition children under age 18, $1 daily. V, MC. **Parking:** At site, or designated lot only.

## FACILITIES

**Number of RV Sites:** 150. **Number of Tent-Only Sites:** 0. **Hookups:** Water, electric (30 amps). **Each Site:** Picnic table, fireplace. **Dump Station:** Yes. **Laundry:** Yes. **Pay Phone:** Yes. **Rest Rooms and Showers:** Yes, coin-op. **Fuel:** No. **Propane:** Yes. **Internal Roads:** Gravel, in good condition. **RV Service:** No. **Market:** 1–2 mi. south, on Rte. 1. **Restaurant:** 1–2 mi. south, on Rte. 1. **General Store:** Yes. **Vending:** No. **Swimming Pool:** Yes. **Playground:** Yes. **Other:** Rec hall. **Activities:** Mini-golf, basketball, horseshoes, bocce, volleyball, swimming. **Nearby Attractions:** Salisbury Beach amusement area, whale-watching, ocean beaches, golf, outlet shopping (Kittery, Maine). **Additional Information:** North of Boston CVB, (978) 977-7760 or (800) 742-5306; www.northof boston.org.

## RESTRICTIONS

**Pets:** Must be quiet, leashed, & cleaned up after. Must not be left unattended. **Fires:** In fireplaces only. **Alcoholic Beverages:** Yes. **Vehicle Maximum Length:** 40 ft. **Other:** Two night min. stay, from Memorial Day through Labor Day; three night min. on holidays.

## TO GET THERE

From I-95 northbound, take exit 58A. Go 2.4 mi. on Rte. 110 east to Rte. 1. Proceed 1 mi. north on Rte. 1 to campground, on left.

## SALISBURY

### Salisbury Beach State Reservation

P.O. Box 5303, Salisbury 01952. T: (978) 462-4481 or (877) I CAMP MA (reservations); www.state.ma.us/dem/ or www.reserve america.com.

🚐 ★★★★★          ⛺ ★★★

| | |
|---|---|
| Beauty: ★★★★★ | Site Privacy: ★★★ |
| Spaciousness: ★★★★ | Quiet: ★★★ |
| Security: ★★★ | Cleanliness: ★★★★ |
| Insect Control: ★★★ | Facilities: ★★★ |

If this stretch of beach wasn't owned by the state, it would be chock-a-block with high-rise hotels. No wonder Salisbury Beach State Reservation is a favorite of beach-loving campers. It's an "ahh"-inspiring, panoramic vista of sandy shore, lapped by the sparkling waters of the North Atlantic. Located 40 miles north of Boston, at the northeast border of Massachusetts, Salisbury Beach is a destination campground. Why leave, when there's a four-mile ocean beach (swimming permitted), a one-mile river beach, a boardwalk for strolling, fishing gear for rent, and ranger programs in the evenings (in season)? Whether you choose a site alongside the Merrimack River, or a spot near the ocean beach, it's hard to go wrong here. Like a suburban subdivision, campsites are set in rows on "streets" labeled A-H and W-Z, within the park's perimeter loop road. With this set-up, there's not a lot of privacy. Tent campers are likely to feel rather exposed. Sites are grassy, with little shade. The campground is immaculate and well-maintained. You can't beat $20 (or less) per night for an ocean-front setting, and clean rest rooms to boot. While the honky-tonk action of Salisbury Beach (go-carts, skee-ball, dance clubs) is right up the street, it's easy to leave it all behind here.

### BASICS

**Operated By:** Massachusetts State Forests & Parks. **Open:** Mid-Apr.–mid-Oct. Limited winter camping available. **Site Assignment:** Reserve up to 6 months in advance by calling (877) I CAMP MA or on line at www.reserveamerica.com. If you cancel or change dates or type of site, call (877) 422-6762 at least 3 days prior to arrival. $10 cancellation/transfer fee. Full payment w/credit card or check required, 30 days prior to arrival. Cancellation fee, $10. 20 percent of campsites reserved for walk-ins. **Registration:** At office. **Fee:** MA residents, $17 w/electric, $14 without. Non-residents, $20–$17. V, MC. **Parking:** At site.

### FACILITIES

**Number of RV Sites:** 484. **Number of Tent-Only Sites:** 0. **Hookups:** Water, electric (15, 20 amps). **Each Site:** Picnic table, fireplace. **Dump Station:** Yes. **Laundry:** No. **Pay Phone:** Yes. **Rest Rooms and Showers:** Yes. **Fuel:** No. **Propane:** No. **Internal Roads:** Paved, in good condition. **RV Service:** No. **Market:** 4 mi. west. **Restaurant:** Several within 1 mi. **General Store:** Yes. **Vending:** Yes. **Swimming Pool:** No. **Playground:** Yes. **Other:** Boat ramp, boardwalk. **Activities:** Evening ranger programs, swimming, boating, canoeing, fishing in ocean & Merrimack River (ocean fishing prohibited from 10 a.m. to 5 p.m. Rentals & bait available, no license needed). **Nearby Attractions:** Pirate's Fun Park (amusement rides), golf, go-cart track, whale watch boat cruises (out of Newburyport), scenic tours. **Additional Information:** North of Boston CVB, (978) 977-7760 or (800) 742-5306; www.northofboston.org.

### RESTRICTIONS

**Pets:** Must be leashed & cleaned up after. Must not be left unattended. Proof of rabies vaccination required at check-in. No pets allowed on ocean, beach, or in rest rooms. **Fires:** Fireplaces only. **Alcoholic Beverages:** No. **Vehicle Maximum Length:** 35 ft. **Other:** Maximum stay is 14 cumulative days between Memorial Day & Labor Day.

### TO GET THERE

From junction of I-95 and Rte. 110, head east on Rte. 110 to Rte. 1-A North. Follow signs to state resevation.

# SANDWICH

## Peters Pond Park Family Camping

185 Cotuit Rd., P.O. Box 999, Sandwich 02563. T: (508) 477-1775; F: (508) 477-1777; www.camp-cape cod.com; info@peterspond.com.

🚐 ★★★★　　　　▲ ★

Beauty: ★★　　　　　Site Privacy: ★★★
Spaciousness: ★★★　　Quiet: ★★
Security: ★★★★★　　Cleanliness: ★★★★
Insect Control: ★★　　Facilities: ★★★★

This bustling family campground is just seven miles from the Sagamore Bridge, one of two bridges marking the 'entrance' to the vacation-land of Cape Cod. And it's definitely a vacation scene here, complete with nightly campfires, a party tent, and kids whooping it up on aqua bikes and paddle boats. The big drawing card here is a 137-acre springfed pond, stocked with salmon, trout and bass, with a nice, sandy beach. (There are actually two beaches, but one is too small to bother with.) Another nice feature: the campground abuts the Rebel Lot Conservation Area, offering good hiking trails. Campsites, with an average width of 40 feet, are set on small side streets, village-like, off a main road. Not quite half the sites are seasonal. A good number of these are set at the far end of the campground. Sites are lined with pine needles or cedar chips and are very level. Best sites on the pond are C21 and 22. Other than those sites, we'd skip the C loop, though; it's pretty crowded. Nice touch: campers get a handy booklet with campground info and map, discounted tickets to area attractions, restaurant menus, etc.

### BASICS

**Operated By:** Peters Pond Trust. **Open:** Patriot's Day (mid-Apr.)–Columbus Day. **Site Assignment:** Reservations recommended. Call the Sunday before for weekend reservations during summer season. For each week of camping, a deposit of equal to two-day fee is required. For holiday weekends, deposit is three-day fee. Deposit secures reservation. Checks & credit cards OK for deposit. Cancellation notice of two weeks required for refunds, minus service charge. **Registration:** At office. **Fee:** $27–$40. Rate includes up to four people. V, MC. **Parking:** At site.

### FACILITIES

**Number of RV Sites:** 452. **Number of Tent-Only Sites:** 0. **Hookups:** Water, electric (20, 30, 50 amps), sewer, cable TV, modem. **Each Site:** Picnic table. **Dump Station:** Yes. **Laundry:** Yes. **Pay Phone:** Yes. **Rest Rooms and Showers:** Yes, coin-op. **Fuel:** No. **Propane:** Yes. **Internal Roads:** Paved, in good condition. **RV Service:** No. **Market:** 5 mi. north. **Restaurant:** Yes (snack bar). **General Store:** Yes. **Vending:** Yes. **Swimming Pool:** No. **Playground:** Yes. **Other:** Rec hall, boat ramp. **Activities:** Lake swimming, boating (rental rowboats, paddleboats, kayaks, aqua cycles), fishing, basketball, ball field, hiking, shuffle-board, volleyball, horseshoes, planned activities. **Nearby Attractions:** Thornton Burgess Museum, Sandwich Glass Museum, Aptucxet Trading Post, ocean beaches, golf. **Additional Information:** Cape Cod Chamber of Commerce, (888) 33-CAPECOD; (508) 862-0700; www.capecodchamber.org.

### RESTRICTIONS

**Pets:** Pets welcome from opening day until July 1 & Labor Day until closing. Spruce St. camping area can campers w/pets during July & Aug. Must be leashed; must have rabies vaccination certificate. Must be kept on site in July & Aug. **Fires:** No open fires. **Alcoholic Beverages:** At sites only. **Vehicle Maximum Length:** 45 ft. **Other:** Three-day min. stay on holidays.

### TO GET THERE

Take Rte. 3 south to Sagamore Bridge. From bridge, follow Rte. 6 to exit 2, Rte. 130. Turn right, go 3 mi. Turn left at first set of lights, Quaker Meeting House Rd. Turn right at next set of lights (Cotuit Rd.) Then head south 0.5 mi. to campground, on right.

## SANDWICH

### Shawme-Crowell State Forest

42 Main St., P.O. Box 621, Sandwich 02563. T: (508) 888-0351;
www.state.ma.us/dem/parks/shrcr.htm.

🚐 ★★★                    ⛺ ★★★★★

| | |
|---|---|
| Beauty: ★★★★★ | Site Privacy: ★★★★★ |
| Spaciousness: ★★★★ | Quiet: ★★★★★ |
| Security: ★★★★★ | Cleanliness: ★★★★ |
| Insect Control: ★★★ | Facilities: ★★★★ |

Set in Sandwich, the oldest town on Cape Cod, this gorgeous state park camping area is a wonderful option for tent campers and RVers with self-contained units. Campsites are arranged in two loops, Area 1 (hilly, with mixed forest) and Area 2 (piney woods.) Area 1 is closest to the campground entrance and campstore. It's hard to find a bad campsite here. Some have long driveways, though, and would pose a challenge for RVs. Site C26, in Area 1, is pretty and offers easy access for RVs, while site 31 is extra-big. The most appealing sites in Area 1, privacy-wise, are sites C7 and C8, located on a dead end off the main road, but near rest rooms and showers. We prefer pine-scented Area 2, though, especially sites A14 (gorgeous, wide, and near rest rooms and A18. This campground has plenty of rest rooms, by the way, but only one (in Area 2) is open for year-'round campers. Extra bang for your buck: Your camping fee buys you day-use privileges at Scusset Beach State Reservation, located across the Sagamore Bridge. There's camping there, too, but we'd stay here and day-trip to Scusset Beach.

#### BASICS

**Operated By:** Massachusetts State Forests & Parks. **Open:** Year-round. **Site Assignment:** Reservations recommended. Reserve up to six months in advance by calling ReserveAmerica at (877) 1-CAMP MA or online at www.reserveamerica .com. 20 percent of campsites are non-reservable, & available for walk-in campers. To change arrival or departure date, or site type, call at least three dayas prior to arrival date. $10 cancellation/transfer fee. No refunds for amounts less than $5. **Registration:** At office. **Fee:** Massachusetts residents, $10; non-residents, $12. V, MC. **Parking:** At site.

#### FACILITIES

**Number of RV Sites:** 285. **Number of Tent-Only Sites:** 0. **Hookups:** None. **Each Site:** Picnic table, fireplace. **Dump Station:** Yes. **Laundry:** No. **Pay Phone:** Yes. **Rest Rooms and Showers:** Yes. **Fuel:** No. **Propane:** No. **Internal Roads:** Paved & gravel, in good condition. **RV Service:** No. **Market:** 5 mi. south. **Restaurant:** 4 mi. east or west. **General Store:** Yes. **Vending:** No. **Swimming Pool:** No. **Playground:** Yes. **Other:** Hunting, horseback riding trails. **Activities:** Biking (on paved roads, mountain bike trails,and along the Cape Cod Canal), fishing (Cape Cod Canal & Cape Cod Bay), hiking, interpretive programs. **Nearby Attractions:** Thornton Burgess Museum, Sandwich Glass Museum, Aptucxet Trading Post, ocean beaches, golf. **Additional Information:** Cape Cod Chamber of Commerce, (888) 33-CAPECOD; (508) 862-0700; www.capecodchamber.org.

#### RESTRICTIONS

**Pets:** Must be leashed, quiet, & cleaned up after. Current rabies vaccination certificate required. Posted areas are off-limits to pets. **Fires:** In fireplaces only. **Alcoholic Beverages:** No. **Vehicle Maximum Length:** 35 ft. **Other:** Maximum stay is 14 cumulative days between Memorial Day & Labor Day.

#### TO GET THERE

Follow Rte. 6 east to exit 1. Turn right at the traffic light onto Rte. 6A, and another right to Rte. 130. Campground entrance is 0.5 mi. on the right.

## SAVOY

### Shady Pines Campground

547 Loop Rd., Savoy 01256. T: (413) 743-2694;
www.shadypinescampground.com;
shdypnescg@aol.com.

🚐 ★★★★                    ⛺ ★★★

| | |
|---|---|
| Beauty: ★★★ | Site Privacy: ★★★ |
| Spaciousness: ★★★★★ | Quiet: ★★ |
| Security: ★★★★★ | Cleanliness: ★★★★ |
| Insect Control: ★★ | Facilities: ★★★ |

Amidst the rolling hills and farmlands of the Berkshires in Western Massachusetts, this campground is a hub of activity. There's often something going on in the adult lounge—perhaps a polka-and-pierogis fest (as when we visited), complete with live entertainment. (Full bar, too.) It's not just a couples scene, though; the fenced-in playground is school-yard sized. Spacious campsites ring a grassy, open area with a ball park, pavilion, swimming pool, and playground. Adjacent to the pavilion is a ten-acre safari field! Somehow, they manage to keep this huge property nicely mown and landscaped; a nice touch is the sand-and-limestone coating on the roads. No mud or dust here. Campsites are semi-wooded or open. Tent sites are clustered in the far right-hand corner of the property, near some rental cabins. These, and RV sites 197 through 202 are in close proximity to walking trails leading to Savoy Mountain. A unique feature here: piped-in music in rest rooms. All in all, a livelier scene than at nearby Peppermint Park Campground (see listing) and—certainly—Windsor State Park.

## BASICS

**Operated By:** Bill & Edna Daniels. **Open:** Year-round. **Site Assignment:** Reservations recommended. Send one-night's fee deposit to reserve. Three-day min. on holiday weekends; reservation will be accepted only w/payment in full. **Registration:** At office. **Fee:** $22 per day, two people; extra children aged 15-18, $3 per day; age 7-14, $2 per day. V, MC. **Parking:** At site.

## FACILITIES

**Number of RV Sites:** 150. **Number of Tent-Only Sites:** 0. **Hookups:** Water, electric (20 amps). **Each Site:** Picnic table, fireplace. **Dump Station:** Yes. **Laundry:** Yes. **Pay Phone:** Yes. **Rest Rooms and Showers:** Yes, coin-op. **Fuel:** No. **Propane:** No. **Internal Roads:** Gravel, in good condition. **RV Service:** No. **Market:** Yes. **Restaurant:** Yes. **General Store:** Yes. **Vending:** No. **Swimming Pool:** Yes. **Playground:** Yes. **Other:** Rec hall, game room, adult lounge (18 & up). **Activities:** Swimming, walking trails, hourshoes, ball field, planned activities. **Nearby Attractions:** Mt. Greylock, Tanglewood (outdoor concerts), Natural Bridge, Western Gateway Heritage State Park, Mass MOCA (Contemporary Arts museum), Clark Art Institute, Jacob's Pillow (dance). **Additional Information:** Berkshire Hills Visitors Bureau, (413) 443-9186 or (800) 237-5747; www.berkshires.org.

## RESTRICTIONS

**Pets:** Must be leashed & cleaned up after. Must not be left unattended. Walk dogs in woods, away from campsites. **Fires:** Fireplaces only. **Alcoholic Beverages:** Yes. **Vehicle Maximum Length:** 40 ft. **Other:** No motorcycles.

## TO GET THERE

From junction of Rte. 8A and Rte. 116, go 3 mi. southeast on Rte. 116, then 0.25 mi. north on Loop Rd. Campground entrance is on the right.

## SAVOY/FLORIDA

## Savoy Mountain State Forest

260 Central Shaft Rd., Florida 01247. T: (413) 663-8469; www.state.ma.us/dem/parks/svym.htm.

| 🚐 ★★ | 🏕 ★★★★ |
|---|---|
| Beauty: ★★★★ | Site Privacy: ★★★ |
| Spaciousness: ★★★ | Quiet: ★★★★ |
| Security: ★★★ | Cleanliness: ★★★ |
| Insect Control: ★★ | Facilities: ★★ |

A ranger at another state park, with 30 years' experience in the system, deems Savoy Mountain his absolute favorite. It's easy to see why. Located in the Berkshire Hills of Western Massachusetts, this park offers wonderful diversity, with waterfalls, balanced rocks, and scenic vistas galore. Campsites are located in an old apple orchard, which fill the air with scent in springtime. Wooded hills rise in the distance, while fields of moutain laurel are studded with sparkling ponds. Recreational activities including hiking (60 miles of trails), pond swimming, or fishing in trout-stocked North Pond. Campsites, set in a loop, are mostly open and grassy, bordered by trees. Sites 13 through 18, nearest the beach at South Pond, fill up quickly, as do the three nice-looking rustic cabins. Site 43 is fairly open, but near the rest room. Number 29 is very wooded, while sites 21, 22, and 23 are set back for ample privacy. This park offers an inviting wilderness getaway for tent campers and pop-up RVs but note that it's located in bear country (and we saw evidence of same), so practice bear-safe camping.

## BASICS

**Operated By:** Massachusetts State Forests & Parks. **Open:** Mid-May–Columbus Day. **Site Assignment:** Reservations recommended. Reserve up to six months in advance by callingReserveAmerica at (877) I-CAMP-MA or online at www.reservamerica.com. Thirty-six campsites are reservable; nine are non-reservable & held on a first-come, first-served basis. To change arrival or departure date, or site type, call at least three dayas prior to arrival date. $10 cancellation/ transfer fee. No refunds for amounts less than $5. **Registration:** At office. **Fee:** Massachusetts residents, $10; non-residents, $12. Log cabins, $25. V, MC. **Parking:** At site.

## FACILITIES

**Number of RV Sites:** 45. **Number of Tent-Only Sites:** 0. **Hookups:** None. **Each Site:** Picnic table, fireplace. **Dump Station:** No. **Laundry:** No. **Pay Phone:** Yes. **Rest Rooms and Showers:** Yes. **Fuel:** No. **Propane:** No. **Internal Roads:** Paved, in good condition. **RV Service:** No. **Market:** 0.7 mi. north. **Restaurant:** 5 mi. west. **General Store:** No. **Vending:** Yes. **Swimming Pool:** No. **Playground:** No. **Other:** Boat ramp, nature center. **Activities:** Swimming, boating (no gas-powered engines), interpretive programs, fishing. **Nearby Attractions:** Mt. Greylock, Tanglewood (outdoor concerts), Natural Bridge State Park, Western Gateway Heritage State Park, Mass MOCA (contemporary art), Clark Art Institute, Jacob's Pillow (dance). **Additional Information:** Berkshire Hills Visitors Bureau, (413) 443-9186 or (800) 237-5747; www.berkshires.org.

## RESTRICTIONS

**Pets:** Must be leashed & cleaned up after. Must not be left unattended. Proof of rabies vaccination required. **Fires:** In fireplaces only. **Alcoholic Beverages:** At site only. **Vehicle Maximum Length:** 16 ft. **Other:** Maximum stay limit is 14 cumulative days between Memorial Day & Labor Day.

## TO GET THERE

Follow Rte. 2 west through Florida, then bear left on Central Shaft Rd. Head 4 mi. south on Central Shaft Rd. to campground entrance.

## SHELBURNE FALLS

# Springbrook Family Camping Area

Patten Rd., Box 52, Shelburne Falls 01370. T: (413) 625-6618; www.springbrookcamping.com; info@ springbrookcamping.com.

🚐 ★★★          ⛺ ★★

Beauty: ★★★★          Site Privacy: ★★★
Spaciousness: ★★★★     Quiet: ★★★
Security: ★★★★          Cleanliness: ★★★
Insect Control: ★★★     Facilities: ★★

Set in a quiet farming community along the Mohawk Trail in Western Massachusetts, Springbrook boasts a feature that other area campgrounds can't match: sweeping, high-elevation views of the Holyoke Range to the south, New Hampshire's Mt. Monadnock to the north, and Mt. Wachusett in the middle. Granted, these aren't the Tetons, but this rolling panorama is lovely, especially during fall foliage season. The scenic drive into the campground and tall, fragrant pines add to the ambience here. About half the campsites are seasonal, the other half are transient, and, alas, it's the former who nab best views. There's an open field for those who wish to wander over and enjoy the scenery. Set in a north-south loop along the hillside, sites are spacious, and semi-wooded, with a few pull-thrus. Tents are grouped in a separate area at the western edge of the campground. Tent site F, at the end of the loop, offers the most privacy, although it's a bit far from the rest rooms. For RVs, sites 80 and 82 and 49, 50, and 50A, at the far south end of the property, offer plenty of space. Family-run for 40-plus years, Springbrook is the nicest commercial campground in the area, and a good choice for campers looking for a peaceful escape but more services than they'd find at a nearby state park.

## BASICS

**Operated By:** Dean family. **Open:** May 15–Oct. 15. **Site Assignment:** Reservations recommended. Deposit of one night's fee must be received within 7 days. No reservation is confirmed until deposit is received. Three-day min. on holidays; 3-day deposit required. Refunds will be granted w/two week notice of cancellation of if same site can be re-rented. **Registration:** At office. **Fee:** $22–$24 based on two adults w/children under age 17, one car, one camping unit. One day free w/one-week stay. V, MC. **Parking:** At site.

## FACILITIES
**Number of RV Sites:** 69. **Number of Tent-Only Sites:** 11. **Hookups:** Water, electric (30 amps). **Each Site:** Picnic table, fire ring. **Dump Station:** Yes. **Laundry:** No. **Pay Phone:** Yes. **Rest Rooms and Showers:** Yes, coin-op. **Fuel:** No. **Propane:** Yes. **Internal Roads:** Paved & gravel, fair condition. **RV Service:** No. **Market:** 5 mi. east, at junction of Rte. 2 & I-91. **Restaurant:** 5 mi. east, at junction of Rte. 2 & I-91. **General Store:** Yes. **Vending:** No. **Swimming Pool:** Yes. **Playground:** Yes. **Other:** Rec hall. **Activities:** Volleyball, horseshoes, croquet, shuffleboard, swimming. **Nearby Attractions:** Bridge of Flowers, glacial pot holes, Mohawk Trail scenic drive, golf, Historic Deerfield. **Additional Information:** Berkshire Hills Visitors Bureau, (413) 443-9186 or (800) 237-5747; www.berkshires.org.

## RESTRICTIONS
**Pets:** Must be leashed, quiet, & cleaned up after. Proof of rabies vaccination required. **Fires:** In fire rings only. **Alcoholic Beverages:** Sites only. **Vehicle Maximum Length:** 35 ft. **Other:** Quiet hours are from 10:30 p.m. until 7:30 a.m.

## TO GET THERE
From I-91, take exit 26 (Greenfield), heading 5.5 mi. west on Rte. 2 to Shelburne Center. Just before the church, turn right (north) onto Little Mohawk Rd. Go 1.5 mi. to Patten District sign, turn left and keep left. Campground entrance is on left.

## SOUTH CARVER
### Myles Standish State Forest

Cranberry Rd., P.O. Box 66, South Carver 02366. T: (508) 866-2526; www.state.ma.us/dem/parks/mssf.htm.

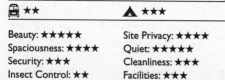

| 🚐 ★★ | ▲ ★★★ |
|---|---|
| Beauty: ★★★★★ | Site Privacy: ★★★★ |
| Spaciousness: ★★★★ | Quiet: ★★★★★ |
| Security: ★★★ | Cleanliness: ★★★ |
| Insect Control: ★★ | Facilities: ★★★ |

It's not easy trying to find it-those helpful blue RV road signs seem to be missing at key points along the route-but this immense state forest is worth sleuthing out. Just 40 miles from Boston, Miles Standish State Forest is the largest remaining pine barrens zone in New England, and one of the largest public open spaces in Massachusetts. Soaring pitch pines, scrub oak, and plantations of white and red pine make this a real wilderness escape. Dozens of gem-like ponds dot the landscape. Campsites are clustered near the ponds, with the best ones overlooking Barrett Pond. Camp near Fearing Pond, though, and you get the benefit of a swimming hole; plus, the pond is stocked with trout. Sites 18 and 19 are spectacular; best for RVs are sites 28, 34, and 35, all flat, wooded, and wide, offering great views of Fearing Pond. Beyond swimming and fishing, the park offers more than 90 miles of biking and hiking trails (15 paved for biking), and nature programs daily in season, perhaps a wildflower walk or edible plant hike. At nearly 18,000 acres, the park is big and difficult to navigate. Pay close attention to your map, or you may end up, as we did, face-to-face with the MCI Plymouth correctional facility, located, curiously enough, on park property.

## BASICS
**Operated By:** Massachusetts State Forests & Parks. **Open:** Mid-Apr.-Columbus Day. Fully open from Memorial Day-Labor Day; sites limited in off-season. Open-self-contained units only, Nov. 1-Apr. 15. **Site Assignment:** Reservations recommended. Reserve up to six months in advance by calling ReserveAmerica at (877) 1-CAMP-MA or online at www.reservamerica.com. Some sites are non-reservable & held on a first-come, first-served basis. Arrive before 11 a.m. to get on waiting list. To change arrival or departure date, or site type, call at least three dayas prior to arrival date. $10 cancellation/transfer fee. No refunds for amounts less than $5. **Registration:** At office. **Fee:** Massachusetts residents, $10; non-residents, $12. V, MC. **Parking:** At sites & parking lots near trailheads.

## FACILITIES

**Number of RV Sites:** 425. **Number of Tent-Only Sites:** 0. **Hookups:** None. **Each Site:** Picnic table, fireplace. **Dump Station:** Yes. **Laundry:** No. **Pay Phone:** Yes. **Rest Rooms and Showers:** Yes. **Fuel:** No. **Propane:** No. **Internal Roads:** Gravel, in good condition. **RV Service:** No. **Market:** 5 mi. north, in Plymouth. **Restaurant:** 5 mi. north, in Plymouth. **General Store:** No. **Vending:** No. **Swimming Pool:** No. **Playground:** No. **Other:** Interpretive center. **Activities:** Bicycling, boating (no gas-powered engines), hiking, swimming in Fearing Pond & College Pond, fishing (trout-stocked Fearing Pond), interpretive programs, wildlife watching (endangered turtles are seen at East Head Reservoir). **Nearby Attractions:** Plimoth Plantation, whale-watching cruises, scenic harbor cruises, Mayflower II, Plymouth National Wax Museum, Pilgrim Hall Museum, winery, Ocean Spray Cranberry World, tours, winery, Edaville Railroad. **Additional Information:** Destination Plymouth, (800) USA-1620 or www.visit-plymouth.com.

## RESTRICTIONS

**Pets:** Must be leashed & cleaned up after. Must not be left unattended. Proof of rabies vaccination required. **Fires:** In fireplaces only. **Alcoholic Beverages:** No. **Vehicle Maximum Length:** 30 ft. **Other:** Maximum stay is 14 cumulative days between Memorial Day & Labor Day.

## TO GET THERE

From Rte. 3, take exit 5; head west on Long Pond Rd. Follow signs to campground; turn right on Alden Rd.

## SOUTH CARVER

### Shady Acres Family Campground

P.O. Box 128, Carver 02366. T: (508) 866-4040.

🚐 ★★★          ⛺ ★★

| | |
|---|---|
| Beauty: ★★ | Site Privacy: ★ |
| Spaciousness: ★★★ | Quiet: ★★★★★ |
| Security: ★★★ | Cleanliness: ★★★ |
| Insect Control: ★★★★★ | Facilities: ★★★ |

This campground is definitely out-of-the-way; you enter via a twisting road lined with cranberry bogs. In fall, when the bogs are flooded, the berries rise to the surface, looking like pools of scarlet. Split-rail fencing adds a nice country feel. The campground itself is pleasant and quiet, if not very fancy (though improvements are being made to the campstore and office.) Thanks to its location, this campground is far quieter than the nearby KOA campground just off the highway in Middleboro. Campsites are set in a series of loops, with two lanes of full-hookup sites right in the middle. The six tent sites are right up front, too. An ice cream shop and mini-golf course are set just outside the campground; a game room, rec hall, and swimming pools are set back, overlooking a good-sized pond. Campsites are nicely shaded, but a couple of tall trees between sites don't offer much buffer. We'd avoid the sites surrounding the rec hall—numbers 15 through 19, 111 through 115, and 8 through 10, unless you like camping with a soundtrack of pop music.

## BASICS

**Operated By:** Denise & Joseph Soares. **Open:** Mid-Mar.–mid-Dec. **Site Assignment:** Reservations recommended. Deposit equal to one-night's stay required; check or credit card OK. 72-hour notice required for cancellation refunds. **Registration:** At office. **Fee:** $22–$31. Rate based on two adults & two children. V, MC, D. **Parking:** At site.

## FACILITIES

**Number of RV Sites:** 175. **Number of Tent-Only Sites:** 6. **Hookups:** Water, electric (30, 50 amps), sewer. **Each Site:** Picnic table, fire ring. **Dump Station:** Yes. **Laundry:** Yes. **Pay Phone:** Yes. **Rest Rooms and Showers:** Yes, coin-op. **Fuel:** No. **Propane:** Yes. **Internal Roads:** Gravel, in fair condition. **RV Service:** Yes. **Market:** 8 mi. north. **Restaurant:** Yes. **General Store:** Yes. **Vending:** Yes. **Swimming Pool:** Yes (2). **Playground:** Yes. **Other:** Rec hall, game room, mini-golf. **Activities:** Boating, canoeing, fishing (private pond, no license required), swimming, basketball, planned activities. **Nearby Attractions:** Plimoth Plantation, whale-watching cruises, scenic harbor cruises, Mayflower II, Plymouth National Wax Museum, Pilgrim Hall Museum, winery, Ocean Spray Cranberry World, tours, winery, Edaville

Railroad. **Additional Information:** Plymouth County CVB, (508) 747-0100 or (800) 231-1620; www.plymouth-1620.com.

## RESTRICTIONS

**Pets:** Must be leashed, quiet, & cleaned up after. Current rabies vaccination certificate required. **Fires:** In fire rings only. **Alcoholic Beverages:** Yes. **Vehicle Maximum Length:** None. **Other:** Two-night min. stay required on weekends from May to Sep.; three-night min. stay required on holidays.

## TO GET THERE

From Rte. 495 north, exit at Rte. 58 north and follow to fork. Bear right onto Tremont St. Campground is on the right, about 1 mi. past US Post Office.

## SOUTH PLYMOUTH

### Sandy Pond Campground

834 Bourne Rd., Plymouth 02360. T: (508) 759-9336 (Apr. to Sep.) or off-season (508) 224-3707; www. sandypond.com.

🚐 ★★                    ▲ ★★

Beauty: ★★                 Site Privacy: ★
Spaciousness: ★            Quiet: ★★
Security: ★★★              Cleanliness: ★★★
Insect Control: ★★★★★       Facilities: ★★

As you drive up to this campground, tucked into a residential area, your first thought might be, "Uh-oh!" Just to the left is a wide-open area, chock-a-block with RVs. Keep driving, though, and you'll realize that was the safari area; among the 300 campsites here are many less-exposed places to pull in for the weekend. Spacious, it's not, but this rather intimate setting has a friendly feel. This is mostly due to the campers, including some seasonal guests, who hang out in groups and meet for campground-run activities like candy bingo, kiddie hayrides, and ice cream socials. A footpath leads to a private, sandy beach, one of the nicest we've seen, on Sandy Pond. Among the tent sites, T-24 and 25 overlook another pond, Covel Pond, but are a hike from the rest rooms. T-6, a corner site, is very secluded. With the RV sites, the higher the number, the far-

ther you are from the action, except for FP-100 to 102 and 78 to 80 (near well-used horseshoe pits.) One caveat: this campground tends to operate in a rather haphazard fashion. Two rigs on the same site? Two different stories with regard to canoe rental availability? It happens! Therefore, the self-sufficient, easy-going camper is likely to manage best here. Like people? All the better.

## BASICS

**Operated By:** Doonan family. **Open:** Apr. 13–Sept. 30. **Site Assignment:** Reservations recommended. Must be accompanied by 50 percent deposit, received at least one week prior to visit. Refunds issued for cancellation if cancellation occurs at least one week prior to visit. **Registration:** At office. **Fee:** $22–$30 based on family of four (two minor children.) V, MC, D. **Parking:** At site.

## FACILITIES

**Number of RV Sites:** 220. **Number of Tent-Only Sites:** 80. **Hookups:** Water, electric (30, 50 amps), sewer. **Each Site:** Picnic table, fire ring. **Dump Station:** Yes. **Laundry:** Yes. **Pay Phone:** Yes. **Rest Rooms and Showers:** Yes, some coin-op. **Fuel:** No. **Propane:** Yes. **Internal Roads:** Gravel, in good condition. **RV Service:** No. **Market:** 5.5 mi. west on Rte. 6W. **Restaurant:** 5.5 mi.west on Rte. 6W. **General Store:** Yes. **Vending:** Yes. **Swimming Pool:** No. **Playground:** Yes. **Other:** Rec hall. **Activities:** Boating (rentals available), canoeing, hiking, swimming, basketball, planned activities. **Nearby Attractions:** Plimoth Plantation, whale-watching cruises, scenic harbor cruises, Mayflower II, Plymouth National Wax Museum, Pilgrim Hall Museum, winery, Ocean Spray Cranberry World, tours, winery. **Additional Information:** Destination Plymouth, (800) USA-1620 or www. visit-plymouth.com.

## RESTRICTIONS

**Pets:** Must have current rabies certificate. No large or aggressive animals (ie. dobermans, pit bulls, shepherds.) $5 fee per day per dog. No pets on holiday weekends. **Fires:** In fire rings only. **Alcoholic Beverages:** Yes, at sites only. **Vehicle Maximum Length:** None. **Other:** Two-night min. stay, Memorial Day through Labor Day. Three-night min. on holidays. 4th of July min. stay; please inquire.

## TO GET THERE

Take Rte. 3 South to exit 3. Right at end of ramp, go 0.2 mi. Head left on Long Pond Rd., go 1.75 mi., turn right at Halfway Pond Rd. Go 0.75 mi. Turn left on Bourne Rd. Follow for 6 mi. to campground (on left.)

## SOUTHWICK

### Sodom Mountain Campground

P.O. Box 702, Southwick 01077. T: (413) 569-3930; F: (413) 569-2987; www.sodommountain.com.

🚐 ★★★                    ⛺ ★★★

| | |
|---|---|
| Beauty: ★★★ | Site Privacy: ★★★ |
| Spaciousness: ★★★ | Quiet: ★★★★ |
| Security: ★★★★★ | Cleanliness: ★★ |
| Insect Control: ★★ | Facilities: ★★ |

Heading to Six Flags New England theme park, or other atttractions in the Springfield area? This campground is a convenient base. Located 12 miles east of Six Flags, it's the closest campground to the park, other than Southwick Acres (owned by the same family, but geared more to seniors and seasonal campers than Sodom Mountain.) Another selling point: they offer discounted tickets to Six Flags—sizable discounts on adult admissions, we found. Factor in your savings on a couple of adult tickets to Six Flags, and it's like you're getting a night of camping for free. Not into wild rides and the whole theme park scene? The campground is located alongside Sodom Mountain, offering marked hiking trails for all abilities. We also sleuthed out Southwick's town beach, on South Pond, with a sandy-bottomed, life-guarded swimming area and lots of picnic tables. The campground offers wooded and open sites, with some pull-thrus. Sites 67A and B are nicest for tents, while site 105 is a shady spot for RVs. The G section is the nicest overall, in our view. The rest room (one serves all) is very basic. Check out the peacock pen near the entrance.

## BASICS

**Operated By:** LaFrance family. **Open:** May 1–Columbus Day. **Site Assignment:** Reservations recommended, especially on weekends.

One nights' fee required for deposit. Refunds for cancellations w/two weeks' notice, minus $7 service fee. **Registration:** At office. **Fee:** $29–$38 for two adults & two children. V, MC. **Parking:** At site.

## FACILITIES

**Number of RV Sites:** 165. **Number of Tent-Only Sites:** 15. **Hookups:** Water, electric (30, 50 amps), sewer. **Each Site:** Picnic table, fire ring. **Dump Station:** Yes. **Laundry:** Yes. **Pay Phone:** Yes. **Rest Rooms and Showers:** Yes, coin-op. **Fuel:** No. **Propane:** Yes. **Internal Roads:** Gravel, in good condition. **RV Service:** No. **Market:** 4.1 mi. south on Rte. 202. **Restaurant:** 4.1 mi. south on Rte. 202. **General Store:** Yes. **Vending:** Yes. **Swimming Pool:** Yes. **Playground:** Yes. **Other:** Lodge, game room. **Activities:** Swimming, hiking, shuffleboard, basketball, volleyball. **Nearby Attractions:** Six Flags New England theme park, Basketball Hall of Fame, Southwick Motocrosse 338, Big E (Eastern States Exposition) fair, late Sept., Southwick Town Beach at South Pond. **Additional Information:** Greater Springfield CVB, (413) 755-1343; www.valleyvisitor.com.

## RESTRICTIONS

**Pets:** Must be leashed, quiet, & cleaned up after. Must not be left unattended. Current rabies certificate required. **Fires:** In fire rings only. **Alcoholic Beverages:** At sites or in lodge only. **Vehicle Maximum Length:** 40 ft. **Other:** Two-night min. stay required from June through Aug. Three-night min. plus advance payment in full for holidays.

## TO GET THERE

From I-90 (Massachusetts Turnpike), take exit 3. Follow Rte. 202 south to Southwick Center. Go through town, then take Rte. 57 west 3 mi. to South Loomis St. Take a left on South Loomis for 0.25 mi. to campground, on right.

## STURBRIDGE

### Jellystone Park Sturbridge

P.O. Box 600, Sturbridge 01566. T: (508) 347-9570; F: (508) 347-2336; www.jellystonestur-bridge.com; rsmith@jellystonesturbridge.com.

 ★★★★                     ★★★

Beauty: ★★★
Spaciousness: ★★
Security: ★★★★★
Insect Control: ★★★

Site Privacy: ★
Quiet: ★★
Cleanliness: ★★★★
Facilities: ★★★★★

If the presence of costumed characters Yogi, Cindy, and Boo Boo Bear don't convince you, perhaps the all-day schedule of kid's activities will—the emphasis here is on family fun. Open year-round, the campground offers non-stop action in summer months, from mini-golf to movies to ice cream-eating contests. Some parents escape to the Bear's Den, a post-and-beam style lounge with a stone fireplace. Campsites are arranged in a series of loops, with the far end devoted to rental cabins. Some sites are pull-thru. The camping area is heavily wooded, but there's not much buffer between sites. Two fairly spacious, pretty sites are 739 and 740, although they're a good trek from the beach, pool, and main building activity hub. The nicest tent sites, grouped together here, are 266 and 267, relatively secluded and leafy, also close to rest rooms, laundry, and the aqua center. (Waterslides, a pool and hot tub; they charge extra for these, which seems rather niggly to us.) This park is on the pricey side, but you get lots of activity, good security, and clean facilities for your money.

## BASICS

**Operated By:** James Leaming, manager. **Open:** May–Oct. **Site Assignment:** Reservations recommended. 50% deposit required. Refund for cancellation w/7 days' notice; beyond 7 days, will transfer deposit to another date for camping. **Registration:** At office. **Fee:** Memorial Day to Labor Day, $40-49. Off-season rates, $26 to $33.50. Extra charge on holiday weekends & weekends in July-Aug. Rates are for two adults at site, per day; extra charge of $3 for children; $5-9 for extra adult. Packages available V, MC, D, AMEX. **Parking:** At site & designated parking areas only.

## FACILITIES

**Number of RV Sites:** 359. **Number of Tent-Only Sites:** 40. **Hookups:** Water, electric (20, 30 amps), sewer, cable TV. **Each Site:** Picnic tables, fire rings. **Dump Station:** Yes. **Laundry:** Yes. **Pay Phone:** Yes. **Rest Rooms and Showers:** Yes.

**Fuel:** No. **Propane:** Yes. **Internal Roads:** Paved & gravel, in fair condition. **RV Service:** No. **Market:** 1 mi. north in Sturbridge. **Restaurant:** Yes. **General Store:** Yes. **Vending:** Yes. **Swimming Pool:** Yes. **Playground:** Yes. **Other:** Mini-golf, aqua center (water slide, hot tub), lounge, game room, petting zoo. **Activities:** Lake swimming, fishing (no license required), boating, pony rides. **Nearby Attractions:** Old Sturbridge Village living history museum. **Additional Information:** Plymouth County CVB, (508) 747-0100 or (800) 231-1620; www.plymouth-1620.com.

## RESTRICTIONS

**Pets:** Must be leashed, quiet & cleaned up after. Unattended pets should be left inside trailers. **Fires:** In fire rings only. **Alcoholic Beverages:** Yes. **Vehicle Maximum Length:** 40 ft. **Other:** Air conditioners & electric heaters not allowed unless prior arrangements are made w/office.

## TO GET THERE

From junction of I-84 and Rte. 20, go 1 mi. west on I-84 to exit 2, then 0.25 mi. on River Rd. Campground entrance is on the right

## STURBRIDGE

## Outdoor World Sturbridge Resort

19 Maushapaug Rd., Sturbridge 01566. T: (508) 347-7156; F: (508) 347-3535; www.campoutdoorworld.com.

🚐 ★★★★                    ⛺ ★★★

Beauty: ★★★★
Spaciousness: ★★★★
Security: ★★★★
Insect Control: ★★★

Site Privacy: ★★
Quiet: ★★★
Cleanliness: ★★★★★
Facilities: ★★★★★

Step into the piney lodge or the indoor pool and hot tub area, and you'd think you were on the property of a resort hotel. Such is the oh-so-luxe life that awaits the happy camper at Outdoor World, a membership resort owned by Resorts USA. Set on Pioneer Lake, the resort employs a social director, who arranges things like live music, storyteller visits, and events like a cardboard boat race, chili cook-off, and theme weekends. Campsites ring the lake, with the nicest spots right on the water, including RV sites S-6 through S-14 (even numbers) and S-21 through 23, the most secluded of the bunch. Ask for tent site S18A for best views. Sites B-1 through 5 are lovely, as well. Steer clear of sites near the busy lodge and pool area. The full hookup sites are more exposed and more tightly packed together than the others. Only two are pull-thru. Sites aren't terribly spacious, but campers are generally quiet here, and the wooded surroundings provide a peaceful quality. It's a far less rollicking, more adult atmosphere than that of nearby Jellystone Park.

## BASICS

**Operated By:** Resorts USA. **Open:** Year-round. **Site Assignment:** Outdoor World is a membership park. Call (800) 222-5557 for information on arranging a visit, or to reserve a campsite. **Registration:** At office. **Fee:** $35 in summer, $25 in winter. No extra charge for additional persons. V, MC, D, Amex. **Parking:** At site or designated parking areas.

## FACILITIES

**Number of RV Sites:** 93. **Number of Tent-Only Sites:** 5. **Hookups:** Water, electric (30, 50 amps), sewer, cable TV. **Each Site:** Picnic table, fire ring. **Dump Station:** Yes. **Laundry:** Yes. **Pay Phone:** Yes. **Rest Rooms and Showers:** Yes. **Fuel:** No. **Propane:** Yes. **Internal Roads:** Gravel, in good condition. **RV Service:** No. **Market:** 5 mi. north in Sturbridge. **Restaurant:** 5 mi. north in Sturbridge or 1 mi. south. **General Store:** Yes. **Vending:** Yes. **Swimming Pool:** Yes (indoor). **Playground:** Yes. **Other:** Mini-golf, game room, lounge, hot tub, beach, boat house. **Activities:** Lake swimming, boating (canoes, row boats, paddle boats), lake fishing, mini-golf, basketball, volleyball, horseshoes, hiking trails, movies, planned activities. **Nearby Attractions:** Old Sturbridge Village living history museum. **Additional Information:** Plymouth County CVB, (508) 747-0100 or (800) 231-1620; www.plymouth-1620.com.

## RESTRICTIONS

**Pets:** Must be kept on a leash. Pets must accompany owner when leaving campsite or trailer. Owners must clean up after pets. **Fires:** Fire pits only. **Alcoholic Beverages:** Yes. **Vehicle Maximum Length:** 35 ft. **Other:** Limit ten people per campsite.

## TO GET THERE

Take the Massachusetts Turnpike west to I-84 (exit 9); follow I-84 to Mass. exit 1 and turn left off exit. Take first right onto Mashapaug Rd. to campground entrance

## STURBRIDGE

## Wells State Park

Walker Mountain Rd., P.O. Box 602, Sturbridge 01566. T: (508) 347-9257; www.state.ma.us/dem/ parks/well.htm.

🚐 ★★          ⛺ ★★★★★

| | |
|---|---|
| Beauty: ★★★★★ | Site Privacy: ★★★★ |
| Spaciousness: ★★★★ | Quiet: ★★★★★ |
| Security: ★★★ | Cleanliness: ★★★★ |
| Insect Control: ★★ | Facilities: ★★★ |

Among the several campgrounds in the Sturbridge area, this one is the 'wilderness' option. If you can do without hookups, you'll enjoy the Old New England beauty of this property. Crisscrossed with stone walls, Wells State Park is a true beauty spot, heavily wooded with a mix of maples and other deciduous trees. Other natural features include a beaver lodge and dam, vernal pools, and a sandy-bottomed pond. The hiking here is exceptional, offering 9.5 miles of marked scenic trails. The 1.5 mile hike to Carpenter's Rocks leads to a cliff face with east-facing views of the park. Interpretive programs include wildflower walks and beaver pond tours. Campsites are set on upper and lower loops, with each loop surrounding a grassy playing field. The lower loop is closest to Walker Pond. On the upper loop, site 51 is spacious and secluded, as is 27, a campsite set far from the road. The best sites on the lower loop feature water views. Sites 15 and 16 are close together, but near the water. Site 19 is a good waterfront RV site, with pull-thru access. A couple of waterfront sites are held for walk-ins and not reservable, so it may be possible, with luck, to get a prime spot here without planning ahead.

## BASICS

**Operated By:** Massachusetts Forest & Park Service. **Open:** May 1–Columbus Day. **Site Assign-**

ment: Reserve up to 6 months in advance through ReserveAmerica by calling (877) CAMP MA or online at www.reserveamerica.com. To change your reservation or site type, or to cancel, you must call at least 3 days prior to your arrival date. $10 cancellation/transfer fee. Refunds for amounts less than $5 cannot be processed. Two night min. stay required on weekends. **Registration:** At park headquarters. **Fee:** Massachusetts residents, $10; non-residents, $12. V, MC. **Parking:** At site & parking lot only.

## FACILITIES

**Number of RV Sites: 58. Number of Tent-Only Sites: 2. Hookups:** None. **Each Site:** Picnic table, fireplace w/grill, lantern pole. **Dump Station:** Yes. **Laundry:** No. **Pay Phone:** Yes. **Rest Rooms and Showers:** Yes. **Fuel:** No. **Propane:** No. **Internal Roads:** Gravel, in good condition. **RV Service:** No. **Market:** 2.3 mi. east in Sturbridge. **Restaurant:** 2.3 mi. east in Sturbridge. **General Store:** No. **Vending:** Yes. **Swimming Pool:** No. **Playground:** No. **Other:** Interpretive center. **Activities:** Swimming in Walker Pond, beach, ball fields, basketball court, hiking, biking, equestrian trails, fishing, interpretive programs for children (must be accompanied by an adult). **Nearby Attractions:** Old Sturbridge Village living history museum, Brimfield Flea Markets (various weekends). **Additional Information:** Plymouth County CVB, (508) 747-0100 or (800) 231-1620; www.plymouth-1620.com.

## RESTRICTIONS

**Pets:** Pets must be leashed & cleaned up after. Proof of rabies vaccination required. Do not leave pets unattended. **Fires:** Fireplaces only. **Alcoholic Beverages:** No. **Vehicle Maximum Length:** 35 ft. **Other:** Maximum stay is 14 cumulative days between Memorial Day & Labor Day.

## TO GET THERE

Take I-90 (Massachusetts Turnpike) to Rte. 20 East. Follow Rte.20E to Rte. 49N, following signs to park access road. Park entrance is 1 mi. north on Rte. 49 (third left.)

## SUTTON

## The Old Holbrook Place

114 Manchaug Rd., Sutton 01590. T: (508) 865-5050.

| 🚐 ★★★★ | 🛖 ★★ |
|---|---|
| Beauty: ★★★★ | Site Privacy: ★★★ |
| Spaciousness: ★★★ | Quiet: ★★★★ |
| Security: ★★★★ | Cleanliness: ★★★ |
| Insect Control: ★★★ | Facilities: ★★★★ |

Located just south of Worcester on 350-acre Lake Manchaug, The Old Holbrook Place is a tiny gem of a campground. Operating the property since 1946, now on their third generation of guests, the Nelsons are delightfully friendly hosts (Mrs. Nelson was making a shell necklace for a camper kid when we visited, typical of the character here.) The property includes a small picnic grove and a hilly, three-sided sandy beach and swim area with raft. One side is a shallow, baby's crib (wading beach.) Campsites are set along both sides of the camp road, with some along the lake and some along the road. About half are seasonal sites (blessedly lacking in lawn art.) The best tent site is at Big Rock, alongside a boulder. Among the waterfront sites, numbers 16 and 17 boast the best views, and get nice breezes off the lake. They're close to rest rooms, but right next to the boat launch. Site 26 is nice, too, facing a marshy area of the lake. Although the picnic area and beach are open for day use, campers use a private rest room (you get a key upon check-in.) Other nice features: books and puzzles to swap, and nice park benches at waters' edge.

## BASICS

**Operated By:** Nelson family. **Open:** Memorial Day–Labor Day. **Site Assignment:** Reservations recommended, at least two weeks in advance. Will try to honor site requests. Deposit required, equal to one night's fee. Deposit is refundable if cancellation is made a week in advance, & if site can be rented. **Registration:** At office. **Fee:** $16–$24 per family (parents & unmarried children.)No credit cards. **Parking:** At site.

## FACILITIES

**Number of RV Sites:** 66. **Number of Tent-Only Sites:** 0. **Hookups:** Water, electric (20 amps), sewer. **Each Site:** Picnic table, fire ring. **Dump Station:** Yes. **Laundry:** No. **Pay Phone:** Yes. **Rest Rooms and Showers:** Yes. **Fuel:** No. **Propane:** No. **Internal Roads:** Gravel, in good condition. **RV Service:** No. **Market:** 2 mi. west. **Restaurant:** 4 mi. east. **General Store:** Yes. **Vending:** No. **Swimming Pool:** No. **Playground:** No. **Other:** Boat ramp. **Activities:** Boating (rentals available), lake swimming. **Nearby Attractions:** New England Science Center, Ecotarium, Worcester Art Museum, outlet shopping. **Additional Information:** Central Massachusetts Tourist Council, (508) 755-7400; www.worcester.org.

## RESTRICTIONS

**Pets:** Must be leashed & cleaned up after. Not allowed on the beach. **Fires:** In fire rings only. **Alcoholic Beverages:** Yes. **Vehicle Maximum Length:** 30 ft. **Other:** Visitors must register upon entering the park.

## TO GET THERE

From Rte. 395, take exit 4A, onto Sutton Ave. Head east 3.6 mi., then take second right (after passing white church) to Manchaug Rd. Campground is exactly 1 mi. in from Central Tpk. (Sutton Ave.), on Manchaug Rd. (Second campground you pass.)

## TAUNTON

### Massasoit State Park

1361 Middleboro Ave., East Taunton 02718. T: (508) 822-7405; www.state.ma.us/dem/parks/mass.htm.

🚐 ★★★★　　　▲ ★★★★

Beauty: ★★★★
Spaciousness: ★★★★★
Security: ★★★
Insect Control: ★★★
Site Privacy: ★★★
Quiet: ★★★★
Cleanliness: ★★★
Facilities: ★★★

Located about 40 miles south of Boston, this campground boasts a unique feature for a state park: water and electrical hookups. This may explain why campers tend to make a vacation of it, and stay for a whole two weeks. Very popular with local urban dwellers, Massasoit State Park is a cool oasis on a sweltering summer day. Pine carpeted, the gravel and grassy campsites are set in four loops, designated by alphabet. Areas E and G, with hookups, have frontage on Middle Pond. The pond offers a rocky, grassy beach with a small, unguarded swimming area. Site E5 is huge, great for RVs. Section H is for self-contained camping units (no rest rooms), while section C has no electrical hookups. Sites C2 and C3 are fairly secluded tent sites, with good proximity to a rest room. (Shy guys take note: the men's showers are open, not curtained.) There's a nice picnic grove, and fishing, on Big Bearhole Pond (off J Rd.) A hiking trail leads to this peachy spot. Trivia tidbit: Stall Island, on park property, was one of Elizabeth Pole's farms. It is said that she traded "a jacknife and a pot of beans" to Native Americans for 5000 acres of land in 1637.

## BASICS

**Operated By:** Massachusetts State Forests & Parks. **Open:** Mid-Apr.–Columbus Day. **Site Assignment:** Reservations recommended. Reserve up to six months in advance by calling ReserveAmerica at (877) 1-CAMP MA or online at www.reservamerica.com. 15 sites are non-reservable, & available for walk-in campers. To change arrival or departure date, or site type, call at least three dayas prior to arrival date. $10 cancellation/ transfer fee. No refunds for amounts less than $5. **Registration:** At park headquarters. **Fee:** Massachusetts residents, $10–$15; non-residents, $12–$17. V, MC. **Parking:** At site.

## FACILITIES

**Number of RV Sites:** 120. **Number of Tent-Only Sites:** 0. **Hookups:** Water, electric (15, 20 amps). **Each Site:** Picnic table, fireplace. **Dump Station:** Yes. **Laundry:** No. **Pay Phone:** Yes. **Rest Rooms and Showers:** Yes. **Fuel:** No. **Propane:** No. **Internal Roads:** Paved, in good condition. **RV Service:** No. **Market:** 3 mi. north on Rte. 44. **Restaurant:** 4–5 mi. northeast. **General Store:** No. **Vending:** No. **Swimming Pool:** No. **Playground:** No. **Other:** Boat ramp. **Activities:** Hiking, horse trails, bicycling, fishing (MA license available in Middleboro), swimming. **Nearby Attractions:** Edaville Railroad, Battleship Cove, New Bedford Whaling Museum, Plimoth Plantation, Cranberry World Visitors Center, Pilgrim Hall Museum, Fuller Museum of Art. **Additional Information:** Plymouth County CVB, (508) 747-0100 or (800) 231-1620; www.plymouth-1620.com.

## RESTRICTIONS

**Pets:** Must be leashed, quiet, & cleaned up after. Current rabies vaccination certificate required. Posted areas are off-limits to pets. **Fires:** In fireplaces only. **Alcoholic Beverages:** No. **Vehicle Maximum Length:** 40 ft. **Other:** Maximum stay is 14 cumulative days between Memorial Day & Labor Day.

## TO GET THERE

Follow Rte. 24 south to Rte. 44 (exit 13); heading east, follow signs on Rte. 44 to campground entrance.

## TEMPLETON

### Otter River State Forest

86 Winchendon Rd., Baldwinville 01436. T: (978) 939-8962; www.state.ma.us/dem/parks/ottr.htm.

🚐 ★        ▲ ★★★

| | |
|---|---|
| Beauty: ★★★★ | Site Privacy: ★★★ |
| Spaciousness: ★★★ | Quiet: ★★★★ |
| Security: ★★★ | Cleanliness: ★★★★★ |
| Insect Control: ★★ | Facilities: ★★ |

Located in a rural area along Rte. 2, northwest of Boston, Otter River State Forest is notable as the first state forest established in Massachusetts (1915.) Criss-crossed with rivers and streams, this wilderness area offers a clutch of campsites clustered near Beamon Pond. Along with its sister campground, Lake Dennison State Recreation Area, to the north, Otter River is a pleasant place to overnight near the beginning of the Mohawk Trail, a 63-mile scenic drive (and former Native American footpath) that officially starts in Orange. Heavily wooded, and very quiet, Otter River offers good hiking, including a section of the Ware River Rail Trail. Beamon Pond has a small, sandy beach and a concrete fishing bridge. Ranger programs, including kids' crafts, games, nature walks, movies, and bike rides, are run on weekends in summer. Lacking hookups, this campground is best for tent campers and pop-ups. Campsites are mostly gravel, softened with pine needles. Least-desirable sites are numbers 73 through 78, as they're small and close to the road. Sites 1 through 27 are open only to self-contained RVs. Site 62 is a great spot, near the beach, as is 81, very secluded on a dead end, but near the beach and showers and a water faucet. There's not a lot of action here, but this campground is a pleasant short-term nature escape, especially if combined with a visit to Lake Dennison State Recreation Area.

## BASICS

**Operated By:** Massachusetts State Parks & Forests. **Open:** Memorial Day–Labor Day. **Site Assignment:** Reservations recommended. Reserve up to six months in advance by calling ReserveAmerica at (877) 1-CAMP MA or online at www.reserveamerica.com. About 20 percent of campsites are non-reservable, & available on first-come, first-served basis. To change arrival or departure date, or site type, call at least three days prior to arrival date. $10 cancellation/transfer fee. No refunds for amounts less than $5. **Registration:** At office. **Fee:** Massachusetts residents, $10; non-residents, $12. V, MC. **Parking:** At site.

## FACILITIES

**Number of RV Sites:** 83. **Number of Tent-Only Sites:** 0. **Hookups:** None. **Each Site:** Picnic table, fireplace. **Dump Station:** No. **Laundry:** No. **Pay Phone:** Yes. **Rest Rooms and Showers:** Yes. **Fuel:** No. **Propane:** No. **Internal Roads:** Paved, good condition. **RV Service:** No. **Market:** 5 mi. north, in Winchendon. **Restaurant:** 5 mi. north, in Winchendon. **General Store:** No. **Vending:** Yes. **Swimming Pool:** No. **Playground:** No. **Other:** Interpretive Center. **Activities:** Hiking, nature walks, campfire programs, fishing, swimming. **Nearby Attractions:** Lake Dennison State Recreation Area, Mohawk Trail scenic drive. **Additional Information:** Central Massachusetts Tourist Council, (508) 755-7400; www.worcester.org.

## RESTRICTIONS

**Pets:** Must be leashed & cleaned up after. Must not be left unattended. Proof of rabies vaccination required. **Fires:** In fireplaces only. **Alcoholic Beverages:** No. **Vehicle Maximum Length:** None (but sites are fairly small, & best for pop-ups & small rigs). **Other:** Maximum stay is 14 cumulative days between Memorial Day & Labor Day.

## TO GET THERE

Follow Rte. 2 west to exit 20 (Baldwinville Rd.) to Rte. 202 north; follow signs

## WALES

### Oak Haven Family Campground

P.O. Box 166, Wales 01081. T: (413) 245-7148; F: (413) 245-4656; www.oakhavencampground.com; oakhaven87@aol.com.

🚐 ★★★★　　　▲ ★

Beauty: ★★★　　　Site Privacy: ★★★
Spaciousness: ★★★★　Quiet: ★★★
Security: ★★★　　　Cleanliness: ★★★★
Insect Control: ★★★　Facilities: ★★★

Wooded, grassy, and set in a rural area between Worcester and Springfield, Oak Haven has become a summer home-away-from-home for its 80 or so seasonal campers. Campers who join them for the weekend or the week will quickly sense the low-key camaraderie here. St. signs reflect a sense of humor; there's Snob Hill and Rowdy Rd., for example. A comedy hypnotist is likely to show up on the activities schedule. There's a activities director on board to plan kids' stuff. Site sizes vary; some are open, some are shaded. All are back-in, and fairly spacious. Campsites are set in a loop, with the smallest numbers closest to the entrance. Higher numbers are in back, near a good-sized ball field. There are only two rest rooms, so you can bet the that's where the tenters are, although this campground attracts far more RVers than tenters. The ambience of the place is wholesome and well-maintained. Bonus for flea market mavens and collectors: this campground is just five minutes away from Brimfield Flea Markets, New England's largest antique flea market.

Events are held on various weekends during spring, summer, and fall.

## BASICS

**Operated By:** Alan & Penny Jalbert. **Open:** May 1–Oct. 15. **Site Assignment:** Reservations accepted year-'round; one night's fee required as deposit except holidays & Shriner's Benefit weekend, which must be paid in full one month in advance. Full refund, less $10 service charge, for reservations cancelled before seven days. **Registration:** At office. **Fee:** $23 –$25. Rates based on two people, one camping unit & two vehicles. Extra adult (18 years & up) $2; children (age 6 & up), $1; air conditioning or electric heat, $3 per day. MC, V. **Parking:** At site.

## FACILITIES

**Number of RV Sites:** 140. **Number of Tent-Only Sites:** 0. **Hookups:** Water, electric (20, 30, 50 amps), sewer. **Each Site:** Picnic table, fireplace. **Dump Station:** Yes. **Laundry:** Yes. **Pay Phone:** Yes. **Rest Rooms and Showers:** Yes (coin-op). **Fuel:** No. **Propane:** Yes. **Internal Roads:** Gravel, in good condition. **RV Service:** No. **Market:** 10 mi. east, in Sturbridge, & 10 mi. west, in Palmer. **Restaurant:** 10 mi. east, in Sturbridge, & 10 mi. west, in Palmer. **General Store:** Yes. **Vending:** Yes. **Swimming Pool:** Yes. **Playground:** Yes. **Other:** Rec hall. **Activities:** Baseball, swimming, volleyball, horseshoes. **Nearby Attractions:** Old Sturbridge Village, Brimfield Flea Markets (various weekends), Norcross Wildlife Sanctuary. **Additional Information:** Greater Springfield CVB, (413) 787-1548 or (800) 723-1548; www.valleyvisitor.com.

## RESTRICTIONS

**Pets:** Maximum two dogs per campsite. Dogs must be kept on leash & picked up after. Dogs should not be left unattended. **Fires:** In grills, campstoves, & fireplaces only. **Alcoholic Beverages:** At site only. **Vehicle Maximum Length:** 40 ft. **Other:** Three night min. stay required on holiday weekends.

## TO GET THERE

From I-90 (Massachusetts Turnpike), take exit 9 (Sturbridge) to US. 20 W. At the center of Brimfield, take S.R. 19S, 4.5 mi. to center of Wales. Campground will be on your left.

## WELFLEET

### Maurice's Campground

80 Rte. 6, Unit 1, Wellfleet 02667. T: (508) 349-2029; F: (508) 349-6704; www.mauricescamp ground.com; stay@mauricescampground.com.

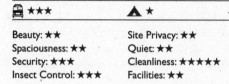

Beauty: ★★
Spaciousness: ★★
Security: ★★★
Insect Control: ★★★

Site Privacy: ★★
Quiet: ★★
Cleanliness: ★★★★★
Facilities: ★★

Located in Wellfleet on the Outer Cape, 20 miles west of Provincetown, this low-key establishment offers tiny cabins and cottages (toward the front of the property), and campsites for tents, tent trailers, trailers and RVS. Set in a grove of native pines, about half the sites are seasonal. The east side of the campground sits right alongside the Cape Cod Rail Trail bike path. We'd skip tent sites 1 and 2, and RV site 32, since they're right next to the access point of the bike trail, so privacy would be impacted. The rest of the tent sites along the bicycle trail are appealing, though, especially sites 6 through 10. RVers would do well to set up on Anchor Dr. (sites 125 through 131), nice and spacious, but we'd avoided tightly-packed sites 106 through 109 and 114 through 116. Everywhere, tall pine trees don't provide much buffer. In some spots, only a split-rail fence separates you from the next site. On the plus side: within a couple of miles of the campground are beautiful stretches of National Seashore, including Nauset Beach, Coast Guard Beach, and Marconi Beach. (The campground office sells car passes for Wellfleet beaches.)

### BASICS

**Operated By:** Martin Gauthier, manager. **Open:** Memorial Day–Columbus Day. **Site Assignment:** Reservations advised for Jul. & Aug. Deposit for 1 to 4 days, $25; 5 to 7 days, $50. Pay in full upon arrival. Two-night min. stay in Jul. & Aug. Cancellations of site reservations must be made at least 48 hours in advance of your arrival date or a one-night reservation fee will be charged to your credit card. Will try to honor specific site requests, but cannot guarantee. **Reg-**istration:** At office. **Fee:** $24–$30 for two people. Extra children age 3 to 18, $2 per night; extra adult, $5. V, MC. **Parking:** At site.

### FACILITIES

**Number of RV Sites:** 200. **Number of Tent-Only Sites:** 0. **Hookups:** Water, electric (20, 30 amps), sewer, cable TV. **Each Site:** Picnic tables. **Dump Station:** Yes. **Laundry:** No. **Pay Phone:** Yes. **Rest Rooms and Showers:** Yes, coin-op. **Fuel:** No. **Propane:** Yes. **Internal Roads:** Paved, in good condition. **RV Service:** No. **Market:** Yes. **Restaurant:** Yes. **General Store:** No. **Vending:** No. **Swimming Pool:** No. **Playground:** Yes. **Other:** Rec area, basketball hoop, horseshoe pits. **Activities:** Basketball, horseshoes, bicycling. **Nearby Attractions:** Cape Cod Rail Trail (bike path), Cape Cod National Seashore, Wellfleet Drive-In (movies), Wellfleet Bay Wildlife Sanctuary. **Additional Information:** Cape Cod Chamber of Commerce, (508) 862-0700 or (888) 33-CAPECOD; www.capecodchamber.org.

### RESTRICTIONS

**Pets:** No. **Fires:** No open fires. Campstoves, & charcoal grills OK. **Alcoholic Beverages:** Yes. **Vehicle Maximum Length:** 32 ft.

### TO GET THERE

Follow Rte. 6 east to the Orleans rotary. From rotary, follow Rte. 6 east towards Provincetown for 6 mi. At Eastham/Wellfleet town line, look for Wellfleet Drive-In on left. Campground is 200 yards farther up on the right. Turn right into driveway just past Maurice's Market.

## WESTFORD

### Wyman's Beach Family Campground

48 Wyman's Beach Rd., Westford 01886. T: (978) 692-6287; F: (978) 692-4155; www.wymanscamp ing .com; ewyman@wymanscamping.com.

★★★★ ▲ ★★★★

Beauty: ★★★
Spaciousness: ★★
Security: ★★
Insect Control: ★★★★★

Site Privacy: ★★★
Quiet: ★★★★
Cleanliness: ★★★
Facilities: ★★★

Time seems to have stood still at Wyman's Beach campground, 30 miles northwest of Boston.

Generations of kids have splashed in sandy-bottomed Long Sought-For Pond, known as, simply, 'the lake.' RVers and tent campers join seasonal campers and cabin-dwellers to relax here on a small campers-only beach, or with the public at a day-use beach. The campground has the feeling of a lakeside resort, with a snack bar, horse-shoe pit, playground, even an activity director who leads the kids in arts-and-crafts projects, and theme nights—perhaps a 1950s party (perfect), Hawaiian Night, or bingo. Site sizes vary; some are 25 feet wide, some as big as 60 × 55 feet or so. The most-requested, most-secluded RV site is 81, on a hill, and semi-secluded 117. Best tent sites by far are 129 and 130, roomy and away from the action. Count on plenty of kids, and grandkids, running around, especially on holiday weekends. Sites are grass, back-in, and mostly shaded, set on short side streets and loop streets off the main road. Wyman's Beach campground offers a pleasant lakeshore experience and a central location, with easy access to Lexington and Concord and Boston.

## BASICS

**Operated By:** Wyman family. **Open:** Early May–early Oct. **Site Assignment:** Reserve two weeks in advance, by phone or on line. Deposit of two days' fee required. Refund w/two week notice prior to arrival date. **Registration:** At office. **Fee:** $20–$24. Fees based on two adults per site; for each child over age 5, add $1 per day. V, MC, D. **Parking:** At site.

## FACILITIES

**Number of RV Sites:** 200. **Number of Tent-Only Sites:** 10. **Hookups:** Water, electric (30, 50 amps), sewer. **Each Site:** Picnic table, fire ring. **Dump Station:** Yes. **Laundry:** Yes. **Pay Phone:** Yes. **Rest Rooms and Showers:** Yes, coin op. **Fuel:** No. **Propane:** Yes. **Internal Roads:** Paved & gravel, good condition. **RV Service:** No. **Market:** 5 mi. south. **Restaurant:** 2 mi. west on Rte. 40. **General Store:** Yes. **Vending:** Yes. **Swimming Pool:** No. **Playground:** Yes. **Other:** Rec hall. **Activities:** Pond swimming, arcade games, horseshoes, bocce, volleyball, basketball, shuffleboard, planned activities. **Nearby Attractions:** Butterfly Place, Lowell National Historic Park. **Additional Information:** Greater Merrimack

Valley CVB, (978) 459-6150 or (800) 443-3332; www.lowell.org.

## RESTRICTIONS

**Pets:** Must be leashed, quiet & cleaned up after. Must not be left unattended. **Fires:** In fire rings only. **Alcoholic Beverages:** At sites only. **Vehicle Maximum Length:** 40 ft.

## TO GET THERE

From I-495, take Exit 35 (Rte. 3N) 4 mi. to Hwy. 40 (Exit 33.) Head west 2.6 mi. to Dunstable Rd. Go north 0.8 mi. Campground entrance is on the right.

## WESTPORT

## Horseneck State Reservation

P.O. Box 328, Westport Point 02791. T: (508) 636-8817 or (508) 636-8816 (off -season); www.state.me.us/dem/parks/hbch.htm.

| 🚐 ★★★ | 🏕 ★★★ |
|---|---|
| Beauty: ★★ | Site Privacy: ★★ |
| Spaciousness: ★★ | Quiet: ★★ |
| Security: ★★ | Cleanliness: ★ |
| Insect Control: ★★★ | Facilities: ★★★ |

Nudging the Rhode Island border to the west and jutting into Buzzards Bay, Horseneck Beach offers a sublime seacoast setting, with campsites directly on the beach or nestled behind sand dunes. Windswept sea oats and rosa rugosa add to the allure. While the campers' beach is rather rocky, campers get free access to the wide, sandy, public beach to the north. There's not much here in the way of amenities (savvy campers know to bring their own firewood, or they'll have to travel 16-plus miles to the nearest supermarket to get it), and the rest rooms can be really grungy (due to staffing shortages, they say.) But, the seaside location is the draw here. Several campsites are directly on the beach, or right across the road from it, but they can get windy. These sites aren't so good for tenters, but fine for RVers, who sort of parallel-park into them. Even-numbered sites 54 through 82 sit right on the water's edge; odd-numbered sites 55 through 81 face the water, too, although the road runs between the campsites and the beach. Avoid site 77; it's oddly tiny. For tenters, sites 97 and 99 sit right behind a dune, but close to the rest rooms and beach path. You're never far from the water here.

## BASICS

**Operated By:** Massachusetts State Forests & Parks. **Open:** Mid-May–mid-Oct. **Site Assignment:** Reservations recommended. Reserve up to six months in advance by calling ReserveAmerica at (877) 1-CAMP MA or online at www.reserv america.com. To change arrival or departure date, or site type, call at least three dayas prior to arrival date. $10 cancellation/ transfer fee. No refunds for amounts less than $5. **Registration:** At office. **Fee:** Massachusetts residents, $12; non-residents, $15. V, MC. **Parking:** At site.

## FACILITIES

**Number of RV Sites:** 100. **Number of Tent-Only Sites:** 0. **Hookups:** None. **Each Site:** Picnic table, fireplace. **Dump Station:** Yes. **Laundry:** No. **Pay Phone:** Yes. **Rest Rooms and Showers:** Yes. **Fuel:** No. **Propane:** No. **Internal Roads:** Gravel, in good condition. **RV Service:** No. **Market:** 16.3 mi. north, on Rte. 88N. **Restaurant:** Yes (snack bar at public beach). **General Store:** No. **Vending:** No. **Swimming Pool:** No. **Playground:** Yes. **Other:** Boat ramp, nature center. **Activities:** Swimming (ocean beach), basketball, volleyball, saltwater fishing, interpretive programs, Jr. ranger program. **Nearby Attractions:** Winery, New Bedford Whaling Museum, Cape Cod. **Additional Information:** Bristol County CVB, (508) 997-1250 or (800) 288-6263; www.bristol-county.org.

## RESTRICTIONS

**Pets:** Must be leashed, quiet, & cleaned up after. Current rabies vaccination certificate required. Beach & swimming areas are off-limits to pets. **Fires:** In fireplaces only. **Alcoholic Beverages:** No. **Vehicle Maximum Length:** 35 ft. **Other:** Maximum stay is 14 cumulative days between Memorial Day & Labor Day.

## TO GET THERE

Take I-95W to Rte. 88, exit 10 south. Follow Rte. 88 south for 10 mi. to state reservation. Campground entrance is just past main entrance on the right.

## WINCHENDON

## Lake Dennison State Recreation Area

86 Winchendon Rd., Baldwinville 01436. T: (978) 939-8962 or (978) 297-1609; www.state.ma.us/ dem/parks/lden.htm.

🚐 ★★★★          ▲ ★★★★

| | |
|---|---|
| Beauty: ★★★★ | Site Privacy: ★★★ |
| Spaciousness: ★★★★ | Quiet: ★★★★★ |
| Security: ★★★ | Cleanliness: ★★★ |
| Insect Control: ★★ | Facilities: ★★ |

Located just to the north of the camping area at Otter River State Forest, the Lake Dennison Recreation Area offers both a day-use beach and a destination campground. As state parks go, this one offers plenty of recreation options, from fishing in the trout-stocked lake (pick up a Mass. license at the Wal-Mart in Gardner), to hiking the 2.5-mile Wilder-McKenzie Nature Trail, to swimming and sunning at the beach. A bicycle is a handy thing to have here, too, since it makes it easier to get around the place. Campsites are arrayed in two loops, along the north and east sides of the lake. Stately rows of pine add to the beauty of the campground. Campsites with the nicest waterfront views are sites 103 to 109; sites 101, 102 and 103 are huge, and great for RVs. Sites 110 to 113 are fairly spacious as well. For tenters, sites 9 and 21 are set at the end of a long driveway, offering maximum privacy. The rest rooms aren't in great shape here, marred by bad mirrors and a bit of graffitti, but at least they are plentiful. If you're into wildlife, follow the dirt roads (shown on the trail map)leading to Swamp Rd. and Beaver Pond. You'll see beavers and perhaps, the river otters for whom Otter River was named. We'd give this camping area higher marks than neighboring Beamon Pond, at Otter River State Park, for visual appeal and the fact that it's easier to navigate with an RV.

## BASICS

**Operated By:** Massachusetts State Forests & Park. **Open:** Mid-May–mid-Sept. **Site Assignment:** Reservations recommended. Reservations may be made up to six months in advance sites and the beach. Avoid site 77; it's oddly tiny. For tenters, sites 97 and 99 sit right behind a dune, but close to the rest rooms and beach path. You're never far from the water here.

## BASICS

**Operated By:** Massachusetts State Forests & Parks. **Open:** Mid-May–mid-Oct. **Site Assignment:** Reservations recommended. Reserve up to six months in advance by calling ReserveAmerica at (877) 1-CAMP MA or online at www.reserv america.com. To change arrival or departure date, or site type, call at least three dayas prior to arrival date. $10 cancellation/ transfer fee. No refunds for amounts less than $5. **Registration:** At office. **Fee:** Massachusetts residents, $12; non-residents, $15. V, MC. **Parking:** At site.

## FACILITIES

**Number of RV Sites:** 100. **Number of Tent-Only Sites:** 0. **Hookups:** None. **Each Site:** Picnic table, fireplace. **Dump Station:** Yes. **Laundry:** No. **Pay Phone:** Yes. **Rest Rooms and Showers:** Yes. **Fuel:** No. **Propane:** No. **Internal Roads:** Gravel, in good condition. **RV Service:** No. **Market:** 16.3 mi. north, on Rte. 88N.

**Restaurant:** Yes (snack bar at public beach). **General Store:** No. **Vending:** No. **Swimming Pool:** No. **Playground:** Yes. **Other:** Boat ramp, nature center. **Activities:** Swimming (ocean beach), basketball, volleyball, saltwater fishing, interpretive programs, Jr. ranger program. **Nearby Attractions:** Winery, New Bedford Whaling Museum, Cape Cod. **Additional Information:** Bristol County CVB, (508) 997-1250 or (800) 288-6263; www.bristol-county.org.

## RESTRICTIONS

**Pets:** Must be leashed, quiet, & cleaned up after. Current rabies vaccination certificate required. Beach & swimming areas are off-limits to pets. **Fires:** In fireplaces only. **Alcoholic Beverages:** No. **Vehicle Maximum Length:** 35 ft. **Other:** Maximum stay is 14 cumulative days between Memorial Day & Labor Day.

## TO GET THERE

Take I-95W to Rte. 88, exit 10 south. Follow Rte. 88 south for 10 mi. to state reservation. Campground entrance is just past main entrance on the right.

# New Hampshire

From coastal beaches, freshwater lakes, northern forests, rolling hills and valleys, and towering mountains, New Hampshire offers campers a diverse landscape, rich in scenic beauty and cultural heritage. The state boasts more than 150 private campgrounds, ranging from rustic sites to resort-style properties, and some of the finest state parks in the nation. Visitors to the Granite State can set up camp on an ocean beach or along the shorelines of a pristine lake; you can camp amid acres of dense pine forest dotted with meandering rivers, cascades, and waterfalls, or in the shadows of New England's tallest mountains. Campgrounds can also be found near the state's top tourist attractions and just outside its bustling cities and resort towns.

The southwest region of the state, dominated by **Mount Monadnock** (the most climbed mountain in North America!) is often called New Hampshire's quiet corner. Campers will find scenic backroads leading to woodlands, lakes, valley villages, and historic sites. It's the perfect place to get away from it all.

The New Hampshire Lakes Region, nestled in the center of the state, is dotted with 273 lakes and ponds, including **Lake Winnipesaukee,** the state's largest. As expected, campers in this region will find that recreation centers around the water: fishing, swimming, and boating are popular pursuits.

The south central region of the state is home to its largest cities: **Manchester, Nashua,** and **Concord,** where campers have museums, theaters, and shopping malls to visit. Just outside the cities, campgrounds are nestled in a rural landscape of rolling hills, fields, and farms.

Campground choices abound in the popular northern White Mountains region. This region encompasses the 780,000-acre **White Mountain National Forest,** the **Kancamagus National Scenic Byway,** 6,288-foot **Mt. Washington** (the tallest mountain in the Northeast), more than 100 waterfalls, and thousands of miles of rivers, streams, and trails. Campers have a delightful blend of busy resort towns (like **North Conway, Lincoln,** and **North Woodstock**), quaint villages and wide expanses of back-to-nature wilderness to explore. Campgrounds in the area run the gamut from small, tucked-away properties to spacious, amenity-laden resorts.

New Hampshire has a mere 18 miles of Atlantic coastline and only one state park campground with oceanfront property. But several top-notch campgrounds are clustered in surrounding inland towns, some set in rural areas, others along freshwater rivers and tidal marshlands. All have quick access to the historic seaport city of **Portsmouth**, ocean beaches and parks (much of the coastline is public land), and popular seacoast attractions.

One very nice bonus for campers visiting small and condensed New Hampshire: no matter where you set up camp, the mountains, lakes, cities, attractions, and ocean, all are just a short drive away.

## The following facilities accept payment in checks or cash only:

Beech Hill, Twin Mountain

Wakeda Family Campground, Hampton Falls

## The following facilities feature 20 or fewer sites:

Cannon Mountain RV Park, Laconia

Twin Mountain Motor Court & RV Park,
   Twin Mountain

# Campground Profiles

## ALBANY

### Jigger Johnson Campground

Kancamagus Hwy., Albany 03818. T: (603) 447-5448.

🚐 ★★★                     ⛺ ★★★★

| | |
|---|---|
| Beauty: ★★★★ | Site Privacy: ★★★★ |
| Spaciousness: ★★★★ | Quiet: ★★★★ |
| Security: ★★★★ | Cleanliness: ★★★★ |
| Insect Control: ★★★ | Facilities: ★★★ |

Jigger Johnson is the largest campground on the Kancamagus, and the only campground along the Kanc that has coin-operated hot showers. Most of the sites along the northeastern end of the campground, near the banks of the Swift River, are spacious and set amid fairly dense forest. There is a series of interpretive programs on Saturday evenings throughout the summer, focusing on a particular aspect of the local flora and fauna, and the campground is very close to some classic White Mountain hiking. The trail that leads down to the banks of the Swift River intersects with a trail that runs along the backside of the campground. This mellow trail follows the Swift both upstream and downstream for quite a distance, passing some beautiful bends in the river and traveling through delightful aromatic groves of birch and pine. It's a great hike to do with kids because it's relatively flat, and there are all sorts of wonderful things to see and experience.

**BASICS**

**Operated By:** US Forest Service. **Open:** Late May–mid-Oct. **Site Assignment:** First come first served. **Registration:** Select site, then pay at self-service fee station. **Fee:** $15. **Parking:** At site.

**FACILITIES**

**Number of RV Sites:** 76. **Number of Tent-Only Sites:** 0. **Hookups:** None. **Each Site:** Fire ring, picnic table. **Dump Station:** No. **Laundry:** No. **Pay Phone:** No. **Rest Rooms & Showers:** Yes. **Fuel:** No. **Propane:** No. **Internal Roads:** Paved. **RV Service:** No. **Market:** No. **Restaurant:** No. **General Store:** No. **Vending:** No. **Swimming Pool:** No. **Playground:** No. **Activities:** Fishing, hiking, scenic byway. **Nearby Attractions:** Historic Russell-Colbath, an 1830s homestead. **Additional Information:** North Conway Chamber of Commerce, (603) 356-3171.

**RESTRICTIONS**

**Pets:** On leash. **Fires:** In fire ring. **Alcoholic Beverages:** At site. **Vehicle Maximum Length:** 2 vehicles per site. **Other:** 8 people per site; 14-day stay limit.

## TO GET THERE

From Lincoln, follow Kancamagus Hwy. to campground on left. From Conway, follow Kancamagus Hwy. to campground on right, shortly after Bear Notch Rd., also on right.

## ASHLAND

### Ames Brook Campground

104 Winona Rd., Ashland 03217. T: (603) 968-7998; amsbrkcg@lr.net.

🚐 ★★★           ▲ ★★★

Beauty: ★★★          Site Privacy: ★★★
Spaciousness: ★★★     Quiet: ★★★★
Security: ★★★         Cleanliness: ★★★
Insect Control: ★★★   Facilities: ★★★

If all you're looking for is a clean, pleasant base to explore the New Hampshire Lakes region and beyond, you can't go wrong here. This rural campground, minutes from downtown Ashland and Lake Winnipesaukee, has flat sites, rectangular sandy swatches laid out in a row, all carved out of the woods. Alas, the campground doesn't have much of a personality, a row of semi-permanent-looking seasonals crowd the front of the campground; further back in the woods, you'll find the narrow, barely-there Ames Brook winding through a small section of the campground. If you like to sleep to the sound of babbling water, request sites numbers 50 to 52. A small row of full hookup sites are also along the brook. We like the library of books and magazines the owners keep in the office and laundromat area; nice touch. The campground offers a quieter, more natural setting than its neighborhood Yogi Bear's Jellystone Park, but with fewer activities and facilities.

## BASICS

**Operated By:** Barbara Marion. **Open:** Memorial Day–Columbus Day. **Site Assignment:** Reservations suggested, one-half of scheduled stay required as deposit, must cancel within 5 days of scheduled visit, MC, V, D, & personal checks accepted. **Registration:** At office. **Fee:** Full hookup, $29; water & electric, $27; no hookup, $22, based on two adults; children 10–17 years

are additional $2, extra adult is $6. **Parking:** At site, one vehicle per site.

## FACILITIES

**Number of RV Sites:** 56. **Number of Tent-Only Sites:** 0. **Hookups:** Water, electric, sewer (30 amps), cable TV. **Each Site:** Table, fire ring. **Dump Station:** Yes. **Laundry:** Yes. **Pay Phone:** Yes. **Rest Rooms & Showers:** Yes. **Fuel:** No. **Propane:** Yes. **Internal Roads:** Gravel, dirt (fair). **RV Service:** No. **Market:** Ashland (1 mi). **Restaurant:** No. **General Store:** Yes. **Vending:** No. **Swimming Pool:** Yes. **Playground:** Yes. **Other:** Small book library, game room, activities hall. **Activities:** Swimming, croquet, basketball. **Nearby Attractions:** Lake Winnipesaukee, Squam Lake, Weirs Beach, outlet shopping, antiquing, quick access to the White Mountain area. **Additional Information:** Greater Laconia/Weirs Beach Chamber of Commerce, 11 Veterans Square, Laconia, NH 03246 (603) 524-5531.

## RESTRICTIONS

**Pets:** Must be on a leash, never left unattended. **Fires:** In grills, stoves, & fire rings only. **Alcoholic Beverages:** At site only. **Vehicle Maximum Length:** None. **Other:** Two tents or one trailer per site; no boats parked on site but may be parked in lot.

## TO GET THERE

From I-93, exit 24, go 0.75 mi. south on Rte. 3, then 0.25 mi. south on Rte. 132, then 0.5 mi. south on Winona Rd. campground is on the right.

## ASHLAND

### Yogi Bear's Jellystone Park

P.O. Box 1926, Ashland 03217. T: (603) 968-9000; www.jellystonenh.com; yogi@jellystonenh.com.

🚐 ★★★★          ▲ ★★

Beauty: ★★           Site Privacy: ★★
Spaciousness: ★★      Quiet: ★★
Security: ★★★         Cleanliness: ★★★★
Insect Control: ★★★   Facilities: ★★★★★

If you're looking for a little peace and quiet, don't even think about coming here. This franchise property is a "happening place," for campers who like a jam-packed, bustling schedule of activities and very close neighbors. The campground features major events throughout the summer, with concerts, dances, parades, contests, and more. This, in addition to the daily schedule of arts and crafts, hayrides, workshops, bingo.whew! We get tired just reading the list and watching the families scurry from event to event. Most sites are small and in the open, with little privacy. The property is set on the pretty Pemigawasset River, but an annoying and unattractive fence separates you from the view. There's a small beach area and a fishing dock. But, if you want to get away from it all, you'll have to rent a boat and paddle the river. Otherwise, let the kids go meet Yogi and BooBoo while you join the country line dancing lessons-right before the ice cream social! Lots of people, especially families, love this place.

## BASICS

**Operated By:** Jane, Marvin, & Erma Cohen. **Open:** Memorial Day–Columbus Day. **Site Assignment:** Reservations strongly urged; full deposit for 2-3 day stay, 50 percent for longer stays. Refunds, less $5 w/ 14 day notice. MC, V, D, & personal checks accepted. **Registration:** At office. **Fee:** Full hookup, $49; water & electric, $45; no hookup, $42, based on two people per site, children, ages 2–17 are $2; grandparents, $6; additional adults, $22.50. **Parking:** At site, one vehicle per site.

## FACILITIES

**Number of RV Sites:** 255. **Number of Tent-Only Sites:** 20. **Hookups:** Water, electric, sewer (20, 30 amps). **Each Site:** Table, fire ring. **Dump Station:** Yes. **Laundry:** Yes. **Pay Phone:** Yes. **Rest Rooms & Showers:** Yes (coin-op). **Fuel:** No. **Propane:** No. **Internal Roads:** Paved (good). **RV Service:** Yes. **Market:** Ashland (2 mi). **Restaurant:** Yes. **General Store:** Yes. **Vending:** Yes. **Swimming Pool:** Yes. **Playground:** Yes. **Other:** Water playground, hot tub, river frontage, boat dock, indoor & outdoor theaters, teen rec hall, arcade, canoe, rowboat, & kayak rentals, 19-hole mini-golf, day trip information center babysitting referral service, ice cream shop, cabin rentals. **Activities:** Swimming, fishing, boating, basketball,

mini-golf, horseshoes, shuffleboard, bolleyball, softball, bocci ball, planned activities including dance workshops, arts & crafts, concerts, live entertainment, hayrides, movies, & more. **Nearby Attractions:** Lake Winnipesaukee, Squam Lake, Weirs Beach, outlet shopping, antiquing, quick access to the White Mountain area. **Additional Information:** Greater Laconia/Weirs Beach Chamber of Commerce, 11 Veterans Square, Laconia, NH 03246 (603) 524-5531.

## RESTRICTIONS

**Pets:** Strongly discouraged; must be on a leash, never left unattended & not allowed in most public areas. **Fires:** In grills, stoves, & fire rings only. **Alcoholic Beverages:** Must be in cup or glass if carried off site. **Vehicle Maximum Length:** 35 ft. **Other:** No motor bikes.

## TO GET THERE

From I-93, exit 23, go 0.5 mi. east on Rte. 104, then 4 mi. north on Rte. 132; campground is on the left

## BARNSTEAD

### Sun River Campground

Rte. 28, P.O. Box 7, Center Barnstead 03225. T: (603) 269-3333; www.ucampnh.com/sunriver; sun river@worldpath.net.

🚐 ★★　　　🏕 ★★★

| | |
|---|---|
| Beauty: ★★★ | Site Privacy: ★★★ |
| Spaciousness: ★★★ | Quiet: ★★★★ |
| Security: ★★★ | Cleanliness: ★★★★ |
| Insect Control: ★★★ | Facilities: ★★★ |

This modest, rural campground will appeal to those looking for quiet days and nights and simple outdoor fun. The campground, nestled in thick woods, along two miles of the meandering Suncook River, has spacious, shaded sites (average width is about 40 feet.) Bring your fishing pole; there's state stocked fishing in the river for trout, bass, pickerel, and perch. The beach is a tiny patch of sand near a pool in the river, ringed by trees-a picturesque place to wet your feet or for the kids to take a dunk. The sites along the river are best but we'd avoid the ones near the beach (site 43 particularly), where you might not get the peace and quiet you crave. Many visitors use the campground as a base to explore the area, heading to southern New Hampshire attractions or north into the mountains.

## BASICS

**Operated By:** Keith & Nancy Bainton. **Open:** May 15–Oct. 15. **Site Assignment:** Reservations suggested. One half of amount due w/ reservation; one week cancellation notice for deposit return. MC, V, AE, & personal checks accepted. **Registration:** At office. **Fee:** Water & electric, $22; no hookups, $18, based on two adults & two children. **Parking:** At site, one vehicle per site.

## FACILITIES

**Number of RV Sites:** 63. **Number of Tent-Only Sites:** 7. **Hookups:** Water, electric (20, 30 amps). **Each Site:** Picnic table, fire ring. **Dump Station:** Yes. **Laundry:** Yes. **Pay Phone:** Yes. **Rest Rooms & Showers:** Yes. **Fuel:** No. **Propane:** No. **Internal Roads:** Gravel, dirt (fair). **RV Service:** No. **Market:** Barnstead (5 mi.). **Restaurant:** No. **General Store:** Yes. **Vending:** No. **Swimming Pool:** No. **Playground:** Yes. **Other:** Two mi. of river frontage, rec hall, beach, group area, pop-up & trailer rentals. **Activities:** Swimming, stocked fishing, ping pong, horseshoes, basketball, volleyball, pot luck suppers, marshmallow roasts on the beach, walking club & story hours. **Nearby Attractions:** Concord, NH International Speedway, quick access to Lakes Region & Seacoast area, antiquing. **Additional Information:** Greater Concord Chamber of Commerce, 244 North Main St., Concord, NH 03301-5078, (603) 224-2508.

## RESTRICTIONS

**Pets:** Must be on a leash, never left unattended, not allowed on the beach. **Fires:** In grills, stoves, & fire rings only. **Alcoholic Beverages:** At site only. **Vehicle Maximum Length:** None. **Other:** No bike riding after dusk, no mini bikes or all terrain vehicles allowed.

## TO GET THERE

From junction of Rtes. 4/202 & 28, go 12 miles north on Rte. 28; campground is on the right.

# BARRINGTON

## Ayers Lake Farm

557 Rte. 202, Barrington 03825. T: (603) 335-1110 (603) 332-5940; www.ucampnh.com/ayerslake.

🚐 ★★★          ▲ ★★★★

| | |
|---|---|
| Beauty: ★★★★ | Site Privacy: ★★★ |
| Spaciousness: ★★★ | Quiet: ★★★★ |
| Security: ★★★★★ | Cleanliness: ★★★★ |
| Insect Control: ★★★ | Facilities: ★★★ |

When we first drove up to the campground, we thought we'd arrived at a very pretty New England country inn. The office is in a beautiful, historic farmhouse, with sweeping lawns and gardens reaching to the water. The campground itself is just south of the farmhouse, with nearly all the sites nestled in a semi-circle along the shoreline. There's a pretty beach on Ayers Lake, and 15 secluded acres of pine forest, fields, and shorefront. It's located between New Hampshire's mountains and ocean, only a short 30- to 45-minute drive to either if you'd like to explore. But you'll be tempted to stay put. That's the good news. The bad news: Only a few sites are available on any given night throughout the season; most are taken by returning seasonal renters who obviously love this place. Call ahead and see if you get lucky. Also, check into the campground's more secluded cottage rentals on the property.

## BASICS

**Operated By:** Bedford family. **Open:** Memorial Day–Columbus Day. **Site Assignment:** Reservations suggested, 50 percent deposit, 3 days paid in advance for holiday weekends, two weeks notice for refund of deposit. **Registration:** At office. **Fee:** Full hookups, $29; waterside, $34; waterfront, $32, no hookups, $25. **Parking:** At site.

## FACILITIES

**Number of RV Sites:** 47. **Number of Tent-Only Sites:** 3. **Hookups:** Water, electric, sewer (20, 30 amps). **Each Site:** Picnic table, fire ring. **Dump Station:** Yes. **Laundry:** No. **Pay Phone:** Yes. **Rest Rooms & Showers:** Yes. **Fuel:** No. **Propane:** No. **Internal Roads:** Dirt (good). **RV Service:** No. **Market:** Barrington (5 mi).

**Restaurant:** No. **General Store:** No. **Vending:** No. **Swimming Pool:** No. **Playground:** Yes. **Other:** Lake frontage, beach, boat ramp, cottage rentals, canoe & rowboat rentals, psorts field. **Activities:** Swimming, boating, fishing, horseshoes. **Nearby Attractions:** New Hampshire seacoast beaches, historic town of Portsmouth, quick access to Lakes region, antiquing. **Additional Information:** Barrington Chamber of Commerce, P.O. Box 363, Barrington, NH 03825, (603) 664-2200; also visit www. SeacoastNH.com.

### RESTRICTIONS

**Pets:** Must be on a leash, never left unattended. Pets are not allowed on beach or playground. **Fires:** In grills, stoves, & fire rings only. **Alcoholic Beverages:** At site only. **Vehicle Maximum Length:** 32 ft. **Other:** No power boats can be landed, launched or docked in the campground.

### TO GET THERE

From junction Hwy. 16 (Spaulding Turnpike) and US 202, go 5 mi. southwest on US 202; campground is on the right

## BARRINGTON

### Barrington Shores

70 Hall Rd., Barrington 03825. T: (603)664-9333; www.barringtonshores.com; bashores@world path.net.

| 🚐 ★★★★ | ⛺ ★★★ |
|---|---|

| | |
|---|---|
| Beauty: ★★★★ | Site Privacy: ★★★ |
| Spaciousness: ★★★ | Quiet: ★★★ |
| Security: ★★★★★ | Cleanliness: ★★★★ |
| Insect Control: ★★★ | Facilities: ★★★ |

Remember busy summer days spent at the lakeside cottage? There was boating, and fishing, and races to the raft. In the evening, there were bonfires and marshmallow roasts. If you're looking for that classic lake vacation, for a fraction of the cost, head to Barrington Shores. This hilly campground on pretty Swain's Lake offers freshwater lake swimming, fishing, boating, and lots of planned activities. There are plenty of lake views from the tiered sites, two large, sandy beaches, boat ramp (many campers bring their own), and

dock. This is a busy place with a festive atmosphere, perfect for hot, summer days. The roads are a bit of a maze, but we like the sandy sites and field stone fire pits. Try to avoid sites No. 116 and No. 117 right off a road, but No. 121 and No. 122 on the lake and with water and electric are especially nice; sites 69–73, with full service, overlook the lake and have a bit of room around them.

### BASICS

**Operated By:** Don & Gail Ziemba. **Open:** Mid-May–late-Sept. **Site Assignment:** Reservations recommended; holiday weekends/three-night stay or less requires payment in full, longer stays a 50% deposit; two-week notice for full refund, less $5 processing fee. **Registration:** At office. **Fee:** Waterfront w/ water, electric, & waterview w/water, electric, cable, $32; waterview w/water & electric, $29; full-service, $30; rates are based on two adlults & up to three children under 18; additional child is $2 per night; additional adult is $10 per night. Maximum four adults per site. **Parking:** At site; one vehicle per site.

### FACILITIES

**Number of RV Sites:** 137. **Number of Tent-Only Sites:** 5. **Hookups:** Water, electric, sewer (20, 30, 50 amps), cable TV, phone. **Each Site:** Picnic table, fireplace. **Dump Station:** Yes. **Laundry:** Yes. **Pay Phone:** Yes. **Rest Rooms & Showers:** Yes (coin-op). **Fuel:** No. **Propane:** Yes. **Internal Roads:** Dirt, gravel (fair). **RV Service:** No. **Market:** Lee (2 mi.). **Restaurant:** No. **General Store:** Yes. **Vending:** No. **Swimming Pool:** No. **Playground:** Yes. **Other:** Game room, safari field for rallies, two lakeside beaches, cottage & cabin rentals. **Activities:** Boat rentals, basketball, fishing, swimming, planned activities on weekends. **Nearby Attractions:** New Hampshire & southern Maine beaches, Portsmouth, factory outlet shopping, golf courses, waterpark, Strawbery Banke historic museum, Seacoast Science Center, antique shops. **Additional Information:** Barrington Chamber of Commerce, P.O. Box 363, Barrington, NH 03825, (603) 664-2200; also visit www.SeacoastNH.com.

### RESTRICTIONS

**Pets:** Must be on a leash & never left unattended. No pets in cottage or cabins. **Fires:** In grills, stoves, & fire rings. **Alcoholic Beverages:** At site only. **Vehicle Maximum Length:** 40 ft. **Other:** No bicycle riding after dark.

## TO GET THERE

From I-95, take Spaulding Turnpike (Rte. 16) in Portsmouth to exit 6W (Rte. 4). Follow Rte. 4 to Lee traffic circle & the junction of Rtes. 4 & 125. Take Rte. 125 north 2.5 mi.; take left onto Beauty Hill Rd. Go 1 mi., take left onto Hall Rd., 1 mi. to campground.

## BARTLETT

### Passaconaway Campground

Rte. 12, Kancamagus Hwy., Bartlett 03812. T: (603) 447-5448.

| 🚐 ★★★ | 🛖 ★★★★ |
|---|---|
| Beauty: ★★★★ | Site Privacy: ★★★★★ |
| Spaciousness: ★★★★ | Quiet: ★★★★ |
| Security: ★★★★ | Cleanliness: ★★★★ |
| Insect Control: ★★★ | Facilities: ★★★ |

Of all the campgrounds along the Kancamagus, Passaconaway is probably most conducive to RVs, though there are no hookups. The spacious sites are well suited to larger groups or families with kids, and the relatively central location along the Kancamagus Hwy. puts you in a good spot if you're not sure what part of the Kanc you want to explore first. You'll be close to Rocky Gorge, Sabbaday Falls, the Swift River picnic area, and the myraid trailheads spread out along the length of this superlative stretch of road. The forest separating the individual sites at Passaconaway is fairly dense, which provides a nice sense of seclusion and helps make this an extremely quiet campground. All you'll hear is an occasional vehicle zipping past on the Kanc and the soft rush of the wind in the evergreens, punctuated by the chatter of the forest birds and animals. There's a trailhead right next to site 18; the campground host is located at site 19. Site 10 or site 24.

## BASICS

**Operated By:** US Forest Service. **Open:** Mid-May–mid-Oct. **Site Assignment:** First come first served; no reservations. **Registration:** Select site, then pay at self-service fee station. **Fee:** $14. **Parking:** At site.

## FACILITIES

**Number of RV Sites:** 33. **Number of Tent-Only Sites:** 0. **Hookups:** None. **Each Site:** Fire ring, picnic table. **Dump Station:** No. **Laundry:** No. **Pay Phone:** No. **Rest Rooms & Showers:** No. **Fuel:** No. **Propane:** No. **Internal Roads:** Paved. **RV Service:** No. **Market:** No. **Restaurant:** No. **General Store:** No. **Vending:** No. **Swimming Pool:** No. **Playground:** No. **Activities:** Fishing, hiking, picnicking, scenic byway. **Nearby Attractions:** Historic Russell-Colbath, an 1830s homestead. **Additional Information:** North Conway Chamber of Commerce, (603) 356-3171.

## RESTRICTIONS

**Pets:** On leash. **Fires:** In fire ring. **Alcoholic Beverages:** At site. **Vehicle Maximum Length:** 2 vehicles per site. **Other:** 8 people per site; 14-day stay limit.

## TO GET THERE

Passaconaway Campground is almost in the center of the Kancamagus Hwy. From Lincoln, follow the Kancamagus Hwy. for 16 mi. to campground on left. From Conway, follow Kancamagus Hwy. for 15 mi. to campground on right.

## BRENTWOOD

### 3 Ponds Campground

146 North Rd., Brentwood 03833. T: (603) 679-5350; www.3pondscampground.com.

| 🚐 ★★★ | 🛖 ★★★ |
|---|---|
| Beauty: ★★★ | Site Privacy: ★★ |
| Spaciousness: ★★★ | Quiet: ★★★★ |
| Security: ★★★ | Cleanliness: ★★★★ |
| Insect Control: ★★★ | Facilities: ★★★ |

If our grandma owned a campground this is probably what it would look like: a sweep of perfectly manicured lawn (think golf course quality) stretching to the banks of three pristine, spring-fed ponds, a white gazebo perched on the banks, ham and bean suppers and afternoon cribbage games. Though only 20 to 30 miles from southern New Hampshire's major attractions, this campground sits off the main drag at the end of a residential street, making it feel a bit out of the way. The property has a friendly, quiet and wholesome appeal with just enough conveniences to make it pleasant, enough outdoor scenery to feel like camping. Most sites are perched in open on a grassy knoll—not a lot of privacy but with good views of the water. If you want more privacy, head to the back of campground where you'll have more space and shade.

## BASICS

**Operated By:** Clarence & Claire Hibbard. **Open:** May 15–Oct. 1. **Site Assignment:** First-come, first-served, reservations recommended on weekends; MC, V, personal checks accepted. **Registration:** At office. **Fee:** $25. **Parking:** At site.

## FACILITIES

**Number of RV Sites:** 136. **Number of Tent-Only Sites:** 0. **Hookups:** Water, electric, sewer (20, 30 amps). **Each Site:** Picnic table, fire ring. **Dump Station:** Yes. **Laundry:** Yes. **Pay Phone:** Yes. **Rest Rooms & Showers:** Yes. **Fuel:** No. **Propane:** No. **Internal Roads:** Dirt (fair). **RV Service:** No. **Market:** Raymond (5 mi). **Restaurant:** No. **General Store:** Yes. **Vending:** Yes. **Swimming Pool:** No. **Playground:** Yes. **Other:** Three spring-fed ponds, sandy beach w/swimming area, safari field, adult gazebo on lake, paddleboat rentals, game room. **Activities:** Swimming, fishing, boating, horshoes, softball, volleyball, basketball, planned activities. **Nearby Attractions:** Portsmouth, New Hampshire beaches, Canobie Lake Park. **Additional Information:** Greater Portsmouth Chamber of Commerce, P.O. Box 239, Portsmoutn, NH 03801 (603) 436-3988; also visit www.SeacoastNH.com.

## RESTRICTIONS

**Pets:** Must be on a leash, never left unattended. **Fires:** In grills, stoves, & fire rings only. **Alcoholic Beverages:** At site only. **Vehicle Maximum Length:** 40 ft. **Other:** Ask on arrival.

## TO GET THERE

From junction Rte. 101 and 125 (in Epping), go south 1 mi. on Rte. 125 to Rockingham County Complex Rd., then east 1 mi. to entrance.

## CAMBRIDGE

### Umbagog Lake Campground

181 North, Errol 03579. T: (603) 482-7795 (603) 271-3628 (reservations); F: (603) 271-2629; www.nhparks.state.nh.us; nhcampres@dred. state.nh.us.

🚐 ★★★          ⛺ ★★★★

| | |
|---|---|
| Beauty: ★★★★ | Site Privacy: ★★★★ |
| Spaciousness: ★★★★ | Quiet: ★★★★ |
| Security: ★★★★ | Cleanliness: ★★★ |
| Insect Control: ★★ | Facilities: ★★ |

This unique, rustic campground in New Hampshire's Great North Woods region offers wilderness sites on remote islands, in addition to its woodsy, lakeside base camp. If you're looking to get away from it all, and enjoy a more natural, wilderness experience, this campground has plenty to offer. The base camp is situated on the shores of still-wild Lake Umbagog, and is popular with canoeists, kayakers, and anglers. In recent years, outdoor enthusiasts have come for its peace and quiet and wildlife watching. Herons, osprey, loons, moose, deer, beavers, and bald eagles are often spotted. The base camp includes 38 spacious sites, some with two-way hookups, clustered in loops from the shoreline. For a more private, remote camping experience, reserve one of the island sites. Transportation, for a nominal fee, can be arranged to these sites. Though, to really appreciate this spot, you'll want to explore in your own boat.

## BASICS

**Operated By:** New Hampshire Division of Parks & Recreation. **Open:** Mid-May–mid-Oct. **Site Assignment:** Reservations suggested & must be made through central reservations (603) 271-3628. Reservations must be made at least seven days in advance; $3 non-refundable fee for each reservation. 24-hour cancellation policy w/$10 service fee. MC,V, D; no personal checks. **Registration:** At office. **Fee:** Water & electric, $24; no hookups, $20. **Parking:** At site, no parking at remote wilderness sites (boat access only).

## FACILITIES

**Number of RV Sites:** 38. **Number of Tent-Only Sites:** 30. **Hookups:** Water, electric (15, 20 amps). **Each Site:** Picnic table, fire ring. **Dump Station:** Yes. **Laundry:** No. **Pay Phone:** No. **Rest Rooms & Showers:** Yes. **Fuel:** No. **Propane:** No. **Internal Roads:** Dirt, gravel (fair). **RV Service:** No. **Market:** Errol (7 mi). **Restaurant:** No. **General Store:** Yes. **Vending:** No. **Swimming Pool:** No. **Playground:** Yes. **Other:** Boat launch, boat slips, canoe rentals, cabin rentals, transportation to remote sites. **Activities:** Swimming, boating, fishing, wildlife watching. **Nearby Attractions:** Connecticut Lakes, Rangley & Sadlleback Mountain area of Maine. **Additional Information:** North Country Chamber of Commerce, P.O. Box 1, Colebrook, NH 03576, (603) 237-8939 or Northern White Mountains Chamber of Commerce, 164 Main St. , P.O. Box 298, Berlin, NH 03570, (603) 752-6060.

## RESTRICTIONS

**Pets:** Must be on a leash; never left unattended. **Fires:** In grills, campstoves, & fire rings only. **Alcoholic Beverages:** At site only. **Vehicle Maximum Length:** None. **Other:** 30 wilderness campsites are accessible by water only; transportation available.

## TO GET THERE

From junction Rtes. 16 and 26 (in Errol), go east 7 mi. on Rte. 26; campground is on the right.

## CHICHESTER

### Hillcrest Campground

78 Dover Rd., Chichester 03234. T: (603) 798-5124 or (508) 695-7391 (winter); www.ucampnh.com/hillcrest; hilcrest@tiac.net.

| 🚐 ★★★★ | 🏕 ★★★★ |
| --- | --- |
| Beauty: ★★★ | Site Privacy: ★★★★ |
| Spaciousness: ★★★★ | Quiet: ★★★ |
| Security: ★★★★★ | Cleanliness: ★★★★★ |
| Insect Control: ★★★ | Facilities: ★★★★★ |

The living is easy at this central New Hampshire campground, one of the prettiest in the area. It also offers plenty of conveniences, including a centralized location and on-site amenities. The hilly campground site features towering pine tree woods and a picturesque pond, with a sandy cove beach. The mostly shaded sites, nestled in the woods, are adequately spaced (about 30 feet in average width) and level. The campground is popular with families, who enjoy the organized activities, the large, modern pool, fishing and boating on the pond, and nature trails. Tenters will like the private and spacious Honeymoon site or No. 10, overlooking the pond. There's also a safari field for larger groups with its own pavilion and recreational hall. Forget your gear? Rent one of the eight heated cabins flanking the front of the campground. During the busy summer months, there's a plethora of planned activities to keep you busy, including dances, dinners, children's activities and games, hayrides, fishing tournaments, bingo, and more.

## BASICS

**Operated By:** Potter family. **Open:** May–mid-Oct. **Site Assignment:** Reservations recommended. One night deposit required, one week cancellation notice. **Registration:** At office. **Fee:** Full hookup w/cable, $30; water & electric w/cable, $28; water & electric, $27; no hookups, $24. **Parking:** At site, one vehicle per site.

## FACILITIES

**Number of RV Sites:** 138. **Number of Tent-Only Sites:** 9. **Hookups:** Water, electric, sewer (20, 30 amps), cable TV. **Each Site:** Picnic table, fire ring. **Dump Station:** Yes. **Laundry:** Yes. **Pay Phone:** Yes. **Rest Rooms & Showers:** Yes (coin-op). **Fuel:** No. **Propane:** No. **Internal Roads:** Paved, gravel (good). **RV Service:** No. **Market:** Epsom (2 mi). **Restaurant:** Yes. **General Store:** Yes. **Vending:** No. **Swimming Pool:** Yes. **Playground:** Yes. **Other:** Small pond, group area, mini-golf, rec room, arcade, boat rentals, nature trails, pavillion, cabin rentals. **Activities:** Swimming, boating, fishing, volleyball, badminton, mini-golf, horseshoes, organized activities throughout Jul.-Aug., including arts & crafts, contests, dances, hayrides, dinners, bingo, & more. **Nearby Attractions:** Concord, NH International Speedway, quick access to Lakes Region & Seacoast area, antiquing. **Additional Information:** Greater Concord Chamber of Commerce, 244 North Main St. , Concord, NH 03301-5078, (603) 224-2508.

## RESTRICTIONS

**Pets:** Must be on a leash, never left unattended. **Fires:** In grills, stoves, & fire rings only. **Alcoholic Beverages:** At site only. **Vehicle Maximum Length:** 40 ft.

## TO GET THERE

From junction Rtes. 4/202 and 28, go west 2 mi. on Rte. 4; campground is on the right

## CONWAY

## The Beach Camping Area

P.O. Box 1007, Rte. 16, North Conway 03818. T: (603) 447-2723; www.ucampnh.com/thebeach; beachcampingarea@yahoo.com.

🚐 ★★★              ⛺ ★★★

Beauty: ★★★              Site Privacy: ★★
Spaciousness: ★★★         Quiet: ★★
Security: ★★★             Cleanliness: ★★★
Insect Control: ★★★       Facilities: ★★

If you have to be in the middle of the action, close to North Conway attractions and outlet shopping, here's one of your choices. (Also see the Eastern Slope Campground and Saco River Camping.) All are on the Saco River, very busy and often noisy. The sites at this campground are set side-by-side in rows. The corner river sites are the best, numbers 1 through 7A, offering a little more room and scenery. Be warned that some of the river sites don't offer access or much of a water view of the river, though you will have beach grass and dunes as your backdrop as opposed to another tent or trailer. The tent-only section, ringed by trees and flanked by the Saco River, offers more privacy than other sites. There's a nice sandy beach area and classic cool water swimming hole, offering a refreshing place to dip and dunk after a busy day touring the area. The rec hall, with a few arcade games, is a dreary afterthought; the laundry is a basic one machine facility. Still, it's clean, economical, and if you're like most of campers here, you'll be off early in the morning exploring the area—or outlet shopping!

## BASICS

**Operated By:** Jeff & Stephanie Moore. **Open:** Mid-May–mid-Oct. **Site Assignment:** Reservations suggested, deposit of $30 per weekend, long holiday weekends (three day min. stay) paid in full. 14 day cancellation policy. MC, V, & personal checks accepted. **Registration:** At office. **Fee:** Full hookups, $25, full hookup water sites, $27; water & electric, $23–$25; no hookups, $20–$22. **Parking:** At site.

## FACILITIES

**Number of RV Sites:** 114. **Number of Tent-Only Sites:** 7. **Hookups:** Water, electric, sewer (20, 30 amps). **Each Site:** Picnic table, fire ring. **Dump Station:** Yes. **Laundry:** Yes. **Pay Phone:** Yes. **Rest Rooms & Showers:** Yes. **Fuel:** No. **Propane:** Yes. **Internal Roads:** Dirt, gravel (good). **RV Service:** No. **Market:** Conway (2 mi). **Restaurant:** No. **General Store:** Yes. **Vending:** No. **Swimming Pool:** No. **Playground:** Yes. **Other:** Rec hall, sports field, river frontage, beach. **Activities:** Swimming, fishing. **Nearby Attractions:** North Conway, White Mountains, outlet shopping. **Additional Information:** Greater Conway Village Area Chamber of Commerce, P.O. Box 1019, Conway, NH 03818, (603) 447-2639; also Mount Washington Valley Chamber of Commerce, P.O. Box 2300, North Conway, NH 03860, (800) 521-2137.

## RESTRICTIONS

**Pets:** On leash, must never be left unattended. Pets are not allowed on the beach or in buildings. **Fires:** In grills, stoves, & fire rings only. **Alcoholic Beverages:** At site only. **Vehicle Maximum Length:** 40 ft.

## TO GET THERE

From junction Rtes. 16 and 113, go north 1.5 mi. on Rte. 16; campground is on the left.

## CONWAY

## Eastern Slope Camping Area

P.O. Box 1127, Conway 03818. T: (603) 447-5092; www.ucampnh.com/easternslope.

🚐 ★★★              ⛺ ★★★

Beauty: ★★★  Site Privacy: ★★
Spaciousness: ★★★  Quiet: ★★★
Security: ★★★  Cleanliness: ★★★
Insect Control: ★★★  Facilities: ★★

This place can really rock and roll on summer weekends when vacationing families head to North Conway and the White Mountains for fun, fun, fun. During the day, the campground is quiet and peaceful; most campers are visiting area attractions or pursuing outdoor activities (hiking, biking, rock climbing, kayaking, and canoeing are all readily accessible.) By late afternoon when folks return, the campground comes alive. The property sites have two personalities: there's the fairly congested side-by-side, row after row of sites in the center of the campground. These sites are under a pine tree cover but back-to-back rows don't offer much privacy. Ringing the beach and playground area are much more secluded and spacious sites. Our favorites: sites one-12 along the river. For recreation, there are two swimming holes with sandy beaches, sports fields, and lots of comraderie around the bonfire.

## BASICS

**Operated By:** Danie & Valerie Boatwright. **Open:** Memorial Day–Columbus Day. **Site Assignment:** Reservations suggested, three night deposit, 14-day cancellation policy w/$5 service charge, MC, V, & personal checks accepted. **Registration:** At office. **Fee:** Full hookups, $25.95; sites 1-32A, 53, 54, $31.95; sites 33–39, $30.95; sites 40–71, $28.95; sites 72–215, $23.95, based on one or two adults & three children under 13. **Parking:** At site.

## FACILITIES

**Number of RV Sites:** 204. **Number of Tent-Only Sites:** 6. **Hookups:** Water, electric, sewer (20, 30 amps). **Each Site:** Picnic table, fire ring. **Dump Station:** Yes. **Laundry:** No. **Pay Phone:** Yes. **Rest Rooms & Showers:** Yes. **Fuel:** No. **Propane:** No. **Internal Roads:** Paved (good). **RV Service:** No. **Market:** North Conway (0.5 mi). **Restaurant:** No. **General Store:** Yes. **Vending:** Yes. **Swimming Pool:** No. **Playground:** Yes. **Other:** River frontage, beach, sports field, canoe rentals. **Activities:** Swimming, horseshoes, shuffleboard, softball. **Nearby Attractions:** Storyland, Santa's Village, Six Gun City, North Conway,

White Mountains, outlet shopping. **Additional Information:** Greater Conway Village Area Chamber of Commerce, P.O. Box 1019, Conway, NH 03818, (603) 447-2639; also Mount Washington Valley Chamber of Commerce, P. O. Box 2300, North Conway, NH 03860, (800) 521-2137.

## RESTRICTIONS

**Pets:** Must be on a leash, never left unattended. Pets not allowed at beach area. **Fires:** In grills, stoves, & fire rings only. **Alcoholic Beverages:** At site only. **Vehicle Maximum Length:** 38 ft.

## TO GET THERE

From junctions Rte. 16 and 113, go 1 mi. north on Rte. 16; campground is on the left

## DEERING

## Oxbow Campground

8 Oxbow Rd., Deering 03244. T: (603) 464-5952; www.ucampnh.com/oxbow; oxbow@conknet.com.

🚍 ★★★  ⛺ ★★★

Beauty: ★★★★  Site Privacy: ★★★★
Spaciousness: ★★★★  Quiet: ★★★
Security: ★★★★★  Cleanliness: ★★★
Insect Control: ★★★  Facilities: ★★★

This peaceful, outdoors-oriented campground in southwestern New Hampshire, less than a mile from downtown Hillsboro, is a favorite among local campers and vacationing families. There are three brook-fed ponds on the property: a three-acre, boating pond (people-powered boats only), a one-acre, sandy bottom swimming pond, and a 0.3-acre catch and release stocked fishing pond (no license needed.) Sites on the property vary from deeply wooded for those who like privacy, to open for sun worshipers. All sites have plenty of space; average width is about 55 feet. More than 140 acres of the campground are open for hiking. The Welcome Hall is especially nice, with reading and video libraries, puzzle making and card-playing tables. The Pine Pavillion, on the beach overlooking the swimming pond, is also a favorite gathering spot.

## BASICS

**Operated By:** John Ramsey. **Open:** May–Columbus Day. **Site Assignment:** Reservations suggested, 1-4 day stay, $20 deposit; 1-2 week stay, $50 deposit; 3 weeks or longer, $100 deposit; three day min. stay on holiday weekends. Three to 13 days cancellation notice, deposit returned less $50; 14 day notice, deposit returned less $10; no refunds for reservations for three week stays or longer. MC, V, & personal checks accepted. **Registration:** At office. **Fee:** Full hookups, $27; electric, $24; no hookups, $21; waterfront sites, $3 extra; based on two adults & two children under 18. **Parking:** At site.

## FACILITIES

**Number of RV Sites:** 86. **Number of Tent-Only Sites:** 13. **Hookups:** Water, electric, sewer (20, 30 amps), cable TV, modem. **Each Site:** Picnic table, fire ring. **Dump Station:** No. **Laundry:** Yes. **Pay Phone:** Yes. **Rest Rooms & Showers:** Yes (coin-op). **Fuel:** No. **Propane:** Yes. **Internal Roads:** Gravel, dirt (fair). **RV Service:** No. **Market:** Hillsboro (0.5 mi). **Restaurant:** No. **General Store:** Yes. **Vending:** No. **Swimming Pool:** No. **Playground:** Yes. **Other:** Three ponds, beach areas, rec hall, pavillion, sports field, hiking trails, cabin rentals. **Activities:** Swimming, fishing, boating, shuffleboard, volleyball, basketball, horseshoes, planned activities on summer weekends, including arts & crafts, food events, & games. **Nearby Attractions:** Hillsboro, Concord, state parks, lakes & fishing streams. **Additional Information:** Greater Concord Chamber of Commerce, 244 North Main St. , Concord, NH 03301-5078, (603) 224-2508.

## RESTRICTIONS

**Pets:** Must have up to date vaccinations, kept on a leash, never left unattended. **Fires:** In grills, stoves, & fire rings only. **Alcoholic Beverages:** No more than one beverage per person open at any time. **Vehicle Maximum Length:** None.

## TO GET THERE

From junction Rtes. 202, 9 and 149, go south 0.75 mi. on Rte. 149; campground is on the left

## EAST WAKEFIELD

# Lake Ivanhoe Inn & RV Resort

631 Acton Ridge Rd., East Wakefield 03830. T: (603) 522-8824; F: (603) 522-9235; www.lakeivanhoe.com; office@lakeivanhoe.com.

🚐 ★★★　　　　🅰 ★★★

| | |
|---|---|
| Beauty: ★★★ | Site Privacy: ★★★ |
| Spaciousness: ★★★★ | Quiet: ★★★★ |
| Security: ★★★ | Cleanliness: ★★★ |
| Insect Control: ★★★ | Facilities: ★★ |

If your idea of the perfect getaway is to get away from it all, this campground could be for you. (Though within an hour's drive, you can be in the White Mountains or on the seacoast of Maine.) This campground, set off the main drag, is pleasantly quiet and relaxing. There's a small historic inn on the property and a 100-foot long private, sandy beach across the street for campers. About half the campground is taken by summer seasonal renters who seem content with the slow life: a morning paddle on the lake, an afternoon nap, bingo at night. Lake pleasures seem to dominate, here. There's swimming, boating and fishing on spring-fed 120-acre Lake Ivanhoe, one of 11 lakes in the Wakefield area. Facilities are clean but basic (chem toilets.) Seasonal renters and large rigs are placed up front, while tenters head to the shaded, back portion of the property.

## BASICS

**Operated By:** Ann & Tony Bettencourt. **Open:** Mid-May–Columbus Day. **Site Assignment:** Reservations suggested, a 50 percent deposit is required, 14 day notice for refund of deposit. Two night min. on weekends. MC, V, & personal checks accepted. **Registration:** At office. **Fee:** Full hookup, $35; water & electric, $31; no hookups, $23–$27. **Parking:** At site.

## FACILITIES

**Number of RV Sites:** 69. **Number of Tent-Only Sites:** 6. **Hookups:** Water, electric, sewer (20, 30 amps), cable TV, modem. **Each Site:** Picnic table, fire ring. **Dump Station:** Yes. **Laundry:** Yes. **Pay Phone:** Yes. **Rest Rooms & Showers:**

Yes. **Fuel:** No. **Propane:** Yes. **Internal Roads:** Dirt, gravel (fair). **RV Service:** No. **Market:** Wakefield (1 mi). **Restaurant:** No. **General Store:** Yes. **Vending:** No. **Swimming Pool:** No. **Playground:** Yes. **Other:** Lake frontage & beach, canoe & paddleboat rentals, adult rec hall, game room, sports field, safari area. **Activities:** Swimming, boating, horseshoes, badminton, volleyball, shuffleboard, planned activities on weekends including hayrides, bingo, socials. **Nearby Attractions:** Lake Winnipesaukee, Lakes region attractions. **Additional Information:** Lakes Region Assoc., Rte. 104, P.O. Box 430, New Hampton, NH 03252, (603) 744-8664.

## RESTRICTIONS

**Pets:** Must be on a leash, never left unattended. Pets are not allowed on the beach. **Fires:** In grills, stoves, & fire rings only. **Alcoholic Beverages:** At site only. **Vehicle Maximum Length:** None.

## TO GET THERE

From junction Rtes. 16 and Wakefield Rd., go 0.5 mi. east on Wakefield Rd. to Rte. 152, then 2.5 mi. north to Acton Ridge Rd., then 1.2 mi. east; campground is on the left.

## EPSOM

### Circle 9 Ranch

Windymere Dr., P.O. Box 282, Epsom 03234. T: (603) 736-9656; www.circle9campground.com; circle9rch@aol.com.

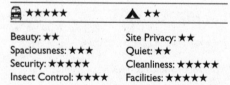

🚐 ★★★★★          ⛺ ★★

| | |
|---|---|
| Beauty: ★★ | Site Privacy: ★★ |
| Spaciousness: ★★★ | Quiet: ★★ |
| Security: ★★★★★ | Cleanliness: ★★★★★ |
| Insect Control: ★★★★ | Facilities: ★★★★★ |

If you're looking for a hootin' and hollerin' time, head to Circle 9, New Hampshire's nod to the west. This popular campground, minutes from downtown Concord and the New Hampshire International Speedway, features live country and western music every Saturday night in its well-known entertainment and commercial bingo center. If you don't meet your fellow campers on the dance floor, you surely will at the campsite, where big rigs are perched side-by-side

in an open central area. There's not a lot of space at individual sites; average width is about 20 feet. We prefer the more private, shaded sites in the back of the campground, clustered around two small ponds or in the woods-and farthest away from the dance hall. Site No. 59 is popular with tenters. You'll find all the amenities here, but not a lot of peace and quiet. Come here for the location and the action.

## BASICS

**Operated By:** Warren & Sheila Rich. **Open:** Year-round. **Site Assignment:** Reservations recommended, MC, V, D, AE, personal checks accepted. Sites must be paid in full during Jul. & Aug., no money returned for cancellations. **Registration:** At office. **Fee:** Full hookup, premium sites, $30; trailer & motor homes, $28; tents & pop-ups, $23, based on two adults & two children. **Parking:** At site, one vehicle per site.

## FACILITIES

**Number of RV Sites:** 113. **Number of Tent-Only Sites:** 12. **Hookups:** Water, electric, sewer (30, 50 amps), cable TV, modem. **Each Site:** Picnic table, fire ring. **Dump Station:** Yes. **Laundry:** Yes. **Pay Phone:** Yes. **Rest Rooms & Showers:** Yes (coin-op). **Fuel:** No. **Propane:** Yes. **Internal Roads:** Paved, gravel (good). **RV Service:** Yes. **Market:** Epsom (1 mi). **Restaurant:** Yes. **General Store:** Yes. **Vending:** Yes. **Swimming Pool:** Yes. **Playground:** Yes. **Other:** Adult-only hot tub, large entertainment center, live country music & western band performances, rec hall, arcade, function hall, pond, safari area. **Activities:** Saturday night concerts & dances, basketball, pond fishing, swimming, horseshoes, commercial bingo. **Nearby Attractions:** Concord, NH International Speedway, quick access to Lakes Region & Seacoast area, antiquing. **Additional Information:** Greater Concord Chamber of Commerce, 244 North Main St., Concord, NH 03301-5078, (603) 224-2508.

## RESTRICTIONS

**Pets:** Must be on a leash, never left unattended. No dogs on holiday weekends; no dogs allowed w/visitors. **Fires:** In grills, stoves, & fire rings only. **Alcoholic Beverages:** At site & at entertainment center. **Vehicle Maximum Length:** 45 ft.

## To Get There

From junction Rtes. 2/202 and 28, go south 0.25 mi. on Rte. 28, then south 0.25 mi. to Windymere Dr.; the campground is on the right.

## EPSOM

### Epsom Valley Campground

990 Suncook Valley Hwy., Epsom 03234. T: (603) 736-9758 or (978) 658-4396 (winter); www.ucampnh.com/epsomvalley.

🚐 ★★★          ▲ ★★★

Beauty: ★★★          Site Privacy: ★★★
Spaciousness: ★★★    Quiet: ★★★★
Security: ★★★         Cleanliness: ★★★★
Insect Control: ★★     Facilities: ★★★

You'll find none of the thrills and frills of some of the more modern campgrounds at Epsom Valley. Come here to settle in the woods, swim in the Suncook River, cast a lure in a rock-strewn river pool. Shaded sites are set under tall pine trees about 25 feet from one another. Not a lot of room, but the woods offer some privacy. There are also a number of open, grassy sites for those who prefer the sun. Activities are centered around simple pleasures: paddling a canoe on the river; fishing from the banks; tossing horseshoes, or playing a game of mini-golf. Most visitors will take time to explore the area; the campground is centrally located, an hour's drive from the seacoast, New Hampshire lakes region, or the mountains. Holiday and race weeks (New Hampshire International Speedway in Loudon is just up the road) are busy and the atmosphere becomes a bit more bustling and noisy, especially with groups filling the campground's Safari Field area.

## Basics

**Operated By:** John & Dwyna Arvanitis. **Open:** Memorial Day–Oct. 12. **Site Assignment:** Reservations suggested. 2 day min. stay during holiday weekends & race weeks. Deposit at your discretion. **Registration:** At office. **Fee:** Full hookups, $25; water & electric, $22; no hookups, $19, based on two adults, two children. **Parking:** At site, one vehicle per site.

## Facilities

**Number of RV Sites:** 67. **Number of Tent-Only Sites:** 3. **Hookups:** Water, electric, sewer (20, 30 amps). **Each Site:** Picnic table, fire ring. **Dump Station:** Yes. **Laundry:** No. **Pay Phone:** Yes. **Rest Rooms & Showers:** Yes (coin-op). **Fuel:** No. **Propane:** No. **Internal Roads:** Gravel, dirt (fair). **RV Service:** No. **Market:** Epsom (1 mi). **Restaurant:** No. **General Store:** No. **Vending:** Yes. **Swimming Pool:** No. **Playground:** Yes. **Other:** Recreational field, baseball diamond, mini-golf course, canoe & paddleboat rentals, safari field. **Activities:** fishing, swimming, horseshoes, volleyball, canoeing, potluck dinners on weekends. **Nearby Attractions:** NH International Speedway, Concord, quick access to Lakes Region & Seacoast area, antiquing. **Additional Information:** Greater Concord Chamber of Commerce, 244 North Main St., Concord, NH 03301-5078, (603) 224-2508.

## Restrictions

**Pets:** Must be on a leash, never left unattended, not allowed beach. One pet per site. **Fires:** In grills, stoves, & fire rings only. **Alcoholic Beverages:** At site only. **Vehicle Maximum Length:** 34 ft.

## To Get There

From junction Rtes. 4/202 and 28, go 0.25 mi. north on Rte. 28; campground is on the right.

## EPSOM

### Lazy River Campground

427 Goboro Rd., Epsom 03234. T: (603) 798-5900.

🚐 ★★★          ▲ ★★★

Beauty: ★★★          Site Privacy: ★★★
Spaciousness: ★★★    Quiet: ★★★★
Security: ★★★         Cleanliness: ★★★
Insect Control: ★★     Facilities: ★★★

One of the clusters of campgrounds in the Concord area, this rural, riverside property offers more activities than its neighbor up the street (Epsom Valley) and a bit more space to roam.

Though, it lacks some of its neighbor's picturesque, woodsy scenery. There's swimming in the Suncook River or take a dip in one of the two pools (one of them is a children's pool.)On holiday weekends, families join in a host of activities, including dances, water balloon tosses, and arts and crafts.You have a choice of wooded, open field sites, or riverfront sites. We like site No. 1 on the river, or site No. 91A, which is larger than most. (The average site width is about 35 feet, so all have a bit of space around them.) If you're traveling in a group, try to rent sites 53–58. These campsites are set off by themselves, situated on a point along the river. This campground, as most in the area, fills up fst during the popular Loudon race car weeks. If you're looking to miss the crowds avoid these summer events (times vary); if you're heading to the races, reserve well in advance, often up to a year.

## BASICS

**Operated By:** Smith family (Ken, Barb, Duane, & Kenny). **Open:** May–Sept. **Site Assignment:** Reservations recommended; 2-day min. stay during holiday weekends & race week. One night deposit required, no fee for cancellation. MC,V, & personal checks accepted. **Registration:** At office. **Fee:** Full hookups, $28; water & electric, $24, based on two adults & three children. **Parking:** At site, one vehicle per site.

## FACILITIES

**Number of RV Sites:** 109. **Number of Tent-Only Sites:** 0. **Hookups:** Water, electric, sewer (20, 30 amps). **Each Site:** Picnic table, fire ring, phone hookup. **Dump Station:** Yes. **Laundry:** Yes. **Pay Phone:** Yes. **Rest Rooms & Showers:** Yes (coin-op). **Fuel:** No. **Propane:** No. **Internal Roads:** Dirt (fair). **RV Service:** No. **Market:** Epsom (0.5 mi). **Restaurant:** No. **General Store:** No. **Vending:** No. **Swimming Pool:** Yes (two). **Playground:** Yes. **Other:** Rec hall, arcade, canoe rentals, riverfront beach, group area. **Activities:** Volleyball, fishing, canoeing, swimming, horsehoes, ping pong, pool,planned activities on holiday weekends including dances, contests, arts & crafts. **Nearby Attractions:** Concord, NH International Speedway, quick access to New Hampshire Lakes Region & Seacoast areas, antiquing. **Additional Information:** Greater Concord Chamber of Commerce, 244 North Main St. , Concord, NH 03301-5078, (603) 224-2508.

## RESTRICTIONS

**Pets:** Must be on a leash, never left unattended. **Fires:** In grills, stoves, & fire rings only. **Alcoholic Beverages:** At site only. **Vehicle Maximum Length:** 35 ft.

## TO GET THERE

From junction of Rtes. 4/202 & 28, go 2 mi. north on Rte. 28, then 0.5 mi. east on Depot Rd.; campground is on the right.

## EXETER

### Exeter Elms

188 Court St. , Exeter 03833.T: (603) 778-7631; www.ucampnh.com/exeterelms; cwaleryszak@aol.com.

| 🚐 ★★★ | 🏕 ★★★★ |
|---|---|
| Beauty: ★★★ | Site Privacy: ★★★★ |
| Spaciousness: ★★★★ | Quiet: ★★★★ |
| Security: ★★★★★ | Cleanliness: ★★★ |
| Insect Control: ★★ | Facilities: ★★★ |

We like the spacious, woodsy feel of this rural campground, set far off the main road, along the Exeter River. The level sites are spacious and private; average width is about 50 feet and most are nestled in trees for extra seclusion with river frontage or views. Many waterfront sites have banks that drop off into deep water so parents with young children may have to keep an eye out; but we particularly like the fact that, unlike some campgrounds, here, there are no annoying, unattractive fences to detract from the natural beauty of the setting. The campground offers a separate wooded tent-only area, but, if you prefer sun and open spaces, you'll have plenty to choose from, too. You'll find a variety of campground activities, plus fishing and canoeing on the river. The town of Portsmouth and the Seacoast region is less than 0.5-hour's drive away.

## BASICS

**Operated By:** Eric & Carol Waleryszak. **Open:** May 15–Sept. 15. **Site Assignment:** Reservations recommended; 50% deposit; refund given if cancelled two weeks prior to check-in, minus 10%

processing fee; three-day min. stay on Memorial Day & Labor Day weekends; four-day min. over Jul. 4th. **Registration:** At office. **Fee:** $21, tents; $27 w/water, electric; $31, full hookup. **Parking:** At site.

## FACILITIES

**Number of RV Sites:** 202. **Number of Tent-Only Sites:** 50. **Hookups:** Water, electric, sewer (15, 30, 50 amps). **Each Site:** Picnic table, fire ring. **Dump Station:** Yes. **Laundry:** Yes. **Pay Phone:** Yes. **Rest Rooms & Showers:** Yes. **Fuel:** No. **Propane:** No. **Internal Roads:** Dirt, gravel (good). **RV Service:** No. **Market:** Exeter (3 mi.). **Restaurant:** No. **General Store:** Yes. **Vending:** Yes. **Swimming Pool:** Yes. **Playground:** Yes. **Other:** Game room, boat rentals, one-mi. river frontage w/access & beach area, recreation field. **Activities:** Swimming, fishing, boating, planned activities w/full-time rec. director, volleyball, basketball, shuffleboard. **Nearby Attractions:** New Hampshire & southern Maine beaches, Portsmouth, Exeter, factory outlet shopping, golf courses, waterpark, Strawbery Banke historic museum, Seacoast Science Center, antique shops. **Additional Information:** Exeter Area Chamber of Commerce, 120 Water St., Exeter, NH 03833, (603) 772-2411; also visit www.Sea-coastNH.com.

## RESTRICTIONS

**Pets:** Must be on a leash, never left unattended. **Fires:** In grills, stoves, & fire rings only. **Alcoholic Beverages:** At site only. **Vehicle Maximum Length:** 40 ft. **Other:** No all terrain vehicles.

## TO GET THERE

From junction Rtes. 111 and 108, go 1.5 mi. south on Rte. 108 to entrance; campground is on the left

## FRANCONIA

### Lafayette Campground

Rte. 3, Franconia Notch State Park, Franconia 03580. T: (603) 823-9513; F: (603) 823-7214; www.nhparks.state.nh.us; nhcampres@dred.state.nh.us.

 ★       ★★★★★

Beauty: ★★★★   Site Privacy: ★★★★
Spaciousness: ★★★★   Quiet: ★★★
Security: ★★★   Cleanliness: ★★★
Insect Control: ★★   Facilities: ★★

This rustic state park campground sits in gorgeous Franconia Notch State Park, surrounding by mountains, streams, and hiking trails. It's best for campers who like to rough it a bit, tenters and pop-up trailers take up the majority of sites. The campground draws lots of outdoorsy types and backpackers, who come to play in the mountains. There are several popular hiking trails that leave directly from the campground and state park attractions, including The Basin, Profile Lake, Old Man in the Mountains, and The Flume are all close by. The woodsy sites, set on hilly terrain and along the Pemigewasset River, are generously spaced with plenty of privacy, but no hookups. Added bonus: new rest rooms with hot showers.

## BASICS

**Operated By:** New Hampshire Division of Parks & Recreation. **Open:** Mid-May–mid-Oct. **Site Assignment:** Reservations suggested. Half the sites can be reserved, half are set aside on a first come, first served basis. Call Reservation Center (603) 271-3628 from Jan.–early Oct., Mon.–Fri. or via email, www.nhparks.state.nh.us. Payment is due within seven days of making reservation. Each reservation is subject to a $3 non-refundable reservation fee. Refunds requests must be received in writing by the reservation office within 14 days of scheduled arrival & are handled on a case by case basis, subject to a $10 handling fee & may be subject to a penalty of a one night cmaping fee. MC, V; no personal checks. **Registration:** At office. **Fee:** $16, based on 2 adults & children under 18. Each additional adult is half the site fee w/a max. of 5 adults per site. **Parking:** At site.

## FACILITIES

**Number of RV Sites:** 98. **Number of Tent-Only Sites:** 0. **Hookups:** None. **Each Site:** Picnic table, fire ring. **Dump Station:** No. **Laundry:** No. **Pay Phone:** Yes. **Rest Rooms & Showers:** Yes (coin-op). **Fuel:** No. **Propane:** No. **Internal Roads:** Dirt, gravel (fair). **RV Service:** No. **Market:** Lincoln (10 mi). **Restaurant:** No. **General**

**Store:** Yes. **Vending:** No. **Swimming Pool:** No. **Playground:** No. **Other:** River frontage, hiking trails. **Activities:** Swimming, hiking. **Nearby Attractions:** Franconia Notch State Park, White Mountains. **Additional Information:** Franconia Notch Chamber of Commerce, P.O. Box 780, Franconia, NH 03580, (800) 237-9007.

## RESTRICTIONS

**Pets:** Not allowed. **Fires:** In grills, stoves, & fire rings only. **Alcoholic Beverages:** At site only. **Vehicle Maximum Length:** None. **Other:** Ask on arrival.

## To Get There

Take Lafayette Campground Exit off Rte. 3, Franconia Notch Parkway

## FRANCONIA NOTCH STATE PARK

### Cannon Mountain RV Park

P.O. Box 1856, Concord 03302. T: (603) 823-8800, (603) 271-3628 (reservations); F: (603) 271-2747; www.nhparks.state.nh.us; nhcampres@dred.state.nh.us.

🚐 ★★★★                        ⛺ na

Beauty: ★★★★            Site Privacy: ★★★
Spaciousness: ★★★        Quiet: ★★★
Security: ★★★              Cleanliness: ★★★★
Insect Control: ★★★        Facilities: ★★★★

The campground itself is meager, only seven sites, stuck in a row at the back of a parking lot. Yet, if you want to camp here you better reserve a spot well in advance—up to a year! The setting, in Franconia Notch State Park, is gorgeous. You'll camp at the base of pristine Echo Lake, elevation 1,931 feet, surrounded by views of Mt. Lafayette and Cannon Mountain. From here, you can walk to the shoreline for boating, swimming, and fishing, take an aerial tram ride to the 4,180-foot summit of Cannon Mountain, visit the New England Ski Museum and the Old Man in the Mountain Museum, and access a handful of popular hiking trails. You can also walk to the Cannon Mountain Ski Resort facilities, including its cafeteria, shops, and restaurant. All this, without ever having to get back in your vehicle. Another bonus: The campground is open year-round (though there's no electric or water hookups after mid-Oct.) Reserve now for next year.

## BASICS

**Operated By:** New Hampshire Division of Parks & Recreation. **Open:** Year-round. **Site Assignment:** Reservations suggested & must be made through central reservation office (603) 271-3628). Reservations must be made at least seven days in advance; $3 non-refundable reservation fee for each reservation. 24-hour cancellation fee w/$10 service charge. MC, V, D; no personal checks. **Registration:** At office. **Fee:** $24. **Parking:** At site.

## FACILITIES

**Number of RV Sites:** 7. **Number of Tent-Only Sites:** 0. **Hookups:** Water, electric, sewer (20, 30 amps). **Each Site:** Picnic table. **Dump Station:** Yes. **Laundry:** No. **Pay Phone:** Yes. **Rest Rooms & Showers:** Yes. **Fuel:** No. **Propane:** No. **Internal Roads:** Paved, gravel (good). **RV Service:** No. **Market:** Franconia (3 mi). **Restaurant:** No. **General Store:** No. **Vending:** No. **Swimming Pool:** No. **Playground:** Yes. **Other:** Access to Franconia Notch State Park & Cannon Ski Resort facilities, boat launch. **Activities:** Swimming, boating, fishing, skiing, hiking, aerial tram. **Nearby Attractions:** Franconia Notch State Park, White Mountains attractions. **Additional Information:** Franconia Notch Chamber of Commerce, P.O. Box 780, Franconia, NH 03580, (800) 237-9007.

## RESTRICTIONS

**Pets:** No pets allowed. **Fires:** No. **Alcoholic Beverages:** At site only. **Vehicle Maximum Length:** None.

## To Get There

At junction of Franconia Notch State Parkway and Echo Lake

## GILFORD

### Ellacoya State Beach & RV Park

Rte. 11, P.O. Box 7277, Gilford 03247. T: (603) 293-7821, (603) 271-3628 (reservations); F: (603) 271-2629; www.nhparks.state.nh.us; nhcampres@dred.state.nh.us.

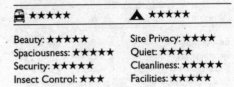

🚐 ★★★                    ▲ n/a

Beauty: ★★★               Site Privacy: ★★★
Spaciousness: ★★★          Quiet: ★★★
Security: ★★★★★            Cleanliness: ★★★
Insect Control: ★★★        Facilities: ★★8

Come summer, it seems that everyone in New Hampshire (and beyond) wants to get on Lake Winnipesaukee, the state's largest lake. Camping here is one way to do it. This small RV campground sits on the southwest shore of the lake, and boasts a 600-foot-long sandy beach, with views of the surrounding Sandwich and Ossipee mountains. Campers must share the space with hordes of day visitors, but come sunset, you'll have it—and the spectacular views— to yourself. Sites all have three-way hookups and are set in rows; amenities are basic (bathouse, small camp store, showers.) But, it's tough to beat this shoreline location, in the heart of the Lakes region.

### BASICS

**Operated By:** New Hampshire Division of Parks & Recreation. **Open:** Early-May–mid-Oct. **Site Assignment:** Reservations suggested & must be made through central reservation office (603) 271-3628); two sites left open on a first-come, first-served basis. Reservations must be made at least seven days in advance; $3 non-refundable reservation fee for each reservation. 24-hour cancellation policy w/$10 service charge. MC, V, D; no personal checks. **Registration:** At office. **Fee:** $35. **Parking:** At site.

### FACILITIES

**Number of RV Sites:** 38. **Number of Tent-Only Sites:** 0. **Hookups:** Water, electric, sewer (20, 30 amps). **Each Site:** Picnic table. **Dump Station:** No. **Laundry:** Yes. **Pay Phone:** Yes. **Rest Rooms & Showers:** Yes. **Fuel:** No. **Propane:** No. **Internal Roads:** Gravel, dirt (fair). **RV Service:** No. **Market:** Laconia (5 mi).

**Restaurant:** No. **General Store:** Yes. **Vending:** No. **Swimming Pool:** No. **Playground:** No. **Other:** Lake frontage, beach, boat launch, canoe rentals. **Activities:** Swimming, boating, fishing, volleyball. **Nearby Attractions:** Weirs Beach, Lakes region attractions. **Additional Information:** Greater Laconia/Weirs Beach Chamber of Commerce, 11 Veterans Square, Laconia, NH 03246, (603) 524-5531.

### RESTRICTIONS

**Pets:** No pets allowed. **Fires:** In communal firepit only. **Alcoholic Beverages:** At site only. **Vehicle Maximum Length:** None. **Other:** No tents allowed.

### TO GET THERE

From junction of I-93 and US 3 at Belmont, take US 3 north 9 mi.; turn east on NH 118 and then east on NH 110 to Ellacoya Beach.

## GLEN

### Glen Ellis Family Campground

P.O. Box 397, Glen 03838. T: (603) 383-4567; www.glenelliscampground.com.

🚐 ★★★★★                 ▲ ★★★★★

Beauty: ★★★★★            Site Privacy: ★★★★
Spaciousness: ★★★★★       Quiet: ★★★★
Security: ★★★★★           Cleanliness: ★★★★★
Insect Control: ★★★        Facilities: ★★★★★

This is top-notch, upscale camping at its finest. Here, campers have the beauty, scenery and economics of outdoor living with the comforts, amenities and services of a resort. Glen Ellis is one of our favorite places to camp. The campground, in New Hampshire's picturesque White Mountains area, lies in the shadows of the Presidential mountain range, nestled between the Ellis and Saco rivers. Facilities, including a large pool, sports fields, laundramat (open to the public), store, playground, and tennis courts are top-of-the-line, immaculately clean and finely landscaped. There are sweeping fields and spacious public areas, offering lots of room to romp and roam. Sites are spacious too, many with river frontage, offering both shade and sun at each site. There are two riverfront beaches for dunks in cool mountain waters (the pool is heated), a few planned activities on Saturday evenings, and White Mountain attractions and outdoor activities at your doorstep. Set your camp on riversite 56, our favorite (if you'd like hookups look at sites 86-100 on the Saco River or 33-51 on the Ellis River) and you won't want to leave.

## BASICS

**Operated By:** Richard & Dick Goff. **Open:** Memorial Day–Columbus Day. **Site Assignment:** Reservations required, one-night deposit; 14-day cancellation policy. **Registration:** At office. **Fee:** Waterfront sites, $24; all other sites, $22, $2 charge for electricity, air conditioning, & sewer, based on two adults & children under 18. **Parking:** At site.

## FACILITIES

**Number of RV Sites:** 130. **Number of Tent-Only Sites:** 73. **Hookups:** Water, electric, sewer (20, 30 amps). **Each Site:** Picnic table, fire ring. **Dump Station:** Yes. **Laundry:** Yes. **Pay Phone:** Yes. **Rest Rooms & Showers:** Yes (coin-op). **Fuel:** No. **Propane:** No. **Internal Roads:** Gravel, dirt (good). **RV Service:** No. **Market:** Gorham (0.5 mi). **Restaurant:** No. **General Store:** Yes. **Vending:** No. **Swimming Pool:** Yes. **Playground:** Yes. **Other:** Rec hall, river frontage & beaches on two rivers, tennis courts, sports fields. **Activities:** Swimming, tubing, basketball, volleyball, baseball, tennis, planned activities on Saturday evening during summer. **Nearby Attractions:** Storyland, Santa's Village, Six Gun City, White Mountains, North Conway. **Additional Information:** Mount Washington Valley Chamber of Commerce, P.O. Box 2300, North Conway, NH 03860, (800) 521-2137.

## RESTRICTIONS

**Pets:** No dogs allowed. **Fires:** In grills, stoves, & fire rings only. **Alcoholic Beverages:** At site only. **Vehicle Maximum Length:** 40 ft.

## TO GET THERE

From junction Rtes. 16 and 302, go west 0.2 mi. on 302; campground is on the left

## GORHAM
## Timberland

P.O. Box 303, Gorham 03581. T: (603) 466-3872; www.ucampnh.com/timberland.

🚐 ★★★　　🏕 ★★★

| | |
|---|---|
| Beauty: ★★★ | Site Privacy: ★★★ |
| Spaciousness: ★★★ | Quiet: ★★★★ |
| Security: ★★★★★ | Cleanliness: ★★★ |
| Insect Control: ★★★ | Facilities: ★★★ |

This campground is a favorite relaxing stopover for those traveling in New Hampshire's northern White Mountains region. Transcient campers who come for a night or two as they tour New England's top attractions make up the bulk of the summer clientele. In fall, the campground becomes a destination, a great place to view New Hampshire's northern fall foliage show. Set in the shadows of the Presidential mountain range, the campground offers shady rows of sites, ultra clean facilities and plenty of convenient full hookup pull-throughs. Nice touches: a 30-minute show on nearby attractions is shown each evening in the rec hall and an adult-only lounge offers a quiet place to read, play cards, watch TV or just relax. Kids have a pool, rec room and sports fields to keep them happily amused.

## BASICS

**Operated By:** Jeff & Sue Davis. **Open:** May–Oct. 20. **Site Assignment:** Reservations suggested, one night deposit, seven day cancellation policy, no refunds on holiday weekends, personal checks accepted. **Registration:** At office. **Fee:** Full hookups (w/cable TV), $24; water & electric (20 amp), $21; no hookups, $18, based on two adults per site, additional child, ages 6-17, $1.50; additional adult, $3. **Parking:** At site.

## FACILITIES

**Number of RV Sites:** 77. **Number of Tent-Only Sites:** 35. **Hookups:** Water, electric, sewer (20, 30 amps), cable TV. **Each Site:** Picnic table, fire ring. **Dump Station:** Yes. **Laundry:** Yes. **Pay Phone:** Yes. **Rest Rooms & Showers:** Yes (coin-op). **Fuel:** No. **Propane:** No. **Internal Roads:** Gravel, dirt (good). **RV Service:** No. **Market:**

Gorham (4 mi). **Restaurant:** No. **General Store:** Yes. **Vending:** No. **Swimming Pool:** Yes. **Playground:** Yes. **Other:** Adult-only lounge, rec hall. **Activities:** Swimming, badminton, volleyball, horseshoes, croquet, basketball. **Nearby Attractions:** Santa's Village, Six Gun City, Storyland, White Mountains, North Conway, outlet shopping. **Additional Information:** Mount Washington Valley Chamber of Commerce, P.O. Box 2300, North Conway, NH 03860, (800) 521-2137.

## RESTRICTIONS

**Pets:** Must be on a leash, never left unattended. **Fires:** In grills, stoves, & fire rings only. **Alcoholic Beverages:** At site only. **Vehicle Maximum Length:** None.

## TO GET THERE

From junction Rtes. 16 and 2, go 4.5 miles on Rte. 2; campground is on the left

## GREENFIELD

### Greenfield State Park Campground

P.O. Box 203, Greenfield 03047. T: (603) 547-3497, (603) 271-3628; F: (603) 547-8361; www.nhparks.state.nh.us.

| 🚐 ★★★ | ▲ ★★★★★ |
|---|---|
| Beauty: ★★★★ | Site Privacy: ★★★★ |
| Spaciousness: ★★★★ | Quiet: ★★★ |
| Security: ★★★ | Cleanliness: ★★★ |
| Insect Control: ★★★ | Facilities: ★★★ |

If you like a lot of elbow room and a woodsy, natural setting, you can't beat this lovely state park campground in southern New Hampshire. The wind in the trees, the heavy smell of pine, a crystal clear lake and plenty of room to roam are enticing features of this 401-acre oasis. We like the extra large sites, all nestled in the woods, and the separate "campers beach." Day visitors and picnickers have their own lake front area, which means campers don't have to share their own slice of sandy beach and swimming area on pretty Otter Lake. Bring your hiking boots and fishing poles: There are nature trails meandering through the woods and skirting Beaver, Mud, and Hogback Ponds, and canoes for rent at the lakeside general store.

## BASICS

**Operated By:** New Hampshire Division of Parks & Recreation. **Open:** May–Columbus Day. **Site Assignment:** Reservations suggested, must be made at least seven days in advance of stay; full payment due, plus $3 non-refundable reservation fee. Seven day cancellation policy. Some sites not reservable but available first come, first served. MC, V accpeted; no personal checks. **Registration:** At office. **Fee:** $16, based on two adults & dependent children under 18. Each additional adult is half the site fee. **Parking:** At site, two cars per site.

## FACILITIES

**Number of RV Sites:** 252. **Number of Tent-Only Sites:** 0. **Hookups:** None. **Each Site:** Picnic table, fire ring. **Dump Station:** Yes. **Laundry:** No. **Pay Phone:** Yes. **Rest Rooms & Showers:** Yes (coin-op). **Fuel:** No. **Propane:** No. **Internal Roads:** Gravel, dirt (good). **RV Service:** No. **Market:** Greenfield (1 mi). **Restaurant:** No. **General Store:** Yes. **Vending:** No. **Swimming Pool:** No. **Playground:** No. **Other:** Lake frontage, beach, nature trails, boat launch, boat rentals. **Activities:** Swimming, boating, fishing, hiking. **Nearby Attractions:** Manchester, Concord, Monadnock State Park. **Additional Information:** Manchester Chamber of Commerce, 889 Elm St., Manchester, NH 03101, (603) 434-7438 or Greater Peterborough Chamber of Commerce, P.O. Box 401, Peterborough, NH 03458, (603) 924-7234.

## RESTRICTIONS

**Pets:** Pets are allowed on designated sites only. Must be on a leash, never left unattended. **Fires:** In grills, stoves, & fire rings only. **Alcoholic Beverages:** At site only. **Vehicle Maximum Length:** None.

## TO GET THERE

From junction Rtes. 31 and 136, go west i mi. on Rte. 136; campground is on the right

## HAMPTON

### Tidewater Campground

160 Lafayette Rd., Hampton 03842. T: (603) 926-5474.

🚐 ★★★          ▲ ★★

Beauty: ★★★          Site Privacy: ★★
Spaciousness: ★★          Quiet: ★★★★
Security: ★★★★★          Cleanliness: ★★★
Insect Control: ★★★          Facilities: ★★★★

This campground, just minutes from Hampton Beach, draws a steady return of vacationing families. There's also a fairly entrenched neighborhood of seasonal renters; more than 140 of its 228 sites are taken by people who've set up their home away from home here. The remaining sites are mainly filled by folks with children, who come to explore the New Hampshire seacoast. Many stay for at least a week or two. Sites vary: there's a section of tent-only sites plopped in the open right behind the office; more attractive sites (16J-16P) back up to an expanse of marsh grasses and tidal water; still others (95C-95H) sit back from busy and noisy Rte. 1. In all, it's a clean, relatively quiet and economical base in the area.

### BASICS

**Operated By:** Wallace Shaw Sr. **Open:** May 15–Oct. 15. **Site Assignment:** Reservations required, min. stay three nights in Jul.–Aug., $50 deposit, full refund w/30 day notice, camping credit towards current year w/15-29 day notice, no refund or credit w/14 days or less. MC, V, personal checks accepted for advance reservations only. **Registration:** At office. **Fee:** Full hookup, $31; electric, $28; no hookups, $26; based on two adults & three children (2–17 years). **Parking:** At site.

### FACILITIES

**Number of RV Sites:** 190. **Number of Tent-Only Sites:** 38. **Hookups:** Water, electric, sewer (20, 30, 50 amps). **Each Site:** Picnic table, fire ring. **Dump Station:** Yes. **Laundry:** No. **Pay Phone:** Yes. **Rest Rooms & Showers:** Yes (coin-op). **Fuel:** No. **Propane:** No. **Internal Roads:** Dirt, gravel (fair). **RV Service:** No. **Market:** Hampton (1 mi). **Restaurant:** No. **General**

**Store:** Yes. **Vending:** No. **Swimming Pool:** Yes. **Playground:** Yes. **Other:** Rec hall, playing field, arcade. **Activities:** basketball, horseshoes. **Nearby Attractions:** Portsmouth, Hampton Beach, New Hampshire seacoast, Odiorne State Park, deep sea fishing, whale-watching. **Additional Information:** Hampton Beach Chamber of Commerce, 490 Lafayette Rd., Hampton, NH 03843, (603) 926-8717; also visit www.seacoastnh.com.

### RESTRICTIONS

**Pets:** no dogs. **Fires:** In grills, stoves, & fire rings only. **Alcoholic Beverages:** At site only. **Vehicle Maximum Length:** 40 ft. **Other:** No weekend visitors, no motocycles.

### TO GET THERE

From I-95 take exit 2, Rt. 101 east towards Hampton Beach, take second right (1.5 mi) on Rte. 1 south; campground is on the right.

## HAMPTON BEACH

### Hampton Beach State RV Park

P.O. Box 606, Rye Beach 03871. T: (603) 926-8990; www.nhparks.state.nh.us.

🚐 ★★★★          ▲ NA

Beauty: ★★★★          Site Privacy: ★★
Spaciousness: ★★★          Quiet: ★★★
Security: ★★★★          Cleanliness: ★★★★
Insect Control: ★★★          Facilities: ★★

The New Hampshire seacoast is a mere 18 miles long (though full of fine state parks and beaches along the way) and this is the only campground on its shoreline. This state park campground, for RVs only, offers few conveniences and fewer comforts. The sites are basic; RVs are set side-by-side on open gravel sites with little privacy and no shade. The office is in a public-works-style building that sits next to a huge parking lot, used for overflow campsites (no hookups in this area.) But the view! Cast your eyes to the east and you'll see swaying sea grasses, a stretch of sugar white beach and the Atlantic Ocean beyond. To your south, is a wide, picturesque tidal inlet. There are sandy paths to th beach and to the state park next door (with a store, rest rooms, and cold showers.) Smack dab on Hampton Beach, you can't beat the locale—or the price—of this real estate. You'll need to reserve one year in advance to get a site for anytime during the summer months.

## BASICS

**Operated By:** NH Division of Parks & Recreation. **Open:** Apr.–Thanksgiving. **Site Assignment:** Reservations required through Reservation Center at (603)271-3628. Reservations can also be made via email at www.nhparks.state.nh.us. Minimum two night stay, three nights on holiday weekends & for a max. of 14 days in a 30-day period. Overflow area accommodates 30 RVs (no hookups) on a first-come, first-served basis. MC, V. **Registration:** At office. **Fee:** $35. **Parking:** At site.

## FACILITIES

**Number of RV Sites:** 58. **Number of Tent-Only Sites:** 0. **Hookups:** Water, electric, sewer (30 amps). **Each Site:** Picnic table, fire ring. **Dump Station:** Yes. **Laundry:** No. **Pay Phone:** Yes. **Rest Rooms & Showers:** Yes, cold showers. **Fuel:** No. **Propane:** No. **Internal Roads:** Gravel (good). **RV Service:** No. **Market:** Hampton (1 mi). **Restaurant:** No. **General Store:** Yes. **Vending:** No. **Swimming Pool:** No. **Playground:** No. **Other:** Boat ramp, direct access to ocean, pavilion & state park adjacent to campground. **Activities:** Ocean swimming, fishing, beach combing. **Nearby Attractions:** Hampton Beach, whale-watching, saltwater fishing, Porstmouth, New Hampshire oceanfront state parks. **Additional Information:** Hampton Beach Chamber of Commerce, 490 Lafayette Rd., Hampton, NH 03843, (603) 926-8717; also NH Division of Parks & Recreation, P.O. Box 1856, Concord, NH 03302-1856, (603) 271-3556, fax (603)271-2629, www.nhparks.state.nh.us.

## RESTRICTIONS

**Pets:** Must be on a leash, never left unattended. **Fires:** In grills, stoves, & fire rings only. **Alcoholic Beverages:** At site only. **Vehicle Maximum Length:** None. **Other:** There are often high winds in this area. Use of awnings, fires, etc. may be restricted.

## TO GET THERE

From I-95 take exit 2, Rte. 101 east towards Hampton Beach. Follow signs to Hampton Beach. Campground is located on Rte. 1A just south of the main part of Hampton Beach near the Seabrook-Hampton town line.

## HAMPTON FALLS

### Wakeda Family Campground

Rte. 88, Hampton Falls 03844. T: (603) 772-5274; www.wakedacampground.com.

🚐 ★★★　　　　▲ ★★★

| | |
|---|---|
| Beauty: ★★★ | Site Privacy: ★★★ |
| Spaciousness: ★★★ | Quiet: ★★★ |
| Security: ★★★★ | Cleanliness: ★★★ |
| Insect Control: ★★★ | Facilities: ★★★ |

This family-friendly campground in the New Hampshire seacoast, offers the best of two worlds: far enough from the maddening crowds and traffic of seacoast beaches and attractions but close enough (only 20-30 minutes) for convenient day trips. The ride back and forth is pleasant, too: you'll pass farms, you-pick-it-orchards, and the sprawling lawns and meandering fieldstone walls of new and historic homes. The campground is a mile off the road, its own large neighborhood of seasonal renters and vacationing families. It's quiet (especially considering that there are more than 400 sites here) and spread out. The kids will like the 18-hole mini-golf course, but miss not having a swimming pool. The adults will appreciate the small hut serving coffee with bagels and donuts on the weekends (nice touch, we think.) There's a variety of sites, open and shaded, all about the same size (average width is about 35 feet.) If you like a bit more privacy and extra space, consider sites 32-47 and 16 East.

## BASICS

**Operated By:** Terry Savage, Jan Humbleton & Karen Bark. **Open:** May 15–Oct. 1. **Site Assignment:** Reservations suggested. No deposit required. No credit cards, personal checks accepted. **Registration:** At office. **Fee:** Full hookup w/50 amp, $35; full w/30 amp, $29.50; full w/20 amp, $28.50; water w/30 amp, $27.50;

water w/20 amp, $24.50; no hookups, $21.50. All fees based on two adults & three children or less. **Parking:** At site.

## FACILITIES

**Number of RV Sites:** 300. **Number of Tent-Only Sites:** 108. **Hookups:** Water, electric, sewer (20, 30, 50 amps). **Each Site:** Picnic table, fire ring. **Dump Station:** Yes. **Laundry:** Yes. **Pay Phone:** Yes. **Rest Rooms & Showers:** Yes (coin-op). **Fuel:** No. **Propane:** No. **Internal Roads:** Paved, gravel (good). **RV Service:** No. **Market:** Hampton (5 mi). **Restaurant:** Yes, small coffee shop. **General Store:** Yes. **Vending:** No. **Swimming Pool:** No. **Playground:** Yes. **Other:** Pavillion, 18-hole mini-golf course, game room, arcade, group facilities, camping cabins, 0.5 court basketball. **Activities:** Mini-golf, horseshoes, volleyball, badminton, basketball, planned activities (ice cream bar, pancake breakfasts) on weekends. **Nearby Attractions:** Portsmouth, seacoast beaches including Hampton Beach, whale-watching, saltwater fishing. **Additional Information:** Hampton Beach Chamber of Commerce, 490 Lafayette Rd., Hampton, NH 03843, (603) 926-8717.

## RESTRICTIONS

**Pets:** Must be on a leash, never left unattended. **Fires:** In grills, stoves, & fire rings only. **Alcoholic Beverages:** At site only. **Vehicle Maximum Length:** 40 ft.

## TO GET THERE

From I-95, take exit 1 (Kingston-Seabrook). Bear right off ramp, turn left at Rte. 1. Go 1 0.5 mi. and take a left on Rte. 88; campground is 4 miles on left.

## HANCOCK

### Seven Maples Campground

24 Longview Rd., Hancock 03449. T: (606) 525-3321; www.sevenmaples.com; sevenmaples@monad.net.

| 🚐 ★★★ | 🏕 ★★★ |
|---|---|
| Beauty: ★★ | Site Privacy: ★★★ |
| Spaciousness: ★★★ | Quiet: ★★★★ |
| Security: ★★★ | Cleanliness: ★★★ |
| Insect Control: ★★★ | Facilities: ★★★ |

This modest campground, tucked in the quiet southwestern corner of New Hampshire, is best for campers who like their pleasures simple and their getaways restful. The pastoral woods setting, framed by grand stand of maple trees, is particularly scenic in the fall. The campground sits on the grounds of an historic 19th-century farm; campers can still walk along side old stone walls built during the 1800s to clear pastures. Within walking distance is the historic town of Hancock, considered one of prettiest towns in New England. Visiting this area is like taking a step back in time. Campground facilities, befitting its setting, are not fancy, but adequate. There are a few welcome concessions to the 20th century: hot showers, heated pool, and small general store. Sites are tucked in the woods or in open pastures. Tenters have sites among the hookups or head to the campground's new open wilderness area.

## BASICS

**Operated By:** Dave & Tina Gullotti. **Open:** Mid-May–Columbus Day. **Site Assignment:** Reservations suggested. One night deposit for stays of less than one week; three night deposit for stays of one week or more; holiday weekends payment in full ;min. three nights on holiday weekends. Two week cancellation policy. MC, V, & personal checks accepted. **Registration:** At office. **Fee:** Full hookups, $29; water & electric, $26; no hookups, $21; wilderness sites, $17, based on family of four. **Parking:** At site.

## FACILITIES

**Number of RV Sites:** 91. **Number of Tent-Only Sites:** 34. **Hookups:** Water, electric, sewer (20, 30 amps). **Each Site:** Picnic table, fire ring. **Dump Station:** Yes. **Laundry:** No. **Pay Phone:** Yes. **Rest Rooms & Showers:** Yes (coin-op). **Fuel:** No. **Propane:** Yes. **Internal Roads:** Gravel, dirt (good). **RV Service:** No. **Market:** Hancock (2 mi). **Restaurant:** No. **General Store:** Yes. **Vending:** Yes. **Swimming Pool:** Yes. **Playground:** Yes. **Other:** Safari group area, sports court, pond. **Activities:** Swimming, hiking, horseshoes, planned activities & theme weekends. **Nearby Attractions:** Monadnock State Park, historic Hancock, Manchester, Keene. **Additional Information:** Manchester Chamber of Commerce,

889 Elm St., Manchester, NH 03101, (603) 434-7438 or Greater Peterborough Chamber of Commerce, P.O. Box 401, Peterborough, NH 03458, (603) 924-7234.

## RESTRICTIONS

**Pets:** Must be on a leash, have current vaccinations, never left unattended. **Fires:** In grills, stoves, & fire rings only. **Alcoholic Beverages:** At site only. **Vehicle Maximum Length:** None.

## TO GET THERE

From junction Rtes. 202 and 123, go northwest 2 mi. on Rte. 123, then north 1 mi. on Rte. 137, then north 0.3 mi. on Longview Rd.; campground is on the left

## HENNIKER

### Keyser Pond Campground

47 Old Concord Rd., Henniker 03242. T: (603) 428-7741; F: (603) 428-8701; www.keyserpond.com; jolly@conknet.com.

| 🚐 ★★★ | ⛺ ★★★ |
|---|---|
| Beauty: ★★★★ | Site Privacy: ★★★ |
| Spaciousness: ★★★ | Quiet: ★★★ |
| Security: ★★★ | Cleanliness: ★★★★ |
| Insect Control: ★★★ | Facilities: ★★★ |

This relaxed and friendly campground in the south central region of New Hampshire is one of two favorites in the area. (Also see Mile-Away listing.) Both are very popular with families, but this is our pick of the two. We like the low-key, slow-paced style of this woodsy destination, sitting on the shores of pretty Keyser Pond. We also like the views from the large, sandy beach and from the waterfront sites: glistening waters surrounded by rolling hills carpeted in dense pine forests. (There is little development along the shoreline.) Days are spent pursuing old-fashioned pleasures, like swim races to a raft, canoe paddles, early morning fishing outings and marshmallow roasts and sing-alongs around the communal campfire circle. There are planned activities and socials offered on summer weekends, too.

## BASICS

**Operated By:** Cal & Jolly Kimball. **Open:** May 15–Oct. 15. **Site Assignment:** Reservations suggested, one night deposit, three day cancellation policy MC, V, D accepted, no personal checks. **Registration:** At office. **Fee:** Waterfront, $30; full hookups, waterfront, $32; full hookups, $27; water & electric, $25; water, $20, based on two adults & their children under 18. **Parking:** At site.

## FACILITIES

**Number of RV Sites:** 107. **Number of Tent-Only Sites:** 9. **Hookups:** Water, electric, sewer (20, 30 amps). **Each Site:** Picnic table, fire ring. **Dump Station:** Yes. **Laundry:** Yes. **Pay Phone:** Yes. **Rest Rooms & Showers:** Yes (coin-op). **Fuel:** No. **Propane:** Yes. **Internal Roads:** Gravel (good). **RV Service:** No. **Market:** Henniker (4.5 mi). **Restaurant:** No. **General Store:** Yes. **Vending:** No. **Swimming Pool:** No. **Playground:** Yes. **Other:** Lake frontage, beach, boat rentals, mini golf course, rec hall, trailer rentals. **Activities:** Swimming, boating, fishing, horseshoes, shuffleboard, volleyball, badminton, planned activities on summer weekends. **Nearby Attractions:** Henniker, Concord, Lakes region. **Additional Information:** Greater Concord Chamber of Commerce, 244 North Main St., Concord, NH 03301-5078, (603) 224-2508 or New London/Lake Sunapee Region Chamber of Commerce, P.O. Box 532, New London, NH 03257, (603) 536-6575.

## RESTRICTIONS

**Pets:** Must be on a leash, never left unattended. **Fires:** In grills, stoves, & fire rings only. **Alcoholic Beverages:** At site only. **Vehicle Maximum Length:** None.

## TO GET THERE

From junction Rtes. 202 and 127 and Old Concord Rd., go south 300 yards on Old Concord Rd.; campground is on the right

## HENNIKER

### Mile Away Campground

41 Old West Hopkinton Rd., Henniker 03242. T: (603) 428-7616, (800) 787-4679 (reservations); www.ucampnh.com/mi.-away.

| 🚐 ★★★★ | ⛺ ★★★ |
|---|---|

Beauty: ★★★
Spaciousness: ★★★
Security: ★★★
Insect Control: ★★★

Site Privacy: ★★★
Quiet: ★★★
Cleanliness: ★★★★
Facilities: ★★★

This well-kept, woodsy campground in the south central region of New Hampshire is one of two favorites in the area (Also see Keyser Pond campground listing.) Both are popular with families and great places to stay. Mile-Away is located on state-stocked French's Pond (trout anglers may want to pack their fly rods) with a picturesque sandy beach area, and a long shallow slope prefect for young swimmers. There are boat rentals and plenty of planned activities offered on weekends throughout the summer. This campground is one of the few in the state that stays open throughout the winter months, with cross country and snowmobile trails accessible from the property, ice skating on the pond and alpine skiing nearby. There are several summer seasonal renters, most clustered near the rec hall and office and toward the beach area. The rest of the sites, mostly shaded with water and electric hookups, are scattered in loops on good-sized lots (average width is about 50 feet.)

## BASICS

**Operated By:** Kate Tenney. **Open:** Memorial Day–Columbus Day. **Site Assignment:** Reservations suggested, one night deposit; no shows forfeit deposit, MC, V, & personal checks accepted. **Registration:** At office. **Fee:** Full hookups, $33; water & electric, $26; based on four people. **Parking:** At site.

## FACILITIES

**Number of RV Sites:** 156. **Number of Tent-Only Sites:** 14. **Hookups:** Water, electric, sewer (20, 30, 50 amps). **Each Site:** Picnic table, fire ring. **Dump Station:** Yes. **Laundry:** Yes. **Pay Phone:** Yes. **Rest Rooms & Showers:** Yes (coin-op). **Fuel:** No. **Propane:** Yes. **Internal Roads:** Gravel, dirt (good). **RV Service:** No. **Market:** Henniker (3 mi). **Restaurant:** No. **General Store:** Yes. **Vending:** No. **Swimming Pool:** No. **Playground:** Yes. **Other:** Pond, beach, boat dock, boat rentals, mini-golf, rec hall, game room, pavillion, safari field. **Activities:** Swimming, boating, fishing, hiking, ice skating, cross country skiing,

snowmobiling, shuffleboard, basketball, horse-shoes, mini golf, badminton, volleyball, planned activities on summer weekends, including socials, bingo, crafts & games. **Nearby Attractions:** Henniker, Lake Sunapee. **Additional Information:** Greater Concord Chamber of Commerce, 244 North Main St.', Concord, NH 03301-5078, (603) 224-2508 or New London/Lake Sunapee Region Chamber of Commerce, P.O. Box 532, New London, NH 03257, (603) 536-6575.

## RESTRICTIONS

**Pets:** Must be on a leash, never left unattended. **Fires:** In grills, stoves, & fire rings only. **Alcoholic Beverages:** At site only. **Vehicle Maximum Length:** None.

## TO GET THERE

From junction I-89 and Rte. 202 (exit 5), go west 5 mi. on Rte. 202, then northeast 1 mi. on Old West Hopkinton Rd.; campground is on the left

## JEFFERSON

## Lantern Motor Inn & Campground Resort

P.O. Box 97, Rte. 2, Jefferson 03583. T: (603) 586-7151; www.thelanternresort.com.

🚐 ★★★                    ▲ ★★★

Beauty: ★★★
Spaciousness: ★★★
Security: ★★★
Insect Control: ★★★

Site Privacy: ★★
Quiet: ★★
Cleanliness: ★★★★★
Facilities: ★★★★★

It's directly across the street from Santa's Village, minutes from Six Gun City and Storyland (New Hampshire's most popular kiddie amusement park attractions) and, as you'd expect, crawling with kids. This campground is a magnet for families and does a nice job of welcoming them and keeping them entertained. The setting is pretty, nestled in the meadows and woods at the foot of the Presidential mountain range. At the end of the day, you'll have stunning views of the sun setting over the craggy mountaintops. Of course, the kids will be too busy to notice: there are two full-size pools (one with piped in underwater music) and a wading pool for young tykes, a large playground and two hot tubs. There are planned activities running from 10 a.m. to 9 p.m. each day, including old-fashioned fun like haywagon rides, face painting, and sing-alongs. At the on-site motor inn, a nightly children's movie is shown followed by a general audience movie (both free.) Everything is clean, bathrooms immaculate. The sites are basic, set in rows, all similar in size (average width is about 35 feet). The tent-only area in the front of the camp-ground backs up to woods facing an open field. Big rigs will find a number of super large, pull-through sites for added ease and convenience.

## BASICS

**Operated By:** John & Norma Ahern. **Open:** May 15–Oct. 15. **Site Assignment:** Reservations suggested, one night deposit, seven day cancellation policy, MC, V, D, AE; no personal checks. **Registration:** At office. **Fee:** Full hook up, super sites, $35; full hookups, $32; water & electric, $27, no hookups, $22, based on a family of four. **Parking:** At site.

## FACILITIES

**Number of RV Sites:** 76. **Number of Tent-Only Sites:** 15. **Hookups:** Water, electric, sewer (30, 50 amps). **Each Site:** Picnic table, fire ring. **Dump Station:** Yes. **Laundry:** Yes. **Pay Phone:** Yes. **Rest Rooms & Showers:** Yes. **Fuel:** No. **Propane:** Yes. **Internal Roads:** Gravel, dirt (good). **RV Service:** No. **Market:** Lancaster (8 mi). **Restaurant:** No. **General Store:** Yes. **Vending:** No. **Swimming Pool:** Yes. **Playground:** Yes. **Other:** Game room, video arcade, trailer rentals, wading pool & two hot tubs, activity tent, on-site motor inn. **Activities:** Swimming, planned activities including hayrides, arts & crafts, contests, kid's programs, & more. **Nearby Attractions:** Santa's Village, Six Gun City, Storyland, North Conway, White Mountains, outlet shopping. **Additional Information:** Mount Washington Valley Chamber of Commerce, P.O. Box 2300, North Conway, NH 03860, (800) 521-2137.

## RESTRICTIONS

**Pets:** Must be on a leash, never left unattended. **Fires:** In grills, stoves, & fire rings only. **Alcoholic Beverages:** At site only. **Vehicle Maximum Length:** None.

## TO GET THERE

From junction Rtes. 2 and 116, go west 0.5 mi. on Rte.2; campground is on the right

## LACONIA

### Gunstock Campground

Rte. 11A, P.O. Box 1307, Laconia 03247. T: (603) 293-4341, (800) 486-7862 or ext 502; F: (603) 293-4318; www.gunstock.com; camping@gunstock.com.

🚐 ★★★★        ⛺ ★★★★

Beauty: ★★★★         Site Privacy: ★★★
Spaciousness: ★★★     Quiet: ★★★
Security: ★★★★        Cleanliness: ★★★★
Insect Control: ★★★   Facilities: ★★★★★

Within a few minutes drive are three mountain ranges, dozens of sparkling lakes (including the Granite State's largest—Lake Winnipesaukee) and a slew of attractions. But, there's no need to ever leave the campground property; we rarely venture out once we've pounded in the stakes. Outside your doorstep (or tent flap) is a top notch year-round resort, complete with a mountain sports center, equestrian center, swimming pools, skate park, archery center, restaurant, and more. In winter, there's cross country and downhill skiing, tubing, nature programs, and snowshoeing. The property also boasts several ponds and a good-sized lake. The campground is large, with more than 250 sites, and often bustling with activity (especially during New Hampshire's popular Race Weeks held in the summer.) Sites are set in rows; the lakeview sites are the prettiest, if you can get one.

## BASICS

**Operated By:** Laconia County. **Open:** Year-round. **Site Assignment:** Reservations suggested & can be made one year in advance. Reservations require a two-night stay, $20 non-refundable deposit in addition to a $2 reservation fee. Holiday stays must be paid in advance & may require three-night min. stay. MC, V, D, AE; no personal checks. **Registration:** At office. **Fee:** Full hookups, $30; water & electric, $28; no hookups, $24. **Parking:** At site.

## FACILITIES

**Number of RV Sites:** 111. **Number of Tent-Only Sites:** 139. **Hookups:** Water, electric, sewer (20, 30 amps). **Each Site:** Picnic table, fire ring. **Dump Station:** Yes. **Laundry:** Yes. **Pay Phone:** Yes. **Rest Rooms & Showers:** Yes. **Fuel:** No. **Propane:** Yes. **Internal Roads:** Gravel, dirt (good). **RV Service:** No. **Market:** Gilford (4 mi). **Restaurant:** Yes. **General Store:** Yes. **Vending:** Yes. **Swimming Pool:** Yes. **Playground:** Yes. **Other:** Mountain sports center, mountain bike center, skate park, equestrian center, group areas, conference center, ski resort, trails, rec hall, ponds & lake access, cabin rentals. **Activities:** Swimming, boating, hiking, horseback riding, archery, biking, alpine & cross country skiing, planned programs. **Nearby Attractions:** Lake Winnipesaukee, Lakes region attractions. **Additional Information:** Greater Laconia/Weirs Beach Chamber of Commerce, 11 Veterans Square, Laconia, NH 03246, (603) 524-5531 or Meredith Area Chamber of Commerce, P.O. Box 732, Meredith, NH 03253-0732, (603) 279-6121.

## RESTRICTIONS

**Pets:** Must be on a leash; never left unattended. **Fires:** In grills, campstoves, & fire rings only. **Alcoholic Beverages:** At site only. **Vehicle Maximum Length:** None.

## TO GET THERE

From junction Rtes. 16 (Spaulding Turnpike) and 11, go 15 mi. north on Rte. 11, then 12 mi. north on Rte. 11A; Gunstock resort and campground is on the left.

## LANCASTER

### Mountain Lake Campground

P.O. Box 475, Rte. 3, Lancaster 03584. T: (603) 788-4509; www.greatnorthwoods.org/mountainlake; mtnlake@ncia.net.

🚐 ★★★　　　🅰 ★★★

| | |
|---|---|
| Beauty: ★★★ | Site Privacy: ★★★ |
| Spaciousness: ★★★ | Quiet: ★★★★ |
| Security: ★★★★ | Cleanliness: ★★★★ |
| Insect Control: ★★★ | Facilities: ★★★ |

This Lancaster campground in the northern White Mountains, close to Santa's Village, Fran-conia Notch State Park and other popular attractions, is suited to families who prefer a quieter, lakeside locale. Situated on the pristine 25-acre Mountain Lake, campers have access to a sandy beach, two boat docks and rental boats (paddleboats, canoes and kayaks.) Campers can also bring their own boats, though no power motors are allowed on the lake. Fishing for perch, bass, pickerel and sunfish is good and a favorite pasttime at the campground. Families will enjoy the short nature trail that runs through the property, skirting a frog pond and tadpole stream. There's also a giant size chess and checker game to play, sports fields, and a rec hall. Level RV sites are set on a hill; the tent area is below towards the lake. There are a number of waterfront sites with water and electric (sites 76-80 are favorites); site 23 is nicely tucked in the woods for extra privacy. We'd stay away from sites 1-15, if you can; they're too close to the road for our liking. Looking for something different? You can rent the teepee on site; the rustic cabins are nice, too.

## BASICS

**Operated By:** Lois & Geert Pesman. **Open:** May–Oct. **Site Assignment:** Reservations suggested in Jul.–Aug., $25 deposit, 7 day cancellation policy, MC, V, & personal checks accepted. **Registration:** At office. **Fee:** Full hookups, $23; water & electric, $20.50; no hookups, $18. **Parking:** At site.

## FACILITIES

**Number of RV Sites:** 100. **Number of Tent-Only Sites:** 1. **Hookups:** Water, electric, sewer (30 amps), cable TV. **Each Site:** Picnic table, fire ring. **Dump Station:** Yes. **Laundry:** Yes. **Pay Phone:** Yes. **Rest Rooms & Showers:** Yes. **Fuel:** No. **Propane:** Yes. **Internal Roads:** Dirt, gravel (good). **RV Service:** No. **Market:** Lancaster (4 mi). **Restaurant:** No. **General Store:** Yes. **Vending:** No. **Swimming Pool:** Yes. **Playground:** Yes. **Other:** Lake frontage, beach, boat rentals, boat docks, rec hall, cabin rentals. **Activities:** Swimming, boating, fishing, shuffleboard, basketball, volleyball, horseshoes. **Nearby Attractions:** Santa's Village, Six Gun City, Storyland, White Mountains, Franconia Notch State Park. **Additional Information:** Northern White Mountains

Chamber of Commerce, 164 Main St. , P.O. Box 298, Berlin, NH 03570, (603) 752-6060, also Franconia Notch Chamber of Commerce, P.O. Box 780, Franconia, NH 03580, (800) 237-9007; Mount Washington Valley Chamber of Commerce, P.O. Box 2300, North Conway, NH 03860, (800) 521-2137.

## RESTRICTIONS

**Pets:** No pit bulls. Certain breeds, including german shepard, rotweiller, & doberman are not allowed during summer months. All pets must be on a leash under 10 ft. long, never left unattended. Pets are not allowed in public buildings, on swimming beach, or docks. **Fires:** In grills, stoves, & fire rings only. **Alcoholic Beverages:** At site only. **Vehicle Maximum Length:** 38 ft.

## TO GET THERE

From junction Rtes. 3 and 2, go south 4 mi. on Rte. 3; campground is on the right.

## LANCASTER

## Roger's Family Camping Resort & Motel

10 Roger's Campground Rd., Lancaster 03584. T: (603) 788-4885; F: (603) 788-3697; www.rogerscampgroundandmotel.usrc.net.

🚐 ★★★★          ▲ ★★★

Beauty: ★★★★          Site Privacy: ★★★
Spaciousness: ★★★     Quiet: ★★
Security: ★★★★★        Cleanliness: ★★
Insect Control: ★★★    Facilities: ★★★★★

Located halfway between Lancaster and Jefferson in the scenic northern White Mountains area, Roger's is New Hampshire's largest campground with 400 sites (not including a large safari group area.) The backdrop is splendid: rolling foothills, forested valleys and craggy summits of the Presidential mountain range surround the campground. There are plenty of nearby attractions and outdoor activities at your doorstep but most campers come to stay put for awhile. This is a destination campground with lots of on-site facilities: hot tub, swimming pool with waterslide, kiddie pool, tennis courts, mini-golf, nature trails, on-site restaurant and a host of planned activities and live entertainment. Kids will love the huge barn-turned-arcade/billiards room and upstairs TV room. RV sites are all pull-throughs, set side-by-side in rows of grassy sites. The tenting area is separate, set behind the pool and motel area, backed by woods. We find the campsites and some facilities a bit bedraggled; it'd all look better with a little sprucing up.

## BASICS

**Operated By:** Crosby Peck/Interlocks Property North. **Open:** May 1–Oct. 15. **Site Assignment:** Reservations suggested, one-half of stay required for deposit, 14 day cancellation policy, MC, V, D, AE & personal checks accepted. **Registration:** At office. **Fee:** Full hookups, $26; water & electric, $21; electric, $20; no hookups, $19, based on two people, additional adult, $5; additional child, $3. **Parking:** At site.

## FACILITIES

**Number of RV Sites:** 300. **Number of Tent-Only Sites:** 100. **Hookups:** Water, electric, sewer (30 amps), modem. **Each Site:** Picnic table, fire ring. **Dump Station:** Yes. **Laundry:** Yes. **Pay Phone:** Yes. **Rest Rooms & Showers:** Yes. **Fuel:** No. **Propane:** Yes. **Internal Roads:** Dirt, gravel (fair). **RV Service:** Yes. **Market:** Lancaster (3 mi). **Restaurant:** Yes. **General Store:** Yes. **Vending:** Yes. **Swimming Pool:** Yes. **Playground:** Yes. **Other:** Cabin & trailer rentals, on-site motel, mini-golf, arcade, waterslide, rec hall, TV room, hot tub, wading pool, tennis courts, safari field, nature trail, sports field. **Activities:** Swimming, tennis, hiking, softball, volleyball, mini-golf, basketball, shuffleboard, horseshoes. **Nearby Attractions:** Santa's Village, Six Gun City, Storyland, White Mountains, Franconia Notch State Park. **Additional Information:** Northern White Mountains Chamber of Commerce, 164 Main St. , P.O. Box 298, Berlin, NH 03570, (603) 752-6060, also Franconia Notch Chamber of Commerce, P.O. Box 780, Franconia, NH 03580, (800) 237-9007; Mount Washington Valley Chamber of Commerce, P.O. Box 2300, North Conway, NH 03860, (800) 521-2137.

## RESTRICTIONS

**Pets:** Must be on a leash, never left unattended. Pets are not allowed in motel units, cabin or trailer rentals. **Fires:** In grills, stoves, & fire rings only. **Alcoholic Beverages:** At site only. **Vehicle Maximum Length:** None.

## To Get There

From junction Rtes. 2 and 3, go 2 mi. east on Rte. 2; campground is on the right

## LEBANON

### Mascoma Lake Campground

92 US Rte. 4A, Lebanon 03766. T: (603) 448-5076, (800) 769-7861; www.mascomalake.com; camping@mascomalake.com.

🚐 ★★★★                  ▲ ★★★★

| | |
|---|---|
| Beauty: ★★★★ | Site Privacy: ★★★ |
| Spaciousness: ★★★ | Quiet: ★★★ |
| Security: ★★★ | Cleanliness: ★★★ |
| Insect Control: ★★★ | Facilities: ★★★★ |

If you're in the mood for old-fashioned pleasures (think: sunsets across the lake, early morning canoe paddles, and sing-alongs around a bonfire), you'll enjoy your stay at this lakeside campground. It's situated in the "quiet corner" of New Hampshire (though there are plenty of those!) straddling the Vermont border. Campground activity centers around pretty Mascoma Lake, with plenty of boating (there are canoe, kayak and paddleboat rentals) swimming, fishing, and lots of lounging on the sandy beach. Campsites are terraced, many overlooking the lake, with a bit of elbow room; average site width is about 35 feet. Type A, active types can happily busy with planned events on the weekend and sports activities, or a trip to nearby attractions (covered bridges, Quechee Gorge, and antiquing are favorites.)

## BASICS

**Operated By:** Carol & Dave Hill. **Open:** May–Oct. **Site Assignment:** Reservations suggested; one night deposit, holiday weekends paid in full; 14-day cancellation policy w/$5 service fee. MC, V. **Registration:** At office. **Fee:** Full hookups, $28; water & electric, $25; no hookups, $22. **Parking:** At site.

## FACILITIES

**Number of RV Sites:** 82. **Number of Tent-Only Sites:** 18. **Hookups:** Water, electric, sewer (20, 30 amps), modem. **Each Site:** Picnic table, fire ring. **Dump Station:** Yes. **Laundry:** Yes. **Pay Phone:** Yes. **Rest Rooms & Showers:** Yes. **Fuel:** No. **Propane:** Yes. **Internal Roads:** Gravel, dirt (good). **RV Service:** No. **Market:** Lebanon (3 mi). **Restaurant:** No. **General Store:** Yes. **Vending:** Yes. **Swimming Pool:** No. **Playground:** Yes. **Other:** Lake frontage, beach, rec hall, boat dock, boat rentals, sports field, planned activities. **Activities:** Swimming, boating, fishing, hiking. **Nearby Attractions:** Hanover, Dartmouth, Sunapee, Quechee Gorge, covered bridges, antiquing. **Additional Information:** Greater Lebanon Chamber of Commerce, 2 Whipple Place, P.O. Box 97, Lebanon, NH 03766, (603) 448-1203.

## RESTRICTIONS

**Pets:** Must be on a leash; never left unattended. **Fires:** In grills, campstoves, & fire rings only. **Alcoholic Beverages:** At site only. **Vehicle Maximum Length:** 35 ft.

## To Get There

From I-89 and exit 17, go east 2 mi. on Rte. 4, then south 0.75 mi. on Rte. 4A; campground is on right

## LEE

### Ferndale Acres

132 Wednesday Hill Rd., Lee 03824. T: (603) 659-5082 (May-Sept.) or, (603) 623-2351 (Oct.-Apr.); www.ferndaleacres.com; fac132.com.

🚐 ★★★                  ▲ ★★

| | |
|---|---|
| Beauty: ★★★ | Site Privacy: ★★ |
| Spaciousness: ★★ | Quiet: ★★★ |
| Security: ★★★ | Cleanliness: ★★ |
| Insect Control: ★★★ | Facilities: ★★★ |

This plain Jane is a bit off the beaten path, set in the middle of a former farmer's field along the Lamprey River. The natural setting is pretty enough but, alas, the best sites, along the river, are taken by a core of regulars who rent for the season. Some of these trailers, including an old beat-up bus, look like they've been around for awhile. Tenters and pop-up campers can pick from a handful of shaded sites in the woods, flanking the property. Still, there is plenty for families to do here, including fishing in the river, swimming in the pool, video games, bonfires, dances, and a plethora of planned activities. Adults have their own recreational hall, often with a disc jockey and potluck dinner. Many visitors use the campground as a base to explore Portsmouth and the Seacoast region (about 0.5-hour's drive away.)

## BASICS

**Operated By:** Walter & Lorraine George. **Open:** May 15–Sept. 15. **Site Assignment:** First-come, first-served; hold w/credit card or one-day deposit reservations required on holiday weekends & must be paid in full prior to arrival; MC, V, AE & personal checks accepted. **Registration:** At office. **Fee:** $25 for a family of 2, $1 extra per child, $5 extra per adult. **Parking:** At site.

## FACILITIES

**Number of RV Sites:** 138. **Number of Tent-Only Sites:** 12. **Hookups:** Water, electric, sewer (30 amps). **Each Site:** Picnic table, fire ring. **Dump Station:** No. **Laundry:** Yes. **Pay Phone:** Yes. **Rest Rooms & Showers:** Yes (coin-op). **Fuel:** No. **Propane:** No. **Internal Roads:** Dirt (fair). **RV Service:** No. **Market:** Lee (5 mi.). **Restaurant:** No. **General Store:** Yes. **Vending:** Yes. **Swimming Pool:** Yes. **Playground:** Y. **Other:** Game room, adult rec. hall, river access. **Activities:** Planned activities on weekends, fishing, boat rentals, horseshoes, volleyball, baseball, basketball. **Nearby Attractions:** New Hampshire & southern Maine beaches, Portsmouth, factory outlet shopping, University of New Hampshire, antique shops. **Additional Information:** Greater Portsmouth Chamber of Commerce, P.O. Box 239, Portsmoutn, NH 03801, 603-436-3988; also visit www.SeacoastNH.com.

## RESTRICTIONS

**Pets:** Must be on a leash, never left unattended. **Fires:** In grills, stoves, & fire rings only. **Alcoholic Beverages:** At site only. **Vehicle Maximum Length:** 36 ft. **Other:** No motorbikes.

## TO GET THERE

From junctions Rte. 4 and 155; go 2.5 mi. south on Rte. 155, then 1.5 mi. east on Wednesday Hill Rd., then 1 mi. south on entry road

# LINCOLN

## Hancock Campground

Kancamagus Hwy., Lincoln 03251. T: (603) 447-5448.

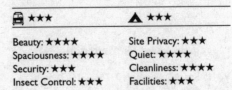

🚐 ★★★                          ⛺ ★★★

Beauty: ★★★★            Site Privacy: ★★★
Spaciousness: ★★★★      Quiet: ★★★★
Security: ★★★             Cleanliness: ★★★★
Insect Control: ★★★       Facilities: ★★★

Hancock Campground is one of two along the Kancamagus that is open all year, and great for those looking to ski on the cheap, with a dash of added adventure. Most all the sites are nicely forested, fairly spacious, well spaced apart, and set within a beautiful birch grove. Right across the street from Hancock is a trail that takes you up and over Potash Knob and Big Coolidge Mountain. Hancock is the campground on the Kancamagus that is closest to civilization, only five miles east of Lincoln, where you can grab a pizza or see a movie if need a little diversion. Another diversionary tactic is to take the short path to the East Branch of the Pemigewasset River (between sites 43 and 45 on the outer side of the loop) and drop a hook in the water. There are also a few spots where you can drop yourself in the water, but be careful. Even late in the summer, that water can be mighty chilly.

## BASICS

**Operated By:** US Forest Service. **Open:** All year. **Site Assignment:** First come first served; no reservations. **Registration:** Select site, then pay at self-service fee station. **Fee:** $16. **Parking:** At site.

## FACILITIES

**Number of RV Sites:** 37. **Number of Tent-Only Sites:** 40. **Hookups:** None. **Each Site:** Fire ring, picnic table. **Dump Station:** No. **Laundry:** No. **Pay Phone:** No. **Rest Rooms & Showers:** Yes. **Fuel:** No. **Propane:** No. **Internal Roads:** Gravel. **RV Service:** No. **Market:** No. **Restaurant:** No. **General Store:** No. **Vending:** No. **Swimming Pool:** No. **Playground:** No. **Other:** Unique swimming hole, Upper Lady's Bath.

**Activities:** Swimming fishing, hiking, picnicking, scenic byway. **Nearby Attractions:** Whale's Tale Water Park, White Mountain Motor Sports Park, Lost River Reservation. **Additional Information:** Lincoln-Woodstock Chamber of Commerce, (603) 745-6621, www.lincolnwoodstock.com.

## RESTRICTIONS

**Pets:** On leash. **Fires:** In fire ring. **Alcoholic Beverages:** At site. **Vehicle Maximum Length:** 2 vehicles per site. **Other:** 8 people per site; 14-day stay limit.

## TO GET THERE

From Lincoln, follow Kancamagus Hwy. to campground on right. It's the first campground you'll come to. From Conway, follow Kancamagus Hwy. to Hancock campground on left. From this side, it will be the last campground you come to.

# LISBON

## Littleton/Lisbon KOA

2154 Rte. 302, Lisbon 03585. T: (603) 838-5525, (800) 562-5836 (reservations); www.koa.com.

| 🚐 ★★★★ | 🏕 ★★★ |
|---|---|
| Beauty: ★★★ | Site Privacy: ★★★ |
| Spaciousness: ★★★ | Quiet: ★★★ |
| Security: ★★★ | Cleanliness: ★★★★★ |
| Insect Control: ★★★ | Facilities: ★★★★ |

This campground is a popular stopover and weekend destination for travelers exploring the scenic Franconia Notch area and beyond. Upon check-in, campers are given a helpful brochure detailing six one-day itineraries, all within an hour of the campground. Conveniently located, the Littleton/Lisbon KOA also offers some nice touches: an adult-only hot tub, frontage on the Ammonoosuc River with swimming holes and pebble beaches (bring your own tubes or kayaks; stocked fishing with license, too), white-glove clean bath facilities and—our favorite—meal delivery! The campground owners work with a local Italian restaurant (pizza, sandwiches, pasta, salads); pick from the menu in the office and the campground will deliver your meal for a nominal fee. Large pull-through sites are clustered in the middle of the property, while tent-only sites back up to the trees and the river. Full hookups are contained in a small loop behind the office and store. All sites are very tidy and uniform.

## BASICS

**Operated By:** Judy & Mike Sullivan. **Open:** First weekend in May–mid-Oct. **Site Assignment:** Reservations suggested in Jul.–Aug., one night deposit, 24-hour cancellation policy, three day min. stay on holiday weekends, MC, V, & personal checks accepted. **Registration:** At office. **Fee:** Full hookups, $31; water & electric, $28; no hookups, $25, based on two adults, additional child, 17 years & under, $2; additional adult, $5. **Parking:** At site.

## FACILITIES

**Number of RV Sites:** 43. **Number of Tent-Only Sites:** 17. **Hookups:** Water, electric, sewer (30 amps), cable TV, modem. **Each Site:** Picnic table, fire ring. **Dump Station:** Yes. **Laundry:** Yes. **Pay Phone:** Yes. **Rest Rooms & Showers:** Yes. **Fuel:** No. **Propane:** Yes. **Internal Roads:** Gravel (good). **RV Service:** No. **Market:** Littleton (5 mi). **Restaurant:** No. **General Store:** Yes. **Vending:** No. **Swimming Pool:** Yes. **Playground:** Yes. **Other:** Adult-only hot tub, river frontage, bike rentals, cabin rentals. **Activities:** Swimming, fishing, horseshoes, basketball. **Nearby Attractions:** White Mountains, Franconia Notch State Park. **Additional Information:** Littleton Area Chamber of Commerce, P.O. Box 105, 120 Main St. , Littleton, NH 03561, (603) 444-6561; Franconia Notch Chamber of Commerce, P.O. Box 780, Franconia, NH 03580, (800) 237-9007.

## RESTRICTIONS

**Pets:** Must be on a leash, never left unattended. **Fires:** In grills, stoves, & fire rings only. **Alcoholic Beverages:** At site only. **Vehicle Maximum Length:** 40 ft.

## TO GET THERE

From I-93, exit 42, go southwest 5.5 mi. on Rte. 302; campground is on the left.

## LITTLETON

### Crazy Horse Campground

778 Hilltop Rd., Littleton 03561. T: (603) 444-2204, (800) 639-4107; F: (603) 444-0776; www.ucampnh.com/crazyhorse; crazyhorse@conriver.net.

🚐 ★★★          ⛺ ★★★★

Beauty: ★★★★              Site Privacy: ★★★
Spaciousness: ★★★         Quiet: ★★★★
Security: ★★★★            Cleanliness: ★★★★
Insect Control: ★★★       Facilities: ★★★

Looking to get away from it all? This White Mountain–area campground offers a picturesque, serene escape, especially appealing to tent campers and outdoor enthusiasts. That's not to say there isn't lots to do in the area: From here you can visit Franconia Notch State Park attractions or head east to the busy North Conway area—easy day trips, if you're looking for some action. But you might be tempted to stay close to the campground, where you'll find hiking and biking trails, planned activities, and a number of nature programs conducted throughout the summer by the New Hampshire Audubon Society. Also nearby is 12-mile long Moore Lake, with a sandy beach, canoe rentals, and good fishing. The tent-only area is separate and remote, tucked in the woods, with the White Mountains as a backdrop (sites C88–96 are especially nice). Full-hookup sites for larger rigs are clustered in loops near the front, with plenty of shade and level ground.

#### BASICS

**Operated By:** Barbara & Joseph DiPierre. **Open:** Year-round. **Site Assignment:** Reservations suggested; one night deposit, 48 hour cancellation policy, 4-day cancellation policy for holiday weekends. MC, V, no personal checks. **Registration:** At office. **Fee:** Full hookups, $25; water & electric, $23; no hookups, $20. **Parking:** At site.

#### FACILITIES

**Number of RV Sites:** 112. **Number of Tent-Only Sites:** 48. **Hookups:** Water, electric, sewer (30, 50 amps), modem. **Each Site:** Picnic table, fire ring. **Dump Station:** Yes. **Laundry:** Yes. **Pay**

**Phone:** Yes. **Rest Rooms & Showers:** Yes. **Fuel:** No. **Propane:** Yes. **Internal Roads:** Gravel, dirt (fair). **RV Service:** No. **Market:** Littleton (2 mi.). **Restaurant:** No. **General Store:** Yes. **Vending:** Yes. **Swimming Pool:** Yes. **Playground:** Yes. **Other:** Boat rentals, rec hall, pavillion, lake access, trailer, teepee & tent rentals. **Activities:** Swimming, boating, fishing, volleyball, horseshoes, basketball, biking, hiking, planned activities, NH Audubon programs, winter activities nearby including skiing, snowmobiling, **Nearby Attractions:** White Mountain attractions, Franconia State Park. **Additional Information:** Littleton Area Chamber of Commerce, P.O. Box 105, 120 Main St., Littleton, NH 03561, (603) 444-6561.

#### RESTRICTIONS

**Pets:** Must be on a leash; never left unattended; current rabies certificate. Pets not allowed in rental units. **Fires:** In grills, campstoves, & fire rings only. **Alcoholic Beverages:** At site only. **Vehicle Maximum Length:** None.

#### TO GET THERE

From junction I-93 and Rte. 135 (exit 43), go south 100 yards on Rte. 135, then northwest (right) 1 mi. on Rte. 135/18, then north (right) 1.5 mi. on Hilltop Rd.; campground is on the right

## MEREDITH

### Clearwater Campground

26 Campground Rd., Meredith 03253. T: (603) 279-7761; www.clearwatercampground.com; info@clearwatercampground.com.

🚐 ★★★          ⛺ ★★★

Beauty: ★★★★              Site Privacy: ★★★
Spaciousness: ★★★         Quiet: ★★★
Security: ★★★★★           Cleanliness: ★★★★
Insect Control: ★★★★      Facilities: ★★★★

This centrally located Lakes-region campground, just minutes off the highway, is a water-lover's paradise. The property bumps up to pretty Pemigewasset Lake, with its own sandy beach, boat launch, slips, and dock. There's plenty of recreation off the water, too, with planned activities, play areas, a rec room, and more. It's easier to get to a number of popular attractions in the area and to explore the region from this base. Still, many campers, especially those with kids in tow, are content to stick around and enjoy the lake and campground activities. Most of the sites are on nicely wooded lots that loop off the main roads; only a handful have water views. The most requested site is site 125 next to a huge granite boulder. It's very picturesque, but we found it a bit busy, next to the docks and beach area. Bigger rigs should consider the Meredith Woods RV resort across the street, owned by the same family.

## BASICS

**Operated By:** John & Sue Mackie. **Open:** May 18–Oct. 9. **Site Assignment:** Reservations recommended, $100 per week deposit is required for holiday period; three nights or less require full payment in advance. Cancellation policy: deposits refunded up to one week before arrival. Minimum stays are often required during summer & holiday weekends. V, MC, D, AE & personal checks accepted. **Registration:** At office. **Fee:** $33, no hookups; $34, electric & water; $37 electric, water, sewer, & cable. From May 18–Jun. 14 (excluding Memorial Day weekend) & from Sept. 3-Oct. 9, fees are $20–$23 per night. **Parking:** At site.

## FACILITIES

**Number of RV Sites:** 146. **Number of Tent-Only Sites:** 4. **Hookups:** Water, electric, sewer (20, 30, 50 amps), cable TV. **Each Site:** Picnic table, fire ring, trash barrel. **Dump Station:** Yes. **Laundry:** Yes. **Pay Phone:** Yes. **Rest Rooms & Showers:** Yes. **Fuel:** No. **Propane:** No. **Internal Roads:** Paved, gravel (good). **RV Service:** No. **Market:** Meredith (2 mi). **Restaurant:** No. **General Store:** Yes. **Vending:** No. **Swimming Pool:** No. **Playground:** Yes. **Other:** Lake frontage, beach area, self-guided nature walk, boat rentals, boat dock, launching & slips, recreation pavilion, trailor & cabin rentals, rec rooms w/library, arcade games, TV. **Activities:** Swimming, boating, ping pong, shuffleboard, planned activities. **Nearby Attractions:** Lake Winnepesaukee, Squam Lake, Weirs Beach, scenic railroad, golf courses, hiking trails. **Additional Information:** Meredith Area Chamber of Commerce, P.O. Box

732, Meredith, NH 03253-0732, (603) 279-6121 or Lakes Region Assoc., Rte. 104, P.O. Box 430, New Hampton, NH 03252, (603) 744-8664.

## RESTRICTIONS

**Pets:** Must be on a leash, never left unattended. **Fires:** In grills, stoves, & fire rings only. **Alcoholic Beverages:** At site. **Vehicle Maximum Length:** 35 ft. **Other:** No motorcycles.

## TO GET THERE

From I-93, exit 23 (Meredith); go 3 mi. east on Rte. 104; campground is on the right.

## MEREDITH

## Harbor Hill

189 Rte. 25 East, Meredith 03253. T: (603) 279-6910; www.ucampnh.com; hhcamp@cyberportal.net.

🚐 ★★★                          ⛺ ★★★★

Beauty: ★★★                Site Privacy: ★★★★
Spaciousness: ★★★★      Quiet: ★★★★
Security: ★★★★★           Cleanliness: ★★★★
Insect Control: ★★★         Facilities: ★★★

Location, location, location. You can't beat Harbor Hill's location if you want to explore New Hampshire's popular Lakes region. The campground is a short distance to the shores of Squam Lake (where *On Golden Pond* was filmed), Lake Winnipesaukee (New Hampshire's largest freshwater lake), and to rollicking Weirs Beach. It's especially popular with families who want a quiet, relaxing place to come home to after a day of exploring area beaches and attractions.

## BASICS

**Operated By:** Barbara Palm. **Open:** Memorial Day–Columbus Day. **Site Assignment:** Reservations suggested, 50 percent deposit, 3-day deposit for holiday weekends, cancellations made less than 7 days before scheduled arrival, the deposit is held as raincheck for a future stay within the same year subject to availability & a $10 service charge. MC, V, & personal checks accepted. **Registration:** At office. **Fee:** Full hookups, $30; water & electric, $28; no hookup, $24. **Parking:** At site, one vehicle per site.

## FACILITIES

**Number of RV Sites:** 107. **Number of Tent-Only Sites:** 33. **Hookups:** Water, electric, sewer (20, 30, 50 amps). **Each Site:** Picnic table, fire ring. **Dump Station:** Yes. **Laundry:** Yes. **Pay Phone:** Yes. **Rest Rooms & Showers:** Yes (coin-op). **Fuel:** No. **Propane:** Yes. **Internal Roads:** Paved, gravel (good). **RV Service:** No. **Market:** Meredith (2 mi). **Restaurant:** No. **General Store:** Yes. **Vending:** Yes. **Swimming Pool:** Yes. **Playground:** Yes. **Other:** Rec hall, arcade, cabin rentals, sport court. **Activities:** Swimming, basketball. **Nearby Attractions:** Lake Winnipesaukee, Squam Lake, Weirs Beach, fishing, boating, quick access to White Mountain area. **Additional Information:** Meredith Chamber of Commerce, P.O. Box 732, Meredith, NH 03253-0732, (603) 279-6121.

## RESTRICTIONS

**Pets:** Must be on a leash, never left unattended. **Fires:** In grills, stoves, & fire rings. **Alcoholic Beverages:** At site only. **Vehicle Maximum Length:** 40 ft.

## TO GET THERE

Rt. 93, exit 23, Rt. 104 east go 12 mi. to Rt. 3, then left on Rt. 3 to Rt. 25 east; campground is 1.5 mi. on right

## MEREDITH

## Meredith Woods

26 Campground Rd., Meredith 03253. T: (603) 279-5449; www.ucampnh.com/meredithwoods; meredithwoods@worldnet.att.net.

| 🚐 ★★★★ | ▲ na |
|---|---|
| Beauty: ★★★ | Site Privacy: ★★★ |
| Spaciousness: ★★★ | Quiet: ★★★ |
| Security: ★★★★★ | Cleanliness: ★★★★ |
| Insect Control: ★★★★★ | Facilities: ★★★★★ |

This year-round RV park is a miniature gated neighborhood of rigs. It's RV heaven, smack-dab in the middle of New Hampshire's popular Lakes region. You won't find much in the way of scenic beauty at this campground: all sites are level, gravel or sandy plots, flanked by a few trees and bushes scattered in between for foliage and privacy. It's all very clean and orderly, albeit a bit bland. The most extraordinary feature of this park is the large (and plush by campground standards) recreational center with a heated indoor pool and hot tub, TV social room, and game room. All the facilities are new and modern. Another bonus: Meredith Woods campers have access to the beach, boating, and all other programs and facilities at Clearwater Campground, across the street. (But not vice versa.)

## BASICS

**Operated By:** Mackie family. **Open:** Year-round. **Site Assignment:** Reservations recommended, $75 deposit per each week of scheduled stay; reservations of 3 nights or less & holiday reservations require full payment in advance. Deposits are refundable up to 7 days of arrival. **Registration:** At office. **Fee:** $37, summer; $23–$33, early spring & winter, based on two adults & 3 children under age of 18; additional adults, $10; additional children, $1. **Parking:** At site, one vehicle per site.

## FACILITIES

**Number of RV Sites:** 101. **Number of Tent-Only Sites:** 0. **Hookups:** Water, electric (50 amps), sewer, cable TV, phone. **Each Site:** Picnic table, fire ring, trash can. **Dump Station:** No, all sites have sewer. **Laundry:** Yes. **Pay Phone:** Yes. **Rest Rooms & Showers:** Yes. **Fuel:** No. **Propane:** No. **Internal Roads:** Paved (good). **RV Service:** No. **Market:** Meredith (2 mi). **Restaurant:** No. **General Store:** Yes. **Vending:** No. **Swimming Pool:** Yes. **Playground:** Yes. **Other:** indoor pool & hot tub, TV social room & game room, boat docking by reservation, canoe rack space available; guests also have use of all activities & facilities at Clearwater Campground, across the street, including lake frontage, beach area, self-guided nature walk, boat rentals, boat dock, launching & slips, recreation pavillion, trailor & cabin rentals, rec rooms w/library, arcade games. **Activities:** Swimming, boating, hiking, ping pong, shuffleboard, planned activities. **Nearby Attractions:** Lake Winnipesaukee, Squam Lake, Weirs Beach, quick access to White Mountain region. **Additional Information:** Meredith Area Chamber of Commerce, P.O. Box 732, Meredith, NH 03253-0732, (603) 279-6121.

## RESTRICTIONS

**Pets:** Must be on a leash, never left unattended. **Fires:** In grills, stoves, & fire rings only. **Alcoholic Beverages:** At site nly. **Vehicle Maximum Length:** 40 ft. **Other:** limit of 7 people per site on an overnight basis, no more than 4 of whom can be adults; limit of 1 RV per site.

## TO GET THERE

From I-93, exit 23 (Meredith), go 3 mi. east on Rte. 104; campground is on the left

## MILTON

### Mi-Te-Jo Campground

P.O. Box 830, Townhouse Rd., Milton 03851. T: (603) 652-9022; www.mi-te-jo.com; mitejo@worldpath.net.

🚐 ★★★★★          ▲ ★★★★★

Beauty: ★★★★★          Site Privacy: ★★★★
Spaciousness: ★★★★          Quiet: ★★★
Security: ★★★★★          Cleanliness: ★★★★★
Insect Control: ★★★          Facilities: ★★★★★

This top-notch lakeside campground, less than one hour from the White Mountains to the north and ocean beaches to the east, is a real gem. There's lots of easy day trips from here, but there is little reason to leave. In fact, most campers rent summer sites a week at a time, Saturday to Saturday. This is a true destination/vacation campground, with plenty of outdoor pleasures. There are two sandy beaches on Northeast Pond. "Pond" is an understatement: 770 acres of fresh water feed into another 371-acre pond. Swimming and fishing are top pursuits, and many campers choose to bring their own boats to park in slips or at the docks ($5 per day charge.) There are lots of nice sites on the water (sites A–D are especially nice); sites 111, 112, and 0 are favorites, too, overlooking the lake. But you really can't go wrong here. Landscaping throughout the campground is well-done; facilities are clean, modern, and top-of-the-line.

## BASICS

**Operated By:** Gary & Susan Marique. **Open:** May 15–Columbus Day. **Site Assignment:**

Reservations recommended; required during Jul.–Aug., 50 percent deposit, cancel within 14 days to avoid $20 service charge MC, V, & personal checks accepted. **Registration:** At office. **Fee:** Premium sites w/full hookup, $34; premium sites w/water & electric, $31; vacation sites w/full hookup, $29; vacation sites w/water & electric, $26, based on two adults & their children ages 18 & under. **Parking:** At site.

## FACILITIES

**Number of RV Sites:** 179. **Number of Tent-Only Sites:** 0. **Hookups:** Water, electric, sewer (30 amps), modem. **Each Site:** Picnic table, fire ring. **Dump Station:** Yes. **Laundry:** Yes. **Pay Phone:** Yes. **Rest Rooms & Showers:** Yes (coin-op). **Fuel:** No. **Propane:** Yes. **Internal Roads:** Dirt (good). **RV Service:** No. **Market:** Milton (1 mi). **Restaurant:** No. **General Store:** Yes. **Vending:** Yes. **Swimming Pool:** No. **Playground:** Yes. **Other:** Two beaches, 1900 ft. of lake frontage, skateboard park, ballfield, pavillion, rec hall, boat slips, docks, cabin rentals, canoe, kayak & paddleboat rentals, arcade. **Activities:** Swimming, boating, fishing, bocci, horseshoes, basketball, volleyball, skateboarding. **Nearby Attractions:** New Hampshire seacoast, Portsmouth, quick access to Lakes region & Lake Winnipesaukee, antiquing, hiking. **Additional Information:** Lakes Region Assoc., Rte. 104, P.O. Box 430, New Hampton, NH 03252, (603) 744-8664, fax (603) 744-8659, or visit www.lakesregion.org.

## RESTRICTIONS

**Pets:** Must be on a leash, never left unattended. Pets are not allowed on the beaches or in cabins. **Fires:** In grills, stoves, & fire rings only. **Alcoholic Beverages:** Responsible consumption. **Vehicle Maximum Length:** None. **Other:** Sites are limited to seven campers of which only four may be adults. One RV per site.

## TO GET THERE

Rte. 16 (Spaulding Turnpike), exit 17, go 0.75 mi. east on Rte. 75, then 3.5 mi. north on Rte. 125. Turn right on Townhouse Rd.; the campground is 1 mi. on the left

## MOULTONBORO

### Long Island Bridge Campground

HCR 62, Box 455, Center Harbor 03226. T: (603) 253-6053.

🚐 ★★★          ⛺ ★★★

Beauty: ★★★★          Site Privacy: ★★★
Spaciousness: ★★★      Quiet: ★★★★
Security: ★★★          Cleanliness: ★★★
Insect Control: ★★★     Facilities: ★★★

Here's your chance to get your own slice of pricey Lake Winnipesaukee waterfront real estate, if only for a few nights. This campground rests on the shores of New Hampshire's largest (and very popular) freshwater lake. Only 15 minutes from Center Harbor, the campground is nestled in a cove, away from the hustle and bustle of many of the busier spots on the lake. (Note: the campground is next to a large marina, so you're likely to see some boat traffic.) Campers have access to a lovely, sandy stretch of beach and, if you reserve well in advance, a choice of sites along the shore facing picturesque Long Island and the setting sun. The rest of the sites and facilities are on a hilly terrace across the street. You won't see much, if any, of the lake from these sites (and those with water views have already been snatched up by long-time seasonal renters), but most of the available sites are spacious and ringed with trees for privacy. There are some open, grassy sites, too, for those who prefer the sun. We like the waterfront sites the best, of course, but sites 55, 55A, and 55B are roomy and private. This campground is a great base to explore the area and enjoy the lake.

### BASICS

**Operated By:** Watson family. **Open:** May 15–Oct. 15. **Site Assignment:** Reservations suggested, one night deposit, refunded on a 2 week notice, MC,V, personal checks accepted. **Registration:** At office. **Fee:** Full hookup, $25; water & electric, $23; no hookus, $21; waterfront, $28, based on one family (mother, father & unmarried children) per site. **Parking:** At site.

### FACILITIES

**Number of RV Sites:** 100. **Number of Tent-Only Sites:** 12. **Hookups:** Water, electric, sewer (20, 30 amps). **Each Site:** Picnic table, fire ring. **Dump Station:** Yes. **Laundry:** Yes. **Pay Phone:** Yes. **Rest Rooms & Showers:** Yes (coin-op). **Fuel:** No. **Propane:** No. **Internal Roads:** Dirt (fair). **RV Service:** No. **Market:** Moultonborough (7 mi). **Restaurant:** No. **General Store:** Yes. **Vending:** No. **Swimming Pool:** No. **Playground:** Yes. **Other:** Lake frontage, beach, boat rentals, **Activities:** Swimming, boating, fishing, basketball, volleyball, horseshoes. **Nearby Attractions:** Lake Winnipesaukee, Squam Lake, Weirs Beach, outlet shopping, antiquing. **Additional Information:** Wolfeboro Chamber of Commerce, P.O. Box 547, 32 Central Ave., Wolfeboro, NH 03894, (603) 569-2200.

### RESTRICTIONS

**Pets:** Must be on a leash, never left unattended. Pets not allowed at waterfront sites or beach area (pets are generally not encouraged here). **Fires:** In grills, stoves, & fire rings nly. **Alcoholic Beverages:** At site nly. **Vehicle Maximum Length:** None.

### TO GET THERE

From the junction of Rtes. 3 and 25 (in Meredith), go 7 mi. northeast on Rte. 25, then 6.5 mi. south on Moultonboro Neck Rd.; the campground is on the left

## NEW BOSTON

### Friendly Beaver Campground

Old Coach Rd., New Boston 03070. T: (603) 487-5570; www.friendlybeaver.com; info@friendlybeaver.com.

🚐 ★★★★★          ⛺ ★★★

Beauty: ★★★          Site Privacy: ★★★
Spaciousness: ★★★      Quiet: ★★★
Security: ★★★★         Cleanliness: ★★★★★
Insect Control: ★★★     Facilities: ★★★★★

We love the facilities at this southern New Hampshire campground; they rival many high-end resorts. A stay at Friendly Beaver is certainly not "roughing it." There's a three-pool outdoor complex, including a children's pool, sports pool (water basketball, anyone?), swim pool, and hot tubs. Next door is the adult-only rec hall and indoor pool complex. Kids have their own rec hall—a huge space with an upstairs activity area, large-screen TV, and games. There are plenty of planned activities for adults and children throughout summer weekends, too. Despite the size and resort-style facilities, the campground remains quite friendly, almost quaint. Seasonal renters are spread throughout the major areas of the campground; transient campers are clustered in a separate circle (full hookups available) in open, sunny sites. Special note: the campground is open year-round, with nearby skiing, ice fishing, and snowmobiling in the winter.

## BASICS

**Operated By:** Christine & Tom Quirk. **Open:** Year-round. **Site Assignment:** Reservations suggested, full payment required as deposit. Three night min. stay during holidays. 14-day cancellation notice, w/a $10 service charge; 7-13 day notice, camoing credit for the same year, 6 days notice or less, no refund or credit. MC, V, & personal checks accepted for deposit; no personal checks accepted upon arrival. **Registration:** At office. **Fee:** Full hookups, $36; water & electric, $33; no hookups, $31, based on two adults & two children under 18. **Parking:** At site.

## FACILITIES

**Number of RV Sites:** 166. **Number of Tent-Only Sites:** 7. **Hookups:** Water, electric, sewer (30, 50 amps). **Each Site:** Picnic table, fire ring. **Dump Station:** Yes. **Laundry:** Yes. **Pay Phone:** Yes. **Rest Rooms & Showers:** Yes. **Fuel:** No. **Propane:** No. **Internal Roads:** Gravel, dirt (good). **RV Service:** No. **Market:** Goffstown (15 mi). **Restaurant:** No. **General Store:** Yes. **Vending:** Yes. **Swimming Pool:** Yes. **Playground:** Yes. **Other:** Adult rec hall & lounge, game room, hiking, biking & snowmobiling trails, outdoor patios & decks, safaria field, hot tubs, sports field, pavillion. **Activities:** Swimming, basketball, volleyball, horseshoes, hiking, biking, snowmobiling, planned activities, including pony rides, arts & crafts, children's programs, socials, contests, dances, live entertainment, & more. **Nearby Attractions:**

Manchester, Concord, Crotched Mountain. **Additional Information:** Manchester Chamber of Commerce, 889 Elm St., Manchester, NH 03101, (603) 434-7438.

## RESTRICTIONS

**Pets:** Must be on a leash, never left unattended. **Fires:** In grills, stoves, & fire rings only. **Alcoholic Beverages:** At site only. **Vehicle Maximum Length:** None.

## TO GET THERE

From the junction of Rtes. 77, 136, and 13, go south 100 feet on Rte. 13, then west 2 mi. on Old Coach Rd.; campground is on the right

## NEW HAMPTON

### Twin Tamarack

Rte. 104, P.O. Box 121, New Hampton 03256. T: (603) 279-4387; www.minbiz.org/tamarack; bevsands@juno.com.

🚐 ★★★★                          ⛺ ★★★

| | |
|---|---|
| Beauty: ★★★ | Site Privacy: ★★★ |
| Spaciousness: ★★★ | Quiet: ★★ |
| Security: ★★★★★ | Cleanliness: ★★★★ |
| Insect Control: ★★★ | Facilities: ★★★★ |

This large, activity-oriented campground in the Lakes region is popular with families and groups. On warm, sunny days, campers gather around the pool, located up front next to the recreational hall and office. Or they head across the street to the sandy beach area on Pemigewasset Lake to swim in spring-fed waters or go boating. Evenings are filled with special events and activities (movies, music, and socials.) There's ping pong, video games, pool, hayrides, fishing contests, and more to keep even the most active in your brood busy and happy. The boulder-strewn, hilly grounds and scattered woods add visual interest, but don't expect too much privacy. Many sites are small, close to the road, and each other. But it's a "more the merrier" attitude here, perfect for social, friendly campers and traveling groups.

## BASICS

**Operated By:** Laurie Osuchowski. **Open:** Memorial Day–Columbus Day. **Site Assignment:**

Reservations suggested, take credit card to reserve site & charges one night's fee if cancelled less than 24 hours before arrival unless site is resold. Groups of four sites or more require nonrefundable $75 deposit. MC, V, D, personal checks not accepted on arrival but can be used to reserve a site. **Registration:** At office. **Fee:** Full hookup, $34; water & electric, $30, based on a family of four or two adults. **Parking:** At site.

## FACILITIES

**Number of RV Sites:** 256. **Number of Tent-Only Sites:** 0. **Hookups:** Water, electric, sewer (30, 50 amps). **Each Site:** Picnic table, fire ring. **Dump Station:** Yes. **Laundry:** Yes. **Pay Phone:** Yes. **Rest Rooms & Showers:** Yes. **Fuel:** No. **Propane:** Yes. **Internal Roads:** Gravel, dirt (good). **RV Service:** No. **Market:** New Hampton (3 mi). **Restaurant:** No. **General Store:** Yes. **Vending:** Yes. **Swimming Pool:** Yes. **Playground:** Yes. **Other:** Hot door hot tub, sports courts, canoe & boat rentals, lake access, boat launch, rec room, arcade, group safari area. **Activities:** Swimming, boating, fishing, basketball, horseshoes, volleyball, planned activities, including arts & crafts, fishing derbies, movies, hayrides, dances & socials. **Nearby Attractions:** Lake Winnipesaukee, Squam Lake, Weirs Beach, quick access to White Mountain region. **Additional Information:** Greater Laconia/Weirs Beach Chamber of Commerce, 11 Veterans Square, Laconia, NH 03246, (603) 524-5531.

## RESTRICTIONS

**Pets:** Must be on a leash, never left unattended. **Fires:** In grills, stoves, & fire rings only. **Alcoholic Beverages:** At site only. **Vehicle Maximum Length:** 40 ft. **Other:** Motorcycles not allowed.

## TO GET THERE

From I-93, exit 23, go 2.5 mi. east on Rte. 104; campground is on the left

## NEWFIELDS

### Great Bay Campground

56 Rte. 108, P.O. Box 390, Newfields 03856. T: (603) 778-0226; www.nebsnow.com/greatbay; greatbay@ttic.net.

 ★★★         ★★★

Beauty: ★★★        Site Privacy: ★★
Spaciousness: ★★        Quiet: ★★★
Security: ★★★        Cleanliness: ★★★
Insect Control: ★★        Facilities: ★★★

If you're an angler, with your own boat, you're going to love this campground, situated on the tidal water Squamscott River. It has its own boat launch and is the only private campground in the state located on a saltwater river. Extra bonus: no fishing license is required if you're casting from campground shores. With a boat, campers have access to pristine Great Bay, and beyond, to the ocean. Anglers fill the campground when the stripers and bluefish are running, but this is also a popular summer spot for area families and those visiting the Seacoast region. Unfortunately, most riverfront sites are taken by a cramped cluster of seasonal rentals, but you'll find a good selection of shady, level sites on the property. There's also a wooded tent-only section, nestled in the pines off the water (mosquitoes and black flies can be a nuisance.) This is a good base and destination campground both; when you're not on the water or visiting area attractions, there are planned suppers, dances, and other activities.

## BASICS

**Operated By:** Pat Elderly. **Open:** May 15–Oct. 1. **Site Assignment:** Reservations required; deposits required: 1-3 days, full amount; 4-7 days, a 3-day deposit; 8-30 days, a 7-day deposit. Cancellations: full refund 7 days before arrival, 75%, 5-6 days before arrival; 50%, 3-4 days before arrival; no refund, 0-2 days before arrival. V, MC, D, AE & personal checks accepted. **Registration:** At office. **Fee:** No hookups, $19; water & electric, $23; water, electric, sewer, $28. Rates based on two adults & their under 18 children or grandchildren per site. **Parking:** At site.

## FACILITIES

**Number of RV Sites:** 68. **Number of Tent-Only Sites:** 17. **Hookups:** Water, electric, sewer (20, 30, 50 amps). **Each Site:** Picnic table, fire ring. **Dump Station:** Yes. **Laundry:** Yes. **Pay Phone:** Yes. **Rest Rooms & Showers:** Yes (coin-op). **Fuel:** Yes. **Propane:** Yes. **Internal Roads:** Gravel, dirt (good). **RV Service:** No. **Market:** Newmarket (5 mi). **Restaurant:** No. **General Store:** Yes. **Vending:** Yes. **Swimming Pool:** Yes.

**Playground:** Yes. **Other:** Game room, separate tent-only area, tidal river access, small beach area, boat rentals, boat ramp. **Activities:** Swimming, salt water fishing, boating, volleyball, tetherball, basketball, planned activities. **Nearby Attractions:** New Hampshire & southern Maine beaches, Portsmouth, Exeter, factory outlet shopping, golf courses, waterpark, Strawbery Banke historic museum, Seacoast Science Center, antique shops. **Additional Information:** Greater Portsmouth Chamber of Commerce, P.O. Box 239, Portsmoutn, NH 03801, (603) 436-3988; also visit www.SeacoastNH.com.

## RESTRICTIONS

**Pets:** Must be on a leash, never left unattended. No pit bulls or rotweillers allowed. **Fires:** In grills, stoves, & fire rings only. **Alcoholic Beverages:** At site. **Vehicle Maximum Length:** 44 ft. **Other:** Maximum 28-day stay for tenters.

## TO GET THERE

From I-95 and Rte. 101 (exit 2), go west on Rte. 101 for 3.5 mi. to Rte. 108, then go 4 mi. north on Rte. 101 to entrance (entrance is at the Citgo gas station).

## NEWPORT

### Crow's Nest

529 S. Main St. , Newport 03773. T: (603) 863-6170; www.crowsnestcampground; camping@crowsnestcampground.com.

🚐 ★★★          ⛺ ★★★

Beauty: ★★★          Site Privacy: ★★★
Spaciousness: ★★★     Quiet: ★★★
Security: ★★★         Cleanliness: ★★★
Insect Control: ★★★   Facilities: ★★★

Located in the Lake Sunapee region, Crow's Nest Campground is a favorite with families and anglers in the summer and snowmobilers and skiers in the winter. It is one of the few campgrounds in New Hampshire that remains open when the mercury drops. The property flanks the meandering Sugar River, with plenty of spots for trout fishing and hot summer day dunks. (Those who prefer a less natural swimming experience can take advantage of the campground's heated pool and kid-friendly wading pool.) There's also a spring-fed pond on the property. In winter, there's downhill and cross country skiing nearby, sledding, and snowmobiling (trails are directly accessible from the campground). You'll have a choice of open, wooded, pond, and riverfront sites. The more primitive tent sites are located near the pond with a convenient footpath to the river. Full hookup sites are set in rows near the front of the campground with easy access to the rec hall and office (both heated in the winter.) Our favorites sites are 56–65, with water and electric, set on the riverbank.

## BASICS

**Operated By:** Howie & Kathy Neuberger. **Open:** May 15–Oct. 15 & Dec. 1–Apr. 1. **Site Assignment:** Reservations suggested; stay of one night requires full deposit; two or more nights, 50% deposit; holiday stays paid in full. 14 day cancellation policy w/a $5 service fee. No refunds for holiday stays. MC, V, D; no personal checks. **Registration:** At office. **Fee:** Full hookups (50 amp), $27; full hookup (30 amp), $25; water & electric (riverfront) $25; water & electric, $22; no hookups, $20, based on two adults & three children. **Parking:** At site.

## FACILITIES

**Number of RV Sites:** 84. **Number of Tent-Only Sites:** 11. **Hookups:** Water, electric, sewer (20, 30, 50 amps), modem. **Each Site:** Picnic table, fire ring. **Dump Station:** Yes. **Laundry:** Yes. **Pay Phone:** Yes. **Rest Rooms & Showers:** Yes (coin-op). **Fuel:** No. **Propane:** Yes. **Internal Roads:** Gravel, dirt (good). **RV Service:** No. **Market:** Newport (2 mi). **Restaurant:** No. **General Store:** Yes. **Vending:** Yes. **Swimming Pool:** Yes. **Playground:** Yes. **Other:** Pond & river frontage, group area, mini-golf, bike rentals, sports fields, rec hall, RV, cabin & tent rentals, planned activities, including arts & crafts, socials, & themed weekends. **Activities:** Swimming, fishing, basketball, biking, mini-golf, badminton, horseshoes, volleyball, snowmobiling. **Nearby Attractions:** Lake Sunapee, Dartmouth, Hanover. **Additional Information:** Greater Lebanon Chamber of Commerce, 2 Whipple Place, P.O. Box 97, Lebanon, NH 03766, (603) 448-1203.

## RESTRICTIONS

**Pets:** Must be on a leash; never left unattended. No pets in rental units. **Fires:** In grills, camp-stoves, & fire rings only. **Alcoholic Beverages:** At site only. **Vehicle Maximum Length:** None.

## TO GET THERE

From the junction of I-89 and Rte. 103 (exit 9), go west 22 mi. on Rte. 103, then south 2 mi. on Rte. 10; campground is on the right.

## NEWPORT

### Loon Lake

P.O. Box 345, Reed's Hill Rd., Newport 03773. T: (603) 863-8176; www.camploonlake.com; fnguilmette@turbont.net.

🚐 ★★★          ▲ ★★★

Beauty: ★★★            Site Privacy: ★★★
Spaciousness: ★★★      Quiet: ★★★
Security: ★★★★★        Cleanliness: ★★★★
Insect Control: ★★★    Facilities: ★★★★

We used to go to Lake Sunapee to vacation, one camper told us. "But it got a bit too busy and crowded for us. Now, we come here, where the pace is a bit slower and more relaxing." These were the sentiments we heard again and again during our visits to Loon Lake Campground. New Hampshire's popular Lake Sunapee is just 15 minutes away, but many campers are content to set up camp here and stay put. Who can blame them? The campground setting is beautiful: 750 acres of pine forest surrounding a mile-long freshwater lake. There are canoes, kayaks, and paddleboats to rent (gasoline motors are not allowed on Loon Lake), a sandy beach for lounging, and plenty of campground activities for the active (mini-golf, sports fields, planned events—even a small fitness room, if you must). There are several sites overlooking the lakeshore; others are placed in loops with plenty of shade and adequate privacy.

## BASICS

**Operated By:** Fred & Nancy Guilmette. **Open:** Mid-May–mid-Oct. **Site Assignment:** Reservations suggested; one night deposit; 30 day cancellation notice; less than 30 day notice, campers receive rain check for future stay within the same year w/a $10 service fee. MC, V; no personal checks. **Registration:** At office. **Fee:** Full hookups, $26 (lakeview), $28; water & electric, $24; no hookups, $20, based on two adults & unmarried children under 18. **Parking:** At site.

## FACILITIES

**Number of RV Sites:** 92. **Number of Tent-Only Sites:** 10. **Hookups:** Water, electric, sewer (20, 30 amps). **Each Site:** Picnic table, fire ring. **Dump Station:** Yes. **Laundry:** Yes. **Pay Phone:** Yes. **Rest Rooms & Showers:** Yes. **Fuel:** No. **Propane:** Yes. **Internal Roads:** Gravel, dirt (good). **RV Service:** No. **Market:** Newport (2 mi). **Restaurant:** No. **General Store:** Yes. **Vending:** Yes. **Swimming Pool:** No. **Playground:** Yes. **Other:** Lake frontage, beach, boat rentals, sports field, rec hall, game room, fitness room, mini-golf course, group area, cabin & tent rentals, planned activities, including arts & crafts, contests, socials, theme weekends. **Activities:** Swimming, boating, fishing, mini-golf, horseshoes. **Nearby Attractions:** Lake Sunapee, Dartmouth, Hanover. **Additional Information:** Greater Lebanon Chamber of Commerce, 2 Whipple Place, P.O. Box 97, Lebanon, NH 03766, (603) 448-1203.

## RESTRICTIONS

**Pets:** Must be on a leash; never left unattended. **Fires:** In grills, campstoves, & fire rings only. **Alcoholic Beverages:** At site only. **Vehicle Maximum Length:** None.

## TO GET THERE

From the junction of I-89 and Rte. 103 (exit 9), go north 19 mi. on Rte. 103, then west 1.5 mi. on Rte. 103/11, then north 2.5 mi. on Reeds Mill Rd.; campground is on the left.

## NORTH CONWAY

### Saco River Camping

P.O. Box 546, Rte. 16, North Conway 03860. T: (603) 356-3360; www.sacorivercamping.com.

🚐 ★★★          ▲ ★★★

Beauty: ★★★            Site Privacy: ★★
Spaciousness: ★★       Quiet: ★★
Security: ★★★★★        Cleanliness: ★★★
Insect Control: ★★★    Facilities: ★★★

In the heart of North Conway, this campground is best suited for families who don't mind a bit of noise and commotion. Like other campgrounds in the area, this one can be action-packed, crowded, and bustling. There's room to roam in the sweeping fields and play areas (look for the horses that are kept on site; kids get pony rides, too), but individual sites don't offer much privacy. Most are laid out side-by-side in long rows, flanking each side of road. They do a nice job of entertaining the kids here, with a full-time activity planner offering a large menu of daily programs. Expect evening bonfires, sing-alongs, hayrides, and more. There's also a small beach on the Saco River for swimming and rock skipping.

## BASICS

**Operated By:** John & Don McClure. **Open:** May 1– Oct. 15. **Site Assignment:** Reservations suggested, one night deposit, two week cancellation policy, MC, V, & personal checks accepted. **Registration:** At office. **Fee:** Full hookups, $25; full hookups (riverfront), $27; water & electric, $21; water & electric (riverfront), $23; no hookups, $19. **Parking:** At site.

## FACILITIES

**Number of RV Sites:** 120. **Number of Tent-Only Sites:** 20. **Hookups:** Water, electric, sewer (20, 30 amps). **Each Site:** Picnic table, fire ring. **Dump Station:** Yes. **Laundry:** Yes. **Pay Phone:** Yes. **Rest Rooms & Showers:** Yes (coin-op). **Fuel:** No. **Propane:** Yes. **Internal Roads:** Gravel, paved (good). **RV Service:** No. **Market:** North Conway (0.25 mi). **Restaurant:** No. **General Store:** Yes. **Vending:** Yes. **Swimming Pool:** No. **Playground:** Yes. **Other:** Game room, river frontage, canoe rentals, group safari area. **Activities:** Swimming, boating, softball, horseshoes, planned activities including children's programs, arts & crafts, contests, hayrides, & more. **Nearby Attractions:** North Conway, White Mountains, outlet shopping. **Additional Information:** Greater Conway Village Area Chamber of Commerce, P.O. Box 1019, Conway, NH 03818, (603) 447-2639.

## RESTRICTIONS

**Pets:** Must be on a leash, never left unattended. **Fires:** In grills, stoves, & fire rings only. **Alcoholic Beverages:** At site only. **Vehicle Maximum Length:** None.

## TO GET THERE

From the junction of Rtes. 16 and 302 south, go north 0.25 mi. on Rte. 16/302; campground is on the left.

## NORTH WOODSTOCK

### Lost River Valley Campground

951 Lost River Rd., Rte. 112, North Woodstock 03262. T: (603) 745-8321, (800) 370-678 (reservations); www.lostriver.com.

| 🚐 ★★★★ | 🏕 ★★★★★ |
| --- | --- |
| Beauty: ★★★★ | Site Privacy: ★★★★★ |
| Spaciousness: ★★★★★ | Quiet: ★★★★ |
| Security: ★★★★★ | Cleanliness: ★★★★★ |
| Insect Control: ★★★ | Facilities: ★★★★ |

We've dubbed this campground, "The Rivers Run Through It." Located on the site of a turn-of-the-century lumber mill (an authentic water wheel still churns), the scenic property is surrounded on three sides by national forest and situated between the Lost River and Walker Brook. It's hard to believe that you're only minutes off the highway and near many of New Hampshire's White Mountains and Franconia Notch State Park attractions. Large sites have been sensitively carved out of the boulder-strewn deep-woods setting, many with river or brook frontage. Recreation areas, including a swimming pond, beach area, playground, and sports fields, are situated across the street. Crossing the street may be an issue for families with small children, but the set-up keeps the campground sites quiet, more natural, and pristine. You'll go to sleep to the sound of running waters.

## BASICS

**Operated By:** Nancy Simmons. **Open:** May 15–Columbus Day. **Site Assignment:** First come, first served w/reservations accepted for three nights stay or longer, three-day deposit or 50 percent for stays of a week or more, 14 day cancellation policy w/$15 service charge. MC, V, D & personal checks accepted. **Registration:** At office. **Fee:** Full hookups, $31.50; water & electric, $26 (wooded), $30 (brookfront); water only,

$22 (wooded), $26.50 (brookfront), based on two adults per site, one camp unit & one car per site, additional children, ages 17 & under, $2; additional adult, $8; limit of four adults per site. **Parking:** At site.

## FACILITIES

**Number of RV Sites:** 100. **Number of Tent-Only Sites:** 32. **Hookups:** Water, electric, sewer (20, 30, 50 amps). **Each Site:** Picnic table, fire ring, water. **Dump Station:** Yes. **Laundry:** Yes. **Pay Phone:** Yes. **Rest Rooms & Showers:** Yes. **Fuel:** No. **Propane:** Yes. **Internal Roads:** Dirt, gravel (good). **RV Service:** No. **Market:** North Woodstock (4 mi). **Restaurant:** No. **General Store:** Yes. **Vending:** Yes. **Swimming Pool:** No. **Playground:** Yes. **Other:** River frontage, beach area, kayak & paddleboat rentals, rec hall, TV/reading room, game room, sports court, tennis court. **Activities:** Swimming, boating, fishing, badminton, tennis, basketball, volleyball. **Nearby Attractions:** Franconia Notch State Park, The Flume, Lost River Gorge, Clark's Trading Post, hiking, biking. **Additional Information:** Lincoln-Woodstock Chamber of Commerce, P.O. Box, 358, Kancamagus Hwy., Lincoln, NH 03251, (603) 745-6621; Franconia Notch Chamber of Commerce, P.O. Box 780, Franconia, NH 03580, (800) 237-9007.

## RESTRICTIONS

**Pets:** Must be on a leash, never left unattended. **Fires:** In grills, stoves, & fire rings only. **Alcoholic Beverages:** At site only. **Vehicle Maximum Length:** 32 ft.

## TO GET THERE

From I-93, exit 32, go 3.5 mi. west on Rte. 112; campground is on the left.

## NOTTINGHAM

### Pawtuckaway State Park

128 Mountain Rd., Nottingham 03290. T: (603) 895-3031; F: (603) 895-2061; www.nhparks.state.nh.us; info@nhparks.state.nh.us.

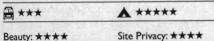

🚐 ★★★　　　　　▲ ★★★★★

Beauty: ★★★★　　　　Site Privacy: ★★★★
Spaciousness: ★★★★　　Quiet: ★★★

Security: ★★★　　　　Cleanliness: ★★★★
Insect Control: ★★★　　Facilities: ★★★

This state park gem in the south central region of New Hampshire is one of our favorite lakeside destinations. Woods and water dominate the scenery and outdoor activities. Forested, primitive-style campsites are clustered on islands dotting pristine Pawtuckaway Lake. Our favorites are the sites on Horse Island (check out sites 16, 41-46, and 67-69 on the island points with great water views), but you can hardly go wrong here—all are spacious and private. This is a popular spot for day visitors; we like that overnight campers have a separate area, removed from the daytime crowds and school and scout groups. There are boat rentals for exploring the lake (fishing is decent, too) and miles of hiking trails. Pack a lunch and head to the top of 908-foot South Mountain, with great views from its summit fire tower. Or walk the Fundy Trail bordering Burnhams Marsh in early morning or evening for a glimpse of beavers, deer, and great herons.

## BASICS

**Operated By:** New Hampshire Division of Parks & Recreation. **Open:** Mid-May–Columbus Day. **Site Assignment:** Reservations suggested by calling Reservation Center (603) 271-3628 from Jan. through early Oct. Reservations must be made seven days in advance of stay, paid in full. Seven day cancellation policy w/a $3 service charge. A number of sites are left open on a first-come, first-served basis. MC, V; no personal checks. **Registration:** At office. **Fee:** Waterview sites on Horse Island & Neals Cove (tents only), $22; Big Island (inland), $16; Big Island (waterview), $22; based on two adults & dependent children under 18. **Parking:** At site.

## FACILITIES

**Number of RV Sites:** 192. **Number of Tent-Only Sites:** 0. **Hookups:** None. **Each Site:** Picnic table, fire ring. **Dump Station:** No. **Laundry:** No. **Pay Phone:** Yes. **Rest Rooms & Showers:** Yes. **Fuel:** No. **Propane:** No. **Internal Roads:** Dirt, gravel (good). **RV Service:** No. **Market:** Raymond (4 mi). **Restaurant:** No. **General Store:** Yes. **Vending:** No. **Swimming Pool:** No.

**Playground:** No. **Other:** Lake frontage, beach, boat rentals, boat launch, hiking trails, group areas. **Activities:** Swimming, hiking, biking, boating, fishing. **Nearby Attractions:** Concord, Manchester, coastal beaches & attractions.

**Additional Information:** Greater Concord Chamber of Commerce, 244 North Main St., Concord, NH 03301-5078, (603) 224-2508 or Manchester Chamber of Commerce, 889 Elm St., Manchester, NH 03101, (603) 434-7438.

## RESTRICTIONS

**Pets:** No. **Fires:** In grills, stoves, & fire rings only. **Alcoholic Beverages:** At site only. **Vehicle Maximum Length:** None.

## TO GET THERE

From the junction of Rtes. 101 and 107 (exit 5 in Raymond), go north 3.5 mi. on Rte. 107, then 0.2 mi. west on Rte. 27, then 1 mi. north on Rte. 156; campground is on the left

## OSSIPEE
### Westward Shores

P.O. Box 308, 110 Nichols Rd., West Ossipee 03890. T: (603) 539-6445; www.wwscamp.com; wwscamp@landmarknet.net.

🚐 ★★★★          ▲ ★

| | | |
|---|---|---|
| Beauty: ★★★ | Site Privacy: ★★★ |
| Spaciousness: ★★★ | Quiet: ★★★ |
| Security: ★★★★★ | Cleanliness: ★★★ |
| Insect Control: ★★★ | Facilities: ★★★★ |

This destination getaway rests on shores of Ossipee Lake, with 1,800 feet of natural sandy beach and a full-service marina on site. Watery pleasures—swimming, boating, and fishing—reign here. You'll find all the supplies you need, including a fleet of boats to rent. Fishing for bass, perch, salmon, and trout is a big draw; Lovell River, one of New England's top trout streams, flows into Ossipee Lake. Families like the gradually sloping, sandy swimming area and the planned activities throughout the summer months. There's also a large rec hall for dances, bingo, and socials, and tennis courts (free to campers). This year-round destination welcomes snowmobilers, cross country skiers, and ice fishers in the winter. You'll have to reserve early to get a site in the summer; most are taken by seasonal renters, so only about 20 are reserved for overnighters. We especially like this campground in the fall, when the surrounding mountain ranges and valleys are ablaze with color, and the lake is still warm enough to enjoy.

## BASICS

**Operated By:** Jim & Patti Gray. **Open:** Year-round. **Site Assignment:** Reservations required, one-night stay deposit, 24-hour cancellation policy. MC, V, & personal checks accepted. **Registration:** At gatehouse. **Fee:** $35 (all sites have full hookups). **Parking:** At site.

## FACILITIES

**Number of RV Sites:** 260. **Number of Tent-Only Sites:** 0. **Hookups:** Water, electric, sewer (20, 30 amps), cable TV. **Each Site:** Picnic table, fire ring. **Dump Station:** Yes. **Laundry:** No. **Pay Phone:** Yes. **Rest Rooms & Showers:** Yes (coin-op). **Fuel:** No. **Propane:** No. **Internal Roads:** Dirt, gravel (good). **RV Service:** No. **Market:** Ossipee (2 mi). **Restaurant:** Yes. **General Store:** Yes. **Vending:** No. **Swimming Pool:** No. **Playground:** Yes. **Other:** Rec hall, marina, launching ramp, boat slips, lake frontage, private beach, boat rentals (including power boats, jet skis, pontoons), cabin rentals, game room, tennis courts, pavillion. **Activities:** Swimming, boating, fishing, snowmobiling, ice skating, tennis, basketball, volleyball, planned activities including arts & crafts, children's games, socials. **Nearby Attractions:** North Conway, White Mountains. **Additional Information:** Greater Conway Village Area Chamber of Commerce, P.O. Box 1019, Conway, NH 03818, (603) 447-2639; also Mount Washington Valley Chamber of Commerce, P.O. Box 2300, North Conway, NH 03860, (800) 521-2137.

## RESTRICTIONS

**Pets:** Must be on a leash, never left unattended. **Fires:** In grills, stoves, & fire rings only. **Alcoholic Beverages:** At site only. **Vehicle Maximum Length:** 32 ft.

## TO GET THERE

From the junction of Rtes. 25 and 16, go 8 mi. north on Rte. 16; campground is on the right.

## RAYMOND

## Pine Acres

74 Freetown Rd., P.O. Box 364, Raymond 03077.
T: (603) 895-2519;
www.pineacresrecreation.com;
camping@pineacresrecreation.com.

🚐 ★★★★★          ⛺ ★★★★

Beauty: ★★★★          Site Privacy: ★★★
Spaciousness: ★★★     Quiet: ★★★
Security: ★★★★         Cleanliness: ★★★
Insect Control: ★★★    Facilities: ★★★★★

This busy, action-packed campground is a mini-resort, popular with vacationing families. It's within a half-hour's drive to New Hampshire's coastal beaches to the east and the Lakes region to the north. But why leave? Most campers don't; they stay to play on the on-site waterslides, swim, fish and boat in the pond, order burgers, fries, and sundaes from Big Daddy's snack bar, and join in non-stop activities (think bingo, hayrides, karoake, crafts, races, contests). This large campground has a natural side, too, as it flanks the pretty Lamprey River. There's a good-sized sandy beach and a wide, still-water section of the river. Most sites are nicely shaded and spaced about 30 feet from one another. Tenters will like sites A1–A4 near the beach. There are cabin and RV rentals on site, too.

### BASICS

**Operated By:** John, Tracy & Stanley Shea. **Open:** May–Nov. **Site Assignment:** Reservations recommended; min. stay five nights in Jul. & Aug. (but check two weeks prior to arrival & they may fit you in for less nights) Cancellation policy: 30 days notice, full refund minus $10 service fee; 9-29 day notice, camping credit toward current year; 9 days notice, no refund or credit. MC, V, D. **Registration:** At office. **Fee:** $34, full hookup; $31, water & electric; $26, no hookup; weekends & holidays an additional $5 per night. Based on a family of five, two adults, 3 children. **Parking:** At site, two vehicles per site.

### FACILITIES

**Number of RV Sites:** 400. **Number of Tent-Only Sites:** 0. **Hookups:** Water, electric, sewer (20, 50 amps). **Each Site:** Picnic table, fire ring.

**Dump Station:** Yes. **Laundry:** Yes. **Pay Phone:** Yes. **Rest Rooms & Showers:** Yes (coin-op). **Fuel:** Yes. **Propane:** Yes. **Internal Roads:** Paved, gravel (good). **RV Service:** No. **Market:** Raymond (2 mi). **Restaurant:** Yes. **General Store:** Yes. **Vending:** Yes. **Swimming Pool:** No. **Playground:** Yes. **Other:** Dual flume waterslide, 18-hole mini-golf, river frontage, beach area, boat rentals, teen rec. hall, adult rec. hall, trailor & cabin rentals, mountain bike rentals, full-time activities director. **Activities:** Swimming, boating, basketball, horseshoes, softball, volleyball, lake & river fishing, planned activities, special themed weekends. **Nearby Attractions:** New Hampshire beaches, Portsmouth, Strawbery Banke museum. **Additional Information:** Greater Portsmouth Chamber of Commerce, P.O. Box 239, Portsmoutn, NH 03801, (603) 436-3988; also visit www.SeacoastNH.com.

### RESTRICTIONS

**Pets:** Must be on a leash, never left unattended. **Fires:** In grills, stoves, & fire rings only. **Alcoholic Beverages:** At site only. **Vehicle Maximum Length:** 40 ft. **Other:** Ask on arrival.

### TO GET THERE

From the junction of Rtes. 101 and 107/102, go south 1 mi. on Rte. 107/102; campground is on the left.

## RICHMOND

## Shir-Roy Camping Area

100 Athol Rd., Richmond 03470. T: (603) 239-4768.

🚐 ★★★          ⛺ ★★★★

Beauty: ★★★★          Site Privacy: ★★★
Spaciousness: ★★★     Quiet: ★★★★
Security: ★★★          Cleanliness: ★★★
Insect Control: ★★★    Facilities: ★★★

This woodsy, rustic campground on pretty, 42-acre, spring-fed Wheeler Pond has been around since 1956. The first time we visited, it was a cool summer night (not unusual for New England) and a warm, roaring log fire was burning in the massive fieldstone fireplace in the main building. This is also where the office and recreational room are housed and where the popular campground potluck dinners are held. Walk out the door, and footsteps away is a 200-foot sandy beach, a kiddie playground, and boats to rent. At night, bring a long stick and marshmallows to roast; there are campfires on the beach. Sounds like summer camp, huh? It feels like it, too. This rustic gem always takes us back to nostalgic, carefree summer days of our youth. Today, families return to share a similar experience with their children and grandchildren. Most of the sites are tucked into the woods, scattered in pods behind the recreation area. Only a handful of sites have lake views, but most are only a short walk away from the beach. The most spacious and private sites are in the "R" section, nestled in the northwest corner of the property. Of the campgrounds in the quiet Monadnock region of New Hampshire, this one is our sentimental favorite.

## BASICS

**Operated By:** Shirley Heise. **Open:** Memorial Day–Columbus Day. **Site Assignment:** Reservations suggested, 50 percent deposit or min. 3 day deposit for holiday weekends, 14 day cancellation notice for return of deposit. MC, V, & personal checks accepted. **Registration:** Office. **Fee:** Full hookup, $24; electric only, $23; no hookup, $20, based on one family (husband, wife & unmarried children) per site. **Parking:** At site, one vehicle per site.

## FACILITIES

**Number of RV Sites:** 106. **Number of Tent-Only Sites:** 2. **Hookups:** Water, electric, sewer (20, 30 amps). **Each Site:** Picnic table, fire ring. **Dump Station:** Yes. **Laundry:** Yes. **Pay Phone:** Yes. **Rest Rooms & Showers:** Yes. **Fuel:** No. **Propane:** No. **Internal Roads:** Gravel, dirt (fair). **RV Service:** No. **Market:** Winchester (7 mi). **Restaurant:** No. **General Store:** Yes. **Vending:** No. **Swimming Pool:** No. **Playground:** Yes. **Other:** Rec. hall, 200 ft. of frontage on spring-fed pond, beach, dock, canoe, rowboat & paddleboat rentals, trailer rentals, group camping area, game room, athletic field. **Activities:** Swimming, fishing, boating, volleyball, horseshoes, potluck suppers. **Nearby Attractions:** Mt. Monadnock, historic towns of Keene, Jaffrey & Peterborough, covered bridges, hiking, antiquing. **Additional Informa-**

**tion:** Greater Keene Chamber of Commerce, 48 Central Square, Keene, NH 03431, (603) 352-1303.

## RESTRICTIONS

**Pets:** Must be on a leash, never left unattended. **Fires:** In grills, stoves, & fire rings only. **Alcoholic Beverages:** At site only. **Vehicle Maximum Length:** None.

## TO GET THERE

From the junction of Rtes. 10 and 119 (in WInchester), go 6 mi. east on Rte. 119, then 0.5 mi. south on Rte. 32; the campground is on the left.

## SOUTH HAMPTON

### Tuxbury Pond Camping Area

88 Whitehall Rd., South Hampton 03827. T: (603) 394-7660, (800) 585-7660; F: (603) 394-7114; www.holipub.com/tuxbury; tuxburypond-camp@aol.com.

| 🚐 ★★★★ | 🏕 ★★★ |
|---|---|
| Beauty: ★★★★ | Site Privacy: ★★★ |
| Spaciousness: ★★★ | Quiet: ★★★ |
| Security: ★★★★★ | Cleanliness: ★★★★ |
| Insect Control: ★★★ | Facilities: ★★★★★ |

This high-energy, action-packed campground is a magnet for vacationing families and a longtime favorite among repeat summer visitors. Located in the popular Hampton Beach area, there's plenty to do on and off this property. The campground is located on a freshwater pond with swimming, boat rentals, and fishing. There's a boat ramp, too, and some campers bring their own boats in tow. (There's a 40-horsepower limit.) Sports fields, rec rooms, mini-golf, two swimming pools, and a variety of planned activities keep youngsters busy while parents relax. There's even a snack bar on the premises for quick meals and munchies. There are many seasonal sites and lots of big rigs, all for campers drawn to the campground for its many facilities and recreation.

## BASICS

**Operated By:** Richard Smith. **Open:** Mother's Day–Columbus Day. **Site Assignment:** Reservations suggested; 50 percent deposit, seven day cancellation policy. MC, V; no personal checks. **Registration:** At office. **Fee:** Full hookups, $31; water & electric, $29, based on two adults & two children. **Parking:** At site.

## FACILITIES

**Number of RV Sites:** 180. **Number of Tent-Only Sites:** 0. **Hookups:** Water, electric (20, 30, 50 amps), sewer, cable TV, modem in office. **Each Site:** Picnic table, fire ring. **Dump Station:** Yes. **Laundry:** Yes. **Pay Phone:** Yes. **Rest Rooms & Showers:** Yes. **Fuel:** No. **Propane:** Yes. **Internal Roads:** Gravel, dirt (good). **RV Service:** No. **Market:** South Hampton (3 mi). **Restaurant:** Yes. **General Store:** Yes. **Vending:** Yes. **Swimming Pool:** Yes. **Playground:** Yes. **Other:** Pond, beach, boat rentals, game room, rec hall, mini-golf, pavillion, group area, sports fields, snack bar. **Activities:** Swimming, boating, fishing, mini-golf, softball, basketball, volleyball, horseshoes, planned activities. **Nearby Attractions:** Hampton Beach, Massachusett's North Shore, Portsmouth, coastal beaches. **Additional Information:** Hampton Beach Area Chamber of Commerce, 490 Lafayette Rd., Hampton, NH 03843, (603) 926-8717.

## RESTRICTIONS

**Pets:** Must be on a leash; never left unattended. **Fires:** In grills, campstoves, & fire rings only. **Alcoholic Beverages:** At site only. **Vehicle Maximum Length:** 40 ft.

## TO GET THERE

From the junction of I-495 and Rte. 150 (exit 54 in Amesbury, MA), go 0.8 mi. north on Rte. 150, then 0.5 mi. northwest on Highland St., then 1.5 mi. west on Lions Mouth Rd., then 1 mi. on Newton road; campground is on the left.

## TAMWORTH

### Tamworth Camping Area

P.O. Box 99, Depot Rd., Tamworth 03886. T: (603) 323-8031, (800) 274-8031 (reservations); www.tamworthcamping.com; tamworthcampingarea.rscs.net.

 ★★★                    ▲ ★★★★

Beauty: ★★★              Site Privacy: ★★★
Spaciousness: ★★★★       Quiet: ★★★

Security: ★★★★★          Cleanliness: ★★★
Insect Control: ★★★       Facilities: ★★★

This pretty riverside campground has been around since 1967 and keeps on improving. Just 30 minutes from popular North Conway and White Mountain area attractions, the campground is close enough for convenient day trips yet away from the hustle and bustle. It boasts about 1,900 feet of Swift River frontage and a pretty, sandy-bottom swimming area perfect for fishing, wading, and river tubing. The 18 river sites, with water and electric hookups, are the most spacious and scenic; reserve them early. We especially like sites 8, 10, and 12. There's also an open group-tent area, nestled in a meadow filled with blueberries and views of Mt. Whittier and the Ossipee Mountains. Families also like the weekend activities that may include arts and crafts, make-your-own-sundae parties, hayrides, and more.

## BASICS

**Operated By:** Dana & Laurie Bonica. **Open:** May 15–Columbus Day. **Site Assignment:** Reservations suggested; two night min. stay for riverfront sites. 50 percent deposit, 100 percent deposit during holiday weekends & motorcycle rally weeks. 14 day cancellation policy w/$5 service fee. MC, V, & personal checks accepted. **Registration:** At office. **Fee:** Full hookups, $33; water & electric, $29; water & electric on river, $33; water, $24; no hookups, $22. **Parking:** At site.

## FACILITIES

**Number of RV Sites:** 87. **Number of Tent-Only Sites:** 13. **Hookups:** Water, electric, sewer (20, 30 amps). **Each Site:** Picnic table, ring. **Dump Station:** Yes. **Laundry:** Yes. **Pay Phone:** Yes. **Rest Rooms & Showers:** Yes (coin-op). **Fuel:** No. **Propane:** Yes. **Internal Roads:** Dirt, gravel (good). **RV Service:** No. **Market:** Ossipee (6 mi). **Restaurant:** No. **General Store:** Yes. **Vending:** No. **Swimming Pool:** No. **Playground:** Yes. **Other:** Rec hall, pavillion, group area, crafts cabin, lending library, 9-hole mini golf course, sports field. **Activities:** Swimming, volleyball, basketball, horseshoes, softball, shuffleboard, badminton, fishing, planned activities, including arts & crafts, hayrides, dances, & more. **Nearby Attractions:** Attitash Bear Peak, Weirs

Beach, Story Land, Conway Scenic Railroad, North Conway, quick access to White Mountains. **Additional Information:** Greater Conway Village Area Chamber of Commerce, P.O. Box 1019, Conway, NH 03818, (603) 447-2639.

## RESTRICTIONS

**Pets:** Must be on a leash, never left unattended. **Fires:** In grills, stoves, & fire rings only. **Alcoholic Beverages:** In a responsible manner. **Vehicle Maximum Length:** None. **Other:** Ask on arrival.

## TO GET THERE

From the junction of Rtes. 25 and 16, go 0.5 mi. north on Rte. 16 to Depot Rd., then 3 mi. west; campground is on the left

## TAMWORTH

## White Lake State Park

Rte. 16, Tamworth 03886. T: (603) 323-7350 (information) (603) 271-3628 (reservations); www.nhparks.state.nh.us.

🚐 ★                          ▲ ★★★★★

Beauty: ★★★★★         Site Privacy: ★★★★
Spaciousness: ★★★★     Quiet: ★★★
Security: ★★★★★         Cleanliness: ★★★★
Insect Control: ★★★       Facilities: ★★

This is New Hampshire's most popular state park and campground for several good reasons. First, there's the lake: gorgeous White Lake, clear, sandy-bottomed, and ringed by picturesque mountains. The state owns all the property you can see surrounding the lake, so there's no development. The shallow, gradually sloping swimming area is popular with families with young children. There's also a lifeguard on duty. The campground sites are rustic (no hookups) but spacious and private, nestled in trees; a handful are on the water. Sites are divided into two separate campground pods, one on each side of the beach and park picnic and day-use area. Both have paths to the large, natural-sand beach. There's also a two-mile walking trail around the lake through the Pitch Pine National Natural Landmark, one of the most virginal stands of northern pitch pines in North America.

Recently, the state has upgraded the park, putting in new showers, rest rooms, and bathouse; these are uncommonly nice for state park campground facilities. Only downside: this gets plenty of day-use visitors, so the beach can get crowded.

## BASICS

**Operated By:** New Hampshire Division of Parks & Recreation. **Open:** Mid-May–Columbus Day. **Site Assignment:** Reservations are suggested but 25 sites are set aside on first-come, first-served basis. Call Reservation Center (603) 271-3628 from Jan. through early Oct., Monday through Friday or via email, www.nhparks.state.nh.us. Payment is due within seven days of making reservation. Refunds requests must be received in writing by the reservation office within 14 days of scheduled arrival & are handled on a case by case basis, subject to a $10 handling fee & may be subject to a penalty of a one night cmaping fee. MC, V are accepted. **Registration:** At office. **Fee:** $16; $22, waterview, based on two adults & children under the age of 18. Each additional adult is half the site fee, max. 5 adults per site. **Parking:** At site.

## FACILITIES

**Number of RV Sites:** 200. **Number of Tent-Only Sites:** 0. **Hookups:** None. **Each Site:** Picnic table, fire ring. **Dump Station:** Yes. **Laundry:** No. **Pay Phone:** Yes. **Rest Rooms & Showers:** Yes (coin-op). **Fuel:** No. **Propane:** No. **Internal Roads:** Gravel (good). **RV Service:** No. **Market:** Tamworth (1 mi). **Restaurant:** No. **General Store:** Yes. **Vending:** Yes. **Swimming Pool:** No. **Playground:** Yes. **Other:** Lake frontage, beach, lifeguards, kayak, canoe & paddleboat rentals, playfield, hiking trails. **Activities:** Swimming, hiking, boating. **Nearby Attractions:** North Conway, White Mountains, Craword Notch Scenic Railroad, outlet shopping. **Additional Information:** Greater Conway Village Area Chamber of Commerce, P.O. Box 1019, Conway, NH 03818, (603) 447-2639.

## RESTRICTIONS

**Pets:** Not allowed. **Fires:** In grills, stoves, & fire rings only. **Alcoholic Beverages:** Not allowed. **Vehicle Maximum Length:** None. **Other:** No car stereos allowed.

## To Get There

From the junction of Rtes. 16 and 25, go north 1.25 mi; campground is on the left.

## TWIN MOUNTAIN

### Beech Hill Campground

P.O. Box 129, Twin Mountain 03595. T: (603) 846-5561; www.beechhill.com; bousquin@ncia.net.

| 🚐 ★★★★ | ⛺ ★★★★★ |
|---|---|

| | |
|---|---|
| Beauty: ★★★★ | Site Privacy: ★★★★★ |
| Spaciousness: ★★★★★ | Quiet: ★★★★ |
| Security: ★★★★ | Cleanliness: ★★★ |
| Insect Control: ★★★ | Facilities: ★★★★ |

We love the spaciousness, privacy, and location of this campground in the White Mountains. Beech Hill caters to folks who like to explore area attractions during the day and return to a lot of elbow room, outdoor scenery, an indoor pool, and planned activities in the evening. The campground is also a favorite with hikers who have some of New Hampshire's best trails nearby (including trails to the summit of Mount Washington, New England's highest peak). Each site is surrounded by trees for privacy; the tent-only sites are especially roomy and secluded. Our favorites: sites 26A–26D. RVers looking for full hookups will like sites 50, 90, and 91. But, really, you can't go wrong here.

## BASICS

**Operated By:** Ed & Linda Bousquin. **Open:** May 15–Oct. 15. **Site Assignment:** Reservations suggested, one night deposit, 10 day cancellation policy, no credit cards, personal checks accepted. **Registration:** At office. **Fee:** Full hookups, $28, water & electric, $26, no hookups, $22, based on two adults & three children under 14. **Parking:** At site.

## FACILITIES

**Number of RV Sites:** 93. **Number of Tent-Only Sites:** 38. **Hookups:** Water, electric, sewer (15, 30 amps). **Each Site:** Picnic table, fire ring. **Dump Station:** Yes. **Laundry:** Yes. **Pay Phone:** Yes. **Rest Rooms & Showers:** Yes. **Fuel:** No. **Propane:** Yes. **Internal Roads:** Dirt, gravel (good). **RV Service:** No. **Market:** Littleton (12

mi). **Restaurant:** No. **General Store:** Yes. **Vending:** No. **Swimming Pool:** Yes. **Playground:** Yes. **Other:** Rec hall, game room, hiking trails, cabin rentals. **Activities:** Swimming, basketball, volleyball, planned activities on summer weekends. **Nearby Attractions:** White Mountains, Franconia Notch State Park. **Additional Information:** Franconia Notch Chamber of Commerce, P.O. Box 780, Franconia, NH 03580, (800) 237-9007; also Twin Mountain Chamber of Commerce, (800) 245-TWIN.

## RESTRICTIONS

**Pets:** Must be on a leash, never left unattended. **Fires:** In grills, stoves, & fire rings only. **Alcoholic Beverages:** At site only. **Vehicle Maximum Length:** None.

## To Get There

From the junction of Rtes. 3 and 302, go west 1.8 mi. on Rte. 302; campground is on the right.

## TWIN MOUNTAIN

### Living Water Campground

P.O. Box 158, Rte. 302 East, Twin Mountain 03595. T: (603) 846-5513; www.livingwatercampground.com.

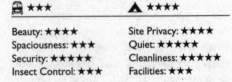

| 🚐 ★★★ | ⛺ ★★★★ |
|---|---|

| | |
|---|---|
| Beauty: ★★★★ | Site Privacy: ★★★★ |
| Spaciousness: ★★★ | Quiet: ★★★★★ |
| Security: ★★★★★ | Cleanliness: ★★★★★ |
| Insect Control: ★★★ | Facilities: ★★★ |

This campground is clean, clean, clean, in more ways than one. "Alcohol-free camping, Experience the Difference!" is their motto, and the owners go the extra mile to ensure a "clean, quiet, family atmosphere." Rules are heavily enforced: absolutely no alcohol, no pets, no radios, no rowdy behavior, quiet time—and they mean quiet—by 10 p.m. "We're only after a niche market, and when they find us, they like it," says owner Jack Catalano. They're very upfront and forward about the rules when taking reservations and when campers check in. If you like a few wine coolers or bottle of ale around the campfire, you better look elsewhere. The campground is located in the center of popular White Mountain attractions set along the Ammonoosuc River. Most families head out during the day to explore the area and return in late afternoon to wade in the river, swim in the pool, and watch the sun set over the mountains. Both open, grassy sites and shaded, wooded sites are available; full hookups are clustered in a half-circle behind the office.

## BASICS

**Operated By:** Jack Catalano. **Open:** Memorial Day–Columbus Day. **Site Assignment:** Reservations suggested, one inght deposit, 48-hour cancellation policy. MC, V; no personal checks. **Registration:** At office. **Fee:** Full hookups, $32; water & electric (30 amp), $30; water & electric (20 amp), $28; no hookups, $26, riverfront sites add $2, based on two persons, additional child 4-11, $1; additional child 12-17, $2; additional adult, family member, $6; additional adult, non-family member, $10. **Parking:** At site.

## FACILITIES

**Number of RV Sites:** 45. **Number of Tent-Only Sites:** 35. **Hookups:** Water, electric, sewer (30 amps). **Each Site:** Picnic table, fire ring. **Dump Station:** Yes. **Laundry:** Yes. **Pay Phone:** Yes. **Rest Rooms & Showers:** Yes (coin-op). **Fuel:** Yes. **Propane:** No. **Internal Roads:** Dirt, gravel (good). **RV Service:** No. **Market:** Littleton (9 mi). **Restaurant:** No. **General Store:** Yes. **Vending:** No. **Swimming Pool:** Yes. **Playground:** Yes. **Other:** Rec hall, river frontage, on-site motel. **Activities:** Swimming, fishing, tetherball, basketball, badminton, volleyball, horseshoes. **Nearby Attractions:** White Mountains, Franconia Notch State Park. **Additional Information:** Franconia Notch Chamber of Commerce, P.O. Box 780, Franconia, NH 03580, (800) 237-9007; Twin Mountain Chamber of Commerce, (800) 245-TWIN.

## RESTRICTIONS

**Pets:** Not allowed. **Fires:** In grills, stoves, & fire rings only. **Alcoholic Beverages:** Not allowed. **Vehicle Maximum Length:** None. **Other:** Lots of restrictions that are strongly enforced: musical instruments & singing must be kept at at low volumes & not permitted after 10 pm or before 7 am; radios, TVs, CD players, etc. permitted only w/earphones; minibikes, scooters, ATVs not permitted.

## TO GET THERE

From the junction of Rtes. 3 and 302, go east 1000 feet on Rte. 302; campground is on the right.

## TWIN MOUNTAIN

## Tarry Ho Campground & Cottages

P.O. Box 369, Rte. 302, Twin Mountain 03595. T: (603) 846-5577; www.tarryho.com; tarryho@loa.com.

🚐 ★★                          ▲ ★★

| | |
|---|---|
| Beauty: ★★★ | Site Privacy: ★★ |
| Spaciousness: ★★ | Quiet: ★★★ |
| Security: ★★★ | Cleanliness: ★★★ |
| Insect Control: ★★★ | Facilities: ★★★ |

We include this campground mainly for its location in the heart of the White Mountains and New Hampshire's popular attractions. It's an excellent base, and the mountain views from the sites are lovely. The campground is relatively small compared to others in the area, sites are a bit cramped, and rest room and showers dated. Still, you have all you need to call home: a small general store for essentials, sports courts, playground, and a swimming pool and river to cool off in at the end of the day. Tenters have better choices in the area (see Beech Hill Campground); tent sites are tiny and clustered near the road, but RVers will find 35 full hookups. Friendly staff, free showers, and free coffee on Saturday mornings are nice touches.

## BASICS

**Operated By:** Bob & Jo Dean. **Open:** Year-round, closed Apr. & Oct. 15-Nov. 15. **Site Assignment:** Reservations suggested, two nights deposit, 14 day cancellation policy, no refunds on weekend & holiday reservations. MC, V, D & personal checks accepted. **Registration:** At office. **Fee:** Full hookups, $27; river sites, $27; water & electric, $24; no hookups, $20, based on two adults & two children to 15 years or three adults. **Parking:** At site, one vehicle per site.

## FACILITIES

**Number of RV Sites:** 47. **Number of Tent-Only Sites:** 8. **Hookups:** Water, electric, sewer (30 amps). **Each Site:** Picnic table, fire ring. **Dump Station:** Yes. **Laundry:** No. **Pay Phone:** Yes. **Rest Rooms & Showers:** Yes. **Fuel:** No. **Propane:** No. **Internal Roads:** Dirt (fair). **RV Service:** No. **Market:** Twin Mountain (0.5 mi). **Restaurant:** No. **General Store:** Yes. **Vending:** No. **Swimming Pool:** Yes. **Playground:** Yes. **Other:** River access, rec hall. **Activities:** Swimming, fishing, tubing, volleyball, basketball, horseshoes. **Nearby Attractions:** White Mountains, Franconia Notch State Park. **Additional Information:** Franconia Notch Chamber of Commerce, P.O. Box 780, Franconia, NH 03580, (800) 237-9007; Twin Mountain Chamber of Commerce, (800) 245-TWIN.

## RESTRICTIONS

**Pets:** Must be on a leash, never left unattended. **Fires:** In grills, stoves, & fire rings only. **Alcoholic Beverages:** At site only. **Vehicle Maximum Length:** None. **Other:** Ask on arrival.

## TO GET THERE

From the junction of Rtes. 3 and 302, go 7 mi. west on Rte. 302; campground is on the left.

## TWIN MOUNTAIN

### Twin Mountain KOA

P.O. Box 148, Twin Mountain 03595. T: (603) 846-5559; F: (603) 846-7762; ucampnh.com/twin-mountain; campkoa@ncia.net.

| 🚐 ★★★★ | ⛺ ★★★ |
|---|---|
| Beauty: ★★★★ | Site Privacy: ★★★ |
| Spaciousness: ★★★ | Quiet: ★★★★ |
| Security: ★★★ | Cleanliness: ★★★★★ |
| Insect Control: ★★★ | Facilities: ★★★★ |

The last time we visited this White Mountain area campground was in the fall, and the surrounding forest of towering pine, poplar, maple, and birch was ablaze with fiery autumn hues. The summit of Mount Washington, visible from our site, had a fresh dusting of powdery white snow. You'll have wonderful mountain views, quick access to outdoor activities (biking, hiking, rock climbing, fishing, boating), and plenty of on-site amenities (swimming pool, planned activities, free movies) at this franchise campground. Most campers explore the surrounding area attractions (check out the popular moose-watching tours in nearby Gorham) before returning to the campground in late afternoon. The facilities and sites are ultra-clean, and the atmosphere friendly and relaxed. For something different, reserve the "kamping kaboose." Where else can you camp in an authentic 19th-century train caboose?

## BASICS

**Operated By:** Barbara & Steve Rabesa. **Open:** May 15–Oct. 15. **Site Assignment:** Reservations suggested; one night deposit, holiday weekends paid in full; seven day cancellation policy w/$10 service fee. MC, V, no personal checks. **Registration:** At office. **Fee:** Full hookups, $32; water & electric, $27.50; no hookups, $25, based on two people; additionl adults, $6; additional children, ages 3-17, $2. **Parking:** At site.

## FACILITIES

**Number of RV Sites:** 30. **Number of Tent-Only Sites:** 30. **Hookups:** Water, electric, sewer (30, 50 amps), cable TV, modem. **Each Site:** Picnic table, fire ring. **Dump Station:** Yes. **Laundry:** Yes. **Pay Phone:** Yes. **Rest Rooms & Showers:** Yes. **Fuel:** No. **Propane:** Yes. **Internal Roads:** Gravel, dirt (good). **RV Service:** No. **Market:** Twin Mountain (2 mi). **Restaurant:** No. **General Store:** Yes. **Vending:** Yes. **Swimming Pool:** Yes. **Playground:** Yes. **Other:** Rec hall, amphitheater, nature trails, cabin & caboose rentals, group area. **Activities:** Swimming, hiking, biking, volleyball, badminton, horseshoes. **Nearby Attractions:** Moose tours, fishing, boating, Storyland, Conway Scenic Railroad, Mount Washington Auto Rd. **Additional Information:** Twin Mountain Chamber of Commerce, Twin Mountain, NH 03595, (800) 245-TWIN.

## RESTRICTIONS

**Pets:** Must be on a leash, never left unattended. Pets not allowed in rental units. **Fires:** In grills, stoves, & fire rings only. **Alcoholic Beverages:** At site. **Vehicle Maximum Length:** None.

## TO GET THERE

From the junction of Rtes. 3 and 302, go north 2 mi. on Rte. 3, then north 1 mi. on Rte. 115; campground is on the right.

## TWIN MOUNTAIN

### Twin Mountain Motor Court & RV Park

P.O. Box 104B, Rte. 3, Twin Mountain 03595. T: (603) 846-5574, (800) 332-8946; www.ucampnh.com/twinmountain.rvpark.

🚐 ★★★                    ⛺ n/a

Beauty: ★★★              Site Privacy: ★★★
Spaciousness: ★★★        Quiet: ★★★★
Security: ★★★            Cleanliness: ★★★★
Insect Control: ★★★      Facilities: ★★★

If you're a self-contained big-rig driver looking for ease and convenience, this campground is a great base when traveling in the White Mountains area. Large 25 × 85–foot sites, all pull-throughs, cater to large RVs; sites are easy to pull in and out of, and all have four-way hookups. Outside, you'll find panoramic views of the mountains, including Mount Washington, Twin Mountains, and Mt. Haystack. There's an outdoor swimming pool for a refreshing dip at the end of the day, or head to the Ammonoosuc River, which flanks the rear of the campground. Bring your fishing rod; the Ammonoosuc is famous for its elusive trout.

## BASICS

**Operated By:** John & Dotty Barber. **Open:** May 15–Oct. 15. **Site Assignment:** Reservations suggested, one night deposit, seven day cancellation policy, MC, V, D & personal checks accepted. **Registration:** At office. **Fee:** $28. **Parking:** At site.

## FACILITIES

**Number of RV Sites:** 18. **Number of Tent-Only Sites:** 0. **Hookups:** Water, electric, sewer (30 amps), cable TV, modem. **Each Site:** Picnic table. **Dump Station:** No. **Laundry:** Yes. **Pay Phone:** Yes. **Rest Rooms & Showers:** No. **Fuel:** No. **Propane:** No. **Internal Roads:** Gravel

(good). **RV Service:** No. **Market:** Littleton (8 mi). **Restaurant:** No. **General Store:** Yes. **Vending:** No. **Swimming Pool:** Yes. **Playground:** Yes. **Other:** River frontage, hiking trails, rec hall, cottage rentals. **Activities:** Swimming, hiking, badminton, horseshoes, basketball, volleyball. **Nearby Attractions:** White Mountains, Franconia Notch State Park. **Additional Information:** Franconia Notch Chamber of Commerce, P.O. Box 780, Franconia, NH 03580, (800) 237-9007; Twin Mountain Chamber of Commerce, (800) 245-TWIN.

## RESTRICTIONS

**Pets:** Must be on a leash, never left unattended. Pets not allowed in cottages. **Fires:** In campground communal bonfire site only. **Alcoholic Beverages:** At site only. **Vehicle Maximum Length:** None.

## TO GET THERE

From the junction of Rtes. 302 and 3, go 1 mi. south on Rte. 3; campground is on the right.

## WARREN

### Moose Hillock Campground

RFD 1, Box 96, Rte. 118 North, Warren 03279. T: (603) 764-5294; www.moosehillock.com.

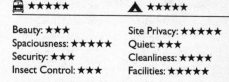

🚐 ★★★★★                 ⛺ ★★★★★

Beauty: ★★★              Site Privacy: ★★★★★
Spaciousness: ★★★★★      Quiet: ★★★
Security: ★★★            Cleanliness: ★★★★
Insect Control: ★★★      Facilities: ★★★★★

Campers with kids in tow will find everything they need—and more!—at this action-packed, family-friendly campground. This place is always squirming with smiling kids—zipping down the waterslide at the themed "Blue Lagoon" swimming pool, fishing the stocked pond, shooting pool, playing games in the large post-and-beam barn turned rec hall, or joining in the organized games, treasure hunts, and arts-and-crafts activities. Nearby are miles of mountain biking and hiking trails. (Two trails leave right from the campground.) Most families come to stay and play and (for the adventurous) to climb nearby

Mt. Moosilauke, one of New Hampshire's 4,000-footers. Facilities are top-notch, and most sites are adequately spaced for elbow room and privacy. Families with young children tend to cluster around the lower loop, close to the pool and playground. RVers wanting more privacy and peace and quiet should select one of the very large full hookup sites that back up to the national forest. Tenters have their own woodsy, private area.

## BASICS

**Operated By:** Ed & Robin Paradis. **Open:** Mid-May –mid-Sept. **Site Assignment:** Reservations suggested. Deposit of full amount for stays of three days or less, 50 percent for stays of one week or longer. 14 day cancellation policy w/$5 service fee. Reservations cancelled 7-14 days prior to scheduled arrival receive 50 percent of deposit; no refunds of deposit for cancellations less than 7 days notice. MC, V, & personal checks accepted. **Registration:** At office. **Fee:** Full hookups, $31 (midweek) $34 (Friday, Saturday & holidays); water & electric, 28–$31; no hookups, $25–$28. **Parking:** At site.

## FACILITIES

**Number of RV Sites:** 195. **Number of Tent-Only Sites:** 25. **Hookups:** Water, electric, sewer. **Each Site:** Picnic table, fire ring. **Dump Station:** Yes. **Laundry:** Yes. **Pay Phone:** Yes. **Rest Rooms & Showers:** Yes (coin-op). **Fuel:** No. **Propane:** Yes. **Internal Roads:** Dirt, gravel (fair). **RV Service:** No. **Market:** Warren (5 mi). **Restaurant:** Yes. **General Store:** Yes. **Vending:** Yes. **Swimming Pool:** Yes. **Playground:** Yes. **Other:** Rec hall, game room, cabin rentals, pavillion, Chapel service, river access, stocked fishing pond, nature trails. **Activities:** Swimming, volleyball, horseshoes, tetherball, basketball, fishing, hiking planned activities including live entertainment, arts & crafts, contests, socials, & more. **Nearby Attractions:** White Mountains, Franconia Notch State Park, Mt. Moosilauke. **Additional Information:** Lincoln-Woodstock Chamber of Commerce, P.O. Box 358, Kancamagus Hwy., Lincoln, NH 03251, (603) 745-6621; also Franconia Notch Chamber of Commerce, P.O. Box 780, Franconia, NH 03580, (800) 237-9007.

## RESTRICTIONS

**Pets:** Must be on a leash, never left unattended. **Fires:** In grills, stoves, & fire rings only. **Alcoholic Beverages:** At site only. **Vehicle Maximum Length:** None.

## TO GET THERE

From I-93, exit 26, go 25 mi. northwest on Rte. 25 to Rte. 118, then north 1 mi. to campground road; campground is 0.5 mi. ahead.

## WEARE

# Cold Springs Camp Resort

22 Wildlife Dr., Weare 03281. T: (603) 529-2528; F: (603) 529-1155; www.coldspringscampresort.com; coldspr@gsinet.net.

| 🚐 ★★★★★ | 🛖 ★★★★ |
|---|---|
| Beauty: ★★★ | Site Privacy: ★★★ |
| Spaciousness: ★★★ | Quiet: ★★★ |
| Security: ★★★★★ | Cleanliness: ★★★★★ |
| Insect Control: ★★★ | Facilities: ★★★★★ |

This high-energy, activity-based campground is one of the top choices for families in the southern New Hampshire region. This is primarily a destination campground. Though the mountains to the north and ocean to the east are just an hour-and-a-half drive away, most folks are content to stay put once they've set up camp. They come to Cold Springs for a quick getaway, to relax at their sites, take part in weekend activities, and use the facilities. There really is no need to leave: everything we wanted was right here. The three-pool complex, complete with hot tubs and waterfall, is the action spot at this property. There's an adult-only pool, a family fun pool for all ages, and another for folks six years and older. There's also a beach area along a slow-moving river if you prefer a more natural and tranquil setting. About half the sites located in the back of the campground are taken by seasonal renters. But there are plenty more to choose from if you wish to come for the weekend or week. Sites are fairly uniform in size and appearance. All are set in level, gravel clearings flanked by trees with an average width of about 25 feet. Tenters have few choices, but we liked sites 147 and 148, set in the woods and backing up to a small (often dry in the summer) creek.

## BASICS

**Operated By:** Bob Silva. **Open:** May–early Oct. **Site Assignment:** Reservations suggested, one night deposit, holiday stays paid in full, 7 day cancellation policy w/$20 service charge. MC, V, D accepted, no personal checks. **Registration:** At office. **Fee:** Full hookups (w/cable), $36; full hookups, $34; water & electric, $32, based on two people; additional adult, $6; additional children under 16, $2. **Parking:** At site.

## FACILITIES

**Number of RV Sites:** 400. **Number of Tent-Only Sites:** 10. **Hookups:** Water, electric, sewer (30, 50 amps), cable TV, modem. **Each Site:** Picnic table, fire ring. **Dump Station:** Yes. **Laundry:** Yes. **Pay Phone:** Yes. **Rest Rooms & Showers:** Yes (coin-op). **Fuel:** No. **Propane:** Yes. **Internal Roads:** Paved (good). **RV Service:** Yes. **Market:** Weare (1 mi). **Restaurant:** Yes. **General Store:** Yes. **Vending:** Yes. **Swimming Pool:** Yes. **Playground:** Yes. **Other:** Hot tubs, river frontage, beach, pavillions, adult, teen & children's rec halls, trailer rentals. **Activities:** Swimming, shuffleboard, basketball, volleyball, horseshoes, planned activities, including children's & adult programs, contests, socials, dances, live entertainment, & more. **Nearby Attractions:** Manchester, Concord. **Additional Information:** Manchester Chamber of Commerce, 889 Elm St. , Manchester, NH 03101, (603) 434-7438.

## RESTRICTIONS

**Pets:** Must be on a leash, never left unattended. Pets are not allowed in beach area. **Fires:** In grills, stoves, & fire rings only. **Alcoholic Beverages:** At site only. **Vehicle Maximum Length:** None.

## TO GET THERE

From the junction of Rte. 149 and 114, go southeast 1 mi. on Rte. 114, then east 0.25 mi. on Barnard Hill Rd.; campground is on the right.

## WENTWORTH

# Pine Haven Campground

P.O. Box 43, Wentworth 03282. T: (603) 786-2900 (information) (800) 370-PINE (reservations); www.pinehavencampground.com; rebele@cyberportal.net.

🚐 ★★★★　　　🛖 ★★★★

| | |
|---|---|
| Beauty: ★★★★ | Site Privacy: ★★★★ |
| Spaciousness: ★★★★ | Quiet: ★★★ |
| Security: ★★★★ | Cleanliness: ★★★★ |
| Insect Control: ★★★ | Facilities: ★★★★ |

If you like the sound of rustling woods and moving waters, you're going to love this pristine campground at the base of the White Mountains. It sits in the quiet and quaint Wentworth area, halfway between popular Lincoln and North Woodstock, with 3,000 feet of frontage on the South Branch of the Baker River. There's a classic river swimming hole for dunks in the clear, cold mountain waters; there's also a heated pool. Families not only flock here for the scenery and clean outdoor living, but also for the daily activities offered throughout July and Aug. These are moonlight swims, horseshoe tournaments, archery, hayrides, crafts, and more. Sites are spacious and nicely tucked in the woods for privacy. Tenters have choice spots along the river; M5 and M6 are our favorites, as is R1. The campground is also popular with rock climbers who come to scale the giant boulders and rock walls in nearby Rumney.

## BASICS

**Operated By:** Rebele family. **Open:** May 15–Oct. 15. **Site Assignment:** Reservations highly suggested. Payment in full for stays of three days or less; or three day deposit for stays longer than three days. Must cancel within 14 days of arrival for deposit refund minus $10 service charge. **Registration:** At office. **Fee:** Full hookups, $29; water & electric, $27; no hookups, $25, based on two adults & their children under the age of 18. **Parking:** At site.

## FACILITIES

**Number of RV Sites:** 67. **Number of Tent-Only Sites:** 35. **Hookups:** Water, electric, sewer

(20, 50 amps). **Each Site:** Picnic table, fire ring. **Dump Station:** Yes. **Laundry:** Yes. **Pay Phone:** Yes. **Rest Rooms & Showers:** Yes. **Fuel:** No. **Propane:** Yes. **Internal Roads:** Dirt, gravel (good). **RV Service:** No. **Market:** Wentworth (0.5 mi). **Restaurant:** No. **General Store:** Yes. **Vending:** No. **Swimming Pool:** Yes. **Playground:** Yes. **Other:** Rec hall, kayak & canoe rentals, river frontage, river swimming, game room, cabin rentals. **Activities:** Swimming, boating, basketball, horseshoes, archery, planned activities throughout the summer including arts & crafts, hayrides, moonlight swims, game nights. **Nearby Attractions:** quick access to White Mountains & Lakes region, hiking, rock climbing, antiquing. **Additional Information:** Lincoln-Woodstock Chamber of Commerce, P.O. Box 358, Kancamagus Hwy., Lincoln, NH 03251, (603) 745-6621.

## RESTRICTIONS

**Pets:** Must be on a leash, never left unattended. **Fires:** In grills, stoves, & fire rings only. **Alcoholic Beverages:** At site only. **Vehicle Maximum Length:** 40 ft. **Other:** Four night min. reservation Jul. & Aug.

## TO GET THERE

On I-93, take exit 26, go 12 mi. west on Rte. 25; campground is on the left.

## WENTWORTH

## Swain Brook Campground

P.O. Box 157, Beech Hill Rd., Wentworth 03282.
T: (603) 764-5537; www.swainbrook.com;
swainbrook1@aol.com.

🚐 ★★★★            ⛺ ★★★★★

| | |
|---|---|
| Beauty: ★★★★★ | Site Privacy: ★★★★ |
| Spaciousness: ★★★★ | Quiet: ★★★★ |
| Security: ★★★★ | Cleanliness: ★★★★ |
| Insect Control: ★★★ | Facilities: ★★★★ |

Nature lovers and outdoor enthusiasts will think they've died and gone to heaven when they check into this modest campground in New Hampshire's quiet countryside. You'll be about 12 miles from a major city (Plymouth to the southeast and Lincoln to the northeast) but at the doorstep of your own private nature preserve. The campground encompasses 417 acres—65 acres of campground and 352 acres of forest, waterfalls, cascades, and swimming holes. There are four miles of hiking trails on the property, with mountain vistas, rest areas, and fishing and swimming spots along the way. Swain Brook is the largest of five mountain brooks in the campground, dropping 520 feet in elevation over a 116-mile stretch. Elevation on the property ranges from 650 feet to 1,290 feet, so bring your hiking boots—and your fishing pole, as the deep hole at the bottom of Freedom Falls is a favorite with campground anglers. The rustic, wilderness sites are our favorites, though RV campers will find a cluster of nicely-spaced, shaded back-in sites near the front of the campground.

## BASICS

**Operated By:** Swain Brook Campground, Inc. **Open:** May–Oct. **Site Assignment:** Reservations suggested; 14-day cancellation policy w/a $10 service fee. MC, V; no personal checks. **Registration:** At office. **Fee:** Full hookup, $25; water & electric (on brook), $27; water & electric, $23; no hookups, $19 (on pond or brook), $22, based on two adults & two children. **Parking:** At site.

## FACILITIES

**Number of RV Sites:** 18. **Number of Tent-Only Sites:** 30. **Hookups:** Water, electric, sewer (30 amps). **Each Site:** Picnic table, fire ring. **Dump Station:** Yes. **Laundry:** No. **Pay Phone:** Yes. **Rest Rooms & Showers:** Yes (coin-op). **Fuel:** No. **Propane:** No. **Internal Roads:** Gravel, dirt (fair). **RV Service:** No. **Market:** Lincoln (12 mi). **Restaurant:** No. **General Store:** Yes. **Vending:** No. **Swimming Pool:** No. **Playground:** Yes. **Other:** nature park, trails, river & pond frontage, swimming holes, mini-golf, trailer, tent & teepee rentals, library, rec hall. **Activities:** Swimming, hiking, biking, mini-golf, horseshoes, tetherball. **Nearby Attractions:** Lincoln, Plymouth, North Woodstock, Mt. Moosilauke, Franconia State Park. **Additional Information:** Lincoln-Woodstock Chamber of Commerce, P.O. Box 358, Kancamagus Hwy., Lincoln, NH

# Rhode Island

New England's smallest state, Rhode Island makes up for its tiny size by packing a lot in. For camping enthusiasts, the state offers a number of choices, and nearly all of them involve the water. With over 400 miles of coastline, it's hard to go anywhere in Rhode that's not near a beach.

Because of that, many of the campsites in the state specialize in water-based activities. There's an enormous amount of choice for boating fans and lots of places to take your canoe out for a spin. There's also plenty of campgrounds in proximity to traditional "lay out in the sand" beaches. For the most part, camping in the state works best during warm weather, but the cities and many historic attractions offer a lot when the water's cold.

Rhode Island has a national reputation for its mansions, and the city of **Newport** has long been a tourist attraction. It has numerous museums, excellent restaurants, and nearby state park land.

Those looking for a more cosmopolitan city will do well in **Providence.** While it's not New York or Boston, Providence combines small-town appeal with many of the amenities of its bigger cousins. The city also has a new park downtown that's the center of activity in the summer, with concerts and other forms of entertainment.

For campers in Rhode Island, there's an easy opportunity to combine relaxation and exploration. Because of the size of the state, everything is close to everything else, and even area attractions like the casinos in Connecticut are easily accessible.

## ASHAWAY

### Frontier Camper Park

180 Maxson Hill Rd., Ashaway 02804. T: (401) 377-4510.

🚐 ★★★★          ⛺ ★★★

Beauty: ★★                 Site Privacy: ★★★
Spaciousness: ★★★          Quiet: ★★
Security: ★★★              Cleanliness: ★★★
Insect Control: ★★★        Facilities: ★★★

If you're looking for a convenient, albeit spartan place to park your trailer or pitch your tent, Frontier is literally right off the highway—and that's pretty much the best thing it has going for it. There's not much to look at here and only slightly more to do than there would be at your average motel. But the facilities are adequate if you're looking to use Frontier only as your base of operations, not a vacation in itself.

#### BASICS

**Operated By:** Janet & Bill Thompson. **Open:** May 1–Oct. 1. **Site Assignment:** Reservations, though space is usually available. **Registration:** Office. **Fee:** Varies depending on season. **Parking:** At site.

#### FACILITIES

**Number of RV Sites:** 50. **Number of Tent-Only Sites:** 60. **Hookups:** Water, electric. **Each Site:** Picnic table, fireplace. **Dump Station:** No. **Laundry:** Yes. **Pay Phone:** Yes. **Rest Rooms and Showers:** Yes. **Fuel:** No. **Propane:** Yes. **Internal Roads:** Gravel. **RV Service:** No. **Market:** Hopkinton City **General Store:** 493 Main St., Hopkinton, RI: Take a left onto Maxson Hill Rd., followed by a right onto Frontier Rd., which becomes Main St. **Restaurant:** 32 Main St., Ashaway, RI 02804: Take a left onto Maxson Hill Rd., followed by a right onto Frontier Rd., which becomes Main St. **General Store:** Yes. **Vending:** Yes. **Swimming Pool:** Yes. **Playground:** Yes. **Other:** Volleyball. **Activities:** Fishing, hiking nearby. **Nearby Attractions:** Mystic Seaport, Foxwood Casino. **Additional Information:** Beaches, I-95.

#### RESTRICTIONS

**Pets:** Allowed. **Fires:** Allowed. **Alcoholic Beverages:** Allowed. **Vehicle Maximum Length:** 35 ft. **Other:** Ask on arrival.

#### TO GET THERE

Take I-95 Exit 1, then go south on Rte. 3. Take a left onto Frontier Rd. and follow the camping signs.

## ASHAWAY

### Hollytree Campground

109 Ashaway Rd./Rte. 216, Ashaway 02804. T: (401) 596-2766.

🚐 ★★★          ⛺ n/a

Beauty: ★★                 Site Privacy: ★★★
Spaciousness: ★★★          Quiet: ★★★
Security: ★★★★             Cleanliness: ★★★
Insect Control: ★★★        Facilities: ★★

Leave your tent at home when visiting this fairly unspectacular but well-located campground. While not downright unattractive, the place does have a bit of a parking-lot feel. And there's really not much to do here, but there's a casino just down the road, and swimming, boating, and outdoor activities within an easy drive.

#### BASICS

**Operated By:** Private operator. **Open:** May 1–Sept. 30. **Site Assignment:** Reservation. **Registration:** At office. **Fee:** $20 & up per night. **Parking:** At site.

#### FACILITIES

**Number of RV Sites:** 140. **Number of Tent-Only Sites:** 0. **Hookups:** Water, electric, sewer. **Each Site:** Picnic tables, fireplace. **Dump Station:** Yes. **Laundry:** Yes. **Pay Phone:** Yes. **Rest Rooms and Showers:** Yes. **Fuel:** No. **Propane:** No. **Internal Roads:** None. **RV Service:** No. **Market:** Pete's Grocery, 244b Ashaway Rd., Bradford, RI 02808: Take a right on Ashaway Rd. & follow for 1.2 mi. **Restaurant:** Brick Oven, 209 Main St., Ashaway, RI 02804: Take a right on Ashaway Rd. & follow for 0.9 mi., then take a right onto Main St. **General Store:** Yes. **Vending:** Yes. **Swimming Pool:** No. **Playground:** Yes.

## CHEPACHET

### Oak Leaf Campground

43 OakleafWay, P.O. Box 521, Chepachet 02814.
T: (401) 568-4446.

🚐 ★★★★          ⛺ ★

Beauty: ★★★            Site Privacy: ★★★
Spaciousness: ★★         Quiet: ★★★
Security: ★★★★          Cleanliness: ★★★
Insect Control: ★★★       Facilities: ★★★★

As far as trailer parks go, this is a fairly nice one.
Plenty of green and lots of trees break up the
parking-lot feel that many RV parks have. If
you're looking for an idyllic natural setting,
plenty of state-controlled land lies nearby, with
places to fish, hike, and swim.

### BASICS

**Operated By:** Private operator. **Open:** Apr.
15–Oct. 31. **Site Assignment:** Reservations.
**Registration:** At office. **Fee:** Starting at $18.
**Parking:** At site.

### FACILITIES

**Number of RV Sites:** 60. **Number of Tent-
Only Sites:** 0. **Hookups:** Water, electric, sewer.
**Each Site:** Picnic table, fireplace. **Dump Sta-
tion:** Yes. **Laundry:** No. **Pay Phone:** Yes. **Rest
Rooms and Showers:** Yes. **Fuel:** No. **Propane:**
No. **Internal Roads:** Paved. **RV Service:** No.
**Market:** Stop & Shop, 60 ProvidenceTurnpike,
Putnam, CT:Take a left onto Old Snake Hill Rd.,
then a right onto Rte. 94. Follow for 4.3 mi. &
take a left onto Rte. 44 & follow for about 2 mi.
**Restaurant:** McDonald's 6 Providence Turnpike,
Putnam, CT:Take a left onto Old Snake Hill Rd.,
then a right onto Rte. 94. Follow for 4.3 mi. &
take a left onto Rte. 44 & follow for about 1.6
mi. **General Store:** Yes. **Vending:** No. **Swimming Pool:** Yes. **Playground:** Yes. **Other:** Rec
hall, basketball courts. **Activities:** Boating, fishing,
golf nearby. **Nearby Attractions:** Historic landmarks. **Additional Information:** Call ahead.

### RESTRICTIONS

**Pets:** Allowed. **Fires:** Allowed. **Alcoholic Beverages:** Allowed. **Vehicle Maximum Length:** 40
ft. **Other:** Ask on arrival.

### TO GET THERE

Rte. 44 to 94 South to Old Snake Hill Rd. to
Oak Leaf Way (follow the signs)

## COVENTRY

### Colwell's Family Campground

Rte. 177, 119 Peckham Ln., Coventry 02816.T:
(401) 397-4614.

🚐 ★★          ⛺ ★★★

Beauty: ★★★★          Site Privacy: ★★★
Spaciousness: ★★★       Quiet: ★★★
Security: ★★★          Cleanliness: ★★★★
Insect Control: ★★★      Facilities: ★★★

This basic campground is well located in the
center of the state. Unfortunately, other than
being situated on Johnson's Pond—a reservoir
that's great for swimming—there's not much to
do here. Still, if you're not looking for campground to entertain the kids, this makes a nice
base of operations, with plenty to do in the surrounding area.

### BASICS

**Operated By:** The Colwell Family. **Open:** May
1–Sept. 30. **Site Assignment:** At time of registration. **Registration:** Reservation. **Fee:**
$12–$15 a night. **Parking:** At site.

### FACILITIES

**Number of RV Sites:** 75. **Number of Tent-
Only Sites:** 0. **Hookups:** Water, electric. **Each
Site:** Picnic table, fireplace. **Dump Station:** Yes.
**Laundry:** No. **Pay Phone:** Yes. **Rest Rooms and
Showers:** Yes. **Fuel:** No. **Propane:** No. **RV Ser-
vice:** No. **Market:** Roch's Supermarket, 1475
Main St.,WestWarwick, RI:Take a right onto
Peckham Ln., followed by a slight left onto Rte.
117. Follow for just over 6 mi. until Rte. 117
becomes Main St. **Restaurant:** Jeffrey's Restau-
rant, 2260 Flat River Rd. Frnt, Coventry, RI:Take
a right onto Peckham Ln., followed by a slight left
onto Flat River Rd. **General Store:** No. **Vending:** No. **Swimming Pool:** No. **Playground:** No.
**Other:** Pond swimming. **Activities:** Boating.
**Nearby Attractions:** Rodger William's Park &
Zoo. **Additional Information:** Call ahead.

## RESTRICTIONS

**Pets:** Allowed. **Fires:** Allowed. **Alcoholic Beverages:** Allowed. **Vehicle Maximum Length:** None. **Other:** Ask on arrival.

## TO GET THERE

I-95 North to Exit 6, left onto Rte. 3, left on Rte. 33 to Rte.117, west 4 mi. to Peckham Ln.

## COVENTRY

### Westwood Family Campground

2093 Harkney Hill Rd., Coventry 02816. T: (401) 397-7779.

| 🚐 ★★★★ | ⛺ ★★★ |
|---|---|
| Beauty: ★★★ | Site Privacy: ★★★ |
| Spaciousness: ★★★ | Quiet: ★★ |
| Security: ★★★ | Cleanliness: ★★★★ |
| Insect Control: ★★★ | Facilities: ★★★★ |

A cross between a campground and a sports summer camp, Westwood is for the active camper. You'll find myriad games in progress at all the fields and courts, plus a golf course, batting cages, and mini-golf within easy driving distance. The campground itself is nothing special, with RVs packed in fairly tightly; even the tent areas are a bit bleak. But for families this makes an excellent choice.

## BASICS

**Operated By:** Don Thomassen. **Open:** May 1–Sept. 30. **Site Assignment:** Reservations. **Registration:** Office. **Fee:** $23 night. **Parking:** At site.

## FACILITIES

**Number of RV Sites:** 60. **Number of Tent-Only Sites:** 10. **Hookups:** Water, electric, sewer. **Each Site:** Fireplace, picnic table. **Dump Station:** Yes. **Laundry:** No. **Pay Phone:** Yes. **Rest Rooms and Showers:** Yes. **Fuel:** No. **Propane:** No. **Internal Roads:** Gravel. **RV Service:** No. **Market:** P J's Country Store, 2246 Flat River Rd., Coventry, RI 02816: Take a left onto Harkney Hill Rd., followed by a right onto Rte. 102, then a right onto Flat River. Rd., which you should follow for 4.7 mi. **Restaurant:** Jeffrey's Restaurant, 2260 Flat River Rd. Frnt, Coventry, RI 02816: Take a left onto Harkney Hill Rd., followed by a right onto Rte. 102, then a right onto Flat River Rd., which you should follow for 4.7 mi. **General Store:** No. **Vending:** No. **Swimming Pool:** No. **Playground:** No. **Other:** Sports fields of all kinds—tennis, volleyball, basketball, etc. **Activities:** Water-based activities on the nearby reservoir. **Nearby Attractions:** Quidnick Reservoir. **Additional Information:** Call ahead.

## RESTRICTIONS

**Pets:** Allowed. **Fires:** Allowed. **Alcoholic Beverages:** Allowed. **Vehicle Maximum Length:** 35 ft. **Other:** Ask on arrival.

## TO GET THERE

Take I95 to Exit 5B (Rte. 102) and follow for 6.4 mi. before taking a right onto Harkeny Hill Rd.

## EXETER

### Peeper Pond Campground

P.O. Box 503, 159 Liberty Church Rd., Exeter 02822. T: (401) 294-5540.

| 🚐 ★★ | ⛺ ★★★★ |
|---|---|
| Beauty: ★★★★ | Site Privacy: ★★★★★ |
| Spaciousness: ★★★★★ | Quiet: ★★★★ |
| Security: ★★★★ | Cleanliness: ★★★★ |
| Insect Control: ★★★ | Facilities: ★★★ |

If you're looking for space, you'll find plenty of it at Peeper Pond. If you want activities and many facilities, however, you're out of luck, as this is a relatively bare-bones campground. In addition to having huge sites with more space than any camper would need, Peeper Pond borders beaches, a national park, and a wildlife preserve. Restaurants and the Tomaquag Indian Memorial Museum in Exeter are also relatively close.

## BASICS

**Operated By:** Private operator. **Open:** May 1–Sept. 30. **Site Assignment:** Reservations taken, but often not required. **Registration:** At office. **Fee:** $18 per night. **Parking:** At site.

## FACILITIES

**Number of RV Sites:** 29. **Number of Tent-Only Sites:** 6. **Hookups:** None. **Each Site:** Picnic tables, fireplace. **Dump Station:** Yes.

**Laundry:** No. **Pay Phone:** Yes. **Rest Rooms and Showers:** Yes. **Fuel:** No. **Propane:** No. **Internal Roads:** Gravel. **RV Service:** No. **Market:** L C Mart, 345 Nooseneck Hill Rd., Exeter, RI: Take a left onto Liberty Church Rd., then a left onto Sheffield Hill Rd. & a right onto Hallville Rd. Take a right onto Ten Rod Rd., which becomes Rte. 102. Follow for about 4 mi. & turn left onto Nooseneck Hill Rd. **Restaurant:** Middle of Nowhere Diner, 222 Nooseneck Hill Rd., Exeter, RI: Take a left onto Liberty Church Rd., then a left onto Sheffield Hill Rd. & a right onto Hallville Rd. Take a right onto Ten Rod Rd., which becomes Rte. 102. Follow for about 4 mi. & turn left onto Nooseneck Hill Rd. **General Store:** Limited. **Vending:** No. **Swimming Pool:** No. **Playground:** No. **Other:** Badminton, horseshoes. **Activities:** Hiking. **Nearby Attractions:** Fisherville Brook Wildlife Refuge. **Additional Information:** Call ahead.

### RESTRICTIONS

**Pets:** Allowed. **Fires:** Allowed. **Alcoholic Beverages:** Allowed. **Vehicle Maximum Length:** 34 ft. **Other:** Ask on arrival.

### TO GET THERE

Located off Rte. 2 between Rtes. 102 & 138. Follow blue-and-white camping signs on Rte. 2 to Mail Rd. 1.5 mi. to Liberty Church Rd., 0.8 mi. to campground. Exit 3A off I-95 North, east on Rte. 138 North (left) on Rte. 2.

## FOSTER

### Ginny-B Campground

46 Johnston Rd., Foster 02825. T: (401) 397-9477; gnnyb@aol.com.

🚐 ★★★★          ▲ ★

| | |
|---|---|
| Beauty: ★★★ | Site Privacy: ★★★ |
| Spaciousness: ★★★ | Quiet: ★★★★ |
| Security: ★★★ | Cleanliness: ★★★ |
| Insect Control: ★★★ | Facilities: ★★★★ |

Near the Connecticut border, Ginny-B offers a nice mix of facilities and nature. Although much of the 90 acres are covered with tall oak trees, there are still plenty of cleared areas for activities. Though it's not quite a destination in itself like many of the Connecticut areas, Ginny-B is a pretty lively campground offering many diversions, and on weekends there are usually plenty of people to share the fun. The public golf course located next to Ginny-B can get quite busy, so if you're visiting here to play golf, you might want to consider a nontraditional tee time.

### BASICS

**Operated By:** Private operator. **Open:** May 1–Sept. 30. **Site Assignment:** Reservations recommended. **Registration:** At office. **Fee:** $16–$20. **Parking:** At site.

### FACILITIES

**Number of RV Sites:** 200. **Number of Tent-Only Sites:** 0. **Hookups:** Water, electric (20), sewer. **Each Site:** Picnic table, fireplace. **Dump Station:** Yes. **Laundry:** Yes. **Pay Phone:** Yes. **Rest Rooms and Showers:** Yes. **Fuel:** No. **Propane:** No. **Internal Roads:** Gravel. **RV Service:** No. **Market:** P J's Country Store, 2246 Flat River Rd., Coventry, RI: Take a left onto S. Killingly Rd., followed by a slight right onto Rte. 94, then a right onto Rte. 102. Follow for 3.5 mi., then take a left onto Maple Valley Rd. & follow for 3.2 mi. Take a left onto Flat River Rd. & follow for 2 mi. **Restaurant:** Countryside Pizza & Backdraft, 110 Danielson Pike, Foster, RI: Take a left onto S. Killingly Rd., followed by a slight right onto Rte. 94 & follow for 2.2 mi. Take left onto Rte. 6 & a left onto Danielson Pike. **General Store:** Yes. **Vending:** Yes. **Swimming Pool:** Yes. **Playground:** No. **Other:** Rec rooms, pond, volleyball & basketball courts, softball diamond. **Activities:** Planned activities. **Nearby Attractions:** Next to a public golf course. **Additional Information:** Call ahead.

### RESTRICTIONS

**Pets:** Allowed. **Fires:** Allowed. **Alcoholic Beverages:** Allowed. **Vehicle Maximum Length:** 40 ft. **Other:** Ask on arrival.

### TO GET THERE

East or west on Rte. 6 (RI/CT state line): turn at the flashing light onto Cucumber Hill Rd. Follow 3.5 mi. and take a left onto Harrington Rd. Drive 0.5 mi. to Ginny-B.

# FOSTER

## Whippoorwill Hill Family Campground

106 Old Plainfield Pike, Foster 02825. T: (401) 397-7256; whiphicp@aol.com.

🚐 ★★★★          ⛺ ★★

Beauty: ★★★
Spaciousness: ★★★★
Security: ★★★★
Insect Control: ★★★

Site Privacy: ★★★★★
Quiet: ★★★★
Cleanliness: ★★★★
Facilities: ★★★★

Surrounded by tall pines and situated next to the huge George B. Parker Woodland, this beautiful campground caters equally to tent and RV campers. Though you'll definitely find more RVers, the large sites give everyone enough space, and some of the tent spots are very remote and private. With the preserve and its numerous trails right next door, Whippoorwill is a hiker's paradise—you could literally spend a week here and walk a new trail every day.

### BASICS

**Operated By:** Private operator. **Open:** Apr. 15–Sept. 30. **Site Assignment:** Reservations recommended. **Registration:** At office. **Fee:** Some tent sites under $20 a night, most RV sites start at $20. **Parking:** At site.

### FACILITIES

**Number of RV Sites:** 150. **Number of Tent-Only Sites:** 0. **Hookups:** Water, electric, sewer. **Each Site:** Fireplace, picnic table. **Dump Station:** Yes. **Laundry:** Yes. **Pay Phone:** Yes. **Rest Rooms and Showers:** Yes. **Fuel:** No. **Propane:** Yes. **Internal Roads:** Gravel. **RV Service:** No. **Market:** P J's Country Store, 2246 Flat River Rd., Coventry, RI 02816: Take a right onto Old Plainfield Pike, then a right onto Tunk Hill Rd. & a right onto Matteson Rd., which you should follow for 3 mi. Take a left onto Maple Valley Rd., followed by a left onto Flat River Rd. **Restaurant:** Jeffrey's Restaurant, 2260 Flat River Rd. Frnt, Coventry, RI 02816: Take a right onto Old Plainfield Pike, then a right onto Tunk Hill Rd. & a right onto Matteson Rd., which you should follow for 3 mi. Take a left onto Maple Valley Rd.,

followed by a left onto Flat River Rd. **General Store:** No. **Vending:** No. **Swimming Pool:** Yes. **Playground:** Yes. **Other:** Arcade, hiking trails, mini-golf course. **Activities:** Live bands, dances. **Nearby Attractions:** Foxwood Casino, beaches, Roger Williams Zoo. **Additional Information:** Call ahead.

### RESTRICTIONS

**Pets:** Allowed. **Fires:** Allowed. **Alcoholic Beverages:** Allowed. **Vehicle Maximum Length:** 40 ft. **Other:** Ask on arrival.

### TO GET THERE

Take Rte. 95 Exit 5 North onto Rte. 102 North—at third caution light (about 9 mi.) turn right onto Old Plainfield Pike (camp is 2 mi. in on the right).

# GREENE

## Hickory Ridge Family Campground

584 Victory Hwy., Greene 02827. T: (401) 391-7474; www.angelfire.com/ma2/hickoryridge camp/; hickoryridge@angelfire.com.

🚐 ★★★★★          ⛺ n/a

Beauty: ★★
Spaciousness: ★★★
Security: ★★★★
Insect Control: ★★★

Site Privacy: ★★★
Quiet: ★★★
Cleanliness: ★★★★
Facilities: ★★★★

A family campground catering to the same campers year after year, Hickory Ridge is a wonderful place if you're planning a long stay or looking for a regular spot to visit every summer. Run by the Pomfret family with a sizable staff, Hickory Ridge is like a big summer camp where everyone seems to know each other. The sites themselves are nothing special and some are even a little crowded, but this gives Hickory Ridge a sort of small-town neighborhood feel. There are no tent sites here, so this isn't the place for quiet contemplation.

### BASICS

**Operated By:** The Pomfret family. **Open:** Apr. 1–Oct. 10. **Site Assignment:** Reservations by phone only. **Registration:** Check in at office. **Fee:** $22. **Parking:** At site.

## FACILITIES

**Number of RV Sites:** 200. **Number of Tent-Only Sites:** 0. **Hookups:** Water, electric, sewer. **Each Site:** Picnic table, fireplace. **Dump Station:** Yes. **Laundry:** Yes. **Pay Phone:** Yes. **Rest Rooms and Showers:** Yes. **Fuel:** No. **Propane:** Yes. **Internal Roads:** Gravel. **RV Service:** No. **Market:** P J's Country Store, 2246 Flat River Rd., Coventry, RI 02816: Take a left onto Rte. 102 & follow for 1.3 mi. Turn left onto Rte. 117 & follow for 4.7 mi. **Restaurant:** Jeffrey's Restaurant, 2260 Flat River Rd. Frnt, Coventry, RI: Take a left onto Rte. 102 & follow for 1.3 mi. Turn left onto Rte. 117 & follow for 4.7 mi. **General Store:** Yes. **Vending:** No. **Swimming Pool:** Yes. **Playground:** Yes. **Other:** Softball field, volleyball, horseshoes, cool-mist tent, rec hall. **Activities:** Planned events in the rec hall on weekends. **Nearby Attractions:** Golf, benches, casinos. **Additional Information:** www.angelfire.com/ma2/HickoryRidgeCamp/.

## RESTRICTIONS

**Pets:** Allowed. **Fires:** Allowed. **Alcoholic Beverages:** Allowed. **Vehicle Maximum Length:** None. **Other:** Ask on arrival.

## TO GET THERE

Take 95 to Exit 5, then go approximately 7 mi. on Rte. 102.

# GREENWICH

## Pine Valley RV Campground

64 Bailey Pond Rd. West, Greenwich 02817. T: (401) 397-7972.

🚐 ★★★                          ⛺ ★★★

| | |
|---|---|
| Beauty: ★★★★ | Site Privacy: ★★★★ |
| Spaciousness: ★★★ | Quiet: ★★★★ |
| Security: ★★★ | Cleanliness: ★★★ |
| Insect Control: ★★★ | Facilities: ★★★★ |

Located between the Arcadia Management Area and Beach Pond State Park, Pine Valley has an unbelievable amount of natural scenery nearby. You could spend an entire season here and still not explore every hiking trail or see even a small selection of the wildlife. Three nearby lakes offer a variety of water-based activities. Since this is a year-round facility, Pine Valley would also make an excellent base camp for anyone who enjoys cross-country skiing.

## BASICS

**Operated By:** Private operator. **Open:** Year-round. **Site Assignment:** Reservations. **Registration:** Office. **Fee:** $10. **Parking:** At site.

## FACILITIES

**Number of RV Sites:** 20. **Number of Tent-Only Sites:** 50. **Hookups:** Water, electric. **Each Site:** Picnic table, fireplace. **Dump Station:** No. **Laundry:** Yes. **Pay Phone:** No. **Rest Rooms and Showers:** Yes. **Fuel:** No. **Propane:** No. **Internal Roads:** None. **RV Service:** No. **Market:** Better Val-U Supermarket, 104 Beach Pond Rd., Voluntown, CT 06384: Take a right onto Bailey Pond Rd., followed by a right onto Hazard Rd. & a right onto Rte. 165, which becomes Beach Pond Rd. **Restaurant:** Town Pizza & Restaurant, 104 Beach Pond Rd., Voluntown, CT 06384: Take a right onto Bailey Pond Rd., followed by a right onto Hazard Rd. & a right onto Rte. 165, which becomes Beach Pond Rd. **General Store:** Yes. **Vending:** No. **Swimming Pool:** Yes. **Playground:** No. **Other:** Volleyball, tennis court, horseshoes. **Activities:** Some planned activities. **Nearby Attractions:** Beach Pond State Park. **Additional Information:** Call ahead.

## RESTRICTIONS

**Pets:** Allowed. **Fires:** Allowed. **Alcoholic Beverages:** Allowed. **Vehicle Maximum Length:** None. **Other:** Ask on arrival.

## TO GET THERE

Take I-395 North to Rte. 14A, which becomes Rte. 14, then take a right onto Flat River Rd., followed by a right onto Hopkins Hollow Rd., then a left onto Sand Hill Rd., which becomes Plain Rd. Take a right onto Seth Brown Rd., followed by a right onto Muddy Brook Rd. and a left onto Hazard Rd., then a right onto Bailey Pond Rd.

## HOPE VALLEY

### Greenwood Hill Family Campground

13 A Newberry Ln. P.O. Box 141, Hope Valley 02832. T: (401) 539-7154; RathbunGHCamp@aol.com.

🚐 ★★★          ⛺ ★★★

Beauty: ★★                  Site Privacy: ★★★
Spaciousness: ★★★          Quiet: ★★★
Security: ★★★              Cleanliness: ★★★
Insect Control: ★★★        Facilities: ★★

This small campground with fairly spacious sites offers group activities as well as a chance for seclusion. Though most campers at Greenwood seem to know each other and enjoy socializing, there are a handful of spartan, completely secluded sites for tents that allow complete privacy. Campers can fish and canoe nearby and enjoy easy access to most of the major attractions in the area.

### BASICS

**Operated By:** George & Ruth Rathbun. **Open:** May 15–Oct. 15. **Site Assignment:** Reservations accepted. **Registration:** Office. **Fee:** $20 & up. **Parking:** At site.

### FACILITIES

**Number of RV Sites:** 40. **Number of Tent-Only Sites:** 10. **Hookups:** Water, electric. **Each Site:** Picnic table, fireplace. **Dump Station:** Yes. **Laundry:** No. **Pay Phone:** No. **Rest Rooms and Showers:** Yes. **Fuel:** No. **Propane:** No. **Internal Roads:** Gravel. **RV Service:** No. **Market:** Spring St. Market, 1 Spring St., Hope Valley, RI: Take a left onto Newberry Ln., followed by a right onto Spring St. **Restaurant:** 14 Spring St. Restaurant, 14 Spring St., Hopkinton, RI: Take a left onto Newberry Ln., followed by a right onto Spring St. **General Store:** No. **Vending:** No. **Swimming Pool:** Yes. **Playground:** Yes. **Other:** Sports fields. **Activities:** Planned weekend events & special dinners. **Nearby Attractions:** Mystic seaport, Newport, RI. **Additional Information:** Trailer rentals & camping equipment rentals.

### RESTRICTIONS

**Pets:** Allowed. **Fires:** Allowed. **Alcoholic Beverages:** Allowed. **Vehicle Maximum Length:** None. **Other:** Ask on arrival.

### TO GET THERE

From I-95 north or south just take Exit 3B (Hope Valley/Wyoming), then RI Rte. 138 west for 3.5 mi. and follow our signs to the campground.

## HOPE VALLEY

### Legrand G. Reynolds Horsemen's Camping Area

260 Arcadia Rd., Hope Valley 02832. T: (401) 539-2356.

🚐 n/a          ⛺ ★★★

Beauty: ★★★★              Site Privacy: ★★★★
Spaciousness: ★★★          Quiet: ★★★★★
Security: ★★★              Cleanliness: ★★★★★
Insect Control: ★★★        Facilities: none

Not for everyone, this campground was created specifically for campers with horses—you must have a horse to be allowed in. RVs are welcome (there's parking for horse trailers). Once here, you and your horse can explore miles of trails or practice for competitions in the show ring. The Arcadia Management Area, most of which is open to horses, is nearby. For those times when you need a little space from your horse, Beach Pond State Park offers swimming and other water-based recreation.

### BASICS

**Operated By:** State of Rhode Island. **Open:** Year-round. **Site Assignment:** First come, first served, max stays apply. **Registration:** By mail. **Fee:** $3 plus $10 for use of show ring. **Parking:** At site.

### FACILITIES

**Number of RV Sites:** 0. **Number of Tent-Only Sites:** 20. **Hookups:** None. **Each Site:** Fireplace, picnic table. **Dump Station:** No. **Laundry:** No. **Pay Phone:** No. **Rest Rooms and Showers:** Rest room, running water. **Fuel:** No. **Propane:** No. **Internal Roads:** Gravel. **RV Service:** No.

**Market:** Stop & Shop Supermarket, 3 Stillson Rd., Wyoming, RI 02898: Take a right onto Arcadia Rd., followed by a left onto Bridge St. & a left onto Rte. 3/Rte. 138, then take a left onto Stillson Rd. **Restaurant:** 3410, 1139 Main, Hope Valley, RI 02832: Take a right onto Arcadia Rd., followed by a left onto Bridge St. & a left onto Rte. 3/Rte. 138 (Main St.). **General Store:** No. **Vending:** No. **Swimming Pool:** No. **Playground:** No. **Other:** Show ring, horse trails. **Activities:** Horseback riding. **Nearby Attractions:** Beach Pond State Park. **Additional Information:** Call ahead.

## RESTRICTIONS

**Pets:** Allowed. **Fires:** Allowed. **Alcoholic Beverages:** Allowed. **Vehicle Maximum Length:** None. **Other:** Ask on arrival.

## TO GET THERE

Take 95 to Exit 5A and follow Rte. 102 South, then take a right onto Rte. 3. Follow until Rte. 165 and take a right onto Escoheag Rd. Follow to the campground.

## HOPE VALLEY

## Whispering Pines Family Campground

Box 425 Saw Mill RD, Hope Valley 02832. T: (401) 539-7011; www.whisperingpinescamping.com/; wpinesri@aol.com.

🚐 ★★★★                    ⛺ ★★

| | |
|---|---|
| Beauty: ★★★★ | Site Privacy: ★★★ |
| Spaciousness: ★★★ | Quiet: ★★★ |
| Security: ★★★ | Cleanliness: ★★★★ |
| Insect Control: ★★★ | Facilities: ★★★★ |

The name Whispering Pines is appropriate since the entire campground is filled with these enormous trees. Most sites are tucked in between the pines, which can make some of them a little dark—though on a sunny day the light manages to shine through, and the trees make this a wonderful place to get out of the heat. Remote yet convenient, Whispering Pines is a fairly self-contained area with many activities, but there's not so much going on that you won't want to check out the nearby beaches or casino.

## BASICS

**Operated By:** Private operator. **Open:** June 1–Oct. 31. **Site Assignment:** Reservations. **Registration:** Office. **Fee:** $25–$29 a night depending on facilities/time of year. **Parking:** At site.

## FACILITIES

**Number of RV Sites:** 180. **Number of Tent-Only Sites:** 0. **Hookups:** Water, electric, sewer. **Each Site:** Picnic table, fireplace. **Dump Station:** Yes. **Laundry:** Yes. **Pay Phone:** Yes. **Rest Rooms and Showers:** Yes. **Fuel:** No. **Propane:** Yes. **Internal Roads:** Gravel. **RV Service:** No. **Market:** Spring St. Market, 1 Spring St., Hope Valley, RI: Take a left onto Highview Ave., then a left onto Main St. & follow for 0.2 mi. **Restaurant:** 3410, 1139 Main, Hope Valley, RI: Take a left onto Highview Ave., then a left onto Main St. & follow for 1.1 mi. **General Store:** Yes. **Vending:** Yes. **Swimming Pool:** Yes. **Playground:** No. **Other:** Sports field, swimming pond, rec room, tennis court, shuffleboard, beach. **Activities:** Planned recreational activities, canoe trips, swimming lessons. **Nearby Attractions:** Foxwoods Casino. **Additional Information:** www.whisperingpinescamping.com.

## RESTRICTIONS

**Pets:** Allowed. **Fires:** Allowed. **Alcoholic Beverages:** Allowed. **Vehicle Maximum Length:** None. **Other:** Ask on arrival.

## TO GET THERE

Take I-95 to Exit 3B west and follow for 3 mi.

## JAMESTOWN

## Fort Getty Recreation Area

P.O. Box 377, Jamestown 02835. T: (401) 423-7211.

🚐 n/a                    ⛺ ★★★

| | |
|---|---|
| Beauty: ★★★★ | Site Privacy: ★★★ |
| Spaciousness: ★★★★ | Quiet: ★★★★ |
| Security: ★★ | Cleanliness: ★★★ |
| Insect Control: ★★★ | Facilities: ★★★ |

Fort Getty Recreation Area, set on windswept bluff near the southern tip of Jamestown Island in the middle of Narragansett Bay, is a beautiful oceanside campground that can be reached by car. Salty sea breezes, sunrises and sunsets to die for, and rocky beach fronts for hours of exploring all recommend it. For the historically minded, there are a couple of bunkers remaining from when Fort Getty was an ammunition depot during World War II. These are also cool little spots for older kids to play in. The land on which the campground is perched is surrounded by several other small islands dotting Narragansett Bay. In a place like this, the environment is captivating, regardless of the weather. It's brilliant on bright sunny days, cool and refreshing when the mainland is sweltering. The stars at night are crystal clear, and you'll see deeper into the universe because there isn't much light pollution out here.

## BASICS

**Operated By:** Jamestown township. **Open:** Mid-May–Oct. 1. **Site Assignment:** First come, first served. **Registration:** At ranger station. **Fee:** $20–$30. **Parking:** At site.

## FACILITIES

**Number of RV Sites:** 0. **Number of Tent-Only Sites:** 30. **Hookups:** Water, electric (30 amps). **Each Site:** Fire ring. **Dump Station:** Yes. **Laundry:** No. **Pay Phone:** Yes. **Rest Rooms and Showers:** Yes. **Fuel:** No. **Propane:** No. **Internal Roads:** Paved. **RV Service:** No. **Market:** No. **Restaurant:** No. **General Store:** No. **Vending:** No. **Swimming Pool:** No. **Playground:** No. **Activities:** Fishing, boating, walking trails. **Nearby Attractions:** Lighthouse at Beaver Tail. **Additional Information:** Call ahead.

## RESTRICTIONS

**Pets:** On leash. **Fires:** In fire ring. **Alcoholic Beverages:** At site. **Vehicle Maximum Length:** 45 ft. **Other:** Ask on arrival.

## TO GET THERE

From Jamestown, take N. Main St. to the south (toward Beavertail State Park). This road will cross Narragansett Rd. and turn into Southwest Ave. Follow Southwest Ave. to Beavertail Rd. The entrance for the state park and campground is on the right.

## NARAGANSETT

### Breakwater Village Campground

P.O. Box 563, Naragansett 02882. T: (401) 783-9527; F: (401) 783-9454.

🚐 ★★★                     ▲ n/a

Beauty: ★★★             Site Privacy: ★★★
Spaciousness: ★★★       Quiet: ★★★
Security: ★★★★          Cleanliness: ★★★★
Insect Control: ★★★     Facilities: ★★

Visitors to Breakwater Village better enjoy spending time on the beach, because that's all there is to do here. For swimming, surfing, boating, and fishing, you have your choice of five town beaches. You're also close to the heart of Narragansett, which is a traditional resort community offering a variety of activities. The actual campground offers more than a place to park your RV—it's a nice (actually quite pretty) parking lot.

## BASICS

**Operated By:** Private operator. **Open:** Apr. 15–Oct. 15. **Site Assignment:** Reservations accepted. **Registration:** At office. **Fee:** $30. **Parking:** At site.

## FACILITIES

**Number of RV Sites:** 38. **Number of Tent-Only Sites:** 0. **Hookups:** Water, electric. **Each Site:** None. **Dump Station:** Yes. **Laundry:** No. **Pay Phone:** No. **Rest Rooms and Showers:** No. **Fuel:** No. **Propane:** No. **RV Service:** No. **Market:** Seaview Marketplace, 682 Matunuck Beach Rd., Wakefield, RI 02879: Take a left onto Point Judith Rd., followed by a left onto Woodruff Ave. & a left onto Salt Pond Rd. Merge onto Rte. 1 & follow for 5 mi. to Matunuck Beach Rd. **Restaurant:** Charlie O's Tavern-The Point, 2 Sand Hill Cove Rd., Narragansett, RI 02882: Take a right onto Point Judith Rd., followed by a right onto Sand Hill Cove Rd. **General Store:** Snack bar. **Vending:** No. **Swimming Pool:** No. **Playground:** No. **Activities:** No planned activities. **Nearby Attractions:** Lots of beaches. **Additional Information:** Call ahead.

**Pets:** On leash. **Fires:** Allowed. **Alcoholic Beverages:** Allowed. **Vehicle Maximum Length:** None. **Other:** Ask on arrival.

**TO GET THERE**

Take interstate Rte. 95 South, to Rte. 4 South, to Rte.1 South, to Rte. 108 South, 4 mi. along 108 on right-hand side.

## NARAGANSETT

### Fisherman's Memorial State Park

Rte. 108, 1011 Point Judith Rd., Narragansett 02882. T: (401) 789-8374; www.riparks.com/fisherma.htm.

🚐 ★★★★          ▲ ★★★

| | |
|---|---|
| Beauty: ★★★ | Site Privacy: ★★★ |
| Spaciousness: ★★★★ | Quiet: ★★★ |
| Security: ★★★ | Cleanliness: ★★★ |
| Insect Control: ★★★ | Facilities: ★★★★ |

Fisherman's Memorial State Park looks like a suburban housing development with trailers and tents instead of ranches and capes. Though there are trees separating some of the sites, most are just empty patches of grass laid out along winding roads. This layout gives the campground—at least during the busy summer season—the feel of a 1950s small town. Many people stay here for more than a couple of days, and at night adults sit out on their "front porches" talking, eating, and drinking while the kids play on the street. The state of Rhode Island runs the park and keeps it well groomed despite the large crowds that can often be found.

**BASICS**

**Operated By:** Rhode Island Division of Parks & Recreation. **Open:** Year-round. **Site Assignment:** Reservations by mail only, form available on website. **Registration:** By mail or at park office. **Fee:** $8–12 for residents, $12–$16 for nonresidents. **Parking:** At site.

**FACILITIES**

**Number of RV Sites:** 150. **Number of Tent-Only Sites:** 35. **Hookups:** Water, electric, sewer. **Each Site:** Picnic table, fireplace. **Dump Station:** Yes. **Laundry:** Yes. **Pay Phone:** Yes. **Rest Rooms and Showers:** Yes. **Fuel:** No. **Propane:** No. **Internal Roads:** Asphalt. **RV Service:** No. **Market:** Seaview Marketplace, 682 Matunuck Beach Rd., Wakefield, RI 02879: Take a left onto Point Judith Rd., followed by a left onto Woodruff Ave. & a left onto Salt Pond Rd. Merge onto Rte. 1 & follow for 5 mi. to Matunuck Beach Rd. **Restaurant:** Charlie O's Tavern-The Point, 2 Sand Hill Cove Rd., Narragansett, RI 02882: Take a right onto Point Judith Rd., followed by a right onto Sand Hill Cove Rd. **General Store:** No. **Vending:** No. **Swimming Pool:** No. **Playground:** Yes. **Other:** Tennis courts, basketball courts, horseshoe pit. **Activities:** Farmer's market on site, other planned activities. **Nearby Attractions:** Four beaches, city of Newport. **Additional Information:** www.riparks.com/fisherma.htm#FishermansTop.

**RESTRICTIONS**

**Pets:** Not allowed. **Fires:** Allowed. **Alcoholic Beverages:** Allowed. **Vehicle Maximum Length:** None. **Other:** Ask on arrival.

**TO GET THERE**

Take interstate Rte. 95 South, to Rte. 4 South, to Rte.1 South, to Rte. 108 South, 4 mi. along 108 on right-hand side.

## NORTH SCITUATE

### Holiday Acres Campground

591 Snake Hill Rd., North Scituate 02857. T: (401) 934-0789.

🚐 ★★★★          ▲ ★★★

| | |
|---|---|
| Beauty: ★★★ | Site Privacy: ★★★ |
| Spaciousness: ★★★ | Quiet: ★★★ |
| Security: ★★★ | Cleanliness: ★★★ |
| Insect Control: ★★★ | Facilities: ★★★★ |

Located on a busy freshwater lake (though motorboats aren't permitted), Holiday Acres offers a nice mix of facilities and wildlife. There are many planned activities, and the sports areas here offer a nice change from the lake, which is pretty much the center of the action for most visitors. Some sites have waterfront views, but folks looking for more privacy and a break from the action might choose a site a bit away from the lake.

## BASICS

**Operated By:** Private operator. **Open:** Year-round. **Site Assignment:** Reservations. **Registration:** At office. **Fee:** $20–$35, depending on facilities/time of year. **Parking:** At site.

## FACILITIES

**Number of RV Sites:** 200. **Number of Tent-Only Sites:** 25. **Hookups:** Water, electric, sewer. **Each Site:** Picnic table, fireplace. **Dump Station:** Yes. **Laundry:** Yes. **Pay Phone:** Yes. **Rest Rooms and Showers:** Yes. **Fuel:** No. **Propane:** No. **RV Service:** No. **Market:** Dino's Park-N-Shop, 1020 Putnam Pike, Chepachet, RI 02814: Take a right onto Snake Hill Rd., then a right onto Tourtellot Hill Rd. Follow for 2.4 mi., then take a right onto Rte. 44 & follow for 0.2 mi. **Restaurant:** Harmony Restaurant, 401 Putnam Pike, Chepachet, RI 02814: Take a right onto Snake Hill Rd., followed by a left onto Sawmill Rd., then a left onto Rte. 44. **General Store:** Yes. **Vending:** Yes. **Swimming Pool:** No. **Playground:** No. **Other:** Mini-golf, horseshoes, volleyball courts. **Activities:** Canoe & paddle boat rentals. **Nearby Attractions:** Inquire at campground. **Additional Information:** Call ahead.

## RESTRICTIONS

**Pets:** On leash only. **Fires:** Allowed. **Alcoholic Beverages:** Allowed. **Vehicle Maximum Length:** None. **Other:** Ask on arrival.

## TO GET THERE

Take Rte. 6 to a left onto Rte. 102, follow for 3.2 mi. and take a left onto Snake Hill Rd.

## PASCOAG

### Buck Hill Family Campground

464 Wakefield Rd., Pascoag 02859. T: (800) 387-5224; F: (828) 765-1700; www.buckhill.20m.com/contact.html; buckhill@m-y.net.

🚐 ★★★★          ⛺ ★★★

Beauty: ★★            Site Privacy: ★★
Spaciousness: ★★       Quiet: ★★

Security: ★★★          Cleanliness: ★★★
Insect Control: ★★★     Facilities: ★★★★

Located alongside the North Toe River, Buck Hill is a fairly large campground, but many of its RV sites are cramped together. This is the case mainly along the river, where camping is most desirable and you're practically bumper to bumper with other RVs. If you're looking to meet people, this proximity to your neighbor adds to the atmosphere, but you won't find much peace and quiet. For tenters and RVers looking for more privacy, there are some sites set a bit off the beaten path. An odd mix of nature and people, this campground is scenic if you get away from the crowds. The stocked river has excellent fishing.

## BASICS

**Operated By:** Private operator. **Open:** May 1–Oct. 31. **Site Assignment:** Reservations. **Registration:** Office. **Fee:** $21 w/ full hookup, discounts for extended stays. **Parking:** At site.

## FACILITIES

**Number of RV Sites:** 98. **Number of Tent-Only Sites:** 0. **Hookups:** Water, electric. **Each Site:** Picnic table, fire ring. **Dump Station:** Yes. **Laundry:** Yes. **Pay Phone:** Yes. **Rest Rooms and Showers:** Yes. **Fuel:** No. **Propane:** Yes. **Internal Roads:** Gravel. **RV Service:** No. **Market:** Stop & Shop, 60 Providence Turnpike, Putnam, CT 06260: Take a left onto Wakefield Rd., followed by a left onto Buck Hill Rd. & a right onto Quaddick Town Farm Rd. Follow for around 5 mi. until it turns into Quaddick Town Farm Rd., which becomes East Putnam Rd. Follow for 1 mi. & turn left onto Rte. 44. **Restaurant:** McDonald's, 6 Providence Turnpike, Putnam, CT 06260: Take a left onto Wakefield Rd., followed by a left onto Buck Hill Rd. & a right onto Quaddick Town Farm Rd. Follow for around 5 mi. until it turns into Quaddick Town Farm Rd., which becomes East Putnam Rd. Follow for 1 mi. & turn left onto Rte. 44. **General Store:** Yes. **Vending:** No. **Swimming Pool:** No. **Playground:** Yes. **Other:** Rec room, rifle range, river. **Activities:** Swimming, fishing. **Nearby Attractions:** Mt. Mitchell. **Additional Information:** www.buckhill.20m.com/contact.html.

**Pets:** On leash only. **Fires:** Allowed. **Alcoholic Beverages:** Allowed. **Vehicle Maximum Length:** None. **Other:** Ask on arrival.

## TO GET THERE

Take Rte. 100 to Buck Hill Rd., following for 1.75 mi., and then take a left onto Croft Rd., following for 1.5 mi. to the campground.

## RICHMOND

## Wawaloam Campground

510 Gardinier Rd., Richmond 02892. T: (401) 294-3039; www.wawaloam.com; wawaloam99@aol.com.

| 🚐 ★★★★ | 🏕 n/a |
| --- | --- |
| Beauty: ★★★ | Site Privacy: ★★★ |
| Spaciousness: ★★★★ | Quiet: ★★★★ |
| Security: ★★★★ | Cleanliness: ★★★★ |
| Insect Control: ★★★ | Facilities: ★★★★ |

Yet another enormous campground in Rhode Island that caters to trailers, this one might be the best of the bunch. Sites are fairly spacious, and the scenery is pleasant (with lots of trees); it's better than your average "giant parking lot," which is what many campgrounds tend to feel like. A huge swimming pool complete with water slide is as nice as anything you'd find at a resort. This makes Wawaloam a good stop for families because you can spend at least one day parked by the water without having to do anything to entertain the kids.

## BASICS

**Operated By:** Jim & Maureen Smith. **Open:** Year-round. **Site Assignment:** Reservation. **Registration:** Office. **Fee:** $32 ($2 extra for sewer hook-up). **Parking:** At site.

## FACILITIES

**Number of RV Sites:** 300. **Number of Tent-Only Sites:** 0. **Hookups:** Water, electric (about half have sewer). **Each Site:** Picnic table, fireplace. **Dump Station:** Yes. **Laundry:** Yes. **Pay Phone:** Yes. **Rest Rooms and Showers:** Yes. **Fuel:** Yes. **Propane:** Yes. **Internal Roads:** Gravel. **RV Service:** No. **Market:** L C Mart 345 Noose-

neck Hill Rd., Exeter, RI: Take a left onto Gardner Rd., followed by a right onto Ten Rod Rd., then a left onto Town Hall Rd., a left onto Rte. 102 & a left onto Nooseneck Hill Rd. **Restaurant:** Middle of Nowhere Diner, 222 Nooseneck Hill Rd. Exeter, RI: Take a left onto Gardner Rd., followed by a right onto Ten Rod Rd., then a left onto Town Hall Rd., a left onto Rte. 102 & a left onto Nooseneck Hill Rd. **General Store:** Yes. **Vending:** Yes. **Swimming Pool:** Yes. **Playground:** Yes. **Other:** Sports field, mini-golf, horseshoes. **Activities:** Friday night dinner, Sunday morning breakfast, fishing derbies, lots of planned activities. **Nearby Attractions:** Fairly close to Arcadia Management area, a really large state park w/ fishing, hiking, etc. **Additional Information:** www.wawaloam.com.

## RESTRICTIONS

**Pets:** Allowed. **Fires:** Allowed. **Alcoholic Beverages:** Allowed. **Vehicle Maximum Length:** None. **Other:** Ask on arrival.

## TO GET THERE

I-95 Exit 5A to Rte. 3. Bear right on Rte. 3, take first left onto Rte. 1025, go 1.5 mi. to Town Hall Rd., bear right; Gardiner Rd. is first left after old Town Hall—follow 1.5 mi. to campground on right.

## SOUTH KINGSTON

## Wakamo Park Resort

697 Succotash Rd., South Kingston 02879. T: (401) 783-6688.

| 🚐 ★★★★ | 🏕 n/a |
| --- | --- |
| Beauty: ★★★★ | Site Privacy: ★★★★ |
| Spaciousness: ★★★ | Quiet: ★★★★ |
| Security: ★★★★ | Cleanliness: ★★★★ |
| Insect Control: ★★★ | Facilities: ★★ |

A beachfront resort, Wakamo Park is located near East Matunuck State Beach and the Great Swamp Management Area. The beach is one of the nicest in the state, and when it's warm it gives Wakamo a tropical island feel. For colder days and more active vacationers, the Great Swamp Management area offers hiking trails, canoeing, fishing, and more. Wakamo's small size (only 30 sites) gives it a homey feel for an RV park, making it more inviting than most.

## BASICS

**Operated By:** Private operator. **Open:** Apr. 15–Oct. 15. **Site Assignment:** Reservations accepted. **Registration:** At office. **Fee:** $40. **Parking:** At site.

## FACILITIES

**Number of RV Sites:** 30. **Number of Tent-Only Sites:** 0. **Hookups:** Water, electric, sewer. **Each Site:** None. **Dump Station:** No. **Laundry:** No. **Pay Phone:** No. **Rest Rooms and Showers:** No. **Fuel:** No. **Propane:** No. **RV Service:** No. **Market:** Seaview Marketplace, 682 Matunuck Beach Rd., Wakefield, RI 02879: Take a left onto Succotash Rd., followed by a slight right onto Rte. 1 & a slight right onto Matanuck Rd. **Restaurant:** Cap'n Jack's **Restaurant:** 706 Succotash Rd., Wakefield, RI 02879: Take a right onto Succotash Rd. **General Store:** Yes. **Vending:** No. **Swimming Pool:** No. **Playground:** No. **Other:** Canoe & paddleboat rentals. **Activities:** Some planned activities. **Nearby Attractions:** Great Swamp Management Area. **Additional Information:** Call ahead.

## RESTRICTIONS

**Pets:** Not allowed. **Fires:** Allowed. **Alcoholic Beverages:** Allowed. **Vehicle Maximum Length:** None. **Other:** Ask on arrival.

## TO GET THERE

Take I-295 south to Exit 9, Rte. 4. Take a slight right onto Tower Hill Rd., which becomes Rte. 1. Follow for about 13 mi. until it becomes Succotash Rd.

## WAKEFIELD

### Card's Camps

1065 Worden's Pond Rd., Wakefield 02879. T: (401) 783-7158; F: (401) 783-5267; www.cardscamps.com.

| 🚐 ★★★★★ | ⛺ n/a |
|---|---|
| Beauty: ★★★ | Site Privacy: ★★★ |
| Spaciousness: ★★★★ | Quiet: ★★★ |
| Security: ★★★ | Cleanliness: ★★★ |
| Insect Control: ★★★ | Facilities: ★★★★ |

An enormous campground catering entirely to RVers, Card's Camp is a nicer-than-average RV park. Because it's so large and borders a nature preserve, there's enough open space here to make you feel involved in nature even though you're not sleeping outside in a tent. The campground also lies right on Worden Pond, the largest pond in the state, and pond-side campsites are available.

## BASICS

**Operated By:** Private operator. **Open:** May 1–Oct. 1. **Site Assignment:** Reservations normally required. **Registration:** At office. **Fee:** $38-45 for the first night, $22-32 for each additional. **Parking:** At site.

## FACILITIES

**Number of RV Sites:** Over 250. **Number of Tent-Only Sites:** 0. **Hookups:** Water, electric, sewer. **Each Site:** Picnic table, fireplace. **Dump Station:** Yes. **Laundry:** No. **Pay Phone:** Yes. **Rest Rooms and Showers:** Yes. **Fuel:** No. **Propane:** Yes. **RV Service:** No. **Market:** 4071 Old Post Rd., Charlestown, RI: Take a right onto Wordens Pond Rd., followed by a left onto Shannock Rd., a right onto Old Coach Rd., & a left onto Narrow Ln. Then take a slight right onto Post Rd. & follow for 0.6 mi. **Restaurant:** Rojelio's Railway 3769 Old Post Rd. A, Charlestown, RI: Take a right onto Wordens Pond Rd., followed by a left onto Shannock Rd., a right onto Old Coach Rd., & a left onto Narrow Ln. Then take a slight right onto Post Rd. & follow for 0.6 mi. **General Store:** No. **Vending:** No. **Swimming Pool:** Yes. **Playground:** Yes. **Other:** Volleyball, basketball, horseshoes, freshwater pond. **Activities:** Boat rentals, fishing, hunting. **Nearby Attractions:** Great Swamp Management Area preserve. **Additional Information:** www.cardscamps.com.

## RESTRICTIONS

**Pets:** Allowed. **Fires:** Allowed. **Alcoholic Beverages:** Allowed. **Vehicle Maximum Length:** None. **Other:** Ask on arrival.

## TO GET THERE

Take I-95 South to Exit 9 for Rte. 4 South. Take Rte. 4 South to Rte. 1 South. Take Rte. 1 South for approximately 12 mi. to Rte. 110 North. Take Rte. 110 North (also the U.R.I. Exit) and continue to the intersection with a flashing red light at Worden's Pond Rd. Then take a left and continue on Worden's Pond Rd. for about 2 mi. to Card's Camps on your right.

## WEST GREENWICH
## Oak Embers Campground

219 Escoheag Hill Rd., West Greenwich 02817. T: (401) 397-4042; F: (401) 397-4446; www.oakembers.com; info@oakembers.com.

🚐 ★★★          ⛺ ★★★

Beauty: ★★★★          Site Privacy: ★★★
Spaciousness: ★★★★    Quiet: ★★★★
Security: ★★★★         Cleanliness: ★★★★
Insect Control: ★★★     Facilities: ★★★★

Though it's set next to one of the more picturesque parts of the state, Oak Embers is not much to look at. The surrounding scenery is beautiful, but the campground itself feels much like an old summer camp, though this might be intentional on the part of the owners. Still, once you get away from the most crowded areas of the campground, you'll find plenty of trees and solitude and more than enough nature in which to lose yourself. Oak Embers combines the best of both worlds—it's near a lot of noncamping activities yet offers all the outdoor amenities as well.

## BASICS
**Operated By:** Jack & Fran Smith. **Open:** May 1–Sept. 30. **Site Assignment:** By reservation. **Registration:** Reservations required. **Fee:** $20 per night (electric), $18 (no hookups), 3 nights min. during weekends on peak season. **Parking:** At site.

## FACILITIES
**Number of RV Sites:** 37. **Number of Tent-Only Sites:** 23. **Hookups:** Water, electric. **Each Site:** Picnic table, fireplace. **Dump Station:** Yes. **Laundry:** Yes. **Pay Phone:** Yes. **Rest Rooms and Showers:** Yes. **Fuel:** No. **Propane:** No. **Internal Roads:** Gravel. **RV Service:** No. **Market:** Better Val-U Supermarket, 104 Beach Pond Rd., Voluntown, CT: Take a right onto Escoheag Hill Rd., followed by a right onto Ten Rod Rd. Follow for

about 4 mi. as it becomes Beach Pond Rd. **Restaurant:** Town Pizza & Restaurant, 104 Beach Pond Rd., Voluntown, CT: Take a right onto Escoheag Hill Rd., followed by a right onto Ten Rod Rd. Follow for about 4 mi. **General Store:** No. **Vending:** Yes. **Swimming Pool:** Yes. **Playground:** No. **Other:** Rec room, sports field. **Activities:** Hayrides, horseback riding, volleyball, theme weekends. **Nearby Attractions:** Arcadia Management Area. **Additional Information:** www.oakembers.com.

## RESTRICTIONS
**Pets:** Allowed. **Fires:** Allowed. **Alcoholic Beverages:** Allowed. **Vehicle Maximum Length:** 40 ft. **Other:** Ask on arrival.

## TO GET THERE
Take Rte. 95 South to Exit 5A onto Rte. 5, Right onto Rte. 3 to Rte. 165. Right on Rte. 165 to Escoheag Hill Rd. Right on Escoheag Hill Rd.

## WESTERLY
## Timber Creek RV Resort

118 Dunns Corners Rd., Westerly 02891. T: (401) 322-1877; www.timbercreekrvresort.com; timbercreek@efortress.com.

🚐 ★★★★          ⛺ n/a

Beauty: ★★★          Site Privacy: ★★★
Spaciousness: ★★★★    Quiet: ★★★
Security: ★★★         Cleanliness: ★★★
Insect Control: ★★★     Facilities: ★★★★★

With a summer camp–like setting, this RV-only park caters to families looking for a resort-type RV park. Numerous sports fields, a swimming pool, and other top-notch facilities make Timber Creek an active place to visit. Many planned activities and droves of people make this a fun place for kids. The camp is only a few years old, so most facilities are in good shape. Nature lovers might want to pick another campground since you must venture far off the grounds to hike.

## BASICS
**Operated By:** Private operator. **Open:** May 1–Oct. 31. **Site Assignment:** Reservations rec-

ommended, 7-day cancellation policy. **Registration:** Office.  **Fee:** $32 . **Parking:** At site.

## FACILITIES

**Number of RV Sites:** 200. **Number of Tent-Only Sites:** 0. **Hookups:** Water, electric (50 amps), sewer. **Each Site:** Picnic table, fire ring. **Dump Station:** Yes. **Laundry:** Yes. **Pay Phone:** Yes. **Rest Rooms and Showers:** Yes. **Fuel:** No. **Propane:** Yes. **Internal Roads:** Gravel. **RV Service:** No. **Market:** W. B. Cody's, 265 Post Rd., Westerly, RI 02891: Take a right onto Dunns Croner Bradford Rd. & follow for 1.4 mi., followed by a left onto Post Rd. **Restaurant:** On site. **General Store:** Yes. **Vending:** Yes. **Swimming Pool:** Yes. **Playground:** Yes. **Other:** Kids rec room, driving range, fishing pond, sports fields, adult lodge. **Activities:** Paddle boats, hayrides. **Nearby Attractions:** Beaches, golf courses. **Additional Information:** www.timbercreekrvresort.com.

## RESTRICTIONS

**Pets:** Allowed. **Fires:** Allowed. **Alcoholic Beverages:** Allowed. **Vehicle Maximum Length:** None. **Other:** Ask on arrival.

## TO GET THERE

Take RI Exit 1, Rte. 3 south approximately 1.5 mi. Take left on Rte. 216, follow to end, bear right on Rte. 91. At traffic islands go straight through onto Dunns Corners Rd.; Resort is 0.5 mi. on right.

# Vermont

When people think of Vermont they think of the outdoors. It's hard not to picture any part of the state without seeing trees, undeveloped space, mountains, and water. That reputation is deserved, as Vermont has enormous amounts of unpopulated terrain. There are forests, mountains, lakes, and a seemingly endless amount of land—making this one of the better states for camping in the nation.

Camping in Vermont is fairly popular, and most campers in the state seek to encounter nature. Though there are some super-developed commercial campgrounds, most offer outdoors activities as the prime appeal. Even at the big RV parks with pools, rec halls, and other amenities its very rare that excellent hiking and a non-man made place to swim aren't nearby.

Vermont also has a large number of state-run campgrounds. Most of these are bare-bones facilities. For the most part, they accommodate RVs, but offer no hookups and only the barest amenities. These sites do, however, offer nature at its best. The state has maintained an enormous amount of public land—all of which remains undeveloped.

Those looking for campgrounds near a bustling metropolis will, for the most part, not find that in Vermont. Even the big "cities" in the state are relatively small, and Boston is pretty far away. Vermont does have lots of little towns with folksy charm and interesting local residents. The state is also so large that many areas don't get a lot of tourists, making them ideal spots to visit if you're looking to stay off the beaten path.

In many of the bigger towns, Vermont does have a shocking amount of antique and curiosity shops. Small cities like **Brattleboro** offer enough for a days worth of browsing, and many have regional theaters or small concert venues. In the winter months, Vermont also has some of the best skiing in the country. There are actually campgrounds affiliated with or nearby some of the mountains—though you'd have to be pretty hearty to camp in a tent during the dead of winter.

Basically, Vermont offers traditional camping with an almost endless amount of sites to choose from. Simply hiking all the trails in the state would take years, and canoeing all the rivers, climbing all the mountains, and fishing every lake would take a lifetime.

**The following facilities feature 20 or fewer sites:**

Knight Island State Park, St. Albans Bay

## ACUSTNEY

### Getaway Mountain and Campground

P.O. Box 372, Ascutney 05030. T: (802) 674-2812.

🚐 ★★★★　　　▲ ★★

Beauty: ★★★　　　　Site Privacy: ★★★
Spaciousness: ★★★　　Quiet: ★★★
Security: ★★★　　　　Cleanliness: ★★★
Insect Control: ★★★　　Facilities: ★★★

A small, pleasant RV park, Getaway Mountain offers a nice alternative to large RV parking lot–type campgrounds. Most of the sites have shade trees, and though tents aren't the norm, it wouldn't be completely ridiculous to pitch one here. There's canoeing available on the nearby Connecticut River as well as easy access to hiking at Wilgus State Park.

#### BASICS

**Operated By:** Dave Fraczk. **Open:** May 1–Oct. 31. **Site Assignment:** Reservations accepted. **Registration:** At office. **Fee:** $18. **Parking:** At site.

#### FACILITIES

**Number of RV Sites:** 38. **Number of Tent-Only Sites:** 0. **Hookups:** Water, electric, sewer. **Each Site:** Fireplace. **Dump Station:** Yes. **Laundry:** No. **Pay Phone:** Yes. **Rest Rooms and Showers:** Yes. **Fuel:** No. **Propane:** No. **Internal Roads:** Entrance paved, Remainder is gravel. **RV Service:** No. **Market:** Country Village Store, Rte. 131, Ascutney, VT 05030. **Restaurant:** Mr. G's Restauraunt: 202 Rte. 131 Ext 8 Ascutney, VT 05030 (802) 674-2486. **General Store:** No. **Vending:** No. **Swimming Pool:** Yes. **Playground:** Yes. **Other:** Rec room, canoe rentals. **Activities:** Arcade, holiday events (hayrides, bonfires). **Nearby Attractions:** Arts & Historical Society, Fletcher Farm, Black River Academy Museum. **Additional Information:** Call ahead.

#### RESTRICTIONS

**Pets:** Allowed. **Fires:** Allowed. **Alcoholic Beverages:** Allowed. **Vehicle Maximum Length:** 30 ft. & plus. **Other:** Ask on arrival.

#### TO GET THERE

Take I-91 to Exit 8 then take Rte. 131 to Rte. 5. Go south on Rte. 5 for 2 mi.

## ALBURG

### Alburg RV Resort

P.O. Box 50, Blue Rock Rd., Alburg 05440. T: (802) 796-3733.

🚐 ★★★★　　　▲ ★★★

Beauty: ★★★★　　　Site Privacy: ★★★★
Spaciousness: ★★★★　Quiet: ★★★
Security: ★★★★　　　Cleanliness: ★★★★
Insect Control: ★★★　　Facilities: ★★★★

The grassy sites here are located just off Lake Champlain set back in between trees. The lake is their major appeal, as there's a beach with swimming and boat access. The prime attraction, however, might be that the lake offers excellent sailing conditions. Guests with boats can hit the water right from the shore. If you have a bigger boat, there's a dock nearby. Some sites have a view of the Green Mountains—though whether you can actually see them depends on the weather. Most sites are private and there are tent-only sites, but the campground is dominated by large RVs parked for the whole season. There are a few sites available on a short term basis, you'll want to reserve early.

#### BASICS

**Operated By:** Gilles R. & Francoise H. Gravel. **Open:** May 1–Oct. 1. **Site Assignment:** Reservations recommended. **Registration:** At office. **Fee:** $22–$25. **Parking:** At site.

#### FACILITIES

**Number of RV Sites:** 150. **Number of Tent-Only Sites:** 25. **Hookups:** Water, electric (20, 30 amps), sewer. **Each Site:** Fire ring, picnic table. **Dump Station:** Yes. **Laundry:** Yes. **Pay Phone:** Yes. **Rest Rooms and Showers:** Yes. **Fuel:** No. **Propane:** Yes. **Internal Roads:** paved/ gravel. **RV Service:** No. **Market:** Grand Union Co, 39 1st St., Swanton, VT 05488: Take a right onto Rte. 2 followed by a right onto Rte. 78. Follow for 10.6 mi. **Restaurant:** Anchorage, 164 Lake St., Rouses Point, NY 12979: Take a right onto Rte. 2 & follow it for 7.2 mi. then take a left onto Rte. 11/9-B & continue for 1.3 mi. **General Store:** Yes. **Vending:** Yes. **Swimming Pool:** Yes. **Playground:** Yes. **Other:** Lake, softball field, volleyball court, basketball court, shuffleboard, rec hall. **Activities:** Windsurfing, sailing. **Nearby Attractions:** Vermont Maple Festival (Apr.), Ethan Allen Homestead Aquarium, Moritime Museum, Lake Champlain. **Additional Information:** Call ahead.

## RESTRICTIONS

**Pets:** Allowed.. **Fires:** Allowed. **Alcoholic Beverages:** Allowed. **Vehicle Maximum Length:** 40 ft.

## TO GET THERE

From the junction of US 2 and Hwy. 78, go 2 mi. east on Hwy. 78, then 0.5 mi. south on Blue Rock Rd.

## ALBURG
### Goose Point

526 US Rte. 2 South, Alburg 05440. T: (802) 796-3711.

🚐 ★★★★　　　🏕 ★★

| | |
|---|---|
| Beauty: ★★★★ | Site Privacy: ★★★★ |
| Spaciousness: ★★★★★ | Quiet: ★★★ |
| Security: ★★★ | Cleanliness: ★★★★ |
| Insect Control: ★★★ | Facilities: ★★★★ |

Goose Point is big, and feels bigger. The campground, because of it size, offers something for everyone. RV sites range from grassy open spots to shaded private ones. Most of the tent sites are wooded and set off from the RVs. There's a lot of sailing done in the Missiquoi Bay of Lake Champlain, which also offers fishing—and not just your normal drop-a-line-to-catch-a-sunfish type, but the real catch-a-pike-or-trout-for-dinner variety. For tent campers who don't want to risk having their trip ruined by rain, there's also a bed-and-breakfast on the grounds where you can stay if Mother Nature doesn't cooperate.

## BASICS

**Operated By:** Gordie & Pauline Beyor. **Open:** May 1–Oct. 15. **Site Assignment:** At time of registration. **Registration:** Entrance Gate. **Fee:** $18–$20. **Parking:** At site.

## FACILITIES

**Number of RV Sites:** 96. **Number of Tent-Only Sites:** 47. **Hookups:** Water, electric, sewer. **Each Site:** Picnic table, fire ring. **Dump Station:** Yes. **Laundry:** No. **Pay Phone:** Yes. **Rest Rooms and Showers:** Yes. **Fuel:** No. **Propane:** Yes. **Internal Roads:** Paved/gravel. **RV Service:** No. **Market:** Grand Union Co., 39 1st St., Swanton, VT: Take a left onto Rte. 2 then a right onto Rte. 78 & follow it for 10.8 mi. until it becomes Rte. 7. Then take a right back onto Rte. 78. **Restaurant:** Northern, Rte. 2, Alburg, VT 05440: Take a left onto Rte. 2. **General Store:** Yes. **Vending:** Yes. **Swimming Pool:** Yes. **Playground:** No. **Other:** Bait & tackle sold. **Activities:** Boating, fishing. **Nearby Attractions:** Ben & Jerry's Factory, Shelburne Museum, Appalachian Trail, Fletcher Farm. **Additional Information:** Call ahead.

## RESTRICTIONS

**Pets:** Allowed. **Fires:** Allowed. **Alcoholic Beverages:** Allowed. **Vehicle Maximum Length:** 35 ft. **Other:** Ask on arrival.

## TO GET THERE

On Rte. 2 go 3 mi. south of the junction with Rte. 78.

## BARTON
### Belview Campground

P.O. Box 222, Rte. 16E, Barton 05822. T: (802) 525-3242.

🚐 ★★★　　　🏕 ★★★★

| | |
|---|---|
| Beauty: ★★★★★ | Site Privacy: ★★★★ |
| Spaciousness: ★★★★ | Quiet: ★★★★ |
| Security: ★★★★ | Cleanliness: ★★★★ |
| Insect Control: ★★★ | Facilities: ★★★ |

A truly beautfiul campground, Belview has the advantage of being located a stone's throw from Crystal Lake but being set back in the woods a little bit. Though the sites are flat and fairly private, the park is offset by rolling hills on one side and farmland on the other—giving a variety of views. Though there aren't many facilities on site, there's a lot to do nearby. The lake also offers motor boating and fishing. Additionally, for those looking for smaller crowds and no power boats, there's May Pond nearby. Next to May Pond is May Pond Mountain, which offers a challenging hike.

## BASICS

**Operated By:** Bob & Joyce Morse. **Open:** May 15–Oct. 15. **Site Assignment:** Reservations accepted. **Registration:** Office Entrance. **Fee:** $14–$20. **Parking:** At site.

## FACILITIES

**Number of RV Sites:** 50. **Number of Tent-Only Sites:** 0. **Hookups:** Water, electric, sewer, cable TV. **Dump Station:** Yes. **Laundry:** No. **Pay Phone:** Yes. **Rest Rooms and Showers:** Yes. **Fuel:** No. **Propane:** Nearby, but not on site. **Internal Roads:** Paved/gravel in good condition. **RV Service:** No. **Market:** Cole's Markets, 52 Main St., Orleans, VT 05860: Take a left onto Rte. 16 & follow it for 2.5 mi. to I-91 N. Follow it for 5.6 mi. to Exit 26. Take a left at the fork in the ramp & a left onto Rte. 58 East. **Restaurant:** Nickelodeon, 95 Main St., Newport, VT 05855: Take a left onto Rte. 16 & follow it for 2.5 mi. to I-91 N. Continue for 5.6 mi. to Exit 26. Take a left at the fork in the ramp & a left onto Rte. 58 East. **General Store:** No. **Vending:** No. **Swimming Pool:** No. **Playground:** Yes. **Activities:** Hiking, biking, fishing (3 lakes & ponds). **Nearby Attractions:** Concerts, Orleans County Fair (seasonal), Orleans Country Club & Barton Golf Course, Crystal Lake. **Additional Information:** Call ahead.

## RESTRICTIONS

**Pets:** Allowed. **Fires:** Allowed. **Alcoholic Beverages:** Allowed. **Vehicle Maximum Length:** 40 ft. **Other:** Ask on arrival.

## TO GET THERE

Belview is located on Rte. 16E, 2 mi. from I-91 Exit 25. Go one mi. into the village, bear right on Rte. 5S for 0.5 mi., turn left over railroad tracks onto 16E. 0.5 mi. on right before going up hill.

# BRANDON

## Country Village Campground

40 Rte. 7, Brandon 05733. T: (802) 247-3333. cvcjb@juno.com

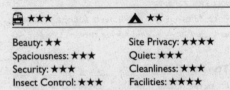

| Beauty: ★★ | Site Privacy: ★★★★ |
| Spaciousness: ★★★ | Quiet: ★★★ |
| Security: ★★★ | Cleanliness: ★★★ |
| Insect Control: ★★★ | Facilities: ★★★★ |

A pretty wide open campground, Country Village is supposed to be some sort of rural town. Mostly, it has RVs parked for the season in a fairly pleasant, albeit nothing special to look at setting. There's also not much at the actual campground, but there's a lot nearby. Lake Dunmore is within easy driving or long hiking distance. The campground is more of a summer camp, as most of the residents stay for the season.

## BASICS

**Operated By:** The Ceccoli Family. **Open:** May 15–Oct. 15. **Site Assignment:** Reservations recommended. **Registration:** Entrance. **Fee:** $13. **Parking:** At site.

## FACILITIES

**Number of RV Sites:** 41. **Number of Tent-Only Sites:** 0. **Hookups:** Water, electric. **Each Site:** Picnic table, fire ring. **Dump Station:** Yes. **Laundry:** No. **Pay Phone:** Yes. **Rest Rooms and Showers:** Yes. **Fuel:** No. **Propane:** No. **Internal Roads:** Compressed gravel. **RV Service:** No. **Market:** Brandon Discount Foods: 2598 Franklin St. Brandon, VT 05733. **Restaurant:** Blueberry Hill Inn: Forest Rd. 32, Brandon, VT 05733, (802) 247-6735. **General Store:** Limited. **Vending:** No. **Swimming Pool:** Yes. **Playground:** Yes. **Other:** Mini golf, horseshoe pit. **Activities:** Mini Golf, Shuffleboard, Canoeing (nearby), dog walking, Fall Foliage. **Nearby Attractions:** Marble Exhibit, Wilson Castle, Antique Shopping, Lake Dunmole, Otter Creek. **Additional Information:** E-mail the campground.

## RESTRICTIONS

**Pets:** Allowed. **Fires:** Allowed. **Alcoholic Beverages:** Allowed. **Vehicle Maximum Length:** 40 ft. **Other:** Ask on arrival.

## TO GET THERE

Take Rte. 7 to Rte. 73 and follow to campground

## BRATTLEBORO

### Fort Dummer State Park

434 Old Guilford Rd., Brattleboro 05301. T: (802) 254-2610; www.state.vt.us.

🚐 ★★★          ▲ ★★★

| | |
|---|---|
| Beauty: ★★★ | Site Privacy: ★★★ |
| Spaciousness: ★★★ | Quiet: ★★★ |
| Security: ★★★ | Cleanliness: ★★★★ |
| Insect Control: ★★★ | Facilities: ★★ |

The best part about Fort Dummer is location. The campground offers easy access to Brattleboro, which is one of Vermont's more interesting cities. The campground itself isn't very active. The facilities are sparse and there's not much there other than hiking trails. Nearby, however, there's fishing, boating, and just about everything else. The sites are well-maintained, and though the campground does not stand out, it's a perfectly pleasant home base for a Brattleboro-area trip.

## BASICS

**Operated By:** State of Vermont. **Open:** late May–Sept. (Labor Day). **Site Assignment:** Reservations accepted. **Registration:** Entrance Station. **Fee:** $11. **Parking:** At site.

## FACILITIES

**Number of RV Sites:** 51. **Number of Tent-Only Sites:** 10. **Hookups:** None. **Each Site:** Picnic table, fireplace. **Dump Station:** Yes. **Laundry:** No. **Pay Phone:** No. **Rest Rooms and Showers:** Yes. **Fuel:** No. **Propane:** No. **Internal Roads:** Paved, gravel. **RV Service:** No. **Market:** Price Chopper, 499 Canal St., Brattleboro, VT 05301: Take a right onto S. Main St. followed by a right onto Rte. 5 & a slight right onto Rte. 142. **Restaurant:** Ray's Diner, 105 Canal St., Brattle-

boro, VT 05301: Take a right onto S. Main St. followed by a left onto Rte. 5. **General Store:** No. **Vending:** No. **Swimming Pool:** No. **Playground:** Yes. **Other:** Dog walking Trail. **Activities:** Hiking Trails, Wildlife- & bird-watching, open field for games. **Nearby Attractions:** Green Mountains, Bennington Battle Monument, Townshend Dam, Basketville. **Additional Information:** Call ahead.

## RESTRICTIONS

**Pets:** Allowed. **Fires:** Allowed. **Alcoholic Beverages:** Allowed. **Vehicle Maximum Length:** 30 ft. **Other:** Ask on arrival.

## TO GET THERE

Take Exit 1 on I-91 to Rte. 5 and turn right on Fairground Rd. then go right on Main St. until Old Guilford Rd.

## BRATTLEBORO

### Moss Hollow Campground

RD 4, Box 723, Brattleboro 05301. T: (802) 368-2418.

🚐 ★★★          ▲ ★★★

| | |
|---|---|
| Beauty: ★★★ | Site Privacy: ★★★★ |
| Spaciousness: ★★★★ | Quiet: ★★★★ |
| Security: ★★★ | Cleanliness: ★★★★ |
| Insect Control: ★★★ | Facilities: ★★★ |

Located in a very rustic area, the prime attraction of this campground has to be the stream that runs through it. There's lots of fishing available as well as a swimming hole. If you're looking for more active sports, nearby Mount Snow offers hiking, mountain biking, and some trails for four-wheel ATVs. There's also an enormous network of hiking trails available as well as chair lift to the top of the mountain.

## BASICS

**Operated By:** Private operator. **Open:** May 15–Oct. 15. **Site Assignment:** Reservations recommended. **Registration:** At office. **Fee:** $15. **Parking:** At site.

## FACILITIES

**Number of RV Sites:** 50. **Number of Tent-Only Sites:** 0. **Hookups:** Water, electric. **Each**

**Site:** Picnic table, fire ring. **Dump Station:** Yes. **Laundry:** No. **Pay Phone:** Yes. **Rest Rooms and Showers:** Yes. **Fuel:** No. **Propane:** No. **Internal Roads:** Paved, dirt. **RV Service:** No. **Market:** Avenue Grocery, 82 Western Ave., Brattleboro, VT 05301: Take a right onto Abbot Rd., which becomes Greenleaf St., then take a right onto Rte. 9 & follow it for 1.5 mi. **Restaurant:** Dalem's Chalet Inc., 78 South St., Brattleboro, VT 05301: Take a right onto Abbot Rd. which becomes Greenleaf St. then take a right onto Rte. 9 & follow it for 0.3 mi. **General Store:** Yes. **Vending:** No. **Swimming Pool:** No. **Playground:** No. **Other:** Horseshoe pits. **Activities:** Fishing, swimming, biking. **Nearby Attractions:** ATV Trails. **Additional Information:** Mountain bikers must wear helmets.

## RESTRICTIONS

**Pets:** Allowed. **Fires:** Allowed. **Alcoholic Beverages:** Allowed. **Vehicle Maximum Length:** None. **Other:** Ask on arrival.

## TO GET THERE

Take I-91 to Rte. 9 and follow for 1.5 mi. Turn left onto Green Leaf St. and follow until the end of the road. Cross the bridge and follow the dirt road to the campground.

## BROWNINGTON

### Will-O-Wood Campground

227 Will-O-Wood Ln., Brownington 05860. T: (802) 525-3575; www.will-o-woodcampground.com.

| 🚐 ★★★★ | 🏕 ★★★ |
| --- | --- |
| Beauty: ★★★ | Site Privacy: ★★★★ |
| Spaciousness: ★★★★ | Quiet: ★★★ |
| Security: ★★★ | Cleanliness: ★★★★ |
| Insect Control: ★★★ | Facilities: ★★★★ |

Not quite on Lake Willoughby, Will-O-Wood offers large sites and excellent facilities. The campground is basically sits atop a grassy hill, with lots of nearby mountains for hiking as well as the lake only a half mile away. Though RVs dominate the campground, the tent sites have decent privacy and the overall spaciousness makes it a good mix for both types of campers.

The campground also makes a good choice for families, as there's lots to do in and within easy access of the facility.

## BASICS

**Operated By:** Bob, Fran, Jeff, & Dave LaBerge. **Open:** May 1–Oct. 15. **Site Assignment:** Reservations accepted. **Registration:** At office. **Fee:** $18–$23. **Parking:** At site.

## FACILITIES

**Number of RV Sites:** 84. **Number of Tent-Only Sites:** 33. **Hookups:** Water, electric, sewer. **Each Site:** Picnic table, fire ring, grill. **Dump Station:** Yes. **Laundry:** Yes. **Pay Phone:** Yes. **Rest Rooms and Showers:** Yes. **Fuel:** No. **Propane:** Yes. **Internal Roads:** Paved. **RV Service:** No. **Market:** Cole's Markets, 52 Main St., Orleans, VT 05860: Take a right onto Rte. 58 & go 0.1 mi. **Restaurant:** Delightful Dairy, 3556 Schoolhouse Rd. Orleans, VT 05860. **General Store:** Yes. **Vending:** Yes. **Swimming Pool:** Yes. **Playground:** Yes. **Other:** On-site trailor rental, special weekly, monthly, & seasonal rates, rec hall. **Activities:** Hiking, hunting, golf, bicycling, horseshoes. **Nearby Attractions:** Orleans Country Club, Crystal Lake, Mount Pisgah, Mount Hor, Lake Willoughby, golf courses. **Additional Information:** Call ahead.

## RESTRICTIONS

**Pets:** Allowed. **Fires:** Allowed. **Alcoholic Beverages:** Allowed. **Vehicle Maximum Length:** No limit. **Other:** Ask on arrival.

## TO GET THERE

Take I-91 to Exit 26, then follow Rte. 58E for 7 mi. to Rte. 5A S and go 0.5 mi.

## BURLINGTON

### Burlington's North Beach Campground

60 Institute Rd., Burlington 05401. T: (802) 862-0942 or 800-571-1198; F: (802) 865-7087; www.holidayjunction.com/usa/vt/cvt0014.html.

| 🚐 ★★★ | 🏕 ★★★ |
| --- | --- |
| Beauty: ★★★★ | Site Privacy: ★★★★ |
| Spaciousness: ★★★★ | Quiet: ★★★★ |

Security: ★★★     Cleanliness: ★★★★
Insect Control: ★★★     Facilities: ★★★

Burlington's North Beach Campground actually offers a nice mix of private campsites and a crowded lakefront. Though they're not secluded, the grassy sites are of a decent size and are nestled into the woods. Though it's near the busy (at least by Vermont standards) city of Burlington, North Beach feels like its in the woods. Lake Champlain, which abuts the park, has a large beach that can get quite crowded. There's also a large bike path and numerous hiking trails.

## BASICS

**Operated By:** City of Burlington. **Open:** May 1–Oct. 15. **Site Assignment:** Reservations accepted. **Registration:** At office. **Fee:** $15–$25 (additional tents are $5 each, 2 per site max.). **Parking:** At site.

## FACILITIES

**Number of RV Sites:** 16. **Number of Tent-Only Sites:** 137. **Hookups:** Water, electric, sewer. **Each Site:** Fireplace. **Dump Station:** Yes. **Laundry:** No. **Pay Phone:** Yes. **Rest Rooms and Showers:** Yes. **Fuel:** No. **Propane:** No. **Internal Roads:** Paved. **RV Service:** No. **Market:** Grand Union Co, 1134 North Ave., Burlington, VT 05401: Take a left onto North Ave. & follow it for 1 mi. **Restaurant:** Jimbo's Subs Wings & Things, 1130 North Ave., Burlington, VT 05401: Take a left onto North Ave. & follow it for 1 mi. **General Store:** Snack bar. **Vending:** Yes. **Swimming Pool:** No. **Playground:** Yes. **Other:** Bike path. **Activities:** Swimming, biking. **Nearby Attractions:** Historic downtown Burlington, Starr Farm Park (off-leash dog area), Paquett Arena at Leddy Park, Flynn Center. **Additional Information:** http://ci.burlington .vt.us/departments/parks/burlingtonparksandrec reation.htm.

## RESTRICTIONS

**Pets:** Allowed. **Fires:** Allowed. **Alcoholic Beverages:** Allowed. **Vehicle Maximum Length:** 55 ft. **Other:** Ask on arrival.

## TO GET THERE

From 1-89 to US 2W, take a left onto Pearl St., followed by a right onto N. Champlain St., a left onto Manhattan Dr., a left onto Pickin St., a right onto North St., and a right onto North Ave.

## COLCHESTER

### Lone Pine Campsites

52 Sunset View Rd., Colchester 05446. T: (802) 878-5447; www.lonepine.together.com.

🚐 ★★★★          ⛺ ★

Beauty: ★★★          Site Privacy: ★★★
Spaciousness: ★★★     Quiet: ★★★
Security: ★★★★          Cleanliness: ★★★★
Insect Control: ★★★     Facilities: ★★★★

Yet another enormous RV park, this one feels like a planned community for RVs. Sites are laid out on a grid, each with one shade tree. Campsites are grassy, and though I-89 is nearby, there's enough tree buffer to keep the camoground pretty much shielded form the noise of passing trucks. The major advantage here are the planned activities, which include a summer camp during the week for younger kids. Burlington is also pretty close by and has restaurants and shopping.

## BASICS

**Operated By:** Bradd Rubman. **Open:** May 1–Oct. 15. **Site Assignment:** Reservations accepted. **Registration:** At office. **Fee:** $26–$35 daily or $180–$220 weekly. **Parking:** At site.

## FACILITIES

**Number of RV Sites:** 265. **Number of Tent-Only Sites:** 0. **Hookups:** Water, electric, sewer. **Each Site:** Picnic table, fire ring, grill. **Dump Station:** Yes. **Laundry:** Yes. **Pay Phone:** Yes. **Rest Rooms and Showers:** Yes. **Fuel:** No. **Propane:** Yes. **Internal Roads:** Paved. **RV Service:** No. **Market:** Supervalu, Creek Farm Plz, Colchester, VT 05446: Take a left onto Rte. 127 & follow it for 0.2 mi. **Restaurant:** New York Pizza Oven, 288 Lakeshore Dr., Colchester, VT 05446: Take a right onto Rte. 127 & follow it for 0.9 mi. **General Store:** Yes. **Vending:** Yes. **Swimming Pool:** Yes. **Playground:** Yes. **Other:** Rec hall, game room, basketball courts, mini golf, tennis courts. **Activities:** Planned activities, fire truck rides.

**Nearby Attractions:** Shelburne Museum, Vermont Teddy Bear Factory, Ben & Jerry's Factory, shopping malls, fishing charters. **Additional Information:** Call ahead.

## RESTRICTIONS

**Pets:** Allowed. **Fires:** Allowed. **Alcoholic Beverages:** Allowed. **Vehicle Maximum Length:** None. **Other:** Ask on arrival.

## TO GET THERE

I-89 to Exit 16, then take Rtes. 2 and 7 north for 3 mi. followed by a left onto Bay Rd. for 1 mi.

## COLCHESTER

### Malletts Bay Campground

88 Malletts Bay Campground Rd., Colchester 05446. T: (802) 863-6980.

🚐 ★★★★          ⛺ ★★

| | |
|---|---|
| Beauty: ★★★ | Site Privacy: ★★★ |
| Spaciousness: ★★ | Quiet: ★★★ |
| Security: ★★★★ | Cleanliness: ★★★ |
| Insect Control: ★★★ | Facilities: ★★★ |

On the positive side, Malletts Bay is well-located if you want to be next to a town that has a lot going on. It's also on Lake Champlain, which offers every imaginable water-based activity. The negative side is that the sites are laid out fairly close together in a grid. RVers can pick from both open and wooded spots, while tent campers are relegated to grassy fields that sometimes are a little too close to the RVs. This is not a wonderful place for tent campers—adequate at best. Still, with the lake on one side and Bayside Park on the other and the busy town nearby, there's a lot around to make this campground appealing.

## BASICS

**Operated By:** The Handy family. **Open:** May 15–Oct. 15. **Site Assignment:** Reservations accepted. **Registration:** At office. **Fee:** $22–$29. **Parking:** At site.

## FACILITIES

**Number of RV Sites:** 119. **Number of Tent-Only Sites:** 71. **Hookups:** Water, electric, sewer. **Each Site:** Fireplace, picnic table. **Dump Sta-**

**tion:** Yes. **Laundry:** Yes. **Pay Phone:** Yes. **Rest Rooms and Showers:** Yes. **Fuel:** No. **Propane:** Yes. **Internal Roads:** Paved. **RV Service:** No. **Market:** Bayside Square Quick Stop, 336 Malletts Bay Ave., Colchester, VT 05446: Take a right onto Mallets Bay Ave. & follow it for 0.9 mi. **Restaurant:** Edgewater Pub, 340 Malletts Bay Ave., Colchester, VT 05446: Take a right onto Mallets Bay Ave. & follow it for 0.9 mi. **General Store:** No. **Vending:** No. **Swimming Pool:** Yes. **Playground:** Yes. **Other:** Game room, public beach. **Activities:** Tennis, boating, swimming, fishing. **Nearby Attractions:** St. Annes Shrine, Ethan Allen Homestead, Shelburne Museum, Ben & Jerry's Factory, shopping malls, tennis courts. **Additional Information:** Call ahead.

## RESTRICTIONS

**Pets:** Allowed. **Fires:** Allowed. **Alcoholic Beverages:** Allowed. **Vehicle Maximum Length:** 40 ft. **Other:** Ask on arrival.

## TO GET THERE

Take I-89 to Exit 16. Go north 1.5 mi. on Rte. 7. At the stop light, go left 3 mi. on Blakely Rd. Then go left on Lakeshore Dr. at the light

## CONCORD

### Breezy Meadows Campground

23 Wendel Rd., Concord 05824. T: (802) 695-9949 or 603-788-3624; www.gocampingamerica.com/breezymeadows; breezy@together.net.

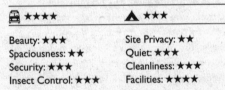

| | |
|---|---|
| Beauty: ★★★ | Site Privacy: ★★ |
| Spaciousness: ★★ | Quiet: ★★★ |
| Security: ★★★ | Cleanliness: ★★★ |
| Insect Control: ★★★ | Facilities: ★★★★ |

Basically a grassy parking lot inset from the woods, Breezy Meadows is surrounded by scenery more impressive than the campground itself. RV sites tend to be a little bit close together, packed in small groups in little cutouts from the woods. Still, walk a few feet away from your vehicle and you have almost picture-perfect views of Moose River and the surrounding wilderness. Though it's a fairly small campground (additional sites are planned), Breezy Meadows has a fair amount of planned activities and the amenities of a bigger campground.

**BASICS**

**Operated By:** James & Anita Matott. **Open:** May 1–Oct. 1. **Site Assignment:** Reservations accepted. **Registration:** At office. **Fee:** $17 tent, $22-27 full hookups. **Parking:** At site.

**FACILITIES**

**Number of RV Sites:** 51. **Number of Tent-Only Sites:** 0. **Hookups:** Water, electric (20, 30, 50), sewer, cable TV. **Dump Station:** Yes. **Laundry:** Yes. **Pay Phone:** Yes. **Rest Rooms and Showers:** Yes. **Fuel:** No. **Propane:** Yes. **Internal Roads:** Gravel. **RV Service:** No. **Market:** Shop 'n' Save, 129 Portland St., St. Johnsbury, VT 05819: Take a left onto Rte. 2 & follow it for 12.5 mi. **Restaurant:** Village Pizza, 124 Portland St., St. Johnsbury, VT 05819: Take a left onto Rte. 2 & follow it for 12.5 mi. **General Store:** Yes. **Vending:** Yes. **Swimming Pool:** Yes. **Playground:** Yes. **Other:** Basketball, volleyball (sand & grass), shuffleboard. **Activities:** Canoe & paddleboat rentals. **Nearby Attractions:** Maple Groves Farms, Fairbanks Museum & Planetarium, White Mountains. **Additional Information:** Call ahead.

**RESTRICTIONS**

**Pets:** Allowed. **Fires:** Allowed. **Alcoholic Beverages:** Allowed. **Vehicle Maximum Length:** Unlimited. **Other:** Ask on arrival.

**TO GET THERE**

From I-91 take Exit 19 to I-93. From I-93 take Exit 1 to Rte. 2E approximately 8 mi.

## CONCORD

## Rustic Haven Campground

1111 Main St., Concord 05824. T: (802) 695-9933; www.campsites411.com.

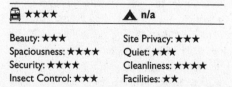

🚐 ★★★★  ⛺ n/a

| | |
|---|---|
| Beauty: ★★★ | Site Privacy: ★★★ |
| Spaciousness: ★★★★ | Quiet: ★★★ |
| Security: ★★★★ | Cleanliness: ★★★★ |
| Insect Control: ★★★ | Facilities: ★★ |

Small, but surprisingly full-service, Rustic Haven's a pretty good choice for a family that wants some amneities but doesn't want to deal with a huge park. Sites are large, grassy, and shaded by pine trees. The campground is also well-located, with stores and restaurants out-of-sight but nearby and hiking on Kirby mountain close as well. There are also fishing spots within a few minutes away.

**BASICS**

**Operated By:** The Bacon family. **Open:** May 15–Oct. 15. **Site Assignment:** Reservations accepted. **Registration:** At office. **Fee:** $18–$24. **Parking:** At site.

**FACILITIES**

**Number of RV Sites:** 38. **Number of Tent-Only Sites:** 0. **Hookups:** Water, electric, sewer. **Each Site:** Picnic table, fireplace. **Dump Station:** Yes. **Laundry:** No. **Pay Phone:** Yes. **Rest Rooms and Showers:** Yes. **Fuel:** No. **Propane:** Yes. **Internal Roads:** Paved/good condition gravel. **RV Service:** No. **Market:** Walking distance: Goodwins' Grocery, Main St. & East St. Johnsbury, VT 05838. **Restaurant:** Walking distance: Mooselook Restaurant, 1058 Main St., Concord, VT 05824. **General Store:** Yes. **Vending:** No. **Swimming Pool:** Yes. **Playground:** Yes. **Other:** Horseshoe pits, basketball, shuffleboard, volleyball. **Activities:** Hiking, fishing. **Nearby Attractions:** White Mountains, Lake Willoughby, Fairbanks Museum & Planetarium. **Additional Information:** Call ahead.

**RESTRICTIONS**

**Pets:** Allowed. **Fires:** Allowed. **Alcoholic Beverages:** Allowed. **Vehicle Maximum Length:** 60 ft. **Other:** Ask on arrival.

**TO GET THERE**

From I-91 take Exit 20, St. Johnsbury, to Rte. 2E and follow for 7 mi.

## DANVILLE

## Sugar Ridge RV Village & Campground

24 Old Stagecoach Rd., Danville 05828. T: (802) 684-2550; F: (802) 684-1006; www.sugarridgerv park.com; SugRidge@aol.com.

🚐 ★★★★                    ⛺ ★★★

Beauty: ★★★★              Site Privacy: ★★★★
Spaciousness: ★★★★        Quiet: ★★★★
Security: ★★★             Cleanliness: ★★★★
Insect Control: ★★★       Facilities: ★★★★

A new campground, Sugar Ridge is located amongst a variety of trees and has some stunning natural settings along its many hiking trails. There are secluded tent sites, and even the RV locations have good privacy, as most sites are cut out from the woods. The campground, despite its natural surroundings, does not skimp on the amenities. Everything here is top-notch and has the advantage of being barely broken in. Most sites are even modem-ready. That might be more than your average camper is looking for, but it actually makes this a place you could spend the summer, working from your RV. Reservations are a must and minimum stays apply during some busy weekends.

### BASICS

**Operated By:** Kirk Fenoss. **Open:** May 1–Oct. 31. **Site Assignment:** Reservations recommended. **Registration:** At office. **Fee:** $22.50–$29.50. **Parking:** At site.

### FACILITIES

**Number of RV Sites:** 111. **Number of Tent-Only Sites:** 0. **Hookups:** Water, electric, sewer. **Dump Station:** Yes. **Laundry:** Yes. **Pay Phone:** Yes. **Rest Rooms and Showers:** Yes. **Fuel:** No. **Propane:** Yes. **Internal Roads:** Paved/gravel. **RV Service:** No. **Market:** White Market, 78 Portland St., St. Johnsbury, VT 05819: Take a left onto Rte. 2 then a slight right onto Rte. 28 & follow it for 2.8 mi. Turn right onto Rte. 2 & follow it for 1.5 mi. **Restaurant:** Creamery Restaurant, 46 Hill St., Danville, VT 05828: Take a right onto Rte.

2 & follow it for 2.1 mi. Then take a right onto Hill St. **General Store:** Yes. **Vending:** No. **Swimming Pool:** Yes. **Playground:** Yes. **Other:** Organized activities, crafts shop, rec hall, mini-golf course, tennis, basketball, horseshoe pits, shuffleboard, sand volleyball. **Activities:** Horse-drawn carriage rides, paddle boats. **Nearby Attractions:** Summer playhouse, Santa's Village, White mountains, Harvey's Lake, Six Gun City, Rock of Ages Granite Quarry. **Additional Information:** Information and registration available online.

### RESTRICTIONS

**Pets:** Allowed. **Fires:** Allowed. **Alcoholic Beverages:** Allowed. **Vehicle Maximum Length:** Large RVs welcome (pease check ahead of time for accomodation). **Other:** 2 trailers & 2 pop-up tents available for rent.

### TO GET THERE

From I-91, Exit 21, go 4.5 mi. west on Rte. 2; the campground is a half mi. east of Danville town.

## DERBY

## Fireside Campground

Box 340, Derby 05829. T: (802) 766-5109.

🚐 ★★★                    ⛺ ★★★

Beauty: ★★★               Site Privacy: ★★★★
Spaciousness: ★★★         Quiet: ★★★
Security: ★★★             Cleanliness: ★★★★
Insect Control: ★★★       Facilities: ★★★

The best thing about Fireside Campground may very well be its proximity to the town of Derby, which has restaurants, tennis courts, a bowling alley, and more. The campsites aren't much to look at, but they're flat and at least somewhat private. There's not that much to do here. Being able to walk to town, is nice, but doesn't really make up for the lack of traditional campground activities. You are pretty close to the Canadian border and there's hiking and swimming nearby, but that's basically true for any location in Vermont. If however, you have friends in the area or want to attend a concert at the opera in Derby

Line, where the stage is in Canada and the audience sits in the U.S.

## BASICS

**Operated By:** Liz Willey. **Open:** May 15–Oct. 1. **Site Assignment:** First come, first served. **Registration:** At office. **Fee:** $14. **Parking:** At site.

## FACILITIES

**Number of RV Sites:** 24. **Number of Tent-Only Sites:** 10. **Hookups:** Water, electric, sewer. **Dump Station:** Yes. **Laundry:** No. **Pay Phone:** No. **Rest Rooms and Showers:** Yes. **Fuel:** No. **Propane:** No. **Internal Roads:** Grass/gravel. **RV Service:** No. **Market:** Derby Village Store, 483 Main St., Derby, VT 05829: Take a right onto Rte. 5 & follow it for 1.6 mi. **Restaurant:** Border Restaurant, 135 Main St., Derby, VT 05829: Take a right onto Rte. 5 & follow it for 0.9 mi. **General Store:** Right off site. **Vending:** No. **Swimming Pool:** No. **Playground:** No. **Activities:** Tennis & bowling immediately nearby. **Nearby Attractions:** Derby is within walking distance. **Additional Information:** Call ahead.

## RESTRICTIONS

**Pets:** Allowed. **Fires:** Allowed. **Alcoholic Beverages:** Allowed. **Vehicle Maximum Length:** 40 ft. **Other:** Ask on arrival.

## TO GET THERE

Take I-91 to Exit 28 and go 0.25 mi. east on Rte. 105.

## DERBY

### Char-Bo Campground

P.O. Box 438, Derby 05829. T: (802) 766-8807; charbo@together.net.

| 🚐 ★★★ | ⛺ ★★★★ |
|---|---|

| | |
|---|---|
| Beauty: ★★★★ | Site Privacy: ★★★ |
| Spaciousness: ★★★ | Quiet: ★★★ |
| Security: ★★★ | Cleanliness: ★★★★ |
| Insect Control: ★★★ | Facilities: ★★★ |

Located on top of a hill, Char-Bo offers excellent views of what seems like the entire state. You can see nearby Lake Salem, Lake Willoughby, and numerous mountains. Sites for RVs are nothing special—patches of grass with another RV close by. Tent sites are a lot better, private with trees offering shade. One oddball attraction that's basically walking distance away is the state's only elk farm.

## BASICS

**Operated By:** Private operator. **Open:** May 1–Oct. 15. **Site Assignment:** Inquire at registration. **Registration:** At office. **Fee:** $21–$23. **Parking:** At site.

## FACILITIES

**Number of RV Sites:** 33. **Number of Tent-Only Sites:** 11. **Hookups:** Water, electric, sewer. **Each Site:** Picnic table, fire ring, grill. **Dump Station:** Yes. **Laundry:** Yes. **Pay Phone:** Yes. **Rest Rooms and Showers:** Yes. **Fuel:** No. **Propane:** Yes. **Internal Roads:** Paved/gravel. **RV Service:** No. **Market:** Derby Village Store, 483 Main St., Derby, VT 05829: Take a right onto Rte. 105 & follow it until it becomes Rte. 5. Continue for 3.9 mi. **Restaurant:** Border Restaurant, 135 Main St., Derby, VT 05829: Take a right onto Rte. 105 & follow it until it becomes Rte. 5. Follow it for 3.2 mi. **General Store:** Yes. **Vending:** Yes. **Swimming Pool:** Yes. **Playground:** Yes. **Other:** Mini golf, rec hall, boat rentals. **Activities:** Swimming, boating, canoeing. **Nearby Attractions:** Green Mountains, Fairbanks Museum & Planetarium, Craftsbury. **Additional Information:** Planned activities (weekends only).

## RESTRICTIONS

**Pets:** Allowed. **Fires:** Allowed. **Alcoholic Beverages:** Allowed. **Vehicle Maximum Length:** 50 ft. **Other:** Boat, Canoe, & Paddleboat Rental.

## TO GET THERE

Take Exit 28 off I-91 and go three mi. east of Derby Center on Rte. 105.

# ENOSBURG FALLS

## Brookside Campground

680 Sand Hill Rd., Enosburg Falls 05450. T: (802) 933-4376.

🚐 ★★★　　　　▲ ★★★★

Beauty: ★★★　　　　Site Privacy: ★★★★
Spaciousness: ★★★　　Quiet: ★★★★
Security: ★★★　　　　Cleanliness: ★★★
Insect Control: ★★★　　Facilities: ★★★

This entire campground was cut out from the woods along the Bogue Brook. The sites themselves are little slivers of land where the trees have been beaten back. When making a reservation here, it's best to specify what type of site you're looking for, as there's a mix of sunny and shady as well as some that are a little more private than others. Tent campers can get even more privacy, as there are some sites that are very much set away from the action.

**BASICS**

**Operated By:** Private operator. **Open:** May 1–Oct. 1. **Site Assignment:** Reservations recommended. **Registration:** Entrance office. **Fee:** $10–$14. **Parking:** At site.

**FACILITIES**

**Number of RV Sites:** 35. **Number of Tent-Only Sites:** Unnumbered, but numerous. **Hookups:** Water, electric (20, 30), sewer. **Dump Station:** Yes. **Laundry:** Yes. **Pay Phone:** Yes. **Rest Rooms and Showers:** Yes. **Fuel:** No. **Propane:** No. **Internal Roads:** Varies. **RV Service:** No. **Market:** Uncle Floyd's, 182 Main St., Enosburg Falls, VT 05450: Take a left onto Tyler Branch Rd. & follow it for 2.9 mi. Take a right onto Rte. 108, which becomes Rte. 105. Continue 2.8 mi. **Restaurant:** Carney's Restaurant, 98 Main St., Enosburg Falls, VT 05450: Take a left onto Tyler Branch Rd. & follow it for 2.9 mi. Take a right onto Rte. 108, which becomes Rte. 105. Continue 2.5 mi. **General Store:** No. **Vending:** No. **Swimming Pool:** No. **Playground:** Yes. **Other:** Horseshoes, volleyball, **Activities:** Fishing, 2 golf courses, horseshoes. **Nearby Attractions:** Lake Champlain, historic villages, University of Ver-

mont, Fleming Museum, cruises on the *Spirit of Ethan Allen.* **Additional Information:** Call ahead.

**RESTRICTIONS**

**Pets:** Allowed. **Fires:** Allowed. **Alcoholic Beverages:** Allowed. **Vehicle Maximum Length:** Welcomes large campers. **Other:** Ask on arrival.

**TO GET THERE**

Go 0.5 mi. south across the Iron Bridge from Rte. 105, then follow signs from 108S north to Boston Post Rd. and follow signs to campground.

# FAIR HAVEN

## Half Moon Pond State Park

1621 Black Pond Rd., Fair Haven 05743. T: (802) 273-2848; www.vtstateparks.com.

🚐 ★★★★　　　　▲ ★★★★

Beauty: ★★★★★　　Site Privacy: ★★★★★
Spaciousness: ★★★★　Quiet: ★★★★
Security: ★★★★★　　Cleanliness: ★★★★★
Insect Control: ★★★　　Facilities: ★★★

If you're looking for a campground that will have you feeling like you've really gotten away, Half Moon State Park definitely fits the bill. And if the absolute stillness and remote location of the park are not reason enough to go, the pristine Half Moon Pond for which the park is named should convince you. Its beach area is an exceptional starting point for some relaxed paddling, fishing, and swimming. In addition, there is a fairly elaborate network of hiking trails accessible from within the park, which is surrounded by dense forest and is adjacent to the Bomoseen Wildlife Preserve. A string of ponds, marshlands, and abandoned quarry sites in the area are interconnected by hiking trails ranging in length from 0.3 mile to 4.5 miles. Both sides of the campground have some sites perched right on the shore of Half Moon Pond. These are the primo sites.

**BASICS**

**Operated By:** Vermont Agency of Natural Resources. **Open:** Mid-May–Columbus Day. **Site Assignment:** Reservations or first come, first served. **Registration:** At ranger station. **Fee:** $13–$17. **Parking:** At site.

## FACILITIES

**Number of RV Sites:** 60. **Number of Tent-Only Sites:** 0. **Hookups:** None. **Each Site:** Stone hearth, picnic table. **Dump Station:** Yes. **Laundry:** No. **Pay Phone:** Yes. **Rest Rooms and Showers:** Yes. **Fuel:** No. **Propane:** No. **Internal Roads:** Paved/gravel in good condition. **RV Service:** No. **Market:** No. **Restaurant:** No. **General Store:** No. **Vending:** No. **Swimming Pool:** No. **Playground:** Yes. **Other:** Boat rentals. **Activities:** Hiking, boating (no motors) limited swimming. **Nearby Attractions:** Horseback riding, Hubbardton Battlefield, Wilson Castle, Vermont Marble Exhibit, Morgan Horse Farm, Lake Champlain Ferries, Devil's Bowl Speedway, Shelburne Museum. **Additional Information:** Call ahead.

## RESTRICTIONS

**Pets:** On leash. **Fires:** In fire hearth. **Alcoholic Beverages:** Ask on arrival. **Vehicle Maximum Length:** None. **Other:** Reservations 800-658-1622 (V & MC accepted).

## TO GET THERE

Between Fair Haven and Rutland on Rte. 4, take Exit 4. Go north on Rte. 30 for 6.5 mi. Turn left on Hortonia Rd. and continue for 2 mi. Turn left on Black Pond Rd. and continue for 2 mi.

## FAIRFAX

### Maple Grove Campground

1627 Main St., Rte. 104, Fairfax 05454. T: (802) 849-6439; www.vtwebs.com/maplegrove; heyjo@together.net.

🚐 ★★★★          ⛺ ★★★★

| | |
|---|---|
| Beauty: ★★★★ | Site Privacy: ★★★★ |
| Spaciousness: ★★★ | Quiet: ★★★★ |
| Security: ★★★ | Cleanliness: ★★★★ |
| Insect Control: ★★★ | Facilities: ★★★ |

Maple Grove may be small, but it offers a surprisingly nice mix of full-service RV sites and grassy, wooded sites for tent campers. There's a fair amount of privacy for all of campers because,

though the sites are level, they are large and have enough trees to add privacy. The Lamoille River runs through the campground and canoers can actually take that all the way to Lake Champlain.

## BASICS

**Operated By:** Private operator. **Open:** May 1–Oct. 12. **Site Assignment:** At registration. **Registration:** Reservations accepted. **Fee:** $16–$22. **Parking:** At site.

## FACILITIES

**Number of RV Sites:** 26. **Number of Tent-Only Sites:** 0. **Hookups:** Water, electric (20, 50), sewer. **Each Site:** Picnic table, fireplace. **Dump Station:** Yes. **Laundry:** Yes. **Pay Phone:** Yes. **Rest Rooms and Showers:** Yes. **Fuel:** No. **Propane:** No. **Internal Roads:** Paved/gravel in good condition. **RV Service:** No. **Market:** Lyn's Market, Main St., East Fairfield, VT 05448: Take a right onto Main St. **Restaurant:** Country Pantry, 951 Main St., Fairfax, VT 05454: Take a right onto Main St. **General Store:** Yes. **Vending:** No. **Swimming Pool:** No. **Playground:** Yes. **Other:** Horseshoes, volleyball. **Activities:** Lake Champlain, Long Trail, Green Mountains. **Nearby Attractions:** Stables, fishing, mini golf. **Additional Information:** Horseshoes, games, hiking, canoeing, fishing, rafting.

## RESTRICTIONS

**Pets:** Allowed. **Fires:** Allowed. **Alcoholic Beverages:** Allowed. **Vehicle Maximum Length:** None. **Other:** Ask on arrival.

## TO GET THERE

From the north take Exit 19 off I-89 and go south on Rte. 104 for 8 mi. From the south, take Exit 18 off I-89 and go east on Rte. 104A for 5 mi. At a stop sign, go north on Rte. 104 for 1 mi.

## FRANKLIN

## Mill Pond Campground

RR No. I Box 2335 Mill Pond Rd., Franklin 05457. T: (802) 285-2240.

🚐 ★★★★　　　　　🏕 n/a

Beauty: ★★★★　　　Site Privacy: ★★★
Spaciousness: ★★★　Quiet: ★★★
Security: ★★★　　　Cleanliness: ★★★
Insect Control: ★★★　Facilities: ★★★

Leave your tent at home, this campground only serves RVs. The primary clientele at Mill Pond is families looking for access to Lake Carni, which is the prime attraction here. The busy lake offers swimming, boating, and fishing and is the focal point of a stay here. You can choose from wooded or open sites (though reservations are needed if you're picky), and the campground is better looking and quieter than your average RV park.

### BASICS

**Operated By:** Phil & Doreen LeGrand. **Open:** May 1–Oct. 1. **Site Assignment:** Reservations accepted. **Registration:** At office. **Fee:** $16–$20. **Parking:** At site.

### FACILITIES

**Number of RV Sites:** 58. **Number of Tent-Only Sites:** 0. **Hookups:** Water, electric. **Dump Station:** No. **Laundry:** No. **Pay Phone:** No. **Rest Rooms and Showers:** Yes. **Fuel:** No. **Propane:** No. **Internal Roads:** Compressed gravel. **RV Service:** No. **Market:** Sheldon Creek Market, 94 Bridge St., Sheldon, VT 05483. **Restaurant:** Lake Carmi. Snack Bar, 2395 Lake Rd., Franklin, VT 05457. **General Store:** Limited. **Vending:** No. **Swimming Pool:** Yes. **Playground:** Yes. **Other:** Volleyball, horseshoes, basketball, baseball, badminton, arcade, lounge. **Activities:** Planned activities, fishing, boating. **Nearby Attractions:** Shelburne Farms, University of Vermont, Fleming Museum, cruises on the *Spirit of Ethan Allen*. **Additional Information:** Call ahead.

### RESTRICTIONS

**Pets:** Allowed. **Fires:** Allowed. **Alcoholic Beverages:** Allowed. **Vehicle Maximum Length:** 40 ft. (sometimes varies). **Other:** Ask on arrival.

## To Get There

Go east on Rte. 105 out of St. Albans to the junction of Rte. 120, north of the small town of Franklin. Continue 4 mi. from Franklin east on Rte. 120.

## GRAND ISLE

## Champlain Adult Campground

Champlain Landing, Grand Isle 05458. T: (802) 372-5938; champlaina@aol.com.

🚐 ★★★　　　　　🏕 ★★★

Beauty: ★★★★　　　Site Privacy: ★★★★
Spaciousness: ★★★★　Quiet: ★★★★★
Security: ★★★　　　Cleanliness: ★★★★
Insect Control: ★★★　Facilities: ★★★

If you're looking for a campground that isn't overrun by hyperactive kids, this might be the place for you. Champlain requires guests to be over 18, and because of that gets a lot of retirees and guests looking to camp away from kids. Not surprisingly, the campground is very quiet and doesn't have much in the way of planned actiivities. There's a public golf course nearby as well as a dock for fishing, and you can take a swim in Lake Champlain if you want. The campground is set back from the lake with the private sites seperated by cedar trees.

### BASICS

**Operated By:** Emma & Jean Claude Guillon. **Open:** May 15–Oct. 15. **Site Assignment:** At time of registration. **Registration:** Entrance, reservations accepted. **Fee:** $18, no charge for WWI & WWII veterans. **Parking:** At site.

### FACILITIES

**Number of RV Sites:** 79. **Number of Tent-Only Sites:** 0. **Hookups:** Water, electric, sewer. **Each Site:** Picnic table, fireplace. **Dump Station:** Yes. **Laundry:** Yes. **Pay Phone:** Yes. **Rest Rooms and Showers:** Yes. **Fuel:** No. **Propane:** No. **Internal Roads:** Paved/compressed gravel. **RV Service:** No. **Market:** Less than 2 mi. away. **Restaurant:** Less than 2 mi. away **General Store:** No. **Vending:** No. **Swimming Pool:** No. **Playground:** No. **Other:** Rec hall. **Activities:** None. **Nearby Attractions:** Hyde Log Cabin

Historical Site, Shakespeare Festival, outlet center. **Additional Information:** Call ahead.

## RESTRICTIONS

**Pets:** Allowed. **Fires:** Allowed. **Alcoholic Beverages:** Allowed. **Vehicle Maximum Length:** 34 ft. **Other:** Ask on arrival.

## TO GET THERE

From I-89 take Exit 17 and follow Rte. 2 to the Lake Champlain Islands and Rte. 314. Follow Rte. 314 for 2.5 mi. to the campground.

## GRAND ISLE
## Grand Isle State Park

36 East Shore Rd. South, Grand Isle 05458. T: (802) 372-4300;
www.state.vt.us/anr/fpr/parks/htm/grandisle.html.

🚐 ★★★          ⛺ ★★★★

| | |
|---|---|
| Beauty: ★★★ | Site Privacy: ★★★ |
| Spaciousness: ★★★★ | Quiet: ★★★ |
| Security: ★★★ | Cleanliness: ★★★ |
| Insect Control: ★★★ | Facilities: ★★★★ |

Grand Isle is somewhat different than the other state parks in Connecticut. Though the sites still lack hookups, there's more going on at and around the campground than at any other state-run property in Vermont. Of course, there's also plenty of natural splendor, including a lake with boating, swimming, and fishing as well as tree-lined hiking trails. Even there, however, there's some development, as the trails have been organized into a fitness course. Grand Isle is also the only state park that has a rec hall—making it a good location for group events.

## BASICS

**Operated By:** State of Vermont. **Open:** May 15–Columbus Day. **Site Assignment:** Reservations recommended. **Registration:** Park office. **Fee:** $14–$20. **Parking:** At site.

## FACILITIES

**Number of RV Sites:** 156. **Number of Tent-Only Sites:** 0. **Hookups:** None. **Each Site:** Table, fire ring. **Dump Station:** Yes. **Laundry:** No. **Pay Phone:** Yes. **Rest Rooms and Showers:** Yes. **Fuel:** No. **Propane:** No. **Internal Roads:** Paved. **RV Service:** No. **Market:** Cumberland Bay Market, 1544 Cumberland Head Rd., Plattsburgh, NY 12901: Take a left onto Rte. 2 followed by a right onto Pearl St. & a left onto Bell Hill Rd. Bell Hill Rd. becomes Grand Isle Ferry Rte. 314 to Plattsburgh. **Restaurant:** Gus' Red Hots, 3 Cumberland Head Rd., Plattsburgh, NY 12901: Take a left onto Rte. 2 followed by a right onto Pearl St. & a left onto Bell Hill Rd. Bell Hill Rd. which becomes Grand Isle Ferry then Rte. 314 to Plattsburgh. **General Store:** No. **Vending:** Yes. **Swimming Pool:** No. **Playground:** Yes. **Other:** Rech hall, boat ramp, fitness trail. **Activities:** Activity center, fitness trail, nature walks, fishing, boat rentals. **Nearby Attractions:** Hyde Log Cabin, Shelburne Museum, State Fish Hatcherie. **Additional Information:** Call ahead.

## RESTRICTIONS

**Pets:** Yes, w/ rabies vaccination. **Fires:** Allowed. **Alcoholic Beverages:** Allowed. **Vehicle Maximum Length:** Unlimited. **Other:** Ask on arrival.

## TO GET THERE

From Grand Isle: Go 1 mi. south on US 2.

## HARDWICK
## Idle Hours Campground

P.O. Box 1053, Mackville Pond Rd., Hardwick 05843. T: (802) 472-6732;
idlehour@together.net.

🚐 ★★★          ⛺ ★★★

| | |
|---|---|
| Beauty: ★★★ | Site Privacy: ★★★★ |
| Spaciousness: ★★★★ | Quiet: ★★★★ |
| Security: ★★★★ | Cleanliness: ★★★★ |
| Insect Control: ★★★ | Facilities: ★★★ |

This small campground caters to seasonal campers, so you almost always need a reservation. Though the activities and facilities are somewhat limited, the sites are remote and hidden by trees for near total privacy. There's also Mackville Pond, which offers a nearly empty alternative to the pool, though even the pool's never that crowded. Fisherman can cast their lines on the nearby Lamoille River. Though RVs are welcome, this is an excellent place for tenters looking for a nice mix of peace and quiet along with a reasonable amount of modern convenience.

## BASICS

**Operated By:** Barb Berthiaume. **Open:** May 27–Sept. 15. **Site Assignment:** Reservations recommended. **Registration:** Entrance. **Fee:** Starts at $15. **Parking:** At site.

## FACILITIES

**Number of RV Sites:** 22. **Number of Tent-Only Sites:** 0. **Hookups:** Water, electric, sewer. **Dump Station:** Yes. **Laundry:** Yes. **Pay Phone:** Yes. **Rest Rooms and Showers:** Yes. **Fuel:** No. **Propane:** No. **Internal Roads:** Paved/gravel. **RV Service:** No. **Market:** Grand Union, Wolcott St., Hardwick, VT 05843. **Restaurant:** Egress Restaurant, 35 South Main St., Hardwick, VT 05843. **General Store:** No. **Vending:** No. **Swimming Pool:** Yes. **Playground:** Yes. **Other:** Canoeing, tubing. **Activities:** Fishing, hiking, wildlife viewing, bird-watching. **Nearby Attractions:** St. Anne Shrine, museums, galleries, Shelburne Farms & Museum. **Additional Information:** Call ahead.

## RESTRICTIONS

**Pets:** Allowed. **Fires:** Allowed. **Alcoholic Beverages:** Allowed. **Vehicle Maximum Length:** Unlimited. **Other:** Ask on arrival.

## TO GET THERE

At junction of Rtes. 14 and 15, take Rte. 14 south for 4/10 mi., turn left onto Mackville Pond Rd. and follow for 1 mi., bearing left at pond to the campground entrance

## HYDE PARK

### Common Ground Camping Resort

Hwy. 100, Box 780, Hyde Park 05655. T: (802) 888-5210.

🚐 ★★★★          ▲ n/a

Beauty: ★★               Site Privacy: ★★
Spaciousness: ★★          Quiet: ★★
Security: ★★★             Cleanliness: ★★★
Insect Control: ★★★       Facilities: ★★★★

Locacted next to a sort of mini amusement park, Common Ground offers a lot for kids to do. It's a small campground with decent sites, but the view is dominated by the go carts and other rides offered at the park. There is, however, access to the nearby Long Trail where—if you can pull the kids away—you can take long hikes. It's also possible to take a day trip up nearby Mount Mansfield. For parents, the main appeal may be that Stowe, which has nice restaurants and shops, is nearby, so they can have some grownup time while the kids play at the amusement park.

## BASICS

**Operated By:** Private operator. **Open:** May 1–Oct. 1. **Site Assignment:** Reservations recommended. **Registration:** At office. **Fee:** $18. **Parking:** At site.

## FACILITIES

**Number of RV Sites:** 20. **Number of Tent-Only Sites:** 0. **Hookups:** Water, electric, sewer. **Dump Station:** Yes. **Laundry:** No. **Pay Phone:** Yes. **Rest Rooms and Showers:** Yes. **Fuel:** No. **Propane:** No. **Internal Roads:** Compressed gravel. **RV Service:** No. **Market:** Hyde Village Market: Main St. Hyde Park, VT 05655 (802) 888-5335. **Restaurant:** Charlmont Restaurant 116 Rte. 15W, Morrisville, VT 05661. **General Store:** No. **Vending:** Yes. **Swimming Pool:** Yes. **Playground:** No. **Other:** Rec hall, mini golf, volleyball. **Activities:** Go carts. **Nearby Attractions:** Ben & Jerry's Factory, museums, galleries, Maple Festival (Spring) Hyde Park Opera House, Long Trail. **Additional Information:** Call ahead.

## RESTRICTIONS

**Pets:** Allowed. **Fires:** Allowed. **Alcoholic Beverages:** Allowed. **Vehicle Maximum Length:** Unlimited. **Other:** Ask on arrival.

## TO GET THERE

Take Rte. 15 to Rte. 100 towards Hyde Park.

## ISLAND POND

### Brighton State Park

102 State Park Road, Island Pond 05846. T: (802) 723-4360 or (800) 658-6934.

🚐 ★★          ▲ ★★★★

Beauty: ★★★★★          Site Privacy: ★★★★
Spaciousness: ★★★★          Quiet: ★★★★
Security: ★★★          Cleanliness: ★★★★★
Insect Control: ★★★          Facilities: ★★★

If you're looking for a wilderness campground, this might be the place for you. Though the actual campsites are on the edge of the woods, most of the surrounding area is rustic. There's no roads to speak of and most of the available activities center around the setting. There's even a naturalist who works at the park who can answer questions about the wildlife and trees. The small private beach only allows boats without a motor and the fishing hole offers some of the best catches in the state. The park headquarters also has a museum and a theater.

#### BASICS

**Operated By:** State of Vermont. **Open:** Oct. 15–Columbus Day. **Site Assignment:** First come, first served. **Registration:** At office. **Fee:** $13–$17. **Parking:** At site.

#### FACILITIES

**Number of RV Sites:** 63. **Number of Tent-Only Sites:** 0. **Hookups:** None. **Each Site:** Picnic table, fireplace, lean-tos at some sites. **Dump Station:** Yes. **Laundry:** No. **Pay Phone:** Yes. **Rest Rooms and Showers:** Yes. **Fuel:** No. **Propane:** No. **Internal Roads:** Paved/gravel. **RV Service:** No. **Market:** John's Market, Main St. Island Pond, VT 05846. **Restaurant:** Loon's Landing, 135 Main St. Island Pond, VT 05846. **General Store:** Snack bar in park. **Vending:** In park. **Swimming Pool:** No. **Playground:** Yes. **Other:** Horsehoes. **Activities:** Hiking trails, beach, nature museum, concession stand. **Nearby Attractions:** Fishing hole, private beach. **Additional Information:** Call ahead.

#### RESTRICTIONS

**Pets:** Allowed, w/ rabies certification. **Fires:** Allowed. **Alcoholic Beverages:** Allowed. **Vehicle Maximum Length:** None. **Other:** Ask on arrival.

#### TO GET THERE

Go 2 mi. east on Rte. 105 from Island Pond, then 0.75 mi. south on State Park Rd.

## ISLAND POND

### Lakeside Camping

1348 Rte. 105, East Brighton Rd., Island Pond 05846. T: (802) 723-6649;
www.lakesidecamping.com;
lakecamp@together.net.

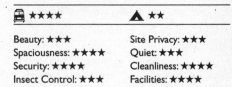

🚐 ★★★★          ▲ ★★

Beauty: ★★★          Site Privacy: ★★★
Spaciousness: ★★★★          Quiet: ★★★
Security: ★★★★          Cleanliness: ★★★★
Insect Control: ★★★          Facilities: ★★★★

Surrounded by red and white pine trees, Lakeside Campground has over 1500 feet of beach. Because of that, water-based activities dominate, but there's plenty of other things to do here, including biking and hiking. Some sites are gathered in clearings, and smaller ones are interespesed with the forest. Some larger RVs can dominate the areas they're parked in, but complete solitude in the vast forest is very close.

#### BASICS

**Operated By:** Private operator. **Open:** May 15–Sept. 12. **Site Assignment:** Reservations recommended. **Registration:** At office. **Fee:** $16–$22. **Parking:** At site.

#### FACILITIES

**Number of RV Sites:** 200. **Number of Tent-Only Sites:** 0. **Hookups:** Water, electric, sewer. **Each Site:** Picnic table, fireplace. **Dump Station:** Yes. **Laundry:** Yes. **Pay Phone:** Yes. **Rest Rooms and Showers:** Yes. **Fuel:** No. **Propane:** Yes. **Internal Roads:** Paved. **RV Service:** No. **Market:** John's Market, Main St., Island Pond, VT 05846. **Restaurant:** Cook Shack, Cross, Island

Pond,VT 05846. **General Store:** No. **Vending:** Yes. **Swimming Pool:** No. **Playground:** Yes. **Other:** Game room, boat rentals. **Activities:** Boat cruises. **Nearby Attractions:** Fairbanks Museum & Planetarium, Gramby Zoo. **Additional Information:** Call ahead.

### RESTRICTIONS

**Pets:** Allowed. **Fires:** Allowed. **Alcoholic Beverages:** Allowed. **Vehicle Maximum Length:** 40 ft. **Other:** Ask on arrival.

### TO GET THERE

Take Rte. 105 to Island Pond and go one mi.

## JEFFERSONVILLE

### Brewster River Campground

110 Campground Dr., Jeffersonville 05464. T: (802) 644-2126; wmckone@sover.net.

| 🚐 ★ | 🅰 ★★★★ |
|---|---|

| | |
|---|---|
| Beauty: ★★★★ | Site Privacy: ★★★★ |
| Spaciousness: ★★★★ | Quiet: ★★★★ |
| Security: ★★★ | Cleanliness: ★★★★ |
| Insect Control: ★★★ | Facilities: ★★ |

Almost entirely domainted by tent campers, Brewster River Campground offers a spartan outdoors experience. Most of the activity here centers around the rive, suitable for swimmers as well as small boats. There are also numerous hiking opportunities nearby, and though you're out in the woods, the town is close enough you can escape the wild if you want to.

### BASICS

**Operated By:** Private operator. **Open:** May 15–Oct. 15 (winter camping by special arrangement). **Site Assignment:** Reservations accepted. **Registration:** At office. **Fee:** $20. **Parking:** At site.

### FACILITIES

**Number of RV Sites:** 3. **Number of Tent-Only Sites:** 17. **Hookups:** Water, electric. **Each Site:** Picnic table, fireplace. **Dump Station:** No. **Laundry:** No. **Pay Phone:** No. **Rest Rooms and Showers:** Yes. **Fuel:** No. **Propane:** No. **Internal Roads:** Paved/gravel. **RV Service:** No. **Market:** Waterville Market, Rte. 109 Main St., Waterville,

VT 05492: Take a right onto Rte. 108 which becomes Rte. 15. Then, take a left back onto Rte. 108 followed by a slight left onto Rte. 109 & follow it for 3.9 mi. **Restaurant:** Diiner's Dunn at the Windridge, Main St., Jeffersonville, VT 05464: Take a right onto Rte. 108 which becomes Rte. 15. Then, take a left back onto Rte. 108 followed by a slight left onto Rte. 109. Follow it for 3.9 mi. **General Store:** No. **Vending:** No. **Swimming Pool:** No. **Playground:** No. **Activities:** Canoeing, fishing, hiking. **Nearby Attractions:** Brewster River. **Additional Information:** Call ahead.

### RESTRICTIONS

**Pets:** No (kennel nearby). **Fires:** Allowed. **Alcoholic Beverages:** Allowed. **Vehicle Maximum Length:** 18. **Other:** Ask on arrival.

### TO GET THERE

Take Rte. 108 and go 3 mi. south of Jeffersonville. The campground is opposite Burnor Rd.

## KILLINGTON

### Gifford Woods State Park

34 Gifford Woods, Killington 05761. T: (802) 775-5354 (in season) or (800) 299-3071 (Jan.–May); www.vtstateparks.com.

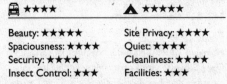

| 🚐 ★★★★ | 🅰 ★★★★★ |
|---|---|

| | |
|---|---|
| Beauty: ★★★★★ | Site Privacy: ★★★★ |
| Spaciousness: ★★★★ | Quiet: ★★★★ |
| Security: ★★★★ | Cleanliness: ★★★★ |
| Insect Control: ★★★ | Facilities: ★★★ |

As at other Vermont state parks, the site arrangement at Gifford Woods is a loosely spaced combination of tent sites and lean-tos named for trees. There are a lot more lean-tos in the lower loop than in the upper. Overall, the upper campground sites are a bit quieter than the lower sites. Perhaps the nicest aspect of Gifford Woods State Park is that you don't have to travel far outside the park, or even within the park for that matter, before you run across some hiking trails. The Appalachian Trail runs right through the park, and reconnects with the Long Trail approximately 1.5 miles north of the park, which makes it a perfectly situated spot from which to launch your adventures into the Green Mountains and the Killington area. Make sure to see the spectacular seven-acre stand of old growth hardwoods, located right across Rte. 100 from the campground. This pristine slice of wilderness has some massive sugar maple, beech, birch, and ash trees.

## BASICS

**Operated By:** Vermont Agency of Natural Resources. **Open:** Mid-May–Columbus Day. **Site Assignment:** Reservations or first come, first served. **Registration:** At ranger station. **Fee:** $11–$15. **Parking:** At site.

## FACILITIES

**Number of RV Sites:** 27. **Number of Tent-Only Sites:** 0. **Hookups:** None. **Each Site:** Fire ring or brick hearth, picnic table. **Dump Station:** Yes. **Laundry:** No. **Pay Phone:** Yes. **Rest Rooms and Showers:** Yes. **Fuel:** No. **Propane:** Yes. **Internal Roads:** Gravel. **RV Service:** No. **Market:** No. **Restaurant:** No. **General Store:** No. **Vending:** No. **Swimming Pool:** No. **Playground:** Yes. **Activities:** Hiking, fishing, wildlife viewing. **Nearby Attractions:** Killington ski gondola, Pico Alpine Slide, Vermont Marble Exhibit, Wilson's Castle, Maple Museum. **Additional Information:** Cross-country skiing is free.

## RESTRICTIONS

**Pets:** Allowed w/ rabies vaccination. **Fires:** In fire ring. **Alcoholic Beverages:** Allowed. **Vehicle Maximum Length:** 30 ft.. **Other:** 2 day min. stay for reservations.

## TO GET THERE

Gifford Woods State Park is located right off Rte. 100, just north of the access road for Killington Ski Area.

## LAKE ELMORE

### Elmore State Park

856 VT Rte. 12, Lake Elmore 05657. T: (802) 888-2982; www.state.vt.us/anr/fpr/parks/htm/elmore.html.

 ★★★           ▲ ★★★★

Beauty: ★★★★           Site Privacy: ★★★★
Spaciousness: ★★★★           Quiet: ★★★★

Security: ★★★           Cleanliness: ★★★★
Insect Control: ★★★           Facilities: ★★★★

A fairly stunning location nestled between forests and mountains, Elmore State Park gets its name from Lake Elmore. The campground sits on the lake which offers boating, swimming, and fishing. For hikers, there's Elmore mountain which offers a challenging climb to the summit as well as some easier paths for less vigorous climbs. Like most of Vermont's state parks, there are no planned activities here, but there's plenty to do as long as the weather stays nice. The sites themselves are very basic with no hookups, but some have lean-tos and they're pretty isolated from each other.

## BASICS

**Operated By:** State of Vermont. **Open:** May 15–Columbus Day. **Site Assignment:** Reservations recommended. **Registration:** At office. **Fee:** $14–$20. **Parking:** At site.

## FACILITIES

**Number of RV Sites:** 60. **Number of Tent-Only Sites:** 0. **Hookups:** None. **Each Site:** Picnic table, fire ring. **Dump Station:** Yes. **Laundry:** No. **Pay Phone:** Yes. **Rest Rooms and Showers:** Yes. **Fuel:** No. **Propane:** No. **Internal Roads:** Paved/gravel. **RV Service:** No. **Market:** Fisher Bridge Discount Grocery, 30 Munson Ave., Morrisville, VT 05661: Take a left onto Rte. 12 & follow it for 4.4 mi. **Restaurant:** House Of Pizza, Munson Ave., Morrisville, VT 05661: Take a left onto Rte. 12 & follow it for 4.4 mi. Then take a right onto Rte. 100 & a right onto Rte. 15. **General Store:** Snack bar. **Vending:** No. **Swimming Pool:** No. **Playground:** Yes. **Other:** Boat ramp, beach. **Activities:** Boat rentals. **Nearby Attractions:** Elmore Mountain. **Additional Information:** Call ahead.

## RESTRICTIONS

**Pets:** Allowed w/ rabies vaccination. **Fires:** Allowed. **Alcoholic Beverages:** Allowed. **Vehicle Maximum Length:** None. **Other:** Ask on arrival.

## TO GET THERE

Go 5 mi. south of Morrisville on Rte. 12.

## LAKESIDE

### Stillwater State Park Campground

Groton State Forest Rd., Groton 05046. T: (802) 584-3822.

🚐 ★★          ⛺ ★★★★

Beauty: ★★★★          Site Privacy: ★★★★
Spaciousness: ★★★★          Quiet: ★★★★
Security: ★★★          Cleanliness: ★★★★
Insect Control: ★★★          Facilities: ★★★

The main attraction here has to be Groton Lake, a very large body of water that offers boating, swimming, and fishing. The only problem is that the lake attracts an awful lot of daytrippers during the summer, making it very crowded. Still, the campsites are wooded and far enough away from the action to be private and quiet. People looking to escape the crowds at the beach can also canoe away to solitary areas or head off on hikes on the abundant trails nearby.

#### BASICS

**Operated By:** State of Vermont. **Open:** May 15–Oct. 15. **Site Assignment:** Reservations recommended. **Registration:** Entrance gate. **Fee:** $13. **Parking:** At site.

#### FACILITIES

**Number of RV Sites:** 62. **Number of Tent-Only Sites:** 14. **Hookups:** None. **Each Site:** Picnic table, fireplace. **Dump Station:** Yes. **Laundry:** No. **Pay Phone:** Yes. **Rest Rooms and Showers:** Yes. **Fuel:** No. **Propane:** No. **Internal Roads:** Paved/gravel. **RV Service:** No. **Market:** Forest Country Store, State Forest Boulder Beach Rd., Groton, VT 05046, (802) 584-4899. **Restaurant:** Upper Valley Grill, 629 Scott Hwy, Groton, VT 05046. **General Store:** Snack bar. **Vending:** No. **Swimming Pool:** No. **Playground:** Yes. **Other:** Boat ramp. **Activities:** Swimming, canoeing, hiking. **Nearby Attractions:** Trails. **Additional Information:** Call ahead.

#### RESTRICTIONS

**Pets:** Yes, on leash. **Fires:** Allowed. **Alcoholic Beverages:** Allowed. **Vehicle Maximum Length:** None. **Other:** Ask on arrival.

#### TO GET THERE

Go 12 mi. west on US Rte. 302, 6 mi. north on Rte. 232 and 0.5 mi. east on Boulder Beach Rd.

## MAIDSTONE

### Maidstone State Park Campground

4858 Maidstone Lake Rd., Maidstone 05905. T: (802) 676-3930.

🚐 ★★          ⛺ ★★★★

Beauty: ★★★          Site Privacy: ★★★★
Spaciousness: ★★★★          Quiet: ★★★★
Security: ★★★          Cleanliness: ★★★★
Insect Control: ★★★          Facilities: ★★★

Situated next to the enormous Maidstone Lake, this campground's prime attraction is water sports. There's incredible fishing, boat rentals are available, and the swimming is excellent. Most of the campsites are right off the water, which offers a nice view, but that can be a mixed blessing since during the day the public nature of the beach makes it a little noisy. The campground is surrounded by thick forest which offers hiking as well as some mountain biking opportunies.

#### BASICS

**Operated By:** State of Vermont. **Open:** May 15–Labor Day. **Site Assignment:** Reservations accepted. **Registration:** Entrance gate. **Fee:** $13. **Parking:** At site.

#### FACILITIES

**Number of RV Sites:** 45. **Number of Tent-Only Sites:** 37. **Hookups:** None. **Each Site:** Picnic table, fireplace. **Dump Station:** Yes. **Laundry:** No. **Pay Phone:** No. **Rest Rooms and Showers:** No. **Fuel:** No. **Propane:** No. **Internal Roads:** Paved/gravel. **RV Service:** No. **Market:** Blue Mountain Variety: 892 US Rte. 3 North Stratford, NH 03590. **Restaurant:** Mountain's Restaurant: State Rte. 3, North Stratford, NH 03590. **General Store:** No. **Vending:** No. **Swimming Pool:** No. **Playground:** Yes. **Other:** Boat rentals. **Activities:** Mountain biking. **Nearby Attractions:** Trails. **Additional Information:** Call ahead.

## RESTRICTIONS

**Pets:** Yes, on leash. **Fires:** Allowed. **Alcoholic Beverages:** Allowed. **Vehicle Maximum Length:** None. **Other:** Ask on arrival.

## TO GET THERE

Take Rte. 102 to State Forest Hwy.

## MARSHFIELD

### Covenant Hills Christian Camp

Town Rd. 49, Marshfield 05658. T: (802) 426-3340.

| | |
|---|---|
| Beauty: ★★★★ | Site Privacy: ★★★ |
| Spaciousness: ★★★ | Quiet: ★★★★ |
| Security: ★★★★ | Cleanliness: ★★★★★ |
| Insect Control: ★★★ | Facilities: ★★★★ |

Obviously a specialty campground, Covenant Hills Christian Camp caters to religious group retreats. Though no attempt is made to convert visitors of differing religious persuasions, this is obviously not the place to go if you're simply looking for a place to sleep. For those interested in a Christian setting, however, the campground is beautiful. The retreat center also rents motel-style rooms for those seeking a less rustic experience.

## BASICS

**Operated By:** Troy Conference of the United Methodist Church. **Open:** Year-round. **Site Assignment:** Reservations required. **Registration:** Main lodge. **Fee:** Varies. **Parking:** At main lodge.

## FACILITIES

**Number of RV Sites:** Unspecified. **Number of Tent-Only Sites:** Unspecified, but numerous. **Hookups:** None. **Dump Station:** Yes. **Laundry:** Yes. **Pay Phone:** Yes. **Rest Rooms and Showers:** Yes. **Fuel:** No. **Propane:** No. **Internal Roads:** Dirt. **RV Service:** No. **Market:** Marshfield Village Store, 1425 US Rte. 2, Marshfield, VT 05658. **Restaurant:** On site. **General Store:** No. **Vending:** No. **Swimming Pool:** No. **Playground:** No. **Other:** Retreat center. **Activities:** Group activities. **Additional Information:** Call ahead.

## RESTRICTIONS

**Pets:** Allowed. **Fires:** Allowed. **Alcoholic Beverages:** No. **Vehicle Maximum Length:** None. **Other:** Ask on arrival.

## TO GET THERE

Located 20 mi. east of Montpelier on US Rte. 2, near the village of South Cabot, about 2 mi. east of Marshfield Dam (Molly's Falls Pond on some maps). Hwy. signs mark the turn onto Houghton Rd. Follow that road 0.8 of a mi., past a sharp left curve, and the camp entrance will be on the right. Signs are posted.

## MARSHFIELD

### Kettle Pond State Park

4239 VT Rte. 232, Marshfield, Marshfield 05658. T: (802) 426-3042; www.state.vt.us/anr/fpr/parks/htm/groton/ketlpond.htm.html.

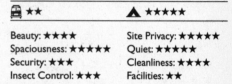

| | |
|---|---|
| Beauty: ★★★★ | Site Privacy: ★★★★★ |
| Spaciousness: ★★★★★ | Quiet: ★★★★★ |
| Security: ★★★ | Cleanliness: ★★★★ |
| Insect Control: ★★★ | Facilities: ★★ |

Located in an enormous state park, the campground at Kettle Pond will accomodate RVs, but the best sites are for tent campers. RVers basically get a place to park, but sites are private and the secenery is impressive. For tenters, there's a handful of remote sites that can give you total privacy. This is not a campground for people looking for a lot of activities. The facilities are sparse and the main draws are the pond, hiking trails, and wildlife.

## BASICS

**Operated By:** State of Vermont. **Open:** May 15–Columbus Day. **Site Assignment:** Reservations accepted. **Registration:** Entrance station. **Fee:** $4/person. **Parking:** At site.

## FACILITIES

**Number of RV Sites:** 27. **Number of Tent-Only Sites:** 6. **Hookups:** None. **Each Site:** Lean-tos. **Dump Station:** No. **Laundry:** No. **Pay Phone:** No. **Rest Rooms and Showers:** No.

**Fuel:** No. **Propane:** No. **Internal Roads:** Paved/gravel. **RV Service:** No. **Market:** Marshfield Village Store, 1425 US Rte. 2, Marshfield, VT 05658. **Restaurant:** River Run Restaurant, 3 Main St., Plainfield, VT 05667. **General Store:** No. **Vending:** No. **Swimming Pool:** No. **Playground:** Yes. **Other:** Pond. **Activities:** Boating, swimming, hiking. **Nearby Attractions:** Trails. **Additional Information:** Call ahead.

## RESTRICTIONS

**Pets:** Allowed. **Fires:** Allowed. **Alcoholic Beverages:** Allowed. **Vehicle Maximum Length:** None. **Other:** Ask on arrival.

## TO GET THERE

From Groton, go 2 mi. west on U.S. 302, then 7.5 mi, northwest on Rte. 232.

## MIDDLEBURY

### Falls of Lana Campground

RR 4, Box 1260, Middlebury 05753. T: (802) 388-4362.

| 🚐 n/a | ⛺ ★★★★ |
|---|---|
| Beauty: ★★★★ | Site Privacy: ★★★★ |
| Spaciousness: ★★★★★ | Quiet: ★★★★★ |
| Security: ★★★ | Cleanliness: ★★★★ |
| Insect Control: ★★★ | Facilities: ★ |

These wooded, secluded sites serve as a base camp for hikers. You can pitch your tent and then set off on day trips over a variety of hiking trails. There's also easy access to Silver Lake, which has swimming and fishing as well as a picnic area. There's absolutely nothing here in terms of facilities, so you'll only want to visit if you're looking to truly "rough it" and spend the day hiking.

## BASICS

**Operated By:** State of Vermont. **Open:** May 15–Oct. 1. **Site Assignment:** First come, first served. **Registration:** Camp entrance. **Fee:** None. **Parking:** At site.

## FACILITIES

**Number of RV Sites:** 0. **Number of Tent-Only Sites:** Unspecified, but numerous. **Hookups:** None. **Dump Station:** No. **Laundry:** No. **Pay Phone:** No. **Rest Rooms and Showers:** Out-

house. **Fuel:** No. **Propane:** No. **Internal Roads:** Paved/compressed gravel. **RV Service:** No. **Market:** A&P: 260 Court St. Middlebury, VT 05753, (802) 388-9028. **Restaurant:** A&W Family Restaurant 1557 Rte. 7 S. Middlebury, VT 05753. **General Store:** No. **Vending:** No. **Swimming Pool:** No. **Playground:** No. **Activities:** None. **Nearby Attractions:** Shops in Middlebury. **Additional Information:** Call ahead.

## RESTRICTIONS

**Pets:** Allowed. **Fires:** Allowed. **Alcoholic Beverages:** Allowed. **Vehicle Maximum Length:** 30 ft. **Other:** Ask on arrival.

## TO GET THERE

Take Rte. 7 to Rte. 125. Turn onto Rte. 32 and follow signs to the Mount Moosalamoo parking area. Go past the parking area and continue to Rte. 27 then follow signs to campgrounds.

## MIDDLEBURY

### Mount Moosalamoo Campground

RR 4, Box 1260, Middlebury 05753. T: (802) 388-4362.

| 🚐 n/a | ⛺ ★★★★★ |
|---|---|
| Beauty: ★★★★★ | Site Privacy: ★★★★★ |
| Spaciousness: ★★★★★ | Quiet: ★★★★★ |
| Security: ★★★★ | Cleanliness: ★★★★★ |
| Insect Control: ★★★ | Facilities: ★ |

If you're looking for absolutely no frills camping, that's what you'll get at Mount Moosalamoo Campground. The "sites" are basically just areas to pitch a tent in between hikes. There's little else to do here excpet hike, but if that's what you're after, the opportunities are endless. This is not a camping area for young kids as there's very little around. Even adults coming here will want to be careful, as it's easy to get lost and, if you get hurt, there's no one to rescue you.

## BASICS

**Operated By:** State of Vermont. **Open:** May 15–Oct. 15. **Site Assignment:** First come, first served. **Registration:** Entrance gate. **Fee:** $5. **Parking:** At site.

## FACILITIES

**Number of RV Sites:** 2. **Number of Tent-Only Sites:** 17. **Hookups:** None. **Dump Station:** No. **Laundry:** No. **Pay Phone:** No. **Rest Rooms and Showers:** Outhouse. **Fuel:** No. **Propane:** No. **Internal Roads:** Paved/compressed gravel. **RV Service:** No. **Market:** A&P: 260 Court St. Middlebury, VT 05753, (802) 388-9028. **Restaurant:** A&W Family Restaurant 1557 Rte. 7 S. Middlebury, VT 05753. **General Store:** No. **Vending:** No. **Swimming Pool:** No. **Playground:** No. **Activities:** Hiking. **Nearby Attractions:** Shops in Middlebury. **Additional Information:** Call ahead.

## RESTRICTIONS

**Pets:** Allowed. **Fires:** Allowed. **Alcoholic Beverages:** Allowed. **Vehicle Maximum Length:** 30 ft. **Other:** Ask on arrival.

## TO GET THERE

Take Rte. 7 to Rte. 125. Turn onto Rte. 32 and follow the signs.

## MILTON

### Homestead Campground

864 Ethan Allen Hwy., Milton 05468. T: (802) 524-2356; heyjo@together.net.

🚐 ★★★          ⛺ ★★★

Beauty: ★★★          Site Privacy: ★★★
Spaciousness: ★★★     Quiet: ★★★
Security: ★★★          Cleanliness: ★★★★
Insect Control: ★★★    Facilities: ★★★★

A campground aimed at families, Homestead offers sites that are level and grassy but packed pretty close together. The main draws here are the planned activities and the fact that there's a lot for kids to do. There's also a flea market on some weekends as well as bingo and wagon rides. Though it's close to Lake Champlain and other outdoor sites, the actual campground is nothing much to look at, but with a mini golf and go-karts facility across the street, there's plenty to keep the kids busy.

## BASICS

**Operated By:** Joe & Sue Monty. **Open:** May 1–Oct. 15. **Site Assignment:** Reservations

accepted. **Registration:** At office. **Fee:** Starts at $21 per night. **Parking:** At site.

## FACILITIES

**Number of RV Sites:** 150. **Number of Tent-Only Sites:** 0. **Hookups:** Water, electric, sewer, cable TV. **Dump Station:** Yes. **Laundry:** Yes. **Pay Phone:** Yes. **Rest Rooms and Showers:** Yes. **Fuel:** No. **Propane:** Yes. **Internal Roads:** Paved/gravel. **RV Service:** No. **Market:** Middle Rd. Market, 69 Middle Rd., Milton, VT 05468: Take a left onto Rte. 7 & go 5.6 mi. **Restaurant:** Lucky Wok, 170 Rte. 7 S, Milton, VT 05468: Take a left onto Rte. 7 & go 5.1 mi. **General Store:** Yes. **Vending:** No. **Swimming Pool:** Yes. **Playground:** Yes. **Other:** Shuffleboard. **Activities:** Planned activities. **Nearby Attractions:** Mini golf, go-carts, & snackbar across the street. **Additional Information:** Call ahead.

## RESTRICTIONS

**Pets:** Allowed. **Fires:** Allowed. **Alcoholic Beverages:** Allowed. **Vehicle Maximum Length:** None. **Other:** Ask on arrival.

## TO GET THERE

From Exit 18 on I-89, go 0.25 mi. south on Rte. 7.

## MORRISVILLE

### Mountain View Campground & Cabins

3154 Rte. 15E, Morrisville 05661. T: (802) 888-2178.

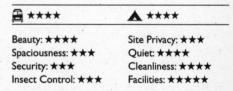

🚐 ★★★★          ⛺ ★★★★

Beauty: ★★★★          Site Privacy: ★★★
Spaciousness: ★★★      Quiet: ★★★★
Security: ★★★           Cleanliness: ★★★★
Insect Control: ★★★     Facilities: ★★★★★

One of the best campgrounds in New England for its size, Mountain View offers a rural location with all the trimmings. In addition to the mountain views that gave the campground its name, there's also the Lamoille River and Bugbee Brook. The tent sites are along the brook, which offers excellent fishing, and the wooded RV sites are closer to the river. This campground has a rare mix of natural beauty and top-notch facilities, with a heated pool, hot tub, and mini golf. If you're looking for nature, the river offers days worth of canoeing.

## BASICS

**Operated By:** The Marceau family. **Open:** June 6–Oct. 15. **Site Assignment:** Reservations accepted. **Registration:** At office. **Fee:** Starts at $22. **Parking:** At site.

## FACILITIES

**Number of RV Sites:** 43. **Number of Tent-Only Sites:** 10. **Hookups:** Water, electric, sewer. **Each Site:** Picnic table, fire ring. **Dump Station:** Yes. **Laundry:** No. **Pay Phone:** Yes. **Rest Rooms and Showers:** Yes. **Fuel:** No. **Propane:** No. **Internal Roads:** Paved. **RV Service:** No. **Market:** Fisher Bridge Discount Grocery, 30 Munson Ave., Morrisville, VT 05661: Take a right onto Rte. 100 & follow it for 1 mi. until it becomes Rte. 12. **Restaurant:** On site. **General Store:** Snack bar. **Vending:** Yes. **Swimming Pool:** Yes. **Playground:** Yes. **Other:** Pavillion, mini golf, jacuzzi. **Activities:** None. **Nearby Attractions:** Alpine slide. **Additional Information:** Call ahead.

## RESTRICTIONS

**Pets:** Allowed. **Fires:** Allowed. **Alcoholic Beverages:** Allowed. **Vehicle Maximum Length:** 40 ft. **Other:** Ask on arrival.

## TO GET THERE

From I-89 take Exit 10 to Rte. 100 and follow it to the junction for Rte. 15. Take a right onto Rte. 15 and continue for 3 mi.

## NEWPORT

### Prouty Beach Campground

Veterans Ave., Newport 05855. T: (802) 334-7951.

🚐 ★★★★          ▲ ★★★

| | |
|---|---|
| Beauty: ★★★★ | Site Privacy: ★★★★ |
| Spaciousness: ★★★★ | Quiet: ★★★★ |
| Security: ★★★ | Cleanliness: ★★★★ |
| Insect Control: ★★★ | Facilities: ★★★★ |

Located along Lake Memphremagog, Prouty Beach Campground offers tremendous fishing. The lake, unfortuantely, can attract quite a crowd, so you won't be casting your line in solitude. But, it's a big body of water, so you might be able to find a quiet spot. The campground offers a lot of facilities without feeling over developed, and sites are fairly large. The big problem you'll find here is crowds at that the public beach, but this might be an ideal spot for families looking for a nice campground with lots to do that's not a barren summer camp.

## BASICS

**Operated By:** Private operator. **Open:** May 15–Oct. 15. **Site Assignment:** Reservations recommended. **Registration:** At office. **Fee:** $20. **Parking:** At site.

## FACILITIES

**Number of RV Sites:** 50. **Number of Tent-Only Sites:** 0. **Hookups:** Water, electric, sewer. **Each Site:** Fire ring, grill, picnic table. **Dump Station:** Yes. **Laundry:** Yes. **Pay Phone:** Yes. **Rest Rooms and Showers:** Yes. **Fuel:** No. **Propane:** No. **Internal Roads:** Paved/gravel. **RV Service:** No. **Market:** East Main Mini Market: 477 East Main St. Newport, VT 05855 (802) 334-8460. **Restaurant:** Brown Cow: 350 East Main St. Newport, VT 05855 (802) 334-7887. **General Store:** Limited. **Vending:** No. **Swimming Pool:** No. **Playground:** Yes. **Other:** Tennis courts, sports field, volleyball courts. **Activities:** Swimming, fishing. **Additional Information:** Call ahead.

## RESTRICTIONS

**Pets:** Allowed. **Fires:** Allowed. **Alcoholic Beverages:** Allowed. **Vehicle Maximum Length:** 40 ft. **Other:** Ask on arrival.

## TO GET THERE

Take I-91 to Rte. 191 and go 3 mi. then take a left onto Freeman followed by a left onto Veterans.

## NORTH HERO

## Kings Bay Campground

1088 Lakeview Dr., North Hero 05474. T: (802) 372-3735.

🚐 ★★★                 ▲ ★★★★

Beauty: ★★★★          Site Privacy: ★★★
Spaciousness: ★★★★    Quiet: ★★★★
Security: ★★★          Cleanliness: ★★★
Insect Control: ★★★    Facilities: ★★

Another campground dominated by seasonal campers, you'll want to make a reseration if you plan to stay here. That might be worth doing, however, as the lakeside sites are shaded and the view can spectacular. To the east you can see the Cold Hollow Mountains, which go all the way into Canada. There's plenty of hiking opportunities as well as fishing.

### BASICS

**Operated By:** Bud Knapp. **Open:** May 15–Sept. 15. **Site Assignment:** Reservations recommended. **Registration:** At office. **Fee:** $15–$18. **Parking:** At site.

### FACILITIES

**Number of RV Sites:** 40. **Number of Tent-Only Sites:** 0. **Hookups:** Water, electric (20), sewer. **Dump Station:** No. **Laundry:** No. **Pay Phone:** No. **Rest Rooms and Showers:** No. **Fuel:** No. **Propane:** No. **Internal Roads:** Compressed gravel. **RV Service:** No. **Market:** Grand Union Co, 39 1st St., Swanton, VT 05488: Take a left onto Lakeview Dr. followed by a right onto Bridge Rd. & a right onto Rte. 2. Continue 5.8 mi. & take a right onto Rte. 78 & follow it for 10.1 mi. then follow Rte. 78 by taking a right then a left. **Restaurant:** River View Dining & Spirits, 5 Merchants Row, Swanton, VT 05488: Take a left onto Lakeview Dr. followed by a right onto Bridge Rd. & a right onto Rte. 2. Continue 5.8 mi. & take a right onto Rte. 78 & follow it for 10.1 mi. **General Store:** No. **Vending:** No. **Swimming Pool:** No. **Playground:** No. **Activities:** None. **Nearby Attractions:** Cold Hollow Mountains. **Additional Information:** Call ahead.

### RESTRICTIONS

**Pets:** Allowed. **Fires:** Allowed. **Alcoholic Beverages:** Allowed. **Vehicle Maximum Length:** 40 ft. **Other:** Ask on arrival.

### TO GET THERE

From North Hero got north on Rte. 2 for 3.3 mi., then take a right onto Lakeview Dr. and go 1 mi.

## ORLEANS

## White Caps Campground

5659 VT Rte. 5A, Orleans 05860. T: (802) 467-3345.

🚐 ★★★★                ▲ ★★★

Beauty: ★★★★          Site Privacy: ★★★
Spaciousness: ★★★      Quiet: ★★★★
Security: ★★★          Cleanliness: ★★★★
Insect Control: ★★★    Facilities: ★★★

A small campground that's built around its access to Lake Willoughby, White Caps has the feel of a small lakeside community. Perhaps that's because though campers do interact with each other, there aren't a lot of planned activities, making for more of an individual trip in a friendly environment. The location is nearly perfect, as the lake offers, fishing, swimming, boating and anything else that can be done on water, while nearby mountains Pisgah and Hor offer hiking for all ability levels. This is an excellent place to take an active vacation, though you could also spend your time just relaxing in front of the lake staring off into the mountains.

### BASICS

**Operated By:** John & Kathleen Binks. **Open:** May 15–Sept. 15. **Site Assignment:** Reservations accepted. **Registration:** At office. **Fee:** $17–$20. **Parking:** At site.

### FACILITIES

**Number of RV Sites:** 35. **Number of Tent-Only Sites:** 15. **Hookups:** Water, electric, sewer. **Each Site:** Picnic tables, fireplace. **Dump Station:** Yes. **Laundry:** Yes. **Pay Phone:** Yes. **Rest Rooms and Showers:** Yes. **Fuel:** No. **Propane:** Yes. **Internal Roads:** Paved/gravel. **RV Service:**

No. **Market:** Cole's Markets, 52 Main St., Orleans, VT 05860: Take a right onto Rte. 58 & follow it for 0.4 mi. **Restaurant:** 3556 School-house Rd., Orleans, VT 05860: Take a right onto Rte. 58 to Orleans. **General Store:** Yes. **Vending:** Yes. **Swimming Pool:** No. **Playground:** No. **Other:** Lake access, hiking trails. **Activities:** Water-based activities. **Nearby Attractions:** Lake Willoughby. **Additional Information:** Call ahead.

## RESTRICTIONS

**Pets:** Allowed. **Fires:** Allowed. **Alcoholic Beverages:** Allowed. **Vehicle Maximum Length:** 40 ft. **Other:** Ask on arrival.

## TO GET THERE

Take I-91 to Exit 23 and follow Rte. 5 north to West Burke, then Rte. 5A for 6 mi.

## PLAINFIELD

## Onion River Campground

RD 1, Box 205, Plainfield 05667. T: (802) 426-3232.

🚐 ★★★                      ▲ n/a

Beauty: ★★★            Site Privacy: ★★★
Spaciousness: ★★★      Quiet: ★★★
Security: ★★★          Cleanliness: ★★★
Insect Control: ★★★    Facilities: ★★★★

With sites lining the water's edge, this is a true fisherman's paradise. You can basically cast your line from your site, and the Winooski River has a nice selection of fish waiting to be caught. The River also has some excellent swimming areas and can be paddled by canoe. The campground is also next to Groton State Forest, which offers easy access to hiking and has mountain bike trails.

## BASICS

**Operated By:** Private operator. **Open:** Apr. 10–Nov. 20. **Site Assignment:** Reservations recommended. **Registration:** At office. **Fee:** $15. **Parking:** At site.

## FACILITIES

**Number of RV Sites:** 48. **Number of Tent-Only Sites:** 0. **Hookups:** Water, electric, sewer. **Each Site:** Picnic table, fire ring, grill. **Dump Sta-**

tion: Yes. **Laundry:** Yes. **Pay Phone:** Yes. **Rest Rooms and Showers:** Yes. **Fuel:** No. **Propane:** Yes. **Internal Roads:** Paved. **RV Service:** No. **Market:** Plainfield Red Store: 230 High St., Plainfield, VT 05667 (802) 454-7886: Take a right onto Brook Rd. followed by a left onto Main St. & a left onto Rte. 2. **Restaurant:** River Run Restaurant, 3 Main St., Plainfield, VT 05667: Take a right onto Brook Rd. followed by a left onto Main St. & a right onto Rte. 2. **General Store:** Limited. **Vending:** No. **Swimming Pool:** No. **Playground:** No. **Other:** Horshoes, badminton, volleyball. **Activities:** Fishing. **Nearby Attractions:** Groton State Forest. **Additional Information:** Call ahead.

## RESTRICTIONS

**Pets:** Allowed. **Fires:** Allowed. **Alcoholic Beverages:** Allowed. **Vehicle Maximum Length:** 40 ft. **Other:** Ask on arrival.

## TO GET THERE

Take Rte.14 to Rte. 2E and follow it for about 5 mi.

## PONWAL

## Pine Hollow Campground

RR 1, Box 343, Ponwal 05261. T: (802) 823-5569.

🚐 ★★★★                    ▲ ★★★

Beauty: ★★★            Site Privacy: ★★★
Spaciousness: ★★       Quiet: ★★★
Security: ★★★★         Cleanliness: ★★★★
Insect Control: ★★★    Facilities: ★★★★

Nature provides the prime attraction at Pine Hollow, which is built around a pond. Though the actual campground is nothing special, with fairly crowded sites and lots of RVs dotting the landscape, the surrounding area is excellent. The main attraction has to be the Long Trail, 265 miles of hiking that offers nearly endless exploration options. There's also lots of fish to be caught in the pond, which also allows swimming and non-motorized boating. Tent campers might wish for a bit more seperation from the RVs, but there's an endless amount of space once you get a little bit away from your actual campsite.

## BASICS

**Operated By:** Ronald & Rachel Lauzon. **Open:** May 15–Oct. 15. **Site Assignment:** Reservations accepted. **Registration:** At office. **Fee:** $14–$18. **Parking:** At site.

## FACILITIES

**Number of RV Sites:** 50. **Number of Tent-Only Sites:** 0. **Hookups:** Water, electric, sewer, cable TV. **Each Site:** Picnic table, fire ring. **Dump Station:** Yes. **Laundry:** No. **Pay Phone:** Yes. **Rest Rooms and Showers:** Yes. **Fuel:** No. **Propane:** No. **Internal Roads:** Paved/gravel. **RV Service:** No. **Market:** Winchester's Store, Rte. 7, Pownal, VT 05261. **Restaurant:** Jaeger House, Rte. 7, Pownal, VT 05261. **General Store:** No. **Vending:** No. **Swimming Pool:** No. **Playground:** Yes. **Other:** Rec hall, badminton, sports field, volleyball, pond. **Activities:** Swimming, boating. **Nearby Attractions:** Long Trail. **Additional Information:** Call ahead.

## RESTRICTIONS

**Pets:** Yes, on leash. **Fires:** Allowed. **Alcoholic Beverages:** Allowed. **Vehicle Maximum Length:** 60 ft. **Other:** Ask on arrival.

## TO GET THERE

Take Rte. 9 to Rte. 7 and go 7.5 mi. to Barbers Pond Rd. Turn right on Old Military Rd. and follow it to the campground

## POULTNEY

### Lake St. Catherine State Park

RD 2 Box 1775, Poultney 05764. T: (802) 287-9158 or (800) 658-1622; www.vtstateparks.com.

🚐 ★★★★          ▲ ★★★★

Beauty: ★★★★
Spaciousness: ★★★★
Security: ★★★
Insect Control: ★★★
Site Privacy: ★★★★
Quiet: ★★★★
Cleanliness: ★★★
Facilities: ★★★

Lake St. Catherine is a good example of the powerful combination of woods and water. The day-use area and the beachfront on the lake draw a lot of people on those hot summer days. A few sites worth noting, for various reasons, include sites 1 and 2, which are right across from one of the bathroom buildings, and site 35, which is one of the most secluded, set within a dense grove of conifers. There is an open grassy area leading in to sites 38 and 39, which makes them suitable for larger groups or for parking a boat trailer. Site 47 is a huge site, set along the side of another small grassy field area, which would make a perfect spot for a volleyball net.

## BASICS

**Operated By:** Vermont Agency of Natural Resources. **Open:** Mid-May–Columbus Day. **Site Assignment:** Reservations or first come first served. **Registration:** At ranger station. **Fee:** $13–$17. **Parking:** At site.

## FACILITIES

**Number of RV Sites:** 51. **Number of Tent-Only Sites:** 0. **Hookups:** None. **Each Site:** Stone hearth, picnic table. **Dump Station:** Yes. **Laundry:** No. **Pay Phone:** Yes. **Rest Rooms and Showers:** Yes. **Fuel:** No. **Propane:** No. **Internal Roads:** Paved/gravel. **RV Service:** No. **Market:** No. **Restaurant:** Snack bar. **General Store:** No. **Vending:** No. **Swimming Pool:** No. **Playground:** Yes. **Activities:** None. **Nearby Attractions:** Equinox Mountain Dr. (Manchester) Wilson's Castle, Vermont Marble Exhibit, Hildene, Bennington Monument & Museum, Orvis. **Additional Information:** Call ahead.

## RESTRICTIONS

**Pets:** On leash. **Fires:** In fire hearth. **Alcoholic Beverages:** Ask on arrival. **Vehicle Maximum Length:** Unlimited. **Other:** Ask on arrival.

## TO GET THERE

From Poultney, go 3 mi. south on Hwy. 30.

## RANDOLPH

### Mobile Acres Trailer Park

Hwy. 12A, Randolph 05060. T: (802) 728-5548.

🚐 ★★★★          ▲ ★★

Beauty: ★★
Spaciousness: ★★
Security: ★★★
Insect Control: ★★★
Site Privacy: ★★★
Quiet: ★★★
Cleanliness: ★★★
Facilities: ★★★

Technically, tent camping is allowed here, but it's impossible to imagine anyone setting up a tent here. With all the RVs tightly packed, it would be a little like camping in a parking lot. Of course, for RVers looking for a friendly community to spend some time in, the park offers full hookups and sites with picnic tables and fire rings (features that do make the park more tent camper–friendly). There are plenty of organized activities, and sometimes impromptu games on the sports field.

## BASICS

**Operated By:** Private operator. **Open:** May 15–Oct. 15. **Site Assignment:** Reservations recommended. **Registration:** Entrance. **Fee:** $18. **Parking:** At site.

## FACILITIES

**Number of RV Sites:** 94. **Number of Tent-Only Sites:** 0. **Hookups:** Water, electric, sewer. **Each Site:** Picnic table, fire ring. **Dump Station:** Yes. **Laundry:** Yes. **Pay Phone:** Yes. **Rest Rooms and Showers:** Yes. **Fuel:** No. **Propane:** Yes. **Internal Roads:** Paved/gravel. **RV Service:** No. **Market:** Grand Union Co., 12 North Main St., Randolph, VT 05060: Take a left onto Braintree Hill Rd. followed by a left onto Rte. 12A & a right onto Rte. 12. **Restaurant:** China Jade, 17 South Main St., Randolph, VT 05060: Take a left onto Braintree Hill Rd. followed by a left onto Rte. 12A & a right onto Rte. 12. **General Store:** No. **Vending:** Yes. **Swimming Pool:** Yes. **Playground:** Yes. **Other:** Sports field, horshoe pit. **Activities:** Lots of organized activities. **Additional Information:** Call ahead.

## RESTRICTIONS

**Pets:** Allowed. **Fires:** Allowed. **Alcoholic Beverages:** Allowed. **Vehicle Maximum Length:** 35 ft. **Other:** Ask on arrival.

## TO GET THERE

From I-89, take Exit 4 to Rte. 66 and go 5 miles west, looking for the campground entrance on the left.

## ROCHESTER
## Mountain Trails Camping Area

1375 Quarry Rd., Rochester 05767. T: (802) 767-3352; www.campusa.com/framemountain trails.cfm.

🚐 ★★★          ⛺ ★★★

Beauty: ★★★★          Site Privacy: ★★★
Spaciousness: ★★★          Quiet: ★★★★
Security: ★★★          Cleanliness: ★★★
Insect Control: ★★★          Facilities: ★★

This is about as basic as camping gets. Though there are hookups for the RV sites, there's not much else here. There's no pool, lake, or stream, and not much to do. The tent sites are fairly wooded and secluded, but primary reason campers use it as a base camp. If you're looking to fish, the White River is nearby, and there's hunting in-season throughout the area. Hikers can also trek from the campground up Mount Cushman, which can be a challenging climb.

## BASICS

**Operated By:** Private operator. **Open:** May 1–Nov. 30. **Site Assignment:** At time of registration. **Registration:** Reservations required. **Fee:** $12–$15. **Parking:** At site.

## FACILITIES

**Number of RV Sites:** 10. **Number of Tent-Only Sites:** 15. **Hookups:** Water, electric, sewer. **Each Site:** Picnic table, fireplace. **Dump Station:** Yes. **Laundry:** No. **Pay Phone:** No. **Rest Rooms and Showers:** Yes. **Fuel:** No. **Propane:** No. **Internal Roads:** Paved/gravel. **RV Service:** No. **Market:** Store of Rochester: Rte. 100, Rochester, VT 05767, (802) 767-3181. **Restaurant:** Huntington House Inn: 1806 East Park St. Rochester, VT 05767. **General Store:** No. **Vending:** No. **Swimming Pool:** No. **Playground:** Yes. **Other:** Horseshoes, badminton. **Activities:** Hiking, fishing. **Nearby Attractions:** Rochester. **Additional Information:** Call ahead.

**TO GET THERE**

Take I-89 to Rte. 107 and continue west to Rte. 100. Follow Rte. 100 north for 2.75 miles.

## RUTLAND

## Green Mountain National Forest Campgrounds

North Main St., Rutland 05701. T: (802) 747-6700.

🚐 n/a　　　　　🔺 ★★★★★

| | |
|---|---|
| Beauty: ★★★★★ | Site Privacy: ★★★★ |
| Spaciousness: ★★★★★ | Quiet: ★★★★★ |
| Security: ★★★ | Cleanliness: ★★★★ |
| Insect Control: ★★★ | Facilities: ★★★★ |

Actually a collection of campsites, rather than one specific area, the Green Mountain National Forest Campgrounds cover an enormous amount of terrain. There are five specific campgrounds connected by 312 miles of hiking trails. This enormous park is an excellent place to travel light and see varying parts of the state on one trip. Areas throughout the campground offer hunting, fishing, hiking, paddling, and basically any outdoor activity you can dream up. In winter, the campground remains open and offers snowshoeing, cross country skiing, and snowmobiling in some places.

**BASICS**

**Operated By:** State of Vermont. **Open:** Year-round. **Site Assignment:** Reservations accepted. **Registration:** At office. **Fee:** $4. **Parking:** Specified at Registration.

**FACILITIES**

**Number of RV Sites:** 0. **Number of Tent-Only Sites:** 94. **Hookups:** None. **Dump Station:** Yes. **Laundry:** No. **Pay Phone:** No. **Rest Rooms and Showers:** Yes. **Fuel:** No. **Propane:** No. **Internal Roads:** Paved/gravel. **RV Service:** No. **Market:** Bedard Cash Market, 137 Library Ave., Rutland,

VT 05701. **Restaurant:** A Crust Above, 134 Woodstock Ave., Rutland, VT 05701. **General Store:** No. **Vending:** No. **Swimming Pool:** No. **Playground:** No. **Activities:** Hiking, fishing, mountain biking. **Nearby Attractions:** Mountains, trails, visitor center. **Additional Information:** Call ahead.

**TO GET THERE**

Take Rte. 4 to Rte. 17 in Rutland

## SHELBURNE

## Shelburne Camping Area

4385 Shelburne Rd., Rte. 7, Shelburne 05482. T: (802) 985-2540; F: (802) 985-8132; shelbcamp@aol.com.

🚐 ★★★　　　　　🔺 ★

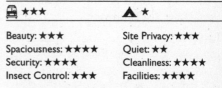

| | |
|---|---|
| Beauty: ★★★ | Site Privacy: ★★★ |
| Spaciousness: ★★★★ | Quiet: ★★ |
| Security: ★★★★ | Cleanliness: ★★★★ |
| Insect Control: ★★★ | Facilities: ★★★★ |

Owned by the same people who own the Dutch Mill Motel and Restaurant, this campground is marked by a Dutch-style windmill at the entrance. Though that makes most people think of mini-golf, there's no course here. However, there is pretty much everything else you'd want in an RV park. Unfortunately, sites are lined up in that boring RV park grid. Still, they're grassy and bigger than average, and most have trees, so it's nice place to stay. Tent campers are technically welcome, but this is not a tent campground. The park is close to Lake Champlain, though not on it, and has access to area beaches.

**BASICS**

**Operated By:** The Bissonette family. **Open:** Apr.–Nov. 1. **Site Assignment:** Reservations accepted. **Registration:** At office. **Fee:** $18–$26. **Parking:** At site.

## FACILITIES

**Number of RV Sites:** 70. **Number of Tent-Only Sites:** 6. **Hookups:** Water, electric, sewer, cable TV. **Each Site:** Picnic table, fire ring. **Dump Station:** Yes. **Laundry:** Yes. **Pay Phone:** Yes. **Rest Rooms and Showers:** Yes. **Fuel:** No. **Propane:** Yes. **Internal Roads:** Paved/gravel. **RV Service:** No. **Market:** Galipeau's Grocery Store, 935 Falls Rd., Shelburne, VT 05482: Take a left onto Rte. 7 followed by a left onto Marsett Rd., which becomes Falls Rd. **Restaurant:** Buono Appetito Italian Restaurant, 3182 Shelburne Rd., Shelburne, VT 05482: Take a right onto Rte. 7 & follow it for 0.7 mi. **General Store:** Yes. **Vending:** Yes. **Swimming Pool:** Yes. **Playground:** Yes. **Other:** Rec room, basketball, volleyball, horseshoes. **Activities:** Swimming & boating. **Nearby Attractions:** Shelburne Museum. **Additional Information:** Call ahead.

## RESTRICTIONS

**Pets:** Allowed. **Fires:** Allowed. **Alcoholic Beverages:** Allowed. **Vehicle Maximum Length:** None. **Other:** Ask on arrival.

## TO GET THERE

Take I-89 Exit 13; follow Rte. 7 south for 5 mi.

## SOUTH HERO

### Apple Tree Bay Campground

P.O. Box 183, 71 Rte. 2, South Hero 05486. T: (802) 372-5398; F: (802) 372-8272; www.appleislandresort.com; atbrcamp@aol.com.

🚐 ★★★★　　　　▲ ★

| | |
|---|---|
| Beauty: ★★★★ | Site Privacy: ★★★ |
| Spaciousness: ★★★ | Quiet: ★★★ |
| Security: ★★★ | Cleanliness: ★★★★ |
| Insect Control: ★★★ | Facilities: ★★★★ |

An all-purpose resort that caters primarily to RVers, Apple Tree has tons of planned activities as well as a very busy lake. Though the lake has its share of motorboats, there's also excellent fishing, and you can hire guides to help you find the fish. It's actually possible to fish for your dinner here, though it's equally likely you'll be throwing back what you catch. Tents are allowed but not reccomended here, as the sites are really meant for RVs. You can see the Green Mountains from here as well as lots of pretty Lake Champlain scenery.

## BASICS

**Operated By:** Paul & Rick Abare. **Open:** May 1–Oct. 20. **Site Assignment:** Reservations recommended. **Registration:** Entrance. **Fee:** $20–$30. **Parking:** At site.

## FACILITIES

**Number of RV Sites:** 200. **Number of Tent-Only Sites:** 0. **Hookups:** Water, electric, sewer. **Each Site:** Picnic tables, fire rings. **Dump Station:** Yes. **Laundry:** Yes. **Pay Phone:** Yes. **Rest Rooms and Showers:** Yes. **Fuel:** No. **Propane:** Yes. **Internal Roads:** Paved/gravel. **RV Service:** No. **Market:** Keeler's Bay Variety Store, 500 Rte. 2, South Hero, VT 05486: Follow Rte. 2 to number 500. **Restaurant:** Sandbar Restaurant on site. **General Store:** Yes. **Vending:** Yes. **Swimming Pool:** Yes. **Playground:** Yes. **Other:** Motel & cabins, 9 hole golf course, clubhouse, volleyball, horshoes. **Activities:** Planned activities, boat rentals, waterskiing. **Nearby Attractions:** Green Mountains. **Additional Information:** Call ahead.

## RESTRICTIONS

**Pets:** Allowed. **Fires:** Allowed. **Alcoholic Beverages:** Allowed. **Vehicle Maximum Length:** 50 ft. **Other:** Ask on arrival.

## TO GET THERE

From I-89, take Exit 17 and turn right. Go 6 mi. on Rte. 2 to the end of the Sand Bar Beach Causeway.

## SOUTH HERO

### Camp Skyland on Lake Champlain

398 South St., South Hero 05486. T: (802) 372-4200.

🚐 ★★★★　　　　▲ ★★★★

| | |
|---|---|
| Beauty: ★★★★★ | Site Privacy: ★★★★ |
| Spaciousness: ★★★★ | Quiet: ★★★★ |
| Security: ★★★★ | Cleanliness: ★★★★ |
| Insect Control: ★★★ | Facilities: ★★★ |

Perhaps the best looking campground in all of Vermont, Camp Skyland offers nature that has virtually undisturbed by man. Located on the Southern part of Grand Isle, the campground offers incredible views of mountains and Lake Champlain. Though RVs are allowed here, you'd be better off bringing a tent. Sites are spacious, secluded and pretty quiet. There's a boat launch as well as lake swimming and nearly endless hiking and exploration options.

## BASICS

**Operated By:** Jack, Priscilla, & Joey Arnold. **Open:** Memorial Day–Sept. 30. **Site Assignment:** Reservations. **Registration:** At office. **Fee:** Starts at $16. **Parking:** At site.

## FACILITIES

**Number of RV Sites:** 22. **Number of Tent-Only Sites:** 11. **Hookups:** Water, electric, sewer. **Each Site:** Picnic tables & fire rings at tent sites. **Dump Station:** No. **Laundry:** Yes. **Pay Phone:** No. **Rest Rooms and Showers:** Yes. **Fuel:** No. **Propane:** No. **Internal Roads:** Paved/gravel. **RV Service:** No. **Market:** Brennan's Quik Stop, 50 Porters Point Ct., Colchester, VT 05446: Take a left onto Rte. 2 & follow it for 12.4 mi. Then, take a right onto Rte. 127 & follow it for 4.8 mi. **Restaurant:** Lee Zachary's Pizza House, Rte. 2 South Hero, VT 05486: Take a left onto Rte. 2 & follow it for 3 mi. **General Store:** No. **Vending:** No. **Swimming Pool:** No. **Playground:** No. **Other:** Rec hall, game room, lending library. **Activities:** Canoe & boat rentals, fishing. **Nearby Attractions:** Trails. **Additional Information:** Call ahead.

## RESTRICTIONS

**Pets:** Allowed. **Fires:** Allowed. **Alcoholic Beverages:** Allowed. **Vehicle Maximum Length:** none. **Other:** Ask on arrival.

## TO GET THERE

Go 10 mi. from I-89, Exit 17, on Rte. 2, then 3.5 mi. to the campground at the end of South St.

## ST. ALBANS BAY

### Burton Island State Park

P.O. Box 123, St. Albans Bay 05481. T: (802) 524-6353; www.state.vt.us/anr/fpr/parks/htm/burton.html.

🚐 n/a     ▲ ★★★★

| | |
|---|---|
| Beauty: ★★★ | Site Privacy: ★★★★ |
| Spaciousness: ★★★ | Quiet: ★★★★★ |
| Security: ★★★★ | Cleanliness: ★★★★ |
| Insect Control: ★★★ | Facilities: ★★★★ |

Only accessible by boat (a ferry makes the trip) Burton Island offers a little something different. For tent campers it offers isolation, as the crowds never get that big due to the location. For boaters, there's electricity at the marina in the boat slips and a chance to get away from the traditional yacht club. The 253 acre park has all sorts of wildlife and a resident naturalist to explain it. There's also a beach for swimming and lots of water-based activities, since this is an island. Hikers can follow the Island's network of nature trails or get lost off the beaten path.

## BASICS

**Operated By:** State of Vermont. **Open:** May 15–Labor Day. **Site Assignment:** Reservations accepted. **Registration:** Entrance gate. **Fee:** $14–$20. **Parking:** At site.

## FACILITIES

**Number of RV Sites:** 0. **Number of Tent-Only Sites:** 42. **Hookups:** None. **Each Site:** Fireplace, picnic table. **Dump Station:** No. **Laundry:** No. **Pay Phone:** Yes. **Rest Rooms and Showers:** Yes. **Fuel:** Yes, for boats. **Propane:** No. **Internal Roads:** Paved/gravel. **RV Service:** No. **Market:** No. **Restaurant:** No. **General Store:** Yes. **Vending:** Yes. **Swimming Pool:** No. **Playground:** Yes. **Activities:** Rowboat & canoe rentals. **Additional Information:** Call ahead.

## RESTRICTIONS

**Pets:** Yes, w/ rabies vaccination. **Fires:** Allowed. **Alcoholic Beverages:** Allowed. **Vehicle Maximum Length:** 60 ft. **Other:** Ask on arrival.

## TO GET THERE

Burton Island State Park is accessible only by boat. Call for ferry information.

## ST. ALBANS BAY

### Knight Island State Park

P.O. Box 123, St. Albans Bay 05481. T: (802) 524-6353; www.state.vt.us/anr/fpr/parks/htm/knighti.html.

🚐 n/a                    ▲ ★★★★★

Beauty: ★★★★★        Site Privacy: ★★★★★
Spaciousness: ★★★★     Quiet: ★★★★★
Security: ★★★          Cleanliness: ★★★★
Insect Control: ★★★     Facilities: ★

It doesn't get much more remote than this, as you have to take a ferry to get here and once you're her you're in the middle of nowhere Of course, the basic appeal of Knight Island is solitude. There are absolutely no facilities, so you'll be completely roughing it, but the scenery might make it worth the extra effort. Each site has a private path to the shore—there's almost no need to see other people if that's what you're looking for. From the various trails that traverse the island, you get amazing views of both the Adirondacks and the Green Mountains. Don't go to Knight Island unless you're looking to get away from it all (except nature), but if that's what you want, this might be the best place in the state.

## BASICS

**Operated By:** State of Vermont. **Open:** Oct. 31–Labor Day. **Site Assignment:** Permit required. **Registration:** Island w/ caretaker. **Fee:** $12, 2 night min. **Parking:** At site.

## FACILITIES

**Number of RV Sites:** 0. **Number of Tent-Only Sites:** 7. **Hookups:** None. **Each Site:** Fire ring. **Dump Station:** No. **Laundry:** No. **Pay Phone:** No. **Rest Rooms and Showers:** No. **Fuel:** No. **Propane:** No. **Internal Roads:** Paved/gravel. **RV Service:** No. **Market:** Hannaford Supermarket, Highgate Shopping Plaza, St. Albans, VT 05478. **Restaurant:** Bayside Pavillion, Lake Rd. St. Albans Bay, VT 05481. **General Store:** No. **Vending:** No. **Swimming Pool:** No. **Playground:** No.

**Activities:** Fishing. **Additional Information:** Call ahead.

## RESTRICTIONS

**Pets:** Yes, w/ rabies vaccination. **Fires:** Allowed. **Alcoholic Beverages:** Allowed. **Vehicle Maximum Length:** 60 ft. **Other:** Ask on arrival.

## TO GET THERE

Must take ferry from Burton Island

## ST. JOHNSBURY

### Moose River Campground

2870 Portland St., St. Johnsbury 05819. T: (802) 748-4334 (summer) or (802) 472-3139 (winter); F: (802) 748-3459 (summer) or (802) 472-6993 (winter); www.gocampingamerica.com/moose rivervt; mooservr@together.net.

🚐 ★★★★               ▲ ★★★

Beauty: ★★             Site Privacy: ★★★
Spaciousness: ★★        Quiet: ★★
Security: ★★★          Cleanliness: ★★★
Insect Control: ★★★     Facilities: ★★★

An adult campground, Moose River has a location that offers both positives and negatives. On the plus side, the campground is between the White and Green Mountains and convenient to the Connecticut River as well as the Moose River, where you can fish. The campground is actually located on a bend in the Moose River on a grassy patch. On the negative side, the sites is a little too close to Rte. 2, which can be noisy and detract from the natural atmosphere. Still, this is one of the few campgrounds that caters strictly to grownups with lots of planned activities. So those seeking such a park can usually ignore the traffic noise.

## BASICS

**Operated By:** Mary & Gary Lunderville. **Open:** May 1–Oct. 22. **Site Assignment:** Reservations accepted. **Registration:** At office. **Fee:** $15–$26. **Parking:** At site.

## FACILITIES

**Number of RV Sites:** 42. **Number of Tent-Only Sites:** 8. **Hookups:** Water, electric, sewer. **Each Site:** Picnic table, fire ring. **Dump Station:**

Yes. **Laundry:** No. **Pay Phone:** Yes. **Rest Rooms and Showers:** Yes. **Fuel:** No. **Propane:** Yes. **Internal Roads:** Compressed gravel. **RV Service:** No. **Market:** Shop 'n' Save, 129 Portland St., St. Johnsbury, VT 05819: Take a right onto Rte. 2. **Restaurant:** Anthony's Diner, 50 Railroad St., St. Johnsbury, VT 05819: Take a right onto Rte. 2 followed by a right onto Rte. 5. **General Store:** No. **Vending:** No. **Swimming Pool:** No. **Playground:** No. **Activities:** Lots of planned activities for grown-ups. **Nearby Attractions:** Golf course, Fairbanks Museum. **Additional Information:** Call ahead.

### RESTRICTIONS

**Pets:** Allowed. **Fires:** Allowed. **Alcoholic Beverages:** Allowed. **Vehicle Maximum Length:** 50 ft. **Other:** No kids allowed.

### To GET THERE

From I-93 take Exit 1, go north on Rte. 18, turn left onto Rte. 2, and follow it for 3 miles.

## STOWE
## Gold Brook Campground

P.O. Box 1028, Rte. 100, Stowe 05672. T: (802) 253-7683.

🚐 ★★★★          ⛺ ★★★★

| | |
|---|---|
| Beauty: ★★★★ | Site Privacy: ★★★★ |
| Spaciousness: ★★★★ | Quiet: ★★★★ |
| Security: ★★★★ | Cleanliness: ★★★★ |
| Insect Control: ★★★ | Facilities: ★★★★ |

Ringed by two small rivers that offer excellent fishing, Gold Brook is the perfect campground for casual fishermen. Most sites touch the water, allowing you to cast your line while barely getting out of bed. Sites are shaded by trees, but there's a fair amount of open field space that's sometimes the scene of pick-up ballgames. Gold Brook does a heavy winter business and has a relationship with the nearby Nichols Lodge. In the winter, snowmobile rentals are available, as is hot breakfast at the lodge. There's also a lot of skiing—both downhill and cross country—easily accessible.

### BASICS

**Operated By:** John, Kay, & Mary Nichols. **Open:** Year-round. **Site Assignment:** Reservations recommended. **Registration:** At office. **Fee:** Starts at $18. **Parking:** At site.

### FACILITIES

**Number of RV Sites:** 50. **Number of Tent-Only Sites:** 29. **Hookups:** Water, electric (30, 50), sewer. **Dump Station:** Yes. **Laundry:** Yes. **Pay Phone:** Yes. **Rest Rooms and Showers:** Yes. **Fuel:** No. **Propane:** Yes. **Internal Roads:** Paved/gravel. **RV Service:** No. **Market:** Gracie's Gourmutt Shop, 20 Main St., Stowe, VT 05672: Take a right onto Rte. 100, which becomes Rte. 108. Continue 1.5 mi. **Restaurant:** Swisspot Restaurant, 128 South Main St., Stowe, VT 05672: Take a right onto Rte. 100, which becomes Rte. 108. Continue 1.3 mi. **General Store:** Limited. **Vending:** Yes. **Swimming Pool:** Yes. **Playground:** Yes. **Other:** Rec hall. **Activities:** Swimming, hunting, fishing, hiking, skiing, snowmobiling. **Nearby Attractions:** Nichols Lodge. **Additional Information:** Call ahead.

### RESTRICTIONS

**Pets:** Allowed. **Fires:** Allowed. **Alcoholic Beverages:** Allowed. **Vehicle Maximum Length:** 40 ft. **Other:** Ask on arrival.

### To GET THERE

Follow Rte. 100 for 7.5 mi. north from Exit 10 off I-89.

## STOWE
## Smugglers' Notch State Park Campground

Box 7248 Mountain Rd., Stowe 05672. T: (802) 253-4014.

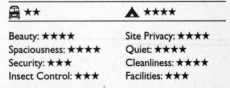

🚐 ★★          ⛺ ★★★★

| | |
|---|---|
| Beauty: ★★★★ | Site Privacy: ★★★★ |
| Spaciousness: ★★★★ | Quiet: ★★★★ |
| Security: ★★★ | Cleanliness: ★★★★ |
| Insect Control: ★★★ | Facilities: ★★★ |

Dotted in between heavy woods, the sites here are fairly spectacular. Like all Vermont state parks, Smugglers' Notch offers very little in the way of amentities—you basically get a table, fireplace, and access to bathrooms and showers—but the natural opportunites are amazing. Even the entrance of the park, a narrow road between two mountains, visually primes visitors for experiencing this wilderness oasis. The campground makes an excellent starting point for all manner of hikes and the location is a state-designated nature area, with lots of rare plants, rock formations, and other natural phenomenons.

## BASICS

**Operated By:** State of Vermont. **Open:** May 15–Oct. 15. **Site Assignment:** Reservations recommended. **Registration:** At office. **Fee:** $12. **Parking:** At site.

## FACILITIES

**Number of RV Sites:** 21. **Number of Tent-Only Sites:** 14. **Hookups:** None. **Each Site:** Picnic table, fireplace. **Dump Station:** Yes. **Laundry:** No. **Pay Phone:** No. **Rest Rooms and Showers:** Yes. **Fuel:** No. **Propane:** No. **Internal Roads:** Paved/gravel. **RV Service:** No. **Market:** Edelweiss Store, 2251 Mountain Rd., Stowe, VT 05672: Take a left onto Rte. 108. **Restaurant:** Backyard Tavern, Mountain Rd., Stowe, VT 05672: Take a left onto Rte. 108. **General Store:** Very limited. **Vending:** No. **Swimming Pool:** No. **Playground:** Yes. **Activities:** Hiking. **Nearby Attractions:** Shops in Stowe. **Additional Information:** Call ahead.

## RESTRICTIONS

**Pets:** Allowed, on leash. **Fires:** Allowed. **Alcoholic Beverages:** Allowed. **Vehicle Maximum Length:** 60 ft. **Other:** Ask on arrival.

## TO GET THERE

From Stowe, follow Rte. 108 to the park entrance.

## SWANTON

### Champlain Valley Campground

600 Mcquam Shore Rd., Swanton 05458. T: (802) 524-5146.

 ★★★★           n/a

Beauty: ★★★★          Site Privacy: ★★★
Spaciousness: ★★★          Quiet: ★★★
Security: ★★★          Cleanliness: ★★★★
Insect Control: ★★★          Facilities: ★★★★

Like all of the Lake Champlain shoreline, this one has impressive views, both of the lake and of the woods around the campground. This one also offers views of Grand Isle, and it's surprisingly uncluttered for a campground that only caters to RVs. Perhaps that's because most of the campers here are staying for the season, which also makes reservations a must since there aren't that many sites available.

## BASICS

**Operated By:** Marc & Linda Bechard. **Open:** May 15–Oct. 15. **Site Assignment:** Reservations recommended. **Registration:** At office. **Fee:** Starts at $20. **Parking:** At site.

## FACILITIES

**Number of RV Sites:** 79. **Number of Tent-Only Sites:** 0. **Hookups:** Water, electric, sewer. **Dump Station:** Yes. **Laundry:** Yes. **Pay Phone:** Yes. **Rest Rooms and Showers:** Yes. **Fuel:** No. **Propane:** Yes. **Internal Roads:** Paved/gravel. **RV Service:** No. **Market:** Cumberland Bay Market, 1544 Cumberland Head Rd., Plattsburgh, NY: Take a right onto Rte. 2 followed by a right onto Pearl St. & a left onto Bell Hill Rd., which becomes Grand Isle Ferry. Continue 4.8 mi. **Restaurant:** Grand Isle Ferry Dock Snackbar, 51 West Shore Rd., Grand Isle, VT 05458: Take a right onto Rte. 2 followed by a right onto Rte. 314 & follow it for 2.1 mi. **General Store:** No. **Vending:** No. **Swimming Pool:** No. **Playground:** Yes. **Other:** Rec hall. **Activities:** Fishing. **Nearby Attractions:** Lake Champlain. **Additional Information:** Call ahead.

## RESTRICTIONS

**Pets:** Allowed. **Fires:** Allowed. **Alcoholic Beverages:** Allowed. **Vehicle Maximum Length:** 32. **Other:** Ask on arrival.

## TO GET THERE

On Rte. 36, go 5 mi. south of Swanton or 10 mi. north of St. Albans

## SWANTON

### Lakewood Campground, Inc.

122 Champlain St., Swanton 05488. T: (802) 868-7270.

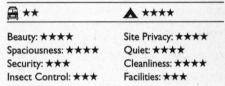

🚐 ★★★★                          ⛺ ★★

| | |
|---|---|
| Beauty: ★★★ | Site Privacy: ★★★ |
| Spaciousness: ★★★ | Quiet: ★★★ |
| Security: ★★★ | Cleanliness: ★★★★ |
| Insect Control: ★★★ | Facilities: ★★★★ |

An enormous RV park, Lakewood is well-maintained. The whole area is manicured and surrounded by trees, with each site carefully alloted at least one tree for shade. The manufactured nature of the place lends a more urban, less wild quality, but otherwise it's a nice, large RV park. There's also the Missiquoi National Wildlife refuge nearby, so unspoiled nature is convenient if not actually within of the campground. The refuge has lots of marshes and can actually get a bit spooky at dusk, but offers tons of hiking and exploration opportunities.

### BASICS

**Operated By:** Origene & Gisele Robitaille. **Open:** May 1–Oct. 1. **Site Assignment:** Reservations accepted. **Registration:** At office. **Fee:** $15–$22. **Parking:** At site.

### FACILITIES

**Number of RV Sites:** 281. **Number of Tent-Only Sites:** 0. **Hookups:** Water, electric, sewer. **Dump Station:** Yes. **Laundry:** Yes. **Pay Phone:** Yes. **Rest Rooms and Showers:** Yes. **Fuel:** No. **Propane:** Yes. **Internal Roads:** Paved. **RV Service:** No. **Market:** On site. **Restaurant:** Murphy's Country Kitchen, 9 Grand Ave., Swanton, VT 05488: Take a left onto Rte. 7 & follow it for 1.4 mi. **General Store:** Yes. **Vending:** Yes. **Swimming Pool:** Yes. **Playground:** Yes. **Other:** Rec hall, baseball field, horseshoes, tennis courts. **Activities:** Planned activities, boat rentals. **Nearby Attractions:** Golf course. **Additional Information:** Call ahead.

### RESTRICTIONS

**Pets:** Allowed. **Fires:** Allowed. **Alcoholic Beverages:** Allowed. **Vehicle Maximum Length:** 35 ft. **Other:** Ask on arrival.

### TO GET THERE

Go 9 miles west of Swanton on Tabor Rd. (off Rte. 78).

## WATERBURY

### Little River State Park Campground

3444 Little River Rd., Waterbury 05676. T: (802) 244-7103.

🚐 ★★                          ⛺ ★★★★

| | |
|---|---|
| Beauty: ★★★★ | Site Privacy: ★★★★ |
| Spaciousness: ★★★★ | Quiet: ★★★★ |
| Security: ★★★ | Cleanliness: ★★★★ |
| Insect Control: ★★★ | Facilities: ★★★ |

Located at the Waterbury Reservoir, the chief appeal here has to be the excellent waterfront area. The reservoir has its own beach and boat launch, though those areas are also open for day use, making them sometimes crowded. The sites themselves are very basic, but they're large and some are remote. If you're looking for privacy, reserve early, because the best sites go quickly. There's a lot of hiking nearby including day-long treks up Mount Mansfield.

### BASICS

**Operated By:** State of Vermont. **Open:** Varies, call ahead. **Site Assignment:** Reservations recommended. **Registration:** At office. **Fee:** $13. **Parking:** At site.

### FACILITIES

**Number of RV Sites:** 100. **Number of Tent-Only Sites:** 20. **Hookups:** None. **Each Site:** Picnic table, fireplace. **Dump Station:** Yes. **Laundry:** No. **Pay Phone:** Yes. **Rest Rooms and Showers:** Yes. **Fuel:** No. **Propane:** No. **Internal Roads:** Paved/gravel. **RV Service:** No. **Market:** Champlain Farms, 1 North Main St., Waterbury, VT 05676: Take a left onto Little River Rd. followed by a left onto Rte. 2. **Restaurant:** Arvad's Spirits & Light Fare, 3 S. Main St., Waterbury, VT

05676: Take a left onto Little River Rd. followed by a left onto Rte. 2. **General Store:** Very limited. **Vending:** No. **Swimming Pool:** No. **Playground:** Yes. **Other:** Beach, boat ramp. **Activities:** Boating, swimming. **Nearby Attractions:** Ben & Jerry's Factory. **Additional Information:** Call ahead.

## RESTRICTIONS

**Pets:** Yes, on leash. **Fires:** Allowed. **Alcoholic Beverages:** Allowed. **Vehicle Maximum Length:** None. **Other:** Ask on arrival.

## TO GET THERE

Take Rte. 2 to Little River Rd., turn and continue for 3.5 mi. to the campground entrance

## WEST BARNET

### Harvey's Lake Cabins & Campground

190 Camper's Ln., West Barnet 05821. T: (802) 633-2213; F: (802) 633-2339; harveys @together.net.

🚐 ★★★★            ▲ ★★★

Beauty: ★★★★            Site Privacy: ★★★★
Spaciousness: ★★★            Quiet: ★★★★
Security: ★★★★            Cleanliness: ★★★★
Insect Control: ★★★            Facilities: ★★★★

Apparently, Jacques Cousteau took his first dive in Harvey's Lake, or at least that's how the locals tell it. Whether it's true or not, it's a beautiful body of water that's perfect for canoeing. You'll have to make reservations early if you want a lakefront campsite, as much of the frontage is taken up by cabins. But fortunately, the non-waterfront sites have plenty of charm. The sites are fairly small, but are surrounded by pine trees, making them private. The enormous lake has no public access, so unlike Lake Champlain it's very quiet, even during the busiest parts of summer.

## BASICS

**Operated By:** Marybeth Vereline. **Open:** May 1–Oct. 15. **Site Assignment:** Reservations recommended. **Registration:** At office. **Fee:** $18–$23. **Parking:** At site.

## FACILITIES

**Number of RV Sites:** 31. **Number of Tent-Only Sites:** 12. **Hookups:** Water, electric, sewer. **Each Site:** Picnic table, fireplace, grill. **Dump Station:** Yes. **Laundry:** Yes. **Pay Phone:** Yes. **Rest Rooms and Showers:** Yes. **Fuel:** No. **Propane:** No. **Internal Roads:** Paved/gravel. **RV Service:** No. **Market:** Bayley Hazen Country Store, 24 Governer Maddocks Rd., Peacham, VT 05862. **Restaurant:** St. J Diner, Rte. 5, St. Johnsbury, VT 05819. **General Store:** No. **Vending:** Yes. **Swimming Pool:** Yes. **Playground:** Yes. **Other:** Rec hall, game room, horseshoes, pool table. **Activities:** Canoe, boat, & bike rentals. **Additional Information:** Call ahead.

## RESTRICTIONS

**Pets:** Allowed. **Fires:** Allowed. **Alcoholic Beverages:** Allowed. **Vehicle Maximum Length:** 35 ft. **Other:** Ask on arrival.

## TO GET THERE

Take Exit 18 off I-91 and go 9 mi. from Danville on Rte. 2, then 9 mi. from Groton off Rte. 302. Go around a white church and over the bridge in West Barnet, then take the first dirt road on the right to the campground.

## WEST DANVILLE

### Injun Joe Court

P.O. Box 27, US Rte. 2, West Danville 05873. T: (802) 684-3430.

🚐 ★★            ▲ n/a

Beauty: ★★★            Site Privacy: ★★★★
Spaciousness: ★★★            Quiet: ★★★
Security: ★★★            Cleanliness: ★★★
Insect Control: ★★★            Facilities: ★★

Primarily a cabin-based resort, Injun Joe Court has seven sites for fully self-contained RVs. Though the cabins themselves are nothing much to look at, the RV sites overlook Joe's Pond and there's a reaonable number of hiking trails around. Still, this is likely a place to stop for a night, not the base for a long stay.

## BASICS

**Operated By:** Beth Perreault & family. **Open:** May 15–Oct. 15. **Site Assignment:** Reservations required. **Registration:** At office. **Fee:** Starts at $22. **Parking:** At site.

## FACILITIES

**Number of RV Sites:** 7. **Number of Tent-Only Sites:** 0. **Hookups:** Water, electric, sewer. **Dump Station:** No. **Laundry:** No. **Pay Phone:** No. **Rest Rooms and Showers:** No. **Fuel:** No. **Propane:** No. **Internal Roads:** Paved/gravel. **RV Service:** No. **Market:** On site. **Restaurant:** On site. **General Store:** Yes. **Vending:** Yes. **Swimming Pool:** No. **Playground:** Yes. **Other:** Rowboats, paddleboats, canoes, private beach. **Activities:** No planned activities. **Nearby Attractions:** Trails. **Additional Information:** Call ahead.

## RESTRICTIONS

**Pets:** Allowed. **Fires:** Allowed. **Alcoholic Beverages:** Allowed. **Vehicle Maximum Length:** 40 ft. **Other:** Ask on arrival.

## TO GET THERE

Ten mi. west of St. Johnsbury on US 2, the campground overlooks Joe's Pond.

## WESTFIELD

### Mill Brook Campground

P.O. Box 133, Westfield 05874. T: (802) 744-6673.

🚐 ★★★          ⛺ ★★★★

| | |
|---|---|
| Beauty: ★★★★ | Site Privacy: ★★★★ |
| Spaciousness: ★★★ | Quiet: ★★★★ |
| Security: ★★★ | Cleanliness: ★★★★ |
| Insect Control: ★★★ | Facilities: ★★★ |

A small and well laid out campground, Mill Brook is an excellent choice for both tent and RV campers. The campground offers large, open, grassy sites for RV campers along Mill Brook, which offers fishing and eventually leads to a waterfall. Tent campers get a lot more seclusion in wooded sites that are far enough away from the RVs to feel like you're at a tents-only campground. There are plenty of hiking trails for all ability levels nearby as well as bike paths.

## BASICS

**Operated By:** The Paxman family. **Open:** May 15–Sept. 15. **Site Assignment:** Reservations accepted. **Registration:** At office. **Fee:** $11.50–$15.50. **Parking:** At site.

## FACILITIES

**Number of RV Sites:** 30. **Number of Tent-Only Sites:** 0. **Hookups:** Water, electric, sewer. **Each Site:** Fireplace, picnic table. **Dump Station:** Yes. **Laundry:** No. **Pay Phone:** Yes. **Rest Rooms and Showers:** Yes. **Fuel:** No. **Propane:** No. **Internal Roads:** Paved/gravel. **RV Service:** No. **Market:** Steve's Discount Center, 149 Main St., Westfield, VT 05874. **Restaurant:** Old Bobbin Mill, Rte. 100, Westfield, VT 05874. **General Store:** No. **Vending:** No. **Swimming Pool:** No. **Playground:** Yes. **Other:** Volleyball, horseshoes, badminton. **Activities:** Fishing, swimming. **Nearby Attractions:** Golf course. **Additional Information:** Call ahead.

## RESTRICTIONS

**Pets:** Allowed. **Fires:** Allowed. **Alcoholic Beverages:** Allowed. **Vehicle Maximum Length:** 40 ft. **Other:** Ask on arrival.

## TO GET THERE

The campground entrance is on Rte. 100 in middle of the village of Westfield

## WILMINGTON

### Molly Stark State Park Campground

705 Hwy. 9 East, Wilmington 05363. T: (802) 464-5460.

🚐 ★★★          ⛺ ★★★★

| | |
|---|---|
| Beauty: ★★★★ | Site Privacy: ★★★★ |
| Spaciousness: ★★★★ | Quiet: ★★★★ |
| Security: ★★★ | Cleanliness: ★★★★ |
| Insect Control: ★★★ | Facilities: ★★★ |

A beautiful park with fairly limited camping facilities, Molly Stark offers quite a bit for those wanting to experience nature unadulterated. Because there are only a small number of sites, the campground never gets crowded and guests have to make their own fun. Much of the opportunity for that comes from the surrounding area, which offers a wide array of choices. There are open lawns for sports as well as forests for exploring. There are also trails up Mount Olga, which offer challenging, but manageable hiking. There's not much in the way of creature comforts here, but there's a lot to do for people looking for a heavy helping of the outdoors.

## BASICS

**Operated By:** State of Vermont. **Open:** May 15–Oct. 15. **Site Assignment:** Reservations accepted. **Registration:** At office. **Fee:** $11. **Parking:** At site.

## FACILITIES

**Number of RV Sites:** 34. **Number of Tent-Only Sites:** 11. **Hookups:** None. **Each Site:** Fireplace, picnic table. **Dump Station:** Yes. **Laundry:** Nearby. **Pay Phone:** No. **Rest Rooms and Showers:** Yes. **Fuel:** No. **Propane:** No. **Internal Roads:** Paved/gravel. **RV Service:** No. **Market:** Shaw's, Rte. 9 Main St. Wilmington, VT 05363. **Restaurant:** Alonzo's Pasta & Grille, 10 West Main St., Wilmington, VT 05363. **General Store:** Nearby. **Vending:** No. **Swimming Pool:** No. **Playground:** Yes. **Other:** Volleyball courts, horseshoe pits. **Activities:** Hiking. **Nearby Attractions:** Mount Olga. **Additional Information:** Call ahead.

## RESTRICTIONS

**Pets:** Allowed. **Fires:** Allowed. **Alcoholic Beverages:** Allowed. **Vehicle Maximum Length:** None. **Other:** Ask on arrival.

## TO GET THERE

Take Rte. 9 to the park entrance.

# Supplemental Directory of Campgrounds

## Baltic

Salt Rock Family Camping, Rte. 97, 06330. T: (860) 822-8728. RV/tent: 125. $20–$25. Hookups: water, electric, sewer.

## Bantam

Looking Glass Hill Campgrounds, 14 Cozy Hill, 06750. T: (860) 567-2050. RV/tent: 50. $15. Hookups: water, electric.

## Bozrah

Odetah, 38 Bozrah St. Ext., 06334. T: (860) 889-4144. RV/tent: 250. $20–$25. Hookups: water, electric, sewer.

## Chaplin

Nickerson Park Camp Grounds, 1036 Phoenixville Rd., 06235. T: (860) 455-0007. RV/tent: 112. $15–$20. Hookups: water, electric, sewer, cable.

## Clinton

River Road Camp Sites, 13 River Rd., 06413. T: (860) 669-2956. RV/tent: 50. $20. Hookups: water, electric.

Riverdale Farm Camp Sites, 111 River Rd., 06413. T: (860) 669-5388. RV/tent: 250. $23. Hookups: water, electric, sewer.

## Cornwall Bridge

Housatonic Meadows State Park, Rte. 7, 06754. T: (860) 676-6772. RV/tent: 95. $10. Hookups: none.

## Deep River

Dale River Camp Sites, River Rd., 06417. T: (860) 669-5388. RV/tent: 96. $25–$32. Hookups: water, electric (30, 50 amps), sewer, cable TV.

## East Hampton

Markham Meadows Campgrounds, 7 Markham Rd., 06424. T: (860) 267-9738. RV/tent: 100. $22. Hookups: water, electric.

Nelson's Family Campground, 71 Mott Hill Rd., 06424. T: (860) 267-5300. F: (860) 267-5312. www.nelsonscampground.com. RV/tent: 90. $27. Hookups: water, electric (30, 50 amps), sewer, cable TV.

## East Killingly

Stateline Campresort, Rte. 101, 06243. T: (860) 774-3016. F: (860) 774-6470. anewman@localnet.com. RV/tent: 226. $25. Hookups: water, electric, sewer, phone.

## Eastford

Silvermine Horse Camp, Star Rte. Pilfershire Rd., 06242. T: (860) 974-1562. RV/tent: 30. No fee. Hookups: none.

## Goshen

Mohawk Campground, 708 Sharon Turnpike, 06756. T: (860) 491-2231. RV/tent: 80. $15. Hookups: water, electric.

Valley in the Pines Campground, Lucas Rd., 06756. T: (860) 491-2032. RV/tent: 30. $25. Hookups: water, electric, sewer.

## Haddam

Devil's Hopyard State Park, 366 Hopyard Rd., 06423. T: (860) 873-8566. RV/tent: 21. $9. Hookups: none.

## Higganum

Little City Campground, 733 Little City Rd., 06438. T: (860) 345-8469. RV/tent: 55. $30–$33. Hookups: water, electric (15, 30 amps), sewer.

## CONNECTICUT (continued)

### Jewett City

Ross Hill Park, 170 Ross Hill Rd., 06351. T: (860) 376-9606. RV/tent: 250. $20. Hookups: water, electric, sewer.

Hopeville Pond State Park, 193 Roode Rd., 06351. T: (860) 376-0313. RV/tent: 82. $13. Hookups: water, electric, sewer.

### Kent

Macedonia Brook State Park, 159 Macedonia Brook Rd., 06757. T: (860) 927-4100. RV/tent: 80. $9. Hookups: none.

### Kent

Treetops Campground, Spectacle Lake, 06757. T: (860) 927-3555. RV/tent: 262. $20. Hookups: water, electric, sewer.

### Lebanon

Waters Edge Family Campground, 271 Leonard Bridge Rd., 06249. T: (860) 642-7470. RV/tent: 170. $23–$26. Hookups: water, electric.

### Litchfield

White Memorial Campground, P.O. Box 368, 06759. T: (860) 567-0069. RV/tent: 65. $8–$15. Hookups: none.

### Madison

Hammonasset Beach State Park/William F. Miller Campground, Box 271, 06443. T: (203) 245-1817. RV/tent: 558. $12. Hookups: water, electric, sewer.

### New Preston

Lake Waramaug State Park, 30 Lake Waramaug Rd., 06777. T: (860) 868-0220. RV/tent: 78. $10. Hookups: water, electric, sewer.

### Niantic

Rocky Neck State Park, Box 676, 06357. T: (860) 739-5471. RV/tent: 160. $12. Hookups: water, electric, sewer.

### North Grosvenor

West Thompson Lake Campground, RFD 1, 06255. T: (203) 923-2982. RV/tent: 30. $20. Hookups: water, electric.

### Oakdale

Laurel-Lock Campgrounds, 15 Cottage Rd., 06370. T: (860) 859-1424. RV/tent: 130. $22. Hookups: water, electric, sewer, cable.

Pequot Ledge Campgrounds, 157 Doyle Rd., 06370. T: (860) 859-0682. RV/tent: 92. $25. Hookups: water, electric, sewer.

### Oneco

River Bend Campground, P.O. Box 23, 06373. T: (860) 564-3440. RV/tent: 160. $25. Hookups: water, electric, sewer.

### Pleasant Valley

American Legion State Forest/Austin F. Hawes Memorial Campground, P.O. Box 161, 06063. T: (860) 379-0922. RV/tent: 30. $10. Hookups: water, electric, sewer.

### Pomfret Center

Mashamoquet Brook State Park/Mashamoquet Brook Campground, 147 Wolf Den Drive, 06259. T: (860) 928-6121. RV/tent: 20. $9. Hookups: water, sewer.

### Preston

Strawberry Park Resort Campground, 42 Pierce Rd., 06365. T: (860) 886-1944. RV/tent: 440. $20–$40. Hookups: water, electric, sewer.

### Salem

Salem Farms Campground Inc., 39 Alexander Rd., 06420. T: (860) 859-2320. RV/tent: 186. $21. Hookups: water, electric, sewer.

Witch Meadow Lake Campsites, 139 Witch Meadow Rd., 06420. T: (860) 859-1542. RV/tent: 280. $23. Hookups: water, electric, sewer.

### Southbury

Kettletown State Park, 175 Quaker Farms Rd., 06488. T: (203) 264-5678. RV/tent: 72. $10. Hookups: water, sewer.

### Stafford Springs

Mineral Springs Family Campground, 135 Leonard Rd., 06076. T: (860) 684-2993. RV/tent: 150. $17. Hookups: water, electric.

### Sterling

Sterling Park Campground, 177 Gibson Hill Rd., 06377. T: (860) 564-8777. RV/tent: 100. $25. Hookups: water, electric, sewer, cable.

### Thomaston

Black Rock State Park, Rte. 6, 06787. T: (860) 283-8088. RV/tent: 96. $10. Hookups: none.

### Torrington

Burr Pond State Park/Taylor Brook Campground, 385 Burr Mountain Rd., 06790. T: (860) 379-0172. RV/tent: 40. $10. Hookups: water, electric, sewer.

## CONNECTICUT (continued)

### Voluntown

Frog Hollow Horse Camp, RFD 1, 06384. T: (860) 376-4075. RV/tent: 18. $9. Hookups: water, electric, sewer.

Nature's Camp Site, Rte. 49, 06384. T: (860) 376-4203. RV/tent: 185. $24. Hookups: water, electric, sewer.

Pachaug State Forest/Green Falls Campground, P.O. Box 5, 06384. T: (860) 376-4075. RV/tent: 18. $13. Hookups: water, electric, sewer.

Pachaug State Forest/Mt. Misery Campground, P.O. Box 5, 06384. T: (860) 376-4075. RV/tent: 22. $11. Hookups: water, electric, sewer.

### Wethersfield

Roaring Brook, 308 Silas Deane Hwy., 06109. T: (860) 563-2199. RV/tent: 400. $12. Hookups: water, electric, sewer.

### Willington

Moosemeadow Camping Resort, 28 Kechkes Rd., 06279. T: (860) 429-7451. RV/tent: 100. $25–$33. Hookups: water, electric (20, 30 amps), sewer, cable TV.

Rainbow Acres Family Campground, 166 Village Hill Rd., 06279. T: (860) 684-5704. RV/tent: 135. $20. Hookups: water, electric.

### Woodstock

Manna Campground, 1728 Hwy. 198, 06281. T: (860) 928-9174. RV/tent: 26. $20. Hookups: water, electric, sewer.

Solair Family Nudist Campground, 65 Ide Perrin Rd., 06281. T: (860) 928-9174. RV/tent: 150. $20. Hookups: water, electric.

## MAINE

### Acton

Apple Valley Campground, P.O. Box 92, 04001. T: (207) 636-2285. RV/tent: 145. $21. Hookups: water, electric (30 amps), sewer, cable TV.

### Addison

Pleasant River RV Park, West Side Rd., 04606. T: (207) 483-4083. www.camp.com/pleasantriver. RV/tent: 6. $20. Hookups: water, electric (20, 30, 50 amps), sewer, phone.

### Alfred

Bunganut Lake Campground, P.O. Box 141, 04002. T: (207) 247-3875. www.camp.com/bunganutlake. RV/tent: 110. $24. Hookups: water, electric (20, 30 amps).

Scott's Cove Camping Area, Box 761, 04002. T: (207) 324-6594. www.scottscovecamping.com. RV/tent: 50. $24. Hookups: water, electric (20, 30 amps), sewer.

Walnut Grove Campground, 599 Gore Rd., 04002. T: (207) 324-1207. www.gocampingamerica.com/walnutgroveme. RV/tent: 93. $18. Hookups: water, electric (20, 30 amps).

### Baileyville

Sunset Acres Campground, 162 Airline Rd., 04694. T: (207) 454-1440. www.camp.com/sunsetacres. RV/tent: 15. $12. Hookups: water, electric (30, 50 amps), sewer.

### Bangor

Shady Acres RV & Campground, RR 2 Box 7890, 04419. T: (207) 848-5515. RV/tent: 50. $18–$20. Hookups: water, electric (30 amps), sewer.

Wheeler Stream Camping Area, RR 2 Box 2800, 04401. T: (207) 848-3713. RV/tent: 25. $16. Hookups: water, electric (20, 30 amps).

### Berwick

Beaver Dam Campground, 551 Rte. 9, 03901. T: (207) 698-2267. www.beaverdamcampground.com. RV/tent: 40. $22. Hookups: water, electric (20, 30, 50 amps), sewer.

### Bethel

Bethel Outdoor Adventures & Campground, 121 Mayville Rd., 04217. T: (207) 824-4224. www.betheloutdooradventure.com. RV/tent: 34. $14. Hookups: water, electric (50 amps), sewer.

### Biddeford

Homestead by the River, Rte. 5, 04072. T: (207) 282-6445. F: (207) 283-1287. www.homesteadbytheriver.com. RV/tent: 110. $20. Hookups: water, electric (30, 50 amps), sewer.

Shamrock RV Park, 391 West St., 04005. T: (207) 284-4282. www.lamere.net/shamrock. RV/tent: 60. $20. Hookups: water, electric (20, 30 amps), sewer.

## MAINE (continued)

### Boothbay

Camper's Cove Campground, P.O. Box 136, 04537. T: (207) 633-5013 or (207) 633-0050. RV/tent: 56. $18. Hookups: water, electric (30 amps), sewer.

### Bridgton

Vicki-Lin Camping Area, RR 2, P.O. Box 449, 04009. T: (207) 647-2630. RV/tent: 87. $25. Hookups: water, electric (30 amps), sewer.

### Brownfield

Shannon's Saco River Sanctuary, Rte. 160 North, 04010. T: (207) 452-2274. www.angelfire.com/me3/shannonsanctuary. RV/tent: 55. $24. Hookups: water, electric (30 amps).

### Bucksport

Masthead Campground, RR 2 Box 1590, 04416. T: (207) 469-3482. RV/tent: 38. $14. Hookups: water, electric (15, 20 amps).

### Calais

Hilltop Campground, RR 1 Box 298, 04671. T: (207) 454-3985. www.hilltopcamping.com. RV/tent: 81. $15. Hookups: water, electric (20, 30, 50 amps), sewer.

### Danforth

Greenland Cove Campground, East Grand Lake, 04424. T: (207) 448-2863. F: (207) 532-4456. www.rec.com/gcc. RV/tent: 85. $21. Hookups: water, electric (20, 30 amps).

### Deer Isle

Sunshine Campground, RR 2 Box 521E, 04627. T: (207) 348-2663. RV/tent: 22. $16. Hookups: water, electric (15, 20 amps).

### Denmark

Granger Pond Camping Area, P.O. Box 47, 04022. T: (207) 452-2342. RV/tent: 45. $12. Hookups: water, electric (15 amps), sewer.

Pleasant Mountain Camping Area, RR 1, 04022. T: (207) 452-2170. RV/tent: 40. $20. Hookups: water, electric (30 amps), sewer.

### Dixfield

Mountain View Campground, 208 Weld St., 04224. T: (207) 562-8285. www.explore.com/~jenndon/mountainview. RV/tent: 45. $19. Hookups: water, electric (50 amps), sewer.

### East Hebron

Hebron Pines Campground, RR 1, 04238. T: (207) 966-2179. RV/tent: 24. $21. Hookups: water, electric (30 amps).

### East Machias

River's Edge Campground, HCR 74, Box 265, 04630. T: (207) 255-5987. RV/tent: 38. $13. Hookups: water, electric (20, 30, 50 amps), sewer.

### Eastbrook

Eastbrook Campground, RR 1 Box 465M, 04634. T: (207) 565-3509 or (888) 565-2319. www.eastbrookcamp.com. RV/tent: 5. $10–$24. Hookups: water, electric (20, 30, 50 amps), sewer.

### Eastport

Seaview Campground, 16 Norwood Rd., 04631. T: (207) 853-4471. www.Eastport.com. RV/tent: 74. $18. Hookups: water, electric (20, 30 amps), sewer, cable TV.

### Ellsworth

Hospitality Woods RV Park, 2 Our Way, 04605. T: (207) 667-2668 or (800) 773-2668. www.cT: net/~dandan. RV/tent: 47. $25. Hookups: water, electric (20, 30, 50 amps), sewer, cable TV, phone.

### Farmingdale

Foggy Bottom RV Campground, 195 AQ Ave., 04344. T: (207) 582-0075. F: (207) 582-8584. RV/tent: 9. $20. Hookups: water, electric (50 amps), sewer.

Troll Valley Campground, RR 4, 04938. T: (207) 778-3656. RV/tent: 25. $17. Hookups: water, electric (50 amps).

### Freeport

Big Skye Acres Campground, 1430 Hallowell, 04222. T: (207) 688-4288. F: Fax (207) 688-3323. www.bigskyeacres.com. RV/tent: 212. $23. Hookups: water, electric (30 amps), sewer.

Blueberry Pond Campground, 218 Poland Range Rd., 04069. T: (207) 688-4421 or (877) 290-1381. F: Fax (207) 688-4063. www.blueberrycampground.com. RV/tent: 97. $19. Hookups: water, electric (20, 30 amps), sewer.

Recompence Shore Campsites, 134 Burnett Rd., 04032. T: (207) 865-9307. www.freeportcamping.com. RV/tent: 104. $14. Hookups: water, electric (15 amps).

### Fryeburg

Canal Bridge Campground, Rte. 5, 04037. T: (207) 935-2286. RV/tent: 50. $20. Hookups: water, electric (20 amps).

## MAINE (continued)

### Georgetown

Sagahadoc Bay Campground, Sagahadoc Bay Rd., 04548. T: (207) 371-2014. www.sagbaycamping. com. RV/tent: 36. $24. Hookups: water, electric (50 amps), sewer.

### Gray

Twin Brooks Camping Area, P.O. Box 194, 04039. T: (207) 428-3832. RV/tent: 52. $20. Hookups: water, electric (20 amps), sewer.

### Greenville

Allagash Gateway Campsite, P.O. Box 675, 04441. T: (207) 723-9215. www.allagashgateway.com. RV/tent: 30. $12. Hookups: none.

Frost Pond Campground, P.O. Box 620, HCR 76, 04441. T: (207) 695-2821. www.frostpondcamps. com. RV/tent: 10. $15. Hookups: none.

Moosehead Family Campground, P.O. Box 307, 04441. T: (207) 695-2210. F: (207) 695-2007. www.mooseheadcampground.com. RV/tent: 35. $15. Hookups: water, electric (50 amps).

### Greenwood

Littlefield Beaches Campground, 13 Littlefield Ln., 04255. T: (207) 875-3290. www.littlefieldbeaches. com. RV/tent: 170. $21. Hookups: water, electric (30 amps), sewer.

### Hanover

Stony Brook Recreation, 42 Powell Pl., 04237. T: (207) 824-2836 or (888) 439-5625 ext 0604. F: (207) 824-6898. www.stonybrookrec.com. RV/tent: 140. $18. Hookups: water, electric (30 amps), sewer, cable TV.

### Harrison

Bear Mountain Village Cabins and Sites, RR 2, P.O. Box 745, 04040. T: (207) 583-2541. RV/tent: 71. $10–$12. Hookups: water, electric (30 amps).

Vacationland Campground, 233 Vacationland Rd., 04040. T: (207) 583-4953. www.vacationlandcamp-ground.com. RV/tent: 90. $18. Hookups: water, electric (30 amps), sewer, phone, modem.

### Hermon

Pumpkin Patch RV Resort, 149 Billings Rd., 04401. T: (207) 848-2231. F: (207) 848-7731. www.pump-kinpatchrv.com. RV/tent: 35. $22. Hookups: water, electric (30, 50 amps), sewer, cable TV.

### Holden

Red Barn RV Park, 602 Main Rd., 04429. T: (207) 843-6011. F: (207) 843-6011. RV/tent: 125. $15. Hookups: water, electric (20, 30, 50 amps), sewer, cable TV, phone.

### Jackman

Jackman Landing, P.O. Box 567, Main St., 04945. T: (207) 668-3301. RV/tent: 24. $15. Hookups: water, electric (30 amps).

John's Four Season Accomodations, 37 John St., 04945. T: (207) 668-7683 or (888) 668-0098. F: (207) 668-7683. RV/tent: 14. $15. Hookups: water, electric (30 amps), sewer, cable TV.

Loon Echo Family Campground, Rte. 201, P.O. Box 711, 04945. T: (207) 668-4829. RV/tent: 15. $16. Hookups: none.

Moose Alley Campground, Rte. 201, P.O. Box 298, 04945. T: (207) 668-2781. RV/tent: 21. $15. Hookups: water, electric (30 amps), cable TV.

### Jefferson

Town Line Campsites, 483 East Pond Rd., 04348. T: (207) 832-7055. RV/tent: 55. $13. Hookups: water, electric (15 amps).

### Kennebunk

Hemlock Grove Campground, 1299 Portland Rd., 04046. T: (207) 985-0398. RV/tent: 54. $18. Hookups: water, electric (30, 50 amps), sewer.

Red Apple Campground, 111 Sinnott Rd., 04046. T: (207) 967-4927. F: (207) 967-8905. www.redapple campground.com. RV/tent: 37. $16. Hookups: water, electric (20, 30 amps), sewer, cable TV, phone.

Salty Acres, 272 Mills Rd., Rte. 9, 04046. T: (207) 967-2483. F: (207) 967-2500. RV/tent: 140. $18. Hookups: water, electric (20, 30 amps), sewer.

### Kezar Falls

Windsong Campground, P.O. Box 547, 04047. T: (207) 625-4389. RV/tent: 35. $13. Hookups: water, electric (20, 30 amps).

### Kingfield

Deer Farm Campground, Tufts Pond Rd., 04947. T: (207) 265-4599. www.deerfarmcamps.com. RV/tent: 47. $16. Hookups: water, electric (30 amps).

### Lebanon

Heavenlee Acres Campground, 75 Cemetery Rd., 04027. T: (207) 457-1260. F: (207) 457-3088. www.gocampingamerica.com/heavenlee. RV/tent: 140. $17. Hookups: water, electric (30, 50 amps), sewer.

King & Queens Court Resort, 21 Flat Rock Bridge Rd., 04027. T: (207) 339-9465. F: (207) 339-9583. www.kingandqueenscamping.com. RV/tent: 70. $30. Hookups: water, electric (20 amps), sewer.

## MAINE (continued)

### Lebanon (continued)

Potter's Place Adult Camping Area, 89 Baker's Grant Rd., 04027.T: (207) 457-1341. RV/tent: 100. $16. Hookups: water, electric (20, 30 amps).

### Lee

Sleeping Bear Camping, P.O. Box 37, 04455.T: (207) 738-3148. RV/tent: 9. $12. Hookups: water, electric (30 amps).

### Lewiston

Lewiston/Auburn North Allen Pond Campground, 102 North Mountain Rd., 04236.T: (207) 946-7439. RV/tent: 65. $18. Hookups: water, electric (30 amps).

### Lincoln

Lakeside Camping and Cabins, P.O. Box 38, 04457. T: (207) 732-4241. RV/tent: 40. $15. Hookups: water, electric (15 amps), sewer.

### Litchfield

Birches Family Campground, Norris Point Rd., 04350.T: (207) 268-4330. www.thebirches.com. RV/tent: 115. $8. Hookups: water, electric (30 amps), modem.

### Livermore

Rol-Lin Hills, RR 2, P.O. Box 3300, 04254.T: (207) 897-6394. RV/tent: 30. $13. Hookups: water, electric (30 amps), sewer.

### Lubec

South Bay Campground, RR 1 Box 6565, 04652. T: (207) 733-1037. F: (207) 733-1038. www.ne.com/southbay. RV/tent: 42. $15. Hookups: water, electric (20, 30 amps), sewer.

Sunset Point Trailer Park, P.O. Box 180, 04652. T: (207) 733-2272. RV/tent: 45. $19. Hookups: water, electric (20, 50 amps).

### Madison

Abnaki Family Camping Center, Abnaki Rd., 04950. T: (207) 474-2070. RV/tent: 95. $13–$20. Hookups: water, electric (20 amps).

### Medway

Pine Grove Campground and Cottages, P.O. Box 604, 04460.T: (207) 746-5172. RV/tent: 43. $16. Hookups: water, electric (30 amps), sewer, modem.

### Millinocket

Abol Bridge Campground, Bowater Great Northern Paper Co. Rd., 04462.T: No phone. RV/tent: 36. $15. Hookups: none.

Hidden Springs Campground, 224 Central St., 04462.T: (207) 723-6337 or (888) 685-4488. www.hiddenspring.com. RV/tent: 103. $15. Hookups: water, electric (50 amps).

Jo-Mary Lake Campground, P.O. Box 329, 04462. T: (207) 723-8117. RV/tent: 60. $15. Hookups: none.

Pray's Big Eddy Campground, P.O. Box 548, 04462. T: (207) 723-9581. www.eastmill.com/pages/pray. RV/tent: 80. $8 per person. Hookups: water, electric (15 amps).

### Moody

Outdoor World-Moody Beach Campground, US 1, 04054.T: (207) 646-4586. F: (207) 646-0637. www.campoutdoorworld.com. RV/tent: 150. $20. Hookups: water, electric (30, 50 amps), sewer.

### Mount Vernon

Five Seasons Family Resort, RR 2, 04352.T: (207) 685-9141. www.5seasonsfamilyresort.com. RV/tent: 54. $24. Hookups: water, electric (30 amps).

### Naples

Brandy Pond Park, P.O. Box 1617, 04055.T: (207) 693-3129. RV/tent: 75. $10–$12. Hookups: water, electric (20 amps), sewer.

Colonial Mast Campground, Kansas Rd., 04055. T: (207) 693-6652. RV/tent: 79. $26. Hookups: water, electric (30 amps), sewer.

Loon's Haven Family Campground, Rte. 114, 04055. T: (207) 693-6881. RV/tent: 37. $23. Hookups: water, electric (20 amps).

### New Harbor

Pemaquid Point Campground, 9 Pemaquid Point Campground Rd., 04554.T: (207) 677-CAMP. RV/tent: 51. $26. Hookups: water, electric (50 amps).

### Newport

Christies Campground, Rte. 2 Box 565, 04953. T: (207) 368-4645. F: (207) 368-4251. www.camp. com/christies. RV/tent: 80. $14. Hookups: water, electric (20, 30 amps), sewer.

Tent Village Travel Trailer Park, RR 2 Box 580, 04953. T: (207) 368-5047 or (800) 319-9333. www.camp. com/village. RV/tent: 52. $15. Hookups: water, electric (20, 30 amps), sewer.

### Nobleboro

Duck Puddle Campground, P.O. Box 176, 04555. T: (207) 563-5608. www.duckpuddlecampground. com. RV/tent: 120. $22. Hookups: water, electric (30 amps), sewer.

## MAINE (continued)

### North Bridgton

Lakeside Pines Campground, P.O. Box 182, 04057. T: (207) 647-3935. www.lakesidepinescamping. com. RV/tent: 185. $31. Hookups: water, electric (30 amps), sewer.

### Old Orchard Beach

Acorn Village, 42 Walnut St., 04064. T: (207) 934-4154. www.camp.com/acornvillage. RV/tent: 75. $23. Hookups: water, electric (20 amps) sewer.

Ne're Beach Family Campground, 38 Saco Ave. (Rte. 5), 04064. T: (207) 934-7614. RV/tent: 58. $27. Hookups: water, electric (20, 30 amps), sewer.

Virginia Tent & Trailer Park, Box 242, 04064. T: (207) 934-4791. www.virginiaparkcampground.com. RV/tent: 130. $24. Hookups: water, electric (20, 30, 50 amps), sewer.

Wagon Wheel Campground & Cabins, 3 Old Orchard Rd., 04064. T: (207) 934-2160. F: (207) 934-4578. www.gocampingamerica.com/wagon wheel. RV/tent: 54. $32. Hookups: water, electric (20, 30 amps), sewer.

### Oxford

Mirror Pond Campground, 210 Tiger Hill Rd., 04270. T: (207) 539-4888. RV/tent: 40. $15. Hookups: water, electric (30 amps).

### Parsonfield

Locklin Camping Area, Tripp Town Rd., 04047. T: (207) 625-8622. RV/tent: 50. $18. Hookups: water, electric (50 amps).

### Patten

Shin Pond Village Campground & Cottages, Shin Pond Rd., 04765. T: (207) 528-2900. www.shin-pond.com. RV/tent: 30. $6–$20. Hookups: water, electric (30 amps).

### Perry

Knowlton's Campground, RR 1 Box 171, 04667. T: (207) 726-4756. RV/tent: 80. $14. Hookups: water, electric (20, 30 amps), sewer.

### Phippsburg

Ocean View Park/Popham Beach, Rte. 209, 04562. T: (207) 389-2564 (summer) or (207) 443-1000 (winter). RV/tent: 48. $21. Hookups: water, electric (20 amps), sewer.

### Poland

Range Pond Campground, 94 Plains Rd., 04274. T: (207) 998-2624. www.rangepondcamp.com. RV/tent: 90. $18. Hookups: water, electric (30 amps), sewer.

### Richmond

Nesowadnehunk Lake Wilderness Campground, Langdon Rd., 04357. T: (207) 458-1551. RV/tent: 46. $8 per person, $16 minimum. Hookups: water, electric (15 amps).

### Rockwood

Old Mill Campground, Cabins & Marina, Rte. 15, 04478. T: (207) 534-7333. F: (207) 534-9792. RV/tent: 50. $16. Hookups: water, electric. (20 amps), sewer.

Seboomook Wilderness Campground, P.O. Box 560, HC 85, 04478. T: (207) 534-8824. www.seboomookwilderness.com. RV/tent: 39. $20. Hookups: water, electric (15 amps), sewer.

### Roxbury

Silver Lake Campground, P.O. Box 32, 04275. T: (207) 545-0416. RV/tent: 25. $14. Hookups: water, electric (30 amps).

### Rumford

Madison Resort Inn & Campground, Rte. 2, 04276. T: (207) 364-7973 or (800) 258-MADISON. F: (207) 369-0341. www.madisoninn.com. RV/tent: 61. $20. Hookups: water, electric (50 amps).

### Sanford

Apache Campground, 165 Bernier Rd., 04073. T: (207) 324-5652. www.camp.com/apachecamp ground. RV/tent: 150. $17. Hookups: water, electric (20, 30 amps) sewer.

Jellystone Park Camp Resort, 1175 Main St., 04073. T: (207) 324-7782. www.jellystoneme.com. RV/tent: 102. $17. Hookups: water, electric (30, 50 amps), sewer.

Sand Pond Campground, P.O. Box 741., 04073. T: (207) 324-1752. F: (207) 324-17. www.sand pond.com. RV/tent: 48. $21. Hookups: water, electric (30, 50 amps), sewer.

### Scarborough

Wild Duck Campground, 39 Dunstan Landing Rd., 04074. T: (207) 883-4432. RV/tent: 70. $23. Hookups: water, electric (30 amps), sewer.

### Sebago

Nason's Beach & Campground, 771 Sebago Rd., 04029. T: (207) 787-2345. RV/tent: 50. $22. Hookups: water, electric (30 amps).

### Skowhegan

Eaton Mountain Ski Area and Campground, HCR 71, P.O. Box 128, 04976. T: (207) 474-2666. www.eatonmountain.com. RV/tent: 32. $15. Hookups: water, electric (30 amps), sewer.

## MAINE (continued)

### Skowhegan (continued)

Two Rivers Campground, HCR 71, P.O. Box 14, 04976. T: (207) 474-6482. www.twors.com. RV/tent: 65. $18. Hookups: water, electric (30 amps), cable TV, phone.

Yonder Hill Campground, 17 Parlin St., 04976. T: (207) 474-7353. RV/tent: 70. $18. Hookups: water, electric (30 amps), sewer.

### Solon

The Evergreens Campground, Rte. 201 A, 04979. T: (207) 643-2324. www.Kynd.com/~evrgrncp. RV/tent: 40. $20. Hookups: water, electric (30 amps).

### South Thomaston

Lobster Buoy Campsites, HC 33, P.O. Box 625, 04858. T: (207) 594-7546. RV/tent: 40. $16. Hookups: water, electric (30 amps).

### Stetson

Stetson Shores, P.O. Box 86M, 04488. T: (207) 296-2041. www.camp.com/stetson. RV/tent: 47. $19. Hookups: water, electric (20, 30 amps), sewer.

### Steuben

Mainayr Campground, 321 Village Rd., 04680. T: (207) 546-2690. F: (207) 546-3780. www.mainayr.com. RV/tent: 100. $17. Hookups: water, electric (20, 30 amps), sewer.

### Stonington

Greenlaw's RV Tent & Rental, P.O. Box 72, 04681. T: (207) 367-5049. RV/tent: 27. $18. Hookups: water, electric (15, 20, 30 amps), sewer.

### The Forks

Indian Pond Campground, HCR 63, P.O. Box 52, 04985. T: (800) 371-7774. F: (207) 237-3269. RV/tent: 27. $14. Hookups: none.

Northern Outdoors Adventure Resort, Rte. 201, 04985. T: (800) 765-7238. F: (207) 663-2244. www.northernoutdoors.com. RV/tent: 10. $11 per person. Hookups: none.

### Tremont

Quietside Campground & Cabins, P.O. Box 10, 04653. T: (207) 244-5992. RV/tent: 35. $18–$22. Hookups: water, electric (20, 30 amps).

### Vassalboro

Green Valley Campground, Cross Hill Rd., 04989. T: (207) 923-3000. RV/tent: 80. $22. Hookups: water, electric (30 amps), sewer.

### Warren

Sandy Shores RV Resort, 459 Sandy Shores Rd., 04864. T: (207) 273-2073. F: (207) 845-2019. www.midcoast.com/sandyshores. RV/tent: 29. $25. Hookups: water, electric (50 amps), sewer, cable TV.

### Waterville

Countryside Campground, West River Rd., 04903. T: (207) 873-4603. RV/tent: 25. $12. Hookups: water, electric (30 amps), sewer, phone, cable TV.

### Weld

Dummer's Beach Campground, P.O. Box 82, 04285. T: (207) 585-2200. RV/tent: 200. $17. Hookups: water, electric (30 amps).

### Wells

Beach Acres Campground, 563M Post Rd., 04090. T: (207) 646-5612. F: Fax (207) 646-2288. www.beachacres.com. RV/tent: 71. $20. Hookups: water, electric (20, 30, 50 amps), sewer.

Gregoire's Campground, 697 Sanford, 04090. T: (207) 646-3711. RV/tent: 100. $15. Hookups: water, electric (20, 30 amps), sewer.

Pinederosa Camping Area, 128 North Village Rd., 04090. T: (207) 646-2492. www.pinederosa.com. RV/tent: 122. $20. Hookups: water, electric (20, 30 amps), sewer.

Riverside Campground, 2295 Post Rd., 04090. T: (207) 646-3145. www.riversidecampground wells.com. RV/tent: 125. $21. Hookups: water, electric (20, 30, 50 amps), sewer, cable TV, phone.

Stadig Mobile Park & Campground, 146 Bypass Rd., 04090. T: (207) 646-2298. www.stadig.com. RV/tent: 150. $18. Hookups: water, electric (20, 30 amps), sewer.

### West Bethel

Pleasant River Campground, P.O. Box 92, 04286. T: (207) 836-2000. RV/tent: 75. $18. Hookups: water, electric (50 amps), sewer.

### West Poland

Hemlocks Camping Area, P.O. Box 58, 04291. T: (207) 998-2384 or (888) 578-9251. www.hemlockscampground.com. RV/tent: 75. $17. Hookups: water, electric (30 amps), sewer.

Mac's Campground, P.O. Box 87, 04291. T: (207) 998-4238. RV/tent: 33. $18. Hookups: water, electric (20 amps), sewer.

## MAINE (continued)

### Wilsons Mills

Aziscoos Valley Camping Area, HCR 10, P.O. Box 302, 03579. T: (207) 486-3271. RV/tent: 31. $9. Hookups: water, electric (30 amps).

### Windham

Highland Lake Park, 19 Roosevelt Trail, 04062. T: (207) 892-8911. RV/tent: 40. $16. Hookups: water, electric (20 amps), sewer, cable TV.

### Winslow

Giordano's Camping and Recreation, RR 2, 04901. T: (207) 873-2408. www.campanddance.com. RV/tent: 45. $16. Hookups: water, electric (15 amps).

### Winthrop

Augusta West Kampground, P.O. Box 232, 04364. T: (207) 377-9993. RV/tent: 81. $19. Hookups: water, electric (30 amps), sewer, phone, modem.

### York Beach

York Beach Camper Park, 11 Cappy's Ln., 03910. T: (207) 363-1343. RV/tent: 39. $25. Hookups: water, electric (30, 50 amps), sewer.

### York Harbor

Camp Eaton, Rte. 1A, 03911. T: (207) 363-3424. www.campeaton.com. RV/tent: 307. $32. Hookups: water, electric (30, 50 amps), sewer, cable TV.

## MASSACHUSETTS

### Amesbury

Powow Cove Campground, 2 Powow Cove Ln., 01913. T: (978) 399-4022. RV/tent: 73. $25. Hookups: water, electric (30 amps).

### Ashburnham

Howe's Camping, 133 Sherbert Rd., 01430. T: (978) 827-4558 or (800) 766-4807. RV/tent: 30. $18. Hookups: water, electric (20 amps).

### Ashby

The Pines, 39 Davis Rd., 01431. T: (978) 386-7702. F: (978) 386-2354. RV/tent: 59. $23. Hookups: water, electric (50 amps).

### Assonet

Forge Pond Campground, 62 Forge Rd., 02702. T: (508) 644-2969. RV/tent: 65. $20. Hookups: water, electric (15 amps).

### Barre

Coldbrook Campground, 864 Old Coldbrook Rd., 01005. T: (978) 355-2090. www.coldbrookcountry.com. RV/tent: 195. $23. Hookups: water, electric (30 amps).

### Becket

Bonny Rigg Campground, P.O. Box 14, 01011. T: (413) 623-5366. www.bonnyrigg.com. RV/tent: 200. $21. Hookups: water, electric (30 amps).

### Bedford

Military Park (Hanscom AFB FAM-CAMP), P.O. Box 479, 02047. T: (617) 377-4670. RV/tent: 73.

$6–$12. Hookups: water, electric (20, 30, 50 amps).

### Bernardston

Purple Meadow Campground, P.O. Box 192, 01337. T: (413) 648-9289. RV/tent: 40. $10–$13. Hookups: water, electric (15, 20, 30 amps).

Travelers Woods of New England, P.O. Box 88, 152 River St., 01337. T: (413) 648-9105. RV/tent: 94. $18. Hookups: water, electric (30 amps), sewer.

### Bolton

Crystal Springs Campground, P.O. Box 279, 01740. T: (978) 779-2711. RV/tent: 200. $17. Hookups: water, electric (30 amps), sewer.

### Brimfield

Village Green Family Campground, 228 Sturbridge Rd. Rte. 20, 01010. T: (413) 245-3504. F: (413) 245-0115. www.villagegreencampground.com. RV/tent: 131. $20. Hookups: water, electric (30 amps).

### Charlemont

Mohawk Park, P.O. Box 668, 01339. T: (413) 339-4470. RV/tent: 81. $20. Hookups: water, electric (20 amps), sewer.

### Dennisport

Grindell's Ocean View Park, 61 Old Wharf Rd., 02639. T: (508) 398-2671. RV/tent: 160. $30. Hookups: water, electric (20 amps), sewer, cable TV.

## MASSACHUSETTS (continued)

### East Douglas

Lake Manchaug Camping, 76 Oak St., 01516. T: (508) 476-2471. RV/tent: 190. $30. Hookups: water, electric (50 amps), sewer.

### East Otis

Laurel Ridge Camping Area, 40 Old Blandford Rd., 01029. T: (413) 269-4804 or (800) 538-CAMP. RV/tent: 181. $22. Hookups: water, electric (30 amps).

### East Wareham

Maple Park Family Campground, RFD. 2, 02538. T: (508) 295-4945 or (508) 291-CAMP. RV/tent: 400. $22. Hookups: water, electric (20 amps), sewer.

### Granville

Granville State Forest, 323 West Hartland Rd., 01034. T: (413) 357-6611. RV/tent: 36. $12. Hookups: none.

### Hancock

Berkshire Vista Nude Resort, P.O. Box 1177, 01237. T: (413) 738-5154. F: (413) 232-7860. www.berkshirevista.com. RV/tent: 180. $57. Hookups: water, electric (50 amps), sewer.

### Hinsdale

Fernwood Forest, P.O. Box 896, 01235. T: (413) 655-2292. www.topcities.com/Busines/fernwood/index.htm. RV/tent: 36. $15. Hookups: water, electric (30 amps).

### Mashpee

Johns Pond Campground/Otis Trailer Village, P.O. Box 586, 02541. T: (508) 477-0444. F: (508) 457-4233. www.johnspondcampground.com. RV/tent: 90. $20. Hookups: water, electric (30 amps), sewer.

### Monson

Partridge Hollow, P.O. Box 41, Munn Rd., 01057. T: (413) 267-5122. RV/tent: 240. $23. Hookups: water, electric (50 amps).

### North Egremont

Prospect Lake Park, 50 Prospect Lake Rd., 02152. T: (413) 528-4158 or (877) 860-4757. F: (413) 528-3666. RV/tent: 140. $24. Hookups: water, electric (30 amps), sewer.

### North Rutland

Pout & Trout Family Campground, 94 River Rd., 01543. T: (508) 886-6677. F: (508) 886-6931. RV/tent: 156. $20. Hookups: water, electric (30 amps).

### North Truro

North of Highland, 52 Head of the Meadow Rd., 02652. T: (508) 487-1191. RV/tent: 237. $20. Hookups: none.

### Northfield

Barton Cove Campground and Canoe Shuttle Service, 90 Millers Falls Rd., 01360. T: (413) 863-9300. RV/tent: 31. $15. Hookups: none.

### Otis

Camp Overflow, P.O. Box 645, 01253. T: (413) 269-4036. RV/tent: 175. $13–$18. Hookups: water, electric (20 amps), dump station.

Mountain View Campground, P.O. Box 162, 01253. T: (413) 269-8928. www.otismass.com; www.berkshire.com. RV/tent: 54. $25. Hookups: water, electric (50 amps), sewer.

### Phillipston

Lamb City Campground, 85 Royalston Rd., 01331. T: (978) 249-2049 or (800) 292-5262. www.lambcity.com. RV/tent: 212. $22. Hookups: water, electric (30 amps), sewer, cable TV.

### Pittsfield

Bonnie Brae Cabins & Campsites, 108 Broadway St., 01201. T: (413) 442-3754. www.hometown.aol.com/honey44/myhomepage/business.html. RV/tent: 42. $26. Hookups: water, electric (30 amps), sewer.

### Plymouth

Indianhead Resort, 1929 State Rd., 02360. T: (508) 888-3688. F: (508) 888-5907. RV/tent: 200. $20. Hookups: water, electric (50 amps).

Shady Pond Campground, 834 Bourne Rd., 02360. T: (503) 759-9336. www.shadypond.com. RV/tent: 200. $22–$28. Hookups: water, electric (50 amps), sewer.

### Rochester

Knight and Look Campground, 241 Marion Rd., 02770. T: (508) 763-2454. RV/tent: 120. $23–$26. Hookups: water, electric (20 amps), sewer.

### Sandwich

Dunroamin' Trailer Park, 5 John Ewer Rd., 02563. T: (508) 477-0541 or (508) 477-0859. F: (508) 477-9659. RV/tent: 64. $30. Hookups: water, electric (30 amps), sewer.

### South Dennis

Airline Mobile Home Park, 310 Chartham Rd., 02660. T: (508) 385-3616. RV/tent: 50. $17–$27. Hookups: water, electric (15, 30 amps).

## MASSACHUSETTS (continued)

### South Wellfleet

Paine's Campground, P.O. Box 201, 02663. T: (508) 349-3007. F: (508) 349-0246. www.camping-capecod.com. RV/tent: 50. $18. Hookups: water, electric (30 amps).

### Southwick

Southwick Acres, College Hwy., 01077. T: (413) 569-6339. F: (413) 569-2987. www.southwickacres.com. RV/tent: 40. $33. Hookups: water, electric (30 amps).

### Townsend

Pearl Hill State Park, New Fitchburg Rd., 01469. T: (978) 597-8802. RV/tent: 51. $12. Hookups: none.

### Vineyard Haven

Martha's Vineyard Family Campground, Inc., Edgartown Rd., 02568. T: (508) 693-3772. F: (508) 693-5767. www.campmvfc.com. RV/tent: 40. $32. Hookups: water, electric (30 amps), sewer, cable TV, modem.

### Warwick

Wagon Wheel Camping Area, 909 Wendell Rd., 01378. T: (978) 544-3425. RV/tent: 102. $18. Hookups: water, electric (30 amps), sewer.

### Washington

Summit Hill Campground, Summit Hill Rd., 01223. T: (413) 623-5761. RV/tent: 106. $20. Hookups: water, electric (15 amps).

### West Brookfield

Highview Campground, 58 John Gilbert Rd., 01585. T: (508) 867-7800. RV/tent: 212. $27. Hookups: water, electric (30 amps).

The Old Sawmill Campground, Long Hill Rd., 01585. T: (508) 867-2427. RV/tent: 120. $19. Hookups: water, electric (20, 30 amps).

### West Sutton

Sutton Falls Camping Area, 90 Manchaug Rd., 01590. T: (508) 865-3898. www.suttonfalls.com. RV/tent: 119. $19. Hookups: water, electric (15 amps).

### Westhampton

Windy Acres Campground, 139 South St., 01027. T: (413) 527-9862. RV/tent: 127. $22. Hookups: water, electric (30 amps).

### Whately/Deerfield

White Birch Campground, 214 North St., 01093. T: (413) 665-4941. RV/tent: 60. $22. Hookups: water, electric (30 amps).

### Windsor

Windsor State Forest, River Rd., 01270. T: (413) 684-0948 (summer) or (413) 442-8928 (Oct.–Apr.). RV/tent: 24. $12. Hookups: water.

### Worthington

Berkshire Park Camping Area, 350 Harvey Rd., 01237. T: (413) 238-5918. F: (413) 238-0132. www.erols.com/bpca. RV/tent: 134. $18. Hookups: water, electric (30 amps).

## NEW HAMPSHIRE

### Alton Bay

Viewland Campground, P.O. Box 26, Bay Hill Rd., 03810. T: (603) 875-7100. RV/tent: 56. $20. Hookups: water, electric, sewer.

### Ashland

Squam Lakes Camp Resort, RFD 1 Box 42, 03217. T: (603) 968-7227. F: (603) 968-3464. RV/tent: 119. $14. Hookups: water, electric (20, 30, 50 amps), sewer, cable TV.

### Bath

Twin River Campground & Cottages, P.O. Box 212, 03740. T: (603) 747-3640 or (800) 811-1040. F: (603) 747-2160. www.ucampnh.com/twinriver. RV/tent: 116. $18. Hookups: water, electric (20, 30, 50 amps), sewer, modem.

### Bethlehem

Apple Hill Campground, P.O. Box 388, 03574. T: (603) 869-2238. www.musar.com/applehill. RV/tent: 66. $18. Hookups: water, electric (20, 30 amps), sewer.

Snowy Mountain Campground & Motel, 1225 Main St., 03574. T: (603) 444-7789. RV/tent: 40. $16. Hookups: water, electric (15 amps).

### Bristol

Davidson's Countryside Campground, 100 Schofield Rd., 03222. T: (603) 744-2403. F: (603) 744-0071. www.worldpath.net/~davcamp. RV/tent: 273. $24. Hookups: water, electric (20, 30 amps), sewer.

## NEW HAMPSHIRE (continued)

### Brookline

Field & Stream Park, 5 Dupaw Gould Rd., 03033.
T: (603) 673-4677. F: (603) 673-6217. www.field-
nstream.hypermart.net. RV/tent: 40. $24.
Hookups: water, electric (20, 30 amps), sewer,
cable TV, modem.

### Campton

Branch Brook Four Season Campground, P.O. Box
390, 03223. T: (603) 726-7001. F: (603) 726-4093.
www.campnh.com. RV/tent: 50. $23. Hookups:
water, electric (20, 30, 50 amps), sewer.

### Canaan

Crescent Campsites, P.O. Box 238, 03741. T: (603)
523-9910 or (800) 494-5118. www.endor.com/
~crescent. RV/tent: 80. $22. Hookups: water, elec-
tric (20, 30 amps), sewer.

### Center Ossipee

Deer Cap Campground, P.O. Box 332, 03814.
T: (603) 539-6030. www.ucampnh.com. RV/tent:
75. $15. Hookups: water, electric (30 amps), sewer.

Terrace Pines Campground, P.O. Box 98 Z, 03814.
T: (603) 539-6210. F: (603) 539-6325. www.
terracepines.com. RV/tent: 65. $27. Hookups:
water, electric (20, 30 amps), sewer, cable TV.

### Chester

Silver Sands Campground, 603 Raymond Rd., 03036.
T: (603) 887-3638. F: (603) 887-3638. RV/tent: 206.
$18. Hookups: water, electric (30 amps), sewer.

### Colebrook

Maplewoods Scenic Campground and Bed & Breakfast, Box 114, 03576. T: (603) 237-4237. F: (603)
237-4237. www.maplewoodsci-cg.com. RV/tent:
450. $15. Hookups: water, electric (30 amps),
sewer.

### Conway Lake

Cove Camping Area, P.O. Box 778A, 03818. T: (603)
447-6734. F: (603) 447-5169. www.covecamping.
com. RV/tent: 155. $20. Hookups: water, electric
(20, 30 amps).

### Derry

Hidden Valley Campground, 81 Damren Rd., 03038.
T: (603) 887-3767. F: (603) 887-8115.
www.ucampnh.com/hiddenvalley. RV/tent: 72. $25.
Hookups: water, electric (20, 30 amps) sewer.

### Dover

Old Stage Campground, 46 Old Stage Rd., 03820.
T: (603) 742-4050. www.ucampnh.com/oldstage.
RV/tent: 157. $24. Hookups: water, electric (20, 30
amps), sewer.

### Durham/Lee

Forest Glen Campground, P.O. Box 676, 03824.
T: (603) 659-3416. RV/tent: 130. $25. Hookups:
water, electric (30 amps), sewer, cable TV.

### East Lempster

Tamarack Trails Campground, P.O. Box 24, 03605.
T: (603) 863-6443. RV/tent: 28. $15. Hookups:
water, electric (30 amps), sewer.

### East Wakefield

Beachwood Shores Campground, HC Box 228,
03830. T: (603) 539-4272 or (800) 371-4282.
www.ucampnh.com/beachwoodshores. RV/tent:
90. $28. Hookups: water, electric (20, 30 amps),
sewer.

Lake Forest Resort, North Shore Rd., 03839.
T: (603) 522-3306. www.ucampnh.com/lakeforest.
RV/tent: 130. $21. Hookups: water, electric (30, 50
amps), sewer.

### Epsom

Blake's Brook Campground, 76 Mountain Rd.,
03234. T: (603) 736-4793 or (888) 425-2537.
F: (603) 736-4083. www.blakesbrook.com. RV/
tent: 68. $21. Hookups: water, electric (20, 30
amps), sewer.

### Errol

Log Haven Campground, P.O. Box 239, 03579.
T: (603) 482-3294. www.loghaven.com. RV/tent: 55.
$15. Hookups: water, electric (20, 30 amps), sewer.

### Exeter

Green Gate Camping Area, P.O. Box 185, 03833.
T: (603) 772-2100. www.greengatecamp.com.
RV/tent: 127. $24. Hookups: water, electric (20, 30
amps), sewer.

### Fitzwilliam

Laurel Lake Campground, P.O. Box 114, 03447.
T: (603) 585-3304. RV/tent: 65. $22. Hookups:
water, electric (20, 30 amps), sewer.

### Franconia

Fransted Campground, P.O. Box 155, 03580. T: (603)
823-5675. F: (603) 823-5676. www.franstedcamp
ground.com. RV/tent: 95. $18. Hookups: water,
electric (20, 30 amps), sewer.

## NEW HAMPSHIRE (continued)

### Franklin

Thousand Acres Campground, 1079 South Main St., 03235. T: (603) 934-4440. www.thousandacres camp.com. RV/tent: 150. $20. Hookups: water, electric (20, 30 amps), sewer.

### Glen

Green Meadow Camping Area, P.O. Box 246, 03838. T: (603) 383-6801. www.ucampnh.com/green meadow. RV/tent: 92. $20. Hookups: water, electric (15 amps), sewer, cable TV.

### Hampstead

Sanborn Shore Acres Campground, Main St., 03841. T: (603) 329-5247. F: (603) 329-9497. RV/tent: 140. $25. Hookups: water, electric (amps), sewer.

Sunset Park Campground, 104 Emerson Rd., 03841. T: (603) 329-6941. RV/tent: 151. $18. Hookups: water, electric (30 amps), sewer.

### Hampton

Shel-Al Camping Area, Rte. 1, 03862. T: (603) 964-5730. www.ucampnh.com. RV/tent: 208. $23. Hookups: water, electric (20, 30 amps), sewer.

### Holderness

Bethel Woods Campground, Rte. 3, 03245. T: (603) 279-6266. F: (603) 279-6266. www.bethelwoods.com. RV/tent: 380. $22. Hookups: water, electric (20, 30 amps), sewer.

### Jaffrey

Emerald Acres, 39 Ridgecrest Rd., 03452. T: (603) 532-8838. RV/tent: 52. $14. Hookups: water, electric (20, 30 amps), sewer.

### Jefferson

Israel River Campground, RR 1 Box 179A, 03583. T: (603) 586-7977. F: (603) 586-7187. RV/tent: 119. $18. Hookups: water, electric (30 amps), sewer.

Jefferson Campground, Box 112A, 03583. T: (603) 586-4510. F: (603) 586-7044. www.jeffersoncamp ground.com. RV/tent: 192. $16. Hookups: water, electric (20, 30 amps), sewer.

### Kingston

Country Shore Camping Area, P.O. Box 550, 03865. T: (603) 642-5072. F: (603) 642-6745. www.ucam pnh.com/countryshore. RV/tent: 100. $27. Hookups: water, electric (20, 30, 50 amps), sewer.

### Laconia

Hack-Ma-Tack Campground, 713 Endicott St. North, 03246. T: (603) 366-5977. RV/tent: 80. $24. Hookups: water, electric (30 amps), sewer.

Paugus Bay Campground, 96 Hilliard Rd., 03246. T: (603) 366-4757. www.geocities.com/weirs_pbc. RV/tent: 173. $30. Hookups: water, electric (20, 30 amps), sewer.

### Lancaster

Beaver Trails Campground, RR 2 Box 315, 03584. T: (603) 788-3815. F: (603) 788-2808. www.great northwoods.org/beavertrails. RV/tent: 350. $20. Hookups: water, electric (20, 30, 50 amps), sewer, modem.

### Lee

Wadleigh Falls Campground, 16 Campground Rd., 03824. T: (603) 659-1751. F: (603) 659-4045. www.wadleighfalls.com. RV/tent: 50. $23. Hookups: water, electric (20, 30, 50 amps), sewer.

### Lincoln

Country Bumpkins Campground & Cabins, Rte. 3, 03251. T: (603) 745-8837. www.countrybumpkins.com. RV/tent: 45. $19. Hookups: water, electric (20, 30 amps), sewer.

### Lochmere

Silver Lake Park Campground, 389 Jamestown Rd., 03252. T: (603) 524-6289. www.ucampnh.com/silverlake. RV/tent: 77. $21. Hookups: water, electric (20, 30 amps), sewer.

### Milan

Nay Pond Campground, 7 Nay Pond Rd., 03588. T: (603) 449-2122. RV/tent: 33. $15. Hookups: water, electric (30 amps), sewer.

### Moultonboro

Pine Woods Campground, P.O. Box 776, 03254. T: (603) 253-6251. www.pinewoods.com. RV/tent: 97. $23. Hookups: water, electric (20, 30, 50 amps), sewer.

### Newport

Northstar Campground, 43 Coonbrook Rd., 03773. T: (603) 863-4001. www.northstar.com. RV/tent: 69. $22. Hookups: water, electric (20, 30 amps), sewer.

### Orford

Jacobs Brook Campground, High Bridge Rd., 03777. T: (603) 353-9210. www.outdoors.at/jacobsbrook. RV/tent: 65. $20. Hookups: water, electric (20, 30 amps), sewer.

### Pittsburg

Mountain View Cabins & Campground, RR 1 Box 30, 03592. T: (603) 538-6305. F: (603) 538-1157. RV/tent: 53. $14. Hookups: water, electric (20 amps), sewer.

## NEW HAMPSHIRE (continued)

### Plymouth

Plymouth Sands Campground, 3 Quincy Rd., 03264.
T: (603) 536-2605. RV/tent: 84. $16. Hookups:
water, electric (20 amps), sewer.

### Rochester

Crown Point Campground, 44 First Crown Point
Rd., 03867. T: (603) 332-0405. RV/tent: 135. $24.
Hookups: water, electric (20, 30 amps), sewer.

Grand View Camping Area, 51 Four Rod Rd., 03867.
T: (603) 332-1263. F: (603) 332- 7947. www.grand-
viewcamping.com. RV/tent: 70. $28. Hookups:
water, electric (20, 30 amps), sewer.

### Rumney

Baker River Campground, 56 Campground Rd.,
03266. T: (603) 786-9707. www.ucampnh.com/
bakerriver. RV/tent: 60. $18. Hookups: water, elec-
tric (20, 30 amps), sewer.

### Sandown

Angle Pond Grove Camping Area, P.O. Box 173,
03826. T: (603) 887-4434. F: (603) 887-4434.
www.anglepondgrove.com. RV/tent: 15. $20.
Hookups: water, electric (30, 50 amps), sewer.

### Shelburne

White Birches Camping Park, 218 SR 2, 03581.
T: (603) 466-2022. F: (603) 466-3441. www.go
campingamerica/whitebirches. RV/tent: 91. $15.
Hookups: water, electric (30 amps), sewer.

### Tamworth

Foothills Campground, 506 Maple Rd., 03886.
T: (603) 323-8322. F: (603) 323-8194. www.the
foothills.com. RV/tent: 40. $18. Hookups: water,
electric (20, 30 amps), sewer.

Tamworth Camping Area, P.O. Box 99, 03886.
T: (603) 323-8031. F: (603) 323-7500. www.
tamworthcampingarea.com. RV/tent: 38. $21.
Hookups: water, electric (20, 30 amps), sewer.

### Thornton

Pemi River Campground, RFD 1 Box 926, 03223.
T: (603) 726-7015. RV/tent: 71. $22. Hookups:
water, electric (15, 30, 50 amps).

### Twin Mountain

Ammonoosuc Campground, P.O. Box 178 North,
03595. T: (603) 846-5527. www.ucampnh.com/
ammonoosuc. RV/tent: 112. $20. Hookups: water,
electric (20, 30 amps), sewer.

### Warren

Scenic View Campground, 193AA South Main St.,
03279. T: (603) 764-9380. www.usastar.com/

scenicview. RV/tent: 98. $23. Hookups: water, elec-
tric (20, 30 amps), cable TV, phone, modem.

### Washington

Happy Days Campground, 928 Valley Rd., 03280.
T: (603) 495-0150. F: (603) 495-0261. www.ucamp
nh.com/happydays. RV/tent: 185. $20. Hookups:
water, electric (20, 30 amps), sewer.

### Weare

Autumn Hills Campground, 285 South Stark Hwy.,
03281. T: (603) 529-2425. F: (603) 529-5877.
www.autumnhillscampground.com. RV/tent: 159.
$21. Hookups: water, electric (20, 30 amps), sewer.

### Webster

Cold Brook Campground, 539 Battle St., 03303.
T: (603) 746-3390. www.coldbrookcampground.
com. RV/tent: 50. $15. Hookups: water, electric
(15, 20 amps), sewer.

### Weirs Beach

Weirs Beach Tent and Trailer Park, 198 Endicott St.,
03246. T: (603) 366-4747. www.wbttp.com.
RV/tent: 184. $22. Hookups: water, electric (30
amps), sewer.

### West Ossipee

Bearcamp River Campground, P.O. Box 104, 03890.
T: (603) 539-4898. F: (603) 539-6025. www.bear
camp.com. RV/tent: 112. $23. Hookups: water,
electric (20, 30 amps), sewer.

### Whitefield

Burns Lake Campground, RR 2 Box 620A, 03598.
T: (603) 837-9037. RV/tent: 70. $14. Hookups:
water, electric (20, 30 amps).

### Winchester

Forest Lake Campground, 331 Keene Rd., 03470.
T: (603) 239-4267. RV/tent: 150. $20. Hookups:
water, electric (20, 30 amps), sewer.

### Wolfeboro

Robie's RV Park, 139 Governor Wentworth Hwy.,
03894. T: (603) 569-2732. F: (603) 569-4354.
RV/tent: 50. $24. Hookups: water, electric (30, 50
amps), sewer.

Willey Brook Campground, 883 Center St., 03894.
T: (603) 569-9493. www.WilleyBrookCamp-
ground.com. RV/tent: 33. $16. Hookups: water,
electric (30 amps), sewer.

## RHODE ISLAND

### Charlestown

Charlestown Breachway, Burlingame State Park, 02908. T: (401) 364-7000. RV/tent: 75. $8–$12. Hookups: water, electric.

Ninigret Conservation Area, East Beach Rd., 02813. T: (401) 322-0450 or (401) 322-8910. RV/tent: 20. $12. Hookups: water, electric.

### Chepachet

Camp Ponagansett, Bungy Rd., 02814. T: (401) 647-7377. RV/tent: 40. $15. Hookups: water, electric.

### Foster

Dyer Woods Nudist Campground, 114 Johnson Rd., 02825. T: (401) 397-3007. RV/tent: 16. $10. Hookups: water, electric.

### Middletown

Meadowlark Park, 132 Prospect Ave., 02842. T: (401) 846-9455. RV/tent: 40. $20. Hookups: water, electric, sewer.

Paradise Motel and Campground, 459 Aquidneck Ave., 02842. T: (401) 847-1500. RV/tent: 16. $25. Hookups: water, electric, sewer.

Middletown Campground, Second Beach, 02842. T: (401) 846-6273. RV/tent: 44. Seasonal rates on request. Hookups: water, electric.

### Narragansett

Long Cove Campsite and Marina, 325 Point Judith Rd., 02882. T: (401) 783-4902. RV/tent: 150. $19. Hookups: water, electric, sewer.

### Pascoag

Echo Lake Campground, 180 Moroney Rd., 02859. T: (401) 568-7109. RV/tent: 150. $20. Hookups: water, electric, sewer.

### Portsmouth

Melville Campground Recreation, 181 Bradford Ave., 02871. T: (401) 682-2424. RV/tent: 133. $15–$23. Hookups: water, electric, sewer.

Melville Ponds Campground, Rte. 114, 02835. T: (401) 849-8212. RV/tent: 128. $21–$25. Hookups: water, electric.

### Wakefield

Worden's Pond Family Campground, 416 Wordens Pond Rd. No. A, 02879. T: (401) 789-9113. RV/tent: 200. $20. Hookups: water, electric, sewer.

## VERMONT

### Addison

Ten Acres Campground, RR 1 Box 356, 05491. T: (802) 759-2662. RV/tent: 87. $16. Hookups: water, electric, sewer.

### Andover

Horseshoe Acres Campgrounds, 1978 Weston Andover Rd., 05143. T: (802) 875-2960. RV/tent: 120. $16–$23. Hookups: water, electric, sewer.

### Arlington

Camping on the Battenkill, Rte. 7A, 05250. T: (802) 375-6663 or (800) 830-6663. RV/tent: 96. $20. Hookups: water, electric, sewer.

Howell's Camping Area, No Name Rd., 05250. T: (802) 375-6469. RV/tent: 77. $17. Hookups: water, electric, sewer.

### Ascutney

Running Bear Camping Area, 6248 Rte. 5, 05030. T: (802) 674-6417. RV/tent: 90. $16–$20. Hookups: water, electric, sewer.

Wilgus State Park Campground, P.O. Box 196, 05030. T: (802) 674-5422. RV/tent: 29. $12. Hookups: none.

### Barnard

Silver Lake Family Campground, Stage Rd., 05031. T: (802) 234-9974. RV/tent: 67. $17. Hookups: water, electric, sewer.

Silver Lake State Park Campground, Town Rd., 05031. T: (802) 234-9451. RV/tent: 47. $13. Hookups: none.

### Barton

Sugar Mill Farm, Box 26, 05822. T: (800) 688-7978. RV/tent: 18. $17. Hookups: water, electric.

### Bennington

Greenwood Lodge and Campsites, Rte. 9, 05201. T: (802) 442-2547. F: (802) 442-2547. RV/tent: 20. $14. Hookups: water, electric, sewer.

## VERMONT (continued)

### Bomoseen

Lake Bomoseen Campground, Rte. 30, 05732.
T: (802) 273-2061. RV/tent: 99. $20. Hookups:
water, electric, sewer, phone.

### Brandon

Branbury State Park, RD 2 Box 242, 05743. T: (802)
247-5925. RV/tent: 39. $3. Hookups: none.

Smoke Rise Farm Campground, Rte. 7 North,
05733. T: (802) 247-6472. RV/tent: 50. $10.
Hookups: water, electric, sewer.

### Brattleboro

Hidden Acres Campground, 792 US Rte. 5, 05301.
T: (802) 254-2098. RV/tent: 40. $19–25. Hookups:
water, electric, sewer.

### Bristol

Elephant Mountain Camping Area, RD 3 Box 850,
05443. T: (802) 453-3123. RV/tent: 50. $15.
Hookups: water, electric, sewer.

Maple Hill Campground, 690 Quaker St., 05443.
T: (802) 453-3687. RV/tent: 13. $16. Hookups:
electric.

### Brookfield

Allis State Park Campground, RD 2 Box 192, 05036.
T: (802) 276-3175. RV/tent: 27. $11. Hookups:
none.

### Burlington

North Beach Campground, Lakeview Terrace,
05401. T: (800) 571-1198. RV/tent: 137. $18–$25.
Hookups: water, electric (30, 50 amps), sewer.

### Cavendish

Caton Place Campground, RR 1 Box 107, 05142.
T: (802) 226-7767. RV/tent: 85. $14–$15.
Hookups: water, electric (15, 20, 30 amps), sewer.

### Charlotte

Mt. Philo State Park, 5425 Mt. Philo Rd., 05445.
T: (802) 425-2390. www.state.vt.us/anr/fpr/parks/
htm/philo.html. RV/tent: 7. $12–18. Hookups:
none.

Old Lantern Campground, P.O. Box 221, 5445.
T: (802) 425-2120. RV/tent: 95. $15–$20.
Hookups: water, electric, sewer.

### Chester

Hidden Valley Campgrounds, 1924 Mattson Rd.,
05143. T: (802) 886-2497. RV/tent: 32. $15.
Hookups: water, electric.

### Danby

Otter Creek Campground, Rte. 7, 05739. T: (802)
293-5041. RV/tent: 50. $14 (higher in winter).
Hookups: water, electric.

### Dorset

Dorset RV Park, 1567 Rte. 30, 05251-9802. T: (802)
867-5754. RV/tent: 40. $10–$19. Hookups: water,
electric, sewer.

### East Burkes

Burke Mountain Campgrounds, Mountain Rd.,
05832. T: (802) 626-1204. RV/tent: 25. $10.
Hookups: water, electric, sewer.

### East Dummerston

KOA Campground, 1238 US 5, 05346. T: (802) 254-
5908. RV/tent: 42. $24–$32. Hookups: water, electric (20, 30, 50 amps), sewer.

### East Montpelier

Green Valley Campground, RR 2, P.O. Box 21,
05651. T: (802) 223-6217. F: (802) 223-1702.
RV/tent: 36. $15–$25. Hookups: water, electric,
sewer, phone.

### East Thetford

Rest n' Nest Campground, Latham Rd., 05043.
T: (802) 785-2997. RV/tent: 90. $20. Hookups:
water, electric, sewer.

### Enosburg Falls

Lake Carmi, 460 Marsh Farm Rd., 05450. T: (802)
933-8383. RV/tent: 140. $13–$17. Hookups: none.

### Fair Haven

Bomoseen State Park, RR 1 Box 2620, 05743.
T: (802) 265-4242. RV/tent: 66. $13. Hookups: none.

### Gaysville

White River Valley Camping, Box 106T, 05746.
T: (802) 234-9115. RV/tent: 40. $17–$22.
Hookups: water, electric, sewer.

### Graniteville

Lazy Lions Campground, 281 Middle Rd., 05654-
9801. T: (802) 479-2823. F: (802) 479-2870.
www.campusa.com/framenorthbeach.cfm.
RV/tent: 180. $20 RV, $15 tent. Hookups: water,
electric, sewer, phone.

### Groton

Ricker Pond State Park, 526 State Forest Rd.,
05046. T: (802) 584-3821. RV/tent: 55. $17.
Hookups: none.

## VERMONT (continued)

### Hartford

Quechee Gorge State Park Campground, 190 Dewey Mills Rd., 05001.T: (802) 295-2990 or (800) 299-3071. RV/tent: 54. $12–$18. Hookups: none.

### Isle La Motte

Lakehurst Campground, 204 Lakehurst Rd., 05463. T: (802) 928-3266. www.campusa.com/frame northbeach.cfm. RV/tent: 160. $15–$20. Hookups: water, electric, sewer.

Summer Place Campground & Cabins, P.O. Box 30, 05463.T: (802) 928-3300. RV/tent: 70. $14. Hookups: water, electric.

### Jamaica

Jamaica State Park Campground, P.O. Box 45, 05343. T: (802) 874-4600. RV/tent: 61. $13. Hookups: none.

### Killington

Gifford Woods State Park, Hwy. 100, 05751. T: (802) 775-5354. RV/tent: 48. $15. Hookups: none.

Killington Campground at Alpenhof Lodge, Box 2880, Killington Rd., 05751.T: (802) 422-9787. RV/tent: 10. $20. Hookups: water, electric.

### Ludlow

Hideaway Squirrel Hill Camp, 176 Bixby Rd., 05149. T: (802) 228-8800. RV/tent: 24. $10–$15. Hookups: water, electric.

### Manchester Center

Greendale Campground, 2539 Depot St., 05255. T: (802) 362-2307. RV/tent: 11. $5. Hookups: water.

### Marshfield

Groton Forest Road Campground, RD 1 Box 402, Hwy. 232, 05658.T: (802) 426-4122. RV/tent: 35. $14. Hookups: water, electric.

Larry & Sons Campground, Rte. 2, 05658.T: (802) 426-3514. RV/tent: 23. $10. Hookups: water, electric.

### Middlebury

Rivers Bend Campground, 1000 Dog Team Rd., 05653.T: (802) 388-9092. RV/tent: 65. $20–$24. Hookups: water, electric (20, 30 amps).

### Newfane

Kenolie Village Campground, 16 Kenolie Campground Rd., 05345. T: (802) 365-7671. RV/tent: 150. $13. Hookups: water, electric (20, 30 amps).

### North Clarendon

Iroquios Land Family, 2334 East Clarendon Rd., 05759.T: (802) 773-2832. RV/tent: 35. $20. Hookups: water, electric, sewer.

### North Dorset

Emerald Lake State Park Campground, RD 485, 05251.T: (802) 362-1655. RV/tent: 105. $13. Hookups: none.

### North Hero

Carry Bay Campground & Cottages, 5289 Rte. 2, 05474.T: (802) 372-8233. RV/tent: 30. $20 RV, $12 tent. Hookups: water, electric, sewer.

Norh Hero State Park, 3803 Lakeview Drive, 05474-9698.T: (802) 372-8727. RV/tent: 99. $12–$17. Hookups: none.

### Perkinsville

Crown Point Camping Area, 131 Bishops Camp Rd., 05151.T: (802) 263-5555. RV/tent: 36. $15. Hookups: water, electric, sewer.

Winhall Brook Camping Area, RR 1 Box 164B, 05151.T: (802) 874-4881. RV/tent: 109. $10. Hookups: none.

### Peru

Green Mountain/Red Mill Brook, 231 North Main St., 05701-2417.T: (802) 362-2307. RV/tent: 20. $5. Hookups: none.

Hapgood Pond Recreation Area, P.O. Box 248, 05152.T: (802) 824-6456. RV/tent: 28. $10. Hookups: water.

### Plymouth

Coolidge State Park, Rte. A, 05056.T: (802) 672-3612. RV/tent: 60. $11–$15. Hookups: none.

Sugarhouse Campground, Rte. 100, 05056.T: (802) 672-5043. RV/tent: 45. $15 (higher rates in winter). Hookups: water, electric.

### Randolph Center

Lake Champagne Campground, Furnace Pt., 05061. T: (802) 728-5293. F: (802) 479-2870. RV/tent: 68. $18–$28. Hookups: water, electric, sewer.

### Rochester

Chittendon Brook Recreation Area, Rte. 100, 05767.T: (802) 767-4261. RV/tent: 17. $9. Hookups: none.

## VERMONT (continued)

### Salisbury

Branbury State Park, 3570 Lake Dunmore Rd., 05769. T: (802) 247-5925. RV/tent: 45. $13–$17. Hookups: none.

Lake Dunmore Kampersville, RR 1, 05769-9801. T: (802) 352-4501 or (877) 250-2568. RV/tent: 120. $17. Hookups: water, electric, sewer.

Waterhouse Campground & Marina, 937 West Shore Rd., 05769. T: (802) 352-4433. RV/tent: 60. $17–$25. Hookups: water, electric, sewer.

### Shaftsbury

Lake Shaftsbury State Park, RR 1 Box 266, 05262. T: (802) 375-9978. RV/tent: 15. $16. Hookups: none.

### South Hero

Apple Island, Rte. 2, 05486-4008. T: (802) 372-5398. F: (802) 372-8272. RV/tent: 200. $25–$30. Hookups: water, electric, sewer.

### South Londonderry

Ball Mountain Lake Project Campground, 98 Reservoir Rd., Springfield, Vermon, 05156-2210. T: (802) 824-4570. RV/tent: 111. $12–$18. Hookups: water, electric (20, 30 amps), sewer.

### Springfield

Tree Farm Campground, 53 Skitchewaug Trail, 05156. T: (802) 885-2889. RV/tent: 118. $17. Hookups: water, electric, sewer.

### Thetford

Thetford Hill State Park Campground, P.O. Box 132, 05074. T: (802) 785-2266. RV/tent: 16. $11. Hookups: none.

### Townshend

Bald Mountain Campground, 1760 State Forest Rd., 05353. T: (802) 365-7510. RV/tent: 200. $18. Hookups: water, electric, sewer.

Camperama, Depot Rd., 05353. T: (802) 365-4315 or (800) 632-2677. RV/tent: 205. $20–$23. Hookups: water, electric, sewer.

Townshend State Park Campground, RD 1 Box 2650, 05353. T: (802) 365-7500. RV/tent: 35. $11. Hookups: none.

### Underhill

South Hill Riverside Campground, RD 2 Box 287, 05489. T: (802) 899-2232. RV/tent: 50. $20. Hookups: water, electric, sewer.

### Vergennes

Button Bay State Park, RD 3 Box 4075, 05491. T: (802) 475-2377. RV/tent: 72. $13–$17. Hookups: none.

D.A.R. State Park, RD 2 Box 3493, 05491. T: (802) 759-2354. RV/tent: 70. $12–$16. Hookups: none.

Whispering Pines Campground, 1072 Panton Rd., 05491. T: (802) 475-2264. RV/tent: 40. $12. Hookups: water, electric.

### Waterbury

Duxbury Campground, 2542 VT 100, 05676. T: (802) 244-7546. RV/tent: 16. $10. Hookups: water, electric.

### Waterbury Center

The Long Trail, 4711 Waterbury-Stowe Rd., 05677. T: (802) 244-7037. RV/tent: 70. $4. Hookups: none.

### Wells River

Pleasant Valley Camp Grounds, 964 Wallace Hill Rd., 05081. T: (802) 584-3884 or (802) 866-5991. RV/tent: 37. $12–$19. Hookups: water, electric, sewer.

### Westfield

Barrewood Campground, 3201 VT 100, 05874-9801. T: (802) 744-6340. RV/tent: 46. $12–$18. Hookups: water, electric, sewer.

### White Junction

Maple Leaf Motel & Campground, Rte. 5 South, 05001. T: (802) 295-2817. RV/tent: 14. $19. Hookups: water, electric, sewer.

### White River Junction

Pine Valley RV Resort, 400 Woodstock Rd., 05001. T: (802) 296-6711. RV/tent: 90. $12–$26. Hookups: water, electric, sewer.

### Williamstown

Limehurst Lake, 4104 Rte. 14, 05679. T: (802) 433-6662 or (800) 242-9876. RV/tent: 76. $18–$23. Hookups: water, electric, sewer.

### Windsor

Ascutney State Park, Box 186, HCR 71, 05089. T: (802) 674-2060. RV/tent: 39. $11. Hookups: none.

### Woodford

Greenwood Lodge and Campsites, Box 246, 05201. T: (802) 442-2547. grnwd@compuserve.com. RV/tent: 20. $16–$22. Hookups: water, electric (30, 50 amps).

Woodford State Park Campground, HCR 65, Box 928, 05201. T: (802) 447-7169. RV/tent: 103. $13. Hookups: none.

# Index

# Notes

# Notes

# Notes

# Notes

# Notes

# Notes

# Notes